중·고등 영어도 역시 **1위 해커스**다.

해커스북 중·고등

HackersBook.com

해커스
수능 독해
불변의 패턴
실전편이 특별한 이유!

최신 경향과 출제 패턴을 반영한 문제로 실전 대비가 가능하니까!

1

최신 수능/모평/학평
출제경향을 그대로 반영한
**양질의 수능 영어 독해
모의고사**

2

한 번만 읽어도 1등급 오르는
**32개의 수능 독해
불변의 패턴**

3

정확한 해석과 오답분석/
구문분석까지 수록한
상세하고 알찬 해설

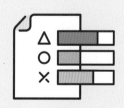

해커스 수능 독해
불변의 패턴
유형편

해커스 수능 독해
불변의 패턴
실전편

어려운 수능에도 끄떡없는 실력을 기를 수 있으니까!

4

난이도 높았던 역대 수능/모평/학평을
기반으로 제작한
고난도 실전모의고사 3회분

5

비연계 수능에 효과적으로
대비할 수 있는
새로운 소재의 지문

해커스
수능독해
불변의
패턴

실전편

모의고사
15회

![해커스 어학연구소 로고] 해커스 어학연구소

Contents

실전 문제로 수능 완벽 대비! 문제집

꼼꼼한 해설로 학습 마무리! 해설집

책의 특징과 구성

최신 출제 경향과 출제 패턴을 반영한 실전모의고사로 실전 대비가 가능합니다.

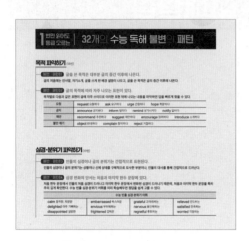

1번만 읽어도 1등급 오르는
32개의 수능 독해 불변의 패턴

기출 기반의 빅데이터에서 추출한 출제 포인트를 '불변의 패턴'으로 정리하였습니다. 32개의 불변의 패턴들만 익혀두면 보다 쉽고 빠르게 수능 영어 독해 문제를 풀 수 있습니다.

최신 출제 경향과 불변의 패턴을 기반으로 제작한
실전모의고사 12회분 + 고난도 3회분

최신 수능, 모평, 학평의 출제 경향과 32개의 불변의 패턴을 반영한 실전모의고사 15회분으로 실전 감각을 끌어올릴 수 있습니다. 다양한 범위의 새로운 소재를 반영한 지문을 수록해 비연계로 출제되는 수능 영어에 효과적으로 대비할 수 있도록 하였습니다. 또한 어렵게 출제되었던 역대 수능의 소재와 난이도를 반영한 고난도 실전모의고사 3회분을 통해 심화학습을 할 수 있습니다.

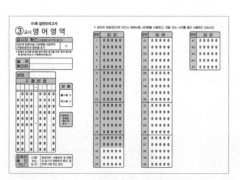

실제 시험처럼 연습할 수 있는
OMR 답안지

실전모의고사를 풀면서 실제 시험처럼 시간 내에 답안지를 작성하는 연습을 할 수 있도록 OMR 답안지를 제공해, 실전 감각을 높일 수 있도록 하였습니다.

2 | 완벽한 이해와 복습을 돕는 해설을 통해 실력을 향상시킬 수 있습니다.

---

32 빈칸 추론하기 정답 ⑤

[해설] 주제문에 해당하는 빈칸 문장에서 이 기제, 즉 자가포식이 '무엇'을 통해서 세포를 재생시키는 방법이라고 하고, 글의 중반에서 제대로 기능을 하지 않는 세포들을 효과적으로 겨냥하여 그것들의 제거를 확실히 한다고 했다. 따라서 빈칸에는 ⑤ '손상된 세포 성분의 제거'가 와서 자가포식이 손상된 세포 성분의 제거를 통해 신체가 새롭고 건강한 세포를 재생시키는 방법이라는 의미가 되어야 한다.

[오답분석] ①의 건강한 장기의 보존은 글의 내용과 관련이 없다. ②은 글에 언급된 proteins를 사용하여 헷갈리게 하는 오답이다. ③의 의료 시술의 적용은 글의 내용과 관련이 없다. ④은 글에서 제대로 기능을 하지 않는 세포는 제거한다고 했으므로 이와 반대되는 내용이어서 오답이다.

[해석] 인간의 신체에서 가장 주목할 만한 측면 중 하나는 스스로를 조절하고 최상의 기능을 유지하는 능력이다. 이를 성취하기 위해, 신체는 자가포식이라는 자기 소화 체계를 포함하는 다양한 자연적 과정들을 이용한다. 이 기제는 손상된 세포 성분의 제거를 통해서 신체가 새롭고 건강한 세포를 재생시키는 방법이다. 인간의 세포들이 스트레스를 받으면, 신체의 정상적인 작용을 확실히 하

정확하고 상세한
해설 · 오답분석 · 해석

모든 문제에 상세한 해설과 정확한 해석을 제공해 혼자서도 효과적인 복습이 가능하게 하였고, 헷갈릴 만한 선택지에 대한 오답분석도 수록하여 정답뿐만 아니라 오답인 이유까지 완벽하게 이해할 수 있게 구성하였습니다.

[해석] 탐욕은 인간 본성에 내재된 생물학적 기반의 행동이다. 욕구는 모든 살아있는 생명체의 생존에 필수적이지만, 인간은 생물학적 관점에서뿐만 아니라 사회적 관점에서의 욕구도 경험한다. 이는 인간이 갖는 충동들을, 번식하려는 본능적 욕구와 같이 동물이 느끼는 것들로부터 구별 짓는다. 사람들은 단순히 살아 있는 것 이상을 원한다; 그들은 또한 물질적 소유물과 부를 원한다. 하지만 현대 사회에서, 탐욕은 다소 역설적인데, 탐욕 자체는 사회에서 비난받는 반면, 탐욕과 유사한 개인의 행동은 당연하게 부추겨지며, 사람들이 할 수 있는 한 부와 번영을 추구하도록 권장되기 때문이다. 이는 탐욕이 실제로 개인을 이롭게 하지만, 제한되지 않을 경우 문명사회가 대가를 치르게 될 수 있기 때문이다. 사회학자들은 사회가 억제되지 않은 탐욕을 악이라 부름으로써 여전히 제한하는 것과 동시에 탐욕을 가진 개인들에게 동기를 부여하는 균형 상태를 찾는 것을 목표로 한다고 주장한다.

[어휘] credit 공로를 인정해주다　enduring 지속되는, 영구적인
practicing (현재) 활동하고 있는　wield (힘을) 행사하다, 휘두르다
phenomena(phenomenon의 복수형) 현상, 경이로운 것
discrete 별개의, 분리된　disorder 장애, 이상　shuttle 실어 나르다, 오가다
one-size-fits-all 일률적인, 두루 적용되도록 만든　clinician 임상의
intertwine 얽히게 하다　holistic 전체론적인, 전체론의

[구문분석] [10행] **Rather than** ①[classifying psychological phenomena as discrete disorders] and ②[shuttling patients into one-size-fits-all treatments], Jung's concept of the "complex" <u>allows</u> _{동사} <u>clinicians</u> <u>to identify</u> how their conflicting problems are 목적어　목적격 보어(to부정사)
intertwined.

→ ①[classifying ~ disorders]와 ②[shuttling ~ treatments]는 전치사 rather than의 목적어 역할을 하는 동명사구이다.

→ 동사 allow의 목적어로 clinicians, 목적격 보어로 to부정사 to identify가 쓰였다.

완벽한 이해와 심화학습을 할 수 있는
정답의 단서 · 어휘 · 구문분석

정답의 단서가 되는 부분을 해석에 표시하여 한눈에 주요 내용을 파악할 수 있도록 하였습니다. 또한 모든 문제에 구문분석을 제공하여 문장구조를 익히고 독해 실력을 향상시킬 수 있게 구성하였습니다.

목적 파악하기 (18번)

불변의 패턴 01 글을 쓴 목적은 대부분 글의 중간 이후에 나온다.

글의 처음에는 인사말, 자기소개, 글을 쓰게 된 배경 설명이 나오고, 글을 쓴 목적은 글의 중간 이후에 나온다.

불변의 패턴 02 글의 목적에 따라 자주 나오는 표현이 있다.

목적별로 다음과 같은 표현이 글에 자주 쓰이므로 이러한 표현 뒤에 나오는 내용을 파악하면 답을 빠르게 찾을 수 있다.

요청	request 요청하다	ask 요구하다	urge 간청하다	hope 희망하다
공지	announce 공지하다	inform 알리다	remind 상기시키다	notify 알리다
제안	recommend 추천하다	suggest 제안하다	encourage 장려하다	introduce 소개하다
불만 제기	object 반대하다	complain 항의하다	reject 거절하다	

심경·분위기 파악하기 (19번)

불변의 패턴 03 인물의 심경이나 글의 분위기는 간접적으로 표현된다.

인물의 심경이나 글의 분위기는 상황이나 신체 상태를 구체적으로 묘사한 부분이나, 인물의 대사를 통해 간접적으로 드러난다.

불변의 패턴 04 심경 변화의 단서는 처음과 마지막 한두 문장에 있다.

처음 한두 문장에서 인물의 처음 심경이 드러나고 마지막 한두 문장에서 변화된 심경이 드러나기 때문에, 처음과 마지막 한두 문장을 특히 주의 깊게 확인한다. 수능 빈출 심경·분위기 어휘를 미리 학습해두면 정답을 쉽게 고를 수 있다.

수능 빈출 심경·분위기 어휘			
calm 침착한, 차분한	embarrassed 쑥스러운	grateful 고마워하는	relieved 안도하는
delighted 아주 기뻐하는	envious 부러워하는	nervous 불안해하는	satisfied 만족하는
disappointed 실망한	frightened 겁먹은	regretful 후회하는	worried 걱정하는

주장·요지 파악하기 (20번·22번)

불변의 패턴 05 주장·요지는 처음과 마지막 두세 문장에서 제시된다.

주장이나 요지는 두괄식으로 글의 처음에 제시된 후 마지막에 다시 한번 언급되는 경우가 많다.

불변의 패턴 06 자주 출제되는 오답의 유형은 정해져 있다.

오답 선택지의 특징을 알아두면 함정을 피해 정답을 선택할 수 있다.
- 글과 반대되거나 다른 내용
- 글과 일부만 일치하고 나머지는 다른 내용
- 글에 나오지 않은 소재를 언급한 내용

밑줄 의미 추론하기 (21번)

불변의패턴07 밑줄이 있는 문장은 주제문을 바꿔 말한 것이다.

밑줄 친 부분이 포함된 문장은 주제문을 다른 말로 바꿔 말한 것인 경우가 많다.

불변의패턴08 밑줄 친 부분은 비유적이거나 상징적인 표현이다.

밑줄 친 부분은 글의 내용을 비유적/상징적으로 표현한 것이기 때문에 글자 그대로 해석해서는 의미 파악이 힘들다. 따라서 글의 처음부터 정독해서 읽고 핵심 내용을 파악한 후 밑줄 문장의 숨은 의미를 추론한다.

★ 3점 문제로 출제될 때는 글의 주제도 추상적이고 매우 함축적인 어구가 출제되므로, 밑줄 친 표현이 글의 주제 및 문맥과 어떻게 연결되는지 집중하여 파악해야 한다.

★ 3점 문제
주제·제목 파악하기 (23번·24번)

불변의패턴09 주제문은 처음이나 마지막 두세 문장에 나온다.

글의 처음과 마지막 두세 문장을 읽으면서 주제문을 찾고, 이 내용을 다른 말로 가장 잘 표현한 정답을 골라야 한다.

★ 3점 문제로 출제될 때는 생소한 주제를 어려운 어휘와 복잡한 구문, 긴 문장을 사용하여 설명하므로, 모든 문장을 완벽히 이해하기는 힘들다. 따라서, 글의 전개 방식을 파악하여 더 집중해서 읽어야 하는 부분을 찾는 연습을 하는 것이 중요하다.

불변의패턴10 주제문과 함께 자주 나오는 표현이 있다.

주제문에 자주 쓰이는 아래의 표현들을 알아두고 글에서 해당 표현을 찾아 그 뒤에 나오는 내용을 집중해서 파악하면 답을 빠르게 찾을 수 있다.

조사/연구	according to ~에 따르면		
중요성 강조	should/must/have to ~해야 한다 make sure ~을 확실히 해라 important 중요한 necessary 필수적인 try to ~ 하도록 노력해라		
대조/반전	but/however 그러나 although 비록 ~이긴 하지만 in fact 사실은 the truth is 사실은		
결론/정리	therefore 그러므로 in other words 즉 thus 따라서		

도표 정보 파악하기 (25번)

불변의패턴11 제목과 첫 문장에 무엇에 관한 도표인지 나온다.

도표의 제목과 첫 문장을 보고 무엇에 관한 도표인지 먼저 파악하면 도표를 더 쉽고 빠르게 이해할 수 있다. 만약 제목만 읽고 파악이 됐다면 첫 문장을 넘기고 바로 선택지부터 읽는다.

불변의패턴12 정답의 단서는 도표의 수치 변화에 있다.

증가, 감소, 비교, 배수 표현이 정답의 단서가 되는 경우가 많다. 따라서 수치의 변화를 나타내는 표현을 알아두고 이를 특히 주의하여 읽는다.

증가	increase 증가하다 rise 오르다 grow 증가하다 soar 치솟다
감소	decrease 감소하다 decline 감소하다 drop 줄다 reduce 감소하다
비교	more/less than ~보다 많은/~보다 적은 higher/lower than ~보다 높은/~보다 낮은
배수	twice/two times 2배 half 절반 a quarter 4분의 1 one-third 3분의 1

세부 정보 파악하기 (26번)

불변의 패턴 13 **선택지는 글의 순서대로 나온다.**

선택지는 글의 내용의 흐름과 동일한 순서로 제시된다. 선택지를 먼저 보고 글에서 해당하는 부분을 찾아서 내용이 일치하는지 확인한다. 정답은 대개 ③~⑤ 중에 있으므로 ⑤부터 역순으로 확인하면 정답을 더 빨리 찾을 수 있다.

불변의 패턴 14 **정답은 글에 나온 정보가 일부 변형된 것이다.**

정답은 글에 나온 정보를 일부만 틀리게 표현한 경우가 많다. 따라서 선택지의 내용 전체가 글의 내용과 일치하는지 꼼꼼히 확인해야 한다.

안내문 정보 파악하기 (27번·28번)

불변의 패턴 15 **정답의 단서는 수치가 포함된 부분에 있는 경우가 많다.**

기간, 날짜, 연도, 나이, 가격 등 수치가 포함된 부분에 정답의 단서가 있는 경우가 많으므로 이를 중점적으로 본다.

불변의 패턴 16 **예외 조항 및 추가 정보와 관련된 선택지가 정답인 경우가 많다.**

안내문에서는 별표, 괄호, Notice, Note, Additional Information 등으로 예외 조항이나 추가 정보를 제공하는데, 이 부분에서 정답이 출제되는 경우가 많으니 주의 깊게 확인한다. 예외 조항과 추가 정보는 보통 글의 중간 이후에 위치하기 때문에 ⑤부터 역순으로 확인하면 정답을 더 빨리 찾을 수 있다.

★3점 문제
어법상 틀린 것 찾기 (29번)

불변의 패턴 17 **밑줄은 동사, 분사, 동명사, to부정사에서 많이 나온다.**

밑줄이 동사, 분사, 동명사, to부정사에서 많이 출제되므로 이러한 어법 포인트를 집중적으로 학습하여 대비한다.

★ 3점 문제는 품사를 한 번에 파악하기 힘든 길고 복잡한 구조의 문장들로 구성된 글이 출제된다. 따라서, 평소에 독해 문제를 풀면서 문장 구조를 분석하는 연습을 꾸준히 해야 한다.

불변의 패턴 18 **밑줄의 품사에 따라 확인해야 하는 것이 정해져 있다.**

동사/준동사 밑줄	• 밑줄 친 자리에 동사와 준동사 중 바른 것이 왔는가? • 동사의 수/시제/태 등이 바른가? • 동명사/to부정사/분사 중 적절한 준동사가 왔는가? • 준동사의 능동형·수동형·부정형 등이 바른 형태로 왔는가?
명사/대명사/한정사 밑줄	• 가산명사 또는 불가산명사가 바른 형태로 쓰였는가? • 단수형과 복수형 중 적절한 것으로 쓰였는가? • 대명사와 한정사는 그것이 가리키거나 수식하는 명사에 맞는 것이 왔는가?
형용사/부사/비교구문 밑줄	• 형용사나 부사 중 바른 것이 왔는가? • 원급/비교급/최상급 비교구문의 형태가 바른가?
전치사/접속사/관계사 밑줄	• 전치사와 부사절 접속사 중 바른 것이 왔는가? • 명사절 접속사와 관계사 중 바른 것이 왔는가?
기타	• 여러 가지를 나열·반복하는 규칙(병렬과 생략)이 바르게 적용되었는가? • 특수한 어순 규칙(어순과 도치)을 잘 따르고 있는가?

어휘 적절성 파악하기 (30번)

불변의패턴 19 쓰임이 적절하지 않은 어휘는 문맥과 반대되는 의미로 나온다.

밑줄 친 단어 중 쓰임이 적절하지 않은 것은 대부분 문맥과 반대되는 의미의 단어로 나온다. 글의 소재와 논리적 맥락을 파악하면서 밑줄 친 단어의 쓰임이 적절하게 쓰였는지에 대한 근거를 찾는다. 근거는 밑줄이 있는 문장의 앞뒤 문장인 경우가 많으니 이를 중점적으로 본다. 정답이라고 생각한 선택지에 적절할 것 같다고 생각되는 의미를 넣어서 다시 읽어보고 자연스러운지 확인한다.

★ 3점 문제는 글 전체의 맥락을 파악해야 쓰임이 적절한지 판단할 수 있는 어휘에 밑줄이 쳐져 있는 경우도 있으므로, 전체적인 내용의 흐름을 정확히 이해하는 것이 중요하다.

불변의패턴 20 네모 안 어휘들은 보통 서로 반의어 관계이다.

각 네모 안의 어휘는 대부분 반의어로 짝지어져 있다. 접사의 유무로 구분되는 반의어 관계 혹은 형태가 전혀 다른 반의어 관계가 있는데, 보통 후자가 더 많이 출제되므로 반의어 관계의 어휘를 폭넓게 익혀 둔다.

반의어 관계의 어휘	
neglect 무시하다 ↔ recognize 인정하다	common 흔한 ↔ unique 독특한
include 포함시키다 ↔ exclude 제외시키다	physical 육체의 ↔ psychological 정신의
support 지지하다 ↔ criticize 비판하다	receptive 수용하는 ↔ resistant 저항하는
allow 허락하다 ↔ forbid 금지하다	frequent 빈번한 ↔ rare 드문
expand 확대되다 ↔ shrink 줄어들다	collective 집단적인 ↔ individual 개별적인

빈칸 추론하기 (31번~34번)

불변의패턴 21 글의 초반부에 나온 빈칸 문장은 주제문이다.

주제문이 초반에 있는 두괄식 글, 또는 주제문이 초반에 나온 후 후반에서 다시 언급되는 양괄식 글이 많이 출제된다. 빈칸이 글의 초반부에 나오면 이어지는 글의 내용을 종합해서 주제문을 완성하는 느낌으로 빈칸에 들어갈 말을 추론해야 한다.

불변의패턴 22 후반부의 빈칸 문장은 주제문을 재진술하는 문장이다.

글의 후반부에 나오는 빈칸 문장은 앞서 나온 주제문을 다시 한번 언급하는 문장인 경우가 많다. 따라서 글의 초중반부에서 주제문을 찾아서 확실히 이해한 후, 이를 다른 말로 바꿔 말한 선택지를 찾아야 한다.

★ 3점 문제는 글의 소재가 생소하거나 내용이 난해한 경우가 많아 전체 내용을 완벽히 이해하기 힘들다. 이때, 글의 전개 방식을 파악하면 더 수월하게 내용을 파악할 수 있다.

흐름과 관계 없는 문장 찾기 (35번)

불변의패턴 23 주제만 파악하면 정답이 보인다.

흐름과 관계 없는 문장을 찾기 위해서는 주제를 정확히 파악해야 한다. 주제문이 초반에 나오는 경우가 많으니 처음 한두 문장에서 주제를 파악하고 이와 관련 없는 문장을 고른다.

불변의패턴 24 핵심 소재만 같고 주제에서 살짝 벗어나는 문장이 정답이다.

흐름과 관계 없는 문장은 보통 글의 핵심 소재 또는 관련 소재에 대해 다루지만 주제에서 살짝 벗어나는 내용인 경우가 많다. 언뜻 보기에 자연스럽게 연결되어 있는 것처럼 보일 수 있으니 주의해야 한다.

글의 순서 배열하기 (36번~37번)

불변의패턴 25 대명사나 연결어를 찾으면 앞뒤 글의 순서가 보인다.

각 문단의 첫 문장에 나온 대명사나 연결어를 찾으면 그 앞에 올 내용을 추측할 수 있다. 글의 순서를 알려주는 아래의 표현을 참고한다.

- it, that/those, this/these 등의 대명사가 가리키는 내용이 어느 문단에 있는지 찾는다.
- but, however, while 등의 역접 연결어가 있는 문장과 반대되는 내용이 어느 문단에 있는지 찾는다.
- for example, also, so 등의 순접 연결어가 있는 문장과 비슷한 내용이 어느 문단에 있는지 찾는다.

★ 3점 문제로 출제될 경우 (A), (B), (C) 사이의 연결 고리가 되는 분명한 단서들이 없을 때가 있다. 이때는 오직 글의 흐름을 통해 순서를 파악해야 하므로, 주어진 글을 정확히 이해하는 것이 중요하다.

불변의패턴 26 주어진 글을 보고 뒤에 나올 글의 구조를 예측할 수 있다.

자주 출제되는 글의 구조를 알아두면, 주어진 글을 통해 글의 구조를 예측하여 글을 더 쉽고 빠르게 이해할 수 있다.

<주어진 글>	주제	문제점	통념
	↓	↓	↓
(A) (B) (C)	부연 설명/예시	해결 방안	반박 ↓ 결론

★ 3점 문제는 주어진 문장과 첫 번째 순서의 글이 연결성이 부족한 경우가 많으므로 (A), (B), (C) 간의 관계에 주목하자!
★ 주어진 문장과 이어지는 첫 번째 순서의 글을 찾은 후, 두 번째 순서의 글을 찾기 힘들 때는, 나머지 두 글의 관계를 파악해 순서를 찾는다.

주어진 문장의 위치 찾기 (38번~39번)

불변의패턴 27 주어진 문장에는 앞뒤 문장에 대한 결정적인 단서가 있다.

주어진 문장에 있는 대명사, 관사, 연결어는 그 문장 앞뒤로 어떤 내용이 오는지 알려주는 중요한 단서이다.

- 대명사와 관사가 있으면 그것이 가리키는 대상이 언급된 문장을 찾는다. 주어진 문장은 그 뒤에 와야 한다.
- 연결어가 있으면, 연결어의 뜻을 바탕으로 논리 관계가 자연스러운 문장을 찾는다.

★ 3점 문제는 주어진 문장에 지시어나 연결어 같은 단서가 없을 때가 많다. 이때는 주어진 문장에서 주제를 파악하고, 글에서 앞뒤 문장 사이의 논리가 부자연스러운 부분이 있는지에 더 중점을 두는 것이 좋다.

불변의패턴 28 뜬금없는 대명사나 지시어, 어색한 연결어가 있는 문장 앞이 정답이다.

글의 흐름상 어색한 부분을 찾는 것이 관건이다. 무엇을 가리키는지 명확하지 않은 대명사나 지시어가 나오는 문장, 연결어의 성격에 맞게 앞뒤 내용이 연결되지 않는 문장, 이전에 언급된 적 없는 명사에 정관사 the가 붙은 문장을 찾아 그 앞에 주어진 문장을 넣어 흐름이 자연스러운지 확인한다.

요약문 완성하기 (40번)

불변의패턴 29 요약문은 글의 핵심 내용을 간추린 요지이다.

요약문은 글의 핵심 내용을 한 문장으로 표현한 요지이다. 문제를 풀 때 먼저 요약문부터 읽고 글의 소재가 무엇인지 파악한 후 글을 읽으면 정답을 더 쉽고 빠르게 찾을 수 있다.

불변의패턴 30 핵심 단어를 다르게 표현한 단어가 정답이다.

요약문의 빈칸에는 글의 핵심 내용을 다른 말로 바꾸어 표현한 단어가 들어간다. 글에서 핵심이 되는 단어나 구절을 파악하여 그 유의어로 조합된 선택지를 고른다.

장문 독해 (41번~45번)

불변의패턴 31 장문 독해 1은 주로 학술적 내용의 설명문이 나온다.

다음 표와 같이 인문·사회, 과학·기술 등 학술적인 분야의 소재를 활용한 설명문이 주로 출제되는데, 이 종류의 글은 마지막에 주제문이 나오는 경우가 많다. 주제를 확실히 이해하면 적절한 제목을 파악하거나 문맥에 맞지 않는 어휘를 찾는 것이 훨씬 수월하다.

인문·사회 기출 소재	• 언어의 고유한 특성인 범주화 • 교육에서 'hands-on'에 의미를 부여하는 'minds-on'의 중요성 • 자본주의에서 여가의 탄생과 진화 • 사생활에 대한 권리의 적용과 제한 범위 • 물을 이용할 권리와 토지 소유권의 분리 • 정치적 도덕주의 정의 및 이상적 사회 실현에서 이 사상의 한계와 이점 • 인간의 적응 방식으로서의 문화
과학·기술 기출 소재	• 동물 행동의 복잡성을 만드는 요소 • 해양생물학 연구의 맹점 • 비타민C 효용성 실험을 통해서 본 실험 통제 방법 • 인간의 창의력과 컴퓨터의 창의력 • 밀폐된 용기 안에서 액체와 증기가 평형 상태를 이루는 현상 • 기회보다 위협에 더 크게 반응하도록 설계된 생물의 특성 • 인간이 다른 포유동물들보다 월등히 큰 뇌를 가지게 된 이유

불변의패턴 32 장문 독해 2는 일상의 에피소드를 다루는 일화가 나온다.

다양한 일상의 에피소드를 다루는 일화가 나오는데, 주로 상황과 등장 인물들을 소개한 뒤 사건이 전개되며 교훈적 결론을 맺는 구조로 이루어진다. 사건의 논리적 흐름을 이해하여 글의 순서를 먼저 파악하면 지칭 추론과 세부 정보 파악 문제를 더 쉽게 해결할 수 있다. 지칭 추론 문제는 선택지의 대명사가 가리키는 등장 인물의 이니셜을 표시하면서 푸는 것이 좋다.

영어 실력을 높여주는 다양한 학습 자료 제공

HackersBook.com

해커스 수능 독해 불변의 패턴
실전편

| 실전모의고사 |

문제풀이 전 확인사항
1. OMR 답안지와 필기도구를 준비했나요?
2. 시계를 준비하고 시작 시간을 기입했나요?
   ☑ 잠깐! 문제를 풀 때 찍은 문제는 따로 체크해 두세요.

매 회 문제를 풀기 전에, 위 사항을 점검하고 모의고사에 임하세요.

01회 실전모의고사

* [3점] 표시가 있는 문제 제외하고는 모두 2점으로 계산합니다.

18 다음 글의 목적으로 가장 적절한 것은?

Dear Valued Customers,

Here at Used Threads, we have always prided ourselves on offering guests a wide selection of second-hand items. By purchasing recycled clothes, customers not only gain unique pieces, but also help to save the environment. Now, we'd like to go a step further, which is why we are launching weekly classes about how to upcycle clothing. These classes will be free and will take place from 3 to 4 p.m. on Saturdays. During the sessions, we will teach customers how to transform their old clothes with techniques like sewing and dyeing. If you're interested in attending a class, please e-mail me at least a day beforehand as spots are limited. We hope to see you there!

Best Regards,
Ari Kim, Used Threads Manager

① 의류 산업이 환경에 해로운 이유를 설명하려고
② 환경 보호를 위한 의류 재활용을 장려하려고
③ 의류 업사이클링 수업 개설을 안내하려고
④ 중고 의류 매장의 영업 시간을 공지하려고
⑤ 업사이클링에 활용할 의류 기부를 요청하려고

19 다음 글에 드러난 Sarah의 심경으로 가장 적절한 것은?

Sarah quietly made her way through the house, her eyes trying to adjust to the darkness that surrounded her. Searching for an escape route or something she could use to defend herself, she could feel her heartbeat hammering in her chest. With every small sound, her muscles tensed up. Sweat poured down her back. Sarah thought she could finally see the front door, but gasped when she realized that a figure stood in front of it. Although his features weren't clear, Sarah knew who it was, and it made her tremble. The person didn't make a sound, but suddenly moved towards her. Screaming for help, Sarah turned to run and sprinted down the hallway. She knew there was little else she could do now.

① anxious and terrified
② annoyed and irritated
③ excited and enthusiastic
④ pleased and content
⑤ bored and lonely

20 다음 글에서 필자가 주장하는 바로 가장 적절한 것은?

When considering the current state of society, many individuals think that conditions are deteriorating and we are facing a crisis. But is this really true? People need to develop a more accurate perspective by relying solely on facts to form their opinions. Of course, it is a natural human instinct to focus on frightening events. This is why people usually remember news stories about serious crimes such as murders much more easily than other types of reports. But this internal filter can easily create the impression that violent acts are occurring with increasing frequency. The truth of the matter is that they are less common now than in the past; in fact, the murder rate in the United States has declined by almost 50 percent over the past 30 years. So, it is important to always ask, "Are my beliefs based on accurate information?"

① 위기가 닥쳤을 때 신속하게 상황을 파악하라.
② 믿음이 아닌 정확한 정보에 기반해서 판단하라.
③ 사회적 문제에 대한 자신만의 입장을 확립하라.
④ 철저한 검증을 통해 정보의 오류를 바로잡아라.
⑤ 외부의 판단보다 내면의 목소리에 귀를 기울여라.

21 밑줄 친 flip the lens가 다음 글에서 의미하는 바로 가장 적절한 것은? [3점]

In recent years, a number of anthropologists have decided to flip the lens. Throughout much of the history of this field, researchers from Western countries focused on the study of cultures that were beyond their own experiences. Being an "objective" outsider was thought to be the best way to draw accurate conclusions about the society being observed. Now, however, some researchers have begun to utilize anthropological techniques to increase their knowledge of the societies that they themselves are a part of. Noted anthropologist Gillian Tett decided to apply the practices of this discipline to better understand corporations — she used the framework of anthropology to immerse herself in the banking sector and came to the conclusion that "risks were building in this strange, shadowy world." Because of her willingness to view an aspect of her own culture with the same level of neutrality that anthropologists traditionally strive for when studying more "exotic" ones, Tett was one of the few people to accurately predict the 2008 financial crisis.

① adopting a variety of techniques when studying a culture
② seeking advice from experts outside their own profession
③ looking at the same subjects from a different perspective
④ analyzing information to develop more detailed predictions
⑤ placing themselves under the same close examination as others

22 다음 글의 요지로 가장 적절한 것은?

There is a common assumption that innovation in business is the result of extensive employee autonomy. Imagine a software company that hopes to create groundbreaking applications that will capture the imagination of consumers. To achieve this goal, it may decide to release several of its best developers from their current projects and allow them to explore different ideas without restraint. Contrary to expectation, granting this freedom will not necessarily stimulate their creativity or produce breakthrough ideas. The key to meaningful innovation is structure — employees need clearly defined goals, extensive support from management, and systems to measure progress. All of this is necessary to ensure that the ideas being generated are practical and fit into the company's business model, as well as to set up an infrastructure to effectively execute any concepts with the potential to develop into successful products.

① 분명한 목표 설정이 기업 성장의 필수 조건이다.
② 구성원의 자발적인 혁신이 기업 발전에 기여한다.
③ 기업 내 진정한 혁신은 체계적인 접근에서 나온다.
④ 기업의 지나친 통제는 구성원의 역량 발휘를 저해한다.
⑤ 자율성을 최대한 보장하는 기업 구조가 혁신을 촉진한다.

23 다음 글의 주제로 가장 적절한 것은?

Have you ever felt depressed but told a friend "Everything is great"? Chances are, the sound of your voice — and perhaps a sigh — gave you away and failed to convince your friend of the truthfulness of your statement. According to the results of research published in *American Psychologist*, up to 24 kinds of emotions are decipherable from the tone of our voice and our non-verbal exclamations, known as vocal bursts. They can reveal complex emotions ranging from surprise (gasp) and realization (ohhh) to interest (ah?) and confusion (huh?). In the study, more than 2,000 vocal bursts were recorded by actors around the world and then evaluated by people recruited online. All of the vocal bursts were then categorized as correlating with a recognizable emotion. This shows that, whether we are aware of our own vocal bursts or not, others pick up on them and can identify them, suggesting that our feelings are difficult to fake.

① an effective way to identify truthful statements
② the ability to conceal feelings during conversation
③ the role of vocal cues in distinguishing sentiments
④ benefits of non-verbal utterances over verbal ones
⑤ categories of vocalizations used to express emotions

24 다음 글의 제목으로 가장 적절한 것은?

NFTs, or non-fungible tokens, are digital tokens that are purchased and sold online and represent real-world objects such as photos, videos, and artwork. NFTs function as certificates of ownership for those items, and these tokens cannot be duplicated, meaning that such a certificate is not interchangeable and there can only be one owner at a time. Although many NFTs are costly, buying them is quickly gaining popularity as doing so gives a collector a unique and special connection to the work, with their purchase being marked on a blockchain. However, as there are currently no regulations governing the making and selling of NFTs, there are copyright threats associated with them. This is due to the fact that anyone — not just the copyright holder — can publish a token for a particular item on the blockchain and put that NFT on the market, a process also known as "minting." This means there is a possibility artists might see an NFT created for their work without their permission, which is comparable to using copyrighted material in your work without securing a license.

① How NFTs Are Revolutionizing the Online Marketplace
② Can Copyright Protection Exist on the Blockchain?
③ The Growing Popularity of Blockchain Technology
④ Legal Repercussions of Stealing Online Content
⑤ NFTs: New Concept, Same Old Threat

25 다음 표의 내용과 일치하지 <u>않는</u> 것은?

Environment-related Patents Granted in U.S.

Year of 2006		Year of 2016	
Segment	Patent (number)	Segment	Patent (number)
Transportation	2,590	Energy	3,390
Environmental Management	2,410	Environmental Management	2,690
Energy	2,280	Transportation	2,140
Production of Goods	1,110	Buildings	1,320
Buildings	1,090	Production of Goods	1,300
Waste	270	Waste	390
Greenhouse Gas	110	Greenhouse Gas	200
Total	9,930	Total	11,240

* Note: Details may not add to totals shown due to rounding.

The tables above show the number of environment-related patents in seven segments granted in the United States in 2006 and 2016. ① The total number of environment-related patents granted in 2016 was greater than the number awarded in 2006. ② The top two segments in terms of patents received in 2006 were Transportation and Environmental Management. ③ On the other hand, in 2016, the number of patents awarded to Energy was first among the seven segments. ④ Although the number of patents granted to Production of Goods increased from 2006 to 2016, its ranking remained the same. ⑤ In 2016, the combined number of patents received by the Waste and Greenhouse Gas segments was less than half of the number of patents received by the Production of Goods segment.

26 Berthe Morisot에 관한 다음 글의 내용과 일치하지 <u>않는</u> 것은?

Berthe Morisot was born in 1841 in Bourges, France, to a wealthy family. From an early age, her mother encouraged a serious education in art. Morisot likewise took her art career seriously and willingly pursued it. She developed her skills by copying masterpieces at the Louvre, and further progressed by studying under the famous painter Jean-Baptiste-Camille Corot. In 1868, she met Édouard Manet and the two cultivated a close working relationship. Alongside Manet and other Impressionist artists of the time, such as Edgar Degas, Claude Monet, and Pierre-Auguste Renoir, Morisot held regular exhibitions at the Paris Salon. She achieved widespread recognition for the themes of modernity she portrayed in her works. She continued to paint up until her death in 1895, when she died of pneumonia at the age of 54.

① 어린 시절부터 미술 교육을 받았다.
② Louvre 박물관에서 명작들을 모사하곤 했다.
③ Édouard Manet와 긴밀한 관계가 아니었다.
④ 다른 인상주의 화가들과 함께 전시를 열었다.
⑤ 1895년 사망 직전까지 꾸준히 그림을 그렸다.

27 Website Maker One-day Class에 관한 다음 안내문의 내용과 일치하지 <u>않는</u> 것은?

Website Maker One-day Class

Do you think making a website is hard? We'll show you how easy it is! This course teaches you how to build and design your very own website.

When: Monday, November 20, 8:00 a.m. to 5 p.m.
Where: Dallas Community College
Who: Dallas residents (Ages 18 and up)
Fee: $120 (does not include lunch)

Schedule:
• 8:00 a.m. – 10:00 a.m.: Basic coding
• 10:00 a.m. – 12:00 p.m.: Web design
• 12:00 p.m. – 1:30 p.m.: Lunch
• 1:30 p.m. – 5:00 p.m.: Web development

By the end of the class, you will have created your own website.

How to register: Visit www.websitemaker.org, or call 515-888-2121 by November 10.

For questions, email faq@websitemaker.org.

① 평일에 진행된다.
② Dallas 주민들을 대상으로 한다.
③ 참가비에 점심이 포함되어 있다.
④ 웹 디자인 수업은 오전 10시에 시작한다.
⑤ 등록 마감일은 11월 10일이다.

28 The Lake City Observatory Stargazing Night에 관한 다음 안내문의 내용과 일치하는 것은?

The Lake City Observatory Stargazing Night

The Lake City Observatory is hosting a stargazing night for community members, friends, and families. Come explore the night sky with us, and learn more about the stars.

Date: Saturday, October 15
Time: 6:30 p.m. – 9:30 p.m.
Location: The parking lot by The Lake City Observatory

What's included:
• Guided stargazing with astronomers
• Telescope viewings of the night sky and stars
• Free star charts

Admission: Free (but donations to The Lake City Observatory are appreciated.)

※ Food and drinks will not be provided, but guests are welcome to bring snacks and beverages themselves.

① 9월 15일에 3시간 동안 진행된다.
② Lake City Observatory 옥상에서 별을 관측한다.
③ 별자리표는 별도로 구매해야 한다.
④ 기부금을 받는다.
⑤ 간식과 음료가 제공된다.

29 다음 글의 밑줄 친 부분 중, 어법상 틀린 것은?

The Ptolemaic System, devised by Ptolemy in the second century AD, is a mathematical model in which an immobile Earth ① is situated at the center of the universe. Other celestial bodies, including the planets, Moon, Sun, and stars, ② revolving around Earth in this system. According to Ptolemy, the universe is composed of fixed, transparent spheres, and heavenly bodies are attached to these spheres ③ which have their own particular rotations. The celestial sphere, which is the largest, exists to hold the stars and marks the boundary of this universe. This concept of spheres ④ making up the universe with Earth at its center endured long after Ptolemy and wasn't overturned until around 1400 years later. It was then ⑤ that Copernicus proposed a heliocentric model of the universe, meaning that Earth and the other planets orbit the Sun.

* celestial: 천체의 ** heliocentric: 태양 중심의

30 다음 글의 밑줄 친 부분 중, 문맥상 낱말의 쓰임이 적절하지 않은 것은? [3점]

John Cage (1912–1992) was a composer known for defying tradition. He experimented with playing instruments in ① unconventional ways and piecing together tones and rhythms that did not follow established musical structures. He is best known for a controversial piece that, from a traditional perspective, can ② hardly be called "music." That piece is *4'33"*, so named because it lasts exactly four minutes and 33 seconds. For its ③ duration, neither instruments nor vocalists produce a single note. The idea for Cage was that, throughout the period of "silence," the audience would find that there was not silence at all; they would become aware of the ambient sounds around them that would typically be ④ perceived. Cage had toyed with the idea of the piece for years, but he became convinced of its value after spending time in an anechoic chamber, where the silence was so ⑤ overwhelming that he was able to hear his own blood circulation.

* anechoic: 반향이 없는

[31~34] 다음 빈칸에 들어갈 말로 가장 적절한 것을 고르시오.

31

"Only in relation to our imagination can things be called beautiful or ugly..." Baruch Spinoza points out the socially constructed nature of beauty and ugliness through his theories, as ideas and definitions related to these concepts have shifted so often over time. Artistically speaking, those words have both had moral and aesthetic implications; "ugly" has denoted the bad while "beautiful" has been applied to the good. But are these terms this simple? Why must "ugly" have a negative connotation? After all, ugly art can be interesting and unique. In fact, pieces that we deem ugly can make those who gaze upon them think, and can trigger a state of being _____ to new ideas: something a typically beautiful piece of art could have a more difficult time accomplishing. By using fine art techniques to make something look "ugly," an artist can encourage more critical discourse between people as they view the piece. They might question their previous assumptions about beauty and embrace new ideas, which is a key characteristic of compelling art anyway. [3점]

* denote: 의미하다

① receptive ② doubtful
③ critical ④ indifferent
⑤ resistant

32

That which is forgotten is not always lost. Research shows that memories _____. Take the brain activity of numerous university students who were observed during memory formation and recall. When students were asked to remember as much as they could about a list of words they'd been given earlier in the study, fMRI scans showed that the brain activity throughout recall was the same as in the course of the learning process. Even when students had forgotten most of what they had learned, the original neurological patterns were still picked up, illustrating that the memories were still there despite being unattainable. Much is still unclear regarding how long memories persist, but evidence like this has shown that it might be longer than we think. Therefore, it would not be wrong to say that memories are just archived in the less accessible parts of our brains.

* fMRI: 기능성 자기공명영상

① disappear after a certain amount of time
② form when we experience intense emotions
③ help form strong relationships between people
④ can affect the meaning we associate with words
⑤ remain stored even if we can't readily retrieve them

33

Assistive technologies allow disabled individuals to perform an array of tasks without the aid of another person, thereby increasing their level of independence. Although recent developments have improved the functionality of assistive technologies, the corresponding increase in complexity necessitates that sufficient training be offered to the people with disabilities who will use them. While some devices can be easily incorporated into a person's life with a minimum of instruction, others are more sophisticated and require a significant amount of knowledge to be utilized effectively. In fact, a number of studies have shown that people who avoid new assistive technologies report feeling intimidated by the complex interfaces and many optional features, which leads them to believe that they are unqualified to operate them. Fortunately, _____ have an increased likelihood of overcoming this barrier and integrating new assistive technologies into their day-to-day routine, greatly enhancing the overall quality of their life. [3점]

* assistive technology: 보조공학(補助工學)

① individuals who are asked to improve the underlying design
② individuals who are provided with access to ongoing support
③ individuals who have agreed to provide additional guidance
④ individuals who have tried to use several different versions
⑤ individuals who are experiencing less severe disabilities

34

In Adam Smith's 1759 work *The Theory of Moral Sentiments*, he posited that, although everyone is driven to a certain extent by self-interest and personal passions, _____. As members of society, we are keenly aware of what behaviors are considered objectionable to the majority and what are not based on the reactions we receive or witness. Because we have a natural ability to empathize and want others to see us as morally accountable, we are taught that we must do what is perceived as the right thing. To help us determine whether we are doing the right thing, Smith suggested that we each have a conscience that informs us of how our behavior will be interpreted. This "impartial spectator," as he called it, prevents us from being overly interested in our own affairs and causes us to do things that are worthy of society's praise rather than its reproach. [3점]

① societal norms frequently undergo change
② we are unable to understand how others feel
③ a guilty conscious makes us seek forgiveness
④ people innately know how they should behave
⑤ we act in accordance with others' expectations

35 다음 글에서 전체 흐름과 관계 <u>없는</u> 문장은?

In a study on hidden anger, researchers observed that certain unintended behaviors often come forward. One group of them consists of repetitive physical acts, such as facial tics and spasmodic foot movements. ① They may also include uncontrollable behaviors such as poor sleeping habits, jaw clenching, and teeth grinding, which others may notice but not associate with anger. ② Other behaviors are deliberate but not directly linked to anger, and these may be expressed as procrastination, habitual lateness, excessive politeness, or inappropriate sarcasm and flippancy in conversation. ③ A clear distinguishing line can be drawn between behavior and personality, with one side of the line representing what we do and the other how we think or feel and why. ④ Whatever the case, these behaviors are often attributed to harmless personality flaws or eccentricities. ⑤ Few if any people ever associate them with deeper issues that might have been provoked by anger.

* spasmodic: 경련성의　** flippancy: 경솔한 언행

[36~37] 주어진 글 다음에 이어질 글의 순서로 가장 적절한 것을 고르시오.

36

In his 1935 essay "The Work of Art in the Age of Mechanical Reproduction," Walter Benjamin contended that the aura of original art had disappeared in the modern age as a result of new forms of replicable media technology.

(A) The destruction of the vital force that gives art its individuality — its spirit — altered the effect of art on viewers. Before the age of mechanical reproduction, viewing an image or an object required one to be in the presence of the original piece, allowing for a more personal experience.

(B) For Benjamin, art possessed an aura that was derived from its physical uniqueness. Making a copy, as one might do with a photograph or a film, he argued, removed the artwork from its original context, destroying its authenticity.

(C) By producing copies and making it possible for many people to see the work simultaneously, however, a viewer could no longer be fully absorbed in it because the individual connection was eliminated. Instead, the viewers, "the distracted mass," collectively absorbed the art. [3점]

① (A) – (C) – (B) ② (B) – (A) – (C)
③ (B) – (C) – (A) ④ (C) – (A) – (B)
⑤ (C) – (B) – (A)

37

The scientific method is based on the principle of methodological naturalism.

(A) The philosophy behind this strategy is that natural things in the physical world can be tested and experimented on, whereas theories about other potential causes for events cannot. Essentially, methodological naturalism embraces the skepticism of the phrase "seeing is believing."

(B) In other words, it does not allow for belief or emotion to be considered. This requirement has formed an essential part of the scientific method since the Enlightenment, when logic and reason began to replace old worldviews.

(C) Proponents of this approach to providing explanations about the universe assert that truths can only be realized by studying natural events and phenomena. In particular, they prefer that the objects of scientific research be tangible so that it is absolutely clear that they are real and not imagined.

① (A) – (C) – (B) ② (B) – (A) – (C)
③ (B) – (C) – (A) ④ (C) – (A) – (B)
⑤ (C) – (B) – (A)

[38~39] 글의 흐름으로 보아, 주어진 문장이 들어가기에 가장 적절한 곳을 고르시오.

38

Still, a relatively new technological trend could be bringing millennials back to television, but via other media.

According to statistics, millennials watch far less television than older generations. The average American over 65 watches almost four and a half hours of television a day; the average millennial, meanwhile, watches just two. (①) Furthermore, the amount of television millennials watch has declined in the last two decades, while older generations are watching more. (②) Several factors may explain this disparity, the most prominent of which is the Internet. (③) While older generations still rely on television for most of their entertainment and news, millennials prefer to consume both online. (④) A recent study has shown that 9 percent more millennials stream online videos than watch television, a trend that shows no signs of slowing. (⑤) As a form of television watching, streaming differs considerably from the analogue viewing style of older generations, but it nonetheless reveals that this younger generation hasn't entirely abandoned the medium.

39

> Regardless of which of these types of cones are deficient, the end result for the affected individual is the same.

In 1794, the English chemist and physicist John Dalton published an academic article that included the first description of colorblindness. (①) In it, he provided a summary of his research regarding red-green colorblindness, which is now known to be caused by a problem with the light-sensitive cells called cones that are found in the retina of the human eye. (②) Typically, a person has three sets of fully functional cones — each responds to different light wavelengths, enabling the eye to perceive the three primary colors. (③) However, in some cases, the cells that detect either red or green are less sensitive than normal or are missing altogether. (④) It becomes difficult or even impossible to distinguish between these two colors. (⑤) This form of colorblindness is usually genetic, but it can also result from physical damage to the eye or even old age. [3점]

40 다음 글의 내용을 한 문장으로 요약하고자 한다. 빈칸 (A), (B)에 들어갈 말로 가장 적절한 것은?

In search of a new, more effective strategy to reduce bullying at schools, Princeton University psychologist Betsy Levy Paluck and her research team turned to students themselves or, more specifically, students who were identified by their classmates as trendsetters, team leaders, and peer role models — known in scientific terms as "social referents." According to social psychology theory, individuals learn what is desirable by observing other people's behavior and seeing what is rewarded or punished. Social referents, Paluck said, might play a significant role in shaping what is considered acceptable behavior. With that in mind, Paluck and her team worked with schools across New Jersey in the 2012–2013 school year and staged bullying intervention programs at half of them. In these intervention programs, student social referents — students with the most connections to other students — were coached to spread anti-conflict messages. At the end of the year, it was found that schools where the intervention programs had taken place reported less violence and more diplomacy among students, demonstrating how powerful peer modeling can be.

↓

Social referents serve as an ___(A)___ for how others in a group should behave, so in a school setting they can be a key factor in preventing ___(B)___ .

	(A)		(B)
①	alternative	······	confusion
②	incentive	······	violence
③	example	······	conflict
④	alternative	······	abuse
⑤	example	······	change

[41~42] 다음 글을 읽고, 물음에 답하시오.

Gaslighting, which involves manipulating a person so that they (a) question their own reality or perceptions, is often thought of in terms of personal relationships. In this case, a single person is the victim, and according to psychologists, it can be extremely dangerous and toxic for them. What is more unsettling is that a manipulator's gaslighting can affect not only a single person but also an entire group of people.

Farah Latif, a communications expert at George Washington University, explains how some politicians utilize gaslighting to "destabilize and disorient public opinion on political issues." Their techniques — inventing false narratives, attempting to discredit their opposition, and continually (b) denying proven facts — are all utilized to "garner support" for their aims and objectives. A politician who gaslights voters might try to (c) emphasize their own mistakes or even blame them on another politician. They spread misinformation and especially target the media and researchers, attempting to portray them as unreliable sources of information. The repercussions of these actions include public distrust, twisted perceptions of reality, and the (d) inability of voters to rationally consider important issues. Gaslighting, therefore, has the very real and terrifying ability to (e) contaminate the normal functioning of politics itself.

* garner: 얻다

41 윗글의 제목으로 가장 적절한 것은?

① How Gaslighting Makes You Doubt Your Political Stance
② Recognize the Signs You Are Being Gaslighted!
③ Do Politicians Intentionally Use Gaslighting?
④ Political Gaslighting: Distorting Election Results
⑤ Gaslighting as a Political Technique to Mislead the Public

42 밑줄 친 (a)~(e) 중에서 문맥상 낱말의 쓰임이 적절하지 않은 것은?

① (a)　　② (b)　　③ (c)　　④ (d)　　⑤ (e)

[43~45] 다음 글을 읽고, 물음에 답하시오.

(A)

There had been a long drought, so a hardworking farmer was looking for a water source for (a) his crops. His neighbor heard about this and saw an opportunity to make some money. "I have a large well on my property," the neighbor said. "I am willing to sell it to you." The farmer happily agreed and paid (b) him a good price. The following day, the farmer went to draw some water. But before he could do so, the neighbor suddenly stopped him.

(B)

The two continued to argue until they finally decided to take the problem to the town's judge. "Sir, he won't let me take any water out from the well that I bought," complained the farmer. The judge asked the neighbor why he wouldn't allow it. "As I told the farmer, I sold my well, not my water, to (c) him, your honor. Therefore, the water is still mine. I did nothing wrong," the neighbor replied.

(C)

After hearing this, the judge thought for a moment. "You're right," he finally said to the neighbor. "You only sold the well." The neighbor felt triumphant because he had succeeded in his trick. But the judge was not finished speaking. "The well is the farmer's and the water is yours. Since you are using the farmer's well to store your water, you must now pay (d) him rent for using that space."

(D)

"What's wrong?" asked the farmer. "Why won't you let me get the water?" The neighbor insisted, "I sold you the well, not the water inside. If (e) you want the water, you must pay me extra for it." Shocked, the farmer replied that this was unfair, but the neighbor would not change his mind.

43 주어진 글 (A)에 이어질 내용을 순서에 맞게 배열한 것으로 가장 적절한 것은?

① (B) – (D) – (C)　　② (C) – (B) – (D)
③ (C) – (D) – (B)　　④ (D) – (B) – (C)
⑤ (D) – (C) – (B)

44 밑줄 친 (a)~(e) 중에서 가리키는 대상이 나머지 넷과 다른 것은?

① (a)　② (b)　③ (c)　④ (d)　⑤ (e)

45 윗글에 관한 내용으로 적절하지 <u>않은</u> 것은?

① 이웃은 농부에게 우물을 팔았다.
② 농부와 이웃은 말다툼 끝에 판사를 찾아갔다.
③ 이웃은 자신에게 잘못이 없다고 말했다.
④ 판사는 농부에게 돈을 더 내라고 말했다.
⑤ 이웃은 농부가 물을 길어가지 못하게 했다.

정답·해설·해석 p. 2

문제풀이 후 확인사항
1. 45분 내에 문제를 풀었다.
2. 체크해둔 문제와 틀린 문제는 해설을 꼼꼼히 확인했다.

수고하셨습니다! HackersBook.com에서 제공하는 어휘리스트로 어휘를 암기하세요.

02회 실전모의고사

목표 시간: 45분 | 시작: ___ 시 ___ 분 ~ 종료: ___ 시 ___ 분 | 점수: ___점 / 63점

* [3점] 표시가 있는 문제 제외하고는 모두 2점으로 계산합니다.

18 다음 글의 목적으로 가장 적절한 것은?

Dear Staff Members,

I am so excited to meet all of you at the upcoming Wild Birch Music Festival. Since the event is next week, I thought I would send you some guidelines about working during the festival. We want to make sure that everyone is prepared and that we can give audience members a great weekend. To accomplish this, staff members are expected to address every complaint and question that event attendees present to them. Please practice patience and positivity when talking to participants, and if you aren't able to answer an inquiry, locate and notify a manager to handle the situation. We know that everyone will do their best to make the event a success. If you have any questions, please contact me.

Sincerely,
Rachel Park
Festival Coordinator

① 행사 진행을 위한 안전 교육 이수를 독려하려고
② 단체 관람 예약이 확정되었음을 알리려고
③ 음악 축제의 변경된 일정을 공지하려고
④ 지역 행사의 진행 요원을 모집하려고
⑤ 행사 진행에 관한 지침을 전달하려고

19 다음 글에 나타난 'I'의 심경 변화로 가장 적절한 것은?

It was the big day of the presentation, and I was running late. I tapped my foot as I waited for my bus, which was taking longer than usual to arrive. I knew my boss would get angry if I arrived in the middle of the meeting. Checking my watch again, I groaned and rolled my eyes. I didn't know what other options I had, so I was about to text my boss. "Chloe!" I heard someone shout, so I looked up. "Do you need a ride?" It was my coworker Rachel! I nodded enthusiastically and jumped into her car. "Rachel, you saved my life!" With a lift to work, I would definitely make it to the meeting on time. I could finally relax.

① anxious → relieved
② concerned → regretful
③ hopeful → discouraged
④ angry → flattered
⑤ annoyed → jealous

20 다음 글에서 필자가 주장하는 바로 가장 적절한 것은?

When parents tell children "don't be shy" or "don't be lazy," the intention is to make their children behave better. However, parents should know that those words actually function as labels that reinforce the negative traits they describe. When parents and educators consistently use certain words to refer to kids, the children come to believe that those words define them. The children unconsciously adopt these characteristics as part of their identity and begin to behave in ways that fit the label they have been given. Furthermore, when children behave in ways that do not match the tags their parents have attached to them, they may have difficulty responding to praise or other unexpected positive reinforcement and revert to their old behavior. This makes it difficult for the children to lose the negative traits that their parents are trying to discourage. That's why it's vital for parents to be aware of the words they use when describing their children.

① 아이들에게 다양한 사람들을 만날 기회를 주어야 한다.
② 아이들을 칭찬하는 긍정적인 표현법을 익혀야 한다.
③ 아이들이 좋은 행동을 모방하도록 격려해야 한다.
④ 아이들을 부정적인 표현에 가두는 것을 경계해야 한다.
⑤ 아이들에게 다른 사람의 말을 경청하는 태도를 가르쳐야 한다.

21 밑줄 친 even when you win, you lose가 다음 글에서 의미하는 바로 가장 적절한 것은? [3점]

In business negotiations, one party often tries to defeat the other. If you do this, however, you might find that <u>even when you win, you lose</u>. The other person will likely feel resentful and might be unwilling to do business with you in the future. This is why many experts advocate a "win-win" mindset when negotiating. It involves a conscious effort to ensure that everyone gets the maximum benefit from whatever agreement is reached. An important element of this approach is a focus on an objective standard that can be used to measure the value that each party receives. In some cases, this will require finding a neutral arbitrator to make the final determination of whether an agreement is fair. It is also often necessary to grant significant concessions so that the other person is able to meet his or her goals. This negotiating strategy is much more likely to result in lasting partnerships rather than one-off deals.

* arbitrator: 중재자

① Knowledge of various strategies is necessary to get the best deal.
② Focusing only on immediate gains may affect long-term relationships.
③ Extended business partnerships often include unforeseen difficulties.
④ Agreements that appear fair could benefit one party over the other.
⑤ Avoiding defeat should be the main goal when involved in negotiations.

22 다음 글의 요지로 가장 적절한 것은?

A lot of anxiety and depression among the youth comes from the ever-growing pressure to succeed. In a national survey, nearly 80% of youths stated that personal achievement was more important to them than caring for others. While much of human history has progressed thanks to the drive for success, in modern times, success has turned into an obsession. Before, prosperity was balanced with other facets of life — health, empathy, family, and friends. Now, the obsession with achievement has led young adults to strive for their own success no matter the cost. It is a drive that pushes them forward to the detriment of other aspects of themselves. Although their drive to achieve is not necessarily a bad thing, problems arise when the youth pursue success solely for individual purposes. This ultimately comes at a cost to their mental health, their character, and morality.

① 모든 사회적 성공에는 어느 정도 물질적 대가가 따른다.
② 목표에 정진하려면 주변 사람들의 적극적인 협조가 필요하다.
③ 성공에 대한 과거의 잣대가 오늘날 청년들의 발전을 가로막는다.
④ 청년들의 정서적 불안은 개인이 아닌 공동체의 문제가 되고 있다.
⑤ 개인적 성공에 대한 강박이 청년들에게 부정적 영향을 미치고 있다.

23 다음 글의 주제로 가장 적절한 것은?

Introduced by Soviet economist Nikolai Kondratiev in his 1925 book *The Major Economic Cycles*, Kondratiev waves are hypothetical cycles in world economies. Kondratiev believed that each wave — representing long-lasting periods of economic rises, plateaus, and falls — resulted from technological innovations and periods of change. While Kondratiev waves are a subject of interest for some investors and a fascinating academic discussion topic, most economists do not accept they are even real, mostly due to the imprecise nature of the theory. There is no formal agreement on the cause of the waves, the standards for identifying the start and end years of a wave cycle, or even any consensus about where an economy is on a wave at any time due to the relatively long duration of each one — between 40 and 60 years. Generally, many suggest Kondratiev's theory was based on recognizing patterns that may not even exist.

* plateau: 안정기

① means of identifying the beginning of a new economic wave
② benefits of technological innovation on economies worldwide
③ importance of predicting the timing of market ups and downs
④ doubts over the existence of identifiable cycles in world economies
⑤ reasons Kondratiev wave theory may be useful for modern investors

24 다음 글의 제목으로 가장 적절한 것은?

Chances are you've had a song get stuck in your head. Words you did not mean to memorize come to mind without any effort, even though you may struggle to retain other information. This is because music is a mnemonic device; a tool that assists with remembering things. Songs often consist of rhymes and rhythm, which neatly organize information into patterns that are simple for the brain to recollect. Yet, because humans process and store a multitude of memories in the hippocampus and frontal cortex, which take in a significant amount of data each minute, remembering specific information is not always so straightforward. Even so, music includes an abundance of cues (hidden in the lyrics and images they evoke) that aid in bringing certain pieces of information to mind. This means that setting a tune to any piece of information you need to remember will improve your ability to recall it.

* hippocampus: (대뇌 측두엽의) 해마　** frontal cortex: 전두엽

① Why Does Music Produce Mental Images?
② Visual Cues: The Key to Remembering Lyrics
③ How Music Contributes to Retrieving Memories
④ Rhyme and Rhythm: Complex Patterns of Data
⑤ Several Effective Tools to Improve Memorization

25 다음 도표의 내용과 일치하지 <u>않는</u> 것은?

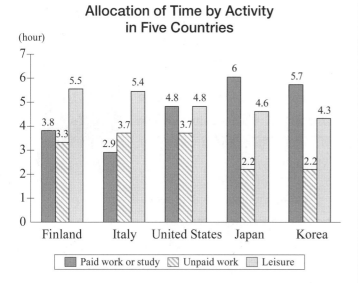

Allocation of Time by Activity in Five Countries

The above graph shows how much time people spend in paid work or study, unpaid work, and leisure in a day. ① Among the five countries, Finland and Italy rank first and second respectively in the amount of time spent on leisure activities. ② In the United States, time spent on paid work or study is 4.8 hours, which is over one hour longer than the time spent on unpaid work in the country. ③ Time spent on paid work or study in Japan is more than twice as long as that in Italy. ④ In the case of Korea, the amount of time allocated for unpaid work is less than half of that devoted to leisure. ⑤ The time spent on unpaid work is the least of the three time-allocation categories in all the countries except Italy.

26 Emmanuel Levinas에 관한 다음 글의 내용과 일치하지 <u>않는</u> 것은?

Emmanuel Levinas was one of the most renowned philosophical thinkers of the 20th century. He was born in Kaunas, Lithuania in 1906 and was raised by a traditional Jewish family. At the age of 18, Levinas left to study at the University of Strasbourg in France where he majored in philosophy. He then went on to attend the University of Freiburg in Germany, where he learned from famed philosophers Edmund Husserl and Martin Heidegger. Eventually, Levinas became an instructor himself, but the Second World War soon began. He was held prisoner for five years in a labor camp and suffered the loss of his family at the hands of the Nazis. Even after the traumatic experience, Levinas returned to teaching and produced some of his most famous pieces. In his work, he commented on the ideas of Husserl and Heidegger and highlighted the importance of ethics, drawing attention to the "face of the Other" and human consciousness.

① 리투아니아의 유대인 집안에서 자랐다.
② Strasbourg 대학에서 철학을 전공했다.
③ Edmund Husserl과 Martin Heidegger의 가르침을 받았다.
④ 전쟁을 겪은 후에 가르치는 일을 그만두었다.
⑤ 윤리학의 중요성을 강조했다.

27 Norwalk City's 2022 Plant a Tree Event에 관한 다음 안내문의 내용과 일치하지 <u>않는</u> 것은?

Norwalk City's 2022 Plant a Tree Event

Norwalk Community Center is hosting the annual Plant a Tree Event on September 26. Come join us with family and friends!

- Participants should gather at the plaza in front of City Hall by 10:00 a.m.
- Trees will be handed out for free.
※ The supply is limited, so it will be first come, first served.
- Participation is free for everyone.

After the planting, refreshments will be provided to all who participated. Children 12 and under will be given a tree-shaped pin in honor of the event.

For more information, visit the Norwalk Community Center website (www.norwalkcc.org) or call 222-3478.

① 매년 개최되는 행사이다.
② 나무는 선착순으로 배분될 것이다.
③ 나무 심기가 끝난 후 간식이 제공될 것이다.
④ 12세 이하 어린이들은 나무 모양 핀을 받을 것이다.
⑤ 관련 문의는 전화로만 할 수 있다.

28 5th Fairfield High School Drama Club Auditions에 관한 다음 안내문의 내용과 일치하는 것은?

5th Fairfield High School Drama Club Auditions

Always dreamed of being on the stage? Then, come to The Drama Club, and make your dream a reality.

• **When:** Monday, September 27 from 5–7 p.m.
• **Where:** Fairfield Auditorium
• **Who:** Any Fairfield High School student
• **What to bring:** a permission form (signed by a guardian)

During the auditions, we will:

1. Participate in icebreakers and warm-up activities
2. Study scripts in small groups
3. Have individual auditions in front of senior club members

The results will be posted outside of room 202 on Friday, October 1.

① 3시간 넘게 진행될 예정이다.
② 학생회관에서 열린다.
③ 담임 선생님의 동의서를 지참해야 한다.
④ 오디션에 소그룹으로 하는 활동이 포함된다.
⑤ 오디션 결과는 202호 내부에 게시될 것이다.

29 다음 글의 밑줄 친 부분 중, 어법상 틀린 것은? [3점]

With the average adult ① spent 11 hours a day using smartphones or computers, playing video games, or watching TV, it is unsurprising that some experts believe the overuse of technology and devices is becoming a problem. Many people agree, saying that technology makes their lives more stressful, prevents them from sleeping, and ② ruins their mental health. That's why some individuals are trying what is being referred to as a "digital detox." This is a period ③ in which they refrain from using electronic devices — whether that means giving up all digital devices for a while or simply avoiding any app or program that takes up too much of their time — in favor of socializing with family and friends. Although the idea of a digital detox might sound impossible or uncomfortable, ④ disconnecting from your devices can have a positive effect. Not only can it ⑤ reverse the issues caused by excessive technology use but it can also help you be more mindful and engaged during real-life experiences.

30 다음 글의 밑줄 친 부분 중, 문맥상 낱말의 쓰임이 적절 하지 않은 것은?

Although, in a broader sense, courage is the ability to take action in the face of risk, there are many different types of courage. Moral courage is a type of courage that calls for ① careful and deliberate thought. The morally courageous tend to have a strong sense of what is right and wrong and want to effect ② positive change in the world. Yet they also understand that there may be negative consequences for their actions, and may experience pressure to ③ acknowledge a problem despite its incidence. For example, an ethical concern may arise in the workplace, and organizational constraints may prevent the majority of people from ④ criticizing it, although they recognize it as wrong. However, a morally courageous person, fully ⑤ aware that they could lose their job or face other consequences, would reason that it is immoral to become complicit and instead choose to say something.

[31~34] 다음 빈칸에 들어갈 말로 가장 적절한 것을 고르시오.

31

Nearly all mammals — excluding sloths and manatees — have seven cervical vertebrae. The number of lumbar and thoracic vertebrae, however, varies more from mammal to mammal. Despite the giraffe's enormously long neck, scientists have always believed that giraffes were similar to most other mammals and that they have seven cervical vertebrae. But research conducted by the University of Tokyo has shown that assumptions related to the unique neck of the giraffe might be wrong; in fact, they discovered that the giraffe's first thoracic vertebra actually functions like a cervical vertebra. This provides the giraffe's neck with more _____, which allows them to reach food in higher places and water in lower ones. The high mobility of the giraffe's first thoracic vertebra, which is comparable to that of a cervical vertebra, indicates that this bone therefore acts as part of the neck rather than the body.

* cervical vertebrae: 경추(頸椎) ** lumbar: 요추의
*** thoracic vertebrae: 흉추(胸椎)

① pressure
② resistance
③ durability
④ disability
⑤ flexibility

32

There seems to be no limit to the things in life that can break our hearts, so we cope by learning to make light of painful situations. But in 1991, doctors discovered that hearts can literally "break" from pain. Heart attacks are fearsome because people die from them, so when people with a broken heart feel chest pain and it worsens by the minute, they wonder if they're having a heart attack. The cardiologist makes an examination and recognizes the electrocardiographic changes that indicate a problem but is usually stumped because the symptoms are only _____. Compared to diseases that happen in people with blocked arteries, the arteries of a person with a broken heart appear normal, and there are no other signs common to heart disease. But that shows how powerful emotions can be when something life-changing occurs, such as the death of a loved one. It's like one's heart is stunned and momentarily doesn't work as it should.

① characteristic of terminal patients
② measurable with advanced equipment
③ mimicking the conditions of heart failure
④ addressable with prolonged treatment
⑤ indicative of something milder

33

The importance of architectural lighting cannot be overstated as it does far more than just help us see well enough to navigate a space. Light is powerful because, in its absence, it creates shadows, which can _____. Just as the size and shape of a human shadow outside varies throughout the day, depending on the position of the sun, the proportions of architectural features like columns or latticework can be influenced by the light source in a room. Positioning a light low to the ground to cast a long shadow, for instance, can evoke a sense of awe and mystery, while a space with large windows that allows natural sunlight to pour through can give one a sense of calm and well-being. Essentially, light has the power to give substance to architecture in the form of shadows while shaping the atmosphere of a space. [3점]

* latticework: 격자

① draw people's attention to a specific point in the room
② minimize the appearance of flaws in a building's design
③ have an emotional impact on the occupant of the space
④ add a sense of depth and texture to an otherwise plain room
⑤ create a cooling effect and make the building more energy efficient

34

The development of modern sociology was heavily influenced by the eminent French intellectual Émile Durkheim and the positivist train of thought that he subscribed to. Positivism, which emerged in the mid-to-late 19th century, was founded on the belief that the social sciences should be treated with the same objective rigor and emphasis on empiricism and causality as the natural sciences. To this end, Durkheim stated, "Our main goal is to extend scientific rationalism to human conduct." In response to this approach, _____ around the turn of the 20th century. Many social scientists openly embraced the idea that sociological investigations must understand cultural behaviors, values, and symbols from very specific — often culturally rooted — perspectives. This approach was adopted by a number of major intellectuals, including the German sociologist and historian Max Weber. Among other things, Weber argued that while the natural sciences may be able to achieve generalizable observations, social sciences would always function as a subjective form of inquiry. [3점]

* positivism: 실증주의

① the role of sociologists changed dramatically
② quantitative research techniques were developed
③ natural science was divided into several categories
④ an antipositivist methodology gradually emerged
⑤ the social sciences became more of a priority

35 다음 글에서 전체 흐름과 관계 없는 문장은?

The task of a project manager is to ensure that a project is completed successfully: the operational budget is maintained, schedules are kept, and the client and all the stakeholders are satisfied. ① To reach this goal, it is vital to reduce potential risks — any events or factors that can threaten the project's success. ② However, since not all risks pose an equal threat and a certain amount of risk is unavoidable in any project, organizations must manage risk by ranking potential threats in order of severity. ③ Sometimes, reducing a risk comes at a cost and can even exceed the cost of the risk itself, in which case, it makes more sense to simply accept the risk. ④ This process, called 'risk prioritization,' involves using metrics to separate mission-critical risks from less impactful ones, which is done by questioning whether taking a risk is worth the reward. ⑤ To determine whether it is, factors that must be considered include the probability of the risk occurring and the likely impact, with the logic being that risks with low probability and positive outcomes are the most desirable to take.

[36~37] 주어진 글 다음에 이어질 글의 순서로 가장 적절한 것을 고르시오.

36

Although science fiction may seem like just a fun way to escape at first glance, the popularity of this genre may be based in something more profound.

(A) But despite their differences from us, they frequently face situations that we can relate to, allowing us to see the problems in our own society. Essentially, by framing modern issues in an exciting context that seems like it has nothing to do with us, we are able to process them more easily.

(B) At the same time, it provides a sense of distance. Since characters in science fiction stories are from a different time or place, they initially seem far removed from us to the extent that we don't view them through the same lens as we might view someone from our own society.

(C) Some suggest that its appeal lies in the fact that it is incredibly relevant to us. That's because it serves as a means of tackling serious issues that affect our society today.

① (A) – (C) – (B) ② (B) – (A) – (C)
③ (B) – (C) – (A) ④ (C) – (A) – (B)
⑤ (C) – (B) – (A)

37

A milestone in artificial intelligence was set when Google's AlphaGo program beat top-ranked player Lee Sedol at the game of Go. Now, building on that achievement, four of the world's best poker players have been defeated by the Libratus program.

(A) However, Libratus's human-like behaviors were based completely on calculations. Through trial and error, Libratus' algorithms had determined that bluffing was an effective strategy and began to incorporate it into its own plays. It was also aware that its opponents could bluff, too, which indicated that it could understand a type of uncertainty that hadn't been expected to be comprehended by programs before.

(B) Designed by researchers at Carnegie Mellon University, Libratus was simply given the rules of a two-player version of the game known as Texas Hold'em. It was then left to play countless versions of the game until it became better at learning and decision-making.

(C) The level of expertise it achieved through this process was astonishing. The fact that poker requires the ability to understand the thought processes of one's opponents and to know whether they are bluffing seemed to suggest that Libratus had gained the power to think intuitively. [3점]

* game of Go: 바둑　** bluff: (포커에서 패가 센 것처럼 꾸며) 속이다

① (A) – (C) – (B)　② (B) – (A) – (C)
③ (B) – (C) – (A)　④ (C) – (A) – (B)
⑤ (C) – (B) – (A)

[38~39] 글의 흐름으로 보아, 주어진 문장이 들어가기에 가장 적절한 곳을 고르시오.

38

There are also around 750 identified chemicals used in the process, 29 of which are known carcinogens and many of which end up in nearby groundwater supplies, threatening the health of local residents.

Fracking is a high-pressure water drilling technique used to extract oil and natural gas from shale rock deep underground. (①) The technique is highly controversial and has inspired activists and scientists to rally against it, highlighting environmental and health concerns. (②) They point out that, for one, the process causes toxic pollutants such as methane to be released into the air. (③) But despite threats like these which impact communities, proponents believe that fracking has positive and practical uses that make up for its potential to cause harm. (④) For example, fracking allows for electricity generation at half of the carbon dioxide-emission levels of coal. (⑤) Additionally, it results in lower energy prices and greater energy security.

* carcinogen: 발암 물질　** fracking: 수압 파쇄법

39

Another difference lies in the tendency of dictators to preside over mass media, propaganda, and rallies so that they can create an idealized image of themselves.

The distinctions between an autocracy and dictatorship are generally disregarded given their subtle nature. (①) Although both forms of government are characterized by an excessive centralization of power, the two systems do differ in several ways. (②) While an autocracy is controlled by a single person, a dictatorship can have either one leader or a group of leaders in power. (③) The term dictatorship also carries extremely negative implications because dictators themselves have historically been connected to crimes against their own people. (④) Autocracies, in contrast, have been viewed favorably in the past because they've been associated with high productivity. (⑤) They attempt this in order to deceive their audiences on a large scale and encourage their people's praise and devotion. [3점]

* autocracy: 전제 정치

40 다음 글의 내용을 한 문장으로 요약하고자 한다. 빈칸 (A), (B)에 들어갈 말로 가장 적절한 것은?

Cultural pluralism has, in recent years, been decried for its potential to undermine social cohesion, rather than reinforce it, and its supposedly adverse effect on the uniqueness of a dominant culture. Critics suggest that instead of promoting a model of inclusivity when it comes to immigration, governments should focus on assimilation, whereby new arrivals are forced to adjust to the dominant culture, shedding most, if not all, of their cultural characteristics along the way. But at the same time, supporters of this view ignore the essentially hybrid nature of every culture on earth, none of which emerged in a vacuum. Each culture was shaped by a centuries-long influx of cultural practices, linguistic structures, and, indeed, immigrants. Cultural pluralism is merely the continuation of this trend, and its complex form of social relation is an extension of prior practices. Culture has always been fostered by diversity, and adopting an exclusive approach to certain traditions and practices is effectively contradicting the very nature of culture.

* decry: 비난하다

↓

While it has been claimed that cultural pluralism can damage a society's _____(A)_____ culture, it has also been noted that the blending of various customs has _____(B)_____ every culture today.

	(A)		(B)
①	total	·····	threatened
②	primary	·····	influenced
③	previous	·····	imitated
④	essential	·····	followed
⑤	expired	·····	determined

[41~42] 다음 글을 읽고, 물음에 답하시오.

Conceived in the aftermath of World War I, and influenced by the Dada art of the previous decade, Surrealism was a cultural movement officially established in 1924 by French poet André Breton. It began as a new form of (a) literary expression heavily inspired by the writings and dream interpretation of father of psychoanalysis Sigmund Freud, and its objective was to give a voice to the private world of the subconscious mind, which was thought to have been repressed by societal conventions and logic. Since Surrealism was originally intended as a means of (b) spontaneous expression, some did not initially believe that it would lend itself well to the slow and labor-intensive processes of painting or sculpting. However, surrealist visual artists are arguably more remembered today than poets involved in the movement due to the dreamlike, sometimes bizarre imagery they created — the artistic depictions of their mind's deepest thoughts.

A leading figure of the movement was Belgian artist René Magritte, whose paintings frequently depicted everyday objects. *The Treachery of Images*, one of his most iconic works, shows a realistic-looking pipe, perhaps (c) similar to one that might be found in an advertisement, with the caption: "This is not a pipe." While a viewer might at first find such a statement curious, they would have to eventually (d) deny that "the pipe" is in fact simply a painting, a combination of colors on canvas, rather than a physical object one could fill with tobacco. Through works like this, Magritte emphasized the paradox of representing objects through art and led viewers to question their preconditioned ideas of (e) reality.

41 윗글의 제목으로 가장 적절한 것은?

① Surrealism and the Dream Imagery of Freud
② Defying Logic: Magritte and an Surrealist Art
③ Tapping into the Subconscious Mind with Psychoanalysis
④ René Magritte: Creating *The Treachery of Images*
⑤ Are Realistic Artistic Depictions Paradoxical?

42 밑줄 친 (a)~(e) 중에서 문맥상 낱말의 쓰임이 적절하지 않은 것은? [3점]

① (a)　　② (b)　　③ (c)　　④ (d)　　⑤ (e)

[43~45] 다음 글을 읽고, 물음에 답하시오.

(A)

Every evening, Laney took a walk around the neighborhood with her two dogs. One day, she saw a lady looking through the garbage bin. Being a kind and generous person, Laney offered the woman some chocolate bars that (a) she had in her pocket. "Thank you so much," the lady replied with a smile. "But I'm afraid that's not something I should give my cat."

(B)

It was about a neighborhood that had a community pet store. People donated whatever they could, and others could take whatever they needed. Some people traded items, like donating unused toys and taking a leash instead. Nobody had to pay for anything; it was a system built on goodwill and trust. Laney couldn't wait to start one in (b) her own neighborhood. She and other volunteers fixed up an old shed near the park. Lots of people dropped by to help or donate. The store became a success, and many pet owners who needed help were grateful.

(C)

Laney was surprised and asked the lady what she meant. The woman said she had been a victim of the recent hurricane. She had lost her house and many of her possessions. She was still recovering financially and did not have much money to spare. "Being on such a tight budget," (c) she said "I have trouble buying supplies for my kitty."

(D)

As she walked home, Laney could not get the woman's story out of (d) her mind. While she often donated clothes and food to people in need, she realized she never thought about all the pets in need. She thought about how she could help for many days. Then, (e) she came across an article with a perfect solution.

43 주어진 글 (A)에 이어질 내용을 순서에 맞게 배열한 것으로 가장 적절한 것은?

① (B) – (D) – (C)   ② (C) – (B) – (D)
③ (C) – (D) – (B)   ④ (D) – (B) – (C)
⑤ (D) – (C) – (B)

44 밑줄 친 (a)~(e) 중에서 가리키는 대상이 나머지 넷과 다른 것은?

① (a)   ② (b)   ③ (c)   ④ (d)   ⑤ (e)

45 윗글의 Laney에 관한 내용으로 적절하지 않은 것은?

① 쓰레기통을 뒤지는 여자를 보았다.
② 오래된 헛간을 수리했다.
③ 반려동물 용품을 교환하는 서비스를 시작했다.
④ 놀라서 여자에게 무슨 사연인지 물었다.
⑤ 도움이 필요한 사람들을 위해 돈을 기부하곤 했다.

정답·해설·해석 p. 12

문제풀이 후 확인사항
1. 45분 내에 문제를 풀었다.
2. 체크해둔 문제와 틀린 문제는 해설을 꼼꼼히 확인했다.

수고하셨습니다! HackersBook.com에서 제공하는 어휘리스트로 어휘를 암기하세요.

03회 실전모의고사

목표 시간: 45분 　시작: ___ 시 ___ 분 ~ 종료: ___ 시 ___ 분 　점수: ___ 점 / 63점

* [3점] 표시가 있는 문제 제외하고는 모두 2점으로 계산합니다.

18 다음 글의 목적으로 가장 적절한 것은?

Dear Ji Ho Kim,

　We received your complaint regarding the noise that affected your stay at our hotel on March 9. I can't imagine how inconvenient that was for you and want you to know that we take issues like these very seriously. Our staff has already been instructed to make reducing disturbances a priority in the future in order to ensure a more comfortable stay for guests. Despite the problems you experienced while you were here last, we hope that you visit us again and give us the opportunity to make up for it. We always appreciate your feedback as a valued customer and express regret again for the noise.

Yours Sincerely,
Brian Smith, The Swan Hotel Manager

① 서비스에 대한 만족도를 조사하려고
② 고객의 예약 일정을 확인하려고
③ 소음의 원인을 설명하려고
④ 불편을 겪은 고객에게 사과하려고
⑤ 무료 숙박권 사용 방법을 안내하려고

19 다음 글에 나타난 'I'의 심경 변화로 가장 적절한 것은?

　I've felt uncertain about this day for a while now. Mystery writer Gavin Hale's most recent thriller, *Down to the Bones*, was released in bookstores nationwide this morning. It's no secret that his last book received overwhelmingly negative reviews from critics like me, especially because of its boring descriptions. So, I was more than cautious about reading his newest offering. But now, after finally finishing the novel, I must say that my opinion has changed. I never imagined Hale had another masterpiece left in him. *Down to the Bones* is an exciting story full of memorable characters and dramatic plot twists. I hope that this marks a turning point in Hale's career and that he builds on the achievement of this latest novel.

① relieved → curious
② doubtful → impressed
③ confused → sorrowful
④ satisfied → frightened
⑤ ashamed → indifferent

20 다음 글에서 필자가 주장하는 바로 가장 적절한 것은?

　You may have experienced a situation in which you had a hunch that a certain course of action was the correct one. But how far can you trust your intuition? While most people would insist it's untrustworthy, it might be more reliable than you think. Recent studies show the human brain is constantly collecting and processing data from the environment. Psychologists believe that our instinctive reactions are based on information that we have processed subconsciously but are not aware of on a conscious level. For example, a businessperson may decide to reject a deal that seems highly advantageous based on gut feeling. This may appear illogical, but it could be that he or she has picked up on subtle cues that the person on the other side of the deal is not trustworthy. Giving your intuitive responses careful consideration will greatly increase your chances of making the best decisions.

① 직관력을 키울 수 있는 환경을 조성하라.
② 문제 해결을 위해 논리적으로 사고하라.
③ 결정을 내릴 때 직감을 무시하지 마라.
④ 협상을 할 때 신뢰를 바탕으로 하라.
⑤ 이성적으로 옳고 그름을 판단하라.

21 밑줄 친 jump the gun이 다음 글에서 의미하는 바로 가장 적절한 것은? [3점]

People who engage in autosuggestion — a psychological technique involving the repeated use of verbal suggestions to modify one's behavior — often <u>jump the gun</u>. They fail to imagine themselves taking the specific steps that will lead them to their objective and instead direct their thoughts to their ultimate desire. A person who repeats the affirmation "I am wealthy" is unlikely to have much success in achieving financial independence because what is being envisioned does not represent a concrete action. Instead, something like "I am reducing my monthly spending" or "I am proving myself worthy of a salary increase" would be much more effective because these are acts that would contribute to measurable progress and are practical based on the person's current circumstances. For its successful implementation, autosuggestion requires that a person continually envision the next stage in the process of realizing his or her dream.

① give up before they make any accomplishments
② lack the imagination to achieve a high level of success
③ use methods that have a positive effect on their actions
④ have objectives that are not of direct benefit to them
⑤ focus on their goals rather than on how to achieve them

22 다음 글의 요지로 가장 적절한 것은?

Teachers are advised to adopt a learning-centric approach to feedback as it enables them to make timely adjustments to students' progress. Rather than simply providing assessments, teachers should specify what students did correctly and incorrectly, and then offer specific suggestions on how to improve. In the case of a presentation, a teacher might say, "You were able to gather a lot of information about your assigned topic; however, you need to present the material in a more orderly fashion and make better use of visuals such as graphs and charts." This not only lets the student know the basis of the grade he or she received on the assignment but also what needs to be done to get better marks on future ones. In other words, feedback should function as a form of instruction that a student can absorb and then apply to other projects.

① 부정적인 피드백은 학생의 학습 동기를 떨어뜨린다.
② 교사는 객관적인 기준으로 학생을 평가해야 한다.
③ 활용 가능한 구체적인 피드백이 학생에게 도움이 된다.
④ 시각 자료가 수반되는 피드백이 더 효과적이다.
⑤ 교사는 학습 목표에 부합하는 과제를 제시해야 한다.

23 다음 글의 주제로 가장 적절한 것은? [3점]

Post hoc, ergo propter hoc is a Latin phrase meaning "after this, therefore because of this." The phrase states that X happened and then Y happened, so therefore, X is the cause of Y. Let's say a car goes off the road during a thunderstorm. We may quickly assume the rain (X) caused the accident (Y). However, later it is revealed that the driver simply dozed off. X and Y are associated only because they occurred at the same time. We make these sorts of conclusions because the human mind is inherently programmed to frame events in terms of cause and effect. Some may think that such a leap in logic matters little. After all, our knowing the driver was sleepy wouldn't have affected the outcome. But consider this: What happens when we do this in a criminal case or medical emergency? What happens during a pandemic or rescue mission? Lives can be ruined or lost.

① the advantages of logical reasoning
② the habit of assuming the worst outcome
③ the thought process of analyzing information
④ the relationship between cause and effect
⑤ the occurrence of an error in reasoning

24 다음 글의 제목으로 가장 적절한 것은?

Skyrocketing housing prices are making it more difficult for entry-level buyers to purchase homes in the US; a development which stems from high numbers of people relocating from urban neighborhoods to suburban and rural areas for more space. In the last decade alone, housing prices have increased by 81.5 percent. Supply hasn't been able to meet demand, as the Great Recession caused a shortage of housing when construction on new homes slowed down exceptionally. This means that many potential buyers have been unable to purchase homes that are quickly appreciating in value. In fact, the housing market hasn't seen such a lack of affordable homes since the 2008 financial crisis, according to US Secretary of Housing and Urban Development Marcia Fudge. This doesn't only impact buyers, but renters as well, as rent prices will continue to increase. Home ownership — an exceedingly effective way to build wealth — has become unattainable for many because of this trend, which shows no signs of abating in the near future.

① An Ongoing Problem: Increasing Housing Prices in the US
② Are Suburban or Rural Properties a Better Investment?
③ Home Ownership: The Best Method to Acquire Wealth
④ Predictions Regarding the Future of the Housing Market
⑤ The Relationship between Rising House Prices and Rents

25 다음 도표의 내용과 일치하지 <u>않는</u> 것은?

Land Area by Land Use Types in 2018

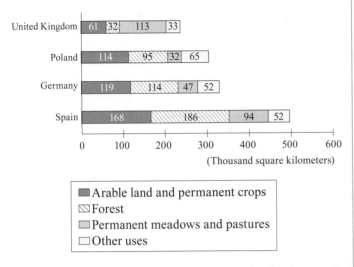

(Thousand square kilometers)

- ■ Arable land and permanent crops
- ▨ Forest
- ▤ Permanent meadows and pastures
- □ Other uses

The graph above shows the land area by land use of four European countries in 2018. ① Among the four countries, Poland had the fewest square kilometers devoted to permanent meadows and pastures, while it had the most square kilometers of land use in other uses. ② As for arable land and permanent crops, Germany ranked the second highest with 119 thousand square kilometers. ③ In Spain, forests took up the largest land area by land use with 186 thousand square kilometers. ④ Although the total land area of the United Kingdom was less than 300 thousand square kilometers, the United Kingdom is the only country where the land area of permanent meadows and pastures was more than 100 thousand square kilometers. ⑤ In the case of Poland and Germany, the land area of forests was the second largest, both of which exceeded 100 thousand square kilometers.

＊ arable land: 경작지

26 Georges Dreyer에 관한 다음 글의 내용과 일치하지 <u>않는</u> 것은?

Georges Dreyer was born in 1873 in Shanghai, where his father was stationed with the Royal Danish Navy. He was a brilliant student from a young age and began studying medicine at the University of Copenhagen, earning his medical degree in 1900. His main research interests were in bacteriology and immunity. He performed numerous studies with vaccines and immunizations. During his studies, he discovered better modifications for the Widal test, which was used for diagnosing typhoid disease. While he was responsible for considerable research into virology, Dreyer also made important contributions to respiratory physiology, which is the study of lung function and how we breathe. He conducted a number of experiments with regards to oxygen and aviation, making his work particularly significant during World War I for fighter pilots. Dreyer was able to develop a device that was capable of supplying sufficient oxygen for airmen who were frequently in environments with low oxygen. Interestingly, Dreyer is seldom acknowledged for these discoveries in physiological studies despite their importance today.

＊ typhoid: 장티푸스 ＊＊ virology: 바이러스학

① Copenhagen 대학에서 의학을 공부했다.
② 백신에 관한 연구를 수행했다.
③ Widal 검사를 개선했다.
④ 호흡기 생리학에 중요한 기여를 했다.
⑤ 환자들에게 산소를 공급할 수 있는 장치를 개발했다.

27 Oil Painting Workshop 101에 관한 다음 안내문의 내용과 일치하지 <u>않는</u> 것은?

Oil Painting Workshop 101

If you've always wanted to paint in oil, this workshop is for you. Beginners are encouraged to join!

Location:
- Weller Community Center
- 2nd floor, Studio 203

Times:
- Every Monday, Wednesday, and Friday
- Morning class: 10 a.m. to 12 p.m.
- Evening class: 8 p.m. to 10 p.m.
* The studio is open on Saturdays from 10 a.m. to 3 p.m. for students who would like to practice.

Registration:
- Sign up at www.painterswork.com.
- Class limit is 7 students max.
- $35 per class

* Wear clothes that can get dirty.
* Parking is available for free.

If you have any questions, you can email Erin Powell at epowell717@painterswork.com.

---

① 초보자들을 위한 수업이다.
② Weller 문화 회관 2층에서 진행된다.
③ 토요일에도 스튜디오가 열려있다.
④ 수강 정원은 5명으로 제한된다.
⑤ 주차 요금은 무료이다.

28 The 7th Annual Charity Dog Walk에 관한 다음 안내문의 내용과 일치하는 것은?

The 7th Annual Charity Dog Walk

The Silverton Animal Shelter is excited to announce the date for its annual Charity Dog Walk. Bring your furry best friends, and take a walk to help our animals in need.

When & Where
• Sunday, June 18 (10:30 a.m. – 3:30 p.m.)
• Jackson Park

Participation Fee
• $15 per person (t-shirt included)
• Free for children under 12

What to Expect
• Coffee and light snacks will be available for purchase.
• The walking trail will be 1.6 km.
• Awards and prizes will be given to the dogs and owners that complete the most trails.

Please Note
• All funds will go to the shelter and caring for un-homed animals.
• Please know that you are responsible for your animal (bring other supplies if necessary).

---

① 일요일에 네 시간 동안 진행된다.
② 참가비에 티셔츠가 포함되지 않는다.
③ 산책로는 2km가 넘는다.
④ 반려견을 위한 상품은 준비되지 않는다.
⑤ 수익금은 동물 보호소에 전액 기부될 것이다.

29 다음 글의 밑줄 친 부분 중, 어법상 틀린 것은?

There are many explanations for why children misbehave, but the one most ① <u>frequently</u> given is that they crave attention. Since children equate attention with parental support, they'll do ② <u>whatever</u> they can to get it, even if this means being disobedient or rude. For instance, a little girl screaming and crying in front of a crowd of people ③ <u>believe</u> she is forcing her parents to redirect their attention to her. Parents should not respond to this sort of behavior by scolding the child for being unable to control their emotions or ④ <u>making</u> a scene themselves. Doing so only reinforces to the child that their bad behavior is an acceptable way ⑤ <u>to get</u> what they desire. Instead, parents should act like the misbehavior doesn't matter, waiting until the child is calm and well-behaved before providing them with praise and other forms of attention.

30 다음 글의 밑줄 친 부분 중, 문맥상 낱말의 쓰임이 적절하지 않은 것은? [3점]

There are some who run away and hide in times of danger, and there are some who would put their lives on the line for others without ① <u>hesitation</u>. When faced with imminent danger, what is it that guides us to one path over another? It may be that courageousness is a ② <u>natural</u> quality; some people are just born to be heroes. Yet, within Aristotelian ethics, it is only a matter of practicality. All the traits we deem to be virtuous — kindness, goodness, bravery — are not ③ <u>abstract</u> concepts but practiced responses that manifest in life. To become good, one must actively cultivate good habits; doing so over and over will automatically lead to living an ethical life. In ④ <u>unexpected</u> situations, we don't have a chance to think things over before acting. But, if we make a concentrated effort to be moral day after day, we will ⑤ <u>consciously</u> react honorably, even when faced with the most surprising events. Morality, for all intents and purposes, is muscle memory.

[31~34] 다음 빈칸에 들어갈 말로 가장 적절한 것을 고르시오.

31

Most people define a "minority" in numerical terms, or as a word that signifies a smaller number or part that is less than half of a total. Because of this designation, which might seem beyond dispute, it is often assumed that a minority has to consist of a group of people that number less than other members of a populace. The term does not always meet this simplified definition though. For example, South Africa has a population that is composed of a numerical majority of black people and a smaller number of white people. However, the country's white people, despite being part of a _____ minority, have historically dominated and oppressed their countrymen, and to this day hold many positions of power. That being the case, black South Africans are a minority, but not in the numerical sense. In spite of comprising a larger group, they can nonetheless be considered a minority because their share of the country's resources, institutions, and mechanisms of control remain smaller in comparison to the share held by whites.

* populace: 대중

① native
② radical
③ religious
④ linguistic
⑤ quantitative

32

The priority in science is not discovery anymore, and the situation is particularly perilous for undirected science. Not being able to promise profitable results means that pure science cannot be done since no investor wants to sink money into something that may prove "useless," at least on the market. Something must be shown at the end of the day, and results must be able to exhibit a price tag. Yet, can anyone say for sure where or when the next big discovery will occur? Do we want to squash the curiosity and creativity of young minds hoping to unlock secrets still hidden from us? Science has left behind its aim of pursuing the truth and is no different than any other large corporation. This leaves thousands of avenues unexplored and ultimately _____. When science has a net worth in dollar signs, we all suffer.

* perilous: 위험한

① means the accuracy of research may decline
② makes scientific research far less competitive
③ limits how we see and understand the universe
④ results in scientists undertaking dangerous experiments
⑤ suggests studies will become more expensive to conduct

33

Technology is no longer simply a part of our lives; it is fundamentally reshaping the way we think, learn, communicate, and play. From this perspective, the significant changes brought about by modern tech culture are viewed with apprehension, a natural human reaction to anything new and different. Specifically, a moral panic is created around what the computer screen can open up — unfiltered and unlimited exposure to violence, cyberbullying, video game addiction, and so forth. Yet, the level of fear this provokes is out of sync with any realistic threat. It is more accurate to say that,

while technology makes us less free in many ways and can be dangerous if overused, it is not doing us serious, long-term harm; our humanity has not been shattered to the extent that we are unwilling or unable to look up from our screens or communicate face-to-face. Yes, _____, but a passive obstruction does not equate to active harm. [3점]

① losing control of technology is a very real possibility
② the costs of technology outweigh the benefits
③ rejecting the modern world may be tempting
④ technology may keep us from living an optimal life
⑤ humanity's limitations can be addressed with technology

34

Approximately half a million years ago, the lineages of Neanderthals and *Homo Sapiens*, or modern humans, split from a common ancestor. Some experts propose that this link was *Homo antecessor*: a species that's roused debates in the scientific community for some time. Remains of what some refer to as *Homo antecessor* were first discovered in the 1990s in Spain. They were found to be around 800,000 years old, and were unique in that the teeth of the uncovered specimens were primitive while aspects of their facial structures were surprisingly similar to those of *Homo sapiens*. This odd combination, which hadn't been yet observed, is what led to researchers _____. But the fact that all of the uncovered *Homo antecessor* specimens have been younger has caused some controversy. Some scientists argue that rather than being part of a distinct species, these remains could actually belong to another species and have these particular features due to not maturing yet. [3점]

* lineage: 혈통

① inferring that they had evolved rather quickly
② designating them as a species of their own
③ establishing them as the common ancestor
④ concluding that they were a superior species
⑤ questioning their views on the lineage of humans

35 다음 글에서 전체 흐름과 관계 없는 문장은?

Bioluminescence is the emission of light by a living organism. Species that exhibit this ability either produce light on their own through a chemical reaction that takes place in their cells or have a symbiotic relationship with light-producing bacteria. ① The firefly is a good example of an organism that produces light independently, mostly for attracting mates and warding off predators. ② It has a light-emitting organ in its abdomen that is triggered when an enzyme called luciferin combines with oxygen and other organic compounds. ③ Another organism that can glow is the Hawaiian bobtail squid, which has an organ that generates light that relies on symbiotic bacteria to function. ④ In fact, most types of organisms, from bacteria to marine vertebrates like sharks, have some species that are capable of bioluminescence. ⑤ These bacteria reside on the underside of the squid, and by interacting with their host's light-emitting organ, produce light for the squid to use when hunting at night.

* symbiotic: 공생의, 공생하는 ** enzyme: 효소

[36~37] 주어진 글 다음에 이어질 글의 순서로 가장 적절한 것을 고르시오.

36

> Sending humans to Mars is a goal shared by many, and government agencies like NASA are currently at the forefront of the quest.

(A) This is where entrepreneurs like Elon Musk come in. His aerospace company SpaceX, and others like it, possess funds the government lacks, allowing for more robust research and financing. When companies can combine their assets with those of the government, the result is advancement in spaceflight.

(B) For instance, SpaceX launched the first-ever flight that was manned entirely by private civilians from NASA's Kennedy Space Center. This was only possible through the collaboration of SpaceX and the US government, a partnership that has provided the first step to the ultimate goal of a manned mission to Mars.

(C) NASA employs experts whose skills and experience are critical. The agency also has decades of experience and data to draw from. But more is needed. Financing is a major concern since federal backing can hardly be expected to completely cover the projected trillion-dollar cost.

① (A) – (C) – (B)　　② (B) – (A) – (C)
③ (B) – (C) – (A)　　④ (C) – (A) – (B)
⑤ (C) – (B) – (A)

37

Ancient civilizations that developed writing systems help us understand history because of all the information they left behind in written documents.

(A) However, there is often little resemblance between these and ancient dialects, which can make decoding incredibly time-consuming and speculative. It is hoped that new technology such as machine translation software could help archaeologists eliminate some of the guesswork.

(B) Even something as simple as a shopping list can be very revealing. Items like these reveal how ancient people lived, and not just in a general sense; they can provide fascinating insight into the everyday details of what they ate, the types of food available in the area, and how much things cost.

(C) Of course, obtaining this kind of information may be dependent on the ability to decipher complex writing systems that haven't been used in a thousand years or more. To do this, archaeologists and linguists may have to turn to more recent forms of a language as references.

* decipher: 판독하다

① (A) – (C) – (B)　　　② (B) – (A) – (C)
③ (B) – (C) – (A)　　　④ (C) – (A) – (B)
⑤ (C) – (B) – (A)

[38~39] 글의 흐름으로 보아, 주어진 문장이 들어가기에 가장 적절한 곳을 고르시오.

38

It would allow for a significant reduction in livestock numbers, and by extension, put less strain on our natural resources.

It is becoming increasingly apparent that raising livestock for meat and milk is no longer sustainable. (①) Not only does animal agriculture require a huge amount of land and water, but it accounts for up to 87% of greenhouse gas emissions. (②) But with the world's population expanding rapidly, along with the demand for meat, can anything be done? (③) One potential solution to the problem may lie in cellular agriculture, a process in which cells are taken from a live animal and cultivated in a lab to become animal products. (④) It could also improve food safety considerably. (⑤) Since food produced via cellular agriculture is closely monitored through all steps of the process, the risk of diseases caused by food contamination is greatly reduced.

39

> Using a MacGuffin sounds harmless, but many writers end up doing so to explain away plot holes or poor writing.

A "MacGuffin" is a plot device that is frequently used in film. (①) It is an object, event, or person that motivates the main characters and drives the story forward but without possessing any meaning itself. (②) A well-known example is in John Huston's 1941 film noir classic *The Maltese Falcon*, in which a statue of a falcon acts as the catalyst for the story. (③) Whether such a device is a helpful tool or a crutch is much debated, but perhaps the inventor of the word can provide a hint. (④) The term MacGuffin is often credited to Angus MacPhail, an English screenwriter and script editor. (⑤) It is thought that MacPhail took the first part of his last name and combined it with "guff," meaning "nonsense," creating a term that represents the "stupid" element in a story. [3점]

* crutch: 지나치게 의지하게 되는 것, 버팀목

40 다음 글의 내용을 한 문장으로 요약하고자 한다. 빈칸 (A), (B)에 들어갈 말로 가장 적절한 것은?

In studying why athletes are so superstitious, with many known to engage in rituals that range from wearing certain clothes to listening to a specific song right before a game, researchers have determined that several factors are at play. Consistent with previous hypotheses about superstitions in sports, it was found that ritual commitment — the carrying out of the same ritual based on the belief that doing so will result in performance success — is more common in situations where both the importance of the game and uncertainty about its outcome is high. A high-stakes championship game, in other words, is more likely to result in athletes executing superstitious rituals than other games in a season. It was also found that the likelihood of ritual commitment increases when an athlete has what is known as an external locus of control — a belief that variables beyond one's power produce outcomes. For sportspersons with such a mindset, ritual commitment provides a way for them to feel as though they have at least some part in influencing future events.

↓

Research indicates that the incidence of superstitious behavior among athletes increases when the outcome of an important game is ___(A)___ and when athletes believe they are not fully ___(B)___ for their results.

	(A)		(B)
①	strategic	······	prepared
②	unpredictable	······	responsible
③	debated	······	responsible
④	indefinite	······	prepared
⑤	unbearable	······	eligible

[41~42] 다음 글을 읽고, 물음에 답하시오.

Our long-held view of domestication — generally, that it's an unnatural process inapplicable to just any species — is currently being challenged by noted changes in various animal populations, yet again emphasizing how (a) limited our understanding of nature truly is. In fact, numerous species of wild animals appear to be domesticating themselves and exhibiting prominent behavioral shifts. This idea is in accordance with the self-domestication hypothesis which posits that "selection against aggression" within a wild species can have (b) similar results to the traditional domestication process. This development is illustrated by the research of Brian Hare, a Duke University evolutionary anthropologist who published a research review related to his observations on the behavior of bonobos. Bonobos are, in the words of Hare, "nice"; they (c) cooperate with one another, spend much of their time playing, and don't fight. This is strikingly different from the behavior of chimpanzees who are genetically close to bonobos. Hare hypothesizes that bonobos, unlike their relatives, underwent domestication due to a lack of competition that took effect millions of years ago. Becoming less (d) gentle, it seems, can have its perks, and Frank Albert, an evolutionary anthropologist at Princeton University, says that the ancestors of bonobos likely "benefited from evolving" in this respect. Adjustments such as these are likely taking place even now, especially for animals that live (e) near humans and densely populated areas. They will continue to evolve, becoming "nicer" in the process.

* posit: 가정하다

41 윗글의 제목으로 가장 적절한 것은?

① Species Cooperate More than We Think!
② The Unnatural Process of Taming an Animal
③ The Behavioral Traits of Undomesticated Animals
④ Why Are Some Species More Evolved than Others?
⑤ Self-Domestication: Evolution Towards Less Violence

42 밑줄 친 (a)~(e) 중에서 문맥상 낱말의 쓰임이 적절하지 않은 것은? [3점]

① (a)　　② (b)　　③ (c)　　④ (d)　　⑤ (e)

[43~45] 다음 글을 읽고, 물음에 답하시오.

(A)

Norma was stuck on the side of the road. Her car had a flat tire and, as she was 70, she didn't have the strength to change the tire herself. She thought about walking towards the nearest town, but it was getting dark and starting to rain. Car after car drove past until one finally stopped. A man stepped out and asked if he could help. She was a little nervous at first. Would he try to rob her? But the man smiled kindly and said, "Why don't (a) you wait over by the streetlight while I fix your flat tire?"

(B)

Norma thanked him again and drove off. A little later, she stopped by a diner for some food. The diner was old and shabby and the food wasn't great. However, the waitress was cheerful and kind, even though she was pregnant. (b) She seemed clearly tired, but she did not let it affect her work. Norma ate, paid for her meal, and waved goodbye as she left.

(C)

In no time at all, the man had changed her tire. "Oh, thank you so much! Let me pay you for your assistance," (c) she said. But the man wouldn't accept it. "If you really want to do something for me," the man said, "Just help someone else when you come across them, the way I helped you."

(D)

The waitress started to clean up the dishes when she noticed a small note Norma had left. It said: "Someone once helped (d) me and asked me to pay it forward. Hopefully, you can do the same one day, too." Underneath the note was a $200 tip! The waitress couldn't believe it. When she arrived home, she told her husband all about it. He was very happy, since any extra cash would be helpful. "Looks like you had an eventful day," he said to his wife. "I did as well. I helped (e) a lady change her tire."

43 주어진 글 (A)에 이어질 내용을 순서에 맞게 배열한 것으로 가장 적절한 것은?

① (B) – (D) – (C)　　　② (C) – (B) – (D)
③ (C) – (D) – (B)　　　④ (D) – (B) – (C)
⑤ (D) – (C) – (B)

44 밑줄 친 (a)~(e) 중에서 가리키는 대상이 나머지 넷과 **다른** 것은?

① (a)　　② (b)　　③ (c)　　④ (d)　　⑤ (e)

45 윗글에 관한 내용으로 적절하지 **않은** 것은?

① Norma는 타이어를 스스로 교체할 힘이 없었다.
② Norma는 처음에는 남자를 경계했다.
③ 식당 종업원은 Norma에게 친절하게 대했다.
④ 남자는 Norma에게 다른 사람을 도우라고 조언했다.
⑤ 식당 종업원은 Norma가 남긴 쪽지를 발견하지 못했다.

정답·해설·해석 p. 23

문제풀이 후 확인사항
1. 45분 내에 문제를 풀었다.
2. 체크해둔 문제와 틀린 문제는 해설을 꼼꼼히 확인했다.

수고하셨습니다! HackersBook.com에서 제공하는 어휘리스트로 어휘를 암기하세요.

04회 실전모의고사

* [3점] 표시가 있는 문제 제외하고는 모두 2점으로 계산합니다.

18 다음 글의 목적으로 가장 적절한 것은?

Dear Mr. Roberts,

First of all, I want to let you know that I'm a huge admirer of your work. I run a local writing club, and many of our members consider themselves your fans. That being said, we would love if you could attend one of our club meetings. Every so often, we invite guest speakers to discuss writing techniques and tips with us. We would be thrilled if you could be the guest speaker at one of our upcoming meetings and share your experiences. Our members are all aspiring writers who would appreciate any advice from such a renowned author. Although we know you must be exceptionally busy, we just wanted to reach out and see if this was feasible. Please let us know if you are interested.

Sincerely,
Julie Chang

① 글쓰기 동아리 개설을 건의하려고
② 글쓰기 동아리 가입 절차를 안내하려고
③ 작가의 작품에 대한 독자 의견을 전달하려고
④ 효과적인 글쓰기 방법에 대해 조언을 구하려고
⑤ 글쓰기 동아리에 초청 연사로 와 줄 것을 요청하려고

19 다음 글에 드러난 Steve의 심경 변화로 가장 적절한 것은?

'This is it,' Steve thought. 'This is the moment I've been waiting for.' He felt himself grin as he once again stretched his legs. Steve had been training for this race for months. Thinking back on all of the early mornings he had spent jogging, he was now ready for the hard work to pay off. He stood at the starting line, waiting for the starting signal. When the race gun fired, everyone began running. Steve launched into a sprint and propelled himself through the crowd. After a while, he started to feel stiff and tired. His legs burned with effort, and his lungs hurt. Steve realized that he had pushed himself too hard at the beginning of the race. It would be difficult to keep his normal pace the rest of the way. Now fearing the miles ahead, Steve could not be sure he would reach the finish line.

① bored → adventurous
② proud → startled
③ tense → touched
④ eager → uneasy
⑤ overjoyed → indifferent

20 다음 글에서 필자가 주장하는 바로 가장 적절한 것은?

Clear communications are valued in all areas of modern society, and this is particularly true in the workplace. Unfortunately, many bosses operate on what is called a "need-to-know basis," providing staff with information only when absolutely necessary. Instead, they must be transparent with their workers, both in good times and bad. Why is this so important? It's because many people want to feel a sense of ownership in the work they do and to believe that they can be a part of the solution if a crisis occurs. Leaders should, therefore, be upfront with their staff about any issues the company or team may be facing, essentially acknowledging that their employees are also their peers. This will help them win the trust and respect of their employees while increasing the level of staff involvement, which benefits the company as a whole.

① 지도자는 직원들과 소통하여 화합을 도모해야 한다.
② 지도자는 어떠한 상황에서도 직원들에게 솔직해야 한다.
③ 직원들이 소속감을 갖도록 주기적인 교육을 실시해야 한다.
④ 지도자는 직원들의 의견을 수용하여 문제를 해결해야 한다.
⑤ 조직은 업무 효율성 증대를 위해 직원 복지 향상에 힘써야 한다.

21 밑줄 친 they have a mind of their own이 다음 글에서 의미하는 바로 가장 적절한 것은?

Brains are incredibly complex structures responsible for an abundance of crucial tasks. Yet, in spite of being such vital organs, they are not perfect; one could even say they have a mind of their own. When it comes to problem-solving, the human brain prefers taking shortcuts (also known as heuristics) to arrive at solutions. It will recall similar past circumstances or depend on prior knowledge in order to bypass critical thinking — it's lazy that way. This can prevent a person from considering other options or contemplating an important matter long enough. Brains can also cause people to think they've had experiences they've never actually had before (false memories). If a person hears a story or watches a video, his or her brain can fool them into thinking that they went through what they heard or saw. With so much information to process, it shouldn't be a surprise that our minds slip up sometimes.

① The brain cannot focus on too many tasks at once.
② Different areas of the brain contradict each other.
③ Humans have difficulty with making decisions.
④ Most people have a very limited attention span.
⑤ The brain is capable of misleading a person.

22 다음 글의 요지로 가장 적절한 것은?

Many people read translated versions of classics like the *Odyssey*. While translations may seem convenient, we can't always be sure that we fully understand what the original writers were trying to say because not all translations are reliable. The thing is, translators must be equally proficient in both languages involved in a translation, and they must have a good understanding of the work itself. Exact translations can be impossible due to the use of figurative language, which can't be translated literally. Furthermore, the words writers use in their work are often chosen very carefully. For instance, poets may select words that rhyme, which may not be possible to duplicate in another language. The original meaning can therefore be lost. The director of the British Centre for Literary Translation commented on the issue, insisting, "There's not a single word in any of the languages I translate that can map perfectly onto a word in English. So it's always interpretative, approximate, creative."

① 비유적 표현의 사용을 통해 시의 작품성이 증대된다.
② 많은 고전 문학이 언어 장벽으로 인해 잘못 이해된다.
③ 번역가는 고전 문학에 대한 해박한 지식이 있어야 한다.
④ 번역본은 원작의 의미를 완전히 반영하지 못할 수도 있다.
⑤ 작가는 번역이 수월하도록 특정 단어를 의도적으로 사용한다.

23 다음 글의 주제로 가장 적절한 것은?

After the devastating flood of 1927, Congress approved the Mississippi River and Tributaries Project, which resulted in the construction of 20,000 miles of levees and floodways. This disrupted the delicate balance of the Mississippi's watercourses, and the surrounding wetlands began to subside. So far, 1,800 square miles of Louisiana wetlands have disappeared. This disaster has taken a heavy toll. The vanishing swamps not only play a vital role in storm surge reduction and nutrient filtration but also are a critical ecosystem. In fact, almost half of the threatened and endangered species in America depend on wetlands. One potential answer is Louisiana's Coastal Master Plan. It aims to recreate the natural processes that built the state's delta, which would protect existing wetlands and restore areas that have been lost. There is an easy way the public can assist, too: eating oysters. Oyster shells can be used to rebuild the reefs. Nearly 5,000 tons of shells have been used for this already, thanks to recycling programs at Louisiana restaurants.

* levee: (강가의) 제방, 부두

① difficulties faced when restoring essential animal habitats
② reasons for the success of Louisiana's Coastal Master Plan
③ mitigating effects of wetlands on storms that lead to floods
④ threat of floods in Louisiana and the need for prevention measures
⑤ importance of wetlands and solutions to prevent their disappearance

24 다음 글의 제목으로 가장 적절한 것은?

Inflation tends to have a negative connotation because it is commonly associated with reduced purchasing power and monetary savings. Some economists, however, insist that a healthy amount of inflation might actually work in the public's favor. Most notably, distinguished economist John Maynard Keynes asserted that moderate inflation is critical to counteract the paradox of thrift, which states that savings can actually be damaging to economic growth. If people are not spending their money, the economy suffers because there is less overall demand. Inflation can also give a financial boost to those in debt, such as mortgage borrowers and people with student loans. The value of loans decreases with inflation and this in turn encourages spending. Inflation targeting — or making adjustments to stick to an inflation rate that is chosen — is used by central banks all over the world with the goal of stimulating the economy and maintaining maximum employment. If people know that prices will rise in the future, it motivates them to buy goods and services now.

* mortgage: (담보) 대출

① Spend Now, Save Later!
② How Do Economic Policies Affect Loans?
③ Inflation as a Means of Economic Growth
④ Inflation: The Harmful Effects of Rising Prices
⑤ The Relationship Between Inflation and Unemployment

25 다음 도표의 내용과 일치하지 <u>않는</u> 것은?

World Population by Region, 2017 and 2050

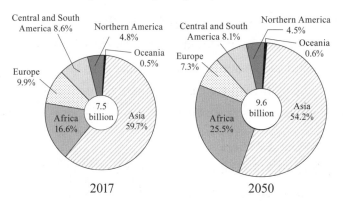

2017   2050

The two pie charts above show the distribution of world population by region in 2017 and 2050. ① Total world population is expected to grow by more than 2 billion from 2017 to 2050. ② Among the six regions, the only two regions that are expected to show increases in their percentage of the total world population between 2017 and 2050 are Africa and Oceania. ③ While Europe ranked third in percentage of total world population in 2017, it is predicted to rank fourth in 2050 with 7.3%. ④ In 2050, the combined percentage of the total world population of Europe and Northern America is expected to be less than half of Africa's. ⑤ Asia's percentage of the total world population is expected to decrease by 5.5% in 2050 compared to 2017, making it less than half of the total world population.

26 Albert Camus에 관한 다음 글의 내용과 일치하지 <u>않는</u> 것은?

Born in November of 1913 to a French family that had relocated to Algeria, Albert Camus would become one of the most famous writers of the 20th century and a Nobel Prize winner. His childhood experience of poverty, as well as his diagnosis of tuberculosis and a lifetime of illness, influenced his work significantly. He is most known for developing absurdism, a philosophy that suggests trying to find the meaning of life is pointless because it does not exist. He put his characters in critical situations in order to demonstrate how the universe, and more specifically human behavior, lacks rationality. He published a number of plays, essays, and short stories revolving around this idea, although his most notable work was the short novel *L'Étranger(The Stranger)*. His life ended in an automobile collision in January 1960, when he was 46.

* tuberculosis: 결핵   ** absurdism: 부조리주의

① 이민자 가정에서 태어났다.
② 일생 동안 병을 앓았다.
③ 인간 행동의 불합리성을 보이고자 했다.
④ 가장 잘 알려진 작품은 수필이다.
⑤ 46세에 자동차 사고로 생을 마감했다.

27 Travel Life Photo Contest에 관한 다음 안내문의 내용과 일치하지 <u>않는</u> 것은?

Travel Life Photo Contest

Travel Life Magazine is holding a photography contest. Amateurs and professionals are welcome to enter.

Rules

- Three photos per entry
- Deadline is May 1.
- All photos must be in JPG format and emailed to photocontest@travellife.org.
  * No digital editing allowed.

Prizes

- First place will receive $10,000 and a feature in our June issue.
- Second place will receive $7,000 plus a trophy.
- Third place will receive $2,500 (no trophy).

Note

- The award ceremony will be held on Friday, May 20. Open to the public.

For more information, visit our website.

① 아마추어와 전문가 모두 참가할 수 있다.
② 출품작은 JPG 형식으로 제출해야 한다.
③ 디지털 편집을 거친 사진은 출품할 수 없다.
④ 3등 입상자는 현금과 트로피를 받을 것이다.
⑤ 시상식은 공개적으로 진행될 것이다.

28 Colin Springs Film Festival에 관한 다음 안내문의 내용과 일치하는 것은?

Colin Springs Film Festival

Do you want a front row seat to experience the latest and greatest cinematic talent? Then be sure to stop by the 9th annual Colin Springs Film Festival for an exclusive first look.

When & Where

• April 3–7 from 10 a.m. to 8 p.m.
• Colin Springs Cinema Center

Tickets

• $150 for an all-access pass
• $50 for a one-day pass

Films

• Over 70 films of every genre
• Movies from over 20 different countries
• Kid-friendly programs

Other Events

• Panel discussions with directors and actors from the films
• Special lectures from celebrity guests

Please visit www.colinspringsfilm.com to learn more about the festival.

① 열 번째 개최되는 행사이다.
② 행사는 4일간 열린다.
③ 일일권의 가격은 150달러이다.
④ 어린이 영화는 상영하지 않는다.
⑤ 유명 인사들의 특강이 있다.

29 다음 글의 밑줄 친 부분 중, 어법상 틀린 것은? [3점]

When looking at the simplicity of human cells, the smallest building blocks of organic life, imagining that viruses — even less complex entities — could overtake them ① is difficult. Yet they can, and they do. The simplest viruses have only two parts: DNA or RNA ② that is a blueprint for making more viruses and a protein shell for protection. However, ③ despite they contain the instructions for reproduction, they lack the proper chemical substances — enzymes — to be able to do so on their own. They need a host to be able to do anything at all. They first infiltrate a cell, and then, once inside, add their genetic blueprint. The cell does not realize the difference and unknowingly begins to produce more of the virus instead of replicating ④ itself. Each new virus can then infect another cell, ⑤ repeating the infection cycle.

30 다음 글의 밑줄 친 부분 중, 문맥상 낱말의 쓰임이 적절하지 않은 것은? [3점]

Populism refers to a political approach that views the world as ① divided, with corrupt government elites on one end controlling everything and good, ordinary people whose expectations are not being met on the other. While it is true that mainstream governments sometimes fail to meet the public's expectations, turning to populism as an alternative can be ② destructive to social order. When a populist leader rises to power, they often suggest that problems have become ③ urgent and that maintaining the status quo will only make matters worse for the people. This creates a sense of panic and causes the people to ④ withdraw their support for the leader, even when leader's solutions for so-called problems like immigration or free trade are not actually in the best interest of all the people. That is because "the people" frequently ⑤ excludes minorities and other marginalized members of the population, which means that populism can turn members of the same society against one another, promote intolerance, and generally create additional problems.

* status quo: 현재 상태

[31~34] 다음 빈칸에 들어갈 말로 가장 적절한 것을 고르시오.

31

Humans are able to envision the future, and interestingly enough, it seems as though some animals can too. In one study, a species of weasel was observed eating ripe bananas immediately but then storing other unripe ones in trees, allowing them to mature. They would then come back to eat the fruit they had saved at a later time. This shows that the weasels were aware to some degree that in the near future, those bananas would become ripe enough to eat. That is, they were able to deduce a(n) _____ outcome and act accordingly. This ability to prepare for the future has been seen in a variety of animal species. It proves that they are not only capable of mental time travel but that they also possess enough reasoning and logic to know the best course of action to take for their own survival.

* weasel: 족제비

① direct   ② immediate

③ probable   ④ negative

⑤ spontaneous

32

One of the most remarkable aspects of the human body is its ability to regulate itself and maintain optimal functioning. It uses a variety of natural processes to achieve this, including the self-digestion system of autophagy. This mechanism is the body's way of regenerating new and healthy cells through the _____. When a person's cells are stressed, autophagy is increased in order to ensure the normal operation of the body and keep it in homeostasis. It efficiently targets dysfunctional cells and ensures their elimination, often through the degradation of damaged and toxic proteins. The parts of the cell that are reused are the cytoplasm — fluid inside the cell — and organelles, which are structures with particular functions. These are broken down into amino acids, which the body utilizes for energy and cellular repair. In this way, autophagy helps prevent numerous health conditions such as Parkinson's and Alzheimer's and can even help fight against infectious diseases.

* autophagy: 자가포식(自家捕食)   ** homeostasis: 항상성(恒常性)

① preservation of healthy organs
② ingestion of certain edible proteins
③ application of medical procedures
④ restoration of dysfunctional cells
⑤ removal of damaged cell components

33

Common-pool resources are goods that are available to a large majority of the public even though _____ _____. For example, although there are plentiful forests, if every person were to collect as much wood as possible from these forests, their decline would be inevitable. A good such as this can be exploited over time, leading to an unreliable supply as individuals consume the resource to the detriment of others. A shortage impacts not only other members of a society or community but the very ones who seek out the supply and are able to consume it, too. This is what's known as the "tragedy of the commons." Preventing the overconsumption or depletion of such goods is accomplished through a number of actions, including government regulation and making the once common-pool resource into a private good. Collective action is also an effective method of controlling the consumption of the resource because individuals work together to preserve it. [3점]

① there isn't a great demand for them
② it is difficult for the public to access them
③ the resources are able to be easily renewed
④ corporations control the overconsumption of them
⑤ they have a limited stock that is vulnerable to abuse

34

Greed is a biologically based behavior intrinsic to human nature. Urges are fundamental to the survival of all living creatures, and yet humans not only experience desire from a biological standpoint, but from a social one as well. This differentiates the impulses humans have from those felt by animals, such as the drive to reproduce. People desire more than to merely stay alive; they also want material possessions and wealth. But in the modern world, _____, since individual behavior that resembles greed is natural and encouraged — people are advised to seek wealth and prosperity to the best of their abilities — while greed itself is condemned by society. This is because while greed actually benefits the individual, it can come at a cost for civilization when unrestricted. Sociologists assert that society aims to find an equilibrium of motivating individuals with greed while still limiting unrestrained greed by labeling it as a vice. [3점]

① greed is somewhat of a paradox
② people can restrain their impulses
③ desires have become unmanageable
④ animalistic urges have all but disappeared
⑤ materialism is no longer a prominent issue

35 다음 글에서 전체 흐름과 관계 <u>없는</u> 문장은?

Cloud computing has already transformed how many businesses operate around the world, and it will also soon shape people's lifestyles. One of the most significant changes has been increased flexibility in the workplace. ① Now that companies have the power to store, process, and manage all of their files on the cloud, employees are able to access data remotely as long as they can connect to the Internet. ② They no longer have to physically visit an office in order to obtain certain information and can virtually collaborate with others rather than setting aside time to meet. ③ Companies should be cautious of external data sharing when they utilize remote access technology. ④ Cloud storage also means that people will not need to rely on as many devices to use or share content. ⑤ A person can simply save their files on the cloud, generate links, and invite others to view them rather than having to go through the process of using a USB drive.

[36~37] 주어진 글 다음에 이어질 글의 순서로 가장 적절한 것을 고르시오.

36

The Swiss psychologist Carl Jung is credited with a great many of the field's most enduring concepts. But for practicing therapists the most useful of these is his approach to diagnosis.

(A) For Jung, the complex is a mass of interrelated ideas that operate in the unconscious mind. This "hidden mass of memories" is formed in our childhood and wields a powerful influence — in both positive and negative ways — over our present and future.

(B) Rather than classifying psychological phenomena as discrete disorders and shuttling patients into one-size-fits-all treatments, Jung's concept of the "complex" allows clinicians to identify how their conflicting problems are intertwined. This approach has been invaluable in understanding the behavior of certain patients who act according to a complex.

(C) Discussing issues in these terms allows therapists to discuss how mechanisms of this sort work in a holistic sense. In addition, it relieves the pressure of delivering unrealistically rapid relief to patients. [3점]

① (A) – (C) – (B)　　　　② (B) – (A) – (C)
③ (B) – (C) – (A)　　　　④ (C) – (A) – (B)
⑤ (C) – (B) – (A)

37

As popular culture has migrated from celebrity-centric to influencer-centric, money has moved along with it. This has led to the establishment of the creator economy.

(A) This resulted in a change in power dynamics. Platforms now must be able to compensate their influencers who bring in millions of users. And even then, it may not be enough, as more and more creators are accumulating wealth on their own terms.

(B) Powered by social media stars, this new ecosystem is in rapid growth; in 2021 alone, the creator economy collected more than 1.3 billion dollars in funding. But it wasn't always such a profitable field, and "Internet celebrities" were once looked down upon by the old guards of traditional marketplaces.

(C) Not much of a surprise, considering they barely made anything and had yet to penetrate their way fully into the consciousness of the public. Then suddenly, Internet platforms began their meteoric rise and became the birthplace for social media giants who amassed huge followings.

① (A) – (C) – (B)　　② (B) – (A) – (C)
③ (B) – (C) – (A)　　④ (C) – (A) – (B)
⑤ (C) –(B) – (A)

[38~39] 글의 흐름으로 보아, 주어진 문장이 들어가기에 가장 적절한 곳을 고르시오.

38

However, unlike science, which only asks how, philosophy asks why.

If science and technology continue on the current trajectory, the end result can only be the extinction of *homo sapiens* as a species or at least civilization as we know it. At some point, Artificial Intelligence will be perfected, which will spawn even more intelligence, and so forth, making humanity irrelevant. (①) Therefore, it is in the interest of our existence to temper our need for discovery with the wisdom of restraint. (②) Philosophy, in this regard, is our best weapon against the untamed dangers of scientific exploration. (③) While often thought of as an opposing force, philosophy is actually closely associated with science and robust enough to ward off crises. (④) Philosophy shares the ideals of logic and rigorous argumentation with science. (⑤) This is a consideration lacking in science but sorely needed. [3점]

* trajectory: 궤도

39

> To get the best results, it helps to engage as many of your senses as you can.

Mental rehearsal describes the technique of practicing an action in your mind before performing it in real life. (①) It is common with athletes but is just as useful in a wide variety of other fields and endeavors. (②) Its benefits are well-known and include increased confidence and concentration, reduced anxiety, and the ability to envision solutions to potential problems. (③) You might visualize yourself crossing the finish line at a race or shaking a client's hand over a successfully completed deal. (④) Then, with your sense of hearing, you might imagine the roar of a cheering crowd or words of congratulations from your colleagues. (⑤) Picturing positive outcomes such as these can help any concerns you might have about your preparedness melt away and give you a sense of control over an upcoming event.

40 다음 글의 내용을 한 문장으로 요약하고자 한다. 빈칸 (A), (B)에 들어갈 말로 가장 적절한 것은?

In the 1950s, Solomon Asch demonstrated the power of peer pressure in an experiment in which participants took a visual perception test requiring them to identify a line that was closest in length to another. This was a simple task, with the correct answer being obvious to participants 99% of the time in independent tests prior to the actual experiment. During the actual experiment, a single study participant was put in a room with several actors. The actors had been told beforehand to provide wrong answers to the questions, and it was found that the effect this had on the actual study participant was to go along with the rest of the group out of fear of being ridiculed. In fact, despite the correct answer being clear to them, many of the participants agreed with the majority and provided the incorrect answer in 12 critical trials of this experiment. However, when two participants were included in the same study instead of just one, and both were aware of what the correct answer was, they almost never followed the majority.

↓

The experiment above suggests that people may do something they know is wrong to ____(A)____ with a group but are more likely to ____(B)____ this behavior when someone else shares their opinion.

	(A)		(B)
①	conform	……	resist
②	conform	……	achieve
③	match	……	allow
④	argue	……	withstand
⑤	argue	……	accept

[41~42] 다음 글을 읽고, 물음에 답하시오.

The earliest types of writing, which were syllabic or logographic, came from the Mayans and Chinese. In these systems, each word or sentence was a self-contained symbol and could stand on its own. Thus, there was no need for spaces, periods, commas, and other such tools that help one understand texts. As alphabetic writing began to develop, though, the (a) absence of punctuation became a real problem. Reading became difficult to say the least, and some form of organization was necessary.

The remedy for this did not appear until around the end of the 3rd century BC when Greek scholar Aristophanes of Byzantium introduced the use of particular marks in order to make the reading of scrolls less (b) time-consuming. He suggested inserting dots to indicate where a passage ended and to show the length of (c) pause needed when reading aloud, which was how text was often conveyed to commoners since only the elite knew how to read. Some (d) praised the practice, especially many famous orators in Rome, but the marks slowly began to appear more and more frequently in documents until they became standardized. Christians in particular played a significant role in establishing punctuation, since they insisted on writing down their key tenets. So as Christianity began to spread across Europe, the incorporation of punctuation further (e) flourished and eventually developed into how we use it today.

* orator: 연설가, 웅변가   ** tenet: 교리

41 윗글의 제목으로 가장 적절한 것은?

① The Spread of Punctuation Worldwide
② The Modern Appeal of Early Writing Systems
③ The Development of Punctuation as a Necessary Reading Aid
④ How Have Ancient Texts Affected Historical Interpretations?
⑤ Punctuation: An Outdated System of Textual Organization

42 밑줄 친 (a)~(e) 중에서 문맥상 낱말의 쓰임이 적절하지 않은 것은? [3점]

① (a)　　② (b)　　③ (c)　　④ (d)　　⑤ (e)

[43~45] 다음 글을 읽고, 물음에 답하시오.

(A)

Once upon a time, a wise priest was headed toward the nearby town. He had been summoned by the king to come see him. As (a) he was walking along the road into town, he found a gold coin on the ground. The priest lived a simple life and was happy with everything he had, even though he was not wealthy. So, he decided to give the coin to someone who needed it more than he did and continued on.

(B)

"What is the meaning of this?" the king asked. "I am the richest man here. What do I need this coin for?" The priest replied, "I had decided to donate it to someone needy, but as (b) I strolled in your kingdom, there was no one. Everyone is living a full and happy life, content with what they have. Only you have the desire to gain more and are not satisfied with what you have. You are in need of this coin more than anyone I have seen."

(C)

It was the king and his army, marching into the square. They were preparing to travel to the neighboring state. The king spotted the priest. "I called (c) you here because I am going to invade another state to expand my kingdom," he said. "Please bless my endeavors, wise priest, so that I may be victorious!" The priest looked at the king thoughtfully, and then gave (d) him the gold coin.

(D)

The priest finally reached the town square. He saw many people busily getting ready for the day. Merchants shouted happily from their stores and customers greeted each other on the street. Children laughed and ran around. 'What a wonderful place,' the priest thought. He walked over and spoke with many people, but none were in need of the gold coin. Suddenly, (e) he heard loud horns.

43 주어진 글 (A)에 이어질 내용을 순서에 맞게 배열한 것으로 가장 적절한 것은?

① (B) – (D) – (C)   ② (C) – (B) – (D)
③ (C) – (D) – (B)   ④ (D) – (B) – (C)
⑤ (D) – (C) – (B)

44 밑줄 친 (a)~(e) 중에서 가리키는 대상이 나머지 넷과 다른 것은?

① (a)   ② (b)   ③ (c)   ④ (d)   ⑤ (e)

45 윗글에 관한 내용으로 적절하지 <u>않은</u> 것은?

① 왕은 사제를 불러들였다.
② 사제는 마을로 가는 길에 금화를 주웠다.
③ 사제는 왕에게 금화가 필요할 것이라 생각했다.
④ 왕은 영토를 확장하고 싶어 했다.
⑤ 마을의 상인들은 아이들에게 화가 나 있었다.

정답·해설·해석 p. 33

문제풀이 후 확인사항
1. 45분 내에 문제를 풀었다.
2. 체크해둔 문제와 틀린 문제는 해설을 꼼꼼히 확인했다.

수고하셨습니다! HackersBook.com에서 제공하는 어휘리스트로 어휘를 암기하세요.

05회 실전모의고사

목표 시간: 45분   시작: ___ 시 ___ 분 ~ 종료: ___ 시 ___ 분   점수: ___ 점 / 63점

* [3점] 표시가 있는 문제 제외하고는 모두 2점으로 계산합니다.

18 다음 글의 목적으로 가장 적절한 것은?

Dear Program Coordinator,

　As summer approaches, I am writing this email about my interest in participating in the summer science camp. I want to ensure that I meet all of the requirements necessary to enroll, so I would appreciate it if you could clarify a point for me. The advertisement I saw said that only a cover letter, a transcript, and an essay were needed for application submission. However, I was wondering if I could also forward a letter of recommendation from my teacher. I feel as though it has valuable insight into what kind of student I am and would be useful as a supplementary document. I hope this is a possibility, and I appreciate your time.

Sincerely,
Grace Evans

① 과학 캠프 준비를 지시하려고
② 과학 캠프 인솔자 모집에 지원하려고
③ 과학 캠프의 주요 일정을 확인하려고
④ 청소년을 위한 과학 캠프 개최를 건의하려고
⑤ 과학 캠프 참가를 위한 제출 서류에 대해 문의하려고

19 다음 글에 나타난 'I'의 심경 변화로 가장 적절한 것은?

I was impatient to get home from the office. It was Friday and I was worn out from a long week at work. Usually I'd have plans, but that evening I just wanted to lie down on my bed. Falling asleep while I was watching television sounded like the ideal night alone. I opened my door and gasped. All of my friends were in my apartment surrounded by colorful balloons. "Happy birthday!" they yelled as I came inside. There were boxes of pizza and a big cake on the table. They'd planned a whole night of activities to celebrate. I quickly forgot my fatigue and looked forward to the fun night ahead.

① lonely → scared
② jealous → pleased
③ exhausted → thrilled
④ horrified → confident
⑤ anxious → encouraged

20 다음 글에서 필자가 주장하는 바로 가장 적절한 것은?

For many people, being vulnerable is frightening as it comes with risks. By being open about your fears and sharing your secrets with others, there is always the chance you will be judged or, worse, rejected. This can be very painful, and to protect yourself from being hurt, you might no longer allow yourself to be vulnerable. On the surface, you might think shutting down and keeping to yourself is a good thing because you feel that avoiding the possibility of criticism from others will eliminate your pain. In reality, this approach merely prevents you from developing genuine connections with others.

According to noted expert Dr. Brené Brown, "Vulnerability is the core and the heart of meaningful human experiences." Without it, you are less likely to receive empathy from others, leading to feelings of isolation and loneliness.

① 외롭지 않으려면 폭넓은 대인 관계를 유지해야 한다.
② 자신에 대한 타인의 비판적 의견을 겸허히 수용해야 한다.
③ 가까운 사이일수록 상대방을 배려하는 자세를 가져야 한다.
④ 타인의 신뢰를 얻기 위해서 때로는 자신의 약점을 숨겨야 한다.
⑤ 유대 관계를 형성하려면 약한 모습을 보이는 것을 두려워해서는 안 된다.

21 밑줄 친 blazed a new trail이 다음 글에서 의미하는 바로 가장 적절한 것은?

Before the creation of environmental, social, and governance (ESG) criteria, the main basis for investing in a company was financial return. Profits were sought through companies no matter how sustainable they were or how they did business. However, as environmental and social issues became more important over time, especially to Millennials and members of Generation Z, so did investing money responsibly. ESG criteria create a point of reference for investors when they want to fund businesses that follow ethical practices. They consider factors like how ecologically friendly a company is, what impact the company has on their employees and customers, and whether the company's long-term strategies are being achieved. The impact of ESG criteria has been profound, with one-third of all professionally managed assets being subject to these standards. They have blazed a new trail, and people, as well as companies, are taking notice.

① made it easier to acquire investments
② doubted how investments are managed
③ invented a new way of enforcing policies
④ redefined how a business becomes successful
⑤ altered the limitations imposed on businesses

22 다음 글의 요지로 가장 적절한 것은?

A common misconception about meditation — that there is a requirement for complete focus on a single idea or action to clear the mind — has led some to give up on this practice because it seems too difficult. What they may not know is that there is a form of meditation called "mindfulness." How does such technique work? It requires that the mind be intensely aware of all sensations and emotions; rather than trying to suppress or ignore these, we should allow ourselves to experience them freely and without judgment. So, if you find thoughts about personal problems or unfinished tasks entering your head while meditating, simply acknowledge them and take note of how they make you feel. This approach allows you to process your emotional responses in an objective manner, which can lessen your overall anxiety.

① 선입견을 갖는 것은 객관적 판단을 흐린다.
② 명상을 할 때는 하나의 주제에 집중하는 것이 좋다.
③ 부정적인 생각을 차단하는 것이 효과적인 명상이다.
④ 감정을 자유롭게 표출하는 것은 스트레스를 완화시킨다.
⑤ 생각과 감정을 온전히 받아들여 정신 건강을 개선할 수 있다.

23 다음 글의 주제로 가장 적절한 것은? [3점]

With regard to its definition, irony has a somewhat simple one: how things appear on the surface opposes what they actually are. It seems like an easy enough concept to grasp, yet it is so subtle and nuanced that there are neuroscientists and psychologists dedicated to studying how irony is understood. It is possible for most people to recognize the irony of a Snowball Fight Festival being canceled due to a blizzard, yet the reason irony cannot be pinned down so easily is because not every coincidence, paradox, or unexpected oddity can be categorized as one. The situation is made more unclear as irony can further be broken down into one of three categories: situational, verbal, and dramatic. And to muddy the waters even further, verbal irony and its cousin sarcasm are often indistinguishable.

① ambiguous nature of the reasoning behind irony
② impact of irony on a situation's dynamics
③ professions related to identifying irony
④ characteristics of the different types of irony
⑤ developments in how irony has been defined over time

24 다음 글의 제목으로 가장 적절한 것은?

According to a University College London study, eating disorders may be a coping tool. For individuals who experienced abuse at a young age, eating disorders might offer them some sense of control when they feel like they have none. If a person is continuously criticized when growing up, it is only natural that they might then begin to view themselves as unworthy. This manner of thinking can lead to the development of disorders as victims are unable to accept that they are good enough. Food can also act as a distraction or a comfort. In the study, some children who were put in stressful situations were unable to eat at all, while others turned to a snack to cope. An obsession with past traumatic episodes can lead to a person experiencing negative emotions easily. As a result, they might seek relief through food, frequently partaking in binge eating to deal with distressing memories.

* partake: (참여)하다

① How Diet Contributes to Stress
② Techniques to Cope with Eating Disorders
③ The Rise in Eating Disorders among Children
④ Childhood Trauma: A Cause of Eating Disorders
⑤ A Healthy Meal: The Solution to Improving Your Mood

25 다음 도표의 내용과 일치하지 <u>않는</u> 것은?

Global Grain Consumption of Food and Feed

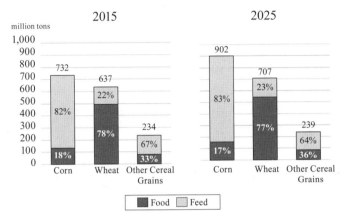

The above graph shows the global grain consumption of food and feed in 2015 and in 2025. ① The combined corn consumption of food and feed is anticipated to increase by 170 million tons, and the combined wheat consumption of food and feed by 70 million tons from 2015 to 2025. ② In 2025, like in 2015, more than 80% of corn is expected to be used on feed while less than 80% of wheat is expected to be consumed as food. ③ Meanwhile, the percentage of corn consumed as food is expected to decrease by 1% from 2015 to 2025. ④ In 2025, the percentage of both corn and wheat consumption of feed is projected to increase by 1%, respectively. ⑤ In both years, the gap between the percentage of other cereal grains consumed as food and that consumed as feed is larger than 30%.

26 Alfred Brendel에 관한 다음 글의 내용과 일치하지 <u>않는</u> 것은?

Noted composer and pianist Alfred Brendel was born in Czechoslovakia on January 5, 1931. Although he took piano lessons as a child, beginning at the age of six, he never studied music formally at an institute. Nevertheless, he gave a public recital as a teenager, performing one of his own pieces and ones by Bach and Brahms. In 1952, he made his first recording and then went on to release a large number of albums with three different record companies. His work has garnered him worldwide fame, and he was made an honorary member of the Vienna

Philharmonic Orchestra. In 2008, Brendel announced his retirement during a concert in Vienna, and his final show was in New York later that year. Since then, he has appeared in an award-winning documentary, and he has also released a book of poetry.

① 6세에 피아노를 배우기 시작했다.
② 10대 시절에 대중 앞에서 자작곡을 연주했다.
③ 세 곳의 음반 회사와 함께 많은 앨범을 발표했다.
④ Vienna에서 마지막 공연을 했다.
⑤ 은퇴 후 시집을 출간했다.

27 Ocean Voyage Aquarium Tour에 관한 다음 안내문의 내용과 일치하지 <u>않는</u> 것은?

Ocean Voyage Aquarium Tour

Enjoy a tour of the most popular exhibits at Ocean Voyage Aquarium. This special tour gives you an up-close look at the animals.

Details:
- Available on Tuesdays and Fridays
- Tour times: 9 a.m., 11 a.m., 3 p.m., 5 p.m.
- Tour lasts 90 minutes.
- Maximum of 10 people per tour (including children)
- Fee: $10 for adults, $5 for children under 12

Activities on tour:
- You will get a chance to feed the sea lions.
- Visit Penguin Island and shake flippers!
- Visit the nursery with baby animals.

This tour is available for members only.

① 동물들을 가까이에서 볼 수 있다.
② 매주 화요일과 금요일에 4회 진행된다.
③ 투어 1회당 인원은 최대 10명까지이다.
④ 바다사자에게 먹이를 줄 수 있다.
⑤ 비회원도 투어에 참여할 수 있다.

28 *Nature and Nurture* Art Exhibition에 관한 다음 안내문의 내용과 일치하는 것은?

Nature and Nurture Art Exhibition

The National Museum of Contemporary Art is debuting its newest exhibition, *Nature and Nurture*, next month.
• From August 11 to December 15
• Open Tuesday to Saturday, 9 a.m.–5 p.m.
• $30 Admission Fee (free for children under 6)

Contents
• Over 60 pieces featured
• Artwork by 25 different renowned artists
• Themes and images that touch on parenting, childhood, and adolescence

More Information
Tickets can be booked by phone or online. Guided tours are only available by reservation.

For a preview of the exhibit, please visit our website at www.NMCA.com.

---

① 두 달 동안 진행된다.
② 6세 미만 어린이의 입장료는 30달러이다.
③ 총 25점의 작품이 전시된다.
④ 입장권은 전화나 온라인으로 예매할 수 있다.
⑤ 예약 없이도 가이드 투어가 가능하다.

29 다음 글의 밑줄 친 부분 중, 어법상 틀린 것은? [3점]

The perception of time varies from culture to culture, which can create challenges when conducting business internationally. For cultures with a linear sense of time, ① alike those of the United States and Germany, time is perceived as moving quickly into the future in a straight line, with the past having little bearing on anything. Because the past cannot be reclaimed, people from such cultures want ② what they do with their time to profit them in some way. Otherwise, it is considered wasted. It is therefore unsurprising that punctuality is key to people who ③ see time in such a fashion. In countries like Spain and Italy, however, the focus is more on the present, with the quality or significance of a meeting ranking higher in importance ④ than maintaining a strict schedule. People from these cultures might see meeting times as irrelevant in comparison to the meeting ⑤ itself and be late for their appointments, potentially causing offense to clients or partners from other cultures.

30 다음 글의 밑줄 친 부분 중, 문맥상 낱말의 쓰임이 적절하지 않은 것은? [3점]

Many Americans blame new arrivals for their nation's economic problems, believing that cutting back on immigration would ① benefit the United States. In reality, however, statistics show that the contributions of immigrants are significant, and the continued success of the United States is reliant on them. One common belief is that immigrants take jobs away from Americans because they're willing to work for ② more money. The fact is, employers pay immigrants the same wage as American workers because doing otherwise would be illegal. Also, some employers would struggle to fill ③ essential jobs in agriculture and manufacturing, industries that drive the US economy if there were no immigrants. Jobs in these industries are increasingly viewed by Americans as ④ undesirable. Furthermore, immigrants are actually more likely to create jobs, whether for themselves or new employees, than to take them away. Immigrants to America ⑤ launch new businesses at twice the rate of people who are US citizens at birth.

[31~34] 다음 빈칸에 들어갈 말로 가장 적절한 것을 고르시오.

31

Humans are creatures of _____, which might explain why we have the tendency to watch our favorite movies and television shows over and over again. Online streaming services have made it easy to access new content, and yet many people still find themselves drawn to older films and shows. But why do we love watching titles we already know from beginning to end? Research actually indicates that this can be a reassuring experience. We crave order and safety, and predictable content delivers these qualities. There's nothing new to mentally process with a familiar past movie or series, and we know how we will emotionally respond to something we've seen before. Our brains are programmed to avoid the unknown, and so we stick to what we're familiar with. This can also be nostalgic for us since people associate old movies and shows with fond memories. Watching a classic Christmas film might remind you of being with your family, or a sitcom could take you back to your childhood. The routine of it is comforting and keeps you coming back for more.

① humor ② intelligence
③ certainty ④ imagination
⑤ relationships

32

Although poor verbal skills are a mark of autism spectrum disorder (ASD), a study has demonstrated that people with ASD _____ a more advanced ability to create and control mental imagery. This skill is fundamental for analyzing and manipulating visual patterns and images and can be assessed through completion of a visuospatial test. One such task was given to the study's participants, prompting them to imagine a letter inside of a circle. Portions of the circle were then highlighted and the test subjects were asked which part would contain most of the letter. The study also included a test in which participants had to compare 3D objects and visualize what they would look like if they were rotated. In both experiments, people with ASD outperformed non-autistic people. They were able to perceive, examine, and judge mental images more quickly and accurately. This aligns with previous research that indicates ASD could result in superior visual detection skills as well as impressive visual memory. [3점]

① slowly lose
② can identify
③ may possess
④ are in need of
⑤ definitely conceal

33

At the center of nearly every observed galaxy lies a black hole, which in turn is flanked by the celestial bodies we see. Surrounding all this is a "halo" of dark matter that is unobservable but nevertheless detectable by its exertion on gravity. Initially, astronomers presumed it was the number of stars that determined the size of a galaxy's black hole; the more stars, the bigger the black hole. However, new evidence suggests that _____. The connection was discovered by analyzing the way elliptical galaxies evolved. When two smaller galaxies combined and became elliptical, the dark matter in each one merged to create a massive black hole. Scientists believe this is what ultimately dictated the new galaxy's shape and guided the growth of its black hole. This is due to the fact that dark matter weighs more than anything else in the process, and so its influence on the other elements is prominent.

* elliptical: 타원형의

① some stars exert more gravity
② black holes can become visible
③ gravity impacts the growth of dark matter
④ dark matter assumes different shapes
⑤ dark matter plays a larger role

34

"Equivocation" refers to two equal voices, and when it appears in political speech, _____ _____. This manner of speaking is often adopted when the speaker wishes to avoid providing a direct answer to a question but does not want to tell an obvious lie. To this end, the speaker purposely makes what they are really saying unclear. For instance, if they say, "I have the *right* to say what I want, so it's only *right* that I do so," it may confuse the listener into thinking that the speaker's legal freedom to voice their opinion is equivalent to their being morally superior. The shift in denotation often goes unnoticed without close scrutiny, and in our minds, we falsely conflate or connect two disparate ideas. If later, the speaker does something immoral, we cannot point back to the statement and find them guilty. The error falls on the listener as the speaker can truthfully claim, "I did not lie." [3점]

① it reflects the ideological beliefs of the listeners
② the intention is to put the listeners' minds at ease
③ the meaning of the statement can be misinterpreted
④ it can directly contradict a speaker's earlier statements
⑤ false statements about an opponent are made by one speaker

35 다음 글에서 전체 흐름과 관계 없는 문장은?

Although guide dogs that work with visually impaired people undergo extensive training, and only the very best are placed into service, some are withdrawn from service for reasons other than retirement. ① According to a study, the most common reasons for early withdrawal are behavioral issues, such as fear and aggression. ② These tend to occur most commonly in male dogs under three and a half years of age. ③ A dog's willingness to work, which is an issue commonly associated with dogs over the age of six, can also warrant removal from service. ④ Owners are usually given the option to keep their guide dogs even after retirement, but most owners are unable to care for them while training with a new dog. ⑤ Studies like this are valuable because being able to predict behavioral changes in dogs at different ages may help in the development of training programs that can reduce the occurrence of service withdrawal.

[36~37] 주어진 글 다음에 이어질 글의 순서로 가장 적절한 것을 고르시오.

36

Despite the negative implications it is often associated with, gentrification is not necessarily bad for low-income families.

(A) With less poverty and safer streets overall, the effect on former residents, particularly children, is significant. Influenced by who and what they see around them, children in gentrifying areas are more likely to develop diverse social networks and pursue a college education, which gives them a chance to achieve upward social mobility.

(B) It is usually assumed that when wealthier people move into impoverished neighborhoods, they use their money to make changes and encourage business development. The consequence of this is an increase in property values, which drives up the cost of rent and forces former residents out.

(C) Yet for those who stay, there are distinct advantages. The influx of funds into a neighborhood inevitably leads to more opportunities for less well-off households to live in dynamic urban areas where jobs are available and crime is lower.

① (A) – (C) – (B) ② (B) – (A) – (C)
③ (B) – (C) – (A) ④ (C) – (A) – (B)
⑤ (C) – (B) – (A)

37

Among the inner planets of the Solar System, only Earth boasts a magnetic field called the magnetosphere. It is crucial to our existence because it protects us from atmospheric erosion caused by the Sun's charged particles.

(A) Solar winds can disrupt it, leading to geomagnetic storms that penetrate the atmosphere and obstruct our satellites. In addition, it weakens considerably when the planet's magnetic poles gradually shift and flip, which can result in numerous repercussions.

(B) In this regard, it acts very much like a shield, as it also holds back cosmic radiation and other unwanted energy harmful to life. While it is an effective gatekeeper, it can be affected by a number of factors.

(C) With a minimal field, compasses would not work and technical issues with satellites would occur. The ozone would likely break down and ultraviolet radiation exposure would increase. While none of these effects would cause an irreversible and immediate disaster, it's safe to say that the consequences would be enough to cause some disorder. [3점]

① (A) – (C) – (B)　　② (B) – (A) – (C)
③ (B) – (C) – (A)　　④ (C) – (A) – (B)
⑤ (C) – (B) – (A)

[38~39] 글의 흐름으로 보아, 주어진 문장이 들어가기에 가장 적절한 곳을 고르시오.

38

Generally, though, monopolies are regarded by most consumers as a negative.

Monopolies are companies that effectively control all or most of the market share in an industry. For companies that have monopoly power, this is undoubtedly a positive situation, in that revenues generated by a market are collected entirely by them. (①) Monopolies not only earn more, but also spend less, since they can more easily achieve "economies of scale" and do not have to spend great sums on marketing themselves against other firms. (②) Monopolies can even confer advantages to consumers since they can provide price stability and invest the money they save in developing better products. (③) For one thing, monopolies face little to no threat of competition, meaning that consumers have no choice but to buy what they offer. (④) They can then set prices at almost any level without worrying that customers will find someone else. (⑤) And monopolies are under no obligation to improve what they offer, which can restrain innovation and lead to products and services of inferior quality.

* economies of scale: 규모의 경제

39

> Though the future this describes may sound utopian to some, it gives significant cause for concern.

In 1997, when AI computer Deep Blue beat chess champion Gary Kasparov, it was the beginning of the end for many. (①) The next step in AI evolution was to go beyond the parameters of such artificial narrow intelligence (ANI) and create artificial general intelligence (AGI). (②) Unlike ANI, AGI means that computers will have the ability to teach themselves; they will evolve, learn, and "reproduce" better versions on their own. (③) Irving Good pointed out that "the first ultra-intelligent machine is the last invention that man need ever make." (④). There is, after all, no reason to presume that an entity with superior intelligence will feel grateful to humans for inventing it and work in our best interests. (⑤) An ultra-intelligent machine could instead realize that humans are inferior in every way and could conclude that humanity is obsolete and eradicate us. [3점]

40 다음 글의 내용을 한 문장으로 요약하고자 한다. 빈칸 (A), (B)에 들어갈 말로 가장 적절한 것은?

When it comes to animals that pass diseases on to humans, bats are especially feared. Not only does their tendency to live in groups facilitate the transfer of pathogens among colony members, but their ability to fly enables these pathogens to be spread fast and efficiently elsewhere. For a long time, it was unknown how bats could host so many deadly viruses without being affected themselves. Recent research has found that their ability to do so is related to their unique response to viruses. Essentially, bats have evolved to prevent their immune systems from reacting strongly to the viruses that they bear, as the immune systems of most land mammals do when encountering a disease. This limits any effects of illness they experience. It may seem counterintuitive for an organism to benefit from an underactive immune system, but it is related to inflammation levels. A moderate amount of inflammation in response to a disease may counteract it, but excessive inflammation can cause extensive and even lifelong damage to an organism, which is often the case in humans.

* pathogen: 병원균 ** inflammation: 염증

⬇

Bats are ____(A)____ of a variety of diseases that are harmful to humans but they do not get sick themselves due to a ____(B)____ immune response.

	(A)		(B)
①	creators	⋯⋯	rapid
②	receivers	⋯⋯	strong
③	carriers	⋯⋯	reduced
④	creators	⋯⋯	slow
⑤	carriers	⋯⋯	raised

[41~42] 다음 글을 읽고, 물음에 답하시오.

Although evolution is a continual and sometimes exceedingly quick process, long-lasting evolutionary changes actually take quite some time. Around a million years, to be exact. When scientists compared data regarding evolutionary changes from short periods of time — 10 to 100 years — to those that occurred over much longer durations, as demonstrated by fossil records, they found that rapid changes often fail to become (a) permanent. In addition, these developments might be restricted to smaller populations. Long-lasting change, in contrast, happens quite (b) slowly in what researchers state is a "remarkably consistent pattern." They are fueled by forces that endure over time and affect populations on a larger scale. This hypothesis (c) supports the theory of punctuated equilibrium — brought forward in the 1970s — which suggests that evolutionary changes follow a pattern of little change, referred to as "stasis", and then "punctuational change." Zoologist Josef Uyeda states that "evolutionary adaptations are caused by some force of natural selection such as environmental change, predation or anthropogenic disturbance, and these forces have to (d) continue and become widespread for the change to persist and accumulate." According to computation biologist Michael Palmer, these changes may also be accurately followed as "there are only a few viable mutations at any point, which makes the dynamics (e) predictable and repeatable, even over the long term." Long-term changes are persistent but slow, and most species only survive less than one to ten million years before dying out or becoming new species altogether.

* anthropogenic: 인위적인, 인간에 의해 발생하는

41 윗글의 제목으로 가장 적절한 것은?

① Predict Future Adaptations for Current Species!
② How Do Long-Term Evolutionary Changes Occur?
③ Natural Selection: Species that Change to Survive
④ Patterns of Adaptations that Have Benefited Animals
⑤ The Relationship Between Population Size and Evolutionary Speed

42 밑줄 친 (a)~(e) 중에서 문맥상 낱말의 쓰임이 적절하지 않은 것은?

① (a)　　② (b)　　③ (c)　　④ (d)　　⑤ (e)

[43~45] 다음 글을 읽고, 물음에 답하시오.

(A)

Ellie Strickland grew up to be a famous scientist who made many important discoveries. She was able to do this by thinking about problems in creative ways that were different from other researchers. A reporter asked her how (a) <u>she</u> was able to be so innovative and think outside the box. Ellie responded by telling the reporter a story from her childhood.

(B)

Ellie chose the sponge. Finally, after they were finished, her mother had one more lesson for (b) <u>her</u>. "This was a failed experiment on how to carry a big bottle with small hands. Now, why don't we fill the bottle with water and try different ways to see how you can carry it without dropping it." This experience taught her that she didn't have to be afraid of making mistakes. That is why now, she uses (c) <u>her</u> mistakes as opportunities to try and discover new things.

(C)

She said that when she was 5 years old, she tried to get a bottle of milk from the fridge by herself. Unfortunately, the bottle was too heavy and she accidentally dropped it on the floor, spilling the milk everywhere. Her mother walked in and saw the mess. But instead of scolding her or punishing her, (d) <u>she</u> said, "What a big mess! Well, the damage is already done. Should we play in it a bit before we clean it up?"

(D)

So the two of them played around in the puddle for a while before her mother said, "Whenever we make a mess, we eventually have to clean it up and make things proper again. But how we do it is not determined. So how would (e) <u>you</u> like to clean this up? We can use a sponge, a mop, or a towel."

43 주어진 글 (A)에 이어질 내용을 순서에 맞게 배열한 것으로 가장 적절한 것은?

① (B) – (D) – (C)　　　　② (C) – (B) – (D)
③ (C) – (D) – (B)　　　　④ (D) – (B) – (C)
⑤ (D) – (C) – (B)

44 밑줄 친 (a)~(e) 중에서 가리키는 대상이 나머지 넷과 다른 것은?

① (a)　　② (b)　　③ (c)　　④ (d)　　⑤ (e)

45 윗글에 관한 내용으로 적절하지 <u>않은</u> 것은?

① 기자는 Ellie에게 창의적 사고를 할 수 있었던 방법을 물었다.
② 어머니는 병에 물을 채워서 다시 옮기자고 했다.
③ 우유병은 Ellie가 들기에 너무 무거웠다.
④ 어머니는 바닥에 쏟아진 우유를 보고 Ellie를 혼냈다.
⑤ 어머니는 쏟아진 우유를 닦을 도구 세 가지를 제시했다.

정답·해설·해석 p. 43

문제풀이 후 확인사항
1. 45분 내에 문제를 풀었다.
2. 체크해둔 문제와 틀린 문제는 해설을 꼼꼼히 확인했다.

수고하셨습니다! HackersBook.com에서 제공하는 어휘리스트로 어휘를 암기하세요.

06회 실전모의고사

* [3점] 표시가 있는 문제 제외하고는 모두 2점으로 계산합니다.

18 다음 글의 목적으로 가장 적절한 것은?

Dear Professor Harlow,

My family will be visiting Cape City next month for our vacation. Recently, I read online about your Stargazing Expedition for kids and thought it would be a wonderful experience. My husband and I have two young boys, ages six and eight. They are very interested in space, and I think they would love your program. It would be a great family activity. I saw on your website that reservations must be made in advance. Could I make a booking for four people for August 13? I hope there are still spaces available for us to join you. Thank you for your time.

Respectfully,
Eleanor Small

① 방문 일정의 변동을 미리 알리려고
② 프로그램 예약이 가능한지 문의하려고
③ 체험 학습을 진행할 강사를 모집하려고
④ 새로운 가족 단위 프로그램을 소개하려고
⑤ 아이들에게 맞는 활동의 추천을 부탁하려고

19 다음 글의 상황에 나타난 분위기로 가장 적절한 것은?

The sailors rushed around, shouting and yelling in panic. The heavy smoke made it difficult to see what was going on, and people were bumping into each other and knocking things over. No one really knew how the fire started, but it spread quickly across the old vessel. The captain looked up at the night sky, but it was clear and filled with stars; there was not even a hint of a rain cloud. "Abandon ship!" he cried. As his command echoed down to the lower decks, the sailors stopped trying to put out the flames and began lowering the life rafts. They went as fast as they could, as the fire was making its way up to where they were.

① boring and monotonous
② eager and enthusiastic
③ hopeful and comforted
④ solemn and sacred
⑤ urgent and desperate

20 다음 글에서 필자가 주장하는 바로 가장 적절한 것은?

With regard to therapy, there is widely held misperception that the client is expected to simply follow the lead of the counselor. In truth, it is vital that the person seeking help express what he or she hopes to accomplish by receiving treatment at the onset of the first session. This should not be interpreted as meaning that the client must request particular therapeutic measures or specify what form of assistance the counselor should provide. Rather, the client must clearly state the problem that needs to be overcome as well as what he or she hopes to accomplish. A person who is experiencing social anxiety might say, "I find it difficult to interact with people I have just met, and I would like to be able to make new friends more easily." By setting a goal in this manner, the client increases the likelihood that the counselor will be able to develop an effective course of treatment.

* client: 내담자

① 내담자도 상담 기법에 대해 정확히 알고 있어야 한다.
② 상담사는 내담자의 요청 사항을 충실히 이행해야 한다.
③ 내담자는 첫 번째 상담에서 감정 표현을 절제해야 한다.
④ 상담사는 내담자에게 치료 방법의 선택권을 보장해야 한다.
⑤ 내담자는 상담사에게 해결하려는 문제를 명확히 밝혀야 한다.

21 밑줄 친 what they see should be what they get이 다음 글에서 의미하는 바로 가장 적절한 것은? [3점]

In the past, generations of schoolchildren grew up with only a tiny fraction of books featuring ethnically diverse characters, many of whom were portrayed in racially insensitive ways. Nowadays, schools are becoming increasingly aware of the need to impart students with knowledge of other cultures and, as a result, are adding books that promote multiculturalism to the curriculum. As one example, *Whoever You Are* by Mem Fox illustrates the fact that although children around the world lead lives that may seem very different, they all have the same emotions. Books like these teach children that diversity should be celebrated rather than feared — a valuable lesson given that the world is more globalized than ever before and the likelihood of having classmates with different backgrounds is high. In this sense, when it comes to the literature available to modern students, <u>what they see should be what they get</u>.

① Children easily get confused by different cultures.
② Schools should be required to purchase works by modern authors.
③ Literature that promotes multiculturalism is now common in schools.
④ Students should have access to books that reflect classroom diversity.
⑤ Classes must always include students from diverse ethnic backgrounds.

22 다음 글의 요지로 가장 적절한 것은?

During a workshop I run for people planning to start their own business, I find it useful to conduct an activity that allows them to precisely perceive themselves. I hand each person a list of adjectives that describe different character traits, along with some blank pieces of paper. On one, I ask them to write down several adjectives that they would apply to themselves. Then, they must do the same for the other members of the group. Once this stage is completed, I have each person create a list with three categories in the following order: "open," "hidden," and "blind spot." For each participant, the first category includes the traits that were included on the person's list and that of another group member; the second contains words that participants used to describe themselves but other people did not use; and the third has only the adjectives that were selected by other group members to describe them. Doing this provides insight into the accuracy of the group members' perceptions of themselves. If you do not know yourself, you are likely to experience significant difficulties when you try to be your own boss.

① 자기 객관화를 위해 정기적인 사업가 훈련이 필요하다.
② 특정한 성격의 특징이 성공적인 사업 운영에 유리하다.
③ 구성원 간의 상호 이해가 조직의 생산성을 향상시킨다.
④ 다양한 단체 활동은 조직 내 협동심 발달에 도움이 된다.
⑤ 사업을 시작하려는 사람들에게는 정확한 자기 인식이 필요하다.

23 다음 글의 주제로 가장 적절한 것은?

When attempting to understand a law that does not fully address a situation or that has ambiguous language, judges are often required to consider legislative intent. This involves identifying the underlying goals of the creators of the law to determine its application to the matter being dealt with by the court. In most cases, the process requires an analysis of the documents connected to the passage of the legislation, such as debate transcripts and early drafts. The information will then be used to figure out the relationship between the law and an issue that it does not explicitly focus on. For instance, legislation created at a time when only male citizens were eligible to vote might include the wording "all men" when granting a specific right regarding participation in elections. A modern judge who examined the relevant documentation and discovered that it was intended to apply to anyone with the right to cast a ballot would then understand the wording to mean "all eligible voters" — including women.

① problems related to ambiguously worded laws
② the importance of creating clear legislation
③ how laws are interpreted by judges
④ the role of judges in creating new legislation
⑤ why legislators need to have realistic objectives

24 다음 글의 제목으로 가장 적절한 것은?

Hygiene has improved considerably since the development of sewage systems. Nevertheless, some research suggests that too much hygiene can actually impair people's immune systems, with children possibly benefiting from a healthy exposure to bacteria, fungi, and viruses. The hygiene hypothesis, which supports this notion, proposes that individuals who grow up in environments that lack these microbes are more likely to contract disorders such as allergies and asthma. Their immune systems have not been conditioned as nature intended since they have not come into contact with a wide variety of microorganisms. This process is instrumental to a person's health and their body's ability to fight infections. In contrast, if children are brought up in a manner that introduces them to a range of microscopic organisms — meaning they are allowed to play outside and get a little dirty — their immune systems can become more resilient.

* microbe: 미생물

① Can a Germ-Free Environment Exist?
② How a Strong Immune System Works
③ How to Eliminate Microscopic Organisms
④ Embracing Microbes for Strong Immunity
⑤ Staying Clean: The Secret to Good Health

25 다음 도표의 내용과 일치하지 <u>않는</u> 것은?

Breakdown of Wastewater Generation in Spain by Point Sources

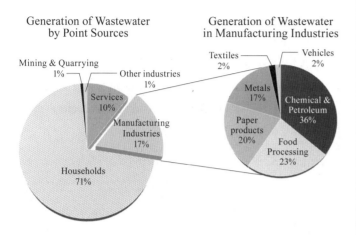

Generation of Wastewater by Point Sources

Generation of Wastewater in Manufacturing Industries

The pie charts above show the breakdown of wastewater generation in Spain by point sources, particularly focusing on manufacturing industries. ① As for the generation of wastewater by point sources, households account for more wastewater than all other categories combined. ② Of wastewater from manufacturing industries, the percentage generated in the manufacture of paper products is ten times as large as that generated in the manufacture of vehicles. ③ The combined proportion of the wastewater generated in the manufacture of paper products and metals is still lower than that generated in chemical and petroleum manufacturing. ④ While there is only a 3% gap between the second- and third-ranked sources of wastewater in manufacturing industries, the difference between the first and second is larger than 10%. ⑤ The proportions of the wastewater generated in the manufacture of both textiles and vehicles are only 2% each.

26 Willis Carrier에 관한 다음 글의 내용과 일치하지 <u>않는</u> 것은?

Born in Angola, New York in 1876, engineer Willis Carrier is known as the inventor of the modern air-conditioning system. Carrier graduated from Cornell University in 1901 with a master's degree in engineering. In 1902, he created a device that could reduce the water content of air to address problems experienced by a publishing company during humid weather. He then spent several years improving it. Carrier received a patent in 1906 for a system that could both lower humidity and cool the air at the same time. Throughout this period, he had been employed as an engineer by a firm called Buffalo Forge Company. However, in 1914, Carrier and several of his coworkers quit their positions at the manufacturer. They pooled their saving to set up their own business producing air conditioners. The Carrier Corporation went on to become one of the biggest employers in New York and is now a multinational corporation.

① Cornell 대학에서 공학 석사 학위를 취득했다.
② 출판사가 겪는 문제를 해결하려고 했다.
③ 습도와 온도를 동시에 낮추는 장치에 관한 특허를 받았다.
④ 1914년에 근무하던 회사에서 해고되었다.
⑤ 설립한 회사는 뉴욕에서 가장 큰 회사 중 하나가 되었다.

27 Sci-Fi Short Story Contest에 관한 다음 안내문의 내용과 일치하지 <u>않는</u> 것은?

Sci-Fi Short Story Contest

Attention all writers of science fiction! Show off your creativity, and submit a sci-fi short story to *Future Worlds Literary Magazine* for a chance to be published and win a prize!

Deadline: November 22, 10 a.m.

Submissions
• Can't be more than 2,000 words
• One submission per entrant
• Must not have been previously published

Judging Guidelines
• Plot
• Setting and atmosphere
• Theme

Prizes
• First Place: publication of the story in the magazine, $100
• Second Place: free annual subscription to the magazine, $50
(The top 10 entrants will also receive thorough feedback from our renowned editors.)

* Submissions must be made online at www. futureworldslitmag.com.

---

① 제출 기한은 11월 22일 오전 10시까지이다.
② 응모작은 2,000 단어를 넘지 않아야 한다.
③ 심사 기준 중에 배경과 분위기 항목이 있다.
④ 2등 수상자는 편집자의 피드백을 받을 수 없다.
⑤ 응모작 제출은 웹사이트에서 진행된다.

---

28 Sense One Virtual Reality Headset 사용에 관한 다음 안내문의 내용과 일치하는 것은?

Sense One Virtual Reality Headset

How to use:
1. Place the device on your head.
2. Use the hand controllers to turn on Sense One.
3. Follow the setup instructions on the screen.
4. Link to your game station.

Caution:
- Do not use if you are feeling dizzy.
- Do not expose the device to high temperatures or moisture.
- Do not clean the device with water or cleaning agents; wipe with a dry cloth.
- Sense One is not to be used by children under 12.

New parts or accessories can be purchased at any Sense One store or online at www.sense1vr.com.
If you have trouble with the headset, call our toll-free number at 1-800-439-9900.

---

① 머리에 쓰면 자동으로 전원이 켜진다.
② 설정 안내는 온라인 사용 설명서를 참고하면 된다.
③ 고온 다습한 곳에서 사용해도 된다.
④ 12세 미만 어린이도 사용할 수 있다.
⑤ 부품은 오프라인 매장과 온라인에서 구할 수 있다.

---

29 다음 밑줄 친 부분 중, 어법상 <u>틀린</u> 것은? [3점]

Craft objects have often been described within Western culture as less sophisticated than artworks of painting and sculpture, despite the beauty of some craft creations and the skill ① <u>that</u> goes into creating them. Before the Renaissance, arts and crafts were considered different parts of a larger industry of makers, who worked in small factories and focused on the quality of their craftsmanship, rather than on their artistic imagination. This changed with the Renaissance, when artists became more ② associated with their work, with each artwork being seen as an emanation of the artist's individual genius. Crafts were further devalued by ③ being labeled women's work or folk culture, while mass production removed many artisans from the production process altogether. More recently, these works of art, and crafts as a whole, ④ have been reevaluated. This is due not only to a reappraisal of their aesthetic qualities and the skill of the makers, but to an understanding ⑤ what these crafts give a voice to marginalized groups that were excluded from mainstream art.

30 (A), (B), (C)의 각 네모 안에서 문맥에 맞는 낱말로 가장 적절한 것은?

Misconceptions about sloths abound — ranging from their misclassification as primates or marsupials to unfounded opinions about their intelligence — but the idea that they are (A) willing / reluctant to be more active, that they are just lazy, is the biggest myth of all. As a matter of fact, given their physical traits, it is (B) apparent / doubtful that they could be any other way. To start, sloths are colorblind due to a rare genetic condition called "rod monochromacy," which would make navigating treetops at a fast pace difficult even for creatures that could — and sloths can't. This is largely due to their slow rate of digestion (a sloth has a four-chambered stomach that fills up quickly and remains full constantly, with experts saying a single leaf can take up to a month to digest). Since they are unable to eat very much, the amount of energy they can exert is seriously limited, making everything they do geared toward (C) saving / wasting as much of it as possible.

* marsupial: 유대류(有袋類)

(A)	(B)	(C)
① reluctant	doubtful	saving
② reluctant	apparent	saving
③ reluctant	apparent	wasting
④ willing	doubtful	wasting
⑤ willing	apparent	wasting

[31~34] 다음 빈칸에 들어갈 말로 가장 적절한 것을 고르시오.

31

A constitutional right is one that is applicable to all citizens. But a right remains a concept enshrined on paper until it is actually exercised. Therefore, it is important that the government ensure that all people are aware of their rights and that everyone has the equal ability to utilize them. Take the right to an education as an example. In many countries, it is a requirement to provide all children with access to schooling. In most cases, this is done by setting up a free public school system. Individuals with disabilities might find it impossible to attend classes, though. If the government does not establish special facilities that meet these students' needs, they will not be able to receive the education they are entitled to under law. In other words, even when a right is entrenched in the constitution, it can remain _____ for some people unless specific actions are taken.

① instituted ② unrealized
③ prohibited ④ designated
⑤ related

32

A model of scientific inquiry derived from the ideas of Greek philosopher Aristotle made it a standard to achieve genuine knowledge. However, in recent decades it has become clear to the scientific community that ＿＿＿＿＿＿＿＿＿＿＿ is under threat. Scientists are being punished for their work if it does not conform to certain agendas, as was the case with a top scientist who was fired from the directorship of a scientific organization in Brazil. The scientist publicly disagreed with the President and helped present evidence that the Amazon was burning due to increased deforestation, which contradicted the government's claim that the number of fires was within historical averages. Erika Berenguer, an expert who helped publish a study on this ecological issue, said she and other researchers were stunned at the dismissal and feared future retribution. Like other scientists around the world, she faces the reality of being fired for seeking transparent, comprehensive, and unbiased inquiry.

* retribution: 응징

① the guidance of traditional authority figures
② the independence of scientific research
③ the consideration of accurate evidence
④ unconditional support of the government
⑤ an attempt to reconstruct scientific knowledge

33

We may ＿＿＿＿＿＿＿＿＿＿＿＿＿＿＿＿＿ without making the most optimal choice. In economics, the idea that we accept "good enough" is explained by the theory of bounded rationality, which contradicts the belief that humans are logical beings who make the best possible decisions because it is in their self-interest to do so. It argues that, to be fully rational, a person would have to be aware of all logical truths about a situation and apply them to their decision-making process. They would also have to know about all potential fallacies in order to correct mistakes in their logic. This is not realistic, so the theory of bounded rationality points to factors such as time constraints, incomplete information, or insufficient mental capabilities. While most of us have many things to take into consideration each day, these limitations make it impossible to do so. It would be more sensible to make tolerable choices that just don't fail to meet some important needs. [3점]

① delay judgment due to a lack of data
② prefer an outcome that is not possible
③ reject options regardless of consequences
④ make decisions that satisfy certain criteria
⑤ seek alternatives to existing arrangements

34

In *The Logic of Scientific Discovery*, philosopher Karl Popper was critical of inductivism, which involves using observation or empirical evidence to verify a hypothesis and develop a theory. He argued that this approach was ineffective and unscientific, because the evidence available at any time and place is limited and all observation would be influenced by our pre-existing understanding. He believed science would be better served through the adoption of a deductive approach, in which scientists made predictions first and then attempted to refute them through observation. This way, old theories could be discarded and updated theories could be introduced, allowing science to progress. He explained this principle, known as falsifiability, by pointing out that in the past, it had been concluded by European scientists that all swans were white. Because this theory has since been found to be false with the discovery of black swans in Australia, Popper felt that _____, putting them more on the level of pseudo-science than actual science. [3점]

* falsifiability: 반증 가능성 ** pseudo-science: 사이비 과학

① theories created new problems for scientists to tackle
② theories were evaluated for their integrity using empirical evidence
③ theories formulated using deductive reasoning were inconclusive
④ theories did more than just describe or predict an event
⑤ theories based on observations risked being disproved at a later time

35 다음 글에서 전체 흐름과 관계 없는 문장은?

Involvement in sports can have a huge impact on the life of a disabled person, and not just due to the physical benefits associated with exercise. ① Able-bodied members of society may have limited knowledge of disabilities, which can cause them to consider all people who have them to be dependent on others or very restricted in their mobility. ② This stigma can lead to the non-inclusion of disabled people in many aspects of community life, depriving them of opportunities. ③ However, sports like wheelchair basketball can help teach society as a whole that people with disabilities can actually be very capable. ④ Players of this form of basketball utilize specialized wheelchairs that are constructed of sturdy yet lightweight materials. ⑤ With this knowledge, able-bodied people may be able to see past a person's disability, allowing disabled individuals to integrate into mainstream society without being discriminated against.

[36~37] 주어진 글 다음에 이어질 글의 순서로 가장 적절한 것을 고르시오.

36

Emotions can often feel overwhelming, and there's a scientific explanation for why this is the case.

(A) The person also has a surge of chemicals such as adrenaline and noradrenaline, their body preparing for a fight since they feel they've suffered an injustice. A similar but unique process would occur with other emotions, too, and vary by degree depending on the person.

(B) Emotions can affect people on a physical level, triggering sensations and reactions in the body. Just as a person might smile when they are happy, each emotion causes its own set of distinct changes.

(C) These collections of reactions are referred to as "affect programs" by researchers and each one consists of different skeletal and nervous system responses, vocalizations, and facial gestures that are brought on by emotions. So, if a person feels angry, for example, they might clench their fists, grind their teeth, experience prickly sensations, and sport a glare.

① (A) – (C) – (B) ② (B) – (A) – (C)
③ (B) – (C) – (A) ④ (C) – (A) – (B)
⑤ (C) – (B) – (A)

37

Curiosity, apart from driving individuals to innovate, absorb new knowledge, and find solutions to problems, is a mechanism of the brain.

(A) In this state, with the brain functioning at an optimal level, an individual is prepared to investigate and search for answers through the use of sensory organs. Gathering this information and boosting intelligence is highly gratifying. In fact, it activates the reward system in the brain.

(B) When encountering something unfamiliar or unexpected, the brain seeks to gather information in order to navigate the situation better. It enters the "curiosity state" — a condition in which the areas of the brain that respond to uncomfortable circumstances become active — because it recognizes a lack of knowledge.

(C) Dopamine is released, resulting in a sense of pleasure after an individual has figured something out. This biological process was integral to the survival of early humans as they discovered new ways to achieve their objectives, and so this trait has been inherited by people today, allowing us to continue this tradition of inquisitiveness. [3점]

① (A) – (C) – (B)   ② (B) – (A) – (C)
③ (B) – (C) – (A)   ④ (C) – (A) – (B)
⑤ (C) – (B) – (A)

[38~39] 글의 흐름으로 보아, 주어진 문장이 들어가기에 가장 적절한 곳을 고르시오.

38

Most people still believe that taking vitamin C supplements during cold and flu season helps us boost immunity or alleviate symptoms.

Thanks to two-time Nobel Prize winner Linus Pauling, the idea that vitamin C can help prevent colds persists. (①) In his 1970 book *Vitamin C and the Common Cold*, he recommended that people take a very high dose of 3,000mg of vitamin C daily to ward off everything from colds to cancer. (②) Needless to say, many medical experts at the time were dismissive of Pauling's assertion, which had no basis in known scientific fact. (③) No matter what criticism he received, Pauling maintained his claim, convincing many of its credibility. (④) As a result, beliefs surrounding the vitamin's capabilities have not disappeared entirely, even though the majority of researchers today no longer consider vitamin C to have any efficacy against serious illnesses. (⑤) After all, the body needs vitamin C to stay healthy — even if most people get enough of it simply from the food they eat.

* efficacy: 효능

39

> Blockchain transactions take place automatically, however, with the data being digitally recorded and stored on numerous networks throughout the world.

Blockchain, or distributed ledger technology (DLT), is the underlying software used for cryptocurrencies such as Bitcoin. (①) Before wide-scale implementation of blockchain can take place, there are various legal issues that must be addressed, almost all of which are concerned with the fact that DLT is decentralized. (②) This means transactions can occur and be recorded without the need for a specially designated authority such as a financial institution or government. (③) In traditional banking, if one were to make a wire transfer from the United States to Hungary, for example, a bank in the United States would be responsible for ensuring that all legal provisions were followed when processing the transaction. (④) Basically, with a decentralized financial system, no one can be held responsible for any issues that may arise. (⑤) This essentially invalidates the laws and regulations that would typically apply to any given transaction, creating legal concerns. [3점]

* cryptocurrency: 암호화폐 ** provision: 규정

40 다음 글의 내용을 한 문장으로 요약하고자 한다. 빈칸 (A), (B)에 들어갈 말로 가장 적절한 것은?

Although both skepticism and cynicism pertain to a person's attitude, they are distinct concepts that vary in a number of ways. Skepticism involves doubting or questioning if something is true or useful. For example, a person can express skepticism about a particular claim; therefore, they are hesitant to accept it as accurate. They might focus on the weaknesses of the declaration and dispute certain assumptions. Being skeptical does not mean that an individual is unable to be swayed by compelling evidence and arguments. Rather, skepticism is a trait that allows a person to stay open minded until he or she is certain about something. On the other hand, cynicism is regarded negatively since people who demonstrate this attitude tend to reject all evidence and remain stubborn in their views. A cynical individual believes that self-interest is the main motivator behind people's actions. Thus, they tend to view things created by other people as unable to be successful or as made for the wrong reasons.

↓

While skepticism is marked by challenging ideas and theories with the ____(A)____ of trusting them, cynicism is shown when a person is ____(B)____ to have faith in other people.

	(A)		(B)
①	certainty	······	unlikely
②	certainty	······	resistant
③	responsibility	······	desperate
④	possibility	······	eager
⑤	possibility	······	unwilling

[41~42] 다음 글을 읽고, 물음에 답하시오.

The idea of behaviorism started with Ivan Pavlov, who learned through his research on dogs that his subjects' behavior could be (a) conditioned; after coming to associate the sound of a bell with food, the dogs would salivate in response to the bell rather than the food itself, implying that expectation can produce results. Not long after, in the early 20th century, psychologists John Watson and B. F. Skinner expanded on the concept, demonstrating how punishment and reward can influence human behavior. They argued that what we experience in our environment determines how we act. Since then, the theory has become vital in helping educators understand how to (b) encourage students to succeed academically and behave well.

In a classroom setting, students who repeatedly receive positive reinforcement in response to good scores or appropriate behavior come to understand that their teacher's reaction is a result of their behavior. Positive reinforcement can take the form of anything that a student considers (c) desirable and wants to receive again, such as praise or a small treat, for instance. It is necessary for a teacher to be (d) inconsistent with their positive reinforcement, however, because when a teacher withholds an anticipated reward, the student may not feel as motivated to perform. Likewise, failing to react to a high score or positive behavior can be construed by as a form of negative reinforcement as it may signify to the student that the quality of their performance is (e) worthless, which can cause them to abandon the pursuit of excellence.

* salivate: 침을 흘리다 ** construe: 이해하다

41 윗글의 제목으로 가장 적절한 것은?

① Teaching by Design: Using Rewards to Motivate Students
② How Rewards Systems Damage Intrinsic Motivation
③ Behaviorism: Outdated or Still Relevant?
④ Tracing the Roots of Behaviorism at School
⑤ Should Negative Reinforcement Be Used in the Classroom?

42 밑줄 친 (a)~(e) 중에서 문맥상 낱말의 쓰임이 적절하지 않은 것은? [3점]

① (a) ② (b) ③ (c) ④ (d) ⑤ (e)

[43~45] 다음 글을 읽고, 물음에 답하시오.

(A)

It was the first day of my university acting class, and I was extremely confident. Looking around the room, I assumed that none of the other students had as much experience as I did. I had already been in multiple productions in high school, so I was positive that this class would be easy and that I would impress my professor with little effort. He was a very successful actor, so I was excited to show (a) him my skills.

(B)

I didn't see the point of preparing too much. The scenes (b) he had outlined were easy, and I was already familiar with them. I knew that when given the chance, I would prove just how advanced my abilities were. On the day of the class, my professor began calling up groups of students to perform. I was blown away because many of them had memorized the lines perfectly, and I had never seen the scenes performed that way. I began to get nervous.

(C)

When the professor discussed what we would learn, I was annoyed to hear that the class would mostly focus on introducing different acting techniques. There wouldn't be many opportunities to perform. I didn't see how the lectures would help me, so I rarely listened to my professor. Just when I thought that we would never have the chance to use our skills, (c) he announced our first acting assignment and gave us a scene to practice.

(D)

The professor called me up and told me to read a scene with another student from my class. I could feel my heart begin to beat faster and my mind seemed to go blank. While my partner remembered all of (d) his lines, I forgot mine. By the time we were done, I knew that I had easily done the worst out of anyone in the class. Although I assumed I'd make a great impression on my teacher, I could tell (e) he was disappointed.

43 주어진 글 (A)에 이어질 내용을 순서에 맞게 배열한 것으로 가장 적절한 것은?

① (B) – (D) – (C)　　② (C) – (B) – (D)
③ (C) – (D) – (B)　　④ (D) – (B) – (C)
⑤ (D) – (C) – (B)

44 밑줄 친 (a)~(e) 중에서 가리키는 대상이 나머지 넷과 다른 것은?

① (a)　② (b)　③ (c)　④ (d)　⑤ (e)

45 윗글에 관한 내용으로 적절하지 <u>않은</u> 것은?

① 연기 수업의 교수는 크게 성공한 배우였다.
② 나는 다른 학생들의 연기를 보고 긴장되기 시작했다.
③ 교수는 다양한 연기 기법을 소개하겠다고 했다.
④ 나는 연기 수업을 열심히 들었다.
⑤ 나는 대사를 잊어버렸다.

정답·해설·해석 p.53

문제풀이 후 확인사항
1. 45분 내에 문제를 풀었다.
2. 체크해둔 문제와 틀린 문제는 해설을 꼼꼼히 확인했다.

수고하셨습니다! HackersBook.com에서 제공하는 어휘리스트로 어휘를 암기하세요.

07회 실전모의고사

18 다음 글의 목적으로 가장 적절한 것은?

Dear Ms. Pearson,

　My name is Henry Lowell. I work at TM Media and one of my clients is Topper Coffee Beans. It is a new local business that is gaining in popularity. The company would like a photo shoot for their newest product and asked me to help them find a location. I think your beautiful coffee shop would be perfect. I would like to ask if we can rent your shop for an entire day for the shoot. You will receive ample compensation, and it would also be free advertising for your store. I look forward to hearing from you soon. Thank you for your consideration.

Yours sincerely,
Henry Lowell

① 촬영 장비 지원을 요청하려고
② 촬영 장소 대여를 문의하려고
③ 지역 행사 참여를 독려하려고
④ 새로운 커피 원두를 홍보하려고
⑤ 제품의 광고 영상 제작을 제안하려고

19 다음 글에 나타난 'I'의 심경 변화로 가장 적절한 것은?

　I thought the rainy weather reflected my mood perfectly. I didn't even care that it was pouring as I slowly walked home from school. That was the worst test grade I'd ever gotten, and I couldn't stop obsessing over it. As I turned the corner, I heard a voice call out, "Sarah!" My neighbor Jenny was standing on her porch, waving me over. "How'd your day go?" she asked. "You looked a bit upset in class. Would you like to come in?" I nodded and followed her in, where Jenny handed me a soft blanket to warm up with, along with a steaming mug of hot chocolate. I smiled warmly at Jenny. She always knew exactly how to brighten my day.

① frightened → lively
② irritated → triumphant
③ depressed → comforted
④ interested → indifferent
⑤ envious → entertained

20 다음 글에서 필자가 주장하는 바로 가장 적절한 것은?

　From time to time, you may face the dilemma of choosing whether to capture something on camera or witness it without the distraction of a screen. Maybe you have felt mild regret about deciding to pass on savoring the moment after you've recorded a video of some awe-inspiring event to share with the public. As if playing a part, you focus on entertaining your peers, but you are unable to fully "take in" what is happening around you as you satisfy the urge to showcase your life and stay socially relevant. All too often, the draw to control one's public image and remain involved prompts people to spend their time carefully curating their profiles and posts via social networks. This causes any sense of contentment they feel to be shallow as individuals place value on advertising their lives through rose-tinted filters that hardly reflect their true realities.

① 소중한 순간들은 영상으로 기록해두어야 한다.
② 타인과의 소통을 위해 소셜 미디어를 적극 활용해야 한다.
③ 소셜 미디어에 자신의 관심사를 정기적으로 업데이트해야 한다.
④ 타인의 시선을 의식하지 않고 자신의 생각을 표현할 수 있어야 한다.
⑤ 소셜 미디어에 공유하는 데 열중하느라 눈앞의 경험을 놓치지 말아야 한다.

21 밑줄 친 move heaven and earth가 다음 글에서 의미하는 바로 가장 적절한 것은?

Modern culture is all about speed, with people wanting quick success, faster technology, and more effective ways to multitask. As individuals constantly rush from one assignment or meeting to the next, the threat of burnout looms. To avoid overexertion, it's important to take a step back. That's where slow living comes in. This mindset is all about recognizing when it's beneficial to pause and catch one's breath. It involves not always trying to fill every hour of the day with engagements. As Socrates realized more than two thousand years ago when he wisely stated, "Beware the barrenness of a busy life," doing more does not always lead to happiness or fulfillment, but focusing on relationships, health, and living in the present just might. People don't need to move heaven and earth in order to prosper.

① gain a new perspective on success
② undertake a task with reluctance
③ try to push oneself too far
④ remove obstacles to achievement
⑤ work for the sake of gratifying someone

22 다음 글의 요지로 가장 적절한 것은?

With the advent of the Fourth Industrial Revolution, the ability to utilize modern technology is becoming an essential life skill, just like communication or critical thinking. Technology should therefore be part of a basic education, especially since future generations will depend on it more and more. Incorporating technology into the learning process supplies pupils with knowledge that will allow them to prosper in a world defined by innovations such as the Internet of Things, augmented reality, and artificial intelligence. This integration can additionally shape education to be more personalized and engaging. A lesson that's based on investigating new technologies is beneficial for participation and cooperation, and multimedia learning environments cater to numerous learning styles. For instance, videos and images can engage visual learners, while smart boards and podcasts can appeal to kinesthetic and auditory learners, respectively.

* augmented reality: 증강 현실

① 학생 수준에 맞는 개인화 교육이 필요하다.
② 교육 과정에 기술을 도입하는 것이 중요하다.
③ 정보화 시대에는 비판적 사고 능력이 필수적이다.
④ 시청각 매체의 활용은 수업 몰입도를 향상시킨다.
⑤ 기술의 발전에 따라 교사는 수업 방식을 바꿀 필요가 있다.

23 다음 글의 주제로 가장 적절한 것은? [3점]

The composition of an art piece can reflect a great deal about society at the time of its creation. Historically speaking, artists from the Classical Period — a period in the history of ancient Greek art ranging from the fifth century BC to the first three-quarters of the fourth century BC — produced work that depicted people and their devotion to deities and idols. The artwork often told stories derived from mythology or religion, which were held in high regard during the period, and conveyed reverence for order and the accomplishments of civilization. Contemporary artists — who came to the fore in the late nineteenth century — rejected these limited themes, focusing instead on the weaknesses of society and expressing their innermost emotions. As time progressed, bringing the World Wars, government reformations, and technological advancements, these pieces increasingly emphasized a world fraught with change and brutality.

* deity: 신(神)

① revival of Classicism in Contemporary art
② purpose of visual art in a rapidly changing world
③ ability of art to transform our understanding of history
④ impact of culture and civilization on the art of the period
⑤ differences between the Classical and Contemporary art

24 다음 글의 제목으로 가장 적절한 것은?

Many of the most notable literary classics portray terrifying future worlds. In these dystopian fictions, society is often collapsing because of a prominent political, religious, or ecological issue. It's widely acknowledged that pieces such as these are written to warn us about problems that could incite disaster in the time to come. They tell us that if we aren't careful, our future could look much the same. But the themes of dystopian fictions also comment on the present, bringing readers' attention to real-world problems and urging reform or a certain degree of change. They also inspire readers to examine constructs that society imposes on people and question beliefs they may not have questioned before. Topics such as morals and ethics are scrutinized and explored through dystopian fiction, giving rise to deep thought and reflection.

① Does the Literature We Read Affect Modern Society?
② Future Crises: How to Avoid Societal Collapse
③ Popular Themes in Literary Dystopias
④ Dystopian Literature: The Rise of a Genre
⑤ How Dystopian Fiction Turns the Mirror on Ourselves

25 다음 도표의 내용과 일치하지 않는 것은?

American Youth Classified as Obese by Three Age Groups

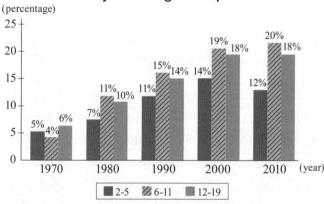

The graph above shows the obesity percentages for three age groups of American youth in five different years. ① In 1990, the obesity percentage of American youth aged 2 to 5 was more than twice as high as that in 1970. ② In all the years except 1970, the obesity percentage of youth aged 12 to 19 was the second highest for all age groups. ③ American youth aged 6 to 11 had the highest rates of obesity among three age groups in 1980, 1990, 2000, and 2010, while those aged 2 to 5 retained the lowest rates for the same years. ④ In the years before 2000, the percentage of youth aged 2 to 5 that were categorized as obese stayed below 8%. ⑤ Meanwhile, the groups of youth aged 6 to 11 and 12 to 19 had increasing percentages in each year from 1970 to 2000.

26 Andrei Tarkovsky에 관한 다음 글의 내용과 일치하지 않는 것은?

Andrei Tarkovsky was a renowned Russian director who received praise from critics around the world for his innovative style of filmmaking. Born in the village of Zavrazhye in 1932, Tarkovsky entered the Soviet film school VGIK in 1954. For his final project prior to graduation, he wrote his first screenplay for a film called *The Steamroller and the Violin*, which was purchased by a major studio. Throughout his long career, he produced many feature-length movies that won awards at prestigious international events such as the Cannes Film Festival. However, his works, which often dealt with overtly religious themes, were heavily censored by Soviet authorities. As a result, he left the Soviet Union in 1980, and, four years later, he formally declared that he would never return. Shortly after this, he was diagnosed with lung cancer, and he passed away in 1986 — the same year that his final film, *The Sacrifice*, was released.

① 혁신적인 영화 제작 방식으로 찬사를 받았다.
② 1954년 VGIK에 입학했다.
③ 학교 졸업 후 첫 영화 대본을 썼다.
④ 그의 영화들은 소련 당국의 심한 검열을 받았다.
⑤ 마지막 영화가 개봉된 해에 세상을 떠났다.

27 Stonybrook Campus Dormitory Fire Drill에 관한 다음 안내문의 내용과 일치하지 않는 것은?

Stonybrook Campus Dormitory Fire Drill

Fire drills are important exercises that may help save your life in the future. It is vital for the safety of all students living in the campus dormitory.

Dates: March 3 (Spring semester), September 20 (Fall semester)
Time: 2 p.m.

During the drill
- All students in the dormitory must participate.
  *If you are unable to participate, please notify staff in advance.
- Follow the evacuation plan posted on each floor.
- Only use the emergency stairs.

After the drill
- Firefighters will explain how to properly use fire extinguishers.
- Staff will explain how to report a fire.

If you have any questions, please contact 982-1100.

① 일 년에 두 번 시행된다.
② 기숙사에 사는 학생은 모두 참여해야 한다.
③ 각 층에 부착된 대피 안내도를 따라야 한다.
④ 비상계단만 이용해야 한다.
⑤ 소방관이 화재 신고 방법을 설명할 것이다.

28 Central Hospital Charity Run에 관한 다음 안내문의 내용과 일치하는 것은?

Central Hospital Charity Run

Central Hospital is excited to announce plans for our first annual charity run. Come out and enjoy some exercise with us for a good cause!

When & Where
- May 19th, 9 a.m.
- Carter Neighborhood Park

Race Details
- Five-kilometer participation fee: $25
- Ten-kilometer participation fee: $35
- Each runner will receive a free T-shirt.
- Prizes will be given to the first, second, and third place runners of each race.

Donations
- All funds will be donated to underprivileged patients of Central Hospital.
- Additional donations can be made at the race site or through the hospital's website, www.centralhospital.org.

Register on our website today to participate!

---

① Central Hospital에서 경주가 진행된다.
② 5킬로미터 코스 참가비는 35달러이다.
③ 각 경주의 1등에게만 상이 주어질 것이다.
④ 모든 기금은 소외 계층 환자에게 기부될 것이다.
⑤ 추가 기부는 온라인으로만 할 수 있다.

29 다음 글의 밑줄 친 부분 중, 어법상 틀린 것은?

Plastics are not biodegradable. That is, they are extremely resistant to the natural decomposition processes that ① break down other substances. Consequently, there is a focus on recycling as a way to prevent plastic containers and packaging from ② accumulating in landfills and wilderness areas. While this approach has proven to be somewhat ③ effectively, it is not ideal because plastics cannot be reused indefinitely; after being recycled only a few times, most plastics degrade to the point that they must be discarded. Plastics are composed of long strands of molecules called polymers that become shorter and shorter after each round of recycling, causing ④ their overall quality to decline. This shortcoming is why most experts agree that governments around the world must ⑤ take action to curtail or even eliminate the use of plastics in the near future.

30 다음 글의 밑줄 친 부분 중, 문맥상 낱말의 쓰임이 적절하지 않은 것은? [3점]

Throughout much of recorded history, myths and folklore have drawn connections between the human experience and celestial activity, yet a new study proves the ① link more concretely than ever. Researchers from three separate colleges in the US and Argentina teamed up to ② track the sleep patterns of nearly 100 indigenous people to determine whether lunar cycles have any notable effect on their ability to rest. The participants were ③ clustered into three control groups: people who lived in rural areas without electricity, people who lived in rural areas with electricity, and people who lived in urban settings with electricity. All three groups experienced the same general trend of sleeping less in the days just before a full moon, as that's when the

④ smallest amount of light is reflected back toward Earth throughout the early nighttime. The results follow the standard assumption that darkness signals the body to sleep. In fact, in findings that suggest a degree of universality in human biology, very ⑤ similar results were recorded among a group of Washington state college students who also took part.

[31~34] 다음 빈칸에 들어갈 말로 가장 적절한 것을 고르시오.

31

Personality may not be as _____ as we think. We all undergo a gradual process of maturation that begins during our teenage years, a period in which many of us seek out new experiences and develop interests in order to find ourselves. For many years, psychologists believed that this process continued into adulthood and ended at about age 30, with factors like personal relationships, performance at school and work, and physical health playing a part in shaping the person that we ultimately become. While it is true that these elements form the basis of each person's distinctive personality, research into the effects of aging now suggests that, in addition to the well-documented physical transformation, we tend to develop into kinder, more altruistic individuals who have more control over our emotions than we did during our younger years. This trend has been observed in all human cultures, indicating that our tendency to adapt as we age is universal.

① unique   ② random
③ complex   ④ significant
⑤ consistent

32

Math is a language known by people across the globe, regardless of nationality and background. It's used to communicate data, make predictions, and understand the world around us. Astronomer Galileo Galilei even went as far as to say, "Mathematics is the language in which God has written the universe." And while it may not be recognized as a language in the traditional sense, math is a written form of communication that utilizes numbers and symbols to convey meaning in a similar way to how vocabulary, grammar, and syntax are used. For example, numbers function the same as nouns and symbols such as the subtraction and multiplication signs act as verbs. A math equation has to be arranged in a certain way to be comprehensible just as a sentence in Spanish or Chinese must be. The only big difference is that math doesn't have to be translated: it is _____ and its rules are unvarying. In this way, math helps people overcome other barriers of communication, making it one of the most useful languages in the world. [3점]

* equation: 방정식

① an innate skill
② an exclusive field
③ a universal dialect
④ the foundation of science
⑤ the origin of communication

33

In *Will Therapy*, Austrian psychoanalyst Otto Rank wrote that all individuals possess will and that will is the faculty that guides people to choose their behavior, whether it is positive or negative. He asserted that will falls somewhere in the middle between impulse and inhibition, two opposing human drives in a constant struggle with each other, and that the management of these two dynamics leads to the development of a personality with its own distinct will. On the basis that each person is unique and that their actions are directed by their will, he argued that this meant _____. This assertion contradicted many prevailing theories at the time — including those of his colleague and friend Sigmund Freud — that claimed humans were deterministic in their thinking, positing that humans cannot help but act as they do. For Rank, however, people make their own choices, and should therefore be held liable for them.

① therapy helps people understand themselves better
② people have to take responsibility for their own actions
③ both internal and external forces determine our behaviors
④ there is a very fine balance between impulse and inhibition
⑤ our power to choose is difficult to recognize within ourselves

34

In the digital era, it is not enough for a business to simply have a website because _____ _____. That's why one of the most effective digital marketing strategies to use is search engine optimization, or SEO. Knowing how search engines work is vital to understanding SEO: search engines scan the internet for content, organize the information they find in an index, and then use the index to generate results. Because the results generated by search engines are ranked, with the most relevant pages appearing first, a business can attempt to improve its website's ranking by using keywords or providing answers to questions potential customers might ask. As the language in the website becomes more relevant to people's searches, the website climbs up the rankings, perhaps even making it to the first page of the search results. This increases the likelihood of people coming across the business's website and potentially becoming customers. [3점]

① traditional advertising is making a comeback
② websites fail to target new customers directly
③ there is no guarantee anyone will be able to find it
④ most people discover new businesses through social media
⑤ websites often fail to connect to customers on a personal level

35 다음 글에서 전체 흐름과 관계 없는 문장은?

The humanities and the sciences are often seen as polar opposites, with many people considering the sciences as critical for future development and the humanities as a waste of time and funding. However, individuals majoring in the sciences should not be so quick to disregard academic subjects related to the humanities. ① Studying the humanities not only provides students with vast knowledge on various topics but also encourages them to be ethical, compassionate, and creative. ② These qualities benefit everyone since they help give us a more complete view of what it means to be human. ③ Although scientists certainly contribute a great deal to the world, so do people who study the humanities. ④ Since scientists are often perceived as clinical and out of touch with the rest of society, it can be helpful for them to take humanities courses as well. ⑤ It can give them a better understanding of the problems they should solve using their knowledge and improve how they communicate their findings with the rest of the world.

[36~37] 주어진 글 다음에 이어질 글의 순서로 가장 적절한 것을 고르시오.

36

When individuals from the same species mate successfully, both the mother and the father provide the offspring with half a pair of an equal number of chromosomes. This allows their young to function normally and, later, produce offspring of their own.

(A) Because a horse has 64 chromosomes and a donkey has 62, a mule inherits 63 chromosomes. Since 63 chromosomes cannot be evenly halved, mules should not be capable of reproducing. Yet, there are cases that defy this logic.

(B) When two different species breed, however, the offspring typically cannot reproduce. This is because it inherits an unequal number of chromosomes from its dissimilar parents. A common example of this is the mule, the offspring of a horse and a donkey.

(C) In 2007, a mule gave birth to a foal that biologists genetically confirmed to be its offspring. Since the mule was tested and found to have exactly 63 chromosomes, the reason she was able to reproduce remains a mystery.

* chromosome: 염색체 ** mule: 노새

① (A) – (C) – (B)　　② (B) – (A) – (C)
③ (B) – (C) – (A)　　④ (C) – (A) – (B)
⑤ (C) – (B) – (A)

37

Collective memory is the idea that memories and attitudes are formed through a social context — that it is not necessary for members of a society to have personally experienced an event for it to form part of their consciousness.

(A) Thus, whether someone wants to spread a message or get elected, evoking a collective memory can help get the job done. The most important thing is that it resonates with prevailing mindsets.

(B) These representations of the past need not necessarily be accurate but instead be interpreted in a way that preserves cohesion within a group. When the masses are unified in their beliefs, it is easy for politicians, or anyone with an agenda, to appeal to the public.

(C) The people and historical events we are taught to respect from a young age, according to theories about collective memory, are selected by those in power. In other words, national histories are manipulated constructs intended to make us feel a certain way. [3점]

① (A) – (C) – (B)
② (B) – (A) – (C)
③ (B) – (C) – (A)
④ (C) – (A) – (B)
⑤ (C) – (B) – (A)

[38~39] 글의 흐름으로 보아, 주어진 문장이 들어가기에 가장 적절한 곳을 고르시오.

38

When people project rather than empathize, they believe that their own emotions and experiences mirror those of the person who is struggling.

Although empathy and projection are two separate reactions to emotional turmoil, the two can also be difficult to differentiate. Empathy requires practice; people must make a conscious effort to listen and observe those who are struggling and they must try their best to understand them. (①) Projection, for most, is a more natural response, especially with the rise of individualism. (②) It occurs when someone transfers his or her own ideas of the other person's experience onto the other person. (③) Essentially, they fail to really see the actual struggles of the person they are interacting with and instead react based on their own biases and opinions about the situation. (④) Modern society has managed to foster citizens more inclined to project by ignoring the need to instill empathy. (⑤) Without empathy, humans lose a true sense of connection and tend to only care about their own worries.

* turmoil: 혼란

39

> In such a case, the process itself would have to be protected, making a utility patent necessary.

Unlike a utility patent, which protects the creation or improvement of a product, process, or machine, a design patent protects the ornamental features of an item. (①) To get approval for such a patent, the design must be original, and if there are similarities to an existing design, they must be unobvious. (②) Another requirement is that the design must be reproducible. (③) If one wished to patent a design produced via a method unable to guarantee the uniformity of the design each and every time, a design patent would be refused. (④) In situations where both the design and the functionality of an object need to be protected, an inventor would have to apply for both utility and design patents. (⑤) Inventions with both types of coverage are generally considered of higher value as they are more strongly protected against being copied. [3점]

40 다음 글의 내용을 한 문장으로 요약하고자 한다. 빈칸 (A), (B)에 들어갈 말로 가장 적절한 것은?

Stanley Milgram's landmark study examined cultural differences between Germans and Americans. He hypothesized that Germans, many of whom had claimed to be "just following orders" during the Holocaust, were more culturally predisposed to obedience. Thus, Milgram devised an experiment to test how far Americans would be willing to follow orders. During the study, each test subject was assigned to be a "teacher" and told to read pairs of words to a "student," who would then be quizzed on how many pairs they remembered. For each wrong answer, the "teacher" was instructed to press a button that would give an electric shock to the "student," with subsequent wrong answers leading to higher voltage shocks. In truth, the button was not sending an electrical current, and the "students" were actors who were working with Milgram. But even as the shocks appeared to cause a great deal of pain, 65 percent of the "teachers" proceeded to the end of the test. This disproved Milgram's theory that over 99.9 percent would defect before reaching the end of the experiment.

⬇

Stanley Milgram's study proved that Americans show just as much ____(A)____ as Germans when instructed to carry out tasks, ____(B)____ his theory that they were more prone to rebel.

	(A)		(B)
①	compliance	······	supporting
②	compliance	······	refuting
③	conformity	······	encouraging
④	resistance	······	challenging
⑤	resistance	······	demonstrating

[41~42] 다음 글을 읽고, 물음에 답하시오.

In George Orwell's revolutionary novel *1984*, characters are threatened with constant government surveillance and the reminder that "Big Brother is Watching You." Of course, Orwell's masterpiece is a work of fiction, illustrating a world in which privacy is nonexistent. Yet critics argue that the idea of "Big Brother" is not really so different from what people are (a) <u>subjected</u> to in modern society. We too, in essence, are always being watched, and most of us are aware that any (b) <u>noticed</u> misconduct can lead to punishment. But surveillance as a means of discipline is not a new concept, and it certainly wasn't invented by George Orwell. In fact, one of the first systems of surveillance was invented in the eighteenth century. The panopticon — a circular structure that allowed supervisors to watch prisoners while (c) <u>revealing</u> the existence of guards — was created by Samuel Bentham. This invention was intended to keep prisoners in line by reminding them that they were being closely observed at all times, without their overseers being visible.

Fast forward 200 years and surveillance, coupled with data gathered from the activity of individuals on the Internet, has marked the advent of what computational psychologist Andrew Kosinski calls the "post-privacy world." Modern institutions are still (d) <u>heavily</u> utilizing a form of the practice Bentham implemented, only now through the use of cameras, lenses, and even people. All of our activity, both physical and digital, can be observed and tracked. The (e) <u>benefits</u> of such a world include increased public safety, easy sources of evidence, and reduced crime. However, many still worry about how this type of system and constant surveillance could be abused. Invading privacy in order to change people's behavior is, after all, exactly what Orwell writes about.

41 윗글의 제목으로 가장 적절한 것은?

① Punishment or Surveillance: Which Is More Effective?
② Ways to Utilize Big Brother for Laborers' Safety
③ Learn to Stand Up to Get Your Privacy Back!
④ Boundless Growth of Surveillance: Good or Bad?
⑤ How to Keep Prisoners in Line without Surveillance

42 밑줄 친 (a)~(e) 중에서 문맥상 낱말의 쓰임이 적절하지 않은 것은? [3점]

① (a)　　② (b)　　③ (c)　　④ (d)　　⑤ (e)

[43~45] 다음 글을 읽고, 물음에 답하시오.

(A)

There were two weeks left before the championship soccer game, so Becky and Hannah had to practice with their team more than usual. One day after practice, their coach called Becky into her office. She reminded (a) her that to play in the championship game, players needed to keep their grades up. Unfortunately, Becky's math grades had fallen, so she wouldn't be able to play unless she did well on her next big test. Becky asked what she should do and her coach replied, "I think you should get a tutor."

(B)

Becky thought that Hannah was a great tutor. She explained everything so clearly. On the day of the big test, Hannah asked Becky if she was ready. "I think so!" Becky said. (b) She felt nervous, but she knew she had studied hard. When Becky finally got her test, she was relieved to find that she knew the answer to every question. She remembered everything Hannah taught her and finished her test before the time had finished.

(C)

Becky was nervous to ask anyone for help because she was embarrassed by her bad grades. She decided to talk to Hannah about (c) her problem. "Who could be my tutor?" asked Becky. "I can!" replied Hannah. "I'm doing well in math and can study with you for the test!" Becky was surprised that Hannah was willing to help her. They planned to meet every day to study after practice. The test was only a week away.

(D)

During the next class, the teacher handed Becky her test and she was amazed to see that she got a perfect score. She went over to hug Hannah. "Thank you so much! I couldn't have done it without (d) you." she told Hannah. Her friend smiled at her and said, "That's what friends are for!" Becky was so happy that (e) she would get to play in her championship soccer game. But what made her even happier was that she had made such a good friend.

43 주어진 글 (A)에 이어질 내용을 순서에 맞게 배열한 것으로 가장 적절한 것은?

① (B) – (D) – (C)　　　② (C) – (B) – (D)
③ (C) – (D) – (B)　　　④ (D) – (B) – (C)
⑤ (D) – (C) – (B)

44 밑줄 친 (a)~(e) 중에서 가리키는 대상이 나머지 넷과 다른 것은?

① (a)　　② (b)　　③ (c)　　④ (d)　　⑤ (e)

45 윗글에 관한 내용으로 적절하지 않은 것은?

① Becky의 수학 성적이 떨어졌다.
② 시험 당일 Becky는 Hannah에게 준비가 되었는지 물었다.
③ Becky는 Hannah가 가르쳐 준 것을 모두 기억했다.
④ Hannah는 기꺼이 Becky를 도와주기로 했다.
⑤ Becky는 시험에서 만점을 받았다.

정답·해설·해석 p. 63

문제풀이 후 확인사항
1. 45분 내에 문제를 풀었다.
2. 체크해둔 문제와 틀린 문제는 해설을 꼼꼼히 확인했다.

수고하셨습니다! HackersBook.com에서 제공하는 어휘리스트로 어휘를 암기하세요.

08회 실전모의고사

목표 시간: 45분   시작: ___ 시 ___ 분 ~ 종료: ___ 시 ___ 분   점수: ___ 점 / 63점

* [3점] 표시가 있는 문제 제외하고는 모두 2점으로 계산합니다.

18 다음 글의 목적으로 가장 적절한 것은?

Dear Stacy Greenwood,

I'm emailing you regarding your café, where I've been a customer for years now. Stacy's is one of my favorite places to enjoy an excellent cup of coffee. I think the changes you've made over the years have all improved the café, and I appreciate your efforts to run your business in a more sustainable way. With that in mind, I want to suggest another way the café could become more environmentally friendly. I believe that Stacy's would really benefit from no longer offering single-use coffee cups. I've seen a few cafés adopt this idea recently, and since I know you want Stacy's to be a green business, I thought it might interest you, too. I hope you take this into consideration, and I look forward to my next visit to your café.

Sincerely,
Ken Rogers

① 커피 메뉴에 대해 문의하려고
② 가맹점 운영의 장점을 홍보하려고
③ 서비스에 대한 불만을 제기하려고
④ 일회용 컵 사용 자제를 제안하려고
⑤ 환경 보호 캠페인을 위한 기부를 부탁하려고

19 다음 글에 나타난 Amy의 심경 변화로 가장 적절한 것은?

Amy looked out the window and saw everyone skiing and having fun. She had come on a trip with her friends to a mountain resort, but she didn't know how to ski! As she had a lot of time to spend by herself, she decided to watch TV. But there wasn't anything interesting on, and she couldn't stop yawning. So, she played with her phone, but she quickly grew tired of that, too. She kept checking what time it was, only to see that she still had a long day ahead of her. She was staring at the ceiling when Keith walked into the room. He asked her if she wanted to go sledding. "Yes!" she said, jumping out of the chair and grabbing her jacket and scarf. The two ran outside into the fresh air. Soon her heart was racing as she flew down the snow-covered slopes.

① lonely → curious
② bored → excited
③ depressed → calm
④ pleased → alarmed
⑤ envious → disappointed

20 다음 글에서 필자가 주장하는 바로 가장 적절한 것은?

According to a recent survey, over 80 percent of executives think good communication is the key to a successful business. Unfortunately, a high number of individuals in management fail to exhibit this skill when interacting with subordinates, showing a tendency to overexplain in the mistaken belief that this qualifies as being thorough. For example, someone giving instructions regarding a new project might also provide unnecessary background details and personal opinions about the undertaking. Doing so often leads to confusion on the part of the listener as it is difficult to identify the objective and any specific requirements. To avoid this situation, managers must always strive to be concise and accurate. Before a meeting with a staff member, they must ask themselves, "If my team member walked away from this conversation understanding one thing, what would I want it to be?" — the answer to this question is what they must focus on conveying.

① 조직이 성장하려면 경영 방식을 혁신해야 한다.
② 어려운 일은 협업을 통해 해결하도록 해야 한다.
③ 관리자는 직원의 능력에 맞게 업무를 배분해야 한다.
④ 관리자는 직원들에게 핵심 정보만 정확히 전달해야 한다.
⑤ 좋은 관리자가 되기 위해서는 직원의 의견을 경청해야 한다.

21 밑줄 친 see yourself through others' eyes가 다음 글에서 의미하는 바로 가장 적절한 것은? [3점]

Most people mistakenly believe that they are less likely to experience negative events than their peers. The underlying cause of this cognitive bias is our inability to accurately evaluate our own abilities in comparison to those of others. We have a natural inclination to overestimate our skills, making us feel unrealistically confident about avoiding the hardships others experience. While an overly optimistic mindset can be beneficial in that it results in greater self-esteem, it can also negatively affect your ability to assess risk, which may lead to harmful behaviors. If you feel sure that you are going to have a successful career and earn great wealth in the future, you may not worry about running up a large credit card debt buying unnecessary luxuries. Therefore, try to see yourself through others' eyes. It may make you more hesitant, but it can also protect you over the long run.

① Develop greater self-confidence by being objective.
② Evaluate the dangers you face in a realistic manner.
③ Find a way to reflect on your behavior without guilt.
④ Avoid comparing yourself negatively with your peers.
⑤ Interact with individuals who understand your needs.

22 다음 글의 요지로 가장 적절한 것은?

When people join together to take collective action, small groups are better able to further common goals than large ones. This results from the underlying tension between shared and individual interests. One factor is the issue of free riding: benefiting from group action without contributing to it. This phenomenon is more pronounced when many people are involved because greater numbers provide greater anonymity. In small groups, though, each person is aware of the contributions made by others — the likelihood of someone not pulling his or her weight is reduced because no one wants to be subject to the negative opinion of the rest of the group. At the same time, all members sense that their individual efforts are necessary for success, which provides additional motivation. For those belonging to large groups, the opposite is true; a failure of one person to contribute will likely have no noticeable effect, resulting in a lack of incentive to participate.

① 개개인의 노력이 집단의 성공에 기여한다.
② 집단의 규모가 집단의 성취도에 영향을 미친다.
③ 빠른 목표 달성을 위해서는 동기 부여가 필요하다.
④ 성공하는 집단에서는 모든 구성원이 결속감을 느낀다.
⑤ 구성원 간의 유대 관계가 팀워크 형성의 필수 요소이다.

23 다음 글의 주제로 가장 적절한 것은?

While there is no doubt solar energy could be integral to solving the world's energy problems, it's not a magic pill. Solar energy actually has considerable environmental ramifications. Large-scale solar power plants cover vast amounts of land and can therefore impact local wildlife by taking up valuable habitat area. Due to the layout and design of such power plants, the land they occupy cannot be simultaneously used for agricultural purposes, and the installation of these facilities can lead to environmental degradation. It's also important to note that the process of manufacturing solar cells requires the use of water, which could potentially threaten an area's local supply. Toxic chemicals such as sulfuric acid and acetone are also utilized during this process and could harm people if not handled properly.

① the process of manufacturing clean energy
② land-use requirements for solar energy plants
③ ideas for addressing the weaknesses of solar cell design
④ land contamination caused by modern agricultural practices
⑤ concerns about the impacts of solar energy on the environment

24 다음 글의 제목으로 가장 적절한 것은?

The comedian Groucho Marx once joked that he wouldn't want to belong to any club that would accept him as a member; the flip side being that he would only want to join a club that wouldn't accept him. This weird longing to belong begins young. Most teens only want to be part of one small group of peers: the "cool kids." They go out of their way to get noticed or approved of, and being rejected by the group just motivates them to try harder. Of course, as adults, we live in a much more complex world and are part of many more social circles. Yet, interestingly, the need for recognition from people who disregard us often lingers. It is important to keep in mind that the toll required to get something does not equate to its merit, so think carefully about who is worth your time and energy.

* toll: 대가

① Social Connections as an Indicator of Status
② Peer Acceptance: A Key Aspect of Childhood
③ Form Relationships with People Who Value You
④ The Benefits of Belonging to an Exclusive Group
⑤ How Can We Make Our Friends Feel Appreciated?

25 다음 도표의 내용과 일치하지 <u>않는</u> 것은?

The Number of Passenger Cars
per 1,000 Inhabitants in 2010 and 2019

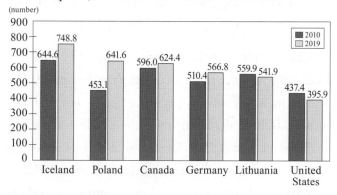

The above graph shows the number of passenger cars per 1,000 inhabitants from selected countries in 2010 and 2019. ① Among the six countries, Lithuania and the United States were the only two countries to experience a decrease in the number of passenger cars per 1,000 inhabitants from 2010 to 2019. ② Iceland and Poland both had an increase of over 100 in the number of passenger cars per 1,000 inhabitants during the period. ③ In Germany, cars never exceeded 600 per 1,000 inhabitants, and it ranked the fourth highest in both 2010 and 2019. ④ Passenger cars in the United States numbered just above 400 per 1,000 inhabitants in 2019 but stayed below 500 both years. ⑤ Iceland had the highest number of passenger cars per 1,000 inhabitants both years and its number in 2019 surpassed that of any other country in either year.

26 Susan Sontag에 관한 다음 글의 내용과 일치하지 않는 것은?

Born in New York in 1933, American author Susan Sontag wrote essays and novels that addressed many aspects of modern culture. She completed two master's degrees from Harvard University. The first was in English literature; the second was in philosophy. In 1951, while still a student, she wrote an article that was published in the prominent journal *Chicago Review*, marking the first time her writing appeared in print. Upon graduation, she traveled in Europe for a few months and then returned to New York to teach at several universities. Her first novel, *The Benefactor*, was released in 1963, and her subsequent works of fiction were critically acclaimed. Sontag was politically active, participating in protests against the Vietnamese War and writing essays in opposition to it. Following her death from leukemia in 2004, she was widely praised as being one of the most influential American intellectuals of her generation.

＊ leukemia: 백혈병

① Harvard University에서 두 개의 석사 학위를 취득했다.
② 1951년에 그녀의 글이 유명 학술지에 처음 기고되었다.
③ 유럽 여행 후 돌아와 여러 대학에서 가르쳤다.
④ 1963년에 마지막 소설을 발표했다.
⑤ 베트남 전쟁에 반대하는 시위에 참여했다.

27 Arrow Chocolate Factory Tour에 관한 다음 안내문의 내용과 일치하지 않는 것은?

Arrow Chocolate Factory Tour

If you love chocolate as much as we do, you can't miss out on our factory tour. Watch how all your favorite treats are made right in front of your eyes!

Tour Schedule:
- Monday to Friday, 10:00 a.m. – 3:00 p.m.
- Saturdays, 10:00 a.m. – 12:00 p.m.
- Tours start at the top of every hour and run for 45 minutes.
* Tours do not run on holidays.

Admission:
- $10 (for 10 and older)
- $5 (for children under 10)

At the factory:
- Full tour of the factory
- Taste-test new products
- Make your own chocolate

General rules:
- Wear a mask that we will provide.
- Follow the tour guide at all times.

Call 1-800-233-6789 for more information.

① 일요일과 공휴일에는 진행되지 않는다.
② 10세 미만의 어린이는 입장료가 5달러이다.
③ 신제품은 시식해볼 수 없다.
④ 자신만의 초콜릿을 만들어 볼 수 있다.
⑤ 반드시 마스크를 착용해야 한다.

28 Jumper Electric Scooter Share에 관한 다음 안내문의 내용과 일치하는 것은?

Jumper Electric Scooter Share

If you are looking for a green and convenient way to get around, look no further. Traveling around the city has never been easier!

How to rent:
1. Download the Jumper app.
2. Open it and become a member.
3. Find the closest scooter and scan the QR code.
4. Start riding!

Price:
- $2 for the first 5 minutes, and 15 cents per minute afterwards.
- First-time users must enter their credit card number into the app before use.
- You will only be charged for the minutes used.

Ending use:
- Press the "Arrive" button on the app once you have finished using the scooter.
- Make sure to park the scooter in a safe place.

---

① 비회원도 이용할 수 있다.
② QR 코드를 스캔한 후 가입한다.
③ 처음 5분은 무료이다.
④ 최초 이용자는 앱에 신용카드 번호를 입력해야 한다.
⑤ 이용 완료 후 스쿠터에 있는 버튼을 누른다.

29 다음 글의 밑줄 친 부분 중, 어법상 틀린 것은?

When movies are filmed, many sounds are too quiet or unclear ① for equipment to record them accurately as they take place on set. To address this issue, special sound-effect artists are required. Known as Foley artists, these individuals ② bring movies to life by looking carefully at camera footage and finding items to create sounds that match it. Being a Foley artist requires a lot of creativity ③ because, despite seeming as though they are authentic, many sounds are replicated in unusual ways. For instance, the sound of a bird ④ flapped its wings might be produced with a leather wallet. Ultimately, the work of a Foley artist is invaluable as it adds a sense of authenticity and mood to films ⑤ that would otherwise have to rely mostly on their visuals.

30 다음 글의 밑줄 친 부분 중, 문맥상 낱말의 쓰임이 적절하지 않은 것은? [3점]

Newton's Three Laws of Motion are the bedrock of physics. Among the three, the third states that for every action there is an equal and opposite reaction. This is something we experience yet ① rarely notice; all forces come in pairs. If a person is walking, their body exerts a force that is ② downwards on the ground. This is something we recognize because we see it and feel it when we walk. Meanwhile, the ground pushes the same upward force. The action-reaction pair represents the ③ asymmetry in nature. And one might think that two such forces would offset each other, but interestingly, this only occurs when ④ both forces are acting on the same object. In the example above, the force of the person acts on the ground while the force of the ground acts on the person. However, if the person stepped on a pillow, the person and ground would exert their force on the pillow, ⑤ cancelling the force.

[31~34] 다음 빈칸에 들어갈 말로 가장 적절한 것을 고르시오.

31

Through selective breeding, offspring can be produced that possess more desirable attributes, including increased size or resistance to disease. However, a side effect of this method is that some plants or animals generated this way inherit unwanted characteristics as well, so the technique is less than perfect. That's where genetically modified organisms (GMOs) come in. Rather than artificially selecting the parents of an organism with the hope of offspring exhibiting certain characteristics, genetic modification makes it possible for engineers to isolate a gene for a specific trait from one living thing, and then insert that same gene into a cell of another. This can be carried out across species and accelerates the development of _____ organisms. Agriculture is one industry in which this technique is commonly used. Crops are altered to be more resilient and nutritious, resulting in cheaper and higher-quality food for consumers.

① rare ② solid
③ peculiar ④ compact
⑤ enhanced

32

Narcissism is far more complicated than simply being vain or having an unwarranted sense of entitlement. While these are certainly symptoms, there is reason to believe that narcissism is actually an internal mechanism for people to _____.
Some theorists argue that the projection of strong attitudes by many narcissists is an affectation that masks the fact that their self-esteem is actually the opposite from how it is presented. Not wanting to reveal this inner fragility, they do everything they can to pretend to be strong and completely justified in their actions. Narcissists are eager to protect themselves from getting too close to others and having their peers learn of their weaknesses, so they avoid forming any true relationships, which could actually be an opportunity to develop empathy. Although they seem to manipulate others skillfully at first, their uncaring behavior drives people away in the end.

* affectation: 가장, 꾸밈

① alter their behavior to appear concerned for others
② raise their self-esteem by connecting with their peers
③ overcome their weaknesses by improving their attitudes
④ deal with shame that stems from issues with self-confidence
⑤ demonstrate their empathy for others to build relationships

33

Freedom of speech is the hallmark of a healthy democratic society. It is particularly championed by those who wish to justify what they say, no matter how unpopular. This is a right of every citizen, but language has the potential to be used as a dangerous tool. Hate speech has the power to plant the seeds of intolerance and hostility that lead to acts of violence. Many advocate the notion that free speech justifies any type of self-expression but this undermines the significance of what it means to speak one's mind; that is, what is essential is not that everyone says whatever they want but that _____. When free speech is substituted for consequence-free speech, we surrender our morality. Hateful rhetoric is subtle and gaslights vulnerable groups, making them feel less worthy. The way it tears down some people and elevates others is proof enough that not every thought needs to be uttered. [3점]

* rhetoric: 수사법, 미사여구

① what they say has good intentions behind it
② the language used is neutral in essence
③ everything that is worth saying is said
④ what is expressed is clear to listeners
⑤ their thoughts are conveyed honestly

34

Ethics consider what is right and wrong, or what is moral and immoral in regards to human behavior or activity. This branch of philosophy can be applied to all manner of situations and questions how matters should be dealt with for the common good. It is no surprise then that _____ since it seems to be advancing so quickly. Bioethics fulfills this role and encompasses ethical issues related to health and biology, from evaluating scientific research to assessing doctor-patient relationships. Controversial issues such as genetic experimentation, organ transplantation, and treating comatose patients all have ethical implications that call for deliberation, and the questions they evoke are often difficult to answer with complete certainty. Medical fees, for instance, are an important point of discussion since the gap between the health of lower-income and higher-income individuals is widening even as more advanced treatment options enter the market. Bioethics reviews how best to help reduce these differences and ensure that more than just the wealthy have access to affordable and effective healthcare. [3점]

* comatose: 혼수상태인

① the conception of morality has fluctuated over time
② the scientific process has become tied to ethics
③ healthcare is becoming a popular career field
④ treatment has become more patient-oriented
⑤ the medical field requires ethical oversight

35 다음 글에서 전체 흐름과 관계 없는 문장은?

Animals have been interacting with human-made technologies for decades, most commonly in behavioral experiments designed to further our understanding of their cognition and in agricultural settings to optimize production. ① But as digital technology becomes increasingly ubiquitous, we are expanding its reach with the hope of using it to improve their lives. ② The face of nature conservation is changing in profound ways thanks to digital technology, with apps and tools progressively shaping our practices. ③ These days, the market is flooded with pet products that allow people to monitor and play with their cats and dogs remotely, and zoos are adopting interactive touchscreens that provide apes the mental stimulation they require. ④ While such innovations may seem harmless, some people are concerned that introducing human-made technologies to other species could make animals reliant on them or reduce the relevance of the natural world. ⑤ Essentially, there is the sense that we may be forcing technology on creatures who may not benefit from it.

[36~37] 주어진 글 다음에 이어질 글의 순서로 가장 적절한 것을 고르시오.

36

Prior to the French Revolution, French units of measurement had not only gone unchanged for about 1,000 years but also varied widely from region to region.

(A) Now known as the metric system, this was a simpler system of measurement that was developed further through conferences with experts from other European nations. Although it would take roughly 50 years for France to make its use mandatory, its impact is undeniable, as it is used today throughout the majority of the world.

(B) Since there were up to 800 different names for units of measurement, many traders used their own measuring devices. This, however, frequently caused conflict and accusation of fraud.

(C) To put an end to the confusion and lack of unity the old system caused, Charles Maurice de Talleyrand suggested replacing it in the 1790s with a new system based on features in nature. The primary unit of measurement in his proposed system was the meter, which was recorded as being one ten-millionth of the distance from the equator to the North Pole.

① (A) – (C) – (B)　　② (B) – (A) – (C)
③ (B) – (C) – (A)　　④ (C) – (A) – (B)
⑤ (C) – (B) – (A)

37

As a fruit matures, it undergoes both external and internal changes, from acquiring a sweeter taste to taking on new colors. These alterations are driven by a variety of hormones and signals including the ethylene gas, which hastens the overall process.

(A) Non-climacteric fruit do not have a surge in ethylene or respiration and do not ripen once picked, relying on the plant for this. Strawberries, cherries, and grapes are examples of fruits that ripen in this way.

(B) The burst of ethylene is accompanied by an increased rate of respiration. These fruits are able to ripen even after being harvested, and can be affected by external ethylene, so if a climacteric fruit with lower levels of the gas is placed next to one with higher levels, its ripening will quicken.

(C) Each fruit differs in how much ethylene is present during its lifecycle, but it generally follows two patterns during development. Climacteric fruits such as apples, bananas, and pears produce more ethylene overall and experience a sudden increase of the gas during ripening. [3점]

* climacteric fruit: 후숙 과일

① (A) – (C) – (B)　　② (B) – (A) – (C)
③ (B) – (C) – (A)　　④ (C) – (A) – (B)
⑤ (C) – (B) – (A)

[38~39] 글의 흐름으로 보아, 주어진 문장이 들어가기에 가장 적절한 곳을 고르시오.

38

It also fails to consider the myriad ways art can be communicated.

Historically, fashion has never really been elevated to the same status as paintings, music, or literature in the art world. This disparity was brought to light at an exhibit at the Metropolitan Museum of Art in 1983. (①) The display of certain iconic clothing items in the same manner as masterpieces by Rembrandt and Picasso angered many critics who did not feel clothes should be categorized as fine art. (②) This assessment narrows the field of artistry to a box that is outdated and restrictive. (③) Fashion, like all art, is a manifestation of the society we live in and an expression of the era we are a part of. (④) It can reflect who we are as a person in the same way a painting we admire reveals to us what we find beautiful or moving. (⑤) Fashion is an industry to be sure, but a creative one that takes as much dedication and craftsmanship as any other artistic endeavor.

39

> Meanwhile, 68% of citizens rely on private coverage through insurance companies, and another 8% lack coverage entirely.

Those who have moved to America from other economically advanced countries have no doubt puzzled over the strange workings of the US healthcare system. (①) Unlike virtually every other industrialized nation in the world, the American government does not offer a form of publicly managed universal health care, instead operating a predominately private system. (②) Under this system, impoverished, disabled, and elderly citizens qualify for some or all of their health care expenses to be covered through publicly funded plans. (③) Moreover, high deductibles — out-of-pocket costs that must be paid in addition to costly monthly premiums before insurance benefits come into effect — prevent many of those enrolled in private insurance policies from being able to reliably access medical services. (④) According to one analysis, the average individual deductible for Americans is $5,940, a sum that exceeds many people's financial means. (⑤) For this reason, critics have put forth a number of different models for the legislature to consider adopting. [3점]

40 다음 글의 내용을 한 문장으로 요약하고자 한다. 빈칸 (A), (B)에 들어갈 말로 가장 적절한 것은?

To determine the role of sleep in spatial learning — an ability that is reliant on the hippocampus — researchers engaged volunteers in an academic sleep experiment that tested how well they could get through a three-dimensional virtual maze. The participants were divided into two groups, both of which received training on how to complete the maze; the first group's session occurred at 10:00 am, while the second group's session took place at 10:00 pm. Both groups were tested on what they learned 11 hours after their training, with the second group demonstrating what they learned the next day following a night of sleep. It was found that the group that slept before being tested outperformed the first group. Although the members of this group were not faster at completing the task, the decisions they made with regards to their movements through the maze were correct more often. The results of the experiment ultimately suggest sleep enhances the processing of spatial information in the hippocampus.

* hippocampus: (뇌의) 해마

↓

> In a test of their ability to _____(A)_____ a virtual maze, participants who slept following their training were more _____(B)_____ than those who did not.

	(A)		(B)
①	design	.....	committed
②	navigate	.....	accurate
③	finish	.....	communicative
④	design	.....	precise
⑤	navigate	.....	observant

[41~42] 다음 글을 읽고, 물음에 답하시오.

Being a successful business today is about more than just offering high quality products. Companies are expected to not only function as profit making organizations, but also as institutions working for the common good. With society facing an abundance of economic, social, and environmental issues, businesses are being more closely analyzed by customers who are wary of where they shop; in other words, a company with a reputation for being eco-friendly is more likely to attract customers than a company notorious for polluting the environment. A business that operates according to the Corporate Social Responsibility (CSR) model keeps this in mind.

One such organization is Lego, which has made numerous sustainability goals in the past few years. It is the only toy company that has been named a World Wildlife Fund Climate Savers Partner, and they have pledged to use environmentally friendly materials for all of their main products and packaging by 2030. CSR has benefited Lego over time, with the company announcing that in the first half of 2021 alone their net profit went up by 140%. So, not only have they cultivated a glowing reputation for investing in sustainability and education, but they've increased profits as well. This shows how CSR is an advantageous business model for companies. Rather than _____ people and habitats, companies that act to foster and care for them will thrive in the future.

41 윗글의 제목으로 가장 적절한 것은?

① Tips for Becoming an Eco-Friendly Company
② The Hidden Costs of Corporate Social Responsibility
③ Sustainability: The Solution to Mending a Reputation
④ Reasons That Socially Responsible Companies Prosper Today
⑤ What Factors Are the Most Important for Maximizing Profit?

42 윗글의 빈칸에 들어갈 말로 가장 적절한 것은? [3점]

① exploiting
② overthrowing
③ replacing
④ indulging
⑤ protecting

[43~45] 다음 글을 읽고, 물음에 답하시오.

(A)

It was Anay's birthday and he received many gifts from his family and friends. But the best present he got was from his older brother: a shiny, new automobile! (a) He was very proud of it and drove it to his office every day. He often saw passersby looking at his prized possession with envy.

(B)

The little boy's eyes lit up! He had never been in an automobile and he was excited. As Anay and the boy drove through town, the boy asked (b) him where he got the car. Anay replied that his older brother gave it to him as a birthday present. "So you didn't have to pay even a penny for it?" the boy asked in amazement. "That's right," replied Anay. "Wow… I wish…" the young boy began, but Anay knew what he was going to say. "You wish you had an older brother like mine, don't you?" (c) he said.

(C)

One day, Anay left his office, and as he headed to his car, he saw that one of the people looking at it was a young boy. He was a little dirty with torn clothes and Anay could see that he was not well-off. Being a kind man, Anay went up to the boy and asked (d) him if he would like a ride home.

(D)

The boy shook his head. "I hope that I can be a brother like that," he said. Anay was surprised at his answer. But, when Anay dropped the boy off at his house, he understood why he said that. "May I get my younger brother? I would like him to see (e) your magnificent car." Soon, he reappeared, carrying a small boy whose legs were paralyzed. "See that shiny car? I will make enough money to buy you one, and you will not have to pay even a penny for it."

43 주어진 글 (A)에 이어질 내용을 순서에 맞게 배열한 것으로 가장 적절한 것은?

① (B) – (D) – (C)　　　② (C) – (B) – (D)
③ (C) – (D) – (B)　　　④ (D) – (B) – (C)
⑤ (D) – (C) – (B)

44 밑줄 친 (a)~(e) 중에서 가리키는 대상이 나머지 넷과 다른 것은?

① (a)　　② (b)　　③ (c)　　④ (d)　　⑤ (e)

45 윗글에 관한 내용으로 적절하지 않은 것은?

① Anay는 형에게 자동차를 선물로 받았다.
② 소년은 한 번도 자동차를 타본 적이 없었다.
③ Anay는 소년에게 집까지 태워 주기를 원하는지 물었다.
④ 소년은 자신도 Anay 같은 형이 될 거라고 말했다.
⑤ 소년의 남동생은 다리가 불편했다.

정답·해설·해석 p. 73

문제풀이 후 확인사항
1. 45분 내에 문제를 풀었다.
2. 체크해둔 문제와 틀린 문제는 해설을 꼼꼼히 확인했다.

수고하셨습니다! HackersBook.com에서 제공하는 어휘리스트로 어휘를 암기하세요.

09회 실전모의고사

목표 시간: 45분   시작: ___ 시 ___ 분 ~ 종료: ___ 시 ___ 분   점수: ___ 점 / 63점

* [3점] 표시가 있는 문제 제외하고는 모두 2점으로 계산합니다.

18 다음 글의 목적으로 가장 적절한 것은?

To Whom It May Concern:

My name is Winnie Anderson. I recently moved to the neighborhood and I was surprised by how many beautiful parks there are. It has been so wonderful to be able to enjoy nature with my family. I've noticed that most of the parks have plenty of exercise equipment and activities for adults but not as many for children. I see children running around all the time and thought they needed a safe space to play. That is why I am submitting this letter. I saw that the city website welcomes suggestions from residents, and I think it would be great if a few playgrounds could be built for the children. Thank you for your consideration.

Sincerely,
Winnie Anderson

① 공원의 소음 방지 대책을 촉구하려고
② 지역 주민을 위한 행사를 홍보하려고
③ 체험 학습 프로그램에 대해 문의하려고
④ 공원 내 운동 기구의 수리를 요청하려고
⑤ 아이들을 위한 놀이터 신설을 건의하려고

19 다음 글에 나타난 'I'의 심경 변화로 가장 적절한 것은?

I ripped open the letter. I couldn't wait to read it. I always thought I'd be an ideal candidate for the university I had applied to. I read the letter aloud to my mother. "Dear Ms. Summers, your application for Crimson University has been received, and you meet all the qualifications for admission." I smiled, thinking "That's it! I'm in!" But then I read the next line. "However, we have already offered admission to the maximum number of incoming freshmen. Therefore, you have been put on our waiting list." My mother tried to comfort me, but I couldn't believe that I had failed. This felt like such a big disaster after so much hard work and dedication. I sighed and threw the letter away in frustration.

① shocked → proud
② worried → relieved
③ confident → disappointed
④ touched → desperate
⑤ calm → envious

20 다음 글에서 필자가 주장하는 바로 가장 적절한 것은?

Anxiety is a form of unwanted time travel. It transports one out of a present that could be cherished into a future that is detested. The English philosopher John Locke stated, "What worries you, masters you." If you focus exclusively on potential negative outcomes, you are in fact experiencing failure in advance. This greatly increases your odds of not succeeding in whatever endeavor you have planned. In effect, you become trapped in a negative feedback loop, whereby your concerns lead you to fail, which makes you more anxious in the future. To avoid this trap, it is vital to remain fully engaged with the present, as it is after all the only time period that truly exists. The future is a fantasy, and the past is a phantom. The trick is to make the most of today in pursuit of a better tomorrow, whether or not it lives up to our expectations from yesterday.

① 과거의 실수에 얽매이지 않고 꿈을 향해 나아가야 한다.
② 미래에 대한 걱정을 하기보다 현재에 집중해야 한다.
③ 불안감을 해소하려면 근본적인 원인을 찾아야 한다.
④ 성공을 위해서는 구체적인 인생 계획을 세워야 한다.
⑤ 예상치 못한 상황에 대비해 항상 대안을 마련해야 한다.

21 밑줄 친 a story without a voice가 다음 글에서 의미하는 바로 가장 적절한 것은? [3점]

In the past, using data and statistics in the form of charts and other visualizations was hit or miss, and some presentations were little more than a story without a voice. Over the last decade, however, more and more organizations have attempted to address this issue by turning to data storytelling, a methodology of communicating information that is specially tailored for a specific audience. Instead of just presenting any information about a company or a product, data storytelling takes advantage of the wealth of information that is now available to businesses thanks to technology and contextualizes it. For instance, the ride-sharing application Uber uses data storytelling to share information such as the number of miles a user has traveled in a year and puts it into perspective in order to show how much value it adds to the user's life. Being told that you've used the service to drive the equivalent of two journeys around Earth is far more compelling and has more of an impact than simply being told how much money you've spent.

① providing unconvincing arguments
② failing to incorporate technology
③ featuring confusing information
④ sharing already known details
⑤ lacking meaning or relevance

22 다음 글의 요지로 가장 적절한 것은?

Majoring in something more "employable" — science, math, computer programming, etc. — is much more attractive than studying literature. Statistics from universities across the country support this assertion, as the number of students with literature degrees has declined by 25 percent over the past decade and this downward trend is likely to continue. It is important to note, however, that literature is much more than just reading books. It fuels the imagination and encourages critical thinking. It improves communication and builds empathy. All are necessary skills to prosper today. Canadian Prime Minister Justin Trudeau has surely made good use of his English degree and there must be a good reason that the first American woman in space studied literature alongside physics. Seeing literature only as a form of entertainment, an outdated subject without practical purpose, is far too short-sighted, as it ultimately informs how well we live.

① 이공계 전공을 선호하는 추세가 점점 더 강해질 것이다.
② 문학은 비판적 사고 능력에 기본이 되는 학문이다.
③ 과학보다 문학 공부의 중요성이 강조되고 있다.
④ 자신의 적성과 능력에 따른 전공 선택이 중요하다.
⑤ 실용성만으로 문학 전공의 가치를 판단해서는 안 된다.

23 다음 글의 주제로 가장 적절한 것은?

The most recent ice age reached its peak nearly 21,000 years ago, resulting in much of the northern hemisphere being covered by thick sheets of ice. Although this posed a challenge for *Homo sapiens*, their large brains made them smart enough to endure the harsh environment. One significant advantage was the use of language, which enabled early humans to share information with each other. According to noted anthropologist Brian Fagan, this also gave them "the ability to conceptualize and plan ahead." As a result, they developed into highly adept hunters who were almost always capable of securing sufficient food. Tool-making was also a major factor, as humans could produce a range of useful implements. In addition to weapons such as spears for hunting, they also had needles to sew tight-fitting clothes that protected against the extreme cold. Another important contributor was the creation of effective shelters. *Homo sapiens* extensively modified caves and other natural formations to make them weatherproof.

① influence of a cold climate on human evolution
② hunting techniques employed by *Homo sapiens*
③ environmental challenges faced by *Homo sapiens*
④ role of intelligence in the survival of early humans
⑤ changes to the human brain during the last ice age

24 다음 글의 제목으로 가장 적절한 것은?

A geographic information system (GIS) is designed to examine trends and patterns related to positions on Earth's surface. It can be used for a multitude of purposes, from forecasting the weather to researching areas with high criminal activity. But one of the most valuable aspects of GIS is its ability to forecast the spread of a disease across large regions. Researchers in Thailand used this system to anticipate areas at risk of avian flu after an outbreak in 2004. The virus is highly contagious and severely impacted poultry farms, causing the deaths of more than 62 million birds — either as a direct result of the virus or through forced slaughter — and extensive damage to the local and national economies. By inputting important information regarding the region, its communities, and cases, scientists were able to gain a better understanding of the disease's potential diffusion patterns so that preventive measures could be put in place.

* avian flu: 조류 독감

① The Technology of GIS: What Does its Future Have in Store?
② Mapping Disease: The Ability of GIS to Predict the Path of a Virus
③ Effects of Mapping Software on the Economy of Thailand
④ Can Thailand's Poultry Industry Recover After Avian Flu?
⑤ Rising Trends and Projections in the GIS Global Market

25 다음 도표의 내용과 일치하지 <u>않는</u> 것은?

Youth Literacy Rate in African Countries

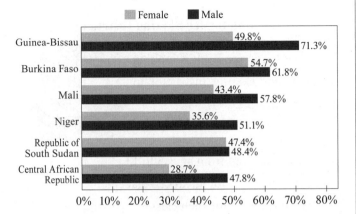

The above graph shows the youth literacy rates of males and females in six African countries. ① Among the six countries, the female youth literacy rate in Burkina Faso is the highest at over 50%. ② The rates of youth literacy for females in the Central African Republic and Niger are both under 40%. ③ The only two countries among the six countries in which the male youth literacy rate does not exceed 50% are the Republic of South Sudan and Central African Republic. ④ In Mali, the youth literacy rate for males is 10% lower than the rate in the Central African Republic. ⑤ While the difference between male and female youth literacy rates in the Republic of South Sudan is only 1%, that in Guinea-Bissau is over 20%.

＊ literacy rate: 식자율(글자를 아는 사람들의 비율)

26 Robert Brown에 관한 다음 글의 내용과 일치하지 <u>않는</u> 것은?

Robert Brown, one of the world's most famous botanists, was born in 1772 in Montrose, Scotland. He is well known for his research into the morphology and geographic distribution of plants, particularly those native to Australia. Although he studied medicine at the University of Edinburgh and spent five years serving as a surgeon in the British Army, he had a strong interest in botany. During his time in the military, he collected many specimens of plants, wrote academic articles, and corresponded with prominent botanists. In 1801, he took the position of naturalist aboard the survey ship *Investigator* which explored the coasts of Australia. When he returned to England in 1805, he had a collection of over 3,900 plants — most of which were previously undiscovered species. During his later research into the fertilization process of orchids, he provided detailed observations of a cell's nucleus and gave it the name that is still used today.

＊ morphology: 형태학

① 세계에서 가장 유명한 식물학자 중 한 명이다.
② Edinburgh 대학에서 의학을 공부했다.
③ 군복무 기간 동안 많은 식물 표본을 수집했다.
④ 식물 채집 후 1801년에 영국으로 돌아왔다.
⑤ 난초의 수정 과정을 연구하며 세포핵을 상세히 관찰했다.

27 Sun Hot Springs에 관한 다음 안내문의 내용과 일치하지 <u>않는</u> 것은?

Sun Hot Springs

Come and relax in our natural geothermal hot springs. All of your worries will melt away.

Entrance Fees:
- $45 for a Day Pass
- $20 for a 2-hour Pass

Outdoor bathing:
- 5:00 a.m. to 10:00 p.m.
- Lounge beds can be rented.
- All food and drink must be consumed in the designated area.

Indoor bathing/spa:
- 5:00 a.m. to 8:00 p.m.
- No loud talking in saunas
- Various massage therapies available (reservations required)

* Overnight guests can use all facilities free of charge.

Please visit www.sunhotsprings.com for more information.

① 2시간 이용권은 20달러이다.
② 야외 온천 이용 시간은 오후 10시까지이다.
③ 음식과 음료는 지정된 구역에서만 섭취해야 한다.
④ 마사지 테라피는 예약해야 이용할 수 있다.
⑤ 투숙객들은 모든 시설을 유료로 이용 가능하다.

28 Looking for Ice Skating Instructor에 관한 다음 안내문의 내용과 일치하는 것은?

Looking for Ice Skating Instructor

The Fargo Ice Rink is looking for an ice skating instructor to teach full time.

Duties:
- Teach children from ages 5 to 13
- Evaluate skills for advanced placement
- Make routines for each class
- Manage ice conditions and skating equipment

Requirements:
- Strong communication and leadership skills
- Prior teaching experience
- First Aid Certification
- At least 25 years of age

Applicants must fill out the online application form at www.ficerink.com. Please include a résumé. For questions, check the Q&A section on our website.

① 5세에서 14세 어린이를 가르친다.
② 스케이트 장비 구입 업무도 담당한다.
③ 지도 경력이 없어도 지원 가능하다.
④ 응급 처치 자격증이 있어야 한다.
⑤ 이력서는 제출하지 않아도 된다.

29 다음 글의 밑줄 친 부분 중, 어법상 틀린 것은? [3점]

Defense mechanisms are unconscious coping techniques used ① to reduce the anxiety caused by unpleasant situations. One example of this is displaced aggression, which occurs ② when a person is angry at someone but chooses a different target to engage in hostile behavior with. Most commonly, the person who ③ initially triggered the anger is in a position of authority and, therefore, immune to retaliation. Displaced aggression is often exhibited by individuals with a narcissistic personality; as they have a high opinion of ④ themselves and lack empathy for others, they are less able to move on from a perceived slight and more willing to take their frustrations out on an innocent. Unfortunately, victims of displaced aggression tend to be the vulnerable members of a group. Many cases of workplace bullying can ⑤ attribute to this psychological phenomenon — a manager feeling the urge to express anger is more likely to target a subordinate than a superior.

30 다음 글의 밑줄 친 부분 중, 문맥상 낱말의 쓰임이 적절하지 않은 것은?

Blindness can cause the ① unexpected symptom of seeing hallucinatory images. Unlike mental problems such as Alzheimer's disease, this phenomenon is not an indication of cognitive instability. Instead, it occurs because of a ② decline in the typical load of sensory information the brain is used to receiving. As the eyes perceive less, the brain cells become overactive in order to fill in missing details. To learn more, neuroscientists scanned the brains of numerous individuals with this condition and discovered that, despite the lack of visual input, the activity in the visual center of their brains remained high. In some cases, there was more activity than in those with ③ regular eyesight. Scientists attribute this outcome to the brain's attempts to ④ delete images from memory rather than passively receive information as it normally would. Furthermore, the images were not static or simple. Patients reported seeing moving parts, people, geometric shapes, and animals, always ⑤ well-defined and in full color.

[31~34] 다음 빈칸에 들어갈 말로 가장 적절한 것을 고르시오.

31

The construction industry has a significant environmental impact that is often overlooked due to how necessary it is; with ever-expanding global populations, just keeping pace with the demand for new construction is a challenge in itself. In an effort to combat the damage caused by construction, the desire for sustainability in building practices has never been greater, and terms like "eco-friendly" and "green" are becoming commonplace within the industry. However, many consider these terms to be exaggerated buzzwords. While buildings being marketed this way may indeed have a smaller environmental footprint than structures of the past, it is believed that truly sustainable architecture is _____. Until more architects and builders take care to incorporate eco-friendly practices into every last aspect of the planning and construction processes, we may be a long way from reducing the negative effects of the building industry on the planet.

① the key for future generations to survive
② too cost-prohibitive to be realistic
③ increasingly difficult to define
④ the exception rather than the rule
⑤ reflected in our modern-day buildings

32

Notwithstanding the immorality of practices such as slavery, the Roman empire was still arguably more progressive with regards to welfare than we are today. The Roman empire was capable of systemizing social programs to benefit the entire population. The empire had 44,850 insulae, blocks of communal housing for the poor, which held shops and stores on the ground level with private residences above. Other programs included handing out grain and pork once a week, providing free bathhouses and drinking water, and even establishing a form of subsidized healthcare. Although what modern society has inherited from such policies is evident in the systems now in place, _____. The scientific and cultural foundation we have had privilege to over the centuries should have resulted in progress far beyond the thousand-year-old Roman systems; instead, we have made meager strides and possibly even regressed.

① it is alarming how much the prices for living expenses have increased

② it is frustrating how people lack the funds to afford basic healthcare

③ it is encouraging that welfare is available to a majority of people

④ it is surprising that social programs have developed so rapidly

⑤ it is disappointing how little has been improved upon them

33

The brain _____.
Although neuroscientists used to believe that neurogenesis — the ability to produce new information-processing neurons in the brain — occurred only during development, it is now understood that our brains are flexible and resilient enough to respond to a variety of situations and challenges throughout our lives. This includes having to replace non-functioning limbs that result from accidents or disabilities with a tool such as a prosthetic device or a wheelchair. When surveying wheelchair-bound participants with debilitating spinal cord injuries for the study, it was found that, rather than viewing devices used to assist with their mobility as external tools, they viewed them as part of themselves. What this means is that the brain adjusts its image of the body to incorporate the wheelchair, allowing those who must use them to carry out activities in natural, automatic ways. [3점]

* prosthetic: 보철의

① is in tune with stimuli produced by the body

② can be permanently damaged by a disability

③ works to offset physical changes when they occur

④ has the unconscious ability to learn how to use tools

⑤ loses the ability to control muscle movement over time

34

Mannerism, an artistic style that emerged in 16th century Italy, marked a departure from the naturalism of the Renaissance and included a shift to a more philosophical approach to pieces. Rather than capturing life-like scenes that featured people as the focal point, mannerist artwork is _____ _____. Bodies are often illustrated with the *figura serpentinata* or "serpentine figure" in these pieces, leaving them with longer limbs, S-shaped forms, and small heads. They are also usually shown in odd and unnatural poses, surrounded by random elements in abnormal settings. These details and components, characterized by artificiality and sophistication, were intended to give the audience an intellectual experience, putting artists on par with poets and scholars since they had mostly been regarded as craftsmen until then. This break from the basic principles of naturalism and classicism, which promoted harmony and balance, could be interpreted as a reflection of the religious and social upheaval that occurred during this era. [3점]

* upheaval: 격변

① distinguished by distorted subjects and asymmetry

② regarded as more realistic for its flawed depictions

③ renowned for its occupation with simplicity in compositions

④ criticized as it fosters an unattainable image of the human body

⑤ known for its devotion to key tenets of the styles that preceded it

35 다음 글에서 전체 흐름과 관계 없는 문장은?

The economic landscape and hyper-competitiveness of professional sports put intense constraints on youth athletes who hope to make a career out of their passion. ① While securing placement on a university team is already a challenge, professional leagues are exponentially more selective. ② As such, only very small percentages of those who are lucky enough to compete at a collegiate level have the abilities to continue on to become top ranked in their respective games, forcing most to transition into other careers once they finish their education. ③ The saying that you shouldn't put all your eggs in one basket is thus a particularly valuable lesson for youth athletes, as they must be willing to diversify their prospects in the event that their ambitions do not come to fruition. ④ They should take time to research

promising fields to specialize in for job security since this is such a significant factor in their future. ⑤ Doing so will ensure that individuals are adaptable — capable of responding to and succeeding in whatever alternative opportunities may present themselves.

[36~37] 주어진 글 다음에 이어질 글의 순서로 가장 적절한 것을 고르시오.

36

The concept of a network of Internet-enabled devices that controls things remotely is known as the Internet of Things (IoT). Although the applications of IoT may seem more apparent in technology-driven sectors, there are potential uses in agriculture, too.

(A) As a result, farmers want to maximize their land's productivity. They are, therefore, turning to technologies like IoT. As IoT is still a new concept, most of the benefits so far come from the huge amounts of data that sensors placed throughout farms can collect.

(B) A significant challenge we face as populations rise is our need to produce more food. This is difficult, as farmland is shrinking due to the expansion of cities and environmental damage has decreased the availability of natural resources.

(C) This information can include the quality of the soil, measurements of temperature and humidity, and even the location of pests. With these details provided to them in real time and with minimal effort, farmers are able to do a better job of assessing the needs of their farms and responding accordingly.

① (A) – (C) – (B)　　　② (B) – (A) – (C)
③ (B) – (C) – (A)　　　④ (C) – (A) – (B)
⑤ (C) – (B) – (A)

37

Although volcanic eruptions are most commonly associated with lava and ash fall, one of the most serious dangers actually comes from lahars — floods of flowing water mixed with large amounts of debris.

(A) Evacuation is the only option for such places and, fortunately, there are sometimes warning signs. If heavy rain is forecast, then the likelihood of a lahar increases as intense rainfall can easily erode loose sediment and send it cascading downward into inhabited areas.

(B) The chance of lahars on volcanoes typically covered in ice and snow is also high as the heat of eruptions can melt it. And with any vegetation and soil being destroyed by the intense heat, there is nothing to slow the water as it engulfs everything in its path.

(C) With enough force to sweep large boulders into surrounding valleys at high speeds, and with the potential for several to occur in quick succession, lahars are a major cause of death in volcanic eruptions. Furthermore, because they can travel great distances, even communities located miles away from volcanoes are at risk. [3점]

* lahar: 화산 이류(火山泥流)

① (A) – (C) – (B) 　　② (B) – (A) – (C)
③ (B) – (C) – (A) 　　④ (C) – (A) – (B)
⑤ (C) – (B) – (A)

[38~39] 글의 흐름으로 보아, 주어진 문장이 들어가기에 가장 적절한 곳을 고르시오.

38

In the Baroque era, the harmonic rhythm was quite fast.

Whereas the Baroque Period was characterized by elaborate and complex compositions, the Classical Period marked a shift toward simplicity. Rather than producing layer upon layer of polyphony, classical composers crafted simple, memorable, "singable" melodies. (①) The melody was often carried in the top line of the music: the soprano voice in a chord or the violin in an orchestra. (②) Below that melody, supporting instruments would expand on the harmony. (③) As part of the movement towards simplicity, there was a relative slowing of harmonic rhythm — the pace at which chords changed within a piece — which was a marked departure from the prior period. (④) Often, the chord would change with nearly every beat. (⑤) In the Classical era, on the other hand, the harmonic rhythm was more relaxed, including a chord change no more than once or twice per measure.

* polyphony: 다성 음악

39

Actions to remedy the violation of informal agreements dealing with other issues only started to be developed in the 15th century.

At its most basic, a contract is a legally binding agreement between two parties. (①) Contract law can be traced back to the Latin principle of *pacta sunt servanda* ("all pacts must be kept"), although the true development of contract law as we understand it today was developed in western Europe as a way to handle disputes between merchants. (②) This meant that, initially, it was created to help parties recover money that was promised under an express, or written, agreement. (③) Eventually, an action known as *assumpsit* ("he has undertaken") was adopted as a form of recovery in the event of the negligent performance of an undertaking. (④) Because this had the potential to encompass many situations, the courts found the need to limit its scope. (⑤) They therefore devised the principle of "consideration," which stated that a contract could only be binding if an exchange was made or promised. [3점]

* consideration: 약인(約因), 대가

40 다음 글의 내용을 한 문장으로 요약하고자 한다. 빈칸 (A), (B)에 들어갈 말로 가장 적절한 것은?

Not wanting to be labeled a troublemaker or too assertive, many take a passive role in their daily interactions. To determine how such an individual is perceived by others, professor Kaitlin Woolley conducted a study wherein 300 participants were presented with a situation: a man ordering ice cream. They were asked to rate three options — he had a weak preference for chocolate, he had a strong preference for maple-bacon, or he had no preference and chose a flavor at random. Interestingly, when the man ordered at random, he was seen as the most robotic and least likeable by the participants. Further investigation revealed that lacking a preference harmed how one was viewed in their professional life. Subjects were less interested in hiring an applicant who stated they had no favorite food or music as opposed to one who did, despite the fact that there was no difference in the quality of their work. Woolley's research shows that, on the whole, someone who just "goes with the flow" is viewed as both less likeable and less capable.

↓

Individuals with no specific ____(A)____ are viewed less favorably and thought to be more ____(B)____ than those who have them.

	(A)	(B)
①	ideas	uninformed
②	opinions	incompetent
③	reasons	compliant
④	plans	particular
⑤	options	arbitrary

[41~42] 다음 글을 읽고, 물음에 답하시오.

If only one piece of scientific knowledge could be passed on to future generations, American physicist Richard Feynman maintained that it should be, "everything is made of atoms." This information, from which so many scientific advancements and discoveries have been developed, finds its origin in the 5th century BC when ancient atomic theory was proposed by Greek philosopher Leucippus and his student Democritus. In fact, Democritus coined the term *atomos* which translates to "uncuttable." His theory was that atoms are indivisible particles of matter that are unchangeable and uniform in composition. This idea, in addition to further reflections on the subject by renowned thinkers such as Aristotle and the poet Lucretius, all had their foundations in philosophy and speculation rather than   (A)   and actual science.

It wasn't until the endeavors of famous chemist John Dalton some 2,000 years later that these assumptions would be scientifically refined. Dalton was able to convert these philosophical notions into scientific theories based on empirical evidence, providing the basis for atomic chemistry. In addition, Dalton's findings   (B)   some of the key concepts of ancient atomic theory. He discovered that atoms of different elements actually vary in size and mass. From his work, more experiments and theories abounded, eventually making up the body of scientific knowledge we possess today.

* coin: (새로운 낱말을) 만들다

41 윗글의 제목으로 가장 적절한 것은?

① Atomic Theory: The Foundation of Empiricism
② The Structure of Matter's Indivisible Particles
③ The Scientific Transition of Atomic Theory
④ Why Modern Scientists are Rooted in Philosophy
⑤ Modern Science: Knowledge with Origins in the Past

42 윗글의 빈칸 (A), (B)에 들어갈 말로 가장 적절한 것은?
[3점]

	(A)	(B)
①	metaphor	······ condemned
②	experimentation	······ disproved
③	experimentation	······ complimented
④	assumptions	······ assessed
⑤	assumptions	······ ignored

[43~45] 다음 글을 읽고, 물음에 답하시오.

(A)

Erica was tired after working a long day at the hospital. She was a nurse's aide, and although it wasn't easy, she loved helping people. As she was getting ready to leave, the head nurse, Jill, noticed how tired (a) she looked. "Hey, Erica. Do you want to grab a cup of coffee?" Erica accepted gratefully.

(B)

"I'm too old for that," she replied. "I'm already 38." Jill smiled and said "That's not too old at all. I will tell (b) you how I know." Then, Jill told Erica about how she became a nurse. She had to drop out of college because her father lost his job and she needed to help her family. She began working as a waitress, since she had no experience or degree. She kept working hard until she became a manager.

(C)

"I kept saving a little money every time I got a paycheck. It wasn't much. But one day, I finally saved enough to go back to school." Jill smiled. "I received my diploma when I was 41 years old." Erica was astonished. "I had no idea it was so difficult for (c) you." "Yes, it was difficult. But I've come to appreciate the hardships in my life," Jill answered. "If my experiences can help others find their way, then I really haven't lost a thing."

(D)

As they sat together, Jill noticed that (d) she was particularly quiet. "Is there anything wrong?" she asked. Erica finally told her the problem. "I don't think I can keep working at the hospital anymore. I'm really struggling financially. My parents look after my children as I work, but they are getting older." Jill knew how much Erica loved working with patients and made a suggestion. "Why don't (e) you go to nursing school? The hospital has a very good financial assistance program. I'm sure your parents would help while you get a degree."

43 주어진 글 (A)에 이어질 내용을 순서에 맞게 배열한 것으로 가장 적절한 것은?

① (B) – (D) – (C)　　　　② (C) – (B) – (D)
③ (C) – (D) – (B)　　　　④ (D) – (B) – (C)
⑤ (D) – (C) – (B)

44 밑줄 친 (a)~(e) 중에서 가리키는 대상이 나머지 넷과 다른 것은?

① (a)　　② (b)　　③ (c)　　④ (d)　　⑤ (e)

45 윗글에 관한 내용으로 적절하지 않은 것은?

① Erica는 사람들을 돕는 일을 좋아했다.
② Jill은 종업원으로 일했었다.
③ Jill은 41세에 대학 졸업장을 받았다.
④ Erica는 병원에서 일하며 많은 돈을 벌었다.
⑤ Jill은 Erica에게 간호 대학을 가라고 제안했다.

정답·해설·해석 p. 83

문제풀이 후 확인사항
1. 45분 내에 문제를 풀었다.
2. 체크해둔 문제와 틀린 문제는 해설을 꼼꼼히 확인했다.

수고하셨습니다! HackersBook.com에서 제공하는 어휘리스트로 어휘를 암기하세요.

10회 실전모의고사

목표 시간: 45분 | 시작: ___ 시 ___ 분 ~ 종료: ___ 시 ___ 분 | 점수: ___점 / 63점

* [3점] 표시가 있는 문제 제외하고는 모두 2점으로 계산합니다.

18 다음 글의 목적으로 가장 적절한 것은?

Dear Residents,

Last week, the city passed a new law to make it easier for the physically disabled to access their homes. It mandates that all multi-unit residential buildings include a wheelchair ramp at the main entrance. Although there is a six-month period to comply with this policy, we have decided to take the necessary steps immediately in order to reduce any difficulties faced in accessing our property for disabled residents and guests as early as possible. Therefore, we would like to notify everyone that from May 15 to 17, workers will be constructing a wheelchair ramp leading up to the front door of our building. We apologize for any inconvenience this may cause and appreciate your patience.

Regards,

David Greer, Greenwoods Apartments Manager

① 입주자 대표 선출 결과를 통보하려고
② 새 법률이 적용될 시점을 안내하려고
③ 아파트 관리비 인상 이유를 설명하려고
④ 휠체어 경사로 설치 공사의 일정을 공지하려고
⑤ 아파트 보안 정책에 관한 주민들의 의견을 물으려고

19 다음 글에 나타난 Melanie의 심경으로 가장 적절한 것은?

Melanie breathed deeply and inhaled the fresh scent of the woods. For the first couple days at the cabin, she hadn't known what to do. She had been working non-stop for more than 20 years, and suddenly having nothing to do was an odd experience. But as her body settled into a slower rhythm, so did her mind and soul. She walked gently through the forest and reached her favorite reading spot — a beautiful patch of grass. She lay down and soaked up the warm sun filtering through the leaves of the trees above. She listened to the nearby stream and the rustling of the small creatures around her. All her senses were in tune with nature, and she felt a peace of mind she hadn't ever felt before.

① relaxed and content
② indifferent and bored
③ sorrowful and depressed
④ confused and puzzled
⑤ proud and delighted

20 다음 글에서 필자가 주장하는 바로 가장 적절한 것은?

When faced with a choice between making a change and keeping things the way they are, there is a natural tendency to ask, "Why rock the boat?" But this predisposition — known as the status quo bias — can lead to missed opportunities, which is why it is important to break free from its shackles. Imagine you had been working in the same position for years; even if it wasn't your dream job, you would likely grow quite comfortable. If one of your close friends suddenly recommended you for an important role at his or her company, you might ask yourself, "Why risk the unknown when things are fine now?" While doing nothing may indeed be the safest course of action, it also precludes the possibility of you ending up in a better situation. Caution is important, but don't let a preference for the familiar prevent you from improving your life.

* shackles: 족쇄

① 목표는 변화하는 상황에 따라 달라져야 한다.
② 일과 여가 생활의 균형을 맞추며 살아야 한다.
③ 현재에 안주하여 도전하는 것을 주저해서는 안 된다.
④ 도전하기 전에 실패의 가능성을 신중히 고려해야 한다.
⑤ 중요한 결정을 내릴 때 타인의 말에 휘둘려서는 안 된다.

21 밑줄 친 providing a ticket to the ball이 다음 글에서 의미하는 바로 가장 적절한 것은? [3점]

Obtaining a bachelor's or master's degree has come to be seen as a prerequisite for achieving professional success and, thereby, financial stability. Given this, most students have a natural response: they apply to universities with the greatest name recognition, major in subjects that will allow them to maximize future earnings, and choose classes based on the ease with which they can obtain high grades. In effect, a degree is viewed as a commodity, and the student's goal is to get the most value at the lowest cost. This poses a significant problem according to noted economist Eamon O'Shea,

who argues that something valuable is missed "by concentrating only on the market-based economic returns to education." Rather than simply providing a ticket to the ball, universities need to reorient themselves to challenge and stimulate young people intellectually so that they can identify their purpose in life and attempt to fulfill it; in other words, students need to be encouraged to pursue real happiness.

① specializing in a certain field of study
② serving as means to achieve a profitable career
③ motivating students to pursue educational goals
④ offering advice regarding how to become wealthy
⑤ providing direct support to the academically gifted

22 다음 글의 요지로 가장 적절한 것은?

There is a widely held belief that humor is primarily a form of escapism in that it relieves stress by allowing people to make light of real-world problems that have a direct impact on their lives. While this is a function of comedy, it can also play a much more important role — it is method to explore social issues in an unconventional way, often providing new insights in the process. Humor can be used to challenge harmful stereotypes about specific groups of people who are in the minority. This is because responding to a joke is a form of social bonding — when humor is centered on presenting the perspective of a marginalized group in a positive manner, it promotes empathy toward people who might otherwise be ignored or even disparaged. In this way, comedy works as a framing mechanism that presents controversial issues as shared experiences, allowing people to see beyond their own prejudices.

① 가벼운 농담은 분위기를 좋게 만드는 역할을 한다.
② 공통된 관심사를 공유하며 친밀감을 형성할 수 있다.
③ 유머를 통해 사회적 문제를 효과적으로 다룰 수 있다.
④ 스트레스를 웃음으로 승화하는 것이 정신 건강에 중요하다.
⑤ 코미디는 때때로 사회적 약자들이 겪는 불평등을 풍자한다.

23 다음 글의 주제로 가장 적절한 것은? [3점]

The Internet has made art more accessible; it is no longer just the domain of ultra-wealthy collectors. The exposure the Internet affords is naturally good for artists, as it gives them the opportunity to showcase their work without having to hope that a dealer might exhibit it in a gallery first. However, while their work is technically out there for all to see, online art curating is overwhelmed with so much content that the lines between good and bad art have been blurred; it's all just art, available to anyone. In addition, the art community itself has turned into a factory of sorts, with the more original art being produced, the higher the potential for profit. Today, artists can be much more commercially successful when they produce 30 mediocre works every month instead of one carefully crafted work a year because art is now just something to be bought and sold rather than something "priceless" to be treasured for its aesthetic or transcendent qualities.

* mediocre: 그저 그런, 썩 좋지 않은

① reasons for the increasing preference for mass-produced art
② the influence of the Internet on how the quality of art is measured
③ the link between the democratization of art and its commodification
④ the consequences of the commercialization of art on artists' profits
⑤ the difficulty of assigning a price to a piece of contemporary art

24 다음 글의 제목으로 가장 적절한 것은?

With the purchasing power of wages remaining relatively constant over the last 40 years, more people are struggling to make ends meet. Workers are using their free time to take on second jobs as a way of paying their bills. For these people, flexibility is a key element of a second job so that it doesn't interfere with their primary job. Technology has helped make this possible, allowing people to work during hours of their own choosing as independent contractors who fulfill the short-term needs of many companies. The "gig economy" is a relatively new term to describe the prevalence of short-term contract work. New platforms have been developed to facilitate contract hiring, like Uber, which allows people to get paid to drive other people around. Numerous websites exist to connect people with short-term jobs in every area imaginable, many of which can be done remotely and without a fixed schedule.

① The Downfall of Professional Careers
② Skills to Succeed in the Gig Economy
③ Flexibility: The Secret to Increased Hiring
④ The Rise of Second Jobs in the Gig Economy
⑤ Hard Work is the Key to Getting a Second Job!

25 다음 표의 내용과 일치하지 <u>않는</u> 것은?

Tourism Employment Figures in Denmark

Year of 2008		Year of 2018	
Divisions	Employment (number)	Divisions	Employment (number)
Food and beverage	83,830	Food and beverage	119,600
Passenger transport	57,810	Sports industry	63,250
Sports industry	28,060	Passenger transport	55,720
Cultural industry	25,850	Cultural industry	27,320
Accommodation services	21,020	Accommodation services	21,380
Travel agencies	6,820	Travel agencies	6,740
Total	223,400	Total	294,020

* Note: Details may not add to totals due to rounding.

The tables above show tourism employment numbers in Denmark in 2008 and 2018. ① The total employment numbers in tourism in Denmark rose by more than 70,000 from 2008 to 2018. ② With regard to the food and beverage division, employment numbers increased by more than 35,000 in the same period. ③ In both 2008 and 2018, the only division in which employment was less than 10,000 was travel agencies. ④ While the divisions of passenger transport and sports industry ranked the second and third highest in 2008 respectively, their ranks switched places with each other in 2018. ⑤ In 2018, employment numbers in the accommodation services division was less than half of that of the cultural industry.

26 Antlions에 관한 다음 글의 내용과 일치하지 <u>않는</u> 것은?

Antlions are insects that belong to the Myrmeleontidae family. Their name is attributed to their larva, which are predatory by nature. An antlion begins its life cycle as an egg, after which it hatches into larval form. An antlion larva is brown with a flat, wingless, oval-shaped body. It has six legs and a head that bears an enormous pair of pincers. Once the larva reaches its maximum size (roughly half an inch long), it forms a cocoon and undergoes metamorphosis, emerging as an adult. An adult antlion is long, slender, and winged, closely resembling a dragonfly. Adult antlions range in size from one-and-a-half to three inches long. They have four long, thin, veined wings, and their heads are topped with two curved antennae.

* Myrmeleontidae: 명주잠자리과 ** metamorphosis: 변태(變態)

① 알에서부터 생애 주기가 시작된다.
② 유충의 몸은 납작하고 날개가 없는 타원형이다.
③ 유충은 여섯 개의 다리를 가지고 있다.
④ 유충이 다 자라면 고치를 만든 후 성충이 된다.
⑤ 성충의 크기는 대략 0.5인치 정도이다.

27 Parson City Library's Borrowing and Renewal Policies에 관한 다음 안내문의 내용과 일치하지 <u>않는</u> 것은?

Parson City Library's
Borrowing and Renewal Policies

Parson City Library would like to announce changes to our borrowing and renewal policies.

Borrowing:

◆ Books

- You can borrow up to a maximum of 7 at a time.
- Each book must be returned within 14 days.

◆ Digital Media

- Includes DVDs, CDs, and audiobooks.
- You can borrow up to a maximum of 5 at a time.
- Each item can be kept up to 30 days (except for DVDs, which can be kept for up to 20 days).

Renewal:

- Books can be renewed 3 times.
- Digital media can be renewed 2 times.
- Each renewal is an extra 10 days.
- The renewal must be made before the due date.

---

① 도서는 한번에 최대 7권까지 대출할 수 있다.

② 대출 도서는 14일 내에 반납해야 한다.

③ DVD는 최대 20일 동안 대출할 수 있다.

④ 도서는 2번 대출 연장이 가능하다.

⑤ 대출 연장 신청은 반납일 전에 해야 한다.

28 Little Chefs Cooking Camp에 관한 다음 안내문의 내용과 일치하는 것은?

Little Chefs Cooking Camp

If you want your child to learn important life skills while still having fun, then sign them up for Little Chefs Cooking Camp today!

• They will discover dishes from around the world.

• They will work with a wide variety of fresh ingredients.

• They will learn about important kitchen safety and equipment.

Instructor: Chef Tim Roberts of The Dinner Table restaurant

Ages: Kids aged 8-12 are welcome.

Session: June 10 to June 14

Cost: $100 (free apron included)

Spaces are limited, so advance registration is required.

For more information on menus and activities, please visit www.littlechefs.com.

---

① 주로 아시안 요리를 배울 것이다.

② 6세 이하의 어린이가 참가할 수 있다.

③ 4일 동안 진행된다.

④ 앞치마는 별도로 구매해야 한다.

⑤ 참가하려면 사전 등록이 필요하다.

29 다음 글의 밑줄 친 부분 중, 어법상 <u>틀린</u> 것은?

The development of technologies to track individuals as they use the Internet has proven to be a boon for companies that market their products online. It allows them ① <u>create</u> personalized advertisements based on specific data points — ranging from age to relationship status to net worth — that target potential customers. However, increased consumer awareness of the threat this poses to privacy ② is leading to significant changes in the advertising industry. Of particular note is the gradual transition from an opt-out model of data collection to an opt-in one. Most social media sites and search engines collect extensive user information by default. Individuals ③ who want to avoid this must scroll through complicated menus to find the appropriate setting to change. ④ Rising complaints over this practice have led some firms to take action. They now create marketing content that encourages consumers to ⑤ voluntarily provide personal details. In particular, well-designed quizzes have a high level of consumer engagement and result in the collection of data that is of great use in advertising.

30 다음 글의 밑줄 친 부분 중, 문맥상 낱말의 쓰임이 적절하지 <u>않은</u> 것은? [3점]

A wolf tone is an unwanted beating or howling sound that is produced when the natural resonating frequency of a stringed instrument's top plate matches a note that is played. Although one might assume that an instrument with a wolf tone is of questionable quality, it's actually the ① high-quality instruments that suffer from it. The reason is quite simple: lower-quality instruments are made of materials that are ② less resonant. Therefore, they are less likely to create a wolf tone, and if they do, the amplitude is often low enough that it is hardly heard. Conversely, higher-quality instruments are extremely resonant and are more apt to support wolf tones that are amplified enough to be ③ noticeable. As ways to reduce the effect also affect the overall sound of the instrument, a balanced method is needed. The goal is to suppress the wolf tone with a ④ maximally invasive solution. This is typically done by attaching a weight to the string below the bridge of the instrument. The placement and mass of the weight must be ⑤ adjusted to find just the right combination, but if done correctly, the howl of the wolf tone can be tamed.

* amplitude: 진폭

[31~34] 다음 빈칸에 들어갈 말로 가장 적절한 것을 고르시오.

31

The popularity of e-commerce, largely driven by our ever-increasing desire for convenience, is only expected to grow on a global scale in the coming years. While a number of factors play into this, including automation and the decline of brick-and-mortar businesses, the growth of emerging markets is also expected to have a notable effect on the future of online sales. Previously, e-commerce penetration in emerging markets lagged behind that of major markets like the United States, but due to recent economic growth, it is expected that three billion people from emerging nations will have access to the Internet by 2022. Given that many of these markets are currently _____, with traditional retailers having long dominated commercial activities, e-commerce in these regions understandably has a lot of potential. With so many opportunities now opening up, it is anticipated that new e-commerce brands will appear, and traditional ones will develop online capabilities to stay relevant as the growth of consumer spending over the Internet intensifies.

① autonomous　　② competitive
③ innovative　　④ untapped
⑤ saturated

32

Of the behaviors that play a central role in _____ _____, solidarity — the process of mutual support within a group — is one of the most widely felt. Neighbors often demonstrate this behavior in small ways when they do favors to help out those who live next door. In work settings, virtually no projects or tasks stand to be accomplished unless colleagues embrace collaboration and reciprocal assistance; indeed, many manual labor jobs physically require joint efforts, such as when construction workers must collectively raise a wall. The realm of politics and social activism offers maybe one of the most explicit examples yet of the need for and implementation of solidarity. Mass social justice movements are perfect manifestations of this behavior, which is demonstrated in the way that people come together to protest oppressive governments or supply food and housing to their fellow citizens during times of economic hardship. All of these cases illustrate how solidarity is a fundamental pillar of life in a community. [3점]

① reinforcing divisions among society members
② motivating people to seek personal success
③ enhancing community awareness of issues
④ preventing large-scale public disasters
⑤ maintaining healthy social structures

33

With the transition to electric vehicles (EV) now underway, the demand for lithium-ion batteries — the power sources for EV — is skyrocketing, creating a new concern: What will we do with them once they reach the end of their life cycle? Unlike other types of batteries, which are shredded into a powder and then melted or dissolved during the recycling process, lithium-ion batteries are more complicated to get rid of. Disposing of them is harmful as they release heavy metals and other environmental contaminants. The current recycling process for them is expensive and results in low-value products, making it cheaper to mine more lithium than to try to reuse it. However, mining the metals needed to make these batteries requires vast amounts of water, the use of which has been linked to declining vegetation, drought, and higher temperatures. While lithium-ion batteries may help pave the way to a more sustainable future eventually, it is clear that _____ _____ through more efficient recycling processes. [3점]

① developing less expensive alternatives for EV can be achieved
② the environmental challenges they pose must be neutralized
③ the high demand for them among EV manufacturers will fall
④ increasing their lifespan may be possible in the near future
⑤ different designs and materials may need to be used

34

Unlike most other microorganisms found in freshwater, *Naegleria fowleri* is fatal to nearly everyone it infects, largely because the infection progresses rapidly and the initial symptoms — headache, fever, and vomiting — are similar to many other illnesses, making it easy to misdiagnose. *Naegleria fowleri* thrives in warm water, which means it was once only found in southern regions, but climate change and the ensuing increase in water temperature has caused the bug to make its way northward in recent years, intensifying concerns among those who enjoy recreational activities in lakes and rivers. The good news is that *Naegleria fowleri* cases are still extremely rare; the Centers for Disease Control and Prevention has only recorded 34 over the past decade. Nonetheless, experts say that _____. As the microorganism is only transmissible when water is inhaled through the nose, at which point it travels up the nasal cavity into the brain where it begins to feed on the tissue, remembering to wear a nose clip can provide effective protection.

* Naegleria fowleri: 파울러자유아메바

① new strains of *Naegleria fowleri* are being discovered
② freshwater activities should be avoided at all costs
③ these cases were never properly diagnosed
④ there is no known cure for the infection
⑤ people should not let their guard down

35 다음 글에서 전체 흐름과 관계 없는 문장은?

Modern society has become increasingly complex, with many measures in place to prioritize the welfare of citizens and encourage progress. ① However, as a result of such safeguards, of the expectation that we will be protected by authorities from any and all potential threats, it can be argued that we live in a "culture of fear." ② This means that our perception of danger has increased, even if the actual level of risk has not, providing an explanation for why many problems in society develop into full-blown crises that policy makers may be limited in their ability to get under control. ③ Part of the difficulty in managing such crises has to do with the fact that they are frequently subjective. ④ For leaders, getting members of the public to accept their definition of the situation can help reduce uncertainty and spread information. ⑤ What may seem entirely innocent to some members of society can be interpreted by others as wrong, leading to the situation getting out of hand.

[36~37] 주어진 글 다음에 이어질 글의 순서로 가장 적절한 것을 고르시오.

36

> Some parents become anxious when faced with having to deal with their child's emotional needs.

(A) This tendency to self-soothe carries over into adulthood. Because people with avoidant attachment have learned to rely on themselves, they may be uncomfortable with receiving emotional support from others or discussing their struggles, which can make it difficult for them to form close relationships.

(B) Knowing that being emotional will be poorly received, the child learns to hold their feelings back. Although they still experience sadness and other emotions, they teach themselves that these feelings do not matter and find ways to comfort themselves that do not involve going to their parents.

(C) Because of their nervousness, they may be unable or unwilling to respond to their child in a comforting way, which may cause them to ignore their child, become angry, or shame them for any emotional displays. This reaction teaches the child that they cannot rely on their parents for emotional support, and they develop an avoidant attachment.

① (A) – (C) – (B)　　② (B) – (A) – (C)
③ (B) – (C) – (A)　　④ (C) – (A) – (B)
⑤ (C) – (B) – (A)

37

The 1993 Pulitzer Prize-winning photo "The Vulture and the Little Girl" was taken by photojournalist Kevin Carter in Sudan. The famous picture shows a famine-stricken child collapsed on the ground as a vulture looks on in the background.

(A) This is a prime example of the high psychological toll of being a photojournalist. Not only is the occupation dangerous — with many photojournalists going headfirst into wars and natural disasters — but there is constant reproach from the public, who expect much more from the person behind the camera than objectivity.

(B) The photo elicited a lot of raw emotion when it was published in *The New York Times*. There was, of course, concern for the starving child, but there was also rage directed at Carter, who many considered heartless for not helping.

(C) Carter did shoo the vulture away after snapping the picture, and the child, who had been crawling to a UN feeding center, eventually did make it there, according to reports. Nonetheless, Carter was bombarded with questions like "Why didn't you help more?" The backlash was incessant.

① (A) – (C) – (B)
② (B) – (A) – (C)
③ (B) – (C) – (A)
④ (C) – (A) – (B)
⑤ (C) – (B) – (A)

[38~39] 글의 흐름으로 보아, 주어진 문장이 들어가기에 가장 적절한 곳을 고르시오.

38

When the law was put into practice, however, a number of challenges emerged.

Once ranked among the top in the world, the US educational system had, by the year 2000, begun to fall behind other nations. To improve its ranking and make students more competitive, educational reforms such as the No Child Left Behind Act (NCLB) were introduced in 2001. (①) The purpose of the legislation was to improve standards and hold schools accountable for underperforming students. (②) In this way, students of every race, background, and economic status would become adequately prepared for college and a career. (③) Among these were difficulties ensuring a consistent application of standards and compliance from different states. (④) Eventually, NCLB was replaced in 2015 with the Every Student Succeeds Act (ESSA). (⑤) Though still imperfect in its implementation, ESSA has provided schools with more flexibility in both the standards they use and how they measure performance.

39

> It is also an example of "technological solutionism" — the widespread notion that all of society's problems can be solved with the invention of a new form of technology.

Medical software is a booming business, with health tech firms rushing to provide hospitals and doctors with AI programs that can carry out a range of diagnostic tasks. (①) Partly, this promotion of medical technology is an attempt to relieve some of the pressure on health care workers and services. (②) But there are various problems with this approach, including that these programs are not infallible and often reflect the biases of those who develop them, putting certain categories of patients at risk. (③) This issue is also exacerbated by the fact that the internal processes of these programs are hidden from everyone but programmers. (④) Many insurance firms that utilize algorithmic assessment programs admit that there is no way to find out how a program reached a conclusion, but they are nonetheless obligated to follow it. (⑤) The lack of accountability — and the biases it could propagate — must be addressed before these programs are more widely utilized. [3점]

40 다음 글의 내용을 한 문장으로 요약하고자 한다. 빈칸 (A), (B)에 들어갈 말로 가장 적절한 것은?

In winter, it is not an uncommon sight to see hundreds or thousands of starlings swooping and swirling as they fly in a coordinated pattern called a murmuration. How the birds are able to form such a cohesive whole as a group composed of so many individual members has long been a subject of interest for scientists, but a study by George F. Young and his team may finally provide an explanation. By carefully examining video footage, they found that individual starlings pay attention to a fixed number of their flying neighbors — seven to be exact — so that they can predict their movements and carry them out themselves, reacting with both incredible speed and precision. According to Young, focusing on these other birds and nothing else allows starlings to maintain the delicate balance between not knowing where or how the group will fly and moving with the group without crashing into others or flying out of the flock. Within this rule of seven, the subgroups combine to form the larger system, the murmuration.

* starling: 찌르레기　** murmuration: 찌르레기 떼

The ___(A)___ of starlings in a murmuration is the result of individual members of the group ___(B)___ the movements of those closest to them.

	(A)	(B)
①	disadvantage	copying
②	harmony	disregarding
③	elegance	comparing
④	certainty	controlling
⑤	unity	anticipating

[41~42] 다음 글을 읽고, 물음에 답하시오.

The English word dialogue is derived from the Greek term *dialogos* with *dia* translating to "through" (or "inter") and *logos* to "word." Today, people define this word as (a) <u>simply</u> meaning a conversation between different parties. However, others have suggested that the term is more nuanced, implying a search for understanding and insight. American physicist and philosopher David Bohm is one such individual; he set out to study the word's philosophical aspects. Eventually, through these efforts, he would propose what is now known as Bohm Dialogue, which is a type of group interaction that aims to reach an (b) <u>understanding</u> between individuals through listening and observation.

Bohm's dialogue can be viewed as a tool; a method for having constructive discussions that aren't (c) <u>disrupted</u> by prior assumptions and judgements. A person must approach this type of dialogue with an open mindset and a non-defensive attitude. They must be able to mindfully think about what is said during a conversation, and recognize when they experience thinking that they have been conditioned to by growing up a certain way and being in particular situations. By recognizing it, they can question it, and therefore be authentically exposed to new ideas and ways of thinking. This way, creativity can (d) <u>flourish</u> within a group as information, views, and feelings are exchanged more freely. Through this type of dialogue, more understanding and insight is gained, (e) <u>disproving</u> that within the right context, there is a deeper meaning for the word.

41 윗글의 제목으로 가장 적절한 것은?

① Methods for Initiating a Dialogue
② Learn to Listen Rather than Speak!
③ The Potential of Meaningful Dialogue
④ How Conversation Can Lead to Judgement
⑤ Interaction: The Basis for Conditioned Thinking

42 밑줄 친 (a)~(e) 중에서 문맥상 낱말의 쓰임이 적절하지 않은 것은? [3점]

① (a)   ② (b)   ③ (c)   ④ (d)   ⑤ (e)

[43~45] 다음 글을 읽고, 물음에 답하시오.

(A)

I was driving home from work and was listening to music on the radio. Bored of the same tiresome pop hits, I decided to browse through the other stations. I somehow ended up on a classical station, and it was then that I heard a heavenly sound from a single piano. The stunning melody reminded me of watching my grandmother play when I was a child. She was exceptionally talented at music, and I knew (a) <u>she</u> would have loved this song.

(B)

I arrived home, and after doing some research, I figured out that the song was "Un Sospiro" by Franz Liszt. I decided to learn how to play it despite not having touched a piano since childhood. My grandmother had taught me a little, but (b) <u>she</u> had never showed me how to play anything so complicated. I was determined to learn it, though.

(C)

On the day of my first lesson, I looked at the dizzying array of notes and once again lost my breath. I thought of my grandmother and how patient she was with me when we learned pieces together during my youth. (c) <u>She</u> always said that as long as I put in the effort, I could achieve whatever I wanted. My piano teacher instructed me to begin, and I nodded at her excitedly. People say that every journey begins with a single step; well, here goes step one.

(D)

The first thing I needed to do was to give my grandmother's old piano a tune-up. She hadn't played it in years, but it was a beautiful instrument. I was sure she would have a smile on (d) <u>her</u> face at the thought of me trying to play. I also ordered the sheet music for the song. Looking over the piece, I knew I wouldn't be able to learn it alone, so I decided to hire a piano teacher to help me. (e) <u>She</u> let me know that while the task would be difficult, we would get through it together. We made plans to have our first meeting soon.

43 주어진 글 (A)에 이어질 내용을 순서에 맞게 배열한 것으로 가장 적절한 것은?

① (B) – (D) – (C)　　　② (C) – (B) – (D)
③ (C) – (D) – (B)　　　④ (D) – (B) – (C)
⑤ (D) – (C) – (B)

44 밑줄 친 (a)~(e) 중에서 가리키는 대상이 나머지 넷과 다른 것은?

① (a)　　② (b)　　③ (c)　　④ (d)　　⑤ (e)

45 윗글의 'I'에 관한 내용으로 적절하지 <u>않은</u> 것은?

① 퇴근길에 라디오에서 음악을 들었다.
② 피아노로 "Un Sospiro"를 연주하기로 결심했다.
③ 어릴 때 할머니께 피아노를 배우다가 혼난 적이 있다.
④ 할머니의 오래된 피아노를 조율해야 했다.
⑤ 피아노를 가르쳐 줄 선생님을 구했다.

정답·해설·해석 p. 93

문제풀이 후 확인사항
1. 45분 내에 문제를 풀었다.
2. 체크해둔 문제와 틀린 문제는 해설을 꼼꼼히 확인했다.

수고하셨습니다! HackersBook.com에서 제공하는 어휘리스트로 어휘를 암기하세요.

11회 실전모의고사

목표 시간: 45분   시작: ___ 시 ___ 분 ~ 종료: ___ 시 ___ 분   점수: ___ 점 / 63점

* [3점] 표시가 있는 문제 제외하고는 모두 2점으로 계산합니다.

18 다음 글의 목적으로 가장 적절한 것은?

The Tallinn Museum of Art announced on Friday that its head curator, Erin Lowe, will be retiring on May 15. Given that Ms. Lowe has worked at the institution for over 20 years and has organized many of its most successful exhibits, she will be greatly missed. The museum is seeking a qualified replacement for her. Duties include managing and directing the museum's various exhibitions, as well as overseeing collections and defining the museum's objectives. Applicants must have previous experience in a similar field. Those interested in the position should send their résumé and a letter of recommendation to humanresources@tallinnmuseum.org.

① 전시 물품 교체 소식을 알리려고
② 큐레이터 교육 일정을 안내하려고
③ 새로운 전시 프로그램을 소개하려고
④ 미술관 큐레이터 채용을 공지하려고
⑤ 미술관 시설의 재정비를 건의하려고

19 다음 글에 나타난 Mia의 심경 변화로 가장 적절한 것은?

After five hours of hiking, Mia was incredibly weary and uncertain about whether she would reach the top of the mountain. She hadn't expected the trail to be this steep. She breathed heavily and willed her heavy legs to keep moving, one foot in front of the other. She was just about to give up and head back down when she rounded a corner and saw something that gave her hope: a sign stating that the summit was just 150 meters ahead. She was so happy to see it that tears almost came to her eyes. She exhaled loudly as she felt a weight drop off her shoulders. Mia smiled and kept climbing until she was standing on the mountaintop, finally able to enjoy the view of the surrounding landscape.

① calm → sorrowful
② pleased → anxious
③ disappointed → angry
④ exhausted → relieved
⑤ excited → discouraged

20 다음 글에서 필자가 주장하는 바로 가장 적절한 것은?

A problem that is commonly encountered during group projects is that everyone involved goes off in a different direction trying to realize diverse and often competing objectives. This can lead to significant levels of inefficiency, which results in time and resources being wasted. If you are a team leader, overcoming the tendency of your subordinates to pursue individual goals will likely be one of the greatest challenges you will face. At the end of the day, the success or failure of your project will rest on whether or not the members of your team have a shared definition of success. Each person on your team needs to clearly understand the ultimate aim and what constitutes its achievement. This necessitates straightforward communication about what you are trying to accomplish and regular follow-ups to make sure all of your staff members are on board.

① 각 구성원 특성에 맞는 피드백을 제공해야 한다.
② 모든 구성원이 공통된 성공의 정의를 가져야 한다.
③ 자유로이 의견을 주고받는 환경이 조성되어야 한다.
④ 구성원들의 업무 진행 상황을 정기적으로 확인해야 한다.
⑤ 자신만의 목표를 설정하도록 구성원을 적극 격려해야 한다.

21 밑줄 친 the very grammar of the film이 다음 글에서 의미하는 바로 가장 적절한 것은? [3점]

In the work of Soviet filmmaker and theorist Sergei Eisenstein, the editing does much more than move the narrative forward — it is the very grammar of the film. Eisenstein was a pioneer of the montage, a technique that involves piecing together a series of images or footage to create a continuous sequence. Most frequently, montages are used in films to depict the passage of time or the progress of the protagonist. However, through the use of another type of montage, known as "the intellectual montage," Eisenstein sought to elicit ideas and emotions; in other words, to produce art. At the end of the 1925 movie *Strike*, for instance, the film switched back and forth between shots of a bull being slaughtered and the violent suppression of a factory workers' strike in pre-revolutionary Russia. The juxtaposition of these disparate images was intended to express the overarching concept that workers were dispensable, much like cattle.

* juxtaposition: 병치(竝置)

① validating a theory that explains the social role of filmmaking
② introducing a protagonist by using disconnected images
③ creating a narrative that appeals to many viewers
④ presenting a montage to convey the passage of time
⑤ employing a technique to evoke a response from viewers

22 다음 글의 요지로 가장 적절한 것은?

The English language is constantly evolving, with thousands of words being created each year. While many of the new additions stem from other languages or are combinations of existing words, some are actually made from scratch. What's interesting is that the speed at which this happens has increased significantly in recent years due to the rise of mass media and the Internet. Writers such as William Shakespeare and John Milton are credited with producing hundreds of words that are still in use today, such as *lonely* and *fragrance*. In those cases, it took many decades, or even centuries, for the new words to be widely used. However, the word *stan* — to be an extremely enthusiastic fan — first appeared in a rap song in 2000 and was given an entry in the Oxford English Dictionary in 2017. This trend is likely to become even more pronounced in the future, meaning that the pace of change will continue to accelerate.

① 현대 영어는 문학에 쓰인 어휘들 위주로 발달하였다.
② 미디어의 발달로 신조어의 전파 속도가 빨라지고 있다.
③ 인터넷에서 만들어진 신조어가 언어 습관을 바꾸고 있다.
④ 근래에 생겨난 영어 어휘들은 대부분 기존 단어들의 결합이다.
⑤ 노래 가사에 쓰인 일부 어휘들은 사전에 등재되지 못하고 있다.

23 다음 글의 주제로 가장 적절한 것은?

When you experience failure, you might tend to respond in one of two ways: deflect the blame for your misfortune or be overly harsh on yourself. Both responses may be natural, but they're hardly helpful for learning from mistakes or pursuing personal growth for future endeavors. While using misfortune as a shield blocks you from improving yourself, being excessively self-critical causes you to suffer from defeatism. To actually enhance performance following a setback, research indicates that you should practice self-compassion instead. This leads to a more realistic evaluation of your behavior and actions through reflection, and therefore helps you in targeting problem areas for the future. By being kind to yourself while still being aware of both your strengths and limitations, you are more likely to develop your skills and improve your well-being. With this mindset, you can work towards achieving your objectives without becoming caught up in failure.

* deflect: 모면하다

① methods for effectively utilizing criticism to motivate peers
② outcomes of adopting a mindset of failure avoidance
③ advantages of self-compassion for achieving growth
④ significance of self-improvement in becoming successful
⑤ drawbacks of practicing kindness while working towards goals

24 다음 글의 제목으로 가장 적절한 것은?

Scientists are people, so they are as prone to different types of bias as anyone else. This inclination can influence their experiments. From data collection to the publication of findings, confirmation bias — the tendency of people to favor information that confirms their existing beliefs or hypotheses — can play a role in any phase of the scientific process. Of course, this is a flaw that should be avoided at all costs during experimentation, even if misleading oneself is a natural urge. But how does one break a habit that is second nature? One method is to conduct research in such a manner that other individuals are able to easily monitor the process. Involving more people in research, in addition to studying and reflecting on opposing conjectures, will ensure less bias. Careful consideration should also be given when designing the experiment and setting the benchmarks for what results actually reinforce or disprove a hypothesis.

① Confirmation Bias: A Subject Worthy of Study
② Keep in Mind the Importance of Benchmarks!
③ Time to Address Flaws in the Scientific Method
④ Identifying Reasoning Errors in an Experiment
⑤ Objectivity: A Constant Challenge for Scientists

25 다음 도표의 내용과 일치하지 <u>않는</u> 것은?

Job Qualification Mismatch
in American Countries

(percentage of the total national employment)

The above graph shows job qualification mismatch, underqualification or overqualification, by percentage in selected countries in North and South America. ① Among the seven countries, the United States and Canada are the only two countries in which the percentages of overqualification do not exceed 20%. ② While the percentages of underqualification in Peru and Brazil are below 10%, those in Canada and Argentina are over 20%. ③ The only country where the combined percentage of underqualification and overqualification is over half of the total national employment is Mexico. ④ In the case of Chile, the percentage of underqualification is less than half of that of overqualification. ⑤ As for the gap between the percentage of underqualification and that of overqualification, the United States showed the smallest gap.

26 Henry Hazlitt에 관한 다음 글의 내용과 일치하지 않는 것은?

Born in 1894, Henry Hazlitt was one of the most important economic journalists in American history. Although he grew up in relative poverty, Hazlitt was able to attend New York's City College. Unfortunately, he had to drop out in order to take care of his mother. Still, the short time he was at university gave him a great desire to learn, and he began reading all kinds of college textbooks on his own. His first job was at a then-newly established newspaper called *The Wall Street Journal*, where his interest in economics began. He went on to write economic editorials for numerous publications, which was quite an achievement for someone who had no formal education. He wrote a total of 15 books during his career, with his first one being published when he was just 21. His literary works earned him renown, and he continued to write about and contribute to economic thinking up until his death in 1993 at the age of 98.

① 미국 역사상 가장 중요한 경제 기자 중 한 명이었다.
② 어머니를 돌보기 위해 대학을 중퇴했다.
③ 대학에 다니는 동안 경제에 관심을 갖게 되었다.
④ 여러 간행물에 경제 사설을 실었다.
⑤ 경력 동안 총 15권의 책을 출간했다.

27 Spanish Exchange Program에 관한 다음 안내문의 내용과 일치하지 않는 것은?

Spanish Exchange Program

Have you always dreamed about going to Spain? Now you can with the Spanish Exchange Program (SEP). Learn the language and culture! Don't miss this once-in-a-lifetime opportunity.

Who: High school students (Grades 10, 11, or 12)
When: June 19 – June 28 (10 days)
Requirements:
• At least a 3.0 GPA
• Have taken at least one Spanish class

While in Spain, students will take part in a variety of activities including:
• Museum trips
• Attending a cultural festival
• Visiting a Spanish food market
• Language exchange with Spanish students
* Students will also have 2 hours of free time every day to explore the city.

Applications must be turned in by April 20th. For more information, please visit www.sep.edu.

---

① 고등학생을 대상으로 한다.
② 6월 19일부터 열흘간 진행된다.
③ 스페인어 수업을 2개 이상 들어야 참가할 수 있다.
④ 문화 축제에 참가하는 활동이 있을 것이다.
⑤ 학생들에게 매일 자유 시간이 주어질 것이다.

28 Halloween Street Parade에 관한 다음 안내문의 내용과 일치하는 것은?

Halloween Street Parade

Lawson City is holding its annual Halloween street parade. There will be many different scary parade balloons sponsored by 50 companies.

Date: Sunday, October 31
Time: 4:00 p.m. to 6:00 p.m.
Place: Main Street (The parade will begin at City Hall and end at Mason Park.)

Events:
• Pumpkin carving　　• Live music
• Costume contest　　• Charity auction

Activities for kids (all free):
• Face painting　　• Candy making
• Obstacle course　　• Haunted house

* Refreshments will be for sale.

For more information, go to www.lawsonparade.com.

① 올해 처음 열리는 행사다.
② 시민들이 후원한 풍선들이 있을 것이다.
③ 퍼레이드는 City Hall에서 끝난다.
④ 사탕 만들기 활동은 유료다.
⑤ 간단한 음식물이 판매될 것이다.

29 다음 글의 밑줄 친 부분 중, 어법상 틀린 것은? [3점]

The caterpillar of the peppered moth (*Biston betularia*) can camouflage itself so ① effectively that it looks indistinguishable from a twig. Although scientists in the past did not understand how exactly the caterpillar was able to do this, it was assumed that the process required the insect to match its appearance with what it saw. However, it is now known that this caterpillar utilizes a ② far more complex form of mimicry, which involves sensors in its skin. Other creatures that use camouflage, such as chameleons and some species of fish, ③ have similar systems. ④ What the caterpillar of the peppered moth does not rely on vision was determined by an experiment in which the eyes of caterpillars were covered with black paint to prevent their use. ⑤ Despite this impediment, the caterpillars were able to match their appearance with the differently shaped twigs they were set on, indicating that this insect's system of mimicry is not based on visual perception.

* mimicry: 의태(擬態)

30 다음 글의 밑줄 친 부분 중, 문맥상 낱말의 쓰임이 적절하지 않은 것은? [3점]

During the Scientific Revolution, people began to regard nature as a machine of sorts — something that could be ① broken down and understood through the application of math and physics. The idea that everything could be figured out was very attractive to scientists and philosophers seeking to ② unlock the mysteries of life and the universe, and French physicist Pierre-Simon Laplace was no exception. In 1814, he conducted a thought experiment that is often referred to as "Laplace's demon." In it, he imagined an entity that knew the ③ precise location and momentum of every atom in existence and, by extension, everything about its past and future. For this hypothetical all-knowing being, nothing was ④ definite. Essentially, Laplace was implying that, by gathering enough information about anything in the world and analyzing it, one can understand its past and predict its future. This would also mean that the future of everything in the universe is ⑤ predetermined, that there is no free will, and that we have no choice in our actions.

* thought experiment: 사고 실험

[31~34] 다음 빈칸에 들어갈 말로 가장 적절한 것을 고르시오.

31

Breaching among humpback whales occurs when a whale picks up speed, leaps almost entirely out of the water, and then whirls around in the air, creating a great splash upon landing on its back or side. While nature documentaries frequently feature footage of this awe-inspiring act, humpback whale breaches are actually quite rare given that performing one takes a large amount of energy for an animal that typically weighs 30 tons. The reasons these giant marine mammals breach are not fully understood, but there are several different theories, most of which revolve around the idea that humpback whales breach in order to _____. Because sound travels faster and further underwater than it does over land or through air, it is thought that the tremendous impact the whale makes upon landing reverberates a great distance through the ocean, thereby notifying other whales of predators, nearby food, or the desire to mate.

* breach: (고래가) 물 위로 뛰어오르다

① deceive ② communicate
③ accelerate ④ navigate
⑤ escape

32

Barriers to effective communication go beyond language. In fact, culture is responsible for miscommunication more often than you might think. When people from different nations meet, a multitude of factors can affect the success of their interaction, including but not limited to body language, gestures, values, and psychology. While these may come across as insignificant, they can account for breakdowns in communication due to individuals becoming confused or insulted by one another. For instance, Americans tend to make strong eye contact during conversation while the Japanese actively avoid it since it makes them feel uncomfortable. If individuals from these two countries are attempting to communicate, this might be a detail to keep in mind so as to _____. Being aware of another culture and its customs is vital for evading any type of barrier to communication.

① reach an agreement
② irritate the other person
③ end the discussion quickly
④ prevent causing any offense
⑤ make the conversation informative

33

It is well established that creativity can take many forms and that the world benefits immensely from the inventions, discoveries, and art that result from it. But is creativity nothing more than the product of a unique mind? For many years, creativity was primarily studied by those interested in psychology and education, with the idea that learning more about the subject could lead to a better understanding of specific people because innovation emerges out of the minds of individuals. At least, that was the assumption. Since then, sociologists and anthropologists have argued that creativity is, in fact, a sociocultural phenomenon, citing examples such as the concept of multiple discovery: an occurrence in which breakthroughs and inventions are made independently by multiple people at the same time. Such incidents, they say, occur because during every period of history, there is a defining spirit or a "zeitgeist" that _____, influencing the amount of creativity that appears and the form it takes. [3점]

① leads some to rethink their personal values
② prompts individuals to advocate for change
③ depends on the ideas of distinctive minds
④ makes people more critical of society
⑤ shapes the collective consciousness

34

How did the concept of otherness take root in society? People have always been wary of civilizations and populations that function differently from their own. With reference to origin, however, perhaps it was the ancient Greeks who popularized this notion, with historical figures such as Hippocrates asserting that some societies were different, and inferior, by nature. The Greeks referred to foreigners from varying societies as "barbarians," which helped them to distinguish themselves and solidify a shared Greek identity. The process of othering, however, is not only useful for establishing identity. At the core of otherness is the suggestion that the Other is second-class to the Self. The dominating group is able to formulate these identities and therefore rationalize measures that discriminate against the Other. For example, the ancient Romans adopted the barbarian perspective from the Greeks, viewing the tribes and people they conquered during the spread of their empire as inferior and therefore justifiably ruled. They distinguished themselves so that _____ and retain power over them. [3점]

① they could learn more about other cultures
② they could promote diversity within society
③ they could devalue those different from them
④ they could encourage tolerance among people
⑤ they could spread their values to other civilizations

35 다음 글에서 전체 흐름과 관계 없는 문장은?

Artificial sweeteners may seem like miraculous substitutes for actual sugar because they do not include calories. Unfortunately, there is strong evidence that both the brain and body have negative reactions to these synthetic substances, and many medical professionals recommend that they should be avoided. ① The stomach includes many beneficial bacteria that digest food, and a study has shown that the efficiency of these microorganisms declines after they interact with artificial sweeteners. ② A person who consumes these substances in large amounts may not be able to get sufficient nutrients from the other foods he or she eats. ③ Growth, energy, and cell repair are all processes that require a balanced intake of nutrients. ④ Artificial sweeteners also bring about hollow satisfaction, which only leads to overeating. ⑤ The combination of high sweetness and no calories triggers a starvation response in the brain, making the person feel very hungry.

[36~37] 주어진 글 다음에 이어질 글의 순서로 가장 적절한 것을 고르시오.

36

In the late 19th century, as old patterns and traditions began to break down and new ideas and forms of expression began to take hold, the Western world entered a new period known as modernism.

(A) With this new concept of art gaining popularity, abstract art emerged. It suggested form itself could inspire feeling — color, line, tone, and texture were enough to evoke emotion. Everything else, including the context of the work or the intention of the artist, was of secondary importance.

(B) One aspect of abstract art was formalism, which is best epitomized by the slogan "art for art's sake." This was the notion that art could be separated from its subject matter and that how paint was actually arranged on a canvas was where its true value was.

(C) Prior to this time, the value of art resided in how well it held a mirror up to the world; the ability to reproduce nature and human civilization was a key indicator of its quality. However, a decline in the appreciation of realism led to art becoming more of a means for individual expression. [3점]

* epitomize: 전형적으로 보여주다

① (A) – (C) – (B)　　② (B) – (A) – (C)
③ (B) – (C) – (A)　　④ (C) – (A) – (B)
⑤ (C) – (B) – (A)

37

Individuals sometimes use the terms socialism and communism interchangeably, considering them identical philosophies. After all, both of these political theories were made with the purpose of creating a more equal society where income differences are not so large.

(A) These two systems are also established in dissimilar ways. Communism is enacted through revolution and an overthrow of the middle and upper classes while socialism is instilled democratically through policy amendments.

(B) In contrast, socialism allows for private property and merely calls for the government to monitor and handle the production of goods. The purpose of this is to guarantee fairer prices and output so the entire population — not just the upper classes — can benefit.

(C) Communism and socialism actually diverge on a few key principles, though. Under communism, all economic resources are publicly owned and people are allocated what they need by a centralized government. Individuals can't hold personal property or assets.

* instill: 주입하다

① (A) – (C) – (B)
② (B) – (A) – (C)
③ (B) – (C) – (A)
④ (C) – (A) – (B)
⑤ (C) – (B) – (A)

[38~39] 글의 흐름으로 보아, 주어진 문장이 들어가기에 가장 적절한 곳을 고르시오.

38

Rather, the astronauts' foremost challenge would be simply surviving the trip to Mars.

By 2030, as part of its plan for the continued exploration of space, NASA hopes to conduct a manned mission to Mars. Before any crewed mission can land on the Red Planet, preparations, including the construction of an underground habitat by robots, need to be made. (①) The prospect of setting up a livable base on Mars, however, is not the most critical hurdle in the journey. (②) That's because space travel is extremely dangerous for humans due to radiation that exists outside the protective cocoon of our atmosphere. (③) Here on Earth, we are shielded by a strong magnetic field produced by the flow of liquid iron in the Earth's core, but the further we move away from our planet, the weaker the magnetic field gets. (④) Given that Earth's magnetic field extends out for approximately 40,000 miles and Mars is 140 million miles away, exposure to radiation is inevitable. (⑤) Consequently, this presents a challenge as radiation has serious effects on the central nervous system and can dramatically increase the chance of cancer developing.

39

Compounding the problem is the improved conditioning of today's players who are scouted from a young age and subjected to training that has become increasingly specialized over the years.

Although the leisurely pace of baseball, with its long intervals of wasted balls and strikes accompanied by trivial achievements, is part of its nostalgic 19th-century charm, some complain that the game is dull, lacking the invigorating action of football and basketball. (①) Recently, however, charges of boredom are emerging not from the game's critics but from its most passionate fans. (②) Team owners have become more focused on statistical pathways to victory that often involve taking as few risks as possible, reducing instances of the stolen base, once one of baseball's most electrifying events. (③) Muscular pitchers throw a steady diet of 100-mile-per-hour fastballs, while hitters consequently have little chance of hitting the ball. (④) The result is an endless parade of strikeouts and walks punctuated by occasional homeruns. (⑤) This absurd state of affairs has led Major League Baseball to change the rules, striving to enliven the proceedings while retaining the fundamental character of the game. [3점]

* stolen base: 도루   ** walk: 포볼에 의한 출루

40 다음 글의 내용을 한 문장으로 요약하고자 한다. 빈칸 (A), (B)에 들어갈 말로 가장 적절한 것은?

In one piece of research, participants were asked to read lists of descriptive words about an individual they had never met. One list included the following: *intelligent*, *industrious*, *impulsive*, *critical*, *stubborn*, and *envious*. The respondents were given these adjectives in exactly the same order. No instruction was given to them other than to read the words on the list. At a later time, when asked to describe the individual, all of them chose the first two words on the list — *intelligent* and *industrious*. Then, another group was given the same list but with the words listed in reverse order, so that *envious* and *stubborn* appeared at the top of the list. Surprisingly, when asked to describe the same individual, this group described the person as *envious* and *stubborn*. Taken together, each group described the same individual differently based on impressions they formed from the first words that they read on the lists.

⬇

The results of a study imply that people's judgment of others may be affected by _____(A)_____ they form based on the information they are provided with _____(B)_____.

	(A)		(B)
①	conflicts	······	instantly
②	perceptions	······	simultaneously
③	perceptions	······	initially
④	concepts	······	formally
⑤	conflicts	······	naturally

[41~42] 다음 글을 읽고, 물음에 답하시오.

Since the late 1990s, the role of institutions in economic development has been a very popular topic in the field of economics, with the consensus being that the quality of institutions is in (a) <u>direct</u> correlation with a country's level of prosperity. In this context, institutions are all the constraints that govern human interaction. They consist of both formal constraints, like regulations and laws, and informal constraints, like societal conventions and behavioral norms. The prevailing view in economics is that high-quality institutions — ones that promote concepts like a free economy, property rights, and a general level of trust — lead to (b) <u>prosperity</u> because they create the right incentives. For instance, in capitalist economies, people are incentivized by profit. Because the rules and regulations in capitalist economies enable entrepreneurs to make profits and ensure that they can keep what they gain from selling goods and services, people are (c) <u>motivated</u> to be innovative and prosperous. As more entrepreneurs succeed, the economy thrives, and the fundamental business values that allowed for their success in the first place, like cooperation and honesty, become societal (d) <u>standards</u>. By contrast, citizens of nations with inferior institutions — like totalitarian states where the economy is centrally planned — do not have the freedom to start their own businesses or to keep future profits. Those people could fail to see a viable reason to (e) <u>preserve</u> the status quo in order to make a profit.

41 윗글의 제목으로 가장 적절한 것은?

① The Next Step: What Happens When Incentives Fail?
② Institutions: The Driving Force Behind Economic Growth
③ Bridging the Gap Between Developed and Developing Nations
④ Rethinking Prevailing Theories to Assist Economic Development
⑤ Institutions and Economic Development: A Strained Relationship

42 밑줄 친 (a)~(e) 중에서 문맥상 낱말의 쓰임이 적절하지 않은 것은?

① (a)　　② (b)　　③ (c)　　④ (d)　　⑤ (e)

[43~45] 다음 글을 읽고, 물음에 답하시오.

(A)

The city was buzzing with activity when Raju and Vinod stepped out of the office building and onto the sidewalk. At this hour, they would normally go straight home. Today, however, they had lost their jobs and feared telling (a) their families. "Let's take a walk by the river," Vinod said.

(B)

It was then that Raju recalled an old lesson that a professor had tried to teach him and Vinod. The professor had presented (b) them with a container filled with rocks, which they agreed was full. Then, he added pebbles that fell between the rocks, filling the container further. Lastly, he added sand, which took up whatever room remained. "The rocks," he said, "represent things of value, like family. Without anything else, (c) they help us have a full life."

(C)

The professor then pointed to the pebbles and said that they represented things of lesser value, such as jobs or money. They are important, but people can also live without them. At last, he explained what the sand stood for. "This represents things with the least value of all, such as the material possessions and trivial concerns we waste our time worrying about. Devoting your time to unimportant matters leaves no room for what is important." Raju finally understood the lesson and shared with Vinod, after which (d) they each went back home to their families.

(D)

As they walked along the riverbank, Raju and Vinod saw a group of children running around. "I think they're playing a game," Raju said. "Let's watch." (e) They saw that each child had a box and that they were trying to fill them with materials they found on the shore. They wanted to see who could fill their box the fastest. The child who won had filled his with rocks. The second one had tried to use pebbles and other small bits of trash, and the last one had used dirt that kept slipping through his fingers.

43 주어진 글 (A)에 이어질 내용을 순서에 맞게 배열한 것으로 가장 적절한 것은?

① (B) – (D) – (C)　　② (C) – (B) – (D)
③ (C) – (D) – (B)　　④ (D) – (B) – (C)
⑤ (D) – (C) – (B)

44 밑줄 친 (a)~(e) 중에서 가리키는 대상이 나머지 넷과 다른 것은?

① (a)　② (b)　③ (c)　④ (d)　⑤ (e)

45 윗글에 관한 내용으로 적절하지 <u>않은</u> 것은?

① Raju와 Vinod는 일자리를 잃었다.
② 교수는 돌멩이가 가치 있는 것들을 상징한다고 말했다.
③ 교수는 직업이나 돈이 없어도 사람은 살아갈 수 있다고 말했다.
④ Raju와 Vinod는 강둑을 따라 걸었다.
⑤ 아이들은 모두 돌멩이로 상자를 채웠다.

정답·해설·해석 p. 103

문제풀이 후 확인사항
1. 45분 내에 문제를 풀었다.
2. 체크해둔 문제와 틀린 문제는 해설을 꼼꼼히 확인했다.

수고하셨습니다! HackersBook.com에서 제공하는 어휘리스트로 어휘를 암기하세요.

12회 실전모의고사

목표 시간: 45분　시작: ___ 시 ___ 분 ~ 종료: ___ 시 ___ 분　점수: ____ 점 / 63점

* [3점] 표시가 있는 문제 제외하고는 모두 2점으로 계산합니다.

18 다음 글의 목적으로 가장 적절한 것은?

To Whom It May Concern:

My husband and I are new residents to the Strickland community. While we love the neighborhood and its available facilities, we have noticed that Seymour Street does not have a place to dispose of trash. This leads to items like plastic bags and old food containers littering the gardens all along the street. I feel like this sends the wrong message to people who visit our community and does not reflect our standards. Other streets have means of trash disposal, and I think this should be consistent throughout the neighborhood. We've discussed this with other residents and they agree that installing a trash can on Seymour Street is a good idea. We hope that you will take this request into consideration and hope to hear from you soon.

Sincerely,
Mr. and Mrs. Davies

① 도로 표지판 보수 작업의 필요성을 주장하려고
② 지역 환경 보호 정책 강화를 요구하려고
③ 거리에 쓰레기통 설치를 요청하려고
④ 쓰레기 분리배출 방법에 대해 문의하려고
⑤ 지역 주민을 위한 문화 센터 건립을 제안하려고

19 다음 글에 나타난 Lisa의 심경 변화로 가장 적절한 것은?

Lisa was sitting at home eating dinner when her roommate came in looking excited. "I got us tickets to a play tonight!" she exclaimed happily. She explained that the play was called *Silent Night* and that it was about a war hero. Lisa frowned because it didn't sound like something she would enjoy, so she was reluctant to go. But after lots of begging, her roommate convinced her to attend. As they sat down in their seats later that night, Lisa sighed and waited for the play to start. She didn't try to pay attention when it began, but she was soon totally immersed in what was happening on the stage. The actors were incredibly talented and the story was dramatic. At the end of the performance, Lisa found herself standing up and clapping. The experience had been unforgettable.

① doubtful → amazed
② pleased → annoyed
③ comfortable → uneasy
④ thrilled → irritated
⑤ stressed → relaxed

20 다음 글에서 필자가 주장하는 바로 가장 적절한 것은?

We are often quick to assess the ethics of any given situation, utilizing our own personal moral compass to appraise a complex scenario with a degree of confidence and finality. For a majority of people, these judgments seem unquestionable and obvious; anyone who believes differently is mistaken. While this approach is often seen as a strength, believing that only our standards are valid can create dilemmas. The central issue with putting our personal standards on a pedestal is that any personal moral assessment is by nature biased. That is to say, our evaluations are based on our preconceived notions about the world and fail to take into consideration other perspectives that may be just as valid. This is why we must avoid making conclusive judgments but instead view a situation from the perspective of others in order not to make the serious mistake of being unfair or unjust.

* pedestal: 근거

① 문제 해결을 위해서는 정확하고 일관성 있는 판단 기준을 세워야 한다.
② 사회적 지위가 높은 사람일수록 더욱 투철한 윤리 의식을 가져야 한다.
③ 중요한 결정을 내릴 때는 어느 정도의 확신과 단호함이 있어야 한다.
④ 문제의 본질을 제대로 파악하기 위해서는 주관적인 의견을 배제해야 한다.
⑤ 타인의 관점을 고려하지 않고 자신의 기준만으로 상황을 판단해서는 안 된다.

21 밑줄 친 planting seeds that never grow가 다음 글에서 의미하는 바로 가장 적절한 것은? [3점]

Oftentimes, individuals who think that they are practicing visualization are in fact planting seeds that never grow. Imagining what you want to accomplish in the future is an important element of success. As author Napoleon Hill said, this technique "converts the brain into the equivalent of an electromagnet which attracts the counterpart of one's dominating thoughts, aims and purposes." Unless you are careful, though, you run the risk of engaging in an activity known as daydreaming, which is merely imagining a different reality. Wistfully fanaticizing about what you would like to achieve is not only unproductive, but it also makes you less prone to carry out your goals. Instead, you need to ensure that you visualize both the scenario that you want to occur and the specific things you must do for it to happen. Then, make certain that you actually perform these tasks so that your dream becomes a reality.

① having negative thoughts that dominate their thinking
② stopping themselves from using their imagination
③ reducing their chances of setting realistic goals
④ failing to take action to attain their objectives
⑤ limiting themselves to uninspiring fantasies

22 다음 글의 요지로 가장 적절한 것은?

No matter how much someone loves their children, any parent can attest to the fact that there are times when kids can become completely infuriating. Perhaps it's a 3-year-old having his fifth temper tantrum of the day, or it might be a teenager refusing to do their chores. Whatever the reason may be, parents can become so exasperated that they even start to wonder whether they might actually dislike their own children, leading to tremendous feelings of guilt. They believe these feelings contradict their natural duty to unconditionally love their kids. Nevertheless, this is a perfectly natural reaction. Instead of feeling ashamed, psychiatrists recommend that parents should realize that such emotions are just a response to certain behaviors rather than the children themselves. That is, the feelings mean "I don't like what my child is doing" rather than "I don't like my child." Keeping this in mind will help parents calm down and accept that such emotions will be as temporary as the behavior.

* temper tantrum: 짜증

① 부모는 때때로 아이와 떨어져서 혼자만의 시간을 가질 필요가 있다.
② 아이의 발달 단계에 맞는 행동 교정 방식을 적용하는 것이 중요하다.
③ 아이의 심리 상담에 부모가 동반하는 것은 오히려 역효과를 낼 수 있다.
④ 부모와의 정서적 교감은 아이가 올바른 가치관을 확립하는 데 필수적이다.
⑤ 아이의 행동에 화가 나는 것은 정상적인 반응이며 나쁜 양육의 징후가 아니다.

23 다음 글의 주제로 가장 적절한 것은?

As GPS-based tools become more widespread, there is mounting evidence to suggest that spatial thinking skills are declining. More than just providing the ability to navigate unknown spaces, spatial thinking involves mental processes that support true understanding; it is a way of connecting the physical environment with what we actually experience, of visualizing the world from new angles and perspectives. Fostering spatial thinking skills among today's students requires that educators go beyond just giving them a loose understanding of where places are. Instead, students must understand geographic representations (maps, globes, and diagrams), collect and organize the information they find, and reinterpret it in maps or through the use of technologies. With practice, they will acquire the tools to better understand relationships between locations and form mental images of spatial patterns while gaining vital skills necessary for solving problems and making decisions in the field of geography.

① the application of spatial thinking in various disciplines
② the integration of new technologies into geography classes
③ the importance of developing students' spatial thinking skills
④ the effect of GPS-based devices on the mental abilities of students
⑤ the causes for the deterioration of spatial reasoning among students

24 다음 글의 제목으로 가장 적절한 것은?

The risks of overconsuming sodium are well known, but this ion serves a crucial purpose: keeping us alive. Because we require it to maintain muscle and nerve function and regulate fluid levels, being low on it triggers "sodium-appetite" neurons, compelling us to seek it out from food. To learn more about what drives our desire for salt, Caltech researchers manipulated the sodium-appetite neurons in the brains of mice, which prompted the animals to lick rock salt until they were satisfied. The researchers found that the activity of the mice's sodium-appetite neurons slowed within seconds of the sodium making contact with their tongues. When they later infused sodium directly into the mice's stomachs or used drugs to suppress salt receptors on their tongues, they found that neural suppression did not occur. This indicates that being able to taste salt plays an integral role in the inhibition of sodium-appetite neurons.

① Is Salt Really as Unhealthy as We Think?
② The Relationship Between Neurons and Salt
③ The Main Reason Behind Excessive Food Cravings
④ Taste: How Inhibiting It Increases Sodium Cravings
⑤ How Manipulating Sodium-Appetite Neurons Can Help Us

25 다음 도표의 내용과 일치하지 <u>않는</u> 것은?

Global Cotton Production in 2009 and 2019

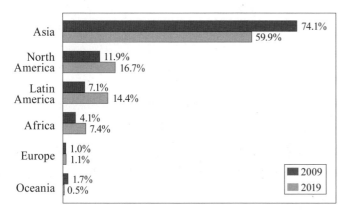

The graph above shows global cotton production by region in 2009 and 2019. ① The only two regions in which the percentage of cotton production decreased between 2009 and 2019 were Asia and Oceania. ② Even though Asia showed the biggest decrease in the percentage of global cotton production from 2009 to 2019, it remained in first place in the amount of cotton production in 2019. ③ Latin America was the region with the third-largest cotton production in both 2009 and 2019, and its percentage of cotton production in 2019 was more than double what it had been in 2009. ④ In 2019, the percentage of cotton production in North America was twice as high as the combined percentage of Africa, Europe, and Oceania. ⑤ Of all regions, Europe had the smallest gap between the percentage of cotton production in 2009 and that in 2019.

26 Edward Sapir에 관한 다음 글의 내용과 일치하지 <u>않는</u> 것은?

Edward Sapir is widely considered to be one of the most important American linguists. Born in Germany, Sapir immigrated with his family to England in 1888 before relocating to the United States in 1890. Sapir attended Columbia University, eventually obtaining a PhD. While studying linguistics and anthropology at this institution, Sapir participated in a seminar that sparked his interest in the languages of the indigenous people of the continent. For several years after graduating, he participated in research projects on Native American languages at the University of California and the University of Pennsylvania. In 1910, Sapir accepted a position at the Canadian National Museum as the head anthropologist. His experience in both linguistics and anthropology shaped his legacy, as he developed an interdisciplinary approach that focused on the relationship between language and culture that continues to influence modern researchers.

① 1890년에 영국에서 미국으로 이주했다.

② Columbia University에서 언어학과 인류학을 연구했다.

③ 졸업 후 아메리카 원주민 언어에 대한 연구 프로젝트에 참여했다.

④ 캐나다 국립 박물관의 수석 인류학자 자리를 거절했다.

⑤ 언어와 문화의 관계에 초점을 맞춘 접근법을 발전시켰다.

27 City Park Naming Contest에 관한 다음 안내문의 내용과 일치하지 <u>않는</u> 것은?

City Park Naming Contest

The new city park has just finished construction and will be open to all on May 15th. In honor of the opening, we are holding a naming contest. The residents of Fairfield will decide what to name our beautiful new park!

Entry Submission:
• One entry per person
• Must not include symbols
• March 1st - 31st on our website (www.cparkname. com)

Voting:
The naming committee will pick the 5 best entries and put them up on the website for voting. Voting will take place from April 20th through May 5th.

Winner:
• There will only be one winner.
• The winner will be awarded a trophy at the ribbon-cutting ceremony.

① 새로운 공원은 5월 15일에 개장할 것이다.
② 한 명당 한 개의 응모작을 제출할 수 있다.
③ 응모작 제출은 3월 한 달간 진행된다.
④ 최상위 응모작 5개가 투표에 부쳐질 것이다.
⑤ 우승자는 개장식에서 상금을 받을 것이다.

28 Arrow Pro Wireless Bluetooth Speaker에 관한 다음 안내문의 내용과 일치하는 것은?

Arrow Pro Wireless Bluetooth Speaker

How to use:
1. Fully charge the speaker.
2. Press the power button once to turn on.
3. Press the blue Bluetooth button.
4. Download the Arrow Pro app on your device.
5. Open the app and sync with Arrow Pro.

Features:
- Compatible with smartphones and tablets
- 5 hours of playback time on a full charge
- Speaker goes into standby mode after 20 minutes

Warning:
- It is not waterproof. Keep away from liquid.
- Stop use immediately if sparks are coming from the product.

* The warranty period is one year. After this period, you will be charged for repairs.

① 전원 버튼을 두 번 누르면 켜진다.
② 태블릿과는 호환되지 않는다.
③ 완충 시 5시간 동안 사용할 수 있다.
④ 방수 기능이 있다.
⑤ 제품 보증 기간은 2년이다.

29 다음 글의 밑줄 친 부분 중, 어법상 틀린 것은? [3점]

According to The Limitation Act 1980, a plaintiff wishing to seek resolution for a dispute must file a claim within the appropriate limitation period. If a plaintiff ① fails to initiate court proceedings within the limitation period, the plaintiff will face financial consequences. Because there is a different limitation period for each type of complaint — for personal injury, the limitation period is three years, while it is six years for rent recovery — determining the limitation period for a specific case is vital, especially ② as limitation periods are subject to change. To this end, it is necessary to keep in mind that all limitation periods ③ begin from the time the action that caused the dispute arises. Plaintiffs ④ who file a claim when the limitation period for their case has expired will find that they have made a mistake as doing so will automatically result in a ruling in the defendant's favor. They may also ⑤ order to pay for the defendant's legal fees in addition to already having paid for their own.

30 (A), (B), (C)의 각 네모 안에서 문맥에 맞는 낱말로 가장 적절한 것은?

One method that smart negotiators use to gain an advantage is to apply time pressure. It has been shown that people become more easily influenced and less (A) rigid / flexible when they feel rushed to make a decision. Imagine needing to buy a new car as soon as possible. If a salesperson recognizes this, the chances of being offered a small discount instead of a big one are high, as is the likelihood of being pressured into (B) accepting / rejecting an inferior deal. Because being under time pressure is a disadvantage, it's best to (C) disclose / conceal this information so you can negotiate from a position of strength. If you believe the other side is under some type of time constraint as well, you should take advantage of this. By recognizing the element of time pressure in any negotiation, you may be able to employ it successfully to reach a better deal or overcome an impasse should one arise.

* impasse: 교착 상태

	(A)		(B)		(C)
①	rigid	·····	rejecting	·····	disclose
②	flexible	·····	accepting	·····	conceal
③	rigid	·····	accepting	·····	conceal
④	flexible	·····	rejecting	·····	conceal
⑤	rigid	·····	accepting	·····	disclose

[31~34] 다음 빈칸에 들어갈 말로 가장 적절한 것을 고르시오.

31

New Criticism pioneers John Crowe Ransom and Cleanth Brooks were quite willing to go up against traditional readings of literature that they felt focused too heavily on the history of the text and its relation to external factors — the author's background, comparative sources, or historical context. Instead, they championed a "close reading," in which analysis is done of the work as it stands on its own. New Critics believed that the author's _____ cannot be determined without asking him or her directly what it is, which makes it pointless to consider while interpreting a piece. Even if they were able to ask the author why they wrote what they wrote, it should not matter because the text carries its own value. It could have a different meaning or significance separate from what the author originally planned. In other words, for the New Critics, the merits of a literary work should be conceived as being entirely contained within the text itself.

① talent
② attitude
③ intention
④ expertise
⑤ credibility

32

Having never been formally trained, Frida Kahlo's art employs a naïve kind of magical realism which she pioneered. This original style is on display in some of her most haunting works, in which she painted numerous self-portraits of her body which expressed the chronic pain she experienced as a result of polio and a bus accident. Kahlo's paintings also stemmed from emotional pain. Political turmoil in Mexico, her split from her husband, and other major events in her life guided her hand on the canvas. As such, in her native land of Mexico, she is referred to as "the heroine of pain," so well does her artwork speak to others who suffer. The torment evident in her paintings resonates deeply with those who have experienced hardships in their own lives. This has led to her personal life becoming inextricable from her work. However, because of the imagination her paintings are imbued with, Kahlo's paintings cannot be distilled down to mere memories. Her legacy is a testament to how beautifully she was able _____ _____. [3점]

* polio: 소아마비 ** turmoil: 혼란

① to suppress her pain to create art
② to ease the suffering of other people
③ to redefine traditional painting styles
④ to weave tragic reality and fantasy into one
⑤ to realistically depict the people around her

33

The discovery of life on a planet that orbits a different star — known as an exoplanet — will most likely occur through the analysis of its atmosphere. The gases that surround the planet can indicate if it is able to support life similar to that on Earth. However, there's always the possibility of organisms from another planet _____ a majority of Earth's life forms, which depend on its oxygen atmosphere. An atmosphere that consists of hydrogen, for example, could also conceivably support life. A bacterium on our own planet (a variety of *E. coli*) has demonstrated the capability of surviving and multiplying in a hydrogen atmosphere devoid of oxygen, and the products of this bacterium generate a number of gases that could act as biosignatures, or evidence of life, in this environment. Hydrogen also has the potential to keep a planet warm enough to feature liquid, and therefore life. This widens the scope of the search for organisms on other planets.

① adapting identical features to
② having a distinct chemistry from
③ lacking a dependency on gas unlike
④ inhabiting the same environment as
⑤ benefiting from research advanced by

34

Facial expressions convey emotion, from raised eyebrows signaling surprise to broad smiles revealing satisfaction. Though this may seem like a behavior people would acquire through the careful observation of others in order to display socially appropriate emotions, facial expressions are actually a natural means of responding to given situations. Our genes cause us to arrange our facial muscles in particular ways depending on how we feel or what type of situation we are in. A study that compared the facial appearance of Olympians during medal ceremonies found that the expressions of blind and sighted athletes did not differ in the same social context. Both blind and sighted individuals receiving silver medals exhibited polite smiles that only utilized their mouth muscles. The blind athletes could not have learned the expression by seeing it first in others, demonstrating that _____.

[3점]

① communication is not always verbal
② facial expressions can be changed with ease
③ they faced great difficulty in mastering this ability
④ they had to have learned it some other way
⑤ they most likely had the innate skill

35 다음 글에서 전체 흐름과 관계 없는 문장은?

According to social psychologists, humans are subject to a phenomenon known as in-group favoritism, meaning that people hold a bias towards other individuals who better reflect their own adopted notions of identity. ① A practical example of this can be seen in the way that sports fans relate to one another, such as fans of the same team sitting together at sporting events rather than consorting with the other team's fans. ② Despite no personal connections, people evaluate those who affiliate with their preferred team more positively because they are in the same cultural group. ③ Culture, or the way of life of a society, helps individuals perceive others from a broader perspective. ④ They have been given a group identity through their love of a sports team, and this has made it easy for them to separate themselves from other fans. ⑤ Therefore, this has also made it easier for them to express favoritism towards certain people who they see as more similar to themselves.

[36~37] 주어진 글 다음에 이어질 글의 순서로 가장 적절한 것을 고르시오.

36

Game theory is a theoretical framework for understanding the decision-making and strategies of competing parties, referred to as players, in social situations.

(A) Both players (the buyer and seller) negotiate based on what they know of one another, using this information to attempt to strategically induce a favorable conclusion. The logic they use is related to game theory and its rules. This does not just apply to financial exchanges but almost any decision that involves interaction.

(B) Players in such interactive situations are prompted to consider each other's prospective decisions because their choices are interdependent. Game theory suggests that a rational player will, through the careful deliberation of what their opponent might do and the utilization of an effective strategy, be able to produce the most beneficial outcome for themselves.

(C) For an individual interested in buying a home, for example, the most advantageous result would be acquiring it at the lowest possible price. The current owner, on the other hand, will need to sell the house for a certain amount of money to turn a profit.

① (A) – (C) – (B)   ② (B) – (A) – (C)
③ (B) – (C) – (A)   ④ (C) – (A) – (B)
⑤ (C) – (B) – (A)

37

> Popularized by anthropologist Franz Boas, historical particularism stands in opposition to evolutionism.

(A) Following this logic, the most advanced societies cannot be viewed as having traveled the furthest; they are in no way superior and should not serve as models for what culture should be. Likewise, less developed societies cannot be seen as slow-moving or as needing to catch up as they are not on the same path or running a race at all.

(B) Instead of suggesting that all human cultures pass through a series of predetermined stages on a path from savagery to civilization, it posits that cultural traits unfold independently based on historical events. Essentially, each society's past dictates where it is on its individual cultural trajectory and where it will one day be.

(C) This is an important distinction because previous theories about social evolution were used to justify the categorization of people into different levels of development. The notion that all cultures are different also led to the understanding that engaging with a culture directly is the most effective way to learn about it. [3점]

* trajectory: 궤적, 궤도

① (A) – (C) – (B)   ② (B) – (A) – (C)
③ (B) – (C) – (A)   ④ (C) – (A) – (B)
⑤ (C) – (B) – (A)

[38~39] 글의 흐름으로 보아, 주어진 문장이 들어가기에 가장 적절한 곳을 고르시오.

38

> Another possibility we might consider is that the Little Ice Age coincided with colonialism.

Most people know about the Ice Age that happened millions of years ago, but few are aware of the Little Ice Age, an event that took place from 1300 to 1850 AD. (①) During this period, temperatures dropped considerably, with the Baltic Sea freezing over and pack ice from the Arctic extending far south into the Atlantic Ocean. (②) Theories abound regarding the Little Ice Age's beginnings, with one interesting contender being the eruption of tropical volcanoes. (③) These geological events would have spewed aerosol into the atmosphere, thereby deflecting light from the sun and making Earth colder. (④) The arrival of Europeans in the Americas during the 15th century resulted in numerous diseases spreading across the continent and the consequent death of an estimated 56 million native inhabitants. (⑤) With so many people suddenly gone, mass reforestation of cultivated land would have taken place, causing CO_2 levels to go down and Earth to cool.

39

Thousands of new words have been added to the lexicon thanks to the myriad dialects and local slang of linguistically inventive Internet users worldwide.

Digital natives are all bilingual to an extent these days — they know both their mother tongue and Internet speak. (①) In fact, on a day-to-day basis, especially for the younger generation, textspeak is likely their main means of communication rather than being supplementary. (②) While it was once thought that this trend would reduce speech to nothing more than emojis and nonsense talk, language has instead become the most spectacular open-source project, which is a project made freely available and may be redistributed and modified. (③) Language has also been bolstered in new and unexpected ways; even the prevalence of poor grammar has led to syntactical rules being learned and shared, and people are speaking more correctly than ever before. (④) To write purposely ungrammatical comments for a laugh or express oneself through GIFs means language itself is already understood well enough by the user. (⑤) Change, in this case, does not equate to decay but evolution. [3점]

* lexicon: 어휘 목록 ** bolster: 보강하다

40 다음 글의 내용을 한 문장으로 요약하고자 한다. 빈칸 (A), (B)에 들어갈 말로 가장 적절한 것은?

Utilitarianism is an ethical theory that determines right from wrong by focusing on the outcome. It holds that the most moral thing to do in any situation is to act in a way that will bring the least pain and the most pleasure to the greatest number of people. In effect, it rejects the notion of egoism and postulates that one must judge what is best not only for oneself but for everyone who might be affected by one's actions, whether that's a single other person or an entire country. Critics of utilitarianism believe it is impractical, as weighing up all the possible outcomes of one's actions is difficult, if not impossible, to do when it is necessary to make a quick choice. It also allows for any action to take place, regardless of how morally questionable it may be — lying, stealing, killing — if it generates the most good in the end. Furthermore, because the doctrine benefits the majority, it makes the concept of justice for the minority irrelevant.

↓

Although utilitarianism seeks to ____(A)____ happiness in the world, it places no limitations on ethically ____(B)____ actions.

	(A)		(B)
①	exploit	……	guided
②	measure	……	partial
③	maximize	……	controversial
④	maximize	……	justifiable
⑤	exploit	……	uncertain

[41~42] 다음 글을 읽고, 물음에 답하시오.

Taken from the Portuguese term "barroco," which means "a pearl of irregular shape," the word "baroque" was initially a pejorative term used to criticize music that appeared to lack a (a) coherent melody and constantly changed key and meter. Today, however, "baroque" is used to describe a diverse and extravagant style of music composed from approximately 1600 to 1750.

It was during this period, as the Western world emerged from the Renaissance and entered what is now known as the "Age of Reason," that new ideas began to spread across all realms. In music, one such idea was that music could be a higher form of communication, a means of (b) arousing emotion in a listener provided the right sounds were produced. Previously, music tended to consist of a single melody, but a new interest in the possibilities music could afford expanded the boundaries of what had been heard up to this point. The tonality in music that we are familiar with today — the use of major and minor keys — became a (c) trivial characteristic of baroque music, as did the use of melodies that featured motifs, or short musical phrases. Composers repeated and developed motifs, elaborately (d) decorating them with trills (rapidly alternating notes). Melodies also became longer, with composers knitting them together through a technique called counterpoint. This involved various instruments being played and different voices singing (e) simultaneously, with an overlapping effect, to build up layers of sound. Composers like Johann Sebastian Bach and George Frideric Handel helped establish such techniques as musical characteristics of the period.

* pejorative: 비난의 뜻을 내포한

41 윗글의 제목으로 가장 적절한 것은?

① Driving Forces Behind Musical Techniques of the Baroque Period
② The Age of Reason: Exploring Renaissance Music
③ The Overlapping Phases of the Baroque Period
④ The Baroque Sound: Can It Truly Be Replicated Today?
⑤ In with the New: How the Baroque Period Revolutionized Music

42 밑줄 친 (a)~(e) 중에서 문맥상 낱말의 쓰임이 적절하지 않은 것은? [3점]

① (a)　　② (b)　　③ (c)　　④ (d)　　⑤ (e)

[43~45] 다음 글을 읽고, 물음에 답하시오.

(A)

Jenny had never traveled outside the US. It was her dream to do so and to visit the place she had always been most interested in: France. Jenny constantly imagined (a) herself visiting the wonderful landmarks and museums there. But she didn't know how she would ever be able to pay for such a trip. She just didn't have that kind of money.

(B)

Jenny couldn't believe it when she made it to France. She was so proud of herself for making it happen. She didn't think she'd ever be able to come, but she had been able to do it with enough hard work and determination. She decided to send her co-worker a post card, thanking her for (b) her encouragement and for showing Jenny that she could do anything if she really set her mind to it.

(C)

One day at work, Jenny's coworker caught (c) her staring at a picture of the Eiffel Tower. She asked Jenny why she didn't book a trip to see it in person. "I can't pay for that. The trip costs too much," replied Jenny sadly. Jenny's coworker smiled at (d) her and said, "Yes, you still can. You just have to start putting away your pennies and it will eventually be enough. Every little bit counts."

(D)

Jenny thought about it and decided it couldn't hurt to try. So, over the next few months, (e) she saved every penny she could. She cut back on buying coffees and going to restaurants. Any time she wanted to buy something new, she looked at the pictures she had saved of France and kept her goal in mind. She started to search for flights, hotels, and tours. In time, Jenny had enough money and she could finally take her dream trip.

43 주어진 글 (A)에 이어질 내용을 순서에 맞게 배열한 것으로 가장 적절한 것은?

① (B) – (D) – (C)　　　② (C) – (B) – (D)
③ (C) – (D) – (B)　　　④ (D) – (B) – (C)
⑤ (D) – (C) – (B)

44 밑줄 친 (a)~(e) 중에서 가리키는 대상이 나머지 넷과 다른 것은?

① (a)　　② (b)　　③ (c)　　④ (d)　　⑤ (e)

45 윗글에 관한 내용으로 적절하지 <u>않은</u> 것은?

① Jenny는 한 번도 미국을 떠난 적이 없었다.
② Jenny는 동료에게 엽서를 보내기로 결심했다.
③ Jenny의 동료는 Jenny가 에펠 탑 사진을 보는 것을 보았다.
④ Jenny는 커피를 사고 식당에 가는 데 드는 비용을 줄였다.
⑤ Jenny의 동료가 항공편을 찾아봐 주었다.

정답·해설·해석 p.113

문제풀이 후 확인사항
1. 45분 내에 문제를 풀었다.
2. 체크해둔 문제와 틀린 문제는 해설을 꼼꼼히 확인했다.

수고하셨습니다! HackersBook.com에서 제공하는 어휘리스트로 어휘를 암기하세요.

13회 고난도 실전모의고사

18 다음 글의 목적으로 가장 적절한 것은?

Dear Mr. Levi,

My name is Donald Miller, and I am a representative of Cast Internet. You are a longtime client of ours, and we would like to thank you for using us as your Internet provider. Unfortunately, our records show that you did not submit payment for your past three monthly bills. We attempted to contact you by phone numerous times to resolve this issue, but you did not answer our calls or return our messages. Please consider this to be your final warning. You need to pay off the outstanding balance for your account by the end of this month. If you do fail to do so, we will have no choice but to disconnect your Internet service. You can pay online or at any of our branch offices. If you have questions, please contact me at 555-0393.

Regards,
Donald Miller

① 잘못 청구된 연체료에 대해 항의하려고
② 인터넷 요금 인하 소식을 전달하려고
③ 연체된 요금의 납부를 요청하려고
④ 요금 납부 기일의 연장을 안내하려고
⑤ 인터넷 서비스 이용 방법을 문의하려고

19 다음 글에 나타난 Noah의 심경 변화로 가장 적절한 것은?

It was finally Noah's turn, and he was shaking like a leaf. It wasn't just because he was on a stage with hundreds of people looking at him. It wasn't just because winning the audition might give him his big break. He would be playing the piano in front of his idol who was the judge! He sat down and placed his trembling fingers on the keys. As he began to play, his heart thumped loudly in his chest, but his beautiful music filled the concert hall. The applause began even before he had finished, and he got up and took a bow with the biggest grin. And his smile grew wider when he saw that his musical hero was giving him a standing ovation! "Bravo!" Noah heard him shout from the first row as he floated off the stage in elation.

① nervous → delighted   ② annoyed → satisfied
③ sorrowful → calm   ④ indifferent → relieved
⑤ embarrassed → puzzled

20 다음 글에서 필자가 주장하는 바로 가장 적절한 것은?

The success of brands today has less to do with being as visible as possible and more to do with being authentic. These days, customers respond not to typical messaging or marketing gimmicks but to consistent stories that come from a place of sincerity and honesty. When brands talk about who they are and the values they stand for, people don't want to hear corporate terminology(*venture capital, market share*, etc) but something that makes them feel like part of the conversation, something that makes them feel like they are talking to a trusted friend. It does not matter how ubiquitous a brand once was; if it fails to connect with modern consumers, who expect the brands they support to have a mission and to mean what they say, it is likely to be crowded out by an up-and-coming brand that can.

① 브랜드를 지지하는 고객의 기대에 부응하는 사업 목표를 설정해야 한다.
② 브랜드의 정체성을 고객에게 각인시키는 마케팅 전략을 수립해야 한다.
③ 브랜드는 진정성 있는 이야기를 통해 고객의 반응을 이끌어내야 한다.
④ 브랜드 인지도를 높이려면 여러 광고 매체를 통해 제품을 알려야 한다.
⑤ 브랜드는 다양한 광고 전략을 활용해 진정성 있는 모습을 보여줘야 한다.

21 밑줄 친 <u>horse that drives the cart of fate</u>가 다음 글에서 의미하는 바로 가장 적절한 것은?

In the genre of tragedy, which is the foremost consideration: plot or character? Put another way, are our lives shaped primarily through the events we encounter or the composition of our personalities? For Aristotle, tragedy was expressed primarily through structure. "Tragedy is an imitation not of men but of an action, and life consists in action," he wrote. Men's lives were shaped by the whims of fate, as when the fortunes of Oedipus were altered by his unwitting involvement in the death of his father. Centuries later, William Shakespeare seemed to support an opposing view when his character Cassius stated, "The fault, dear Brutus, is not in our stars, but in ourselves." In contrast to the Greek playwrights, Shakespeare's art was defined by his detailed and thorough construction of character; he usually borrowed his plots from others. The tragic events that crash down upon the heads of his heroes are precipitated by their own flaws, as when King Lear loses everything because of his pride and arrogance. Shakespeare's tragedy influenced future generations of dramatists for whom personality is the <u>horse that drives the cart of fate</u>.

* unwitting: 자신도 모르는 ** precipitate: 촉발하다

① method for describing the results of actions
② solution to the problems some characters face
③ force that compels man to question his existence
④ victim of a series of extremely tragic events
⑤ cause of the defining incidents in a tragedy

22 다음 글의 요지로 가장 적절한 것은?

The 24-hour news cycle exposes people to a never-ending stream of bad news in the forms of traumatic images and sensationalistic stories. This kind of coverage is hard for people to distance themselves from because of the pervasive nature of technology: negative headlines litter the feeds of social media platforms and allow for constant updates. The expected reactions to such content are empathy and compassion, yet many today suffer from not feeling any type of emotion in response to it at all. People are no longer astonished or horrified by news stories but have instead become numb from reading about tragedy and violence day after day. Over time, the media has sought to cover stories that are more and more shocking in order to gain readership. The result is that people are experiencing compassion fatigue and are now unable to respond to stories that would normally evoke a reaction. It's a widespread phenomenon as people's emotions are worn out by the constant onslaught of bad news, leaving each new disaster to simply blend into the last one.

* sensationalistic: 선정주의적인

① 미디어는 사람들이 공감할 수 있는 사안을 보도해야 한다.
② 부정적인 소식에 무감각해지는 것을 방지하는 감정 훈련이 필요하다.
③ 충격적인 소식에 끊임없이 노출되는 것은 감정적인 마비를 초래한다.
④ 즉각적인 대응을 위해 재난 소식을 신속하게 보도하는 것이 바람직하다.
⑤ 오늘날 소셜 미디어 활용으로 시간에 구애받지 않는 보도가 가능해졌다.

23 다음 글의 주제로 가장 적절한 것은? [3점]

In *Über Sinn und Bedeutung*, Gottlob Frege developed a philosophy of language in which he attempted to explain meaning as consisting of two parts: sense and reference. He proposed that two words or sentences may have the same reference (Bedeutung) but a different sense (Sinn). The "sense" is the manner in which propositions or objects are expressed, and the "reference" is the actual object being discussed. Take the terms "evening star" and "morning star," for instance. Both are commonly used to refer to the planet Venus. Because the two expressions have the same reference but different senses, Frege believed that the meaning of the expressions could be interpreted differently. He developed a system that essentially represented statements in quantifiable mathematical terms. If one distinct expression could be substituted for another (a=b), then logic would dictate that the two expressions had the same meaning.

① a challenge in distinguishing between sense and reference
② a logical approach to deriving meaning from language
③ the influence of Frege on how language is interpreted today
④ the reason some terms fail to be truly synonymous with each other
⑤ the inspiration Frege drew from when applying mathematics to language

24 다음 글의 제목으로 가장 적절한 것은?

Although some researchers have claimed that post-traumatic stress disorder (PTSD) is a social construct — that it's something that only exists because we've collectively accepted that when bad things happen, we will rightfully be traumatized — not everyone who lives through a war, a natural disaster, or any other distressing experience develops it. A recent study suggests this may be because there is a biological basis for PTSD. In the largest study of PTSD to date, a research team at the University of California found that PTSD is polygenic, just like other psychiatric disorders and traits that are passed on via one's lineage, and that the heritability of the disorder is between 5 and 20 percent. The study lends significant weight to previous studies on twins indicating the existence of a link between the development of a psychiatric condition and one's hereditary makeup. Ultimately, the findings could make identifying patients at a higher risk of developing PTSD easier, making them more likely to get help for this debilitating condition.

* polygenic: 다원유전자의

① Is PTSD a Real or Imagined Psychological Condition?
② Through the Bloodline: Understanding PTSD Risk
③ How Trauma Causes Measurable Changes in DNA
④ Does PTSD Have to Impact Family Relationships?
⑤ It Won't End with You: Inherited Family Trauma

25 다음 표의 내용과 일치하지 <u>않는</u> 것은?

Global Expenditure on Information Security by Segment in 2019

Segment	U.S. dollars (billion)	Percentage of total
Security Services	62.0	51.28%
Infrastructure Protection	16.5	13.65%
Network Security Equipment	13.4	11.08%
Identity Access Management	9.8	8.11%
Software	8.5	7.03%
Integrated Risk Management	4.6	3.80%
Application Security	3.1	2.56%
Data Security	2.7	2.23%
Cloud Security	0.4	0.33%
Total	120.9	100%

*Note: Details may not add to totals shown due to rounding.

The above table shows the global expenditure on information security by segment in 2019. ① The segment that the most money was spent on was security services with a proportion of 51.28%. ② While there was a gap of more than 45 billion dollars between the top two segments in terms of expenditure, the gap between the second and the third was 3.1 billion dollars. ③ The proportion of the expenditure for the identity access management segment was 8.11%, which was over twice that of integrated risk management. ④ The combined amount of money spent on the segments of integrated risk management and application security was larger than that of the software segment. ⑤ Application security, data security, and cloud security were the three segments with the least expenditure, accounting for less than three percent of the total respectively.

26 piping plover에 관한 다음 글의 내용과 일치하지 <u>않는</u> 것은?

The piping plover is a shorebird indigenous to North America. Like other shorebirds, it makes its home in sandy areas near large bodies of water. It is small and light-colored with tan, white, and grey feathers. The colors match the area where it nests, providing it with camouflage. The bird mostly eats insects or mollusks. It also eats the eggs of many smaller creatures. When a piping plover is ready to eat, it runs in short bursts, pauses and searches the ground for food, and then runs off again if it does not find anything. These birds are considered endangered, primarily due to changes in habitat. Increased human activity where they live has inhibited the birds' ability to safely nest. Conservation efforts are underway to preserve those regions in an attempt to help piping plover populations recover.

* mollusk: 연체동물

① 북아메리카 토착 조류이다.
② 옅은 털색은 위장 효과를 낸다.
③ 주로 곤충과 연체동물을 먹는다.
④ 먹이를 찾을 때 짧게 이동했다가 멈추기를 반복한다.
⑤ 무분별한 포획으로 멸종 위기에 처했다.

27 Cinema Workshop for Beginners에 관한 다음 안내문의 내용과 일치하지 <u>않는</u> 것은?

Cinema Workshop for Beginners

Do you want to make a movie? All you need is your phone! Join us and learn how to create your own cinematic video.

Where: Walker Community Center
When: Saturday-Sunday, May 10-11
Time: 11:00 a.m. to 4:00 p.m.
Price: $150 per student

What to bring:
- A smartphone (any model)
- Storyline draft

What you will learn:
- Storyboarding
- Methods of filming
- Directing
- Video and sound editing

Note:
- Register on our website, www.cinemaworkshop. com. Registration ends on May 1.
- If you need to cancel, please do so before May 6. After this date, there will be no refunds.
- For further questions, contact Lewis Smith at directorsmith@cinemaworkshop.com.

---

① 이틀간 진행된다.
② 스마트폰 기종에는 제한이 없다.
③ 영상과 음향 편집법을 배울 것이다.
④ 등록 마감일은 5월 6일이다.
⑤ 관련 문의는 이메일로 할 수 있다.

28 Eden Book Festival에 관한 다음 안내문의 내용과 일치하는 것은?

Eden Book Festival

From August 21-30, Eden will be holding its biannual book festival at Eden City Library.

Main Activities:
There will be an introduction to three of the nation's top young authors. They will give speeches on August 21 and 22 in the auditorium from 2:00 p.m. to 5:00 p.m.
Poetry readings will be held every afternoon at 5:00 p.m. Anyone is welcome to attend!

Main Event:
The book market will be open every day from 8:30 a.m. to 4:00 p.m. We will have used and new books, as well as old and rare books. You will be able to buy books or exchange them with other collectors.

The Eden Book Festival is free of charge. Refreshments will be available for purchase. For more information, please visit www.edenbooks. com.

---

① 8월 21일부터 일주일간 개최된다.
② 작가들의 강연은 행사 첫날에만 예정되어 있다.
③ 시 읽기 활동은 매일 오후 두 시에 시작한다.
④ 신간 도서는 판매되지 않는다.
⑤ 입장료는 없다.

29 다음 글의 밑줄 친 부분 중, 어법상 틀린 것은? [3점]

The *Sultana* was a steamboat that sailed on the Mississippi River. On one occasion, its mission was to transport newly ① released Union army prisoners of war from Vicksburg, Mississippi, northward up the Mississippi River to St. Louis, Missouri, a location ② which they would be able to travel home. The legal carrying capacity of the *Sultana* was 376 passengers, but since the government had offered to pay $5 for every enlisted man that ③ was safely returned and $10 for every officer, the Confederates had forced over 2,500 soldiers onto the ship. The ship completed less than half of its intended route before disaster struck. In the middle of the night, one of the boilers suddenly blew up, setting off a chain reaction that caused two other boilers to explode. Soldiers who had ④ been packed in near the boilers on the overcrowded ship died instantly. ⑤ Others perished from fire or shrapnel, while more died later from drowning or exposure. In all, roughly 1,800 people lost their lives in the tragedy.

* enlisted man: 사병(士兵)

30 다음 글의 밑줄 친 부분 중, 문맥상 낱말의 쓰임이 적절하지 않은 것은?

While classical conditioning is frequently associated with physiologist Ivan Pavlov's experiments on dogs, it can also be used in treatments designed to ① alter human behavior. One form of therapy based on classical conditioning is aversion therapy, which is used to help a person stop an ② undesirable habit or addiction. This is done by making them associate it with something unpleasant. For instance, in National Institutes of Health (NIH) studies on the treatment of alcoholism, a doctor administers drugs that ③ inhibit nausea or vomiting whenever the patient drinks alcohol. The drugs are intended to create a conditioned response — not wanting to get sick — to an ordinary neutral stimulus, drinking alcohol. In this type of treatment, because the process of the patient drinking alcohol and getting sick is ④ repeated, eventually, the patient no longer craves alcohol. Even once the nausea-inducing drugs are no longer being administered, the patient may not be willing to ⑤ resume their habit because they have to ask themselves: is even a single drink worth feeling sick over?

* administer: (약을) 투여하다

[31~34] 다음 빈칸에 들어갈 말로 가장 적절한 것을 고르시오.

31

Pop art developed in the late 1950s and early 60s as a reaction to the pomposity of contemporary art. Pop artists presented everyday life by depicting advertising images, mass-produced products, comic books, and celebrities. In doing so, they celebrated the consumer-driven world that had emerged in the post-war period. This form of art was meant to be capable of representing the disposable excess of contemporary culture, just like the material it depicted. The most famous practitioner of pop art, Andy Warhol, epitomized this with his *Campbell's Soup Cans*, in which he painted a type of soup can that millions of Americans purchased regularly. He did this to celebrate its _____, not to suggest that this mass-produced food product had hidden depths. By doing so, Warhol showed that high culture need not necessarily be removed from everyday life and the products that dominated it.

* pomposity: 거만함

① potential   ② feasibility
③ directness   ④ practicality
⑤ superficiality

32

Hysteresis is an economic term defined as an event which continues to have an impact despite the _____. It usually takes place after a significant economic occurrence such as a crash or recession: incidents that are severe in nature and drawn out. For example, following a recession the unemployment rate may persist in rising even though the economy has rebounded. This trend might not appear to make sense, but there is actually an explanation for it. When an economy has recovered, workers may lack the necessary skills required to work in industries; the available expertise doesn't meet the new needs of companies. This was the case in the UK when unemployment went from 1.5 to 2 million over the course of 1980 and 1981 during a recession and then rose to 3 million after its end. Hysteresis can also occur with a stock market crash, as investors feel reluctant to put money back into stocks after such an event. Although the crash is over, the aftershocks of the episode remain.

① removal of factors that caused it
② severity of the effects on workers
③ diversification of professional skills
④ rapidness with which changes occur
⑤ expansion of employment opportunities

33

There is a vast difference between saying that I should save money for retirement and saying that I should give to charity. Both are imperatives pertaining to financial responsibilities. However, the latter imperative represents a moral obligation that affects the whole of society, to the extent that society depends on the generosity of private donors for the remediation of various ills and for the functioning of its participants, whereas the former imperative is only necessary if the individual making the investment cares about having enough money to retire comfortably. A savings deposit is a means to acquiring something I want. Charity is a means of caring for the most vulnerable in my community. Therefore, creating a savings deposit is a hypothetical imperative, which constitutes an objective principal that is _____, rather than a categorical imperative, which is a command that must be obeyed whether the actor in question wishes to do so or not. [3점]

* imperative: 명령

① derived from the dictates of conscience
② arrived at through the application of reason
③ instructive for accomplishing a personal goal
④ essential for an assessment of individual value
⑤ inadvisable under certain financial circumstances

34

The discovery that organisms are made up of atoms and molecules led many biologists to adopt a reductionist paradigm in which the mysteries of biological systems could be unraveled by breaking those systems down into their component parts. But while attempts to "explain all biology in terms of physics and chemistry," as DNA pioneer Francis Crick once advocated, may have an allure of attainability, they _____ _____. Consciousness, as an example, is not merely a series of chemical reactions in the brain but an intricate web of experience and emotion that defies simplification. Diseases are not just symptoms that can be eliminated with targeted pharmaceutical interventions or single gene deletions but complex networks of abnormal functioning that require holistic strategies. Rather than assume that minute chemical or molecular phenomena cause all higher-level occurrences, biologists must focus on the higher-level causes of lower-level phenomena.

It is only by focusing attention on the organism as a whole that complex biological systems can be truly understood. [3점]

* reductionist: 환원주의적인 ** holistic: 전체론적인

① underestimate the unpredictable complexity of biological entities
② recognize that the individual parts of a system have multiple roles
③ focus heavily on chemistry and ignore other possible explanations
④ treat organisms as nothing more than collection of biological functions
⑤ demonstrate the need to focus on genetic factors that caused diseases

35 다음 글에서 전체 흐름과 관계 없는 문장은?

A new study has revealed that the emotional resonance of words can be based solely on how they sound rather than on their significance. ① Building on the "bouba/kiki effect", a correspondence between speech sounds and the visual shape of objects, researchers at Cornell University asked participants to record their emotional reaction to a series of words. ② They found that some words, like *bouba*, were perceived by the participants as having a round shape based on how they sound and that hearing them had a calming effect. ③ Meanwhile, others, like *kiki*, were imagined as being sharp or spiky and recorded as being more emotionally stimulating. ④ For most people, the emotional effect of a word is related as much to the way in which it is delivered as it is to its meaning. ⑤ The researchers claim that this shows how important human emotion is in the development of language, with the implication being that emotional resonance could play a significant role in the encoding of language among infants.

* encoding: 부호화

[36~37] 주어진 글 다음에 이어질 글의 순서로 가장 적절한 것을 고르시오.

36

In American film, road movies are a familiar and popular genre, showing one or two protagonists "hitting the road" in pursuit of an objective. Motion is typically the key feature of the narrative.

(A) Ultimately, the road movie's themes of mobility are paradoxically manifested in an immobile visual style. The focus of the composition is directed toward the center of the screen, and the editing suggests that ensuing images will be repetitive. Thus, the hypnotizing sameness of the road engulfs the protagonists, lulling them into a static and unchanging existence.

(B) It is only natural that the events in road movies serve a broader theme about mobility. Often, the films explore forced motion. Outlaw road movies typically feature characters that are on the run from the law. Other characters are forced into motion by circumstances such as the need to visit a sick relative.

(C) Although travel is the ostensible topic of the road movie, filmic expression goes beyond mere storytelling. Unlike literature, where theme is generally expressed almost exclusively through narrative events, film depends upon visual elements such as composition, the way that images are framed, and editing, the way that images are split and reassembled.

* ostensible: 표면적인

① (A) – (C) – (B)   ② (B) – (A) – (C)
③ (B) – (C) – (A)   ④ (C) – (A) – (B)
⑤ (C) – (B) – (A)

37

> When devising a hypothesis or a theory to explain unexplained phenomena, it is tempting to get lost in intricacy, compounding assumption upon assumption.

(A) It is nevertheless important to recognize that simplicity is no guarantee of accuracy. In 1879, Alfred Kempe attempted to prove the "four color theorem" — that four colors are all that is required to fill in any map in such a way that no two bordering regions share a color. His proof was elegant but wrong.

(B) Complicated predictions that reflect a messy and multifaceted reality are often difficult to test. For that reason, scientists often rely on the principle of Occam's Razor, which states that the simplest explanation is usually the best one. This can be useful for cutting away facts that are true without being relevant because they have an insignificant impact on outcomes.

(C) It might be much easier for researchers if finding the simplest explanation definitely always led to the truth. But as this example shows, Occam's Razor is best used not as a guide to the correctness of a theory but as a criterion for identifying its usefulness. A hypothesis, after all, is a tool for finding the truth, not the truth itself. [3점]

* intricacy: 복잡성   ** four color theorem: 4색 정리

① (A) – (C) – (B)   ② (B) – (A) – (C)
③ (B) – (C) – (A)   ④ (C) – (A) – (B)
⑤ (C) – (B) – (A)

[38~39] 글의 흐름으로 보아, 주어진 문장이 들어가기에 가장 적절한 곳을 고르시오.

38

> Some models of market competition suggest that the two firms in a duopoly make simultaneous decisions.

When market share is divided between two major competitors, the company that leads sets the rules of the game, but it is never a good idea to discount the potential of the follower. (①) The Coca-Colas of the world decide how much product to make available. (②) Their power in the market is derived from a superior brand recognition that increases the competitiveness of their product and leaves their competitors to react to those decisions. (③) A smaller firm in a duopoly or other competitive model, however, can force the leader to react with a clever strategy. (④) Coca-Cola responded to Pepsi's claim to superior results in blind taste tests by reducing production of their longtime market-leading recipe and increasing production of a product that cloned the sweeter flavor of its chief competitor. (⑤) Yet, the reality is that the leader and follower exert influence upon one another, which means that each takes action in turn, responding what the other does. [3점]

39

> The main focus here is to explore the human psyche as the boys descend into chaos and paranoia.

A *deus ex machina* is a literary plot device whereby a seemingly unsolvable problem is suddenly resolved by an unexpected or divine event. The technique is often maligned as being an inept way to wrap things up. (①) Citing William Golding's 1954 classic *Lord of the Flies* as an example, though, some argue that a *deus ex machina* can be used effectively. (②) In the novel, a group of boys who had been marooned on a deserted island and forced to govern themselves is suddenly rescued by a passing ship. (③) Typically, this would be a disappointing resolution since it seems like an overly contrived solution, yet it works because the story is not plot-driven. (④) Thus, the juxtaposition of the group's abrupt return to a civilized world against their savage behavior on the island is what is significant rather than how they got into or out of the situation. (⑤) The *deus ex machina* of the passing ship does not undercut the moral complexities and thematic content of the narrative.

* malign: 비방하다 ** maroon: 고립시키다 *** contrived: 작위적인

40 다음 글의 내용을 한 문장으로 요약하고자 한다. 빈칸 (A), (B)에 들어갈 말로 가장 적절한 것은?

The question of whether machines are intelligent has preoccupied philosophers for decades. The existence of artificial intelligence poses philosophical questions, such as, is there anything that makes human intelligence unique when machines can think? Correspondingly, does the success of artificial intelligence mean that the human mind is simply a type of machine? Perhaps the most influential response is Alan Turing's Turing test, in which a human judges a machine's intelligence through a dialogue between a human and a machine. If the person cannot figure out which speaker is not human, then the machine has successfully passed as human and possesses intelligence. Some believe that this sort of simulation of intelligence is inevitable, since, as the brain obeys the laws of science, the mind's functions must be replicable. However, the majority of people reject the notion that this would be a form of machine intelligence, arguing that the fact that a machine can simulate human intelligence does not actually make it intelligent. Their point is that acting like a human is vastly different from possessing consciousness, which we still know very little about.

↓

Just because a machine is capable of presenting the ___(A)___ of human intelligence, that does not mean that the machine exhibits ___(B)___ intelligence.

	(A)		(B)
①	essence	⋯⋯	imaginary
②	illusion	⋯⋯	genuine
③	beginnings	⋯⋯	sufficient
④	appearance	⋯⋯	fabricated
⑤	definition	⋯⋯	traditional

[41~42] 다음 글을 읽고, 물음에 답하시오.

Dark matter is arguably the most intriguing subject in physics today. For one thing, this invisible stuff is thought to exist because spiral galaxies contain (a) insufficient visible mass to continue spinning at extremely high speeds without breaking up. However, despite the universe being full of (b) signs of dark matter, it remains a mystery; it does not appear to absorb, reflect, or emit any electromagnetic radiation or light — elements on which scientists typically depend to study the workings of the cosmos. Given that dark matter is thought to comprise about 85 percent of the universe's total mass and could help us understand how the cosmos functions at its most basic level, it makes sense to want to hunt it down. But physicists must work with the Standard Model, presently the most (c) viable explanation for how the universe works, which states that the behavior of matter within the universe is governed by how it interacts with four fundamental forces: gravity, electromagnetism, and strong and weak nuclear forces. Although the only component of the Standard Model that is known to interact with dark matter is gravity, scientists are still uncertain whether gravity causes dark matter to behave (d) similarly to visible matter, which gets pulled together to form clusters. If dark matter manifests behaviors that are different from those of visible particles, (e) conventional approaches may be needed to spot it.

* electromagnetic radiation: 전자기 방사선

41 윗글의 제목으로 가장 적절한 것은?

① Is Dark Matter Really Necessary to Explain the Cosmos?
② The Search for New Ways to Measure Dark Matter
③ Why the Standard Model May Be Wrong
④ Missing Matter: Can We Find What We Can't See?
⑤ Dark Matter: Building An Instrument That Can Detect It

42 밑줄 친 (a)~(e) 중에서 문맥상 낱말의 쓰임이 적절하지 않은 것은? [3점]

① (a)　　② (b)　　③ (c)　　④ (d)　　⑤ (e)

[43~45] 다음 글을 읽고, 물음에 답하시오.

(A)

It was the first book club meeting, and the members had decided to throw a party to welcome new members. Josh was hosting the event at his house. (a) He saw his friend Eric and made his way over to say hello. Eric was happy to see Josh and said that he brought someone with him. When Josh asked who it was, Eric pointed to a man standing in a group across the room. "That's David," he said.

(B)

As the night went on, Josh became more and more annoyed as he watched Eric and David joke and laugh together. He didn't understand why David wouldn't talk to (b) him. When Josh saw that Eric was alone, he decided to discuss it with him. "Your friend David was a bit rude to me earlier," Josh said. Eric seemed surprised. "What do you mean?" he asked. Josh told him about what had happened, expecting Eric to see (c) his point of view.

(C)

Josh walked up to David and introduced himself. "Welcome to our club," he said. "What kind of books do you like to read?" David gave him a confused look and didn't answer the question. Josh decided to ask him again, thinking that maybe David hadn't heard him. But still, (d) he didn't reply. Finally, Josh left David and felt annoyed by what had happened. Eric said that David was friendly, but he didn't seem that friendly at all.

(D)

Eric began to laugh and told Josh it was all a big misunderstanding. "David doesn't speak English well," he explained. "He probably didn't understand you or didn't know what to say." David was Spanish, and he had joined the club to improve his English. Eric spoke Spanish too, so they were able to understand each other. Feeling horrible about how (e) he had left David earlier, Josh asked Eric to translate an apology for him. Eric happily agreed, and the three spent the rest of the night laughing about it.

43 주어진 글 (A)에 이어질 내용을 순서에 맞게 배열한 것은 가장 적절한 것은?

① (B) – (D) – (C) 　　② (C) – (B) – (D)
③ (C) – (D) – (B) 　　④ (D) – (B) – (C)
⑤ (D) – (C) – (B)

44 밑줄 친 (a)~(e) 중에서 가리키는 대상이 나머지 넷과 다른 것은?

① (a) 　② (b) 　③ (c) 　④ (d) 　⑤ (e)

45 윗글에 관한 내용으로 적절하지 않은 것은?

① Josh의 집에서 첫 번째 독서 모임 행사를 열었다.
② Josh와 David는 농담을 주고받으며 함께 웃었다.
③ David는 Josh의 물음에 답하지 않았다.
④ Eric은 David가 친절한 사람이라고 말했다.
⑤ David는 영어 실력을 향상시키고자 했다.

정답·해설·해석 p.124

문제풀이 후 확인사항
1. 45분 내에 문제를 풀었다.
2. 체크해둔 문제와 틀린 문제는 해설을 꼼꼼히 확인했다.

수고하셨습니다! HackersBook.com에서 제공하는 어휘리스트로 어휘를 암기하세요.

14회 고난도 실전모의고사

목표 시간: 45분　　시작: ＿＿시 ＿＿분 ~ 종료: ＿＿시 ＿＿분　　점수: ＿＿점 / 63점

* [3점] 표시가 있는 문제 제외하고는 모두 2점으로 계산합니다.

18 다음 글의 목적으로 가장 적절한 것은?

Dear Ms. Wallace,

I'm pleased to hear that you're interested in joining the Lakeview Community Garden. I received your application and can see that you want to lease one of our larger gardens this year. To secure your plot, you will need to submit payment for the year now. Payment guarantees you membership. Please note that it must be done promptly as we currently have numerous applicants on our waiting list. We would prefer that you pay in person so that we can tell you more about how the garden works. Please come by next week, and don't hesitate to contact us with any questions. We look forward to welcoming you.

Yours sincerely,
Mark Gonzalez

① 임대 가능한 텃밭 자리가 있는지 문의하려고
② 텃밭 가꾸기에 필요한 장비를 알려주려고
③ 공동체 텃밭의 운영 방식을 설명하려고
④ 텃밭 임대를 위한 비용 납부를 안내하려고
⑤ 주민을 위한 텃밭 가꾸기 프로그램을 제안하려고

19 다음 글에 나타난 'I'의 심경 변화로 가장 적절한 것은?

It was my first time at a big publishing company. I couldn't believe that my book would be going into print. Having a book published was all I had ever dreamed about. I had worked so hard and tried so many times before, only to have the door slammed in my face, but this time would be different. I was taken up to the editor's office, and I bounded in. But the minute I saw her face, I knew something was wrong. "I'm sorry, but we've decided to go with a different writer this time. Don't worry. With your skills, another opportunity will come up soon." It was such an unexpected blow. I tried not to let it show on my face. I was so close, but my dream had slipped away once again.

① jealous → regretful
② confident → satisfied
③ frustrated → relieved
④ wishful → flattered
⑤ excited → disappointed

20 다음 글에서 필자가 주장하는 바로 가장 적절한 것은?

If every politician in office utilized their powers to the full extent, what would result would barely resemble a democracy. Examples of this can be seen in America now as political polarization has led officials to regularly use what is called "constitutional hardball." This is when representatives do everything in their power, including shutting down the government and packing the Supreme Court, to inhibit their political opponents from achieving anything, which halts progress altogether. While such actions are technically not unconstitutional, in that they are not explicitly forbidden, they hinder the democratic process, which is meant to be protected by a number of constitutional checks and balances and allot specific powers to political actors.

In a broad sense, they do, but they are unable to uphold democracy alone. Institutional forbearance — exercising self-restraint in using available constitutional powers for the benefit of democratic proceedings — is also required.

* checks and balances: 견제와 균형

① 입법을 통해 정치인에게 재량권을 부여해야 한다.
② 헌법에 따른 권리를 행사할 때에도 제도적 자제가 필요하다.
③ 민주주의적 절차는 헌법이 제시하는 기준에 따라 수립되어야 한다.
④ 정치인의 헌법 준수를 감시하는 제도적 장치가 마련되어야 한다.
⑤ 절차를 따르는 한 법적 근거 없이 정치 행위를 견제해서는 안 된다.

21 밑줄 친 the most room to move around가 다음 글에서 의미하는 바로 가장 적절한 것은? [3점]

A trilemma exists when it comes to international economics. In a perfect world, all nations would be able to reap the benefits of a financial trinity that would simultaneously make stable exchange rates, free-flowing capital, and discretionary monetary policy possible. According to the Mundell-Fleming trilemma model, mutual exclusivity makes only one side of the trilemma triangle achievable at any given time in reality. For example, if a country intends to implement an autonomous monetary policy, it should be well aware of the fact that it cannot have a fixed exchange rate and free flow of capital at the same time. If it would like to enjoy the stability of a fixed exchange rate with policy independence, it cannot allow capital to flow freely. Also, choosing to maintain fixed exchange rates with one or more countries as well as having a free flow of capital with others would make having monetary policy free from outside influences next to impossible. Considering the options available to them, governments will most likely choose the one side that gives them the most room to move around.

① the security of set currency values and control over foreign financial matters
② the knowledge to predict the long-term exchange rates between countries
③ the unhindered transfer of assets and the freedom to set economic rules
④ the ability to utilize the three essential elements of international economics
⑤ the implementation of national policies without the approval of outside regulators

22 다음 글의 요지로 가장 적절한 것은?

In spite of the fact that uncertainty is an inevitable facet of the human experiences, the extent to which people accept it can differ greatly. How a person copes in situations where they face unpredictability or are presented with vague information differs depending on their level of tolerance; if they are comfortable and can approach these matters in a neutral way, it is high. The other end of the spectrum would include an aversion to change, disorganization, and straying from a fixed path. When one is forced to accomplish a task in an uncertain environment, this level of tolerance can prove to be a weakness, preventing sound decision-making and overall success. Psychologist Stanley Budner says that people with a higher tolerance for ambiguity are able to work well in erratic conditions because they have "the tendency to perceive unpredictable situations as desirable." From a neurological perspective, this means that when they are presented with insufficient information to make a confident interpretation, anxiety is induced, but to a lesser degree than in someone with a lower tolerance. They can therefore approach an issue with curiosity and open-mindedness rather than dread.

① 섣부른 예측은 판단력을 흐릴 수 있다.
② 의사 결정을 내리기 전에 심사숙고할 필요가 있다.
③ 성공을 위해 삶의 불확실성을 최소화할 것이 요구된다.
④ 모호성에 대한 관용은 낯선 환경에 적응하는 경험을 통해 높아진다.
⑤ 예측 불가능한 상황에 대처할 때 모호성을 받아들이는 태도가 중요하다.

23 다음 글의 주제로 가장 적절한 것은?

If we look to observation as the foundation of science, if we believe that data collection through the senses is the key to a more comprehensive understanding of the universe, then we must grapple with the reality that the hypotheses we seek to evaluate through observation are inextricably tied to the observation itself. Each of us brings to our observations a system of thought, a *theory*, that provides the context for understanding and interpreting those observations. To suggest that empirical data stands alone as uncontested fact is to ignore the fundamental humanity of the scientist. Two observers may look at the same phenomenon and see two different realities, coming as they do from two distinct perspectives. They can, in fact, see two different phenomena even as they seek to discern the truth from a single phenomenon. An observation, then, cannot simply be relied upon to resolve a disagreement between rival theories. The inescapable reality is that observation is influenced by perception.

① the impossibility of arriving at consensus when limited to a single theory
② the role of observation in constructing a hypothesis in experimentation
③ the inability of observation to exist independent of preexisting views
④ the misinterpretation of empirical data due to unknown phenomena
⑤ the difficulty in arriving at new conclusions from existing premises

24 다음 글의 제목으로 가장 적절한 것은?

Russian philosopher Mikhail Bakhtin took the concept of polyphony, which is traditionally associated with musical texture, and applied it to literature. Polyphony describes how some texts include multiple voices or perspectives of characters that are not subverted by the voice of the author. These viewpoints can disagree with each other, and even with the author, loaning a piece of literature a more balanced and diverse quality. Bakhtin based this theory on his interpretation of the writings of Fyodor Dostoevsky, who he claimed illustrates a "profoundly pluralistic" world. His work wasn't dominated by one overarching narrative but rather embraced the contradictions and differences that permeate reality. He asserted that "the fundamental category in Dostoevsky's mode of artistic visualizing was not evolution, but coexistence and interaction." This form of literature offered a more honest reflection of society that didn't try to create an ideology that every character adhered to. People have divergent opinions, and he thought it was better to acknowledge this fact rather than to try and silence their voices.

* subvert: 전복시키다

① Can Novels Truly Capture the Subtle Nuances of Society?
② Writing to Depict Reality: The Inclusion of Diverse Voices
③ The Prioritization of the Omniscient Narrator's Voice in Texts
④ Thematic Expression: Conveying a Novel's Overarching Message
⑤ Building a Consistent Narrative: Methods for Embracing Diversity

25 다음 표의 내용과 일치하지 <u>않는</u> 것은?

Greenhouse Gas Emissions from Waste, in 2013 and 2018

(Tons of CO_2 equivalent, Millions)

Country	Greenhouse Gas Emissions from Waste		2013-2018 (% change)
	2013	2018	
United States	160.8	161.1	0
Russia	86.5	98.2	14
Canada	27.0	27.2	1
Japan	22.6	20.7	-8
United Kingdom	22.3	19.4	-13
Italy	18.6	18.3	-2
France	19.9	18.2	-9
Turkey	18.2	18.1	-1
South Korea	16.2	17.1	6
Spain	15.0	14.1	-6
Australia	12.5	12.6	-1

The table above shows the amount of greenhouse gas (GHG) emissions generated from waste in 2013 and 2018 and the percentage change between the two years for selected countries. ① In both 2013 and 2018, the United States recorded the highest amount of GHG emissions from waste, followed by Russia and Canada. ② Meanwhile, the percentage change of GHG emissions generated from waste in Russia was the highest with a 14 percent change. ③ The amount of GHG emissions from waste in the United Kingdom decreased by 2.9 million tons of CO_2 equivalent from 2013 to 2018. ④ In the case of France and Spain, the amount of GHG emissions from waste in each country decreased by less than 1 million ton of CO_2 equivalent from 2013 to 2018. ⑤ Although the amount of GHG emissions from waste in Australia showed an increase between 2013 and 2018, it ranked the lowest among the selected countries in both years.

26 Clara Haskil에 관한 다음 글의 내용과 일치하지 <u>않는</u> 것은?

Born in Romania in 1895, Clara Haskil began studying the piano with the notable Austrian composer Rudolf Serkin at the age of seven. When she turned 12, she was accepted to the Paris Conservatoire, a prominent college of music in France. She graduated when she was 15, at which point she began to tour Europe and the United States. Haskil received widespread acclaim for her skillful interpretation of the works of classical composers such as Schumann and Mozart. However, her illustrious career almost came to an end in 1942, when she began experiencing severe headaches and a doctor discovered a tumor behind the optical nerve of one eye. Fortunately, this medical issue was resolved through surgery, and she was able to continue playing. Haskil remained a celebrated pianist until her death in 1960.

① 작곡가 Rudolf Serkin에게 피아노를 배웠다.
② 12세에 Paris Conservatoire에 입학했다.
③ 졸업 후 유럽과 미국 순회 공연을 시작했다.
④ 1942년에 심각한 두통을 겪기 시작했다.
⑤ 수술 후 피아노 연주를 계속하지 못했다.

27 Large Trash Collection Services에 관한 다음 안내문의 내용과 일치하지 <u>않는</u> 것은?

Large Trash Collection Services

The Columbus Community Center would like you to observe the following instructions in order to minimize possible environmental pollution.

When: Every Wednesday
Where: In front of your house

What to do:
1) Determine whether the item is reusable or not.
2) Register the item.
   - For reusable items, you don't have to pay a fee.
   - For non-reusable items, you will be required to pay a fee.
3) A collection vehicle will visit your home and take the item.

Collection fee:
- Home appliances (under 10kg): $3
- Home appliances (10kg or more): $5
- Furniture (under 3kg): $2
- Furniture (3kg or more): $5

If you want to register an item, please visit the Columbus Community Center in person or visit our website.

---

① 매주 수요일에 수거한다.
② 재사용이 가능한 물품은 비용을 지불해야 한다.
③ 수거 차량이 집에 방문해서 물품을 수거한다.
④ 10kg 이상의 가전제품과 3kg 이상의 가구의 수거 비용은 같다.
⑤ 주민 센터에 직접 방문해서 수거 신청을 할 수 있다.

28 Swim to Fitness Program에 관한 다음 안내문의 내용과 일치하는 것은?

Swim to Fitness Program

Our eight-week comprehensive swim program will help you get fit in no time. If you are looking to get healthy, our program is right for you!
* Sessions will be held three days a week (Tuesday, Thursday, and Saturday) for eight weeks from October 31 to December 23.

Who it is for:
- Beginner to intermediate students
- Ages 15 and up

What you will learn:
- New swimming styles
- How to improve form

Additional Information:
- The tuition fee is $90 per person.
- The deadline for registration is October 14.
- Please bring your own swimsuits.
- You can register for extra private lessons in addition to taking the program.

Visit www.s2fprogram.com for more information.

---

① 일주일에 2일씩 8주 동안 운영된다.
② 10세 이상을 대상으로 진행된다.
③ 기존에 배운 영법만 연습할 수 있다.
④ 등록 마감일은 10월 14일이다.
⑤ 개인 레슨은 신청할 수 없다.

29 다음 글의 밑줄 친 부분 중, 어법상 틀린 것은?

In modern times, there is a fundamental disagreement on ① what power should rest in the hands of a powerful executive branch or a more diffuse legislative branch. But, rather than ② seeking to resolve this tension, most democracies have built this split into the structure of government. This results in systems ③ in which a battle for sovereignty manifests in a shifting balance of power between these branches. In the eyes of many, splitting sovereignty this way creates an inherently weak system unable to respond effectively to threats, resulting in a preference for a more autocratic system in which the executive holds untrammeled power. Similarly, perceptions of international sovereignty are split between those who see international ties as ④ invariably necessary and those who believe that they dilute national sovereignty. This division between protectionist views of national sovereignty and internationalist views of the world ⑤ has lately caused some countries to abandon international organizations and treaties, purportedly as a means of protecting national sovereignty.

* untrammeled: 속박 받지 않는

30 다음 글의 밑줄 친 부분 중, 문맥상 낱말의 쓰임이 적절하지 않은 것은? [3점]

Let's say that Tom is a waiter at Lucky Dog. If we know that waiters at Lucky Dog are paid on Monday, it is a ① valid conclusion that Tom will be paid on Monday. But what if we only know that waiters at Lucky Dog are paid on Monday and that Tom is paid on Monday? Is it safe to assume that Tom is a waiter at Lucky Dog? Naturally, this conclusion cannot be ② legitimately drawn from the prior two statements. All we know is that we cannot ③ exclude the possibility that Tom might be a waiter at Lucky Dog. We should also consider that there may be numerous other restaurants that pay their waiters on Monday (and Tom might work at one of them), and there is also a chance that Tom works at Lucky Dog but not as a waiter (maybe as a manager). Our ④ premise does not let us determine whether a manager at Lucky Dog is paid on Monday or not. The mistake we have made by assuming Tom is a waiter at Lucky Dog is in ⑤ rejecting an irrelevant consequence of the two initial conditions.

[31~34] 다음 빈칸에 들어갈 말로 가장 적절한 것을 고르시오.

31

When a person's capacity to make sound moral judgements is limited by time constraints, the individual is more likely to rely on _____ to resolve a dilemma. When time pressures are absent, the decision-making process is allowed room for reflection. This observation presents an opportunity for investigating whether human impulse leads naturally to altruistic inclinations. By presenting study participants with stark moral choices in environments that include or do not include time pressures, psychologists can determine whether a utilitarian view of human nature, in which costs and benefits are analyzed by individuals making a consequential choice, bears merit. A participant who has time to consider all facets of a given situation would presumably be more likely to arrive at a utilitarian conclusion. In contrast, the character of a person who must make an instantaneous judgement call is crystallized, revealing whether the individual's impulses are fundamentally moral or not. Ultimately, the time pressure condition provides a testing ground for discerning whether morality is innate.

① reasoning ② talent
③ instinct ④ wisdom
⑤ precision

32

Vsevolod Meyerhold, who was an actor and theater director, sought to redefine the limits of stage expression with his establishment of biomechanics in the early 1920s. Rather than communicating emotions purely through dramatic dialogue or soliloquies, this system of production relied on exaggerated movements to project ideas and messages. Actors did not perform their roles through words or language but through gestures, poses, and acrobatics, their physical presence being of the utmost importance in theatrical scenes. It was Meyerhold's belief that emotions were _____ _____. This was a departure from realistic or natural renditions, as Meyerhold was focused on distancing theatrical performances from written texts, which he believed had too much influence. His method of acting coupled with simplified sets and costumes ensured that the audience's attention remained on the people who traversed the stage with wild, hyperbolic movements. This would give them a new appreciation for bodily motion in theater and elevate the experience.

* soliloquy: 독백

① demonstrated through writing in a more vivid manner
② felt in a way that could not be conveyed on the stage
③ ignored by audiences in favor of aesthetic qualities
④ expressed most convincingly when voiced aloud
⑤ connected to physiology in a rather direct way

33

Karl Polanyi famously noted in 1944 that the classical model of economics expects actors in the market economy to behave as though they existed in a societal vacuum. In other words, participants in the capitalist system are thought by those in the formalist tradition to behave predictably according to their own narrow self-interest without being influenced by the _____. This fixation on the all-powerful "laws" (unnatural laws,

Polanyi would argue) of demand and supply reduced flesh-and-blood social beings to theoretical constructs, members of the generic species *homo economicus* which existed not in nature but merely in the minds of capitalist economists. To support the idea that economics was inevitably embedded in environment, Polanyi studied primitive economies and found that economic behavior therein was fundamentally dependent upon relationships with others. In these precapitalist societies, land and labor were not economic commodities but dependent on the ties of kinship and community, be they marital inheritances or family birthrights. Money was a useful tool for the exchange of certain goods but hardly the defining paradigm for human behavior. [3점]

* embedded: 묻어 들어 있는, 내재된

① broader contexts of society and culture
② flawless dictates of demand and supply
③ open exchange of land and labor for money
④ economic origins of kinship and community
⑤ theoretical constructs of a capitalist economy

34

About 2.35 billion years ago, the wheels were set in motion to _____ thanks to the evolution of oceanic cyanobacteria. This oceanic organism developed the ability to photosynthesize, causing it to outcompete greenhouse gas-producing heterotrophic bacteria in the struggle for survival. Since a byproduct of photosynthesis is oxygen, Earth's atmosphere — which mostly consisted of carbon dioxide, methane, and nitrogen at the time — began to fill with oxygen. As oxygen was toxic to heterotrophic bacteria, the vast majority were wiped out in Earth's first mass extinction. With less greenhouse gases and more oxygen, it is believed that the metabolic strategies of species began to adapt, paving the way for what would eventually lead to the emergence of organisms with more complicated cellular structures. The increase in oxygen also caused Earth to cool to such an extent that it froze over for 300 million years. The conditions during this period, referred to as Snowball Earth, ended with the eruption of underwater volcanoes, which scientists believe led to the evolution of even more complex organisms. [3점]

* cyanobacteria: 남세균(藍細菌)
** heterotrophic bacteria: 종속 영양 세균

① cause the amount of greenhouse gases in the atmosphere to increase

② change the process of photosynthesis in primitive marine organisms

③ enable the development of multicellular lifeforms on Earth

④ lead to the formation of carbon-rich elements on the planet's surface

⑤ kill off the majority of Earth's oxygen-producing heterotrophic bacteria

35 다음 글에서 전체 흐름과 관계 없는 문장은?

For years, the model for treatment of dementia focused on its capacity to rob patients of their identity. The prevailing view of Alzheimer's disease and other types of dementia was that the patient's inhibited memory and diminished capacity for communication resulted in a loss of personhood, or a fundamental sense of self. ① In the 19th century, age-associated mental decline was seen as a form of insanity, and patients were often institutionalized in mental hospitals, preventing them from seeing the people closest to them. ② Today, the model has shifted toward an emphasis on supporting the patient's continuing status as a whole person. ③ Patients suffering from such health conditions often experience behavioral fluctuations as well as an inability to relate to friends and family normally. ④ The key to the conservation of identity is maintaining relationships. ⑤ By keeping older individuals in contact with family members or caretakers who regard them as people rather than victims of a debilitating disease, their dignity and identity can be preserved.

[36~37] 주어진 글 다음에 이어질 글의 순서로 가장 적절한 것을 고르시오.

36

French sociologist Pierre Bourdieu claimed that cultural capital, or a person's skills, education, and familiarity with different elements of "high culture," contributes to both social mobility and the preservation of social classes.

(A) Children acquire cultural capital from their parents, and this capital is expressed through tastes that distinguish them from people lower in the social order. One such representation of this capital is a person's eating habits, since research has shown that individuals in higher social classes tend to emphasize the importance of quality, health, taste, and ethics in regards to food.

(B) A person can gain cultural capital during their lifetime through formal education in addition to activities such as reading and traveling. It is also passed down in families in an attempt to achieve social reproduction, which is the inheritance of social positioning.

(C) What is served on the dinner table could then be just as important as the topic of discussion or etiquette. All of these components help prove that people of certain social classes have "refined" tastes that cement their positions in society.

① (A) – (C) – (B) ② (B) – (A) – (C)
③ (B) – (C) – (A) ④ (C) – (A) – (B)
⑤ (C) – (B) – (A)

37

Theoretically speaking, there is nothing in physics to rule out time travel. While there are certainly obstacles, they are more logical than physical.

(A) Einstein's theory of relativity shows that it's not; space and time can fold to produce curved time loops. In this case, "nothing counts as right now," opening up the possibility that events we regard as occurring in the present may be happening in the future or in the past.

(B) The most famous is illustrated by the Grandfather Paradox. If you were to travel back in time and kill your grandfather, one of your parents would never have been born. In turn, it is impossible for you to have ever been born either, meaning you could not have traveled back in time to kill your grandfather in the first place.

(C) It points to the logical inconsistencies of time travel. Philosopher Tim Maudlin puts it like this: "In a way, that's like asking why I can't be wet and completely dry at the same time." But Maudlin notes that this defense only holds up if time is definitively restricted to a linear line. [3점]

① (A) – (C) – (B)
② (B) – (A) – (C)
③ (B) – (C) – (A)
④ (C) – (A) – (B)
⑤ (C) – (B) – (A)

[38~39] 글의 흐름으로 보아, 주어진 문장이 들어가기에 가장 적절한 곳을 고르시오.

38

As if an anchor were holding it down, a business without well-defined corporate tactics can never leave this area and rise to the top.

In a competitive market, businesses need to have a clear plan of action in order to stand out. The decisions they make in this regard can mean being successful or getting stuck in a state of mediocrity. (①) Michael Porter identifies three strategies for creating and maintaining a high-performing business: cost leadership, differentiation, and focus. (②) A firm must choose a single one of these approaches to pursue. (③) Attempting to balance all the key elements — with the mindset that it is possible to compromise — is a common mistake many business owners make. (④) Doing such a thing essentially equates to having no strategy at all and can lead to a business getting inextricably lodged in what is known as the "middle." (⑤) Instead, quite frequently, low profitability and the inability of management to take decisive action in response to inevitable changes in consumer demand result in bankruptcy and closure.

39

While many entrenched conflicts have been resolved by dividing a disputed territory into distinct political regions, some areas are regarded as indivisible by one or both sides in a conflict.

Given the enormous costs of war in terms of human suffering and economic security, it is a wonder that two nations ever reach the threshold where violent conflict is worth those costs. (①) History has shown, however, that claims of historical territorial ownership are frequently seen as sufficient grounds to risk staggering losses in blood and treasure that may seem irrational to outside observers. (②) Understanding how these sorts of uncompromising, all-or-nothing demands from engaged parties in a contested region shift to an acceptance of shared or divided sovereignty is essential for avoiding the intolerable costs of violence. (③) The factors that brought about a seemingly enduring peace in Northern Ireland following the 1998 Good Friday Agreement, then, may have significant implications for the ongoing clash between Israelis and Palestinians over ownership of Jerusalem. (④) Under what conditions are claims of historical ownership mitigated by other considerations? (⑤) The answer to that question should determine diplomatic strategies in areas where the costs of violent conflict are deemed to be potentially acceptable losses. [3점]

40 다음 글의 내용을 한 문장으로 요약하고자 한다. 빈칸 (A), (B)에 들어갈 말로 가장 적절한 것은?

In an attempt to better understand why some memories are reinforced while others are lost during sleep, researchers focused on two types of brain wave patterns: slow oscillations and delta waves. During an experiment, rats were trained in a new skill, and then, while they slept, the researchers suppressed wave patterns in their brains before testing the animals' ability to recall the skill the next day. The researchers found that whenever they had targeted slow oscillations, the rats' ability to recall the new skill declined, whereas the opposite was true of delta waves. This has led to the idea that slow oscillations solidify memories and delta waves degrade them — that the two types of brain waves are rival forces determining whether we remember or forget. The researchers had not anticipated that there would be any difference between the roles of the two types of waves; in the past, both varieties had been grouped together since they commonly show up simultaneously. However, their findings suggest that there exists a delicate balance between the two that allows us to retain new information while at the same time clear out memories that are no longer necessary.

* slow oscillation: 서파(徐波)

↓

While trying to understand the factors that determine whether or not a memory is ____(A)____, researchers discovered that two types of brain wave patterns ____(B)____.

	(A)	(B)
①	constructive	fluctuate
②	formed	collaborate
③	strengthened	compete
④	accurate	compromise
⑤	eliminated	adjust

[41~42] 다음 글을 읽고, 물음에 답하시오.

In the 11th century, French poets began writing of *l'amour courtois*, or courtly love. The term introduced the world to the idea that pure romantic love was independent of love within a marriage, which was described as ordinary and base. There was little (a) precedent for this conception of love in other cultures. But, once described, this form of passion swept through French society. Did the emotions that (b) fueled courtly love exist before there were words to describe it? Put differently, does language merely describe our experiences, or does it shape our experience of the world? Proponents of linguistic relativity argue that it does play a formative role; cognitive psychologists prefer to think that language arises from (c) unique human understandings. Those in the former camp would suggest that Germans eat junk food when they get sad because they have a word for it (*kummerspeck*). But in fact, English speakers are also likely intimately acquainted with the impulse to overeat when they are depressed, even though they do not have a word to (d) briefly describe the phenomenon. While the language we speak certainly influences us in that it helps to filter our attention towards certain nuances and details expressed in that language, the idea that it constrains thought is difficult to accept. Even though speakers of different languages may have different cognitive processes when expressing themselves linguistically, there is no evidence to suggest that certain concepts are (e) inaccessible when we lack the words and syntax for them.

* courtly love: 궁정풍 연애

41 윗글의 제목으로 가장 적절한 것은?

① Do All Languages Share a Universal Structure?
② Language and Thought Are Dependent on Each Other
③ Where Words Come From: Exploring Linguistic History
④ The Invention of Love: Poems and Courtly Love
⑤ The Flaws Inherent in Linguistic Relativism

42 밑줄 친 (a)~(e) 중에서 문맥상 낱말의 쓰임이 적절하지 않은 것은? [3점]

① (a) ② (b) ③ (c) ④ (d) ⑤ (e)

[43~45] 다음 글을 읽고, 물음에 답하시오.

(A)

Harry wasn't happy to be spending the weekend with his grandparents in the country. Their small farm was surrounded by nothing but fields and forests, and there wasn't another building for miles. Harry knew he needed to find something to keep him busy during his visit, so (a) he asked his grandfather what he should do. "I think we should go on a walk," he replied. "There are some beautiful hiking trails in this area." Harry thought it sounded boring, but agreed to go anyway.

(B)

"Look at how beautiful it is," Harry's grandfather said. Harry stared out at the vast expanse before him. The bright green valley was full of flowers and seemed to go on forever. Harry was in awe at the sight, and just then noticed how perfectly blue the sky was above them. He looked at his grandfather in shock. "This is incredible," (b) he said. "Thank you for bringing me here." Harry felt a new appreciation for where he was and took his time to take in what was right in front of him for the first time.

(C)

Harry and his grandfather made their way through a thick forest with tall trees and sunlight streaming through the leaves. A small river ran next to their walking path, and, although it was peaceful, Harry barely took notice. He kept checking his phone and messaging his friends who were back in the city. (c) He sighed, wishing he were there instead. "Where are we going?" he asked. Harry's grandfather turned and smiled at him. "You'll see."

(D)

They had been walking for hours now, and eventually began making their way up a large hill. Harry had put (d) his phone away and was sweating with the effort of climbing the steep slope. When they finally reached the top, Harry collapsed onto a large rock. The walk had been exactly what he had expected, and he was glad it was nearly over. He pulled out his phone again and began to play a game as his grandfather took (e) his time to enjoy the view. "Harry, come over here. I want to show you something," he said. Harry reluctantly got up and walked to where his grandfather stood.

43 주어진 글 (A)에 이어질 내용을 순서에 맞게 배열한 것으로 가장 적절한 것은?

① (B) – (D) – (C)   ② (C) – (B) – (D)
③ (C) – (D) – (B)   ④ (D) – (B) – (C)
⑤ (D) – (C) – (B)

44 밑줄 친 (a)~(e) 중에서 가리키는 대상이 나머지 넷과 다른 것은?

① (a)   ② (b)   ③ (c)   ④ (d)   ⑤ (e)

45 윗글에 관한 내용으로 적절하지 않은 것은?

① 할아버지는 Harry에게 함께 산책하자고 말했다.
② Harry는 광활한 풍경을 바라보았다.
③ Harry와 할아버지는 울창한 숲을 통과했다.
④ Harry는 가파른 경사를 오르며 땀을 흘렸다.
⑤ Harry는 언덕 꼭대기에서 휴대폰으로 풍경 사진을 찍었다.

정답·해설·해석 p.135

문제풀이 후 확인사항
1. 45분 내에 문제를 풀었다.
2. 체크해둔 문제와 틀린 문제는 해설을 꼼꼼히 확인했다.

수고하셨습니다! HackersBook.com에서 제공하는 어휘리스트로 어휘를 암기하세요.

15회 고난도 실전모의고사

목표 시간: 45분   시작: ___ 시 ___ 분 ~ 종료: ___ 시 ___ 분   점수: ____ 점 / 63점

* [3점] 표시가 있는 문제 제외하고는 모두 2점으로 계산합니다.

18 다음 글의 목적으로 가장 적절한 것은?

Dear Stephanie,

　It has been a long time. How have you been? I went to your last exhibit at the gallery, and it was wonderful. I know how busy you are, but I was wondering if you could spare some time to create a new art piece for the National Children's Hospital. As you know, I've been renovating the National Children's Hospital for the last year. We are planning to fill one wall of the building with paintings by local artists. I hope that you can add your art to this collaboration. I know everyone would love to see your work along with that of other artists. It would be a great honor for the hospital. Please call me or email me at any time if you want further information about the project.

Your friend,
Lily Myers

---

① 보수 공사로 인한 병원 휴업 기간을 공지하려고
② 어린이 병원 개원식에 지역 주민을 초대하려고
③ 벽을 장식할 예술 작품 제작을 의뢰하려고
④ 어린이를 위한 전시 프로그램을 홍보하려고
⑤ 지역 예술가 작품 공모전의 결과를 통보하려고

19 다음 글에 나타난 Hannah의 심경 변화로 가장 적절한 것은?

　Hannah walked into the lunchroom, looking around at her new classmates nervously. It was her first day at a new school, and she didn't know anyone yet. Everyone was already sitting with their groups of friends, and Hannah was too embarrassed to ask anyone if she could join them. She went to an empty table to sit by herself and sighed. At this rate, she'd never make friends. Just as she began to eat her sandwich, a group of girls sat down around her and asked her name. "Nice to meet you, Hannah. I am Amy. This is Milly, and this is Elena." Soon, they were all laughing together, and Hannah felt a huge sense of relief. They asked Hannah to hang out with them again before they said their goodbyes. As she walked to her next class, Hannah smiled and said, "I think I'm going to like it here after all."

① calm → embarrassed
② anxious → pleased
③ irritated → proud
④ satisfied → confused
⑤ nervous → afraid

20 다음 글에서 필자가 주장하는 바로 가장 적절한 것은?

　Schools often tailor their curricula to facilitate the memorization of facts and information during lessons. This encourages students to think within certain parameters rather than giving them the freedom to explore issues creatively. By limiting their ability to evaluate topics carefully, the current education system is not refining the decision-making skills of students but restricting them, which is detrimental to students' futures. Being pressured to make snap judgments based on rushed lessons and material is not beneficial to students, who will be forced to make significant choices throughout their lives. Therefore, lessons should be approached in a way that fosters critical thinking instead of only encouraging the intake and acceptance of basic information. A curriculum with the aim of helping students consider options thoroughly will give them the necessary skills to make the best judgments for themselves when the time comes. This is not something they should just learn during adulthood but early on in their lives.

① 비판적 사고 함양을 위해 학생 참여형 수업의 비중을 늘려야 한다.
② 학교는 시대의 흐름을 반영한 새로운 교과 과정을 마련해야 한다.
③ 교육은 학생들의 판단 능력을 함양하는 데 초점을 맞춰야 한다.
④ 교육은 학생 개개인의 특성에 맞는 지도를 통해 이루어져야 한다.
⑤ 학생들의 독립성과 자율성을 보장하는 교육 정책을 수립해야 한다.

21 밑줄 친 Making more than ends meet이 다음 글에서 의미하는 바로 가장 적절한 것은? [3점]

Making more than ends meet ensures the prolonged existence of social enterprises that aim to tackle societal issues. Their business model depends on it. But they can't take this too far; if they place too much emphasis on maximizing profit, they risk undermining their own objectives of having an authentic social impact. Social enterprises must then strike a delicate balance of being able to sustain themselves through what they earn while still adhering to their mission. More and more businesses are finding themselves in this precarious situation today as it becomes increasingly important to gain social capital through actually helping communities. In fact, a company's dedication to addressing social challenges is often a factor in determining their success in the modern business climate. Good deeds do not always translate to good business, though, and many social enterprises have a difficult time maintaining operations despite a sterling reputation. According to *The Guardian*, 71 percent of social entrepreneurs "struggle to make a living from a social venture," highlighting the dilemma faced by those pursuing this business model. Their objectives are certainly important, but money is too.

① finding ways to reduce business operating expenses
② receiving good publicity for social contributions
③ generating sufficient revenue to make a profit
④ gaining a positive reputation among the public
⑤ attracting investors through sound business models

22 다음 글의 요지로 가장 적절한 것은?

Ethics define what is acceptable behavior and can help people navigate the gray areas between right and wrong. Different professions and institutions have varying ethical standards that act as a loose set of laws that guide activities and interactions. Various fields even apply these codes of conduct to research in order to cultivate public trust and safeguard the honest acquisition of knowledge. These criteria prevent people from tampering with the research process. If someone publishes false or biased data, steals the work of another researcher, or fails to conduct an experiment following the proper protocols, the advancements made are of no real value. Trust and honesty are imperative in the research process so that real progress is made. This means that credit is given to whomever it is owed to, and that there is mutual respect during collaboration and cooperation between researchers. Protocol must be followed so that the public, along with the academic community, can have confidence in research. Without integrity, nothing real is accomplished.

① 대중의 신뢰 확보가 지속 가능한 학문 발전의 요건이다.
② 학문적 성과에 대한 신뢰는 연구 과정에서 윤리를 준수할 때 확보된다.
③ 균형 잡힌 학문의 발전을 위해 분야간 자유로운 교류를 권장해야 한다.
④ 연구 절차에 관한 윤리는 각 학문의 특성에 맞게 정립되어야 한다.
⑤ 연구자의 부도덕한 행위를 규제하는 사회적 조치가 필요하다.

23 다음 글의 주제로 가장 적절한 것은?

We believe we can perceive the flow of time from the locomotion of the hands of a clock. When we say that time flows, we mean that the present moment flows from the past moment and on into the future. What clocks really measure, though, is not a constant flowing of time but the intervals between events. They measure the distance between birth and death, first love and marriage, breakfast and lunch. We have difficulty seeing this and choose to embrace the illusion of time flowing because our experience of time is purely subjective. From a scientific perspective, there is no evidence that any such flow exists. The illusion is a function of our ability to remember the events of the past in a sequence. Our brain edits what happened to us into a narrative so that we feel like there is a flow. What we learn from our experiences is that a broken glass cannot be reassembled and a cup of tea on a table never becomes hot. The irreversibility of events gives us the impression that time moves in one direction, which is not exactly an attribute of time itself.

* locomotion: 이동

① possible explanations for our flawed conception of time
② influence of clocks in shaping our concept of the present
③ differences between subjective and objective experiences
④ difficulty of proving the existence of time through science
⑤ ability of the brain to construct narratives from imaginary events

24 다음 글의 제목으로 가장 적절한 것은?

Throughout most of history, the evolution of species has been a process over which we humans have had little control, governed by a power higher than ourselves. Natural selection has always had a godlike capacity to create new creatures from old ones. But now, humans are finding ways to steer our own evolution by merging with technology, both physically and mentally. If that sounds like science fiction, consider that the modern prosthetics industry can craft limbs controllable with the human mind. Our smartphones have become an extension of our bodies, measuring our heart rates, sensing when we are awake or asleep, and expanding our mental capacities beyond anything thought possible by Socrates or Plato. Over time, perhaps humanity will continue to integrate technology into our own biology until we evolve into a species that would be utterly unrecognizable to our ancestors. This upgraded version of humanity could eventually have less in common with 21st century man than we have in common with Neanderthals. It's hard to say if the resulting species will be human, but it seems nonetheless inevitable.

① Will Robots Replace Humanity as Technology Advances?
② Blurring the Boundaries Between Humans and Machines
③ How Smartphones Have Come to Dominate Human Civilization
④ The Godlike Power of Nature: A History of the Evolution of Humanity
⑤ The Increasing Pace of Integration with Technology

25 다음 도표의 내용과 일치하지 <u>않는</u> 것은?

Adolescents' Attitudes Towards School Life and Education

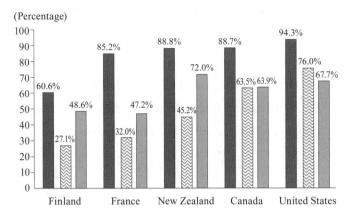

(Percentage)

- ■ Adolescents who want top grades at school
- ▨ Adolescents who expect to complete a university degree
- ▧ Adolescents who feel anxious about school tests even when well-prepared

The graph above shows three indexes regarding adolescents' attitudes towards school life and education in the selected five countries. ① Among the countries in the graph, Finland has the smallest proportion of adolescents who expect to complete a university degree, with 27.1 percent. ② In France, the percentage of adolescents who expect to complete a university degree is less than half of that of adolescents who want top grades at school. ③ The United States is the only country in which the percentage of adolescents who want top grades at school exceeds 90 percent. ④ As for the percentage of adolescents who feel anxious about school tests even when well-prepared, New Zealand ranked first with 72 percent, followed by Canada with 63.9 percent. ⑤ In each of the selected countries, except for the United States, the percentage of adolescents who feel anxious about school tests even when well-prepared is higher than that of adolescents who expect to complete a university degree.

26 Blaise Pascal에 관한 다음 글의 내용과 일치하지 <u>않는</u> 것은?

Blaise Pascal was a 17th-century French scientist, mathematician, and philosopher. His father was highly knowledgeable about math and taught Pascal when he was young. When Pascal was 16 years old, he wrote his first academic article. This work was so sophisticated that some people claimed his father had written it. In 1642, Pascal developed a calculator to help his father with tax collection. Although his calculator was more advanced than any other available at the time, it did not achieve widespread use because of its high cost. From 1646 to 1654, Pascal made important contributions to the field of physics, most notably in areas related to fluid mechanics. However, he became increasingly interested in religion from 1655 onwards, and his writings began to focus more on theology and morality. Pascal died in 1662 following a prolonged illness, but his works continue to influence scholars today.

① 어려서 아버지에게 가르침을 받았다.

② 16세에 처음 학술 논문을 썼다.

③ 1642년 아버지를 돕기 위해 계산기를 발명했다.

④ 물리학 분야에서 중요한 업적을 남겼다.

⑤ 종교에 관심을 가진 후에도 물리학 저술에 집중했다.

27 Coleman Museum's Archaeology Workshops에 관한 다음 안내문의 내용과 일치하지 <u>않는</u> 것은?

Coleman Museum's Archaeology Workshops

This year's workshops will deal with the Roman conquest of the British Isles. Each session will be led by an expert in this field.

Schedule
- Friday, July 15, from 10:00 a.m. to 6:00 p.m.
- A complete list of session topics and times is available at www.coleman.com/workshops.

Location
- Room 201, Coleman Museum Main Building

Registration
- Deadline: June 25
- Fee: $45 (15% discount for university students)
- Contact Denise Miller at 555-3939 to sign up.

Parking
- The $5 daily parking fee will be waived for workshop participants.
- Please request a parking pass at the reception desk when you arrive.

① 해당 분야의 전문가가 진행한다.
② 금요일 오전에 시작된다.
③ 강의 목록은 웹사이트에서 확인할 수 있다.
④ 대학생은 비용 할인이 적용된다.
⑤ 주차권은 나갈 때 요청하면 된다.

28 Norden College English Speech Competition에 관한 다음 안내문의 내용과 일치하는 것은?

Norden College English Speech Competition

Norden College is pleased to announce its fourth annual English Speech Competition. The topic this year will be "The Role of Technology in Social Change." Only students currently enrolled at Norden College are invited to participate.

Venue: Main Hall – Student Services Building
Time and Date: 1:00 p.m. to 6:00 p.m., May 15

Speech Requirements
- Must be entirely in English, completely original, and last six to eight minutes.

Prizes
- First Prize: $150
- Second Prize: $100
- Third Prize: $50

Winners will be announced on the website on May 30. No individual notifications will be made.

Please note: Applications will not be accepted after April 20.

① Norden 지역 주민은 누구나 참가할 수 있다.
② 연설은 10분을 채워야 한다.
③ 1등 상금은 3등 상금의 세 배이다.
④ 수상자는 개별적으로 통보받는다.
⑤ 지원 기한은 5월 15일까지이다.

29 다음 글의 밑줄 친 부분 중, 어법상 틀린 것은?

Serotonin — a brain chemical responsible for transmitting messages between neurons — is believed ① to influence mood and behavior. Higher levels of this "happy chemical" are associated with a more cheerful disposition, while lower levels are conversely connected to symptoms of depression. This relationship first became ② apparent in the 1950s when tuberculosis patients were given the drug *iproniazid* for treatment and subsequently experienced a surprising side effect: elevated moods. It was then discovered ③ that *iproniazid* led to an increase in serotonin due to the fact that it inhibits the normal functioning of the enzyme that breaks the brain chemical down. Medical professionals came to the conclusion that serotonin was inextricably linked to depression in one way or another, and, at the time, this culminated in the development of antidepressants that ④ have targeted this issue. Drugs that impede molecular sponges from absorbing extra neurotransmitters such as serotonin from synapses in the brain ⑤ were generated, and although the validity of the serotonin deficiency theory of depression has been challenged, it unquestionably led to a revolution in the treatment of the condition.

30 다음 글의 밑줄 친 부분 중, 문맥상 낱말의 쓰임이 적절하지 않은 것은?

When one party (the "principal") hires another (the "agent") to act on their behalf, they surrender a certain degree of control with the ① expectation that the other will act in their best interests. In doing so, there are two possible outcomes: the principal will benefit from the work and know-how of the agent or suffer because the agent was ② ineffective or there was a conflict of interests. Known as the principal-agent problem, the dilemma is that there is a risk the agent might ③ disregard his or her own interests. This is possible because the information between both parties is likely to be asymmetrical; the agent tends to know ④ more than the principal, which is why the agent's services are required in the first place. For instance, a lawyer may ⑤ recommend a long and expensive course of action to a potential client — not because it is more likely to result in a better outcome for the client but because it gives the lawyer the chance to make more money in the outcome.

[31~34] 다음 빈칸에 들어갈 말로 가장 적절한 것을 고르시오.

31

Analytical philosophers make the argument that our linguistic descriptions of the world are often vague to the point of uselessness because we have a tendency to conceptualize logical phenomena in terms that are entirely illogical. Let us formulate the hypothesis with the *sorites* paradox: What is a heap? Say you have a heap of sand and remove one grain at a time. Removing a single grain does not make the heap into a non-heap, yet if this process is repeated enough times, at some point, only a single grain will remain. Is the singular grain still a heap? And if not, when did the heap become a non-heap? Within the spectrum of observable phenomena, at some point, the heap of sand constituted a single grain, which is an erroneous conclusion. Thus, the lack of _____ results in a chain of valid arguments that proceeds from a true statement to an obvious falsehood. [3점]

① relevant metaphorical examples
② abstract linguistic descriptions
③ distinction between boundaries
④ repetition of a consistent process
⑤ logical application of thought

32

Marketers often play on the fact that we are innately resistant to extremes in all areas of life and that we feel empowered when we have the ability to choose. That's why employing a marketing technique that offers a number of choices is quite effective; more often than not, we will walk away having purchased something, and much of the time, our choice will have been influenced by the 'Goldilocks Effect', so named for the little girl in the fairy tale who, when presented with choices, opted for selections that were "just right." When presented with three of the same type of product, all with different prices, most of us compare the perceived value of each. We may view the costliest item as too luxurious and the cheapest item as being poor value for money. However, we frequently see the middle item as a product that strikes a good balance between quality and affordability, so we buy it and believe we have reached a rational conclusion, never realizing _____.

① more costly products usually have better features
② our initial selections are typically the best ones
③ we could have easily found a better alternative
④ making a decision requires extensive planning
⑤ our choice was framed by the other options

33

In the process of scientific inquiry, it is inevitable that a dominant theory should sometimes come into conflict with observable fact. The question is not whether a theory is strong enough to avoid such conflicts but how scientists respond when the conflicts arise. To discard a theory instantly upon the discovery of discrepancies between prediction and evidence would be rash. Neither should we dismiss the scientific method as irrational when scientists move from one theory to another upon discovering irregularities in the data. A scientific theory is actually a succession of theories that are refined in response to experimentation. Certainly, paradigm shifts occur when a prevailing theory degenerates over time, but these shifts are not random. Einstein supplants Newton, but first Newton's notion of gravity as an omniscient cosmic force is subjected to numerous experiments revealing that reality aligns with Einstein's view of gravity as a consequence of mass bending space. Both theories are part of the same progression, and neither is wholly discarded. Thus, scientific theories are _____. [3점]

* supplant: 대신하다

① accepted by laypeople who are ignorant of irregularities
② incorporated into the process of scientific inquiry
③ disproved through a process of elimination
④ alternately suggested and dismissed by scientists
⑤ developed by the discovery of conflicting information

34

For centuries, classical mechanics governed physicists' understanding of how objects, such as planets and stars, move within a system. Classical mechanics employs the concept of linearity, which is that effects are proportional to causes. For example, if you were to throw a stone twice as hard as normal, it would travel approximately twice the distance. However, scientists over the last few decades have become aware of a new phenomenon, where unobservable small causes could produce extraordinarily large effects. One such example of this phenomenon is the three-body problem. Unlike linear processes, where if one of the variables were changed a little, the effect would not differ materially, in the three-body problem, a tiny change in a variable could cause a large effect. In essence, the effects are extremely sensitive to the initial conditions that cause them. While these chaotic, non-linear processes are theoretically deterministic, _____. Ultimately, even causes that seem equal can lead to very different effects. [3점]

* linearity: 선형성

① their applications in various disciplines have great potential
② their sensitivities are driven by deterministic forces
③ their outcomes are not dependent on initial conditions
④ their behaviors are actually completely unpredictable
⑤ their results are nearly always consistent with expectations

35 다음 글에서 전체 흐름과 관계 없는 문장은?

Satire in journalism is not meant to be malicious or spread misinformation; it isn't genuine, but it is intended to raise people's awareness about real issues using humor and irony. ① Unlike fake news — information that is created to deliberately deceive people in order to satisfy an agenda — the purpose of satire is to make people laugh, and the factual incorrectness it employs is meant to be understood by audiences. ② Understanding what normal political rhetoric sounds like and being able to recognize exaggeration are key to distinguishing between what is real and what isn't. ③ However, not everyone can tell the difference between the two due to some factors such as declining media literacy and confirmation bias. ④ People are frequently very quick to spread news without checking its credibility simply because a headline may align with their prevailing views. ⑤ Therefore, while satire is not supposed to be taken seriously and can empower audiences to question information and think on their own, it can also be misinterpreted by those who don't get it, thereby shaping public opinion for the worse.

[36~37] 주어진 글 다음에 이어질 글의 순서로 가장 적절한 것을 고르시오.

36

Carbon is required by all living things. Earth is a closed system, which means that the amount of carbon on the planet is always the same, no matter how it is distributed.

(A) To correct this disturbance in the carbon cycle, the amount of carbon released into the atmosphere must be reduced. It would help to slow deforestation as forests can absorb atmospheric carbon. But it is also essential to find alternatives to fossil fuels.

(B) The distribution of carbon, then, becomes imbalanced when underground sediments such as coal and natural gas are burned, releasing carbon into the atmosphere. There, excessive carbon can cause the average temperature of the planet to rise.

(C) The challenge is not removing the amount of carbon on the planet but ensuring that Earth's carbon reservoirs are balanced. Plants and animals, which process carbon through photosynthesis or respiration, represent one reservoir. The sediment underneath Earth's surface, formed when plants and animals decompose, are another reservoir.

* sediment: 퇴적물

① (A) – (C) – (B)   ② (B) – (A) – (C)
③ (B) – (C) – (A)   ④ (C) – (A) – (B)
⑤ (C) – (B) – (A)

37

The votes of state representatives in the Electoral College, rather than those of citizens, are the ones that determine the next president of the United States, although this fact is often overlooked.

(A) Such an idiosyncrasy is becoming harder to ignore as the candidate who won the popular vote lost the election in five of the nation's past general elections. Many presume that the electoral system was the product of meticulous design, but this notion is far from the truth.

(B) The Founding Fathers threw it together at the last minute, and it stopped working as they intended it to almost immediately. And yet, it has remained within the election system because of misguided notions that its inclusion in the Constitution implies it serves an important role in a democratic nation, when in reality it does not.

(C) The current system operates under a winner-take-all rule; whether a candidate wins 100% or 50.1% of the vote in a state, they win the electoral votes for that state. This makes a majority of states safe (they always go for the same party), causing elections to ultimately come down to a handful of "battleground" states that candidates fight over. [3점]

* Electoral College: 선거인단 ** Founding Fathers: 미국 헌법 제정자

① (A) – (C) – (B) ② (B) – (A) – (C)
③ (B) – (C) – (A) ④ (C) – (A) – (B)
⑤ (C) – (B) – (A)

[38~39] 글의 흐름으로 보아, 주어진 문장이 들어가기에 가장 적절한 곳을 고르시오.

38

Some journalists worry about this shift towards individualization since the traditional purpose of the news is to provide citizens with vital information.

A common worry across all industries is the growing prominence of AI and its potential to replace human workers, thereby making various jobs redundant or obsolete. (①) The field of journalism is no exception to this, and with many renowned papers now utilizing AI systems to increase and refine their output, it seems as though technology will only continue to become more fundamental to the journalistic process. (②) These systems are currently limited to interpreting data they're provided with and describing noted patterns, leaving their articles devoid of the personality, wit, and humor that's expressed through the writing of people. (③) AI has allowed papers to cover a wider range of topics, though, and could lead to more personalized coverage for readers in the future, producing stories based on data gathered about readers' interests. (④) This "robot journalism" could even eventually tailor an article for a specific individual, explaining how the information presented relates to that person's own life experiences. (⑤) If papers depend on the preferences of people for their content, they could leave important stories unpublished.

39

Up to that point, it was only possible for one person to view a film at a time.

The very first film contained no action-packed sequences or unexpected twists and turns; instead, it merely showed employees leaving a factory after a long day's work. The movie, which debuted in 1895, was made by Auguste and Louis Lumière and was called *Workers Leaving the Lumière Factory in Lyon*. (①) This was the first of the brothers' "actualités," or "actuality films," which captured scenes involving real people and events, similar to documentaries today. (②) The concept was simple yet groundbreaking. (③) After all, *Workers Leaving the Lumière Factory in Lyon* was the first movie that could be shown to an audience; a feat made possible with the brothers' invention of a device called the Cinematograph. (④) The Cinematograph overcame the limitations of previous technology since it could be used as both a camera and projector. (⑤) The success of *Workers Leaving the Lumière Factory in Lyon* led the brothers to open theaters in London, Brussels, and New York and to send people to shoot scenes of everyday life around the world for audiences to enjoy, jumpstarting cinema as we know it. [3점]

40 다음 글의 내용을 한 문장으로 요약하고자 한다. 빈칸 (A), (B)에 들어갈 말로 가장 적절한 것은?

As diverse as life on Earth is, taxonomy makes understanding and studying such a large range of organisms easier. Plants, animals, and microorganisms are named and classified according to this system, which is based on their form, structure, behavior, and genetic and biochemical analysis. Of the predicted five to thirty million species living on the planet, 1.78 million have been identified and categorized so far. The form of classification most popularly used for this purpose is the Linnaean system, which was established by Swedish naturalist Carolus Linnaeus in the 1750s. It divides organisms into groupings such as kingdom, class, order, and family. Such classification allows people to study the relationships between living things as well as their similarities and differences more efficiently. It also maps plants, animals, and microorganisms out in a way that gives scientists an understanding of all life on Earth, including how and why it has evolved the way it has. This is the key to not only understanding the origin of other species but humankind itself, giving people insight into where they fit in the natural order.

* taxonomy: 분류학

↓

Taxonomy includes the ___(A)___ of plants, animals, and microorganisms into biological categories that help ___(B)___ how all living things are related to one another.

	(A)		(B)
①	unification	······	strengthen
②	arrangement	······	outline
③	illustration	······	demonstrate
④	connection	······	exaggerate
⑤	distribution	······	conceal

[41~42] 다음 글을 읽고, 물음에 답하시오.

The relationship between the artist and the viewer is a sacred bond founded on trust, and the viewer's faith in the sincerity of the artist's intention must be honored for its aesthetic value to be (a) genuine. Imagine that you attend a gallery showing and are struck by the technical proficiency of a Monet painting. You are captivated with the way the intricate brushwork conveys the painter's subjective experience of a landscape, bringing vivid life to a shimmering morning. You spend a sizable portion of your fortune to take the painting home only to learn the next day that it was not, in fact, created by Monet. The work is a forgery.

By commercial standards, the hypothetical counterfeit is considerably (b) less valuable today than it was yesterday. And yet, from an aesthetic standpoint, the skill of the artist is (c) unquestionable. The brush strokes that moved you yesterday still capture the essence of a fleeting moment, even if it was an anonymous watercolorist who experienced the moment and not an established master. However, the supposed intention has altered overnight. Yesterday, the work was designed to capture the truth of a landscape. Today, its painstaking aim was to (d) deceive you. The bond between artist and viewer having been severed, the painting's aesthetic attraction is irreparably marred. The (e) objective purpose of a work is an inextricable element of its aesthetic value.

* forgery: 위작

41 윗글의 제목으로 가장 적절한 것은?

① The Value of Art: Why Good Forgeries Don't Compare to Originals
② The Worthlessness of Authenticity: Forgery as Accomplishment
③ Can Skillful Reproductions Counter Elitism in the Art World?
④ The Reasons Art Appraisal Is Inconsistent and Unreliable
⑤ The Difficulty in Detecting High-Quality Art Forgeries

42 밑줄 친 (a)~(e) 중에서 문맥상 낱말의 쓰임이 적절하지 않은 것은? [3점]

① (a)　　② (b)　　③ (c)　　④ (d)　　⑤ (e)

[43~45] 다음 글을 읽고, 물음에 답하시오.

(A)

As soon as Jane sat down with Louise at the café, she knew something was wrong. Louise was quiet and looked distracted. "Are you okay?" Jane asked. Louise nodded and replied, "I'm just a little worried about the upcoming photography contest. I don't know what to submit." Jane knew that the photography contest was a big deal for Louise and that (a) she wanted to submit the best pictures she possibly could.

(B)

Jane thought about it and said, "Maybe you need to think about making contrast in another way." Louise gave (b) her a puzzled look. "What do you mean?" Jane told her that she could take photographs that showed different subjects to make her pictures more unique. Louise considered her recommendation and said, "That's a good idea, but I still need to figure out what to photograph. (c) I also don't have a lot of time since the pictures are due in only a few days."

(C)

"What about taking some photos around here? We live in the city, but there are parks and trees everywhere," Jane said. "Maybe you should take pictures showing both nature and buildings together." Louise smiled widely at her, knowing that it could work. After they left the café, they walked around so that Louise could take more pictures. Jane noticed that Louise was a lot happier and more confident about her new photos. "These are a lot better," (d) she said, thinking that even if she didn't win the contest, she was finally proud of her work.

(D)

"I don't think any of the photos I've taken are good enough," Louise said sadly. She put a few colorful photographs on the table for them to look over together. They were beautiful, but none of them stood out. "My instructor said that good pictures need contrast," Louise explained. "But all of (e) my photos with different colors and patterns in them look the same. I don't know how else to make contrast." Louise sighed and put her work away.

43 주어진 글 (A)에 이어질 내용을 순서에 맞게 배열한 것으로 가장 적절한 것은?

① (B) – (D) – (C)   ② (C) – (B) – (D)
③ (C) – (D) – (B)   ④ (D) – (B) – (C)
⑤ (D) – (C) – (B)

44 밑줄 친 (a)~(e) 중에서 가리키는 대상이 나머지 넷과 다른 것은?

① (a)   ② (b)   ③ (c)   ④ (d)   ⑤ (e)

45 윗글에 관한 내용으로 적절하지 않은 것은?

① Louise는 다가오는 사진 대회에 관해 걱정했다.
② Jane은 다른 방식으로 사진에 대비를 주라고 말했다.
③ Louise와 Jane은 카페에서 나와 돌아다녔다.
④ Louise는 새로 찍은 사진들이 더 낫다고 여겼다.
⑤ Louise가 찍은 사진들은 흑백이었다.

정답·해설·해석 p.146

문제풀이 후 확인사항
1. 45분 내에 문제를 풀었다.
2. 체크해둔 문제와 틀린 문제는 해설을 꼼꼼히 확인했다.

수고하셨습니다! HACKERSBOOK.com에서 제공하는 어휘리스트로 어휘를 암기하세요.

③교시 영 어 영 역

※ 답안지 작성(표기)은 반드시 컴퓨터용 사인펜을 사용하고, 연필 또는 샤프를 절대 사용하지 마십시오.

결시자 확인 (수험생은 표기하지 말 것)

검은색 컴퓨터용 사인펜을 사용하여 수험번호란과 옆란을 표기	O

※ 문제지 표지에 안내된 필적 확인 문구를 아래 "필적 확인란"에 정자로 반드시 기재하여야 합니다.

필 적 확인란	

성명	

수 험 번 호

문 형

홀수형 O

짝수형 O

※ 문제의 문형을 확인 후 표기

감독관 확인 (수험생은 표기 하지 말 것)

(서명 또는 날 인)	본인여부, 수험번호 및 문형의 표기가 정확한지 확인, 옆란에 서명 또는 날인

문번	답 란	문번	답 란	문번	답 란
1	① ② ③ ④ ⑤	21	① ② ③ ④ ⑤	41	① ② ③ ④ ⑤
2	① ② ③ ④ ⑤	22	① ② ③ ④ ⑤	42	① ② ③ ④ ⑤
3	① ② ③ ④ ⑤	23	① ② ③ ④ ⑤	43	① ② ③ ④ ⑤
4	① ② ③ ④ ⑤	24	① ② ③ ④ ⑤	44	① ② ③ ④ ⑤
5	① ② ③ ④ ⑤	25	① ② ③ ④ ⑤	45	① ② ③ ④ ⑤
6	① ② ③ ④ ⑤	26	① ② ③ ④ ⑤		
7	① ② ③ ④ ⑤	27	① ② ③ ④ ⑤		
8	① ② ③ ④ ⑤	28	① ② ③ ④ ⑤		
9	① ② ③ ④ ⑤	29	① ② ③ ④ ⑤		
10	① ② ③ ④ ⑤	30	① ② ③ ④ ⑤		
11	① ② ③ ④ ⑤	31	① ② ③ ④ ⑤		
12	① ② ③ ④ ⑤	32	① ② ③ ④ ⑤		
13	① ② ③ ④ ⑤	33	① ② ③ ④ ⑤		
14	① ② ③ ④ ⑤	34	① ② ③ ④ ⑤		
15	① ② ③ ④ ⑤	35	① ② ③ ④ ⑤		
16	① ② ③ ④ ⑤	36	① ② ③ ④ ⑤		
17	① ② ③ ④ ⑤	37	① ② ③ ④ ⑤		
18	① ② ③ ④ ⑤	38	① ② ③ ④ ⑤		
19	① ② ③ ④ ⑤	39	① ② ③ ④ ⑤		
20	① ② ③ ④ ⑤	40	① ② ③ ④ ⑤		

✂ 자르는 선

③교시 영 어 영 역

※ 답안지 작성(표기)은 반드시 컴퓨터용 사인펜을 사용하고, 연필 또는 샤프를 절대 사용하지 마십시오.

결시자 확인 (수험생은 표기하지 말 것)

검은색 컴퓨터용 사인펜을 사용하여 수험번호란과 옆란을 표기	O

※ 문제지 표지에 안내된 필적 확인 문구를 아래 "필적 확인란"에 정자로 반드시 기재하여야 합니다.

필 적 확인란	

성명	

수 험 번 호

문 형

홀수형 O

짝수형 O

※ 문제의 문형을 확인 후 표기

감독관 확인 (수험생은 표기 하지 말 것)

(서명 또는 날 인)	본인여부, 수험번호 및 문형의 표기가 정확한지 확인, 옆란에 서명 또는 날인

문번	답 란	문번	답 란	문번	답 란
1	① ② ③ ④ ⑤	21	① ② ③ ④ ⑤	41	① ② ③ ④ ⑤
2	① ② ③ ④ ⑤	22	① ② ③ ④ ⑤	42	① ② ③ ④ ⑤
3	① ② ③ ④ ⑤	23	① ② ③ ④ ⑤	43	① ② ③ ④ ⑤
4	① ② ③ ④ ⑤	24	① ② ③ ④ ⑤	44	① ② ③ ④ ⑤
5	① ② ③ ④ ⑤	25	① ② ③ ④ ⑤	45	① ② ③ ④ ⑤
6	① ② ③ ④ ⑤	26	① ② ③ ④ ⑤		
7	① ② ③ ④ ⑤	27	① ② ③ ④ ⑤		
8	① ② ③ ④ ⑤	28	① ② ③ ④ ⑤		
9	① ② ③ ④ ⑤	29	① ② ③ ④ ⑤		
10	① ② ③ ④ ⑤	30	① ② ③ ④ ⑤		
11	① ② ③ ④ ⑤	31	① ② ③ ④ ⑤		
12	① ② ③ ④ ⑤	32	① ② ③ ④ ⑤		
13	① ② ③ ④ ⑤	33	① ② ③ ④ ⑤		
14	① ② ③ ④ ⑤	34	① ② ③ ④ ⑤		
15	① ② ③ ④ ⑤	35	① ② ③ ④ ⑤		
16	① ② ③ ④ ⑤	36	① ② ③ ④ ⑤		
17	① ② ③ ④ ⑤	37	① ② ③ ④ ⑤		
18	① ② ③ ④ ⑤	38	① ② ③ ④ ⑤		
19	① ② ③ ④ ⑤	39	① ② ③ ④ ⑤		
20	① ② ③ ④ ⑤	40	① ② ③ ④ ⑤		

영어 실력을 높여주는 다양한 학습 자료 제공

HackersBook.com

03회 실전모의고사

③교시 영어영역

결시자 확인 (수험생은 표기하지 말 것)

검은색 컴퓨터용 사인펜을 사용하여 수험번호란과 옆란을 표기	O

※ 문제지 표지에 안내된 필적 확인 문구를 아래 "필적 확인란" 에 정자로 반드시 기재하여야 합니다.

필 적 확인란	

성명	

수 험 번 호

문 형

홀수형 O

짝수형 O

※ 문제의 문형을 확인 후 표기

감독관 확 인 (수험생은 표기 하지 말 것)

(서명 또는 날 인)	본인여부, 수험번호 및 문형 의 표기가 정확한지 확인, 옆 란에 서명 또는 날인

※ 답안지 작성(표기)은 반드시 컴퓨터용 사인펜을 사용하고, 연필 또는 샤프를 절대 사용하지 마십시오.

문번	답 란	문번	답 란	문번	답 란
1	① ② ③ ④ ⑤	21	① ② ③ ④ ⑤	41	① ② ③ ④ ⑤
2	① ② ③ ④ ⑤	22	① ② ③ ④ ⑤	42	① ② ③ ④ ⑤
3	① ② ③ ④ ⑤	23	① ② ③ ④ ⑤	43	① ② ③ ④ ⑤
4	① ② ③ ④ ⑤	24	① ② ③ ④ ⑤	44	① ② ③ ④ ⑤
5	① ② ③ ④ ⑤	25	① ② ③ ④ ⑤	45	① ② ③ ④ ⑤
6	① ② ③ ④ ⑤	26	① ② ③ ④ ⑤		
7	① ② ③ ④ ⑤	27	① ② ③ ④ ⑤		
8	① ② ③ ④ ⑤	28	① ② ③ ④ ⑤		
9	① ② ③ ④ ⑤	29	① ② ③ ④ ⑤		
10	① ② ③ ④ ⑤	30	① ② ③ ④ ⑤		
11	① ② ③ ④ ⑤	31	① ② ③ ④ ⑤		
12	① ② ③ ④ ⑤	32	① ② ③ ④ ⑤		
13	① ② ③ ④ ⑤	33	① ② ③ ④ ⑤		
14	① ② ③ ④ ⑤	34	① ② ③ ④ ⑤		
15	① ② ③ ④ ⑤	35	① ② ③ ④ ⑤		
16	① ② ③ ④ ⑤	36	① ② ③ ④ ⑤		
17	① ② ③ ④ ⑤	37	① ② ③ ④ ⑤		
18	① ② ③ ④ ⑤	38	① ② ③ ④ ⑤		
19	① ② ③ ④ ⑤	39	① ② ③ ④ ⑤		
20	① ② ③ ④ ⑤	40	① ② ③ ④ ⑤		

✂ 자르는 선

04회 실전모의고사

③교시 영어영역

결시자 확인 (수험생은 표기하지 말 것)

검은색 컴퓨터용 사인펜을 사용하여 수험번호란과 옆란을 표기	O

※ 문제지 표지에 안내된 필적 확인 문구를 아래 "필적 확인란" 에 정자로 반드시 기재하여야 합니다.

필 적 확인란	

성명	

수 험 번 호

문 형

홀수형 O

짝수형 O

※ 문제의 문형을 확인 후 표기

감독관 확 인 (수험생은 표기 하지 말 것)

(서명 또는 날 인)	본인여부, 수험번호 및 문형 의 표기가 정확한지 확인, 옆 란에 서명 또는 날인

※ 답안지 작성(표기)은 반드시 컴퓨터용 사인펜을 사용하고, 연필 또는 샤프를 절대 사용하지 마십시오.

문번	답 란	문번	답 란	문번	답 란
1	① ② ③ ④ ⑤	21	① ② ③ ④ ⑤	41	① ② ③ ④ ⑤
2	① ② ③ ④ ⑤	22	① ② ③ ④ ⑤	42	① ② ③ ④ ⑤
3	① ② ③ ④ ⑤	23	① ② ③ ④ ⑤	43	① ② ③ ④ ⑤
4	① ② ③ ④ ⑤	24	① ② ③ ④ ⑤	44	① ② ③ ④ ⑤
5	① ② ③ ④ ⑤	25	① ② ③ ④ ⑤	45	① ② ③ ④ ⑤
6	① ② ③ ④ ⑤	26	① ② ③ ④ ⑤		
7	① ② ③ ④ ⑤	27	① ② ③ ④ ⑤		
8	① ② ③ ④ ⑤	28	① ② ③ ④ ⑤		
9	① ② ③ ④ ⑤	29	① ② ③ ④ ⑤		
10	① ② ③ ④ ⑤	30	① ② ③ ④ ⑤		
11	① ② ③ ④ ⑤	31	① ② ③ ④ ⑤		
12	① ② ③ ④ ⑤	32	① ② ③ ④ ⑤		
13	① ② ③ ④ ⑤	33	① ② ③ ④ ⑤		
14	① ② ③ ④ ⑤	34	① ② ③ ④ ⑤		
15	① ② ③ ④ ⑤	35	① ② ③ ④ ⑤		
16	① ② ③ ④ ⑤	36	① ② ③ ④ ⑤		
17	① ② ③ ④ ⑤	37	① ② ③ ④ ⑤		
18	① ② ③ ④ ⑤	38	① ② ③ ④ ⑤		
19	① ② ③ ④ ⑤	39	① ② ③ ④ ⑤		
20	① ② ③ ④ ⑤	40	① ② ③ ④ ⑤		

영어 실력을 높여주는 다양한 학습 자료 제공

HackersBook.com

문번	답 란		문번	답 란		문번	답 란
1	① ② ③ ④ ⑤		21	① ② ③ ④ ⑤		41	① ② ③ ④ ⑤
2	① ② ③ ④ ⑤		22	① ② ③ ④ ⑤		42	① ② ③ ④ ⑤
3	① ② ③ ④ ⑤		23	① ② ③ ④ ⑤		43	① ② ③ ④ ⑤
4	① ② ③ ④ ⑤		24	① ② ③ ④ ⑤		44	① ② ③ ④ ⑤
5	① ② ③ ④ ⑤		25	① ② ③ ④ ⑤		45	① ② ③ ④ ⑤
6	① ② ③ ④ ⑤		26	① ② ③ ④ ⑤			
7	① ② ③ ④ ⑤		27	① ② ③ ④ ⑤			
8	① ② ③ ④ ⑤		28	① ② ③ ④ ⑤			
9	① ② ③ ④ ⑤		29	① ② ③ ④ ⑤			
10	① ② ③ ④ ⑤		30	① ② ③ ④ ⑤			
11	① ② ③ ④ ⑤		31	① ② ③ ④ ⑤			
12	① ② ③ ④ ⑤		32	① ② ③ ④ ⑤			
13	① ② ③ ④ ⑤		33	① ② ③ ④ ⑤			
14	① ② ③ ④ ⑤		34	① ② ③ ④ ⑤			
15	① ② ③ ④ ⑤		35	① ② ③ ④ ⑤			
16	① ② ③ ④ ⑤		36	① ② ③ ④ ⑤			
17	① ② ③ ④ ⑤		37	① ② ③ ④ ⑤			
18	① ② ③ ④ ⑤		38	① ② ③ ④ ⑤			
19	① ② ③ ④ ⑤		39	① ② ③ ④ ⑤			
20	① ② ③ ④ ⑤		40	① ② ③ ④ ⑤			

✂ 자르는 선

문번	답 란		문번	답 란		문번	답 란
1	① ② ③ ④ ⑤		21	① ② ③ ④ ⑤		41	① ② ③ ④ ⑤
2	① ② ③ ④ ⑤		22	① ② ③ ④ ⑤		42	① ② ③ ④ ⑤
3	① ② ③ ④ ⑤		23	① ② ③ ④ ⑤		43	① ② ③ ④ ⑤
4	① ② ③ ④ ⑤		24	① ② ③ ④ ⑤		44	① ② ③ ④ ⑤
5	① ② ③ ④ ⑤		25	① ② ③ ④ ⑤		45	① ② ③ ④ ⑤
6	① ② ③ ④ ⑤		26	① ② ③ ④ ⑤			
7	① ② ③ ④ ⑤		27	① ② ③ ④ ⑤			
8	① ② ③ ④ ⑤		28	① ② ③ ④ ⑤			
9	① ② ③ ④ ⑤		29	① ② ③ ④ ⑤			
10	① ② ③ ④ ⑤		30	① ② ③ ④ ⑤			
11	① ② ③ ④ ⑤		31	① ② ③ ④ ⑤			
12	① ② ③ ④ ⑤		32	① ② ③ ④ ⑤			
13	① ② ③ ④ ⑤		33	① ② ③ ④ ⑤			
14	① ② ③ ④ ⑤		34	① ② ③ ④ ⑤			
15	① ② ③ ④ ⑤		35	① ② ③ ④ ⑤			
16	① ② ③ ④ ⑤		36	① ② ③ ④ ⑤			
17	① ② ③ ④ ⑤		37	① ② ③ ④ ⑤			
18	① ② ③ ④ ⑤		38	① ② ③ ④ ⑤			
19	① ② ③ ④ ⑤		39	① ② ③ ④ ⑤			
20	① ② ③ ④ ⑤		40	① ② ③ ④ ⑤			

07회 실전모의고사

③ 교시 영 어 영 역

결시자 확인 (수험생은 표기하지 말 것)

| 검은색 컴퓨터용 사인펜을 사용하여 수험번호란과 옆란을 표기 | O |

※ 문제지 표지에 안내된 필적 확인 문구를 아래 "필적 확인란"에 정자로 반드시 기재하여야 합니다.

필 적 확인란

성명

수 험 번 호

문 형

홀수형 O
짝수형 O

※ 문제의 문형을 확인 후 표기

감독관 확인 (수험생은 표기하지 말 것)

(서명 또는 날인)

본인여부, 수험번호 및 문형의 표기가 정확한지 확인, 옆란에 서명 또는 날인

※ 답안지 작성(표기)은 반드시 컴퓨터용 사인펜을 사용하고, 연필 또는 샤프를 절대 사용하지 마십시오.

문번	답 란
1	① ② ③ ④ ⑤
2	① ② ③ ④ ⑤
3	① ② ③ ④ ⑤
4	① ② ③ ④ ⑤
5	① ② ③ ④ ⑤
6	① ② ③ ④ ⑤
7	① ② ③ ④ ⑤
8	① ② ③ ④ ⑤
9	① ② ③ ④ ⑤
10	① ② ③ ④ ⑤
11	① ② ③ ④ ⑤
12	① ② ③ ④ ⑤
13	① ② ③ ④ ⑤
14	① ② ③ ④ ⑤
15	① ② ③ ④ ⑤
16	① ② ③ ④ ⑤
17	① ② ③ ④ ⑤
18	① ② ③ ④ ⑤
19	① ② ③ ④ ⑤
20	① ② ③ ④ ⑤

문번	답 란
21	① ② ③ ④ ⑤
22	① ② ③ ④ ⑤
23	① ② ③ ④ ⑤
24	① ② ③ ④ ⑤
25	① ② ③ ④ ⑤
26	① ② ③ ④ ⑤
27	① ② ③ ④ ⑤
28	① ② ③ ④ ⑤
29	① ② ③ ④ ⑤
30	① ② ③ ④ ⑤
31	① ② ③ ④ ⑤
32	① ② ③ ④ ⑤
33	① ② ③ ④ ⑤
34	① ② ③ ④ ⑤
35	① ② ③ ④ ⑤
36	① ② ③ ④ ⑤
37	① ② ③ ④ ⑤
38	① ② ③ ④ ⑤
39	① ② ③ ④ ⑤
40	① ② ③ ④ ⑤

문번	답 란
41	① ② ③ ④ ⑤
42	① ② ③ ④ ⑤
43	① ② ③ ④ ⑤
44	① ② ③ ④ ⑤
45	① ② ③ ④ ⑤

✂ 자르는 선

08회 실전모의고사

③ 교시 영 어 영 역

결시자 확인 (수험생은 표기하지 말 것)

| 검은색 컴퓨터용 사인펜을 사용하여 수험번호란과 옆란을 표기 | O |

※ 문제지 표지에 안내된 필적 확인 문구를 아래 "필적 확인란"에 정자로 반드시 기재하여야 합니다.

필 적 확인란

성명

수 험 번 호

문 형

홀수형 O
짝수형 O

※ 문제의 문형을 확인 후 표기

감독관 확인 (수험생은 표기하지 말 것)

(서명 또는 날인)

본인여부, 수험번호 및 문형의 표기가 정확한지 확인, 옆란에 서명 또는 날인

※ 답안지 작성(표기)은 반드시 컴퓨터용 사인펜을 사용하고, 연필 또는 샤프를 절대 사용하지 마십시오.

문번	답 란
1	① ② ③ ④ ⑤
2	① ② ③ ④ ⑤
3	① ② ③ ④ ⑤
4	① ② ③ ④ ⑤
5	① ② ③ ④ ⑤
6	① ② ③ ④ ⑤
7	① ② ③ ④ ⑤
8	① ② ③ ④ ⑤
9	① ② ③ ④ ⑤
10	① ② ③ ④ ⑤
11	① ② ③ ④ ⑤
12	① ② ③ ④ ⑤
13	① ② ③ ④ ⑤
14	① ② ③ ④ ⑤
15	① ② ③ ④ ⑤
16	① ② ③ ④ ⑤
17	① ② ③ ④ ⑤
18	① ② ③ ④ ⑤
19	① ② ③ ④ ⑤
20	① ② ③ ④ ⑤

문번	답 란
21	① ② ③ ④ ⑤
22	① ② ③ ④ ⑤
23	① ② ③ ④ ⑤
24	① ② ③ ④ ⑤
25	① ② ③ ④ ⑤
26	① ② ③ ④ ⑤
27	① ② ③ ④ ⑤
28	① ② ③ ④ ⑤
29	① ② ③ ④ ⑤
30	① ② ③ ④ ⑤
31	① ② ③ ④ ⑤
32	① ② ③ ④ ⑤
33	① ② ③ ④ ⑤
34	① ② ③ ④ ⑤
35	① ② ③ ④ ⑤
36	① ② ③ ④ ⑤
37	① ② ③ ④ ⑤
38	① ② ③ ④ ⑤
39	① ② ③ ④ ⑤
40	① ② ③ ④ ⑤

문번	답 란
41	① ② ③ ④ ⑤
42	① ② ③ ④ ⑤
43	① ② ③ ④ ⑤
44	① ② ③ ④ ⑤
45	① ② ③ ④ ⑤

09회 실전모의고사

③교시 영어 영역

※ 답안지 작성(표기)은 반드시 컴퓨터용 사인펜을 사용하고, 연필 또는 샤프를 절대 사용하지 마십시오.

결시자 확인 (수험생은 표기하지 말 것)

검은색 컴퓨터용 사인펜을 사용하여 수험번호란과 옆란을 표기   O

※ 문제지 표지에 안내된 필적 확인 문구를 아래 "필적 확인란"에 정자로 반드시 기재하여야 합니다.

필 적 확인란

성명

수 험 번 호

문 형
- 홀수형 O
- 짝수형 O

※ 문제의 문형을 확인 후 표기

감독관 확인 (수험생은 표기하지 말 것)

(서명 또는 날 인)

본인여부, 수험번호 및 문형의 표기가 정확한지 확인, 옆란에 서명 또는 날인

문번	답란	문번	답란	문번	답란
1	① ② ③ ④ ⑤	21	① ② ③ ④ ⑤	41	① ② ③ ④ ⑤
2	① ② ③ ④ ⑤	22	① ② ③ ④ ⑤	42	① ② ③ ④ ⑤
3	① ② ③ ④ ⑤	23	① ② ③ ④ ⑤	43	① ② ③ ④ ⑤
4	① ② ③ ④ ⑤	24	① ② ③ ④ ⑤	44	① ② ③ ④ ⑤
5	① ② ③ ④ ⑤	25	① ② ③ ④ ⑤	45	① ② ③ ④ ⑤
6	① ② ③ ④ ⑤	26	① ② ③ ④ ⑤		
7	① ② ③ ④ ⑤	27	① ② ③ ④ ⑤		
8	① ② ③ ④ ⑤	28	① ② ③ ④ ⑤		
9	① ② ③ ④ ⑤	29	① ② ③ ④ ⑤		
10	① ② ③ ④ ⑤	30	① ② ③ ④ ⑤		
11	① ② ③ ④ ⑤	31	① ② ③ ④ ⑤		
12	① ② ③ ④ ⑤	32	① ② ③ ④ ⑤		
13	① ② ③ ④ ⑤	33	① ② ③ ④ ⑤		
14	① ② ③ ④ ⑤	34	① ② ③ ④ ⑤		
15	① ② ③ ④ ⑤	35	① ② ③ ④ ⑤		
16	① ② ③ ④ ⑤	36	① ② ③ ④ ⑤		
17	① ② ③ ④ ⑤	37	① ② ③ ④ ⑤		
18	① ② ③ ④ ⑤	38	① ② ③ ④ ⑤		
19	① ② ③ ④ ⑤	39	① ② ③ ④ ⑤		
20	① ② ③ ④ ⑤	40	① ② ③ ④ ⑤		

✂ 자르는 선

10회 실전모의고사

③교시 영어 영역

※ 답안지 작성(표기)은 반드시 컴퓨터용 사인펜을 사용하고, 연필 또는 샤프를 절대 사용하지 마십시오.

결시자 확인 (수험생은 표기하지 말 것)

검은색 컴퓨터용 사인펜을 사용하여 수험번호란과 옆란을 표기   O

※ 문제지 표지에 안내된 필적 확인 문구를 아래 "필적 확인란"에 정자로 반드시 기재하여야 합니다.

필 적 확인란

성명

수 험 번 호

문 형
- 홀수형 O
- 짝수형 O

※ 문제의 문형을 확인 후 표기

감독관 확인 (수험생은 표기하지 말 것)

(서명 또는 날 인)

본인여부, 수험번호 및 문형의 표기가 정확한지 확인, 옆란에 서명 또는 날인

문번	답란	문번	답란	문번	답란
1	① ② ③ ④ ⑤	21	① ② ③ ④ ⑤	41	① ② ③ ④ ⑤
2	① ② ③ ④ ⑤	22	① ② ③ ④ ⑤	42	① ② ③ ④ ⑤
3	① ② ③ ④ ⑤	23	① ② ③ ④ ⑤	43	① ② ③ ④ ⑤
4	① ② ③ ④ ⑤	24	① ② ③ ④ ⑤	44	① ② ③ ④ ⑤
5	① ② ③ ④ ⑤	25	① ② ③ ④ ⑤	45	① ② ③ ④ ⑤
6	① ② ③ ④ ⑤	26	① ② ③ ④ ⑤		
7	① ② ③ ④ ⑤	27	① ② ③ ④ ⑤		
8	① ② ③ ④ ⑤	28	① ② ③ ④ ⑤		
9	① ② ③ ④ ⑤	29	① ② ③ ④ ⑤		
10	① ② ③ ④ ⑤	30	① ② ③ ④ ⑤		
11	① ② ③ ④ ⑤	31	① ② ③ ④ ⑤		
12	① ② ③ ④ ⑤	32	① ② ③ ④ ⑤		
13	① ② ③ ④ ⑤	33	① ② ③ ④ ⑤		
14	① ② ③ ④ ⑤	34	① ② ③ ④ ⑤		
15	① ② ③ ④ ⑤	35	① ② ③ ④ ⑤		
16	① ② ③ ④ ⑤	36	① ② ③ ④ ⑤		
17	① ② ③ ④ ⑤	37	① ② ③ ④ ⑤		
18	① ② ③ ④ ⑤	38	① ② ③ ④ ⑤		
19	① ② ③ ④ ⑤	39	① ② ③ ④ ⑤		
20	① ② ③ ④ ⑤	40	① ② ③ ④ ⑤		

11회 실전모의고사

③교시 영어 영역

※ 답안지 작성(표기)은 반드시 컴퓨터용 사인펜을 사용하고, 연필 또는 샤프를 절대 사용하지 마십시오.

문번	답 란
1	① ② ③ ④ ⑤
2	① ② ③ ④ ⑤
3	① ② ③ ④ ⑤
4	① ② ③ ④ ⑤
5	① ② ③ ④ ⑤
6	① ② ③ ④ ⑤
7	① ② ③ ④ ⑤
8	① ② ③ ④ ⑤
9	① ② ③ ④ ⑤
10	① ② ③ ④ ⑤
11	① ② ③ ④ ⑤
12	① ② ③ ④ ⑤
13	① ② ③ ④ ⑤
14	① ② ③ ④ ⑤
15	① ② ③ ④ ⑤
16	① ② ③ ④ ⑤
17	① ② ③ ④ ⑤
18	① ② ③ ④ ⑤
19	① ② ③ ④ ⑤
20	① ② ③ ④ ⑤

문번	답 란
21	① ② ③ ④ ⑤
22	① ② ③ ④ ⑤
23	① ② ③ ④ ⑤
24	① ② ③ ④ ⑤
25	① ② ③ ④ ⑤
26	① ② ③ ④ ⑤
27	① ② ③ ④ ⑤
28	① ② ③ ④ ⑤
29	① ② ③ ④ ⑤
30	① ② ③ ④ ⑤
31	① ② ③ ④ ⑤
32	① ② ③ ④ ⑤
33	① ② ③ ④ ⑤
34	① ② ③ ④ ⑤
35	① ② ③ ④ ⑤
36	① ② ③ ④ ⑤
37	① ② ③ ④ ⑤
38	① ② ③ ④ ⑤
39	① ② ③ ④ ⑤
40	① ② ③ ④ ⑤

문번	답 란
41	① ② ③ ④ ⑤
42	① ② ③ ④ ⑤
43	① ② ③ ④ ⑤
44	① ② ③ ④ ⑤
45	① ② ③ ④ ⑤

✂ 자르는 선

12회 실전모의고사

③교시 영어 영역

※ 답안지 작성(표기)은 반드시 컴퓨터용 사인펜을 사용하고, 연필 또는 샤프를 절대 사용하지 마십시오.

문번	답 란
1	① ② ③ ④ ⑤
2	① ② ③ ④ ⑤
3	① ② ③ ④ ⑤
4	① ② ③ ④ ⑤
5	① ② ③ ④ ⑤
6	① ② ③ ④ ⑤
7	① ② ③ ④ ⑤
8	① ② ③ ④ ⑤
9	① ② ③ ④ ⑤
10	① ② ③ ④ ⑤
11	① ② ③ ④ ⑤
12	① ② ③ ④ ⑤
13	① ② ③ ④ ⑤
14	① ② ③ ④ ⑤
15	① ② ③ ④ ⑤
16	① ② ③ ④ ⑤
17	① ② ③ ④ ⑤
18	① ② ③ ④ ⑤
19	① ② ③ ④ ⑤
20	① ② ③ ④ ⑤

문번	답 란
21	① ② ③ ④ ⑤
22	① ② ③ ④ ⑤
23	① ② ③ ④ ⑤
24	① ② ③ ④ ⑤
25	① ② ③ ④ ⑤
26	① ② ③ ④ ⑤
27	① ② ③ ④ ⑤
28	① ② ③ ④ ⑤
29	① ② ③ ④ ⑤
30	① ② ③ ④ ⑤
31	① ② ③ ④ ⑤
32	① ② ③ ④ ⑤
33	① ② ③ ④ ⑤
34	① ② ③ ④ ⑤
35	① ② ③ ④ ⑤
36	① ② ③ ④ ⑤
37	① ② ③ ④ ⑤
38	① ② ③ ④ ⑤
39	① ② ③ ④ ⑤
40	① ② ③ ④ ⑤

문번	답 란
41	① ② ③ ④ ⑤
42	① ② ③ ④ ⑤
43	① ② ③ ④ ⑤
44	① ② ③ ④ ⑤
45	① ② ③ ④ ⑤

③교시 영 어 영 역

※ 답안지 작성(표기)은 반드시 컴퓨터용 사인펜을 사용하고, 연필 또는 샤프를 절대 사용하지 마십시오.

결시자 확인 (수험생은 표기하지 말 것)

검은색 컴퓨터용 사인펜을 사용하여 수험번호란과 옆란을 표기	O

※ 문제지 표지에 안내된 필적 확인 문구를 아래 "필적 확인란"에 정자로 반드시 기재하여야 합니다.

필 적 확인란	

성명	

수 험 번 호

문 형

홀수형 O

짝수형 O

※ 문제의 문형을 확인 후 표기

감독관 확인 (수험생은 표기하지 말 것)	(서명 또는 날 인)	본인여부, 수험번호 및 문형의 표기가 정확한지 확인, 옆란에 서명 또는 날인

문번	답란		문번	답란		문번	답란
1	① ② ③ ④ ⑤		21	① ② ③ ④ ⑤		41	① ② ③ ④ ⑤
2	① ② ③ ④ ⑤		22	① ② ③ ④ ⑤		42	① ② ③ ④ ⑤
3	① ② ③ ④ ⑤		23	① ② ③ ④ ⑤		43	① ② ③ ④ ⑤
4	① ② ③ ④ ⑤		24	① ② ③ ④ ⑤		44	① ② ③ ④ ⑤
5	① ② ③ ④ ⑤		25	① ② ③ ④ ⑤		45	① ② ③ ④ ⑤
6	① ② ③ ④ ⑤		26	① ② ③ ④ ⑤			
7	① ② ③ ④ ⑤		27	① ② ③ ④ ⑤			
8	① ② ③ ④ ⑤		28	① ② ③ ④ ⑤			
9	① ② ③ ④ ⑤		29	① ② ③ ④ ⑤			
10	① ② ③ ④ ⑤		30	① ② ③ ④ ⑤			
11	① ② ③ ④ ⑤		31	① ② ③ ④ ⑤			
12	① ② ③ ④ ⑤		32	① ② ③ ④ ⑤			
13	① ② ③ ④ ⑤		33	① ② ③ ④ ⑤			
14	① ② ③ ④ ⑤		34	① ② ③ ④ ⑤			
15	① ② ③ ④ ⑤		35	① ② ③ ④ ⑤			
16	① ② ③ ④ ⑤		36	① ② ③ ④ ⑤			
17	① ② ③ ④ ⑤		37	① ② ③ ④ ⑤			
18	① ② ③ ④ ⑤		38	① ② ③ ④ ⑤			
19	① ② ③ ④ ⑤		39	① ② ③ ④ ⑤			
20	① ② ③ ④ ⑤		40	① ② ③ ④ ⑤			

✂ 자르는 선

③교시 영 어 영 역

※ 답안지 작성(표기)은 반드시 컴퓨터용 사인펜을 사용하고, 연필 또는 샤프를 절대 사용하지 마십시오.

결시자 확인 (수험생은 표기하지 말 것)

검은색 컴퓨터용 사인펜을 사용하여 수험번호란과 옆란을 표기	O

※ 문제지 표지에 안내된 필적 확인 문구를 아래 "필적 확인란"에 정자로 반드시 기재하여야 합니다.

필 적 확인란	

성명	

수 험 번 호

문 형

홀수형 O

짝수형 O

※ 문제의 문형을 확인 후 표기

감독관 확인 (수험생은 표기하지 말 것)	(서명 또는 날 인)	본인여부, 수험번호 및 문형의 표기가 정확한지 확인, 옆란에 서명 또는 날인

문번	답란		문번	답란		문번	답란
1	① ② ③ ④ ⑤		21	① ② ③ ④ ⑤		41	① ② ③ ④ ⑤
2	① ② ③ ④ ⑤		22	① ② ③ ④ ⑤		42	① ② ③ ④ ⑤
3	① ② ③ ④ ⑤		23	① ② ③ ④ ⑤		43	① ② ③ ④ ⑤
4	① ② ③ ④ ⑤		24	① ② ③ ④ ⑤		44	① ② ③ ④ ⑤
5	① ② ③ ④ ⑤		25	① ② ③ ④ ⑤		45	① ② ③ ④ ⑤
6	① ② ③ ④ ⑤		26	① ② ③ ④ ⑤			
7	① ② ③ ④ ⑤		27	① ② ③ ④ ⑤			
8	① ② ③ ④ ⑤		28	① ② ③ ④ ⑤			
9	① ② ③ ④ ⑤		29	① ② ③ ④ ⑤			
10	① ② ③ ④ ⑤		30	① ② ③ ④ ⑤			
11	① ② ③ ④ ⑤		31	① ② ③ ④ ⑤			
12	① ② ③ ④ ⑤		32	① ② ③ ④ ⑤			
13	① ② ③ ④ ⑤		33	① ② ③ ④ ⑤			
14	① ② ③ ④ ⑤		34	① ② ③ ④ ⑤			
15	① ② ③ ④ ⑤		35	① ② ③ ④ ⑤			
16	① ② ③ ④ ⑤		36	① ② ③ ④ ⑤			
17	① ② ③ ④ ⑤		37	① ② ③ ④ ⑤			
18	① ② ③ ④ ⑤		38	① ② ③ ④ ⑤			
19	① ② ③ ④ ⑤		39	① ② ③ ④ ⑤			
20	① ② ③ ④ ⑤		40	① ② ③ ④ ⑤			

15회 고난도 실전모의고사

③교시 영 어 영 역

※ 답안지 작성(표기)은 반드시 컴퓨터용 사인펜을 사용하고, 연필 또는 샤프를 절대 사용하지 마십시오.

결시자 확인 (수험생은 표기하지 말 것)

| 검은색 컴퓨터용 사인펜을 사용하여 수험번호란과 옆란을 표기 | O |

※ 문제지 표지에 안내된 필적 확인 문구를 아래 "필적 확인란"
 에 정자로 반드시 기재하여야 합니다.

필 적 확인란

성명

수 험 번 호

문 형

홀수형 O
짝수형 O

※ 문제의 문형을 확인 후 표기

감독관 확인 (수험생은 표기하지 말 것)

(서명 또는 날 인)

본인여부, 수험번호 및 문형의 표기가 정확한지 확인, 옆란에 서명 또는 날인

문번	답 란
1	① ② ③ ④ ⑤
2	① ② ③ ④ ⑤
3	① ② ③ ④ ⑤
4	① ② ③ ④ ⑤
5	① ② ③ ④ ⑤
6	① ② ③ ④ ⑤
7	① ② ③ ④ ⑤
8	① ② ③ ④ ⑤
9	① ② ③ ④ ⑤
10	① ② ③ ④ ⑤
11	① ② ③ ④ ⑤
12	① ② ③ ④ ⑤
13	① ② ③ ④ ⑤
14	① ② ③ ④ ⑤
15	① ② ③ ④ ⑤
16	① ② ③ ④ ⑤
17	① ② ③ ④ ⑤
18	① ② ③ ④ ⑤
19	① ② ③ ④ ⑤
20	① ② ③ ④ ⑤

문번	답 란
21	① ② ③ ④ ⑤
22	① ② ③ ④ ⑤
23	① ② ③ ④ ⑤
24	① ② ③ ④ ⑤
25	① ② ③ ④ ⑤
26	① ② ③ ④ ⑤
27	① ② ③ ④ ⑤
28	① ② ③ ④ ⑤
29	① ② ③ ④ ⑤
30	① ② ③ ④ ⑤
31	① ② ③ ④ ⑤
32	① ② ③ ④ ⑤
33	① ② ③ ④ ⑤
34	① ② ③ ④ ⑤
35	① ② ③ ④ ⑤
36	① ② ③ ④ ⑤
37	① ② ③ ④ ⑤
38	① ② ③ ④ ⑤
39	① ② ③ ④ ⑤
40	① ② ③ ④ ⑤

문번	답 란
41	① ② ③ ④ ⑤
42	① ② ③ ④ ⑤
43	① ② ③ ④ ⑤
44	① ② ③ ④ ⑤
45	① ② ③ ④ ⑤

- - - - ✂ 자르는 선 - - - - - - - - - - - - - - - - - - -

해커스 수능 독해 불변의 패턴 실전편

③교시 영 어 영 역

※ 답안지 작성(표기)은 반드시 컴퓨터용 사인펜을 사용하고, 연필 또는 샤프를 절대 사용하지 마십시오.

결시자 확인 (수험생은 표기하지 말 것)

| 검은색 컴퓨터용 사인펜을 사용하여 수험번호란과 옆란을 표기 | O |

※ 문제지 표지에 안내된 필적 확인 문구를 아래 "필적 확인란"
 에 정자로 반드시 기재하여야 합니다.

필 적 확인란

성명

수 험 번 호

문 형

홀수형 O
짝수형 O

※ 문제의 문형을 확인 후 표기

감독관 확인 (수험생은 표기하지 말 것)

(서명 또는 날 인)

본인여부, 수험번호 및 문형의 표기가 정확한지 확인, 옆란에 서명 또는 날인

문번	답 란
1	① ② ③ ④ ⑤
2	① ② ③ ④ ⑤
3	① ② ③ ④ ⑤
4	① ② ③ ④ ⑤
5	① ② ③ ④ ⑤
6	① ② ③ ④ ⑤
7	① ② ③ ④ ⑤
8	① ② ③ ④ ⑤
9	① ② ③ ④ ⑤
10	① ② ③ ④ ⑤
11	① ② ③ ④ ⑤
12	① ② ③ ④ ⑤
13	① ② ③ ④ ⑤
14	① ② ③ ④ ⑤
15	① ② ③ ④ ⑤
16	① ② ③ ④ ⑤
17	① ② ③ ④ ⑤
18	① ② ③ ④ ⑤
19	① ② ③ ④ ⑤
20	① ② ③ ④ ⑤

문번	답 란
21	① ② ③ ④ ⑤
22	① ② ③ ④ ⑤
23	① ② ③ ④ ⑤
24	① ② ③ ④ ⑤
25	① ② ③ ④ ⑤
26	① ② ③ ④ ⑤
27	① ② ③ ④ ⑤
28	① ② ③ ④ ⑤
29	① ② ③ ④ ⑤
30	① ② ③ ④ ⑤
31	① ② ③ ④ ⑤
32	① ② ③ ④ ⑤
33	① ② ③ ④ ⑤
34	① ② ③ ④ ⑤
35	① ② ③ ④ ⑤
36	① ② ③ ④ ⑤
37	① ② ③ ④ ⑤
38	① ② ③ ④ ⑤
39	① ② ③ ④ ⑤
40	① ② ③ ④ ⑤

문번	답 란
41	① ② ③ ④ ⑤
42	① ② ③ ④ ⑤
43	① ② ③ ④ ⑤
44	① ② ③ ④ ⑤
45	① ② ③ ④ ⑤

MEMO

MEMO

수능 1등급을 완성하는 독해 실전서

해커스 수능 독해 불변의 패턴 실전편

초판 2쇄 발행 2022년 7월 4일
초판 1쇄 발행 2022년 4월 28일

지은이	해커스 어학연구소
펴낸곳	㈜해커스 어학연구소
펴낸이	해커스 어학연구소 출판팀

주소	서울특별시 서초구 강남대로61길 23 ㈜해커스 어학연구소
고객센터	02-566-0001
교재 관련 문의	publishing@hackers.com
	해커스북 사이트(HackersBook.com) 고객센터 Q&A 게시판
동영상강의	HackersBook.com

ISBN	978-89-6542-467-3 (53740)
Serial Number	01-02-01

한국 브랜드선호도 교육그룹 1위,
해커스북 HackersBook.com

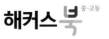

· 효과적인 단어 암기를 돕는 **어휘리스트** 및 **어휘테스트**
· 교재 내 수록된 모든 단어의 출제가 가능한 **단어시험지 제작 프로그램**

한경비즈니스 선정 2019 한국 브랜드선호도 교육(교육그룹) 부문 1위

가장 쉽고 효율적인 영단어 암기법!

해커스 보카
암기 트레이너

✓ **카드, 퀴즈학습** 중 골라서 영단어 암기!

✓ 암기한 **단어 체크**하고,
   나만의 단어장으로 추가 복습까지!

해커스 보카
암기 트레이너
바로가기 ▶

점수
올려주는

해커스
보카

암기 트레이너

inconvenience

+ 암기 할래요   ··· 뜻 보기   ✓ 암기 했어요

**암기했는지 선택해서
단어 암기 완료하기**

불편(한 것/사람)
~에게 불편함을 주다

inconvenience

trouble

disrupt

**영/한 단어를
보고 뜻 맞추기**

카드학습

영단어 카드를 뒤집어
뜻을 확인하고 암기 여부 확인!

퀴즈게임

영한 제시어를 보고
정답을 찾는 퀴즈게임

수능 1등급을 완성하는 독해 실전서

해커스
수능독해
불변의 패턴

실전편 | 정답 및 해설

해커스
수능독해
불변의
패턴

실전편 | 정답 및 해설

■ 해커스 어학연구소

01회 / 실전모의고사

정답

18	③	19	①	20	②	21	⑤	22	③	23	③	24	⑤	25 ④	26 ③	27 ③

문제집 p.14

18	③	19	①	20	②	21	⑤	22	③	23	③	24	⑤	25	④	26	③	27	③
28	④	29	②	30	④	31	①	32	⑤	33	②	34	④	35	③	36	②	37	④
38	④	39	④	40	③	41	⑤	42	③	43	④	44	②	45	④				

18 목적 파악하기
정답 ③

(해설) 글의 중간 이후에서 중고 물품점의 고객들에게 옷을 업사이클링하는 방법에 대한 주 1회 수업이 시작될 것임을 알려주고 있으므로, 정답은 ③이다.

(해석) 소중한 고객님들께,

이곳 Used Threads에서, 저희는 손님들께 다양한 종류의 중고 물품을 제공해드리는 것에 대해 항상 자부심을 느껴왔습니다. 재활용되는 옷을 구매함으로써, 고객님들은 독특한 것들을 구할 뿐만 아니라, 환경을 보호하는 것을 돕습니다. 이제, 저희는 한 걸음 더 나아가고 싶고, 이것이 바로 저희가 옷을 업사이클하는 방법에 대한 주 1회 수업을 시작하는 이유입니다. 이 수업들은 무료이고 토요일마다 오후 3시부터 4시까지 열릴 것입니다. 이 수업 동안, 저희는 고객님들께 바느질과 염색과 같은 방법들로 오래된 옷을 완전히 바꿔놓는 방법을 가르쳐드릴 것입니다. 만약 수업에 참여하는 것에 관심 있으시면, 자리가 한정되어 있기 때문에 적어도 하루 전에 미리 제게 이메일을 보내주십시오. 여러분들을 그곳에서 만나 뵙기를 바랍니다!

Used Threads 매니저 Ari Kim 드림

(어휘) pride oneself on ~에 대해 자부심을 느끼다
upcycle 업사이클하다, 더 나은 것으로 만들다   transform 완전히 바꿔놓다

(구문분석) [6행] Now, we'd like to go a step further, which is [why we are
                                         동사
launching weekly classes about (how to upcycle clothing)].
                            주격 보어

→ [why ~ clothing]은 의문사 why가 이끄는 명사절로, be동사 is의 주격 보어 역할을 한다.

→ (how ~ clothing)은 '~하는 방법'이라는 의미의 'how + to부정사' 구문이다.

19 심경 파악하기
정답 ①

(해설) 심경은 간접적으로 표현된다. 글의 초반부의 Searching for an escape ~ down her back을 통해 어두운 집 안에서 무서워하는 Sarah의 모습을, 후반부의 it made her tremble, Screaming for help를 통해 현관에서 누군가를 발견하고 그에게서 도망치면서 불안함이 극에 달한 Sarah의 심경을 느낄 수 있으므로, Sarah의 심경으로 가장 적절한 것은 ①이다.

(해석) Sarah의 눈은 그녀를 둘러싼 어둠에 적응하려 애쓰며, 그녀는 그 집에서 조용히 앞으로 나아갔다. 탈출할 길이나, 그녀 자신을 지키기 위해 사용할 수 있는 무언가를 찾으면서, 그녀는 자신의 심장 박동이 쿵쾅거리는 것을 가슴에서 느낄 수 있었다. 모든 작은 소리에도, 그녀의 근육은 긴장했다. 등에는 땀이 흘러내렸다. Sarah는 마침내 현관을 발견할 수 있겠다고 생각했지만, 그 앞에 어떤 사람이 서 있다는 것을 알았을 때 숨이 막혔다. 그의 얼굴이 선명하지는

않았지만, Sarah는 그것이 누구인지 알았고 그것은 그녀를 떨리게 했다. 그 사람은 소리를 내지 않았지만 갑자기 그녀 쪽으로 움직였다. 도와달라고 소리지르면서, Sarah는 몸을 돌려 뛰었고 복도를 따라 전속력으로 달렸다. 그녀는 이제 그녀가 달리 할 수 있는 것이 거의 없다는 것을 알았다.

① 불안하고 겁에 질린
② 짜증 나고 화가 난
③ 신이 나고 열광적인
④ 기쁘고 만족한
⑤ 지루하고 외로운

(어휘) adjust to ~에 적응하다   tense up 긴장하다
gasp (놀람 등으로) 숨 막히다, 헐떡거리다   feature 얼굴, 이목구비

(구문분석) [1행] **Sarah** quietly made her way through the house, [**her
eyes** trying to adjust to the darkness that surrounded her].

→ [her eyes ~ her]는 분사구문의 주어(her eyes)와 주절의 주어(Sarah)가 달라서, 분사구문의 주어를 생략하지 않은 형태이다.

[3행] [Searching for an escape route or something she
could use to defend herself], **she** could feel her heartbeat
hammering in her chest.

→ [Searching ~ herself]는 '~하면서'라는 의미의 분사구문으로, 분사구문의 주어가 주절의 주어(she)와 같아서 생략되었다.

20 주장 파악하기
정답 ②

(해설) 글의 첫 세 문장에서 의견을 구성하기 위해서 정확한 정보에 근거한 사실에만 의존함으로써 문제에 대한 좀 더 정확한 관점을 발달시켜야 한다고 주장하고 있으므로 정답은 ②이다.

(해석) 사회의 현재 상태를 생각할 때, 많은 사람들은 상황이 악화되고 있고 우리가 위기에 직면하고 있다고 생각한다. 하지만, 이것이 정말로 사실인가? 사람들은 그들의 의견을 구성하기 위해서 사실에만 의존함으로써 좀 더 정확한 관점을 발달시켜야 한다. 물론, 무서운 사건들에 집중하는 것은 타고난 인간의 본성이다. 이것이 바로 사람들이 대개 다른 종류의 보도보다 살인과 같은 심각한 범죄에 대한 뉴스 소식을 더 쉽게 기억하는 이유이다. 하지만, 이러한 내면의 필터는 폭력적인 행위들이 점점 더 빈번하게 발생하고 있다는 인상을 쉽게 갖게 할 수 있다. 그 문제의 진실은 그것들이 과거보다 현재 덜 흔하다는 것이다; 실제로, 미국의 살인율은 지난 30년 동안 거의 50퍼센트 감소했다. 따라서, "내 생각들이 정확한 정보에 근거하는가?"를 항상 묻는 것이 중요하다.

(어휘) deteriorate 악화되다, 저하하다   rely 의존하다   instinct 본성, 본능
with frequency 빈번하게

구문분석 [11행] The truth of the matter is [that they are less common now than in the past]; ~

주어 / 동사 / 주격 보어

→ [that ~ past]는 접속사 that이 이끄는 명사절로, be동사 is의 주격 보어 역할을 한다.

---

21 밑줄 의미 추론하기　　　정답 ⑤

해설 이전에는 인류학자들이 객관성을 위해 그들이 경험할 수 없었던 문화들을 중점적으로 연구했지만, 이제는 그들 자신이 속한 사회들에 대한 지식을 확대하기 위해 인류학적 기법들을 이용해 연구하기 시작했다고 말하고 있다. 따라서 글의 주제를 비유적으로 표현한 flip the lens(렌즈를 뒤집다)가 의미하는 것은 ⑤ '그들 자신을 다른 사람들과 동일한 면밀한 조사 아래에 두는 것'이다.

오답분석 ①은 글의 핵심 어구 study와 culture를 사용하여 헷갈리게 하는 오답이다. ③은 동일한 관점으로 다른 대상들을 본다고 한 글의 내용과 반대되는 내용이므로 오답이다.

해석 최근 몇 년 동안, 많은 인류학자들이 렌즈를 뒤집기로 했다. 이 분야의 역사의 대부분 동안, 서구 국가들의 연구자들은 그들이 경험할 수 없었던 문화들에 대한 연구에만 중점을 두었다. "객관적인" 제3자가 되는 것이 관찰되고 있는 사회에 대한 정확한 결론을 도출하는 최선의 방법이라고 여겨졌다. 하지만, 이제는 일부 연구자들은 그들 자신이 일원으로 있는 사회들에 대한 지식을 확대하기 위해 인류학적 기법들을 이용하기 시작했다. 유명한 인류학자인 Gillian Tett(질리언 텟)은 기업들을 더 잘 이해하기 위해 이 학문의 관행들을 이용하기로 했는데, 그녀는 금융 분야에 몰두하기 위해 인류학의 틀을 이용했고 "이 이상하고 잘 알려지지 않은 세계에서 위험이 형성되고 있었다"라는 결론에 이르렀다. 인류학자들이 좀 더 "색다른" 것들을 연구할 때 통상적으로 얻으려고 노력하는 동일한 정도의 중립성으로 그녀 자신의 문화의 한 측면을 보려는 의지 때문에, Tett은 2008년의 금융 위기를 정확하게 예측한 소수의 사람들 중 한 명이었다.

① 문화를 연구할 때 다양한 기법들을 쓰는 것
② 그들 자신들의 직종 외의 전문가들에게서 조언을 구하는 것
③ 다른 관점으로 동일한 대상들을 보는 것
④ 좀 더 자세한 예측을 하기 위해 정보를 분석하는 것
⑤ 그들 자신을 다른 사람들과 동일한 면밀한 조사 아래에 두는 것

어휘 anthropologist 인류학자　flip 뒤집다　discipline 학문, 규율　framework 틀, 구성　immerse 몰두하게 하다　banking sector 금융 분야　shadowy 잘 알려지지 않은　neutrality 중립(성)　exotic 색다른, 이국적인　[선택지] profession 직종, 직업

구문분석 [7행] Now, however, some researchers **have begun** ①[to utilize anthropological techniques] ②[to increase their knowledge] of the societies that they themselves are a part of.

→ ①[to ~ techniques]는 to부정사의 명사적 용법(~하기)으로 동사 have begun의 목적어 역할을 하고, ②[to ~ knowledge]는 to부정사의 부사적 용법으로 목적을 의미한다.

[15행] Because of her willingness to view an aspect of her own culture with the same level of **neutrality** [that anthropologists traditionally strive for (when studying more "exotic" **ones**)], ~

→ [that ~ ones]는 선행사 neutrality를 수식하며, 목적격 관계대명사 that이 이끄는 관계대명사절이다.

→ (when ~ ones)는 분사구문의 의미를 분명하게 하기 위해 부사절 접속사 when이 분사 앞에 온 형태이다.

→ ones는 cultures 대신 쓰인 대명사이다.

---

22 요지 파악하기　　　정답 ③

해설 글의 마지막 두 문장으로 미루어 보아 기업 내 의미 있는 혁신은 분명하게 정의된 목표들, 경영진의 광범위한 지원, 진행 상태를 평가할 제도 등의 체계에서 나온다는 내용의 글이므로, 이 글의 요지로 가장 적절한 것은 ③이다.

오답분석 ①은 글의 일부만을 다루고 있기 때문에 오답이다. ⑤는 자율성이 반드시 혁신을 불러일으키지는 않는다는 글의 내용과 반대되는 내용이므로 오답이다.

해석 기업 내 혁신은 폭넓은 직원 자율성의 결과라는 일반적인 가정이 있다. 소비자들의 마음을 사로잡을 획기적인 애플리케이션을 만들고 싶어하는 소프트웨어 회사를 상상해보아라. 이 목표를 이루기 위해, 그 회사는 최고의 개발자들 중 몇몇을 그들의 현재 프로젝트에서 내보내기로 하고 그들이 제한 없이 여러 가지 아이디어들을 탐구하게 할 수도 있다. 기대에 반해서, 이러한 자유를 부여하는 것은 반드시 그들의 창의성을 자극하거나 획기적인 아이디어를 낳지는 않을 것이다. 의미 있는 혁신의 핵심은 체계이고, 직원들은 분명하게 정의된 목표들, 경영진의 광범위한 지원, 진행 상태를 평가할 제도가 필요하다. 이 모든 것은 성공적인 제품으로 발전할 가능성이 있는 모든 콘셉트를 효과적으로 실행할 기반을 마련하기 위해서뿐만 아니라, 만들어지고 있는 아이디어가 실용적이며 회사의 사업 모델에 적합한지를 확실히 하기 위해서 필수적이다.

어휘 assumption 가정　extensive 폭넓은, 광범위한　autonomy 자율(성), 자치　groundbreaking 획기적인　breakthrough 획기적인, 대발명의　execute 실행하다

구문분석 [1행] There is **a common assumption** [that innovation in business is the result of extensive employee autonomy].

→ [that ~ autonomy]는 a common assumption과 동격을 이루는 명사절이다.

[3행] Imagine **a software company** [that hopes to create **groundbreaking applications** (that will capture the imagination of consumers)].

→ [that hopes ~ consumers]와 (that will ~ consumers)는 각각 선행사 a software company와 groundbreaking applications를 수식하며, 주격 관계대명사 that이 이끄는 관계대명사절이다.

[8행] ~ granting this freedom will **not necessarily** stimulate their creativity ~

→ not necessarily는 '반드시 ~은 아닌'이라는 의미로 부분 부정을 나타내는 구문이다.

---

23 주제 파악하기　　　정답 ③

해설 글의 마지막 문장으로 미루어 보아 목소리의 어조와 비언어적 감탄사를 통해 감정들을 구별할 수 있고 모든 소리 내는 감정의 표출은 인식 가능한 감정과 서로 관련된다는 내용의 글로, <American Psychologist>에 게재된 연구 결과를 예를 들어 설명하고 있다. 따라서 이 글의 주제로 가장 적절한 것은 ③ '감정을 구별하는 데 있어 음성 단서의 역할'이다.

(오답분석) ①은 글의 핵심 내용을 바꿔 표현한 to identify truthful statements를 사용했지만 '방법'에 대해서는 언급되지 않았으므로 오답이다. ②은 목소리의 어조와 비언어적 감탄사를 통해 감정들을 식별할 수 있다는 글의 주제와 반대되는 내용이기 때문에 오답이다. ④은 글의 핵심 어구 non-verbal을 사용하여 헷갈리게 하는 오답이다. ⑤은 발성의 범주(종류)에 대해서는 언급되지 않았으므로 오답이다.

(해석) 당신은 우울함을 느끼는데도 친구에게 "모든 게 다 좋다"고 말한 적이 있는가? 아마 당신 목소리의 느낌, 그리고 어쩌면 한숨이 당신의 비밀을 드러내고 당신의 친구에게 당신 발언의 진실성을 확신시키지 못했을 것이다. <American Psychologist>에 게재된 연구 결과에 따르면, 최대 24가지의 감정들이 목소리의 어조와 소리 내는 감정의 표출이라고 알려진 비언어적 감탄사에서 해독 가능하다. 그것들은 놀람(숨이 멎음)과 깨달음(오오)에서부터 관심(어?)과 당혹(허?)에 이르는 복잡한 감정들을 드러낼 수 있다. 그 연구에서, 2천 개가 넘는 소리 내는 감정의 표출이 전 세계의 배우들에 의해 녹음되었고 그리고 나서 온라인에서 모집된 사람들에게 평가되었다. 그 후에 모든 소리 내는 감정의 표출은 인식 가능한 감정과 연관성이 있는 것으로 분류되었다. 이는 우리가 자신의 소리 내는 감정의 표출을 인지하든 안 하든, 다른 사람들은 그것들을 알아차리고 식별할 수 있다는 것을 보여주어, 우리의 감정들은 꾸며내기 어렵다는 것을 시사한다.

① 진실된 발언을 식별하는 효과적인 방법
② 대화 중에 감정을 숨기는 능력
③ 감정을 구별하는 데 있어 음성 단서의 역할
④ 언어적 발화 대비 비언어적인 발화의 이점
⑤ 감정을 표현하는 데에 사용되는 발성의 범주

(어휘) give A away (A의 비밀을) 드러내다   decipherable 해독 가능한
exclamation 감탄사   vocal 소리 내는, 음성의   burst 감정의 표출
pick up on ~을 알아차리다   fake 꾸며내다; 가짜의
[선택지] conceal 숨기다, 감추다   cue 단서, 신호   sentiment 감정, 정서
utterance 발화, 표현함   vocalization 발성

(구문분석)
[15행] This shows that, ①[whether we are aware of our own vocal bursts or not], others pick up on them and can identify them, suggesting that our feelings are difficult ②[to fake].

→ ①[whether ~ not]은 whether ~ or not(~하든 안 하든)이 이끄는 양보의 부사절이다.
→ ②[to fake]는 to부정사의 부사적 용법으로, 형용사 difficult의 의미를 한정한다.

24 제목 파악하기   정답 ⑤

(해설) 온라인에서 사진, 영상, 예술품 등에 대한 소유권 증명서 기능을 하는 디지털 토큰인 NFT에 대해 설명하는 글이다. 아직 NFT를 관리하는 규제가 없어 저작권상의 위험이 있고, 이는 허가 없이 저작권 보호를 받는 자료를 사용하는 것과 유사하다고 설명하고 있다. 따라서 글의 제목으로 가장 적절한 것은 ⑤ 'NFT: 새로운 개념, 늘 똑같은 위험'이다.

(오답분석) ①은 글의 핵심 소재 NFTs를 사용하여 헷갈리게 하는 오답이다. ②은 글의 일부만을 다루고 있는 오답이다. ③은 글에서 언급된 Blockchain을 사용하여 헷갈리게 하는 오답이다. ④은 글에서 언급되고 있지 않다.

(해석) NFT, 즉 대체 불가능한 토큰은 온라인에서 구매되고 팔리며, 사진, 영상, 예술품과 같이 현실에 존재하는 것들을 나타내는 디지털 토큰이다. NFT는 그러한 물건들에 대한 소유권 증명서의 기능을 하고, 이러한 토큰은 복제될 수 없는데, 이는 그러한 증명서가 교환 불가능하고 한 번에 한 명의 소유주만이 있

을 수 있다는 것을 의미한다. 비록 많은 NFT가 비싸지만, 그것들을 구매하는 것은 빠르게 인기를 얻고 있는데, 그들의 구매가 블록체인에 표시되면서 그렇게 하는 것(구매하는 것)이 수집가들에게 그 작품과의 유일하고 특별한 관계성을 부여하기 때문이다. 하지만, NFT의 제작과 판매를 관리하는 규제가 현재 없기 때문에, 그것들과 관련된 저작권상의 위험이 있다. 이는 "주조"라고도 알려진 과정인, 저작권 소유자뿐만 아니라 누구나 블록체인에서 특정 물건에 대한 토큰을 발행하여 그 NFT를 시장에 내놓을 수 있다는 사실 때문이다. 이는 예술가들이 그들의 허가 없이 그들의 작품에 대해 만들어진 NFT를 발견할 가능성이 있다는 것을 의미하는데, 이는 허가받지 않고 당신의 작품에 저작권 보호를 받는 자료를 사용하는 것과 유사하다.

① NFT가 온라인 시장에서 어떻게 혁신을 일으키고 있는가
② 저작권 보호가 블록체인에서 있을 수 있는가?
③ 블록체인 기술의 증가하는 인기
④ 온라인 콘텐츠를 도용하는 것의 법적 영향
⑤ NFT: 새로운 개념, 늘 똑같은 위험

(어휘) fungible 대체 가능한   token 토큰, 표시   certificate 증명서, 자격(증)
duplicate 복제하다   copyright 저작권   mint (화폐를) 주조하다; 조폐국
comparable 유사한, 비교할 만한   [선택지] revolutionize 혁신을 일으키다
repercussion 영향

(구문분석)
[9행] ~ gives a collector a unique and special connection to the work, [with their purchase being marked on a blockchain].
        명사구   과거분사 수동형

→ [with ~ blockchain]은 'with + 명사(구) + 분사' 형태의 분사구문으로, '~하면서'라는 의미로 해석한다.

25 도표 정보 파악하기   정답 ④

(해설) 2006년의 제품 생산 부문의 특허 수의 순위는 4위이고 2016년은 5위로, 순위가 동일한 것이 아니라 낮아졌으므로, 수치의 비교 표현이 잘못 반영되었다. 따라서 도표의 내용과 일치하지 않는 것은 ④이다.

(해석)
미국에서 승인된 환경 관련 특허

2006년		2016년	
부문	특허 (수)	부문	특허 (수)
교통	2,590	에너지	3,390
환경 관리	2,410	환경 관리	2,690
에너지	2,280	교통	2,140
제품 생산	1,100	건축물	1,320
건축물	1,090	제품 생산	1,300
폐기물	270	폐기물	390
온실가스	110	온실가스	200
합계	9,930	합계	11,240

* 참고: 반올림으로 인해 세부 항목들이 제시된 합계에 더해지지 않을 수도 있음

위의 표는 2006년과 2016년에 미국에서 승인된 7개 부문의 환경 관련 특허의 수를 보여준다. ① 2016년에 승인된 환경 관련 특허의 총계는 2006년에 부여된 수보다 더 많았다. ② 2006년에 받은 특허에 관하여 상위 2개 부문은 교통과 환경 관리였다. ③ 반면에, 2016년에는 에너지 부문에 부여된 특허의 수가 7개 부문들 중에서 가장 많았다. ④ 제품 생산 부문에 승인된 특허의 수는 2006년에서 2016년으로 갈 때 증가했지만, 그것의 순위는 동일했다. ⑤ 2016년에, 폐기물과 온실가스 부문에 부여된 특허를 합친 수는 제품 생산 부문에 부여된 특허의 수의 절반보다 더 적었다.

(어휘) grant 승인하다, 부여하다   greenhouse gas 온실가스
rounding 반올림; 어림수의   in terms of ~에 관하여

구문
분석

[12행] In 2016, the combined number of patents received by the Waste and Greenhouse Gas segments was [less than] half of the number of patents received by the Production of Goods segment.

→ [less than]은 '비교급 + than'(~보다 -한)의 형태로 비교를 나타내는 구문이다.

- 오전 10시 - 오후 12시: 웹 디자인
- 오후 12시 - 오후 1시 30분: 점심시간
- 오후 1시 30분 - 오후 5시: 웹 개발

수업이 끝날 무렵에는, 여러분들은 자신만의 웹사이트를 제작했을 것입니다.

등록 방법: 11월 10일까지 www.websitemaker.org로 방문하시거나 515-888-2121로 전화하십시오.

문의 사항은, faq@websitemaker.org로 이메일을 보내주십시오.

---

26 세부 정보 파악하기 정답 ③

해설 she met Édouard Manet and the two cultivated a close working relationship에서 Berthe Morisot가 Édouard Manet와 긴밀한 작업 관계를 쌓았다는 것을 알 수 있는데, ③은 Édouard Manet와 긴밀한 관계가 아니었다고 일부 정보를 잘못 나타냈으므로 글의 내용과 일치하지 않는 것은 ③이다.

해석 Berthe Morisot(베르트 모리조)는 1841년에 프랑스 부르주아 한 부유한 가정에서 태어났다. 어린 나이부터, 그녀의 어머니는 예술에 대한 진지한 교육을 장려했다. Morisot 또한 그녀의 예술 진로를 진지하게 생각했고 그것을 기꺼이 추구했다. 그녀는 Louvre 박물관에서 명작들을 모사함으로써 그녀의 기량을 발전시켰고, 유명한 화가인 Jean-Baptiste-Camille Corot (장 밥티스트 카미유 코로)에게 가르침을 받아 더 발전했다. 1868년에, 그녀는 Édouard Manet(에두아르 마네)를 만났고, 그 둘은 긴밀한 작업 관계를 쌓았다. Manet와, Edgar Degas(에드가 드가), Claude Monet(클로드 모네), 그리고 Pierre-Auguste Renoir(피에르 오귀스트 르누아르)와 같은 당대의 다른 인상주의 화가들과 함께, Morisot는 파리 살롱에서 정기적인 전시들을 열었다. 그녀는 작품에서 그녀가 묘사한 근대성의 주제에 대해 널리 인정을 받았다. 그녀는 1895년, 54세의 나이에 폐렴으로 사망했을 때까지 계속해서 그림을 그렸다.

어휘 cultivate 쌓다, 일구다 modernity 근대성, 현대적임 pneumonia 폐렴

구문
분석

[12행] She achieved widespread recognition for **the themes of modernity** [(that/which) she portrayed in her works].

→ [she ~ works]는 선행사 the themes of modernity를 수식하는 관계대명사절이며, 목적격 관계대명사 that/which가 생략되었다.

---

27 안내문 정보 파악하기 정답 ③

해설 수치가 포함된 부분인 Fee: $120 (does not include lunch)를 통해 수업 비용에 점심이 포함되지 않는다는 것을 알 수 있으므로, 글의 내용과 일치하지 않는 것은 ③이다.

해석

웹사이트 제작자 일일 수업

웹사이트를 만드는 것이 어렵다고 생각하시나요? 그것이 얼마나 쉬운지 저희가 여러분께 보여드리겠습니다! 이 강좌는 자신만의 웹사이트를 제작하고 디자인하는 방법을 여러분께 가르쳐드립니다.

일시: 11월 20일 월요일, 오전 8시에서 오후 5시
장소: Dallas 전문 대학
대상: Dallas 주민들 (18세 이상)
비용: 120달러 (점심은 포함하지 않음)
일정:
- 오전 8시 - 오전 10시: 기초 코딩

어휘 community college 전문 대학 resident 주민

구문
분석

[2행] Do you think [(that) making a website is hard]?

→ 명사절 [making ~ hard]는 동사 think의 목적어이며, 명사절 접속사 that이 생략된 형태이다.

---

28 안내문 정보 파악하기 정답 ④

해설 donations to The Lake City Observatory are appreciated를 통해 Lake City 천문대에 대한 기부를 받는다는 것을 알 수 있으므로, 글의 내용과 일치하는 것은 ④이다.

해석

Lake City 천문대의 별 관측의 밤

Lake City 천문대는 지역 주민, 친구, 가족들을 위한 별 관측의 밤을 주최할 예정입니다. 오셔서 저희와 함께 밤하늘을 탐구해보고 별들에 대해 더 배워보세요.

날짜: 10월 15일 토요일
시간: 오후 6:30-오후 9:30
위치: Lake City 천문대 옆 주차장

포함되는 것:
- 천문학자와 함께하는 안내가 있는 별 관측
- 망원경으로 밤하늘과 별 관찰하기
- 무료 별자리표

입장: 무료 (하지만 Lake City 천문대에 대한 기부는 환영됩니다.)

※ 음식과 음료는 제공되지 않을 것이지만, 손님들은 직접 간식과 음료를 가져오셔도 됩니다.

어휘 observatory 천문대 stargaze 별을 관측하다, 별을 쳐다보다 astronomer 천문학자 telescope 망원경 star chart 별자리표

구문
분석

[17행] ①[Food and drinks will not be provided], but ②[guests are welcome to bring snacks and beverages themselves].

→ 절 ①[Food ~ provided]와 ②[guests ~ themselves]는 등위접속사 but으로 연결된 병렬 구조이다.

---

29 어법상 틀린 것 찾기 정답 ②

해설 복수명사 Other celestial bodies가 주어이고 revolving이 동사 자리를 차지하고 있는데, 현재분사는 단독으로 동사의 역할을 할 수 없으므로, ②의 revolving을 복수동사 revolve로 고쳐야 한다. including the planets, Moon, Sun, and stars는 수식어(삽입구)이다.

어휘 defy 거부하다, 반항하다　unconventional 관습에 얽매이지 않는
piece together 짜맞추다, 종합하다　ambient 주위의
chamber 방, 회의실　toy 장난 삼아 생각해보다　overwhelming 압도적인
circulation 순환

구문분석

[5행] He **is** best **known for** a controversial piece ~

→ be known for'는 '~으로 유명하다'라는 의미로, by 이외의 전치사를 쓰는 수동태 구문이다.

[16행] ~ in an anechoic chamber, where the silence was [**so** overwhelming **that** he was able to hear his own blood circulation].

→ [so ~ circulation]은 '너무 ~해서 -하다'라는 의미를 나타내는 'so + 형용사 + (that) -'으로, that절은 결과를 나타낸다.

오답분석 ①은 주어인 an immobile Earth가 동사 situate가 나타내는 '위치하는' 행위의 대상이므로 수동태 is situated를 사용한 것은 어법상 적절하다. ③은 선행사 spheres를 수식하는 형용사절을 이끄는 주격 관계대명사 which를 사용하여 어법상 적절하다. ④은 앞의 명사를 수식하고 있으며, 수식 받는 명사 spheres가 '구성하는' 행위의 주체이므로 현재분사 making을 사용한 것은 어법상 적절하다. ⑤은 부사 then을 강조하는 it is(was) ~ that 구문을 쓰기 위해 that을 사용한 것은 어법상 적절하다.

해석 서기 2세기에 Ptolemy(프톨레마이오스)에 의해 고안된 천동설은 고정된 지구가 우주의 중심에 위치해있다는 수학적 모델이다. 행성, 달, 태양, 별을 포함하는 다른 천체들은 이 체계 내에서 지구 주위를 돈다. Ptolemy에 따르면, 우주는 고정된 투명한 구들로 구성되어 있고, 천체들이 그것들 각각의 회전이 있는 이 구들에 붙어 있다. 천구는 가장 큰 구로, 별들을 잡아 두기 위해 존재하고, 이 우주의 경계를 표시한다. 지구가 중심에 있는 우주를 구성하는 구들에 대한 이 관념은 Ptolemy 이후에 오랫동안 지속되었고, 약 1400년 후까지 뒤집히지 않았다. 바로 그때 Copernicus(코페르니쿠스)가 지구와 다른 행성들이 태양 주위를 궤도를 그리며 도는 것을 의미하는 태양 중심의 우주 모델을 제안했다.

어휘 Ptolemaic System 천동설　immobile 고정된　revolve 돌다
heavenly body 천체　rotation 회전, 자전　attached 붙어 있는
overturn 뒤집다

구문분석

[1행] The Ptolemaic System, devised by Ptolemy in the second century AD, is **a mathematical model** [in which an immobile Earth is situated at the center of the universe].

→ [in ~ universe]는 선행사 a mathematical model을 수식하며, '전치사 + 관계대명사' in which가 이끄는 관계대명사절이다.

---

30 어휘 적절성 파악하기 정답 ④

해설 John Cage는 <4분 33초>를 통해 관객들에게 "침묵"의 시간 동안 침묵이란 전혀 없다는 것을 알게 하고자 하였고, 그 자신이 반향이 없는 방에서 자신의 혈액이 순환하는 소리도 들었다고 했다. 따라서 보통은 무시되는 주변의 소리들을 의식하게 될 것이라는 맥락이 되어야 하므로, ④의 perceived(인식되는)를 그와 반대되는 의미의 ignored(무시되는), overlooked(간과되는)와 같은 단어로 바꾸어야 문맥상 적절하다.

오답분석 ②은 논란의 작품이 전통적인 관점에서 "음악"이라고 거의 불릴 수 없다는 문맥이 되어야 하므로 hardly가 오는 것이 적절하다. ⑤은 방 안의 침묵이 너무 압도적이어서 혈액이 순환하는 소리를 들을 수 있을 정도라는 문맥이 되어야 하므로 overwhelming이 오는 것이 적절하다.

해석 John Cage(존 케이지)(1912-1992)는 전통을 거부하는 것으로 유명한 작곡가였다. 그는 ① 관습에 얽매이지 않는 방식들로 악기를 연주하고 정해진 음악적 형식들을 따르지 않는 음조와 리듬을 짜맞추는 것을 실험했다. 그는 전통적인 관점에서 "음악"이라고 ② 거의 불릴 수 없는 논란의 작품으로 가장 유명하다. 그 곡은 <4분 33초>인데, 그것이 정확히 4분 그리고 33초 동안 지속되기 때문에 그렇게 이름이 지어졌다. 그 ③ 지속 시간 동안, 악기도 성악가도 단 하나의 음도 내지 않는다. Cage에게 그 의도는 "침묵"의 시간 동안 관객들은 침묵이 전혀 없다는 것을 알게 될 것이라는 점이었다; 그들은 보통 ④ 인식되는(→ 무시되는/간과되는) 그들 주위의 소리들을 의식하게 될 것이다. Cage는 몇 년간 그 작품의 아이디어를 재미 삼아 생각해 보았지만, 그가 반향이 없는 방에서 시간을 보낸 후에 그것의 가치를 확신하게 되었는데, 그 방에서 침묵은 너무 ⑤ 압도적이어서 그는 자신의 혈액이 순환하는 소리도 들을 수 있었다.

---

31 빈칸 추론하기 정답 ①

해설 주제문을 재진술하는 빈칸 문장에서 우리가 추하다고 여기는 작품들은 그것들을 보는 사람들이 새로운 생각들에 '무엇한' 상태를 유발할 수 있다고 하고, 글의 후반에서 추해 보이도록 만들기 위해 예술 기법을 사용한 작품을 보는 사람들이 아름다움에 대한 이전의 가정들에 의문을 가지고 새로운 사상들을 받아들일 수도 있다고 했다. 따라서 빈칸에는 ① '수용적인'이 와서 새로운 생각들에 수용적인 상태를 유발할 수 있다는 의미가 되어야 한다.

오답분석 ⑤의 resistant는 정답인 receptive와 반대 의미의 단어이다.

해석 "오직 우리의 상상력과 관련해서만 어떤 것들이 아름답거나 추하다고 일컬어질 수 있다…"며 Baruch Spinoza(바뤼흐 스피노자)는 그의 이론들을 통해서 아름다움과 추함의 사회적으로 만들어진 특성을 지적했는데, 이는 개념과, 이러한 개념과 관련된 정의는 시간에 따라 매우 자주 바뀌기 때문이다. 예술적으로 말하자면, 그러한 단어들은 윤리적인 암시와 미학적인 암시 모두를 지닌다; "추한"은 나쁜 것을 의미하는 반면, "아름다운"은 좋은 것에 쓰여왔다. 하지만, 이 용어들이 이렇게 단순한가? 왜 "추한"은 부정적인 의미를 가져야만 하는가? 결국, 추한 예술은 흥미롭고 특별할 수 있다. 실제로, 우리가 추하다고 여기는 작품들은 그것들을 보는 사람들이 생각하게 만들 수 있고, 새로운 생각들에 수용적인 상태를 유발할 수 있다: 이는 전형적으로 아름다운 예술 작품이 성취하기에 더 어려움을 겪을 수 있는 것이다. 무언가가 "추해" 보이도록 만들기 위해 예술 기법들을 사용함으로써, 예술가는 사람들이 그 작품을 볼 때 그들 사이에서 더 비판적인 담화가 일어나게 할 수 있다. 그들은 아름다움에 대한 이전의 가정들에 의문을 가지고 새로운 생각들을 받아들일 수도 있는데, 어쨌든 이는 눈을 뗄 수 없는 예술품의 주요한 특징이다.

① 수용적인　　　② 의심하는
③ 비판적인　　　④ 무관심한
⑤ 저항하는

어휘 in relation to ~과 관련하여　implication 암시, 함축
connotation (함축된) 의미　trigger 유발하다　discourse 담화, 담론
embrace 받아들이다, 포용하다　compelling 눈을 뗄 수 없는

구문분석

[1행] ["**Only in relation to our imagination** <u>can</u> <u>things</u> <u>be called</u>] beautiful or ugly…"
　　　　　　　　　　　　　　　　　조동사　주어　동사

→ [Only ~ called]는 제한을 나타내는 부사구 Only ~ imagination이 강조되어 문장 맨 앞에 나왔기 때문에, 주어와 조동사가 도치되어 '조동사(can) + 주어(things) + 동사(be called)'의 어순으로 쓰였다.

[11행] In fact, pieces that we deem ugly can make those who gaze upon them think, and can trigger ~
목적어　　목적격 보어　　동사

→ 사역동사 make의 목적어로 those ~ them, 목적격 보어로 동사원형 think가 쓰였다.

32 빈칸 추론하기   정답 ⑤

[해설] 주제문에 해당하는 빈칸 문장에서 연구는 기억들이 '어떠하다'는 것을 보여준다고 하고, 글의 중반에서 학생들이 외웠던 걸 잊어버렸을 때에도 원래의 신경 양상이 여전히 포착되어 기억에 도달하기 어려울 뿐 기억은 여전히 그곳에 있음을 보여주었다고 했다. 글의 마지막 문장에서는 기억이 우리 뇌의 접근하기 덜 쉬운 부분에 보관되어 있다고 하는 것이 틀리지 않을 것이라고 했다. 따라서 빈칸에는 ⑤ '우리가 쉽게 그것들을 생각해내지 못하더라도 저장된 상태로 있다'가 와야 한다.

[오답분석] ①은 잊어버린 기억이 우리 뇌의 접근하기 덜 쉬운 부분에 보관된다는 글의 내용과 반대되는 내용이므로 오답이다. ②의 감정 관련 내용은 글에서 언급되고 있지 않다. ③의 긴밀한 관계 형성과 관련된 내용은 글에서 언급되고 있지 않다. ④은 글에서 언급된 words를 사용하여 헷갈리게 하는 오답이다.

[해석] 잊혀진 것이 항상 잃어버린 것은 아니다. 연구는 기억들이 우리가 쉽게 그것들을 생각해내지 못하더라도 저장된 상태로 있다는 것을 보여준다. 기억 형성과 회상 동안에 관찰되었던 수많은 대학생들의 뇌 활동을 살펴보자. 학생들이 그 연구에서 앞서 제시되었던 단어 목록에 대해 그들이 할 수 있는 한 많이 기억하도록 요구되었을 때, 기능성 자기공명영상은 회상 동안의 뇌 활동이 암기 과정에서와 동일했음을 보여주었다. 심지어 학생들이 외웠던 것의 대부분을 잊어버렸을 때에도, 원래의 신경 양상이 여전히 포착되어, 도달하기 어려움에도 불구하고 기억들이 여전히 그곳에 있음을 분명히 보여주었다. 기억이 얼마나 오래 지속되는지에 대해서는 많은 것들이 여전히 불확실하지만, 이와 같은 증거는 그것(얼마나 오래 지속되는지)이 우리가 생각하는 것보다 길 수도 있음을 보여주었다. 따라서, 기억은 단지 우리 뇌의 접근하기 덜 쉬운 부분에 보관되어 있다고 하는 것이 틀리지 않을 것이다.

① 일정 정도의 시간 후에 사라진다
② 우리가 강렬한 감정을 경험할 때 형성된다
③ 사람들 간에 긴밀한 관계를 형성하는 것을 돕는다
④ 우리가 단어들과 연관시키는 의미에 영향을 미칠 수 있다
⑤ 우리가 쉽게 그것들을 생각해내지 못하더라도 저장된 상태로 있다

[어휘] neurological 신경의   pick up 포착하다, 알아채다
illustrate 분명히 보여주다   unattainable 도달하기 어려운, 얻기 힘든
archive (기록 보관소 등에) 보관하다; 기록 보관소
[선택지] retrieve 생각해내다, 되찾다

[구문분석] [1행] **That** [which is forgotten] is not always lost.

→ [which is forgotten]은 선행사인 지시대명사 That을 수식하는 관계대명사절이다. that which는 what, the thing which(~하는 것)의 의미로 해석한다.

[15행] Therefore, it would not be wrong [to say that memories
가주어　　　　　　　　　　　　진주어(to부정사구)
are just archived in the less accessible parts of our brains].

→ 가주어 it이 길이가 긴 진주어 to부정사구 [to ~ brains] 대신 주어 자리에 쓰인 형태이다.

33 빈칸 추론하기   정답 ②

[해설] 장애가 있는 사람들의 자립을 돕기 위한 보조공학이 발전함에 따라, 그에 상응하는 복잡성의 증가로 인해 충분한 훈련이 제공될 필요성도 증가한다는 내용의 글이고, 글의 중반에서 연구에 따르면 장애가 있는 사람들이 복잡한 인터페이스와 많은 선택 기능들로 인해 새로운 보조공학에 겁을 먹고 피한다고 하였다. 따라서 빈칸에는 ② '지속적인 지원에 접근할 기회가 주어진 사람들' 이 와서 다행히도 지속적인 지원에 접근할 기회가 주어진 사람들은 이러한 장벽을 극복하고 새로운 보조공학을 일상에 통합시킬 가능성이 증가한다는 의미가 되어야 한다.

[오답분석] ④의 몇 가지 다른 형태에 대한 내용은 글에서 언급되고 있지 않다. ⑤의 장애의 심각한 정도에 대한 내용은 글에서 언급되고 있지 않다.

[해석] 보조공학은 장애가 있는 사람들이 다른 사람의 도움 없이 다수의 일들을 수행하게 하고, 그렇게 함으로써 그들의 자립 수준을 높인다. 최근의 발전이 보조공학의 기능성을 향상시켰더라도, 그에 상응하는 복잡성의 증가는 그것들을 사용할 장애가 있는 사람들에게 충분한 훈련이 제공되는 것을 필요로 한다. 몇몇 기기들은 최소한의 교육으로 한 사람의 삶에 쉽게 통합될 수 있는 반면, 다른 기기들은 좀 더 복잡해서 효과적으로 사용되려면 상당한 양의 지식을 필요로 한다. 실제로, 많은 연구들은 새로운 보조공학을 피하는 사람들이 복잡한 인터페이스와 많은 선택 기능들로 인해 겁을 먹는다는 것을 보여주었고, 이는 그들이 그것들을 조작하기에 부적합하다고 생각하게 한다. 다행히도, 지속적인 지원에 접근할 기회가 주어진 사람들은 이러한 장벽을 극복하고 새로운 보조공학을 그들의 하루하루 일상에 통합시켜, 그들 삶의 전반적인 질을 크게 향상시킬 가능성이 증가한다.

① 근본적인 설계를 개선시키도록 요구되는 사람들
② 지속적인 지원에 접근할 기회가 주어진 사람들
③ 추가 안내를 제공하기로 동의한 사람들
④ 몇 가지 다른 형태들을 사용하려고 노력해온 사람들
⑤ 덜 심각한 장애를 겪고 있는 사람들

[어휘] an array of 다수의   independence 자립, 독립
functionality 기능(성)   necessitate 필요로 하다
sophisticated 복잡한, 정교한   intimidated 겁을 먹은
unqualified 부적합한, 자격이 없는   [선택지] underlying 근본적인, 밑에 있는
ongoing 지속적인, 진행 중인

[구문분석] [5행] ~ the corresponding increase in complexity **necessitates** that sufficient training (should) **be offered** to the people ~

→ 주절에 당위·필요성을 나타내는 동사 necessitates가 와서, that절에서 should가 생략되고 be offered가 쓰인 형태이다.

[15행] ~ which leads them to believe that they are unqualified
동사　　목적어　　목적격 보어
to operate them.

→ 동사 leads의 목적어로 them, 목적격 보어로 to부정사 to believe가 쓰였다.

34 빈칸 추론하기   정답 ⑤

[해설] 주제문에 해당하는 빈칸 문장에서 Adam Smith에 따르면 모든 사람이 어느 정도 이기심과 개인적 욕망으로 움직이더라도 '어떠하다'고 하고, 이어서 우리는 어떤 행동이 대다수에게 못마땅하게 여겨지고 어떤 건 그렇지 않은지 예민하게 의식하고 있다고 했다. 글의 후반에서는 우리의 양심, 즉 "공정한 관찰자"가 우리로 하여금 사회의 칭찬을 받을 만한 일들을 하게 한다고 하였다. 따라

서 빈칸에는 ⑤ '우리가 다른 사람들의 기대에 부합되게 행동한다'가 와서 모두가 어느 정도 이기심과 개인적 욕망으로 움직이더라도 우리가 다른 사람들의 기대에 부합되게 행동한다는 의미가 되어야 한다.

(오답분석) ①의 사회적 규범이 변화한다는 내용은 글에서 언급되고 있지 않다. ②은 우리에게 타고난 공감 능력이 있다는 글의 내용과 반대되는 내용이므로 오답이다. ③의 죄의식에 대한 내용은 글에서 언급되고 있지 않다. ④은 우리가 옳은 일이라 인식되는 것을 해야 한다고 배운다는 글의 내용과 반대되는 내용이므로 오답이다.

(해석) Adam Smith(애덤 스미스)의 1759년 책 <도덕감정론>에서, 그는 모두가 어느 정도 이기심과 개인적 욕망으로 움직이더라도, 우리가 다른 사람들의 기대에 부합되게 행동한다는 것을 사실로 가정했다. 사회 구성원으로서, 우리는 우리가 받거나 목격하는 반응들에 근거하여 어떤 행동이 대다수에게 못마땅하게 여겨지고 어떤 건 그렇지 않은지 예민하게 의식하고 있다. 우리는 타고난 공감 능력이 있고, 다른 사람들이 우리가 도덕적인 책임을 지고 있다고 여기기를 바라기 때문에, 우리는 옳은 일이라 인식되는 것을 해야 한다고 배운다. 우리가 옳은 일을 하고 있는지 판단하는 것을 돕기 위해, Smith는 우리 각자가 우리 행동이 어떻게 이해될지 우리에게 알려주는 양심을 가지고 있다고 말했다. 그가 일컫기를, 이 "공정한 관찰자"는 우리가 자신의 문제에 지나치게 관심을 가지는 것을 막고, 우리가 사회의 비난보다는 칭찬을 받을 만한 일들을 하게 한다.

① 사회적 규범은 자주 변화를 겪는다
② 우리는 다른 사람이 어떻게 느끼는지를 이해할 수 없다
③ 죄의식은 우리가 용서를 구하게 만든다
④ 사람들은 그들이 어떻게 행동해야 하는지를 선천적으로 안다
⑤ 우리가 다른 사람들의 기대에 부합되게 행동한다

(어휘) **posit** 사실로 가정하다 **self-interest** 이기심, 사욕
keenly 예민하게, 날카롭게 **objectionable** 못마땅한
accountable 책임을 지는, 설명할 수 있는 **conscience** 양심
impartial 공정한, 공평한 **spectator** 관찰자, 관중
reproach 비난, 책망 [선택지] **conscious** 의식; 의식하고 있는
innately 선천적으로 **in accordance with** ~에 부합되게

(구문분석)
[10행] To help us **determine** ①[whether we are doing the right thing], Smith **suggested** ②[that we each have **a conscience**] ③[that informs us of how our behavior will be interpreted].
→ ①[whether ~ thing]은 접속사 whether가 이끄는 명사절로, 동사 determine의 목적어 역할을 한다.
→ ②[that ~ conscience]는 접속사 that이 이끄는 명사절로, 동사 suggested의 목적어 역할을 한다.
→ ③[that ~ interpreted]는 선행사 a conscience를 수식하며 주격 관계대명사 that이 이끄는 관계대명사절이다.

35 흐름과 관계 없는 문장 찾기 정답 ③

(해설) 숨겨진 분노가 유발하는 반복적인 신체적 행동이나 통제 불가능한 행동 등의 구체적인 예시를 나열한 뒤, 다른 사람들은 이러한 행동들이 분노 때문이라고 연관 짓지 못하고 성격상 결함이나 별남 때문이라 여긴다고 설명하는 글이다. 그런데 ③은 행동과 성격 사이의 구분선에 대한 내용이므로 핵심 소재는 같지만 주제에서 벗어나 있어 글의 흐름과 무관하다.

(오답분석) ④은 Whatever the case를 통해 숨겨진 분노가 유발하는 세 가지 유형의 행동들을 언급한 첫 문장과 ①~②의 내용을 포괄하여 부연 설명을 하고 있으며, these behaviors는 각 유형의 구체적인 예시들을 가리키고 있으므로 ② 뒤

에 이어지는 것이 적절하다. ⑤의 them은 these behaviors를 가리키고 있으므로 ④ 뒤에 오는 것이 적절하다.

(해석) 숨겨진 분노에 대한 한 연구에서, 연구원들은 의도되지 않은 특정한 행동들이 흔히 나타난다는 것을 발견했다. 그것들 중 일부는 안면 경련이나 경련성 발움직임과 같은 반복적인 신체적 행동들로 이루어진다. ① 그것들은 또한 나쁜 잠버릇, 턱 악물기, 이 갈기와 같은 통제 불가능한 행동들을 포함할 수 있는데, 그것들은 다른 사람들이 알아차릴 수는 있지만 분노와 연관 짓지 못할 수도 있다. ② 다른 행동들은 고의적이지만 분노와 직접적으로 연결되지 않고, 이것들은 미루는 버릇, 습관적인 지각, 과도한 공손함, 또는 대화 중의 부적절한 비꼬기와 경솔한 언행으로 나타날 수도 있다. (③ 행동과 성격 사이에는 명확한 구분선이 그어질 수 있는데, 선의 한쪽은 우리가 하는 것을, 그리고 다른 쪽은 우리가 생각하거나 느끼는 방법과 이유를 나타낸다.) ④ 어떤 경우든, 이러한 행동들은 보통 해롭지 않은 성격상 결함이나 별남에 원인이 있다고 여겨진다. ⑤ 그것들을 분노에 의해 유발되었을지도 모르는 더 심각한 문제들과 연관 짓는 사람들은 만약 있더라도 조금밖에 없다.

(어휘) **come forward** 나타나다, 나서다 **tic** 경련, 틱
clench 악물다, (주먹을) 꽉 쥐다 **grind** 갈다, 빻다
deliberate 고의적인 **procrastination** 미루는 버릇, 꾸물거림
sarcasm 비꼼, 풍자 **flippancy** 경솔한 언행 **eccentricity** 별남, 기이함
provoke 유발하다, 자극하다

(구문분석)
[14행] Whatever the case, these behaviors **are** often **attributed to** harmless personality flaws or eccentricities.
→ be attributed to는 '~에 원인이 있다고 여겨지다'라는 의미로, by 이외의 전치사를 쓰는 수동태 구문이다.

36 글의 순서 배열하기 정답 ②

(해설) 주어진 글은 Walter Benjamin을 인용해 현대에 복제 가능한 미디어 기술로 인해 원본 예술 작품의 아우라가 사라졌다는 주제를 제시한다. (B)는 Benjamin에게 있어서 예술 작품은 그것의 물리적 유일함에서 나오는 아우라를 지니는데 복제품을 만듦으로써 예술 작품의 진본성을 파괴했다는 내용이고, 주어진 글에서 현대에 원본 예술 작품의 아우라가 사라졌다고 했으므로 그 뒤에 와야 한다. (A)의 The destruction of the vital force(그 중요한 힘의 파괴)는 (B)의 '예술 작품의 진본성을 파괴한 것'을 가리키므로 (B) 바로 다음에 오는 것이 적절하다. (C)는 역접 연결어 however를 통해 기술 복제 시대 이전 상황을 설명한 (A)의 내용에 대한 반전 설명으로, 복제품을 만들어 많은 사람이 동시에 한 작품을 보는 것이 가능해진 상황에 대해 언급하고 있으므로 (A) 뒤에 오는 것이 적절하다. 따라서 글의 순서로 가장 적절한 것은 ② (B) - (A) - (C)이다.

(해석) Walter Benjamin(발터 벤야민)은 그의 1935년 논문 <기술 복제 시대의 예술 작품>에서 복제 가능한 미디어 기술이라는 새로운 형태로 인해 원본 예술 작품의 아우라가 현대에서 사라졌다고 주장했다.

(B) Benjamin에게 있어서, 예술 작품은 그것의 물리적인 유일함에서 나오는 아우라를 지녔다. 그가 주장하기를, 사진이나 영화로 할 수 있는 것처럼, 복제품을 만드는 것은 그 예술 작품을 그것의 원래의 맥락에서 없애고, 그것의 진본성을 파괴했다.

(A) 예술에 그것의 영혼인 개성을 부여하는 그 중요한 힘의 파괴는 보는 사람에게 미치는 예술의 영향력을 바꿨다. 기술 복제 시대 이전에, 이미지나 사물을 보는 것은 보는 이가 원본 작품이 존재하는 곳에 있는 것을 필요로 하여, 보다 개인적인 경험을 허용했다.

(C) 하지만, 복제품을 만들고 많은 사람들이 동시에 그 작품을 보는 것을 가능

하게 함으로써, 개별적인 연결성이 없어졌기 때문에 보는 사람은 더 이상 그것에 완전히 몰입할 수 없었다. 대신에, "분산된 대중"인 보는 사람들이 집합적으로 그 예술 작품을 받아들였다.

[어휘] contend 주장하다, 겨루다 aura 아우라, 분위기 replicable 복제 가능한
individuality 개성, 특성 alter 바꾸다, 변화시키다 reproduction 복제
authenticity 진본성, 진짜임 simultaneously 동시에
collectively 집합적으로, 전체적으로 absorb 받아들이다, 흡수하다

[구문분석]
[8행] Before the age of mechanical reproduction, [viewing an image or an object] required one to be in the presence ~

→ [viewing ~ object]는 문장의 주어 역할을 하는 동명사구이다.

[17행] By producing copies and making it possible for many people [to see the work simultaneously], ~
(가주어) (의미상 주어) (진주어(to부정사구))

→ 가주어 it이 길이가 긴 진주어 to부정사구 [to ~ simultaneously] 대신 주어 자리에 쓰인 구조이며, to부정사구의 의미상 주어가 'for + 명사(구)'의 형태로 쓰였다.

---

37 글의 순서 배열하기   정답 ④

[해설] 주어진 글은 과학적 방법은 방법론적 자연주의의 원리에 근거한다는 주제를 제시한다. (C)의 this approach(이 연구법)는 주어진 글의 '방법론적 자연주의'를 가리키므로 주어진 글 바로 다음에 오는 것이 적절하다. (A)의 this strategy는 (C)의 '오로지 자연적인 사건과 현상들을 연구하는 것'을 가리키므로 (C) 바로 다음에 오는 것이 적절하다. (B)는 In other words를 통해 (A)의 "보는 것이 믿는 것이다"라는 구절에 대한 부연 설명을 하고 있으므로 (A) 뒤에 오는 것이 적절하다. 따라서 글의 순서로 가장 적절한 것은 ④ (C) - (A) - (B)이다.

[해석] 과학적 방법은 방법론적 자연주의의 원리에 근거한다.

(C) 세계에 대한 설명을 제공하는 것에 대한 이러한 접근법의 지지자들은 진실이 오로지 자연적인 사건과 현상들을 연구함으로써 인식될 수 있다고 주장한다. 특히, 그들은 과학적 연구의 대상들이 진짜이고 상상된 것이 아니라는 게 틀림없이 확실하도록 그것들이 실재하는 것을 선호한다.

(A) 이 방법 이면의 철학은 물리적 세계에서 자연적인 것들은 검사되고 실험될 수 있는 반면, 사건의 다른 잠재적인 원인들에 대한 이론들은 그럴 수 없다는 것이다. 근본적으로, 방법론적 자연주의는 "보는 것이 믿는 것이다"라는 구절의 회의론을 포함한다.

(B) 다시 말해서, 그것은 믿음이나 감정이 고려되는 것을 허용하지 않는다. 이 요건은 논리와 이성이 이전의 세계관들을 대체하기 시작했던 계몽주의 시대 이후로 과학적 방법의 중요한 부분을 형성해왔다.

[어휘] methodological 방법론적인 naturalism 자연주의
theory 이론 skepticism 회의론 Enlightenment 계몽주의 시대
logic 논리 proponent 지지자 tangible 실재하는, 만질 수 있는

[구문분석]
[3행] ~ is that natural things in the physical world can be tested and experimented on, [whereas theories about other potential causes for events cannot].

→ [whereas ~ cannot]은 접속사 whereas(반면에)가 이끄는 양보의 부사절이다.

→ cannot 뒤에는 be tested and experimented on이 생략되어 있는데, 앞서 natural ~ on에서 이미 언급되었기 때문이다.

---

38 주어진 문장의 위치 찾기   정답 ④

[해설] 주어진 문장의 연결어 Still(그래도)로 보아, 주어진 문장 앞에는 텔레비전과 멀어진 밀레니얼에 대한 내용이 나와야 한다는 것을 알 수 있다. 이 글에서는 ①~③ 뒤 문장까지 이전 세대와 비교하여 밀레니얼 세대들이 텔레비전을 훨씬 더 적게 보고 있으며 대신 온라인을 더 많이 이용한다고 설명하고 있고, 주어진 문장의 상대적으로 새로운 기술적 경향과 다른 매체는 ④ 뒤 문장의 온라인 영상 스트리밍으로 이어지고 있으므로 주어진 문장이 들어가기에 가장 적절한 곳은 ④이다.

[오답분석] ⑤ 뒤 문장은 ④ 뒤 문장에 이어서 새로운 텔레비전 시청의 한 형태로서의 온라인 스트리밍에 대해 언급하고 있다.

[해석] 통계 자료에 따르면, 밀레니얼 세대는 이전 세대들보다 텔레비전을 훨씬 더 적게 본다. 65세 이상의 평균적인 미국인은 텔레비전을 하루에 약 4.5시간 본다; 반면에, 평균적인 밀레니얼 세대는 겨우 2시간만 본다. (①) 게다가, 밀레니얼 세대가 텔레비전을 보는 시간은 지난 20년간 감소한 반면에, 이전 세대들은 더 많이 보고 있다. (②) 여러 요인들이 이 차이를 설명할 수 있을 것인데, 그 중 가장 두드러지는 것은 인터넷이다. (③) 이전 세대들이 오락과 뉴스의 대부분을 위해 여전히 텔레비전에 의존하는 반면, 밀레니얼 세대들은 두 가지 모두를 온라인으로 소비하는 것을 선호한다. (④ 그래도, 상대적으로 새로운 기술적 경향은 밀레니얼 세대가 텔레비전으로 되돌아오게 할 수도 있겠지만, 다른 매체를 통해서일 것이다.) 최근의 조사는 9퍼센트 더 많은 밀레니얼 세대가 텔레비전 시청보다 온라인 영상 스트리밍을 한다는 것을 보여주었는데, 이 추세는 감소의 조짐을 보이지 않는다. (⑤) 텔레비전 시청의 한 형태로서, 스트리밍은 이전 세대의 아날로그적 시청 방식과 상당히 다르지만, 그럼에도 불구하고 그것은 더 젊은 세대가 그 매체를 완전히 떠나지는 않았음을 보여준다.

[어휘] millennial 밀레니얼 세대 disparity 차이 prominent 두드러진

[구문분석]
[10행] Several factors may explain this disparity, the most prominent of which is the Internet.
= and the most prominent of them is the Internet.

→ 선행사 this disparity가 사물이고, the most prominent of 뒤에서 전치사 of의 목적어 역할을 하므로 목적격 관계대명사 which가 쓰였다.

---

39 주어진 문장의 위치 찾기   정답 ④

[해설] 주어진 문장의 Regardless of which of these types of cones are deficient(이러한 추상체 종류들 중 어느 것에 결함이 있는지와 상관없이)로 보아, 주어진 문장 앞에는 결함이 있는 추상체의 종류들이 무엇인지에 대한 내용이 나와야 한다는 것을 알 수 있다. 이 글에서는 ③ 뒤 문장에서 적색이나 녹색을 감지하는 추상체에 결함이 있는 경우에 대해 설명하고 있고, 주어진 문장의 the end result for the affected individual은 ④ 뒤 문장의 '이 두 색깔 간에 구별하는 것이 어렵거나 심지어 불가능해진다'는 내용으로 이어지고 있으므로 주어진 문장이 들어가기에 가장 적절한 곳은 ④이다.

[해석] 1794년에, 영국의 화학자이자 물리학자인 John Dalton(존 돌턴)은 색맹에 대한 최초의 설명을 포함한 학술 논문을 발표했다. (①) 거기서, 그는 적록 색맹에 대한 그의 연구의 개요를 제시했는데, 그것은 사람 눈의 망막에서 발견되는 추상체라고 불리는 빛에 민감한 세포의 문제에 의해 야기된다고 현재 알

려져 있다. (②) 일반적으로, 사람은 완전한 기능을 하는 세 종류의 추상체가 있고, 각각은 다른 빛 파장에 반응해서 눈이 세 가지의 주요한 색들을 인식할 수 있게 한다. (③) 하지만, 일부 경우에서는, 적색이나 녹색을 감지하는 세포들이 정상보다 덜 민감하거나 완전히 결여되어 있다. (④ 이러한 추상체 종류들 중 어느 것에 결함이 있는지와 상관없이, 영향받은 사람에게 최종 결과는 동일하다.) 이 두 색깔 간에 구별하는 것이 어렵거나 심지어 불가능해진다. (⑤) 이러한 유형의 색맹은 보통 유전적이지만, 눈의 물리적 손상이나 노령이 원인일 수도 있다.

[어휘] cone 추상체(눈의 망막 중심부에 있는 감광 세포) deficient 결함이 있는
colorblindness 색맹 retina 망막 wavelength 파장, 주파수
altogether 완전히

[구문분석]
> [6행] In it, he provided a summary of his research regarding **red-green colorblindness**, [which is now known to be caused by a problem with the light-sensitive cells called cones that are found in the retina of the human eye].
>
> → [which ~ eye]는 선행사 red-green colorblindness를 수식하는 주격 관계대명사절로, 콤마 뒤에서 계속적 용법으로 쓰였다.

40 요약문 완성하기
정답 ③

[해설] 글의 전반부에서는 학교 내 따돌림을 줄이기 위한 연구에서 반 친구들에게 유행을 이끄는 사람, 팀 리더, 그리고 또래의 역할 모델로 인정되는 학생들, 즉 "사회적 준거"로 알려진 이들에게 의지했다고 했고, 글의 후반부에서 따돌림 중재 프로그램을 진행한 학교들에서 학생들 간 더 적은 분쟁과 더 많은 사교를 보고했다고 했다. 따라서 role models를 example로, violence를 conflict로 바꾸어 표현한 ③이 정답이다.

[오답분석] 사회적 준거는 역할 모델로 인정되는 사람이고, 용인되는 행동으로 여겨지는 것을 정하는 데에 중요한 역할을 한다고 했으므로 ①과 ④의 alternative, ②의 incentive는 (A)에 들어갈 단어로 적절하지 않다.

[해석] 학교에서의 따돌림을 줄이는 새롭고 좀 더 효과적인 방법을 모색하기 위해, Princeton 대학교의 심리학자인 Betsy Levy Paluck(벳시 레비 팔럭)과 그녀의 연구팀은 학생들 자체에게, 혹은 보다 구체적으로는, 반 친구들에게 유행을 이끄는 사람, 팀 리더, 그리고 또래의 역할 모델로 인정되는 학생들, 즉 과학적 용어로 "사회적 준거"로 알려진 이들에게 의지했다. 사회 심리학 이론에 따르면, 개인은 다른 사람들의 행동을 관찰하고 어떤 것이 보상을 받거나 벌을 받는지를 보면서 무엇이 바람직한지 알게 된다. Paluck이 말하기를, 사회적 준거는 무엇이 용인되는 행동으로 여겨지는지 정하는 데에 중요한 역할을 할지도 모른다. 그 점을 염두에 두고, Paluck과 그녀의 팀은 2012-2013학년도에 뉴저지 전역의 학교들과 연구하고 그 중 절반에서 따돌림 중재 프로그램을 실시했다. 이 중재 프로그램들에서, 다른 학생들과의 가장 많은 접촉이 있는 학생들인 사회적 준거 학생들은 갈등을 반대하는 메시지를 전하도록 지도되었다. 그해의 말에, 중재 프로그램을 진행했던 학교들이 학생들 간에 더 적은 분쟁과 더 많은 사교를 보고했음이 드러났고, 이는 또래 모델링이 얼마나 강력할 수 있는지를 보여주었다.

↓

사회적 준거는 집단 내의 다른 사람들이 어떻게 행동해야 하는지에 대한 (A) 본보기의 역할을 하므로, 학교 환경에서 그들은 (B) 갈등을 막는 핵심 요인이 될 수 있다.

	(A)	(B)
①	대안	혼란
②	유인	폭력
③	본보기	갈등
④	대안	폭행
⑤	본보기	변화

[어휘] bullying 따돌림, 괴롭히기 identify 인정하다, 식별하다
trendsetter 유행을 이끄는 사람 referent 준거, 지시물
shape 정하다, 형성하다 intervention 중재, 조정
diplomacy 사교 능력, 외교(술)

[구문분석]
> [20행] At the end of the year, it was found [that schools where 가주어
> the intervention programs had taken place reported less 진주어(that절)
> violence and more diplomacy among students], ~
>
> → 가주어 it이 길이가 긴 진주어 that절 [that ~ students] 대신 주어 자리에 쓰인 형태이다.

41~42 장문 독해 1

[해석] 사람들을 조종해서 그들이 자신의 현실이나 인식에 (a) 의심하게 하는 것을 뜻하는 가스라이팅은 흔히 사적인 관계의 관점에서 생각된다. 이 경우, 한 사람이 피해자이고, 심리학자들에 따르면, 그것은 그들에게 매우 위험하고 치명적일 수 있다. 더 우려되는 것은 [41]조종자의 가스라이팅이 한 사람뿐만 아니라 한 집단의 사람들 전체에도 영향을 끼칠 수 있다는 것이다.

George Washington 대학교의 커뮤니케이션학 전문가인 Farah Latif(파라 라티프)는 일부 정치인들이 "정치적 사안들에 대한 여론을 동요시키고 방향을 잃게 하기" 위해 어떻게 가스라이팅을 사용하는지를 설명한다. [41, 42]사실이 아닌 이야기를 지어내고, 반대당의 평판을 나쁘게 하려고 시도하며, 끊임없이 입증된 사실들을 (b) 부정하는 그들의 기술들은 모두 그들의 목표와 목적에 대한 "지지를 얻기" 위해 사용된다. 유권자들을 가스라이팅하는 정치인은 그들 자신의 실수를 (c) 강조하거나(→축소하거나) 심지어 그것들을 다른 정치인의 탓으로 돌리려고 할 수도 있다. 그들은 허위 정보를 퍼뜨리고 특히 미디어와 조사원들을 겨냥하여 그들을 정보의 신뢰할 수 없는 출처로 묘사하려 한다. [41]이러한 행동들의 영향은 대중의 불신, 왜곡된 현실 인식, 유권자들이 중요한 사안들에 관해 합리적인 생각을 (d) 할 수 없는 것을 포함한다. 따라서, 가스라이팅은 정상적인 정치 작용 자체에 (e) 악영향을 주는 매우 실질적이고 무서운 능력을 지닌다.

[어휘] manipulate 조종하다, 다루다 question 의심하다 destabilize 동요시키다
disorient 방향을 잃게 하다 public opinion 여론
discredit 평판을 나쁘게 하다 opposition 반대당
twisted 왜곡된, 뒤틀어진 contaminate 악영향을 주다, 오염시키다
[선택지] stance 입장 distort 왜곡하다, 비틀다

[구문분석]
> [6행] [What is more unsettling] is that a manipulator's gaslighting can affect not only a single person but also an entire group of people.
>
> → [What ~ unsettling]은 관계대명사 what(~하는 것)이 이끄는 명사절로, 문장의 주어 역할을 한다.

41 제목 파악하기 정답 ⑤

해설 가스라이팅은 인간 관계에서 한 명의 사람을 대상으로 할 뿐만 아니라 집단의 사람들 전체에도 영향을 끼칠 수 있다고 했다. 마지막 부분으로 미루어 보아 정치인이 "지지를 얻기" 위해 대중을 상대로 가스라이팅을 이용할 경우 대중의 불신, 왜곡된 현실 인식을 초래하고 유권자들이 합리적으로 중요한 사안들에 관해 생각할 수 없게 만든다는 내용의 글로, Farah Latif의 설명을 인용하여 뒷받침하고 있다. 따라서 글의 제목으로 가장 적절한 것은 ⑤ '대중을 잘못된 방향으로 이끄는 정치적 기술로서의 가스라이팅'이다.

오답분석 ①, ③은 글의 일부만을 다루고 있는 오답이다. ②, ④는 글의 핵심 소재 Gaslighting을 사용하여 헷갈리게 하는 오답이다.

해석 ① 가스라이팅이 당신의 정치적 입장을 의심하게 만드는 방법
② 당신이 가스라이팅 당하고 있다는 신호를 알아차려라!
③ 정치인들이 의도적으로 가스라이팅을 이용하는가?
④ 정치적 가스라이팅: 선거 결과를 왜곡하는 것
⑤ 대중을 잘못된 방향으로 이끄는 정치적 기술로서의 가스라이팅

42 어휘 적절성 파악하기 정답 ③

해설 정치인이 자신의 목표와 목적에 대한 "지지를 얻기" 위해 가스라이팅을 이용하여 자신의 실수를 축소하거나 심지어 그것의 잘못을 다른 정치인에게 돌리려 할 수 있다는 맥락이 되어야 하므로, ③의 emphasize(강조하다)를 그와 반대되는 의미의 downplay(축소하다, 경시하다)와 같은 어휘로 바꾸어야 문맥상 적절하다.

오답분석 ②은 정치인들이 사실이 아닌 이야기를 지어내고 끊임없이 입증된 사실을 부정함으로써 지지를 얻으려 한다는 문맥이 되어야 하므로 denying이 오는 것이 적절하다. ④은 정치인의 가스라이팅의 결과 유권자들이 중요한 사안에 관해 합리적인 생각을 할 수 없음이 초래된다는 문맥이 되어야 하므로 inability가 오는 것이 적절하다. ⑤은 가스라이팅이 정치의 정상적인 작용 자체에 악영향을 주는 실질적이고 무서운 능력을 갖고 있다는 문맥이 되어야 하므로 contaminate이 오는 것이 적절하다.

43~45 장문 독해 2

해석 (A) 오랜 가뭄이 있었고, 그래서 한 근면한 농부는 (a)그의 농작물들을 위한 수원을 찾고 있었다. [44]그의 이웃이 이것에 대해 듣고는 돈을 좀 벌 기회를 포착했다. "제 땅에 큰 우물이 하나 있어요"라고 [44]그 이웃이 말했다. "저는 그것을 당신에게 팔 의사가 있어요." 농부는 기꺼이 제안에 응했고 (b)그에게 후한 가격을 지불했다. 다음 날, 농부는 물을 길으러 갔다. 하지만, 그가 그렇게 하기 전에, 이웃이 갑자기 그를 멈춰 세웠다.

(D) "무슨 일인가요?"라며 농부가 물었다. "왜 제가 물을 가져가지 못하게 하는 건가요?" 이웃은 "제가 당신에게 그 우물을 팔았지만, 그 안의 물은 아니에요. 만약 (e)당신이 물을 원한다면, 그것에 대해 추가로 제게 지불해야 합니다"라고 주장했다. 충격을 받고, 농부는 이것이 부당하다고 답했지만, 이웃은 생각을 바꾸지 않았다.

(B) 그 둘은 결국 마을의 판사에게 그 문제를 맡기기로 할 때까지 계속해서 말다툼을 했다. "판사님, 그는 제가 산 우물에서 제가 물을 가져가지 못하게 합니다"라며 농부가 불평했다. 그 판사는 이웃에게 왜 그가 그것을 허락하지 않는지를 물었다. "제가 농부에게 이야기했듯이, 저는 제 물이 아니라 제 우물을 (c)그에게 팔았습니다, 판사님. 따라서, 그 물은 여전히 제 것입니다. 저는 잘못한 것이 없습니다"라며 이웃이 답했다.

(C) 이를 들은 후, 판사는 잠시 동안 생각했다. "당신이 맞습니다"라며 그가 마침내 이웃에게 말했다. "당신은 우물만 팔았습니다." 이웃은 그의 속임수를 성공시켰기 때문에 의기양양했다. 하지만 판사는 말을 끝마친 것이 아니었다. "우물은 농부의 것이고 물은 당신의 것입니다. [45]당신이 물을 보관하기 위해 농부의 우물을 사용하고 있으므로, 당신은 이제 그 공간을 사용하는 것에 대해 (d)그에게 임대료를 지불해야만 합니다."

어휘 hardworking 근면한, 부지런히 일하는 water source 수원 well 우물 property 땅, 부동산 triumphant 의기양양한, 승리를 거둔

구문분석

[13행] The judge asked the neighbor [why he wouldn't allow
　　　　　　　　동사　　간접 목적어　　　직접 목적어
it].

→ [why ~ it]은 의문사 why가 이끄는 명사절로, 동사 asked의 직접 목적어 역할을 한다.

43 글의 순서 배열하기 정답 ④

해설 (A)는 농부가 이웃에게서 우물을 샀지만 이웃이 물을 가져가지 못하게 했다는 내용이다. (D)는 농부가 왜 물을 가져가지 못하게 하는지 묻자, 이웃은 자신은 우물만 판 것이므로 물을 가져가려면 추가로 돈을 지불하라고 했다는 내용이므로 이웃이 물을 가져가지 못하게 했다고 한 (A) 뒤에 와야 한다. (B)는 농부와 이웃이 말다툼을 하다가 판사에게 그 문제를 맡겼다는 내용이므로 두 사람이 서로 말다툼하기 시작한 (D) 다음에 오는 것이 적절하다. (C)는 판사가 판결을 내리는 내용이므로 판사를 찾아갔다고 한 (B) 다음에 오는 것이 적절하다. 따라서 글의 순서로 가장 적절한 것은 ④ (D) - (B) - (C)이다.

44 지칭 대상 파악하기 정답 ②

해설 (a), (c), (d), (e)는 모두 농부를 가리키지만 (b)는 농부의 이웃을 가리키므로, ②이 정답이다.

45 세부 정보 파악하기 정답 ④

해설 (C)의 Since you are using the farmer's well to store your water, you must now pay him rent for using that space를 통해 판사가 이웃에게 돈을 더 내라고 말한 것을 알 수 있는데, ④은 농부에게 말했다고 일부 정보를 잘못 나타냈으므로 글의 내용과 일치하지 않는 것은 ④이다.

18	⑤	19	①	20	④	21	②	22	⑤	23	④	24	③	25	④	26	④	27	⑤
28	④	29	①	30	③	31	⑤	32	③	33	③	34	④	35	③	36	⑤	37	③
38	③	39	⑤	40	②	41	②	42	④	43	③	44	③	45	⑤				

18 목적 파악하기
정답 ⑤

해설 send you some guidelines(지침을 전달하다)라는 표현을 이용해 축제 책임자가 음악 축제에서 일할 진행 요원들에게 축제에서 지켜야 할 근무 관련 지침을 전달하고 있으므로, 정답은 ⑤이다.

해석 진행 요원들께,

저는 다가오는 Wild Birch 음악 축제에서 여러분 모두를 만날 것에 매우 들떠 있습니다. 그 행사가 다음 주이기 때문에, 저는 여러분들에게 축제 동안 근무하는 것과 관련된 몇 가지 지침들을 전해드려야겠다고 생각했습니다. 저희는 모두가 준비되었고 관객들에게 좋은 주말을 선사할 수 있다는 것을 확실하게하고 싶습니다. 이를 이루기 위해, 진행 요원들은 행사 참석자들이 진행 요원에게 제기하는 모든 항의와 문의를 처리하도록 요구됩니다. 참가자들에게 이야기할 때 인내와 적극성을 실천해주시고, 만약 당신이 문의에 답변을 할 수 없다면 그 상황을 처리할 수 있도록 운영자를 찾아서 알려주십시오. 저희는 축제가 성공적이게 하기 위해 모두가 최선을 다할 것임을 알고 있습니다. 어떠한 질문이라도 있으면, 제게 연락해주십시오.

축제 책임자 Rachel Park 드림

어휘 accomplish 이루다, 해내다   expect 요구하다, 예상하다
address 처리하다, 연설하다   patience 인내   positivity 적극성, 확실함
inquiry 문의   locate 찾아내다   coordinator 책임자, 조정자

구문분석 [2행] I am so **excited** [to meet all of you at the upcoming Wild Birch Music Festival].
→ [to ~ Festival]은 to부정사의 부사적 용법으로, 감정의 원인을 나타낸다.

[10행] Please practice patience and positivity [**when** talking to participants] ~
→ [when ~ participants]는 분사구문의 의미를 분명하게 하기 위해 부사절 접속사(when)가 분사(talking) 앞에 온 형태이다.

19 심경 파악하기
정답 ①

해설 심경은 간접적으로 표현된다. 글의 중반부의 Checking my watch again, I groaned and rolled my eyes를 통해 'I'가 발표에 늦을까 봐 불안해하는 것을 알 수 있고, 후반부의 I could finally relax를 통해 제시간에 회의에 도착할 수 있게 되어서 안도감을 느꼈다는 것을 알 수 있으므로, 'I'의 심경 변화로 가장 적절한 것은 ①이다.

해석 발표가 있는 중요한 날이었고, 나는 늦어지고 있었다. 나는 버스를 기다리면서 발을 굴렀고, 버스는 도착하는 데에 평소보다 오래 걸리고 있었다. 만약 내가

회의 중간에 도착한다면 내 상사가 화를 낼 것임을 나는 알고 있었다. 내 시계를 다시 확인하고, 나는 끙 하는 소리를 내며 눈을 굴렸다. 내게 어떤 다른 방법들이 있는지 몰라서, 내 상사에게 문자 메시지를 보내려던 참이었다. "Chloe!" 누가 큰 소리로 부르는 것을 듣고 나는 올려다보았다. "태워 드릴까요?" 그건 내 동료인 Rachel이었다! 나는 매우 열심히 고개를 끄덕였고, 그녀의 차에 뛰어 올라탔다. "Rachel, 당신이 내 목숨을 구했어요!" 직장까지 차를 타고 간다면, 나는 확실히 제시간에 회의에 도착할 수 있을 것이다. 나는 마침내 안심할 수 있었다.

① 불안한 → 안도하는
② 걱정하는 → 후회하는
③ 희망에 찬 → 낙담한
④ 화난 → 우쭐해하는
⑤ 짜증 난 → 질투하는

어휘 groan (고통, 절망 등으로) 끙 하는 소리를 내다, 신음하다
enthusiastically 매우 열심히, 열광적으로   make it to ~에 도착하다, 이르다

구문분석 [7행] I <u>heard</u> <u>someone</u> <u>shout</u>, so I looked up.
　　　　　　동사　　목적어　목적격 보어
→ 지각동사 heard의 목적어로 someone, 목적격 보어로 동사원형 shout가 쓰였다.

20 주장 파악하기
정답 ④

해설 글의 첫 두 문장과 마지막 문장에서 아이들이 더 바르게 행동하도록 하기 위해 부모들이 하는 말이 아이들의 부정적인 특성들을 강화하는 꼬리표가 될 수 있으므로, 부모들은 아이들을 묘사할 때 사용하는 말들을 의식하고 있어야 한다고 주장하고 있다. 따라서 정답은 ④이다.

오답분석 ②은 아이들의 부정적인 특성을 묘사하는 말을 의식하고 있어야 한다는 글의 주장과 무관하게 아이들을 칭찬하는 것에 대한 내용이므로 오답이다.

해석 부모들이 아이들에게 "부끄러워하지 마라"나 "게으름 피우지 마라"라고 말할 때, 그 의도는 아이들이 더 바르게 행동하도록 하기 위함이다. 하지만, 부모들은 그 말들이 실제로는 그들이 묘사하는 부정적인 특성들을 강화하는 꼬리표로 작용한다는 것을 알아야 한다. 아이들을 부르기 위해 부모들과 교육자들이 특정 단어들을 지속적으로 사용할 때, 그 아이들은 그러한 단어들이 그들을 정의한다고 믿게 된다. 그 아이들은 무의식적으로 이 특징들을 그들의 정체성의 일부로서 받아들이고 그들에게 부여된 꼬리표에 어울리는 방식으로 행동하기 시작한다. 게다가, 아이들이 그들의 부모가 그들에게 붙인 꼬리표에 어울리지 않는 방식으로 행동할 때, 그들은 칭찬이나 다른 예상 밖의 긍정적 강화에 반응하는 데에 어려움을 느끼고 그들의 원래의 행동으로 되돌아갈 수도 있다. 이는 아이들이 그들의 부모가 말리려고 하는 부정적인 특성들을 없애는 것을 어렵게 만든다. 그것이 바로 부모들이 아이들을 묘사할 때 그들이 사용하는 말들을 의식하고 있는 것이 중요한 이유이다.

어휘 label 꼬리표, 라벨   reinforce 강화하다   trait 특성, 특징

unconsciously 무의식적으로 adopt 받아들이다, 채택하다
praise 칭찬하다 revert 되돌아가다, 회복하다
discourage 말리다, 좌절시키다

[1행] When parents tell children "don't be shy" or "don't be lazy," the intention is [to make their children behave better].
　　　　　　　　　　　　　 주어　　동사　　　　 주격 보어

→ [to ~ better]는 to부정사의 명사적 용법(~하는 것)으로, be동사 is의 주격 보어 역할을 한다.

[14행] This makes it difficult for the children [to lose the
　　　　　　　　 가목적어　　 의미상 주어
negative traits] that their parents are trying to discourage.
진목적어(to부정사구)

→ 가목적어 it이 길이가 긴 진목적어 to부정사구 [to ~ traits] 대신 동사 makes의 목적어 자리에 쓰인 형태이다.

→ for the children은 'for + 명사' 형태로, to부정사구의 의미상 주어이다.

21　밑줄 의미 추론하기　　정답 ②

(해설) 비즈니스 협상을 할 때는 양측 모두가 최대의 이득을 얻도록 해야 하고, 상대방을 이기려고만 한다면 지속적인 거래로 이어질 수 없다고 말하고 있다. 따라서 글의 주제를 비유적으로 표현한 even when you win, you lose(당신이 이겨도 당신은 진다)가 의미하는 것은 '② 목전의 이득에만 초점을 두는 것은 장기간의 관계에 영향을 미칠 수도 있다'이다.

(오답분석) ①은 글의 핵심 소재 negotiation과 유사한 의미인 deal과, 글에 언급된 strategy를 사용하여 헷갈리게 하는 오답이다. ③의 장기간 협력의 문제점에 대해서는 글에서 언급되지 않았다. ④은 글에서 공정한 합의가 가질 수 있는 부정적인 결과에 대해 다루고 있지 않으므로 오답이다. ⑤은 협상할 때 이기려고 하지 않아야 한다고 한 글의 내용과 반대되는 내용이므로 오답이다.

(해석) 비즈니스 협상에서, 한쪽 당사자는 흔히 상대방을 이기려고 한다. 하지만, 만약 당신이 이렇게 한다면, 당신이 이겨도 당신은 진다는 것을 알 수 있을 것이다. 상대방은 아마 분개할 것이고 앞으로 당신과 거래하기를 꺼릴 것이다. 이는 많은 전문가들이 협상할 때 "모두에게 유리한" 사고방식을 지지하는 이유이다. 그것은 어떤 합의가 이루어지든 모두가 최대의 이득을 얻는 것을 보장하기 위한 의식적인 노력을 수반한다. 이 접근법의 중요한 요소는 각 당사자가 얻는 가치를 측정하는 데에 사용될 수 있는 객관적인 기준에 중점을 두는 것이다. 일부 경우들에서, 이것은 합의가 공평한지에 대한 최종 판정을 할 중립적인 중재자를 찾는 것을 필요로 할 것이다. 상대방이 그 또는 그녀의 목표를 달성할 수 있도록 상당한 양보를 하는 것 또한 종종 필요하다. 이 협상 전략은 일회성의 거래들 대신 지속적인 협력으로 이어질 가능성이 훨씬 더 높다.
① 다양한 전략들에 대한 지식은 최상의 거래를 성사시키는 데에 필수적이다.
② 목전의 이득에만 초점을 두는 것은 장기간의 관계에 영향을 미칠 수도 있다.
③ 장기간의 비즈니스 협력은 종종 예기치 않은 문제들을 수반한다.
④ 공정해 보이는 합의들이 상대방보다 한쪽 당사자에게 이득이 될 수도 있다.
⑤ 협상에 참여할 때, 패배를 피하는 것이 주요한 목적이어야 한다.

(어휘) party 당사자, 관계자 resentful 분개하는 advocate 지지하다, 옹호하다
win-win 모두에게 유리한 mindset 사고방식 conscious 의식적인
arbitrator 중재자 grant a concession 양보하다
one-off 일회성의, 한 사람만의 [선택지] immediate 목전의, 즉각적인
extended 장기간의, 광범위에 걸친

[8행] An important element of this approach is a focus on **an objective standard** ①[that can be used to measure **the value**] ②[that each party receives].

→ ①[that ~ value]는 선행사 an objective standard를 수식하며 주격 관계대명사 that이 이끄는 관계대명사절이고, ②[that ~ receives]는 선행사 the value를 수식하며 목적격 관계대명사 that이 이끄는 관계대명사절이다.

[11행] In some cases, this will require finding a neutral arbitrator to make the final determination of [whether an agreement is fair].

→ [whether ~ fair]는 접속사 whether가 이끄는 명사절로, 전치사 of의 목적어 역할을 한다.

22　요지 파악하기　　정답 ⑤

(해설) 글의 첫 문장과 마지막 문장에서 오늘날 청년들의 개인적 성취에 대한 강박은 그들의 정신 건강, 성격, 그리고 도덕성의 희생이 따르더라도 그들이 자신만의 성공을 위해 노력하게 만든다는 요지가 제시되어 있으므로, 이 글의 요지로 가장 적절한 것은 ⑤이다.

(오답분석) ③은 성공에 대한 과거의 잣대에 대해서는 글에서 다루고 있지 않으므로 오답이다. ④은 이 글은 청년들의 개인적 정서 불안을 야기시킨 성공에 대한 강박이라는 문제에 대해 말하고 있으므로 오답이다.

(해석) 청년들 사이의 많은 불안과 우울은 성공에 대한 계속 커지는 압박감에서 기인한다. 전국적인 조사에서, 거의 80퍼센트 청년들은 개인적인 성취가 다른 사람들에게 마음을 쓰는 것보다 그들에게 더 중요하다고 말했다. 인류 역사의 많은 부분이 성공에 대한 욕구 덕분에 진보해 왔지만, 현대에 들어서 성공은 강박으로 변했다. 이전에, 성공은 건강, 공감, 가족, 그리고 친구와 같은 삶의 다른 측면들과 균형을 이뤘다. 지금은, 성취에 대한 그 강박은 청년들이 어떤 대가를 치르더라도 그들 자신의 성공을 위해 노력하게 만들었다. 그들 자신이 가진 다른 모습들을 해치도록 그들을 밀어붙이는 것은 욕구이다. 성취하고자 하는 그들의 욕구가 반드시 나쁜 것은 아니지만, 청년들이 오로지 개인적 목표만을 위해 성공을 추구할 때 문제들이 발생한다. 이는 궁극적으로 그들의 정신 건강, 성격, 그리고 도덕성의 희생이 따른다.

(어휘) obsession 강박 prosperity 성공, 번영 facet 측면 empathy 공감
drive 욕구, 충동 detriment 해치기, 손상 morality 도덕성

[11행] **It is** a drive **that** pushes them forward to the detriment of other aspects of themselves.

→ a drive를 강조하는 it is ~ that 강조 구문이 쓰였다.

[12행] Although their drive to achieve is **not necessarily** a bad thing, problems ~

→ not necessarily는 '반드시 ~은 아닌'이라는 의미로 부분 부정을 나타내는 구문이다.

23　주제 파악하기　　정답 ④

(해설) 마지막 세 문장으로 미루어 보아 경제 상승, 안정, 하락이 길게 지속되는 기간을 나타내는 각 파동의 원인, 주기를 식별하는 기준 등에 대한 합의가 없으므로 많은 이들이 Kondratiev 파동 이론을 인정하지 않는다는 내용의 글이다.

따라서 이 글의 주제로 가장 적절한 것은 ④ '세계 경제의 식별 가능한 주기의 존재에 대한 의구심'이다.

(오답분석) ①은 경제적 파동 주기가 시작하고 끝나는 해를 식별하는 기준에 대한 합의가 없다는 글의 내용과 반대되는 내용이기 때문에 오답이다.

(해석) 구소련의 경제학자인 Nikolai Kondratiev(니콜라이 콘드라티예프)에 의해 그의 1925년 책 <주요 경제 주기>에서 소개된 Kondratiev 파동은 세계 경제의 가설상 주기이다. Kondratiev는 경제 상승, 안정기, 하락이 길게 지속되는 기간을 나타내는 각 파동이 기술 혁신과 변화의 시기들에서 비롯되었다고 생각했다. Kondratiev 파동은 일부 투자자들에게 흥미 있는 사안이자 매력적인 학문적 논의 주제이지만, 대부분의 경제학자들은 주로 그 이론의 불명확한 본질 때문에 그것들이 실재한다는 것조차 인정하지 않는다. 40에서 60년 사이인 각 파동의 상대적으로 긴 지속 기간으로 인해, 파동의 원인에 대한 공식적인 동의, 파동 주기가 시작하고 끝나는 해를 식별하는 기준들 혹은 어느 시점에 경제가 파동의 어디에 있는지에 대한 합의조차도 없다. 일반적으로, 많은 이들은 Kondratiev의 이론이 존재하지도 않을 수 있는 패턴을 알아본 것을 기반으로 했다고 말한다.

① 새로운 경제적 파동의 시작을 식별하는 방법들
② 세계적으로 경제에 미치는 기술 혁신의 혜택들
③ 시장의 성쇠 시기를 예측하는 것을 중요성
④ 세계 경제의 식별 가능한 주기의 존재에 대한 의구심
⑤ Kondratiev 파동 이론이 현대 투자자들에게 유용할 수 있는 이유들

(어휘) cycle 주기, 순환 wave 파동, 물결 hypothetical 가설상의, 가정된 imprecise 불명확한, 부정확한 identify 식별하다, 알아보다 consensus 합의, 일치 [선택지] ups and downs 성쇠, 오르내림

(구문분석)
[13행] ~ any consensus **about** [where an economy is on a wave at any time] due to the relatively long duration of each one — between 40 and 60 years.
→ [where ~ time]은 의문사 where가 이끄는 명사절로, 전치사 about의 목적어 역할을 한다.

24 제목 파악하기   정답 ③

(해설) 첫 세 문장과 마지막 두 문장으로 미루어 보아 노래의 운과 리듬은 뇌가 기억해내기에 단순한 패턴으로 정보를 적절하게 정리하고, 가사와 이미지에 특정 정보를 기억하는 데에 도움이 되는 단서들이 숨겨져 있기 때문에 음악이 무언가를 기억하는 것을 돕는 도구가 된다는 내용의 글이다. 따라서 글의 제목으로 가장 적절한 것은 '③ 음악이 어떻게 기억을 불러오는 데에 도움이 되는가'이다.

(오답분석) ①은 글에서 음악이 환기시키는 이미지에 숨겨진 단서들이 특정 정보를 기억하는 데에 도움을 준다고 했지만, 왜 음악이 이미지를 만들어내는지에 대해서는 언급하지 않았다. ②은 글에서 언급된 cues와 remembering을 사용하여 헷갈리게 하는 오답이다. ⑤은 글에서 언급되고 있지 않다.

(해석) 아마 한 노래가 당신의 머릿속에 박히게 된 적이 있었을 것이다. 다른 정보는 잊지 않으려고 애쓸지도 모르지만, 당신이 외우려고 의도하지 않았던 가사들은 노력 없이도 생각난다. 이는 음악이 기억 장치이기 때문이다; 이는 무언가를 기억하는 것을 돕는 도구이다. 노래는 흔히 운과 리듬으로 구성되고, 운과 리듬은 뇌가 기억해내기에 단순한 패턴으로 정보를 적절하게 정리한다. 하지만, 사람은 해마와 전두엽에 많은 기억을 처리하고 저장하며, 해마와 전두엽은 매분 상당한 양의 정보를 받아들이기 때문에, 특정 정보를 기억하는 것은 언제나 그렇게 간단하지 않다. 그렇기는 하지만, 음악에는 특정 정보를 기억하는 데에 도움을 주는 많은 단서들(그것들이 환기시키는 가사와 이미지들에 숨겨

진)이 포함되어 있다. 이는 당신이 기억할 필요가 있는 어떤 정보에든 멜로디를 붙이는 것은 그것을 기억해 내는 당신의 능력을 향상시킬 것이라는 점을 의미한다.

① 음악은 왜 머릿속의 이미지를 만들어내는가?
② 시각적 단서들: 가사를 기억하는 것의 비결
③ 음악이 어떻게 기억을 불러오는 데에 도움이 되는가
④ 운과 리듬: 정보의 복잡한 패턴
⑤ 암기를 향상시키는 여러 가지 효과적인 수단

(어휘) word 가사, 말 come to mind 생각나다, 기억나다 retain 잊지 않고 있다, 유지하다 mnemonic 기억의, 기억을 돕는 device 장치 rhyme (시의) 운 neatly 적절히, 솜씨 있게 recollect 기억해내다 straightforward 간단한, 직접의 cue 단서, 신호 evoke 환기시키다, 떠올려 주다 bring A to mind A를 기억하다, 상기하다 tune 멜로디, 선율 [선택지] contribute 도움이 되다, 기여하다 memorization 암기, 기억

(구문분석)
[1행] **Chances are** you've had a song get stuck in your head.
→ chances are (that)은 '아마 ~할 것이다'라는 의미의 관용 구문이다.

[6행] Songs often consist of **rhymes and rhythm**, [which neatly organize information into patterns that are simple for the brain to recollect].
→ [which ~ recollect]는 선행사 rhymes and rhythm을 수식하는 주격 관계대명사절로, 콤마 뒤에서 계속적 용법으로 쓰였다.

25 도표 정보 파악하기   정답 ④

(해설) 한국에서 무급 근무에 배분된 시간은 2.2시간으로, 여가에 배분된 시간인 4.3시간의 절반(2.15)보다 더 적은 것이 아니라 반대로 더 많으므로 수치의 비교 표현이 잘못 반영되었다. 따라서 도표의 내용과 일치하지 않는 것은 ④이다.

(해석)

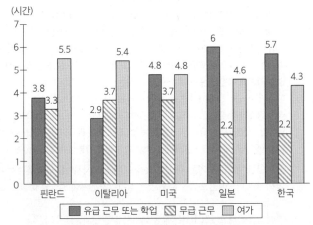

5개국에서의 활동별 시간 배분

위 도표는 사람들이 하루에 얼마나 많은 시간을 유급 근무 또는 학업, 무급 근무, 그리고 여가에 쓰는지를 보여준다. ① 5개국 중에서, 핀란드와 이탈리아가 여가 활동에 들이는 시간의 양에서 각각 1위와 2위를 차지한다. ② 미국에서, 유급 근무 또는 학업에 들이는 시간은 4.8시간이고, 이는 그 국가에서 무급 근무에 들이는 시간보다 1시간 이상 더 길다. ③ 일본에서 유급 근무 또는 학업에 들이는 시간은 이탈리아의 그것(유급 근무 또는 학업에 소비되는 시간)의 2배보다 더 길다. ④ 한국의 경우, 무급 근무에 배분된 시간의 양은 여가에 쏟은 시간의 절반보다 더 적다. ⑤ 이탈리아를 제외한 모든 나라에서 무급 근무에 사용된 시간은 세 개의 시간 배분 범주들 중 가장 적다.

어휘 allocation 배분, 할당 devote (시간을 ~에) 쏟다, 바치다

구문 분석

[8행] Time spent on paid work or study in Japan is more than twice as long as **that** in Italy.

→ 지시대명사 that은 앞의 명사구 Time spent on paid work or study 를 가리키며, 비교 구문에서 동일한 명사구가 반복되는 것을 피하기 위해 사용되었다.

[11행] The time spent on unpaid work is [the least of three time-allocation categories in] all the countries except Italy.

→ [the ~ in]은 'the + 최상급 + in'(-에서 가장 ~한)의 형태로 최상급을 나타내는 구문이다.

---

26 세부 정보 파악하기 정답 ④

해설 the Second World War soon began과 Even after the traumatic experience, Levinas returned to teaching을 통해 2차 세계대전 이후에 Emmanuel Levinas가 가르치는 일에 복귀했다는 것을 알 수 있는데, ④은 가르치는 일을 그만두었다고 일부 정보를 잘못 나타냈으므로 글의 내용과 일치하지 않는 것은 ④이다.

해석 Emmanuel Levinas(에마뉘엘 레비나스)는 20세기의 가장 유명한 철학 사상가들 중 한 명이었다. 그는 1906년 리투아니아의 카우나스에서 태어났고, 전통적인 유대인 집안에서 자랐다. 18세의 나이에, Levinas는 그가 철학을 전공했던 프랑스의 Strasbourg 대학에서 공부하려고 떠났다. 그리고 나서 그는 독일에 있는 Freiburg 대학을 다니기 시작했고, 그곳에서 그는 유명한 철학자들인 Edmund Husserl(에드문트 후설)과 Martin Heidegger(마르틴 하이데거)에게서 가르침을 받았다. 결국, Levinas 자신이 강사가 되었지만, 제2차 세계대전이 곧 시작되었다. 그는 5년 동안 강제 노동 수용소에서 포로로 잡혀 있었고, 나치 당원의 손에 의해 그의 가족들의 죽음을 겪었다. 대단히 충격적인 경험 이후에도, Levinas는 가르치는 일에 복귀했고 그의 가장 유명한 작품들 몇 가지를 출판했다. 그의 작품에서, 그는 Husserl과 Heidegger의 사상들에 대해 견해를 밝히고 윤리학의 중요성을 강조하면서, "타자의 얼굴"과 인간의 의식에 대한 관심을 끌어냈다.

어휘 renowned 유명한 thinker 사상가, 사색가 Jewish 유대인의, 유대교의 hold A prisoner A를 포로로 잡아두다 labor camp 강제 노동 수용소 traumatic 대단히 충격적인, 정신적 외상을 초래할 정도의 ethics 윤리학, 도덕 consciousness 의식

구문 분석

[4행] At the age of 18, Levinas left to study at **the University of Strasbourg in France** [where he majored in philosophy].

→ [where ~ philosophy]는 선행사 the University of Strasbourg in France를 수식하며, 장소를 나타내는 관계부사 where가 이끄는 관계부사절이다.

[15행] In his work, he commented on the ideas of Husserl and Heidegger and highlighted the importance of ethics, [drawing attention to the "face of the Other" and human consciousness].

→ [drawing ~ consciousness]는 '~하면서'라는 의미의 분사구문으로, 분사구문의 주어가 주절의 주어(he)와 같아서 생략되었다.

---

27 안내문 정보 파악하기 정답 ⑤

해설 For more information, visit the Norwalk Community Center website (www.norwalkcc.org) or call 222-3478을 통해 더 많은 정보는 웹사이트 나 전화로 얻을 수 있다는 것을 알 수 있으므로, 글의 내용과 일치하지 않는 것은 ⑤이다.

해석

Norwalk 시 2022년 나무 심기 행사

Norwalk 시민 문화 회관은 9월 26일에 연례 나무 심기 행사를 열 것입니다. 가족 및 친구들과 오셔서 저희와 함께하세요!

- 참가자들은 오전 10시까지 시청 앞 광장에 모여야 합니다.
- 나무는 무료로 배분될 것입니다.
※ 물량이 한정되어 있으므로, 선착순일 것입니다.
- 참가는 모두에게 무료입니다.

나무 심기 후에, 참가한 모두에게 다과가 제공될 것입니다. 12세 이하 어린이들은 행사를 기념하여 나무 모양 핀을 받을 것입니다.

더 많은 정보를 원하시면, Norwalk 시민 문화 회관 웹사이트(www. norwalkcc.org)를 방문하시거나 222-3478로 전화해주십시오.

어휘 community center 시민 문화 회관, 주민 센터 annual 연례의 first come, first served 선착순 refreshments 다과, 음식물 in honor of ~을 기념하여, 축하하여

구문 분석

[8행] Trees [will be handed out] for free.

→ [will ~ out]은 조동사(will)가 있는 '조동사 + be + p.p.' 형태의 수동 태이다.

[12행] After the planting, refreshments will be provided to **all** [who participated].

→ [who participated]는 선행사 all을 수식하며, 주격 관계대명사 who 가 이끄는 관계대명사절이다.

---

28 안내문 정보 파악하기 정답 ④

해설 During the auditions, we will: 2. Study scripts in small groups를 통해 오디션 중에 소그룹으로 대본을 살펴보는 활동을 한다는 것을 알 수 있으므로, 글의 내용과 일치하는 것은 ④이다.

해석

제5회 Fairfield 고등학교
연극 동아리 오디션

무대에 서는 것을 항상 꿈꾸셨나요? 그렇다면, 연극 동아리에 오셔서 당신의 꿈을 현실로 만드세요.

- **언제**: 9월 27일 월요일 오후 5시-7시
- **어디에서**: Fairfield 강당
- **누가**: Fairfield 고등학교 학생은 누구나
- **가져올 것**: 동의서 (보호자의 서명이 되어 있어야 함)

오디션 중에, 우리는 다음을 할 것입니다:
1. 긴장을 풀고 준비하는 활동에 참여합니다.
2. 소그룹으로 대본을 살펴봅니다.
3. 선배 동아리 부원들 앞에서 개별 오디션을 봅니다.

결과는 10월 1일 금요일에 202호 밖에 게시될 것입니다.

어휘 auditorium 강당 guardian 보호자, 관리자
icebreaker 긴장을 깨는 것, 딱딱한 분위기를 푸는 것

구문분석
[3행] Always dreamed **of** [being on the stage]?
→ [being ~ stage]는 전치사 of의 목적어 역할을 하는 동명사구이다.

[10행] [What to bring]: a permission form (signed by a guardian)
→ [What to bring]은 '~할 것'이라는 의미의 'what + to부정사' 구문이다.

29 어법상 틀린 것 찾기   정답 ①

해설 '일반 성인이 11시간을 소비하므로'라는 의미가 되는 것이 자연스러우므로 「with + (대)명사 + 분사」를 써야 한다. 분사의 의미상 주어 the average adult는 spend가 나타내는 '소비하는' 행위의 주체이므로 ①의 과거분사 spent를 현재분사 spending으로 고쳐야 한다.

오답분석 ②은 명사절 접속사 that이 이끄는 종속절 안에서 technology가 주어이고 등위 접속사 and로 연결되어 앞의 makes, prevents와 병렬 구조를 이뤄야 하므로 단수동사 ruins를 사용한 것은 어법상 적절하다. ③은 뒤에 주어 they, 동사 refrain, 전치사의 목적어 using electronic devices가 모두 있는 완전한 절이 왔으므로 '전치사 + 관계대명사' in which를 사용한 것은 어법상 적절하다. ④은 주절의 주어 자리에 명사 역할을 하는 동명사 disconnecting을 사용한 것은 어법상 적절하다. ⑤은 부정어 not only가 문장 앞으로 온 도치 구문으로, 어순이 '조동사(can) + 주어(it) + 동사원형'이 되어야 하므로 동사원형 reverse를 사용한 것은 어법상 적절하다.

해석 일반 성인이 하루에 11시간을 스마트폰이나 컴퓨터를 사용하고, 비디오 게임을 하고, TV를 시청하는 데에 소비하므로, 일부 전문가들이 기술과 기기의 남용이 문제가 되고 있다고 생각하는 것은 놀랍지 않다. 많은 사람들은 기술이 그들의 삶을 더 스트레스가 많게 만들고 그들이 잠을 자는 것을 방해하며 그들의 정신 건강을 해친다고 말하며 동의한다. 그것이 바로 일부 사람들이 "디지털 디톡스"라고 일컬어지는 것을 시도하고 있는 이유이다. 이것은 가족이나 친구들과 어울리기 위해, 잠시 동안 모든 디지털 기기들을 포기하는 것을 의미하든 단순히 너무 많은 시간을 잡아먹는 어떤 애플리케이션이나 프로그램을 피하는 것을 의미하든지 간에, 그들이 전자기기를 사용하는 것을 자제하는 기간이다. 디지털 디톡스라는 발상이 불가능하거나 불편하게 들릴지도 모르지만, 당신의 기기에서 손을 떼는 것은 긍정적인 효과가 있을 수 있다. 그것은 과도한 기술 사용으로 인해 야기되는 문제들을 전환할 수 있을 뿐만 아니라, 당신이 실제 경험들을 하는 동안 더 주의를 기울이고 몰두하는 데에 도움이 될 수도 있다.

어휘 overuse 남용; 남용하다 ruin 해치다, 망가뜨리다
refrain 자제하다, 억제하다 socialize (사람들과) 어울리다
disconnect 떼다, 연결을 끊다 reverse 전환하다, 반전시키다
mindful 주의하는, 염두하는 engaged 몰두하는, 바쁜

구문분석
[3행] ~ <u>it</u> is unsurprising [that some experts believe the
가주어   진주어(that절)
<u>overuse of technology and devices is becoming a problem</u>].
→ 가주어 it이 길이가 긴 진주어 that절 [that ~ problem] 대신에 주어 자리에 쓰인 형태이다.

[5행] Many people agree, saying that technology makes their lives more stressful, [prevents them from sleeping], ~

→ [prevents ~ sleeping]은 prevent A from V-ing의 형태로 'A가 ~하는 것을 방해하다'라는 의미의 동명사 관용 표현이다.

30 어휘 적절성 파악하기   정답 ③

해설 직장에서 윤리적 문제가 발생함에도 불구하고 그것을 비판하는 것을 막으려는 조직의 제약으로 인해 문제를 무시해야 하는 압박을 경험할 수 있다는 맥락이 되어야 하므로, ③의 acknowledge(인정하다)를 그와 반대되는 의미의 ignore(무시하다)와 같은 어휘로 바꾸어야 문맥상 적절하다.

오답분석 ②은 도덕적으로 용감한 사람은 세상에 긍정적인 변화를 가져오고 싶어 하지만 그들의 행동에 부정적인 결과가 있을 수 있음을 또한 이해하고 있다는 문맥이 되어야 하므로 positive가 오는 것이 적절하다. ⑤은 자신이 일자리를 잃거나 다른 결과를 직면할 수 있음을 충분히 인지하면서도 목소리를 내기를 선택한다는 문맥이 되어야 하므로 aware가 오는 것이 적절하다.

해석 넓은 의미로 용기는 위험에 맞서서 행동을 취하는 능력이지만, 용기에는 많은 다양한 유형들이 있다. 도덕적 용기는 ① 주의 깊고 신중한 숙고를 필요로 하는 용기의 한 가지 유형이다. 도덕적으로 용감한 사람은 무엇이 옳고 그른지에 대한 강한 인식을 지니고 세상에 ② 긍정적인 변화를 가져오기를 원하는 경향이 있다. 하지만, 그들은 또한 그들의 행동들에 부정적인 결과가 있을 수도 있음을 이해하고, 문제의 발생에도 불구하고 그것을 ③ 인정해야 하는(→무시해야 하는) 압박을 경험할 수도 있다. 예를 들어, 직장에서 윤리적 문제가 발생할 수 있고, 대다수의 사람들이 그것을 잘못된 것으로 인정하더라도 조직의 제약이 그들이 그것을 ④ 비판하는 것을 막을 수도 있다. 하지만 자신들이 일자리를 잃거나 다른 결과를 직면할 수 있다고 충분히 ⑤ 인지한 도덕적으로 용감한 사람은 공모하는 것은 부도덕하다고 판단하고 대신 무언가 말하기를 선택할 것이다.

어휘 deliberate 신중한 effect (결과를) 가져오다; 효과 incidence 발생, 범위
immoral 부도덕한 reason 판단하다, 추리하다 complicit 공모한, 연루된

구문분석
[13행] However, **a morally courageous person**, [(who is) fully aware that they could lose their job or face other consequences], would reason that ~
→ [fully ~ consequences]는 a morally courageous person을 설명하는 관계절로, '주격 관계대명사(who) + be동사(is)'가 생략되었다.

31 빈칸 추론하기   정답 ⑤

해설 기린의 목의 첫 번째 흉추가 사실 경추처럼 기능한다는 내용의 글이다. 주제와 관련된 빈칸 문장에서는 이것이 기린의 목에 더 많은 '무엇'을 주어서, 그들을 더 높은 곳의 먹이와 더 낮은 곳의 물에 닿을 수 있게 한다고 하였다. 따라서 빈칸에는 ⑤ '유연성'이 와서 기린의 첫 번째 흉추가 경추처럼 기능하는 것은 기린의 목에 더 많은 유연성을 준다는 의미가 되어야 한다.

오답분석 ①, ②, ③, ④은 기린의 목이 높은 곳과 낮은 곳에 더 잘 닿게 하는 특성을 설명하는 단어로 적절하지 않다.

해석 나무늘보와 해우를 제외한 거의 모든 포유류에는 7개의 경추가 있다. 하지만, 요추와 흉추의 수는 포유류에 따라 더 다양하다. 기린의 엄청나게 긴 목에도 불구하고, 과학자들은 기린이 대부분의 다른 포유류와 유사했고, 그들이 7개의 경추가 있다고 항상 생각했었다. 하지만, Tokyo 대학교에 의해 진행된 연구는 기린의 독특한 목에 관련된 추정들이 틀릴 수도 있음을 보여주었다; 실제로, 그들은 기린의 첫 번째 흉추가 실은 경추처럼 기능한다는 것을 발견했

다. 이것은 기린의 목에 더 많은 <u>유연성</u>을 주는데, 이는 그들이 더 높은 곳의 먹이와 더 낮은 곳의 물에 닿을 수 있게 한다. 따라서 경추의 운동성에 필적하는 기린의 첫 번째 흉추의 높은 운동성은 이 뼈가 몸통보다는 목의 일부로 기능한다는 것을 보여준다.

① 압력 　　　　　　　　 ② 저항력
③ 내구성 　　　　　　　　 ④ 장애
⑤ 유연성

 어휘 sloth 나무늘보　manatee 해우, 바다소　assumption 추정, 가정
mobility 운동성, 움직이기 쉬움　comparable to ~에 필적하는
[선택지] durability 내구성

구문분석

> [4행] Despite the giraffe's enormously long neck, scientists have always **believed** ①[that giraffes were similar to most other mammals] **and** ②[that they have seven cervical vertebrae].
>
> → 동사 believed의 목적어 역할을 하는 that절 ①[that ~ mammals]와 ②[that ~ vertebrae]는 등위접속사 and로 연결된 병렬 구조이다.
>
> [14행] The high mobility of the giraffe's first thoracic vertebra, ①[which is comparable to that of a cervical vertebra], **indicates** ②[that this bone therefore acts as part of the neck rather than the body].
>
> → ①[which ~ vertebra]는 선행사 The high ~ thoracic vertebra를 수식하는 주격 관계대명사절로, 콤마 뒤에서 계속적 용법으로 쓰였다.
>
> → ②[that ~ body]는 접속사 that이 이끄는 명사절로, 동사 indicates의 목적어 역할을 한다.

32 빈칸 추론하기 　　　　　　　　정답 ③

해설 상심한 사람이 심장마비처럼 보이는 가슴 통증을 겪는 것으로 보아 고통스러운 상황에 심장이 말 그대로 "고장 날" 수 있다는 내용의 글이고, 빈칸 뒤 문장에서 동맥이 막힌 사람들과 달리 상심한 사람의 동맥은 정상으로 보이고 심장 질환의 징후가 없다고 설명했다. 따라서 주제와 관련된 빈칸에는 ③ '심장마비 질환처럼 보인다'가 와서 증상들이 심장마비 질환처럼 보일 뿐이기 때문에 심장병 전문의가 보통 당황한다는 의미가 되어야 한다.

오답분석 ①, ④, ⑤은 글의 내용과 관련이 없다. ②은 상심한 사람에게는 심장 질환에 흔히 나타나는 징후가 보이지 않는다고 하고, 어떠한 증상들로 인해 전문의들이 당황한다고 했으므로 최신 장비로 측정할 수 있다는 내용은 빈칸에 적절하지 않다.

해석 우리의 마음을 아프게 하는 인생의 일들에는 한계가 없는 듯해서, 우리는 고통스러운 상황들을 가볍게 여기는 것을 배우면서 대처한다. 하지만, 1991년에 의사들은 심장이 말 그대로 고통으로 "고장 날" 수 있다는 것을 발견했다. 사람들이 심장마비로 죽기 때문에 심장마비는 무섭고, 따라서 상심한 사람들이 가슴 통증을 느끼고 그것이 시시각각으로 악화될 때 그들이 심장마비를 겪고 있는 것은 아닌지를 의심한다. 심장병 전문의가 검사를 하고 문제를 암시하는 심전계의 변화들을 인지하지만, 증상들이 심장마비 질환처럼 보일 뿐이기 때문에 보통 당황한다. 동맥이 막힌 사람들에게 일어나는 질병들과 비교할 때, 상심한 사람의 동맥은 정상처럼 보이고 심장 질환에 흔한 다른 징후가 전혀 없다. 하지만, 그것은 사랑하는 사람의 죽음과 같이 인생을 바꿀만한 일이 일어났을 때 감정들이 얼마나 강력해질 수 있는지를 보여준다. 그것은 누군가의 심장이 망연자실하여, 순간적으로 해야 하는 대로 기능하지 않는 것과 같다.

① 말기 환자들의 특징

② 진보된 장비로 측정할 수 있는
③ 심장마비 질환처럼 보이는
④ 장기적인 치료로 다룰 수 있는
⑤ 더 가벼운 것을 암시하는

 어휘 make light of ~을 가볍게 여기다, 경시하다　literally 말 그대로, 실제로
heart attack 심장마비, 심근 경색　by the minute 시시각각으로
cardiologist 심장병 전문의, 심장학자　electrocardiographic 심전계의
stump 당황하게 하다, 난처하게 하다　artery 동맥
stun 망연자실하게 하다, 기절시키다　[선택지] terminal 말기의, 불치의
mimic ~처럼 보이다　heart failure 심장마비　addressable 다룰 수 있는
indicative ~을 나타내는

구문분석

> [15행] But that **shows** [how powerful emotions can be] when something life-changing occurs, ~
>
> → [how ~ occurs]는 동사 shows의 목적어 역할을 하는 명사절이다. 이 명사절은 'how + 형용사(powerful)' 뒤에 '주어(emotions) + 동사(can be)'가 온 구조이다.

33 빈칸 추론하기 　　　　　　　　정답 ③

해설 주제문에 해당하는 빈칸 문장에서 빛은 강력한데, 왜냐하면 그것의 부재로 그림자를 만들며 이는 '어떠하기' 때문이라고 했다. 글의 중반에서 조명을 바닥에 낮게 두어서 긴 그림자를 드리우는 것은 경외심과 신비감을 일깨울 수 있는 반면, 자연 일광이 쏟아져 들어오게 하는 큰 창문들은 차분함과 행복감을 줄 수 있다고 했다. 따라서 빈칸에는 ③ '공간의 점유자에게 감정적 영향을 끼친다'는 내용이 오는 것이 적절하다.

오답분석 ①, ②, ⑤은 글의 내용과 관련이 없다. ④의 빛이 방에 깊이감과 질감을 더한다는 내용은 글에서 언급되고 있지 않다.

해석 건축상 빛의 배치의 중요성은 단지 우리가 어떤 공간에서 걸어 다니기 위해 충분히 잘 보도록 돕는 것보다 훨씬 더 많은 일을 하기 때문에 아무리 과장되어도 지나치지 않는다. 빛은 강력한데, 왜냐하면 그것의 부재로 그림자를 만드는데, 이는 공간의 점유자에게 감정적 영향을 끼칠 수 있기 때문이다. 밖에서는 사람 그림자의 크기 및 모양이 태양의 위치에 따라 온종일 다른 것처럼, 기둥이나 격자와 같은 건축상 특징들의 비율은 방 안의 광원에 의해 영향을 받을 수 있다. 예를 들어, 긴 그림자를 드리우기 위해 조명을 바닥에 낮게 두는 것은 경외심과 신비감을 일깨울 수 있는 반면, 자연 일광이 쏟아져 들어오게 하는 큰 창문들이 있는 공간은 한 사람에게 차분함과 행복감을 줄 수 있다. 근본적으로, 빛은 공간의 분위기를 형성하면서 그림자의 형태로 건축물에 실재성을 부여하는 능력을 지니고 있다.

① 사람들의 주의를 방 안의 특정한 곳으로 끈다
② 건물 디자인의 결점이 드러나는 것을 최소화한다
③ 공간의 점유자에게 감정적 영향을 끼친다
④ 그렇지 않았더라면 평범했을 방에 깊이감과 질감을 더한다
⑤ 냉각 효과를 일으켜 건물이 더 에너지 효율적이게 만든다

어휘 lighting 빛의 배치, 조명법　overstate 과장하다
navigate 걸어 다니다, 항해하다　proportion 비율, 균형　column 기둥, 열
light source 광원　cast a shadow 그림자를 드리우다　evoke 일깨우다
awe 경외심, 두려움　natural sunlight 자연 일광　substance 실재성, 물질
[선택지] occupant 점유자, 거주자　texture 질감, 감촉
otherwise 그렇지 않았더라면 ~인

구문
분석
[10행] Positioning a light low to the ground to cast a long shadow, for instance, can evoke a sense of awe and mystery, [**while** a space with large windows that allows natural sunlight to pour through can give one a sense of calm and well-being].

→ [while ~ well-being]은 접속사 while(반면에)이 이끄는 양보의 부사절이다.

[14행] Essentially, light has the power to give substance to architecture in the form of shadows [**while** shaping the atmosphere of a space].

→ [while ~ space]는 분사구문의 의미를 분명하게 하기 위해 부사절 접속사(while)가 분사구문 앞에 온 형태이며, 이 문장에서는 while이 시간을 나타내는 접속사로 쓰였다.

구문
분석
[4행] Positivism, which emerged in the mid-to-late 19th century, was founded on **the belief** ①[that the social sciences ②[should be treated with] the same objective rigor and emphasis on empiricism and causality as the natural sciences].

→ ①[that ~ sciences]는 the belief와 동격을 이루는 명사절이다.

→ ②[should ~ with]는 조동사(should)가 있는 '조동사 + be + p.p.' 형태의 수동태이다.

[8행] To this end, Durkheim stated, "Our main goal is [to extend scientific rationalism to human conduct]." 동사
주격 보어

→ [to ~ conduct]는 to부정사의 명사적 용법(~하는 것)으로, be동사 is의 주격 보어 역할을 한다.

34 빈칸 추론하기 정답 ④

해설 글의 초반에서 현대 사회학에 영향을 준 실증주의는 사회 과학이 자연 과학처럼 객관적인 엄밀함을 갖추고 경험론 및 인과성을 중시해야 한다는 믿음에 기반을 두었다고 설명했다. In response to this approach(이러한 접근에 대응하여)로 시작하는 빈칸 뒤에서 사회학적 연구는 특정한 관점에서 이해해야 하고, 주관적인 형태의 탐구로서 기능할 것이라고 하며 실증주의적 사회학과 대조적인 개념을 설명하고 있다. 따라서 주제와 관련된 빈칸에는 ④ '반실증주의적 방법론이 점차 대두되었다'가 와야 한다.

오답
분석 ①, ③, ⑤번은 19세기 중후반의 실증주의적 생각의 맥락에 영향을 받은 사회학과 20세기 반실증주의적 방법론에 근거한 사회학을 대조하는 글의 내용과 관련이 없다. ②은 실증주의적 사회 과학과 반대되는 내용이 나와야 하는 글의 흐름과 반대되는 내용이므로 오답이다.

해석 현대 사회학의 발전은 프랑스의 저명한 지식인 Émile Durkheim(에밀 뒤르켐)과 그가 지지한 실증주의적 생각의 맥락의 영향을 크게 받았다. 19세기 중후반에 나타난 실증주의는 사회 과학도 자연 과학과 같은 객관적인 엄밀함을 가지고 그리고 경험론 및 인과성에 중점을 두고 다뤄져야 한다는 믿음에 기반을 두었다. 이를 위해서는, Durkheim은 "우리의 주된 목표는 과학적 합리주의를 인간 행위로 확장하는 것이다."라고 말했다. 이러한 접근에 대응하여, 20세기로 들어설 무렵에 반실증주의적 방법론이 점차 대두되었다. 많은 사회 과학자들은 사회학적 연구는 흔히 문화적으로 고착된, 매우 특정한 관점에서 문화적 행동, 가치, 상징을 이해해야 한다는 생각을 공공연히 받아들였다. 이 접근법은 독일의 사회학자이자 역사가인 Max Weber(막스 베버)를 포함한 많은 주요 지식인들에 의해 받아들여졌다. 그 중에서도 Weber는 자연 과학이 일반화할 수 있는 지식을 얻을 수 있을지도 모르지만, 사회 과학은 항상 주관적인 형태의 탐구로서 기능할 것이라고 주장했다.

① 사회학자들의 역할이 크게 바뀌었다
② 양적 연구 기법들이 개발되었다
③ 자연 과학은 여러 범주로 나뉘었다
④ 반실증주의적 방법론이 점차 대두되었다
⑤ 사회 과학이 더욱 중요해졌다

어휘 sociology 사회학 eminent 저명한 intellectual 지식인
positivist 실증주의의 train 맥락, 흐름 subscribe to ~을 지지하다
emerge 나타나다 rigor 엄밀함, 엄격함 empiricism 경험론
causality 인과성 rationalism 합리주의 embrace 받아들이다
generalizable 일반화될 수 있는 observation (관찰하여 얻은) 지식
inquiry 연구, 조사 [선택지] quantitative 양적인, 양에 관한
antipositivist 반실증주의적인

35 흐름과 관계 없는 문장 찾기 정답 ③

해설 사업을 반드시 성공적으로 완료하기 위해, 사업 관리자들은 잠재적 위험들의 심각성의 순위에 따라 위험 요인들을 관리하고 줄여야 한다는 내용의 글이다. 그런데 ③은 위험을 줄이는 데에 위험 자체의 대가 이상을 지불하게 된다면 위험을 받아들이는 것이 낫다는 내용이므로 핵심 소재는 같지만 주제에서 벗어나 있어 글의 흐름과 무관하다.

오답
분석 ①은 사업을 성공시키려면 잠재적 위험들을 줄여야 한다는 내용으로 이 글의 주제문에 해당하는 문장이다. ②은 However를 통해 ①의 내용에 대한 반전 설명을 하고 있으므로 ① 뒤에 오는 것이 적절하다. ④의 This process는 ranking potential threats in order of severity를 가리키고 있으므로 ② 뒤에 이어지는 게 적절하다. ⑤의 whether it is의 it은 taking a risk is worth the reward를 가리키고 있으므로 ④ 뒤에 이어지는 게 적절하다.

해석 사업 관리자의 임무는 사업이 반드시 성공적으로 완료되게 하는 것이다: 운영 예산이 관리되고, 일정이 지켜지며, 고객 및 모든 이해 당사자들이 만족하도록 말이다. ① 그 목적을 달성하기 위해서, 사업의 성공을 위협할 수 있는 어떠한 사건이나 요인, 즉 잠재적 위험들을 줄이는 것이 중요하다. ② 하지만, 모든 위험들이 동일한 위협을 가하는 것이 아니고, 어떤 사업에서든 어느 정도의 위험은 불가피하기 때문에, 조직들은 심각성 순으로 잠재적 위협들의 순위를 매김으로써 위험을 관리해야 한다. (③ 때때로, 위험을 줄이는 것에는 대가를 지불하게 되고, 심지어 위험 그 자체의 대가를 초과할 수도 있는데, 그 경우에는 위험을 그저 받아들이는 것이 더 타당하다.) ④ '위험 우선순위 결정'이라고 일컬어지는 이 과정은 사업 수행에 필수적인 위험들을 영향력이 덜한 위험들과 구별하는 측정 기준들을 이용하는 것을 수반하는데, 이는 위험을 감수하는 것이 그 대가의 가치가 있는지를 검토함으로써 수행된다. ⑤ 그것이 그러한지를 판단하기 위해, 가능성이 낮은 위험과 긍정적인 결과가 받아들이기에 가장 바람직하다는 논리에 따라, 고려되어야 하는 요인들은 위험의 발생 가능성과 있을 법한 영향을 포함한다.

어휘 stakeholder 이해 당사자, 주주 severity 심각성, 엄격함
make sense 타당하다, 말이 되다
prioritization 우선순위를 결정하기, 우선순위를 매김
metric 측정 기준; 미터법의 mission-critical (조직의) 임무 수행에 필수적인
question 검토하다, 의심하다 probability 가능성, 있을 법함
desirable 바람직한

(해설) 주어진 글은 AlphaGo 프로그램에 이어, Libratus 프로그램이 세계 최고의 포커 선수 4명을 이겼다는 인공 지능 분야의 성취에 관한 주제를 제시한다. (B)는 Libratus 프로그램이 처음에 어떻게 설계되었는지에 관한 내용이고, 주어진 글 마지막에 Libratus 프로그램이 세계 최고의 포커 선수 4명을 이 겼다고 했으므로 그 뒤에 와야 한다. (C)의 this process는 (B)의 '학습과 의 사 결정을 더 잘하게 될 때까지 그 게임의 무수한 형식들을 플레이하는 것'을 가리키므로 (C)는 (B) 바로 다음에 오는 것이 적절하다. (A)는 역접 연결어 However에 이어 Libratus의 인간 같은 행동들은 모두 계산에 기반하고 있 다고 하며 Libratus가 직감적으로 사고하는 것 같았다는 (B)의 내용에 대한 반전 설명을 하고 있으므로, (B) 뒤에 오는 것이 적절하다. 따라서 글의 순서로 가장 적절한 것은 ③ (B) - (C) - (A)이다.

(해석) 구글의 알파고 프로그램이 바둑에서 최상위 기사인 이세돌을 이겼을 때 인공 지능에서의 대기록이 세워졌다. 현재, 그 성취를 기반으로 해서, 세계 최고의 포커 선수 4명이 Libratus(리브라투스) 프로그램에 패배했다.

(B) Carnegie Mellon 대학교의 연구원들에 의해 설계된 Libratus는 Texas Hold'em으로 알려진 게임의 2인 형식의 규칙들만 주어졌다. 그리고 나서 그 것은 학습과 의사결정을 더 잘하게 될 때까지 그 게임의 무수한 형식들을 플 레이하도록 남겨졌다.

(C) 이 과정을 통해 그것이 얻은 전문 지식의 수준은 정말 놀라웠다. 포커가 상대들의 사고 과정을 이해하고 그들이 속이고 있는지 알아내는 능력을 요 한다는 사실은 Libratus가 직감적으로 사고하는 능력을 습득했음을 암시하 는 것 같았다.

(A) 하지만, Libratus의 인간 같은 행동들은 전적으로 계산에 기반했다. 시행 착오를 통해, Libratus의 알고리즘은 속이는 것이 효과적인 전략임을 알아냈 고, 그것을 그들의 경기에 포함시켰다. 그것은 또한 상대 역시 속일 수 있다는 것을 인식했는데, 이는 그것이 이전에는 프로그램에 의해 이해되리라고 예상 되지 않았던 일종의 불확실성을 이해할 수 있음을 나타냈다.

(어휘) milestone 대기록, 획기적인 사건   calculation 계산, 산출
trial and error 시행착오   incorporate 포함시키다, 끌어넣다
opponent 상대; 대립하는   expertise 전문 지식   intuitively 직감적으로

(구문분석) [15행] [**Designed** by researchers at Carnegie Mellon University], Libratus was simply given the rules of a two-player version of the game known as Texas Hold'em.

→ [Designed ~ University]는 과거분사 Designed로 시작하는 수동 형 분사구문이다.

[22행] The fact that poker requires the ability to understand the thought processes of one's opponents and to know whether they are bluffing [seemed to suggest] that Libratus had gained the power to think intuitively.

→ [seemed to suggest]는 'seem + to부정사'의 형태로, '~하는 것 같 다'라는 의미의 to부정사 표현이다.

左段

(구문분석) [6행] However, since **not all** risks pose an equal threat ~

→ not all은 '반드시 ~하지 않다'라는 의미로 부분 부정을 나타내는 구 문이다.

[10행] Sometimes, reducing a risk comes at a cost and can even exceed the cost of the risk itself, in which case, it makes more sense [to simply accept the risk].
    가주어
    진주어(to부정사구)

→ 가주어 it이 길이가 긴 진주어 to부정사구 [to ~ risk] 대신 주어 자리 에 쓰인 형태이다.

(해설) 주어진 글은 과학 공상 소설의 인기가 재미보다 좀 더 심오한 것에 기반을 두 기도 한다는 주제를 제시한다. (C)는 공상 과학이 우리와 관련이 있으며, 사회 의 심각한 문제들을 다루는 수단으로서의 역할을 한다는 내용이고, 이는 주어 진 글의 '좀 더 심오한 것'을 가리키므로 그 뒤에 와야 한다. (B)는 공상과학은 거리감을 느끼게 한다는 내용으로, At the same time을 통해 공상과학이 우 리와 매우 관련 있다고 한 (C)와 대조적인 내용을 이야기하고 있으므로 (C)뒤 에 오는 것이 적절하다. (A)의 their differences는 (B)의 '공상 소설의 이야기 속 등장인물들이 다른 시대나 공간에서 온 것'을 가리키므로 (B) 바로 다음에 오는 것이 적절하다. 따라서 글의 순서로 가장 적절한 것은 ⑤ (C) - (B) - (A) 이다.

(해석) 과학 공상 소설이 언뜻 보기에는 단순히 탈출하는 재미있는 수단처럼 보일 수 도 있지만, 이 장르의 인기는 좀 더 심오한 것에 기반을 두었을지도 모른다.

(C) 일부 사람들은 그것의 매력은 그것이 우리와 매우 관련 있다는 사실에 있 다고 말한다. 이는 그것이 오늘날 우리 사회에 영향을 미치는 심각한 문제들 을 다루는 수단으로서의 역할을 하기 때문이다.

(B) 동시에, 그것은 거리감을 준다. 과학 공상 소설의 이야기 속 등장인물들 은 다른 시대나 공간에서 오기 때문에, 우리가 우리 사회의 누군가를 보는 것 과 같은 시각으로 그들을 보지 않는 정도로 그들은 처음에 우리에게서 멀리 동떨어진 것처럼 보인다.

(A) 하지만, 우리와 그들의 차이에도 불구하고, 그들은 우리가 공감할 수 있는 상황에 자주 직면해, 우리가 우리 사회의 문제들을 보게 한다. 근본적으로, 우 리와 관련이 없어 보이는 흥미진진한 상황 속에서 오늘날의 문제들을 그려봄 으로써, 우리는 그것들을 좀 더 쉽게 처리할 수 있다.

(어휘) science fiction 과학 공상 소설   at first glance 언뜻 보기에는, 처음에
relate to ~에 공감하다, ~과 관련되다   frame 마음속으로 그리다, 표현하다
removed 동떨어진, 다른   serve as ~의 역할을 하다
tackle 다루다, (일에) 부딪히다

(구문분석) [12행] ~, they initially seem far removed from us **to the extent that** we don't view them through the same lens as we might view someone from our own society.

› to the extent that은 '~힐 징도까지'라는 의미의 관용 표현이다.

[16행] Some suggest that its appeal lies in **the fact** [that it is incredibly relevant to us].

→ [that ~ us]는 the fact와 동격을 이루는 명사절이다.

(해설) 주어진 문장의 also로 보아, 주어진 문장 앞에는 그 과정(수압 파쇄법)이 해로 운 이유에 대한 내용이 나와야 한다는 것을 알 수 있다. 이 글에서는 ①~② 뒤 문장까지 수압 파쇄법에 대한 반대 입장과 그것이 해로운 이유에 대해 설명하 고 있지만, ③ 뒤 문장에서 역접 연결어 But을 통해 앞 문장들에 대한 반전 설

명인 수압 파쇄법을 지지하는 사람들의 입장과 장점에 대해 이야기하기 시작한다. 따라서 주어진 문장이 들어가기에 가장 적절한 곳은 ③이다.

(오답분석) ① 뒤 문장의 The technique는 첫 번째 문장의 a high-pressure water drilling technique(고압수 시추 기술)을 가리키므로 주어진 문장이 들어가기에 적절하지 않다. ② 뒤 문장의 They는 ① 뒤 문장의 activists and scientists(활동가들과 과학자들)를 가리키고, ② 뒤 문장은 그들의 주장을 소개하는 내용이므로 주어진 문장은 이 내용이 끝난 이후에 들어가야 한다. ④ 뒤 문장은 ③ 뒤 문장에서 이야기한 긍정적이고 실질적인 용도의 예시를 언급하고 있다. ⑤ 뒤 문장은 ④ 뒤 문장에 이어서 수압 파쇄법의 장점에 대해 언급하고 있다.

(해석) 수압 파쇄법은 지하 깊은 곳의 셰일 바위에서 석유나 천연가스를 추출하는 데에 이용되는 고압수 시추 기술이다. (①) 이 기술은 매우 논란이 되고 있고, 활동가들과 과학자들이 환경적 및 건강상 우려를 강조하며 그것에 반대하여 결집하게 했다. (②) 그들은 한 예로, 그 과정이 메탄과 같은 독성의 오염 물질들이 공기 중으로 방출되게 한다고 지적한다. (③) 또한 그 과정에 사용되는 약 750가지의 확인된 화학 물질들이 있는데, 그 중 29가지는 알려져 있는 발암 물질이며 그 중 다수는 결국 지하수 공급에 들어가 지역 주민들의 건강을 위협한다.) 하지만 지역 사회에 영향을 미치는 이것들과 같은 위험에도 불구하고, 지지자들은 수압 파쇄법은 그것이 피해를 일으킬 가능성을 만회할 긍정적이고 실질적인 용도를 가지고 있다고 생각한다. (④) 예를 들어, 수압 파쇄법은 석탄의 이산화탄소 배출 수준의 절반으로 전기 발생을 가능하게 한다. (⑤) 추가로, 그것은 더 낮은 에너지 가격과 더 높은 에너지 안보라는 결과로 이어진다.

(어휘) groundwater 지하수   drilling 시추(試錐), 구멍 뚫기   extract 추출하다
shale 셰일, 이판암   rally 결집하다, 집결하다   pollutant 오염 물질
methane 메탄   make up 만회하다   carbon dioxide 이산화탄소
energy security 에너지 안보

(구문분석) [10행] They point out that, for one, the process <u>causes</u> <u>toxic pollutants such as methane</u> <u>to be released</u> into the air.
                 동사 목적어 목적격 보어

→ 동사 causes의 목적어로 toxic pollutants such as methane이, 목적격 보어로 to be released가 쓰였다. 여기서 목적격 보어 to be released는 to부정사의 수동형(to be + p.p.)으로 쓰였다.

[13행] ~ proponents **believe** ①[that fracking has **positive and practical uses** ②[that make up for its potential to cause harm]].

→ ①[that ~ harm]은 접속사 that이 이끄는 명사절로, 동사 believe의 목적어 역할을 한다.

→ 명사절 안의 ②[that ~ harm]은 선행사 positive and practical uses를 수식하며, 주격 관계대명사 that이 이끄는 관계대명사절이다.

39 주어진 문장의 위치 찾기   정답 ⑤

(해설) 주어진 문장의 Another difference로 보아, 주어진 문장 앞에는 전제 정치와 독재 정권의 차이점에 대한 내용이 나와야 한다는 것을 알 수 있다. 이 글에서는 ①~④ 뒤 문장까지 전제 정치와 독재 정권의 지배 형태, 인식의 차이에 대해 설명하고 있고, ⑤ 뒤 문장의 this는 주어진 문장의 to preside over mass media, propaganda, and rallies so that they can create an idealistic image of themselves(그들 자신에 대한 이상적인 이미지를 만들 수 있도록 대중 매체, 선전 운동, 집회를 주도하는 것)를 가리키므로 주어진 문장이 들어가기에 가장 적절한 곳은 ⑤이다.

(오답분석) ② 뒤 문장은 ① 뒤 문장에 이어서 차이점 중 한 가지로 지배자의 수를 언급하고 있다. ③~④ 뒤 문장은 ② 뒤 문장에 이어서 두 번째 차이점으로 전제 정치와 독재 정권의 인식에 대한 내용을 다루고 있으므로 주어진 문장은 이 내용이 끝난 이후에 들어가야 한다.

(해석) 전제 정치와 독재 정권 간의 차이는 그것들의 미묘한 본질을 고려할 때 일반적으로 무시된다. (①) 두 형태의 정권 모두 권력의 과도한 집중화로 특징 지어지더라도, 두 체제는 여러 측면에서 다르다. (②) 전제 정치는 한 사람에 의해 지배되는 반면, 독재 정권은 권력의 자리에 한 명의 지도자나 한 무리의 지도자들이 있을 수 있다. (③) 또한 독재자들 자체가 역사적으로 그들 민족에 반하는 범죄들과 결부되어왔기 때문에 독재 정권이라는 용어는 매우 부정적인 암시를 지닌다. (④) 그에 반해서, 전제 정치는 높은 생산성과 연관되었기 때문에 과거에 좋게 여겨졌다. (⑤ 또 다른 차이는 독재자들이 그들 자신에 대한 이상화된 이미지를 만들 수 있도록 대중매체, 선전 운동, 집회를 주도하는 독재자들의 경향에 있다.) 그들은 지지자들을 대규모로 속이고 국민의 찬사와 헌신을 조장하기 위해 이것을 시도한다.

(어휘) preside 주도하다, 주인 노릇을 하다   propaganda 선전 (운동)
rally 집회, 결집   disregard 무시하다   centralization 집중화, 중앙 집권
in power 권력의 자리에 있는, 정권을 쥐고 있는   favorably 좋게, 호의적으로
audience 지지자, 관객   praise 찬사, 칭찬

(구문분석) [9행] ~ the two systems **do** <u>differ</u> in several ways.
→ do는 동사 differ의 의미를 강조한다.

[10행] ~ a dictatorship can have **either** ①[one leader] **or** ②[a group of leaders] in power.
→ ①[one leader]와 ②[a ~ leaders]는 상관접속사 either A or B(A이거나 B인)로 연결된 병렬 구조이다.

40 요약문 완성하기   정답 ②

(해설) 글의 전반부에서 문화적 다원주의가 사회적 화합을 약화시키고 지배적인 문화의 고유함에 악영향을 끼칠 수 있다고 비난받았다고 했고, 글의 후반부에서는 각 문화는 수 세기에 걸친 문화적 관습, 언어 구조, 그리고 사실상 이주자들의 유입에 의해 형성되었고, 문화는 항상 다양성에 의해 발전해왔다고 했다. 따라서 dominant를 primary로, fostered를 influenced로 바꾸어 표현한 ②이 정답이다.

(오답분석) 지배적인 문화의 고유함에 끼칠 추정상의 악영향 때문에 문화적 다원주의가 비난받아왔다고 했으므로 ③의 previous와 ⑤의 expired는 (A)에 들어갈 단어로 적절하지 않다. 각 문화는 문화적 관습, 언어 구조, 이주자들의 오랜 유입에 의해 형성되었고 문화적 다원주의는 이러한 현상의 지속이라고 했으므로 ①의 threatened와 ④의 followed는 (B)에 들어갈 단어로 적절하지 않다.

(해석) 문화적 다원주의는 최근 몇 년 동안 사회적 화합을 강화하기보다는 그것을 약화시킬 가능성과, 지배적인 문화의 고유함에 끼칠 추정상의 악영향 때문에 비난받아왔다. 비판자들은 이민에 관한 한 포용의 방식을 장려하는 대신에, 정부가 동화에 중점을 두어야 하며, 그것으로 인하여 새로 들어오는 사람들은 지배적인 문화에 적응하도록 강요받고 그 과정 중에 전부는 아니더라도 그들의 문화적 특성의 대부분을 포기하게 된다고 시사한다. 하지만, 동시에 이러한 견해의 지지자들은 지구상의 모든 문화의 근본적으로 혼합적인 본질을 간과하는데, 그 중 어느 것도 진공 상태에서 발생하지 않았다. 각 문화는 수 세기에 걸친 문화적 관습, 언어 구조, 그리고 사실상 이주자들의 유입에 의해 형성되었다. 문화적 다원주의는 그저 이러한 현상의 지속이고, 그것의 복합적인 형태의 사회적 관계는 이전 관습들의 연장이다. 문화는 항상 다양성에 의해 발전

해왔고, 특정 전통과 관습에 배타적인 접근 방식을 취하는 것은 사실상 문화의 진정한 본질을 부정한다.

↓

문화적 다원주의가 한 사회의 (A) 주요한 문화를 훼손할 수 있다고 주장되었던 반면, 또한 다양한 관습의 혼합이 오늘날의 모든 문화에 (B) 영향을 끼쳤다고 지적되었다.

	(A)		(B)
①	전체의	……	위협했다
②	주요한	……	영향을 끼쳤다
③	이전의	……	모방했다
④	필수의	……	따랐다
⑤	만료된	……	결정했다

[어휘] cultural pluralism 문화적 다원주의, 문화적 다원성
undermine 약화시키다, 몰래 해치다   cohesion 화합, 결합
supposedly 추정상, 아마   adverse effect 악영향, 역효과
inclusivity 포용, 포괄성   assimilation 동화, 소화
whereby 그리고 그것으로 인하여, ~하는   arrival 도착하는 사람, 도착
shed 포기하다, 버리다   hybrid 혼합의   vacuum 진공 상태
influx 유입, 밀려듦   continuation 지속, 연속   foster 발전시키다, 조성하다
diversity 다양성   effectively 사실상, 효과적으로

[구문분석]

[1행] Cultural pluralism has, in recent years, been decried for its **potential** [to undermine social cohesion], rather than reinforce it, ~

→ [to ~ cohesion]은 to부정사의 형용사적 용법(~할)으로, 앞의 명사 potential을 수식한다.

[7행] ~ assimilation, whereby new arrivals are forced to adjust to the dominant culture, [shedding most if not all of their cultural characteristics along the way].

→ [shedding ~ way]는 '(그 결과) ~하게 된다'라는 의미의 분사구문으로, 분사구문의 주어가 주절의 주어(new arrivals)와 같아서 생략되었다.

41~42 장문 독해 1

[해석] 제1차 세계대전의 여파 속에서 시작되고 이전 10년의 다다이즘 예술에 영향을 받은 초현실주의는 프랑스 시인 André Breton(앙드레 브르통)에 의해 1924년 정식으로 확립된 문화적 사조였다. 그것은 정신 분석의 아버지인 Sigmund Freud(지그문트 프로이트)의 저술과 꿈 해석에 의해 크게 영향을 받은 새로운 형태의 (a) 문학적 표현법으로 시작되었으며, ⁴¹그 목적은 잠재의식이라는 사적 세계에 발언권을 주는 것이었는데, 이는 사회적 관습들과 논리에 의해 억제되었다고 여겨졌다. 초현실주의는 원래 (b) 즉흥적인 표현법으로 의도되었기 때문에, 몇몇 사람들은 처음에는 그것이 회화와 조각의 더디고 노동 집약적인 과정에 적합하지 않다고 생각했다. 하지만 초현실주의 시각 예술가들은 그들이 창조한 꿈같으면서 때때로 특이한 이미지, 즉 그들 마음속 가장 깊은 곳에 있는 생각들의 예술적 묘사 덕분에, 오늘날 그 사조에 참여했던 시인들보다 거의 틀림없이 더 많이 기억된다. ⁴¹그 사조의 주요한 인물은 벨기에 예술가 René Magritte(르네 마그리트)였는데, 그의 그림들은 일상의 물건들을 자주 묘사했다. 그의 가장 상징적인 작품들 중 하나인 <이미지의 배반>은 광고에서 볼 수 있을 것 같은 파이프와 (c) 유사한 진짜처럼 보이는 파이프를 설명 문구와 함께 보여준다: "이것은 파이프가 아닙니다." 감상자는 처음에 그러한 설명이 특이하다고 생각할지도 모

르지만, 그들은 결국에 ⁴²"그 파이프"가 사실은 누군가가 담배로 채울 수 있는 실제의 물건이기보다 단순히 캔버스 위의 색채의 조합인 그림임을 (d) 부정해야(→인정해야/동의해야) 할 것이다. 이와 같은 작품들을 통해, Magritte는 예술을 통해 물체들을 표현하는 것의 모순을 강조했고 ⁴¹감상자들이 (e) 현실에 대한 그들의 조건화된 관념들에 의문을 제기하게 했다.

[어휘] conceive 시작하다, 상상하다   aftermath 여파, 후유증   Dada 다다이즘
Surrealism 초현실주의   psychoanalysis 정신 분석
subconscious 잠재의식의, 거의 무의식의   repress 억제하다, 억누르다
societal 사회의, 사회 활동의   spontaneous 즉흥적인, 저절로 일어나는
lend 적합하다, 도움이 되다   labor-intensive 노동 집약적인
arguably 거의 틀림없이, 주장하건대   imagery 이미지, 형상
depiction 묘사, 서술   caption 설명문, 캡션   physical 실제의, 물리적인
precondition 미리 조건을 갖추다; 전제 조건
[선택지] defy 도전하다, 저항하다   tap into ~에 접근하다, ~을 활용하다

[구문분석]

[20행] A leading figure of the movement was Belgian artist **René Magritte**, [whose paintings frequently depicted everyday objects].

→ [whose ~ objects]는 선행사 René Magritte를 수식하며, 소유격 관계대명사 whose가 이끄는 계속적 용법으로 쓰인 관계대명사절이다.

[22행] *The Treachery of Images*, [one of his most iconic works], shows a realistic-looking pipe, perhaps ~

→ [one ~ works]는 'one of + 소유격 + 최상급 + 복수명사'(가장 ~한 - 중 하나)의 형태로 최상급을 나타내는 구문이다.

---

41 제목 파악하기   정답 ②

[해설] 초현실주의는 사회적 관습과 논리에 억제되는 잠재의식을 표현하기 위한 문학적 표현법으로 시작되었으나 오늘날에는 시각 예술가들이 더 많이 기억된다는 내용의 글로, 이 사조의 주요 예술가인 René Magritte를 예를 들어 설명하고 있다. 또한 글의 후반부에서 Magritte는 감상자들이 현실에 대한 그들의 조건화된 관념들에 의문을 제기하게 했다고 했으므로, 글의 제목으로 가장 적절한 것은 ② '논리에 도전하기: Magritte와 초현실주의 예술'이다.

[오답분석] ①은 글의 초반에서 Freud의 꿈 해석이 초현실주의에 영향을 끼쳤다고만 언급되고 있으므로 글의 일부만을 다루는 오답이다. ③은 초현실주의는 논리에 억제되는 잠재의식을 표현하기 위한 목적으로 시작되었다는 글의 내용과는 관련이 없으므로 오답이다. ④, ⑤은 글의 일부만을 다루고 있는 오답이다.

[해석] ① 초현실주의와 Freud의 꿈 이미지
② 논리에 도전하기: Magritte와 초현실주의 예술
③ 정신 분석으로 잠재의식에 접근하기
④ René Magritte: <이미지의 배반>의 창작
⑤ 진짜 같은 예술의 묘사가 역설적인가?

---

42 어휘 적절성 파악하기   정답 ④

[해설] 그림 속의 파이프가 진짜처럼 보이더라도 그 파이프가 실제의 물건이 아니라 단순히 캔버스 위의 색채의 조합인 그림임을 인정해야 한다는 맥락이 되어야 하므로, ④의 deny(부정하다)를 그와 반대되는 의미의 concede(인정하다) 또는 agree(동의하다)와 같은 어휘로 바꾸어야 문맥상 적절하다.

오답분석 ①은 초현실주의가 프랑스 시인에 의해 확립된 문화적 사조이며 문학적 표현의 새로운 형태로 시작되었다는 문맥이 되어야 하므로 literary가 오는 것이 적절하다. ⑤은 진짜처럼 보이는 그림 속 물체들이 실제의 물건이 아니라 단순히 그림일 뿐임을 보여주는 René Magritte의 작품들이 현실에 대한 관념들에 의문을 제기하게 했다는 문맥이 되어야 하므로 reality가 오는 것이 적절하다.

43~45 장문 독해 2

해석 (A) 매일 저녁, Laney는 그녀의 개 두 마리와 함께 동네 주변을 산책했다. 어느 날, 그녀는 쓰레기통을 뒤지고 있는 한 여성을 보았다. Laney는 친절하고 후한 사람이었기에, (a)그녀가 주머니 속에 가지고 있던 초콜릿 바 몇 개를 그 여성에게 주었다. "정말 고맙습니다"라며 그 여성이 미소와 함께 답했다. "하지만 그게 제 고양이에게 줄 만한 것이 아니라 안타깝네요."

(C) Laney는 놀라서 ⁴⁴그 여성에게 무슨 말인지 물었다. 그 여성은 그녀가 최근 허리케인의 이재민이었다고 말했다. 그녀는 집과 많은 재산을 잃었다. 그녀는 아직 재정적으로 회복하는 중이었고, 할애할 충분한 돈이 없었다. "돈이 너무 없어서, 제 고양이를 위한 물품들을 사는 것이 힘들어요"라고 (c)그녀가 말했다.

(D) Laney는 집으로 걸어가면서, (d)그녀의 머릿속에서 그 여성의 이야기를 떨쳐낼 수가 없었다. ⁴⁵그녀는 종종 어려운 처지의 사람들에게 옷과 음식을 기부했지만, 그녀가 어려움에 처한 모든 반려동물들에 대해서는 생각하지 않았음을 깨달았다. 그녀는 여러 날 동안 그녀가 어떻게 도울 수 있을지에 대해 생각했다. 그리고 나서, (e)그녀는 완벽한 해결책이 있는 기사를 우연히 발견했다.

(B) 그것은 지역의 반려동물용 상점이 있는 한 동네에 관한 것이었다. 사람들은 가능한 건 무엇이든 기부했고, 다른 사람들은 그들이 필요한 건 무엇이든지 가져갈 수 있었다. 일부 사람들은 사용하지 않는 장난감을 기부하고 대신에 가죽끈을 가져가는 식으로 물건들을 교환했다. 아무도 무언가에 대해 지불하지 않아도 됐다; 그것은 선의와 신뢰에 기반을 둔 체계였다. Laney는 당장 (b)그녀의 동네에서 하나를 시작하고 싶었다. 그녀와 다른 자원봉사자들이 공원 근처에 있는 오래된 헛간을 수리했다. 많은 사람들이 돕거나 기부하기 위해 들렀다. 그 상점은 성공했고, 도움이 필요했던 많은 반려동물 주인들이 고마워했다.

어휘 **look through** 뒤지다 **leash** (개를 매어 두는) 가죽끈, 밧줄 **build on** ~을 기반으로 하다 **shed** 헛간, 보관하는 곳 **victim** 이재민, 희생자 **possessions** 재산, 소유물 **on a tight budget** 돈이 없는, 빈곤한 **in need** 어려움에 처한, 궁핍한 **come across** 우연히 발견하다, 이해되다

구문분석 [3행] [Being a kind and generous person], Laney offered the woman some chocolate bars that she had in her pocket.

→ [Being ~ person]은 '~하므로, ~때문에'라는 의미의 분사구문으로, 분사구문의 주어가 주절의 주어(Laney)와 같아서 생략되었다.

[9행] People **donated** ①[whatever they could], and others could **take** ②[whatever they needed].

→ ①[whatever they could]와 ②[whatever they needed]는 복합관계대명사 whatever가 이끄는 명사절로, 각각 동사 donated와 take의 목적어 역할을 한다.

43 글의 순서 배열하기 정답 ③

해설 (A)는 Laney가 산책하다가 쓰레기통을 뒤지는 여성을 만났고 초콜릿 바를 주었다는 내용이다. (C)는 Laney가 무슨 말인지 묻자 그 여성은 돈이 없어 고양이 물품을 사는 것이 힘들다는 것을 이야기했다는 내용이므로, 그 여성이 초콜릿을 받고 고양이에게 줄 만한 것이 아니라 안타깝다고 말한 (A) 뒤에 와야 한다. (D)는 Laney가 빈곤한 여성의 이야기에 대해 계속 생각하고 도와줄 방법을 찾았다는 내용이므로 Laney가 만난 여성이 자신의 어려운 상황에 대해 이야기한 (C) 뒤에 와야 한다. (B)의 It was about a neighborhood에서 It은 (D)의 an article with a perfect solution을 가리키므로 (D) 다음에 오는 것이 적절하다. 따라서 글의 순서로 가장 적절한 것은 ③ (C) - (D) - (B)이다.

44 지칭 대상 파악하기 정답 ③

해설 (a), (b), (d), (e)는 모두 Laney를 가리키지만 (c)는 Laney가 만난 허리케인 이재민을 가리키므로, 정답은 ③이다.

45 세부 정보 파악하기 정답 ⑤

해설 (D)의 While she often donated clothes and food to people in need를 통해 Laney가 도움이 필요한 사람들을 위해 옷과 음식을 기부했다는 것을 알 수 있는데, ⑤은 돈을 기부했다고 일부 정보를 잘못 나타냈으므로 Laney에 관한 내용과 일치하지 않는 것은 ⑤이다.

문제집 p. 38

정답

18	④	19	②	20	③	21	⑤	22	③	23	⑤	24	①	25	⑤	26	⑤	27	④
28	⑤	29	③	30	⑤	31	⑤	32	③	33	④	34	②	35	④	36	④	37	③
38	④	39	③	40	②	41	⑤	42	④	43	②	44	②	45	⑤				

18 목적 파악하기   정답 ④

(해설) express regret(사과하다)이라는 표현을 이용해 호텔의 매니저가 투숙 중 소음으로 인해 불편을 겪었던 고객에게 사과하고 있으므로 정답은 ④이다.

(해석) 김지호 님께,

3월 9일 귀하의 호텔 투숙에 영향을 주었던 소음에 대한 불만 사항을 접수하였습니다. 그것이 얼마나 불편하셨을지 상상도 할 수 없고, 저희가 이런 문제들을 매우 심각하게 받아들인다는 것을 알아주셨으면 합니다. 저희 직원들은 고객님들의 좀 더 편안한 투숙을 책임지기 위해 앞으로 소란을 줄이는 것을 우선 사항으로 삼으라는 교육을 이미 받았습니다. 지난번 이곳에 계시는 동안에 귀하께서 겪은 문제에도 불구하고, 저희는 귀하께서 다시 방문하셔서 저희에게 그것을 만회할 수 있는 기회를 주시길 바랍니다. 저희는 소중한 고객으로서의 귀하의 의견에 항상 감사드리며 소음에 대해 다시 한번 사과드립니다.

The Swan Hotel 매니저 Brian Smith 드림

(어휘) regarding ~에 대한 instruct 교육하다 disturbance 소란, 방해 priority 우선 사항 ensure 책임지다, 보증하다 make up for ~을 만회하다

(구문분석)
[6행] Our staff has already been instructed to make reducing disturbances a priority in the future **in order** [to ensure] a more comfortable stay for guests.

→ 목적의 뜻을 분명히 하기 위해 to부정사 [to ensure] 앞에 in order를 쓴 형태이다.

19 심경 파악하기   정답 ②

(해설) 심경은 간접적으로 표현된다. 글의 초반부의 So, I was more than cautious about reading his newest offering을 통해 Hale의 최신 소설을 읽기 전 확신이 없는 화자의 심경을 알 수 있고, 후반부의 I never imagined Hale had another masterpiece left in him을 통해 Hale의 최신 소설에 감명받았다는 것을 알 수 있다. 따라서 'I'의 심경 변화로 가장 적절한 것은 ②이다.

(해석) 나는 이 날에 대해 한동안 확신이 없었다. 미스터리 작가 Gavin Hale의 최신 스릴러물인 <뼛속까지>가 오늘 오전 전국 서점에 출간되었다. 그의 전작이 특히 지루한 묘사로 인해 나와 같은 비평가들로부터 극도로 부정적인 평가를 받았다는 것은 비밀이 아니다. 그래서 나는 그의 최신작을 읽기가 조심스러운 것 이상이었다. 하지만 지금, 마침내 그 소설을 다 읽고 난 뒤 내 생각이 바뀌었다고 말해야겠다. Hale에게 또 다른 걸작이 남아있을 줄은 상상도 못했다. <뼛속까지>는 인상적인 등장인물들과 극적인 반전들로 가득 찬 흥미진진한 이야기이다. 나는 이것이 Hale의 경력에 전환점이 되기를 바라고, 그가 이 최신 소설의 성공을 발판으로 삼기를 바란다.

① 안도한 → 궁금한   ② 확신이 없는 → 감명받은
③ 혼란스러운 → 슬픈   ④ 만족한 → 겁먹은
⑤ 부끄러운 → 무관심한

(어휘) uncertain 확신이 없는 overwhelmingly 극도로, 압도적으로 cautious 조심스러운, 신중한 offering 작품, 내놓은 것 masterpiece 걸작 memorable 인상적인 plot twist 반전 turning point 전환점 build on ~을 발판으로 삼다

(구문분석)
[4행] It's no secret [that his last book received (가주어) overwhelmingly negative reviews from critics like me] (진주어(that절)), especially because of its boring descriptions.

→ 가주어 it이 길이가 긴 진주어 that절 [that ~ me] 대신 주어 자리에 쓰인 형태이다.

[12행] I **hope** ①[that this marks a turning point in Hale's career] **and** ②[that he builds on the achievement of this latest novel].

→ 동사 hope의 목적어 역할을 하는 ①[that ~ career]와 ②[that ~ novel]은 접속사 that이 이끄는 명사절로, 등위접속사 and로 연결된 병렬 구조이다.

20 주장 파악하기   정답 ③

(해설) 글의 마지막 문장에서 직감이 대부분의 사람들이 생각하는 것보다 믿을 만한 것이며, 직감적인 반응들을 신중하게 고려하면 최고의 결정을 내릴 가능성을 높일 것이라고 주장하고 있으므로 정답은 ③이다.

(오답분석) ①은 글의 핵심 소재인 '직관력'을 사용하여 헷갈리게 하는 오답이다.

(해석) 당신은 특정 행동 방침이 적절한 것이라는 예감이 들었던 상황을 경험해 본 적이 있을 것이다. 하지만 당신은 어느 정도까지 당신의 직감을 믿을 수 있는가? 대부분의 사람들은 그것을 믿을 수 없다고 주장하겠지만, 그것은 당신이 생각하는 것보다 더 믿을 만한 것일 수 있다. 최근 연구들은 인간의 뇌가 주위로부터 끊임없이 데이터를 수집하고 처리한다는 것을 보여준다. 심리학자들은 우리의 직감에 따른 반응들이 우리는 잠재의식적으로 처리했지만 의식 수준에서 알아차리지 못하는 정보에 근거를 두고 있다고 여긴다. 예를 들어, 사업가는 매우 유리한 것처럼 보이는 거래를 직감에 근거하여 거절하기로 결정할지도 모른다. 이것은 비논리적으로 보일 수도 있지만, 그 사람은 상대방이 믿을 만하지 않다는 미묘한 단서를 알아차린 것일 수도 있다. 당신의 직감적인 반응들을 신중하게 고려하는 것은 당신이 최고의 결정을 내릴 가능성을 크게 높일 것이다.

어휘 hunch 예감 course of action 행동 방침 intuition 직감, 직관
untrustworthy 믿을 수 없는 instinctive 직감에 따른, 본능적인
subconsciously 잠재의식적으로 conscious 의식하는 gut feeling 직감
pick up on ~을 알아차리다 subtle 미묘한 cue 단서

구문
분석

[1행] You may have experienced a situation **in which** you had a hunch that a certain course of action was the correct one.

→ '전치사 + 관계대명사' in which는 관계부사 where를 대신할 수 있고, 완전한 절 앞에 온다.

[15행] [Giving your intuitive responses careful consideration] will greatly increase your chances of making the best decisions.

→ [Giving ~ consideration]은 주어 역할을 하는 동명사구이다.

21 밑줄 의미 추론하기   정답 ⑤

해설 자기 암시를 하는 사람들은 자신들의 목표를 이루기 위한 구체적인 행동을 취하는 것은 생각하지 못하고 그 대신 자신들의 생각을 궁극적인 욕망으로 돌린다고 말하고 있다. 따라서 글의 주제를 비유적으로 표현한 jump the gun(성급하게 굴다)이 의미하는 것은 ⑤ '목표를 달성하는 방법보다는 목표에 초점을 맞춘다'이다.

오답
분석
①은 글에서 언급된 내용이 아니다. ②은 글에서 언급된 success를 사용하여 헷갈리게 하는 오답이다. ③은 구체적인 행동을 보여주지 않는 자기 암시는 목표 달성으로 이어지지 않을 것이라는 부정적 영향을 말하는 글의 내용과 반대되므로 오답이다. ④은 글의 일부만을 다루고 있는 오답이다.

해석 자신의 행동을 바꾸기 위한 구두 암시의 반복된 사용을 수반하는 심리적 기법인 자기 암시를 하는 사람들은 종종 성급하게 군다. 그들은 자신들을 목표에 이르게 해줄 구체적인 조치를 취하는 것을 생각하지 못하고 그 대신 그들의 생각을 궁극적인 욕망으로 돌린다. "나는 부유하다"라는 확언을 반복하는 사람은 마음속에 그려지고 있는 것이 구체적인 행동을 나타내는 것이 아니기 때문에 경제적 독립을 성취하는 데 큰 성공을 거두지 못할 것이다. 그 대신, "나는 월 지출을 줄이고 있다"나 "나는 임금 인상을 받을 자격이 있음을 스스로 증명하고 있다"와 같은 것이 훨씬 더 효과적일 수 있는데, 이러한 것들이 눈에 띄는 진전에 기여할 수 있고, 그 사람의 현재 상황에 기반을 둔 실용적인 행동들이기 때문이다. 그것의 성공적인 이행을 위해, 자기 암시는 한 사람이 그 또는 그녀의 꿈을 실현하는 과정에서 계속하여 다음 단계를 마음속에 그릴 필요가 있다.

① 어떤 성취를 거두기도 전에 포기한다
② 높은 수준의 성공을 이루기 위한 상상력이 부족하다
③ 그들의 행동에 긍정적인 영향을 미치는 방법들을 사용한다
④ 그들에게 직접적인 이익이 되지 않는 목표들을 가지고 있다
⑤ 목표를 달성하는 방법보다는 목표에 초점을 맞춘다

어휘 autosuggestion 자기 암시 psychological 심리적인, 정신적인
modify 바꾸다, 수정하다 jump the gun 성급하게 굴다
affirmation 확언, 단언 envision 마음속에 그리다 concrete 구체적인
measurable 눈에 띄는, 측정 가능한 practical 실용적인
implementation 이행 [선택지] have an effect on ~에 영향을 미치다

구문
분석

[7행] A person ①[who repeats the affirmation "I am
주어 1
wealthy"] is unlikely to have much success in achieving
동사 1

financial independence ②[because what is being envisioned
주어 2
does not represent a concrete action].
동사 2

→ ① [who ~ wealthy"]는 주절의 주어인 선행사 A person을 수식하며, 주격 관계대명사 who가 이끄는 관계대명사절이다.

→ ②[because ~ action]은 접속사 because(~ 때문에)가 이끄는 부사절이며, 명사절 what ~ envisioned가 부사절의 주어로 쓰였다.

22 요지 파악하기   정답 ③

해설 글의 첫 두 문장과 마지막 문장에서 교사들은 학생들에게 무엇을 옳게 혹은 그르게 했는지 구체적으로 말하고 개선을 위한 구체적인 제안을 내놓아야 하며, 피드백은 학생들이 다른 프로젝트에 적용할 수 있는 일종의 가르침이 되어야 한다는 글의 요지가 제시되어 있다. 따라서 이 글의 요지로 가장 적절한 것은 ③이다.

오답
분석
①은 글의 핵심 어구 '피드백'을 사용하여 헷갈리게 하는 오답이다. ②은 교사들이 학생들에게 구체적인 평가 결과를 제공해야 한다고 했지 객관적인 평가 기준에 대해 말하고 있는 것은 아니므로 오답이다. ⑤의 '학습 목표'는 글의 내용과 관련이 없으므로 오답이다.

해석 교사들은 피드백에 대한 학습 중심적인 접근법을 취하도록 권고받는데, 그것은 그들이 학생들의 발달에 시기적절한 조정을 할 수 있게 해주기 때문이다. 단순히 평가를 제공하기보다는, 교사들은 학생들이 무엇을 옳게 혹은 그르게 했는지 구체적으로 말하고 그리고 어떻게 개선할지 구체적인 제안을 해야 한다. 발표의 경우, 교사는 "너는 정해진 주제에 관해 많은 정보를 수집할 수 있었어; 하지만 너는 보다 정돈된 방식으로 자료를 제시하고 그래프나 표와 같은 시각 자료를 더 잘 활용할 필요가 있어"라고 말할 수 있다. 이는 그 학생이 그 또는 그녀가 그 과제에서 받았던 성적의 근거뿐만 아니라 향후 과제에서 더 좋은 점수를 얻기 위해 무엇이 이루어져야 하는지를 알게 한다. 다시 말해, 피드백은 학생이 받아들이고 나서 다른 프로젝트에 적용할 수 있는 일종의 가르침으로 작용해야 한다.

어휘 adopt ~을 취하다, 채택하다 approach 접근법 timely 시기적절한
assessment 평가 specify 구체적으로 말하다 assign 지정하다, 부여하다
orderly 정돈된 basis 이유, 근거 mark 점수 instruction 가르침, 지시
absorb 받아들이다, 흡수하다

구문
분석

[11행] This not only lets the student know ①[the basis of the
동사   목적어 1
grade he or she received on the assignment] but also ②[what
목적어 2
needs to be done to get better marks on future ones].

→ 동사 know의 목적어로 ①[the basis ~ assignment]와 ②[what ~ ones]가 쓰였다.

23 주제 파악하기   정답 ⑤

해설 인간의 마음이 본질적으로 인과 측면에서 사건을 구성하도록 설정되어 있기 때문에 오류, 즉 논리적 비약이 발생할 수 있다는 글로, 뇌우 중에 발생한 자동차 사고의 예시를 들어 설명하고 있다. 따라서 이 글의 주제로 가장 적절한 것은 ⑤ '추론에서의 오류의 발생'이다.

오답
분석
③은 글에서 정보를 분석하는 것이 아니라 가정을 할 때 발생하는 오류에 대해 말하고 있으므로 오답이다. ④은 글의 핵심 어구인 cause and effect를

사용하여 헷갈리게 하는 오답이다.

(해석) 'Post hoc, ergo propter hoc'은 "이 뒤에, 따라서 이 때문에"라는 의미의 라틴어 구절이다. 이 구절은 X가 일어나고 나서 Y가 일어났고, 그래서 X는 Y의 원인이라고 말한다. 뇌우가 치는 동안 자동차가 도로를 이탈한다고 가정해보자. 우리는 비(X)가 그 사고(Y)를 일으켰다고 빠르게 가정할지도 모른다. 그러나, 이후에 그 운전자가 단순히 졸았다는 것이 밝혀진다. X와 Y는 단지 그것들이 동시에 발생했기 때문에 연관 지어진 것이다. 인간의 마음은 본질적으로 원인과 결과의 측면에서 사건들을 구성하도록 설정되어 있기 때문에 우리는 이러한 종류의 결론을 내린다. 몇몇 사람들은 이러한 논리의 비약이 거의 문제가 되지 않는다고 생각할 수도 있다. 어쨌든, 운전자가 졸았다는 것을 우리가 아는 것이 결과에 영향을 미치지 않았을 것이다. 하지만 이를 고려해보라: 형사 사건이나 의료 응급 상황에서 우리가 그렇게 한다면 무슨 일이 벌어질까? 전 세계적인 유행병 기간 혹은 구조 임무 동안에는 무슨 일이 일어날까? 삶이 파괴되거나 목숨을 잃을 수도 있다.

① 논리적 추론의 이점들
② 최악의 결과를 가정하는 습관
③ 정보를 분석하는 사고 과정
④ 원인과 결과 간의 관계
⑤ 추론에서의 오류의 발생

(어휘) doze off 졸다   inherently 본질적으로   program 설정하다
frame 구성하다   in terms of ~의 측면에서   leap 비약   rescue 구조, 구출
[선택지] reasoning 추론   occurrence 발생

(구문분석)
[12행] After all, our knowing the driver was sleepy wouldn't
                  의미상 주어 동명사(주어)
have affected the outcome.
→ 소유격 대명사 our가 동명사 주어 knowing의 의미상 주어로 쓰였다.

24 제목 파악하기   정답 ①

(해설) 글의 첫 문장과 마지막 문장으로 미루어 보아 치솟는 주택 가격은 미국에서 주택을 소유하는 것을 힘들게 만들었고, 이 추세는 가까운 미래에 줄어들 것 같지 않다는 내용의 글로 계속되는 미국의 주택 가격의 급증에 대해 설명하고 있다. 따라서 글의 제목으로 가장 적절한 것은 ① '계속 진행 중인 문제: 미국의 상승하는 주택 가격'이다.

(오답분석) ②은 글에서 언급된 suburban과 rural을 사용하여 헷갈리게 하는 오답이다. ③, ④, ⑤은 글의 일부만을 다루고 있는 오답이다.

(해석) 치솟는 주택 가격은 미국에서 신규 구매자들이 주택을 매입하기 더 어렵게 만들고 있다; 이는 더 넓은 공간을 얻기 위해 도시 지역에서 교외와 지방으로 이주하는 많은 수의 사람들에게서 기인한 새로운 사태다. 지난 10년 동안에만, 주택 가격은 81.5퍼센트 올랐다. 신규 주택 건설이 매우 둔화되었을 때, 대침체가 주택 부족을 발생시킴에 따라 공급이 수요를 충족시키지 못하고 있다. 이는 많은 잠재적인 구매자들이 빠르게 가치가 오르고 있는 주택을 구입하지 못하고 있다는 것을 의미한다. 미국 주택도시개발부 장관인 Marcia Fudge(마르시아 퍼지)에 따르면, 사실 주택 시장은 2008년 금융 위기 이후 이렇게나 알맞은 가격의 주택이 부족한 적이 없었다. 임대료가 계속 상승할 것이기 때문에, 이는 구매자들뿐만 아니라 세입자들에게도 영향을 미친다. 부를 축적하는 매우 효과적인 방법인 주택 소유는 이러한 추세로 인해 많은 사람들에게 달성할 수 없게 되었고, 이 추세는 가까운 미래에 약해질 기미가 보이지 않는다.

① 계속 진행 중인 문제: 미국의 상승하는 주택 가격
② 교외 혹은 지방의 부동산이 더 나은 투자인가?
③ 주택 소유: 부를 얻는 가장 좋은 방법
④ 주택 시장의 미래에 대한 예측

⑤ 주택 가격 상승과 임대료의 관계

(어휘) skyrocket 치솟다   entry-level 신규의   development 새로운 사태, 발달
stem from ~에서 기인하다   relocate 이주하다   Great Recession 대침체
appreciate 가치가 오르다   affordable (가격이) 알맞은   renter 세입자
exceedingly 매우, 대단히   unattainable 달성할 수 없는   abate 약해지다
[선택지] property 부동산   ongoing 계속 진행 중인

(구문분석)
[16행] Home ownership — an exceedingly effective **way**
①[to build wealth] — has become unattainable for many
because of **this trend**, ②[which shows no signs of abating
in the near future].
→ ①[to build wealth]는 to부정사의 형용사적 용법(~할)으로 앞의 명사 way를 수식한다.
→ ②[which ~ future]는 선행사 this trend를 수식하는 주격 관계대명사절로, 콤마 뒤에서 계속적 용법으로 쓰였다.

25 도표 정보 파악하기   정답 ⑤

(해설) 폴란드의 경우 2018년 삼림의 토지 면적이 9만 5천 평방 킬로미터로, 10만 평방 킬로미터를 넘지 않으므로, 수치의 비교 표현이 잘못 반영되었다. 따라서 도표의 내용과 일치하지 않는 것은 ⑤이다.

(해석)

2018년 토지 이용 유형에 따른 토지 면적

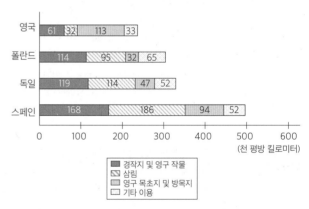

위의 그래프는 2018년 유럽 4개국의 토지 이용에 따른 토지 면적을 나타낸다. ① 4개국 중 폴란드에는 영구 목초지와 방목지로 사용되는 가장 적은 평방 킬로미터가 있는 반면, "기타 이용"으로는 토지 이용에서 가장 많은 평방 킬로미터가 있다. ② 경작지와 영구 작물에 대해서는 독일이 11만 9천 평방 킬로미터로 2위를 차지했다. ③ 스페인에서는, 삼림이 18만 6천 평방 킬로미터로 토지 이용에 있어서 가장 넓은 토지 면적을 차지했다. ④ 영국의 총 토지 면적은 30만 평방 킬로미터보다 적지만, 영국은 영구 목초지와 방목지의 토지 면적이 10만 평방 킬로미터를 넘는 유일한 나라이다. ⑤ 폴란드와 독일의 경우 삼림의 토지 면적이 두 번째로 가장 넓었고, 두 나라 모두 10만 평방 킬로미터를 넘었다.

(어휘) permanent 영구적인   crop 작물   meadow 목초지
pasture 방목지, 초원   take up 차지하다

(구문분석)
[11행] ~ the United Kingdom is **the only country** [where the
land area of permanent meadows and pastures was more
than 100 thousand square kilometers].
→ [where ~ kilometers]는 선행사 the only country를 수식하며, 장소를 나타내는 관계부사 where가 이끄는 관계부사절이다.

26 세부 정보 파악하기 — 정답 ⑤

[해설] Dreyer was able to develop a device that was capable of supplying sufficient oxygen for airmen을 통해 환자가 아닌 비행사들에게 충분한 산소를 공급하는 장치를 개발했다는 것을 알 수 있는데, ⑤은 환자들에게 산소를 공급하는 장치라고 일부 정보를 잘못 나타냈으므로 글의 내용과 일치하지 않는 것은 ⑤이다.

[해석] Georges Dreyer(조르주 드헤이에)는 1873년에 상하이에서 태어났는데, 그곳은 그의 아버지가 덴마크 왕립 해군으로 배치되어 있던 곳이었다. 그는 어려서부터 뛰어난 학생이었고 코펜하겐 대학에서 의학을 공부하기 시작해 1900년에 의학 학위를 받았다. 그의 주된 연구 관심사는 세균학과 면역에 있었다. 그는 백신과 예방 주사에 관한 수많은 연구를 수행했다. 그의 연구 동안, 그는 장티푸스를 진단하는 데 사용되었던 Widal 검사의 더 나은 변형들을 발견했다. Dreyer가 바이러스학에 대한 중요한 연구를 책임지고 있었던 한편, 그는 또한 호흡기 생리학에 중요한 기여를 했는데, 그것은 폐 기능과 우리가 호흡하는 방법에 대한 연구이다. 그는 산소와 항공술에 관한 많은 실험을 실시하며, 제1차 세계대전 동안 전투기 조종사들에게 그의 연구를 특히 의미 있게 만들었다. Dreyer는 산소가 부족한 환경에 자주 있는 비행사들을 위해 충분한 산소를 공급할 수 있는 장치를 개발할 수 있었다. 흥미롭게도, Dreyer는 오늘날 그것들(발견들)의 중요성에도 불구하고 생리학 연구에서 이러한 발견들에 대해 거의 인정받지 못한다.

[어휘] station 배치하다 bacteriology 세균학 immunity 면역
immunization 예방 주사, 면역법 modification 변형, 수정된 것
respiratory physiology 호흡기 생리학 lung 폐 aviation 항공술
airman 비행사 acknowledge 인정하다

[구문분석] [3행] He ~ began studying medicine at the University of Copenhagen, [earning his medical degree in 1900].
→ [earning ~ 1900]는 '~하고'라는 의미의 연속동작을 나타내는 분사구문으로, 분사구문의 주어가 주절의 주어(He)와 같아서 생략되었다.

27 안내문 정보 파악하기 — 정답 ④

[해설] 수치가 포함된 부분인 Class limit is 7 students max를 통해 수강 정원이 최대 7명인 것을 알 수 있으므로, 글의 내용과 일치하지 않는 것은 ④이다.

[해석]

유화 워크숍 101

당신이 늘 유화를 그리고 싶으셨다면, 이 워크숍은 당신을 위한 것입니다. 초보자분들의 참여가 권장됩니다!

장소:
- Weller 문화 회관
- 2층, 203호 스튜디오

시간:
- 매주 월요일, 수요일, 금요일
- 오전 수업: 오전 10시부터 오후 12시까지
- 저녁 수업: 오후 8시부터 오후 10시까지
* 스튜디오는 연습을 원하는 학생들을 위해 토요일마다 오전 10시부터 오후 3시까지 개방됩니다.

등록:
- www.painterswork.com에서 등록하십시오.
- 수강 정원은 최대 7명입니다.

- 수업당 35달러
* 더러워져도 되는 옷을 입으세요.
* 무료로 주차가 가능합니다.
  문의 사항이 있다면 Erin Powell에게 epowell717@painterswork.com으로 이메일을 보내시면 됩니다.

[어휘] paint in oil 유화를 그리다

[구문분석] [21행] [If you have any questions], you can email Erin Powell at epowell717@painterswork.com.
→[If ~ questions]는 접속사 if(만약 ~한다면)가 이끄는 조건의 부사절이다.

28 안내문 정보 파악하기 — 정답 ⑤

[해설] 추가 정보와 관련된 부분인 All funds will go to the shelter and caring for un-homed animals를 통해 모든 기금이 보호소에 전달되어 집 없는 동물들을 돌보는 데 사용될 것임을 알 수 있으므로, 글의 내용과 일치하는 것은 ⑤이다.

[해석]

제7회 연례 자선 반려견 산책

Silverton 동물 보호소는 연례 자선 반려견 산책 날짜를 발표하게 되어 기쁩니다. 여러분의 털로 덮인 단짝 친구들을 데려와서 어려움에 처한 동물들을 돕기 위해 산책을 하세요.

일시 및 장소
• 6월 18일 일요일(오전 10시 30분 - 오후 3시 30분)
• Jackson 공원

참가비
• 1인당 15달러(티셔츠 포함)
• 12세 미만 어린이는 무료

기대할 수 있는 것
• 커피와 가벼운 간식을 구매할 수 있을 것입니다.
• 산책로는 1.6km일 것입니다.
• 가장 많은 산책로를 완보한 반려견과 주인에게는 상과 상품이 주어질 것입니다.

참고사항
• 모든 기금은 보호소에 전달될 것이고, 집 없는 동물들을 돌보는 데 사용될 것입니다.
• 여러분은 여러분의 반려동물에 대한 책임이 있음을 인지해주세요 (필요 시 다른 용품들을 챙겨오세요).

[어휘] furry 털로 덮인 in need 어려움에 처한 walking trail 산책로
be responsible for ~에 책임이 있다

[구문분석] [16행] Awards and prizes [will be given] to the dogs and owners that complete the most trails.
→ [will be given]은 조동사(will)가 있는 '조동사 + be + p.p.' 형태의 수동태이다.

29 어법상 틀린 것 찾기 정답 ③

(해설) 주어 자리에 단수명사 a little girl이 왔으므로 ③의 복수동사 believe를 단수동사 believes로 고쳐야 한다. 참고로, 주어와 동사 사이의 screaming ~ people은 수 일치에 영향을 주지 않는 수식어(분사구)다.

(오답분석) ①은 most의 수식을 받으면서 분사(given)를 수식하는 자리이므로 부사 frequently를 사용한 것은 어법상 적절하다. ②은 목적어가 없는 불완전한 절(they can (do))을 이끌며 동사(do)의 목적어 자리에 올 수 있는 복합관계대명사 whatever를 사용하여 어법상 적절하다. 참고로 can 뒤에 생략된 동사 do는 they'll do에서 이미 언급되었기 때문에 생략되었다. ④은 접속사 or 앞에서 전치사 by의 목적어로 쓰인 동명사 scolding과 병렬 구조를 이루는 동명사 making을 사용하여 어법상 적절하다. for being과 병렬이 아니라는 점도 알아 두자. ⑤은 명사 way를 수식하는 형용사 역할을 하는 to부정사 to get을 사용하여 어법상 적절하다.

(해석) 아이들이 버릇없이 구는 이유에 대해서는 여러 가지 설명이 있지만, 가장 흔히 제시되는 것은 그들이 관심을 몹시 원한다는 것이다. 아이들은 관심을 부모의 지지와 동일시하기 때문에, 비록 그것(그들이 할 수 있는 무엇이든 하는 것)이 반항하거나 무례한 것을 의미할지라도, 그것(관심)을 얻기 위해 그들이 할 수 있는 무엇이든 할 것이다. 예를 들어, 많은 사람들 앞에서 소리를 지르고 우는 한 어린 소녀는 그녀의 부모가 그들의 관심을 그녀에게로 다시 향하게 만들고 있다고 믿는다. 부모는 이런 종류의 행동에 아이가 감정을 주체하지 못한다고 꾸짖거나 그들 자신이 야단법석을 떨면서 반응해서는 안 된다. 그렇게 하는 것은 아이들에게 그들의 나쁜 행동이 그들이 원하는 것을 얻기 위한 용인되는 방법임을 강화할 뿐이다. 대신, 부모는 아이들에게 칭찬과 다른 형태의 관심을 주기 전에 아이가 침착하고 예의 바르게 될 때까지 기다리며 그 잘못된 행동이 문제가 되지 않는 것처럼 행동해야 한다.

(어휘) misbehave 버릇없이 굴다　crave 몹시 원하다, 갈망하다
equate 동일시하다　parental 부모의　disobedient 반항하는
redirect 다시 향하게 하다　scold 꾸짖다　make a scene 야단법석을 떨다
reinforce 강화하다　well-behaved 예의 바른

(구문분석) [7행] ~ she is forcing her parents to redirect their attention to her.
　동사　목적어　목적격 보어
→ 동사 is forcing의 목적어로 her parents, 목적격 보어로 to부정사 to redirect가 쓰였다.

30 어휘 적절성 파악하기 정답 ⑤

(해설) 선해지기 위해서는 계속해서 선한 습관을 길러야 하고, 이는 자동적으로 윤리적인 삶을 살게 할 것이라고 했다. 따라서, 우리가 날마다 도덕적이기 위해 노력하는 것은 뜻밖의 사건들에 직면했을 때에도 무의식적으로 올바르게 반응하도록 해준다는 맥락이 되어야 하므로, ⑤의 consciously(의식적으로)를 그와 반대되는 의미의 unconsciously(무의식적으로)와 같은 어휘로 바꾸어야 문맥상 적절하다.

(해석) 위험한 순간에 도망쳐 숨는 사람도 있고, 다른 사람을 위해 ① 주저 없이 자신의 목숨을 바치는 사람도 있다. 일촉즉발의 위험에 직면했을 때, 우리를 다른 길보다 어느 한 길로 인도하는 것은 무엇인가? 용감함은 ② 타고난 특성일지도 모른다; 어떤 사람들은 그저 영웅이 되기 위해 태어난다. 그러나, 아리스토텔레스 윤리학에서, 그것은 실현 가능성의 문제일 뿐이다. 친절함, 선함, 용기와 같이 우리가 도덕적이라고 여기는 모든 특성들은 ③ 추상적인 개념이 아니라 삶에서 나타나는 경험으로 얻은 반응들이다. 선해지기 위해서는 적극적으로 선한 습관을 길러야 한다; 계속해서 그렇게 하는 것은 자동적으로 윤리적

인 삶을 살게 할 것이다. ④ 예상치 못한 상황에서, 우리는 행동하기 전에 숙고할 기회가 없다. 하지만, 우리가 날마다 도덕적이기 위해 집중적인 노력을 한다면, 우리는 가장 뜻밖의 사건들에 직면했을 때조차도 ⑤ 의식적으로(→무의식적으로) 올바르게 반응할 것이다. 도덕성은 사실상 몸이 기억한다.

(어휘) put one's life on the line 목숨을 바치다　imminent 일촉즉발의
courageousness 용감함　natural 타고난　practicality 실현 가능성
deem 여기다　virtuous 도덕적인　manifest 나타나다
cultivate 기르다, 함양하다　consciously 의식적으로
morality 도덕성, 도덕　for all intents and purposes 사실상, 모든 면에서
muscle memory 몸이 기억하는 것, 근육 기억

(구문분석) [8행] All the traits we deem to be virtuous — kindness, goodness, bravery — are **not** ①[abstract concepts] **but** ②[practiced responses that manifest in life].
→ ①[abstract concepts]와 ②[practiced ~ life]는 상관접속사 not A but B(A가 아니라 B)로 연결된 병렬 구조이다.

31 빈칸 추론하기 정답 ⑤

(해설) "소수 집단"이 항상 수적으로 적은 집단을 뜻하는 게 아니라는 내용의 글이다. 빈칸 앞 문장에서, 남아프리카 공화국은 수적으로 다수인 흑인들과 더 적은 수의 백인들로 인구가 구성되어 있다고 했고, 빈칸 뒤 문장에서 남아프리카 공화국 흑인들은 소수 집단이지만 수적인 의미로는 소수가 아니라고 설명하고 있다. 따라서 빈칸에는 ⑤ '양적인'이 와서 남아프리카 공화국의 백인들은 양적으로 소수 집단임에도 불구하고 오늘날까지 많은 권력이 있는 자리를 차지하고 있다는 의미가 되어야 한다.

(해석) 대부분의 사람들은 "소수 집단"을 수와 관련된 용어로써, 또는 더 작은 숫자나 전체 절반 이하의 부분을 나타내는 단어로 정의한다. 이 논란의 여지가 없어 보이는 명칭 때문에, 소수 집단은 다른 대중 구성원보다 더 적은 수에 달하는 사람들 무리로 구성되어야 한다고 종종 여겨진다. 그러나 그 용어가 항상 이 단순화된 정의를 충족시키는 것은 아니다. 예를 들어, 남아프리카 공화국은 수적으로 다수인 흑인들과 더 적은 수의 백인들로 인구가 구성되어 있다. 하지만, 이 나라의 백인들은 양적 소수 집단임에도 불구하고 역사적으로 같은 나라 사람들을 지배하고 억압해왔으며, 오늘날까지 많은 권력이 있는 자리를 차지하고 있다. 그렇기 때문에, 남아프리카 공화국 흑인들은 소수 집단이지만 수적인 의미로는 그렇지 않다. 더 큰 집단을 구성함에도 불구하고, 그들은 국가의 자원, 제도, 지배 구조에 대한 그들의 몫이 백인들이 가진 몫에 비해 여전히 더 적기 때문에 그럼에도 불구하고 소수 집단으로 간주될 수 있다.

① 토착의　　　　　　　② 급진적인
③ 신앙심이 강한　　　　④ 언어의
⑤ 양적인

(어휘) minority 소수 집단　numerical 수와 관련된, 수적인　signify 의미하다
designation 명칭, 지정　beyond dispute 논란의 여지가 없는
compose 구성하다　dominate 지배하다　oppress 억압하다
countryman 같은 나라 사람, 동포　comprise 구성하다　institution 제도
mechanism 구조, 절차

(구문분석) [6행] The term does **not always** meet this simplified definition though.
→ not always는 '항상 ~인 것은 아니다'라는 의미로 부분 부정을 나타내는 구문이다.

[14행] [That being the case], black South Africans are a minority, but not in the numerical sense.

→ [That ~ case]는 Because that is the case(그렇기 때문에)에서 접속사 Because를 생략하고 동사 is를 현재분사 being으로 바꾼 분사구문 표현이다. 분사구문의 주어(That)가 주절의 주어(black South Africans)와 달라서 생략되지 않았다.

32 빈칸 추론하기   정답 ③

[해설] 과학의 목적이 더 이상 발견에 있는 것이 아니라 이익을 창출하는 것에 있는 상황을 경고하는 내용의 글이다. 글의 중반에서 우리는 아직 숨겨져 있는 비밀을 풀고 싶어하는 젊은이들의 호기심과 창의력을 억누를 것인지 질문을 던지고 있고, 주제문을 재진술하는 빈칸 문장에서 과학의 목적인 진리를 뒤로하는 것은 결국 수천 개의 길을 탐험되지 않은 상태로 남겨놓을 것이라고 했다. 따라서 빈칸에는 ③ '우리가 세계를 보고 이해하는 방법을 제한한다'는 내용이 오는 것이 적절하다.

[오답 분석] ①의 연구의 정확성은 글의 내용과 관련이 없다. ②, ⑤는 글에서 언급되고 있지 않다. ④의 과학자들이 위험한 실험을 한다는 것은 글의 내용과 관련이 없다.

[해석] 과학의 우선순위는 더 이상 발견이 아니며, 그 상황은 목표가 불명한 과학에 특히 위험하다. 수익성 있는 결과를 약속할 수 없다는 것은 순수 과학이 행해질 수 없다는 것을 의미하는데, 적어도 시장에서는 어떠한 투자자도 "쓸모가 없다"고 판명될지도 모르는 무언가에 돈을 투자하고 싶어하지 않기 때문이다. 결국에는 무언가가 증명되어야 하고, 결과는 가격표를 제시할 수 있어야 한다. 하지만, 다음 큰 발견이 어디서 혹은 언제 일어날지 확실하게 말할 수 있는 사람이 있을까? 우리는 아직 우리에게 숨겨져 있는 비밀을 열어 보이고 싶어 하는 젊은이들의 호기심과 창의력을 억누르고 싶은가? 과학은 진리를 추구하는 그것의 목적을 뒤로 해왔고 여느 대기업과 다를 바가 없다. 이것은 수천 개의 길을 탐험되지 않은 상태로 남겨놓고, 궁극적으로는 우리가 세계를 보고 이해하는 방법을 제한한다. 과학에 달러 표시의 순자산이 있을 때, 우리는 모두 고통받는다.

① 연구의 정확성이 떨어질 수 있다는 것을 의미한다
② 과학 연구를 훨씬 덜 경쟁력 있게 만든다
③ 우리가 세계를 보고 이해하는 방법을 제한한다
④ 과학자들이 위험한 실험을 하는 결과를 낳는다
⑤ 연구를 수행하는 데 더 많은 비용이 들 것임을 암시한다

[어휘] undirected 목표가 불명한 profitable 수익성이 있는
sink money 돈을 낭비하다 squash 억누르다 unlock 열어 보이다
avenue (나아갈) 길 net worth 순자산 [선택지] accuracy 정확성

[구문 분석] [3행] [Not being able to promise profitable results] means that pure science cannot be done ~

→ [Not ~ results]는 동사 means의 주어인 동명사구이며, 동명사의 의미를 부정하는 Not이 동명사 being 앞에 온 형태이다.

33 빈칸 추론하기   정답 ④

[해설] 주제문을 재진술하는 빈칸 문장에서 '무엇이 어떠하지만' 소극적인 방해가 적극적인 피해와 일치하지 않는다고 하고, 글의 중반에서 기술이 우리를 덜 자유롭게 만들고 남용된다면 위험할 수 있지만, 그것은 우리에게 심각하고 장기

적인 해를 끼치고 있지 않다고 했다. 따라서 빈칸에는 ④ '기술이 우리가 최상의 삶을 사는 것을 막을지도 모른다'가 와서, 기술이 우리가 최상의 삶을 사는 것을 막을지도 모르지만 소극적인 방해가 적극적인 피해와 일치하지 않는다는 의미가 되어야 한다.

[오답 분석] ①은 글의 핵심 어구 technology를 사용하여 헷갈리게 하는 오답이다. ②은 기술이 끼치는 피해는 그다지 심각하지도 않고 장기적이지도 않다고 한 글의 내용과 반대되는 내용이므로 오답이다. ③은 글에서 언급된 modern을 사용하여 헷갈리게 하는 오답이다. ⑤의 인류의 한계에 대한 내용은 글에서 언급되고 있지 않다.

[해석] 기술은 더 이상 단순히 우리 삶의 일부가 아니다; 그것은 우리가 생각하고, 배우고, 소통하고, 노는 방식을 근본적으로 새로운 모양으로 만들고 있다. 이러한 관점에서 현대 기술 문화가 가져온 중요한 변화는, 어떤 새롭고 색다른 것에 대한 인간의 자연스러운 반응인, 불안함을 가지고 보아진다. 특히, 컴퓨터 화면이 이용할 수 있게 만드는 것, 즉 폭력, 사이버 폭력, 비디오 게임 중독 등에 대한 여과되지 않고 무제한적인 노출을 둘러싸고 도덕적 공황 상태가 조성된다. 그러나, 이것이 야기하는 두려움의 수준은 어떠한 현실적인 위협과도 안 맞는다. 기술이 많은 면에서 우리를 덜 자유롭게 만들고, 남용된다면 위험할 수 있지만, 그것은 우리에게 심각하고, 장기적인 해를 끼치지 않고 있다고 말하는 것이 더 정확하다; 우리의 인간성은 우리가 화면에서 눈을 들어 쳐다보거나 마주보고 소통하는 것을 꺼리거나 할 수 없을 정도로 파괴되지는 않았다. 그렇다, 기술이 우리가 최상의 삶을 사는 것을 막을지도 모르지만, 소극적인 방해가 적극적인 피해와 일치하지는 않는다.

① 기술의 통제력을 잃는 것은 매우 현실적인 가능성이 있다
② 기술의 대가가 이익보다 크다
③ 현대 세계를 거부하는 것은 유혹적일 수 있다
④ 기술이 우리가 최상의 삶을 사는 것을 막을지도 모른다
⑤ 인류의 한계는 기술로 해결될 수 있다

[어휘] fundamentally 근본적으로 reshape 새로운 모양으로 만들다
apprehension 불안 panic 공황 unfiltered 여과되지 않은
cyberbullying 사이버 폭력 provoke 야기하다
out of sync 안 맞는, 조화되지 않는 humanity 인간성 shatter 파괴하다
equate 일치하다 [선택지] outweigh ~보다 크다 optimal 최상의, 최적의
address 해결하다

[구문 분석] [6행] Specifically, a moral panic is created **around** [what the computer screen can open up] ~

→ [what ~ up]은 관계대명사 what이 이끄는 명사절로, 전치사 around의 목적어 역할을 한다.

[10행] Yet, **the level of fear** [(that/which) this provokes] is out of sync with any realistic threat.

→ [this provokes]는 선행사 the level of fear를 수식하는 관계대명사절로, 목적격 관계대명사 that/which가 생략되었다.

[11행] It is more accurate to say that, while technology makes us less free in many ways and can be dangerous (if (technology is) overused), it is not doing us serious, long-term harm

→ (if overused)는 주절과 부사절의 주어가 같을 때 부사절에서 '주어(technology) + be동사(is)'가 생략된 형태이다.

34 빈칸 추론하기 정답 ②

(해설) 1990년대에 처음 발견된 잔해가 네안데르탈인과 '호모 사피엔스'의 공통 조상인 '호모 안테세소르'라는 별개의 종으로 추정되었으나 논란이 있었다는 내용의 글이다. 빈칸 앞에서 '호모 사피엔스'와 유사한 모양의 안면 구조와 덜 발달한 치아의 특이한 조합이 관찰된 적이 없었다고 했고, 글의 후반에서 별개의 종이라서가 아니라 다 자라지 않아서 그런 특징들을 지닌다는 일부 과학자들의 반론을 언급했다. 따라서 주제와 관련된 빈칸에는 ② '그들을 고유한 종으로 지정하도록'이라는 내용이 오는 것이 적절하다.

(오답분석) ①의 다소 빠르게 진화했다는 추측은 글의 내용과 관련이 없다. ③은 일부 전문가들이 네안데르탈인과 '호모 사피엔스'의 공통된 조상이 '호모 안테세소르'였다고 주장했으나 이는 한동안 논쟁을 일으킨 종이었다는 글의 내용과 반대되는 내용이므로 오답이다. ④의 우세한 종인지 여부는 글에서 언급되고 있지 않으며, 글에서 언급된 species를 사용하여 헷갈리게 하는 오답이다. ⑤는 글에서 언급된 lineage를 사용하여 헷갈리게 하는 오답이다.

(해석) 약 50만 년 전에, 네안데르탈인과 '호모 사피엔스', 즉 현대 인류의 혈통들이 공통된 조상에서 갈라졌다. 일부 전문가들은 이 연결 고리가 '호모 안테세소르'였다고 제안한다: 이는 과학계에서 한동안 논쟁을 일으킨 종이다. 일부 사람들이 '호모 안테세소르'로 부르는 것의 잔해들이 1990년대에 스페인에서 처음으로 발견되었다. 그것들은 80만 년 정도가 된 것으로 밝혀졌고, 그들의 안면 구조의 모양이 '호모 사피엔스'의 그것과 놀랍도록 유사하지만 발견된 표본의 치아가 발달되지 않았다는 점에서 독특했다. 아직 관찰된 적이 없던 이러한 특이한 조합이, 연구자들이 그들을 고유한 종으로 지정하도록 한 것이다. 하지만, 발견된 모든 '호모 안테세소르' 표본들이 나이가 어렸다는 사실은 논란을 야기했다. 일부 과학자들은 이 잔해들이 별개의 종의 일부이기보다는 사실상 다른 종의 것일 수 있고 아직 다 자라지 않았기 때문에 이러한 특정한 특징들을 지닌다고 주장한다.

① 그들이 다소 빠르게 진화했다고 추측하도록
② 그들을 고유한 종으로 지정하도록
③ 그들이 공통된 조상임을 확고히 하도록
④ 그들이 우세한 종이라고 결론짓도록
⑤ 인류의 혈통에 대한 그들의 관점에 이의를 제기하도록

(어휘) rouse 일으키다, 불러일으키다 remain 잔해, 나머지
primitive 발달하지 않은, 원시적인 aspect 모양, 측면
controversy 논란, 논쟁 [선택지] designate 지정하다, 칭하다
establish 확고히 하다, 설립하다

(구문분석)
> [6행] Remains **of** [what some refer to as *Homo antecessor*] were first discovered in the 1990s in Spain.
> → [what ~ *antecessor*]는 관계대명사 what(~하는 것)이 이끄는 명사절로, 전치사 of의 목적어 역할을 한다.

> [7행] They were found to be around 800,000 years old, and were unique **in that** the teeth of the uncovered specimens were primitive while aspects of their facial structures were surprisingly similar to those of *Homo sapiens*.
> → in that은 '~라는 점에서, ~이므로'라는 의미의 부사절 접속사이다.

35 흐름과 관계 없는 문장 찾기 정답 ④

(해설) 생물 발광의 두 가지 유형과 이에 대한 각각의 예시로 반딧불이와 하와이 짧은꼬리오징어에 대해 설명하고 있는 글이다. 그런데 ④은 대다수 유기체들의 종

류 중에 생물 발광을 할 수 있는 종들이 있다는 내용이므로 핵심 소재는 같지만 주제에서 벗어나 있어 글의 흐름과 무관하다.

(오답분석) ①은 화학 반응을 통해 스스로 빛을 내는 생물의 예시로 반딧불이를 언급하고 있고, ②의 It은 ①의 '반딧불이'를 가리키고 있으므로 ① 뒤에 이어지는 게 적절하다. ③은 ①, ②에 이어서 빛을 내는 박테리아와 공생 관계를 맺는 생물의 예시로 하와이 짧은꼬리오징어를 언급하고 있고, ⑤의 These bacteria는 ③의 '공생하는 박테리아'를 가리키고 있으므로 ③ 뒤에 이어지는 게 적절하다.

(해석) 생물 발광은 살아있는 유기체에 의한 빛의 방출이다. 이런 능력을 보이는 종들은 자신들의 세포에서 일어나는 화학 반응을 통해 스스로 빛을 내거나 빛을 내는 박테리아와 공생 관계를 맺고 있다. ① 반딧불이는 주로 짝을 유혹하고 포식자들이 가까이 오지 못하게 하려고 독립적으로 빛을 내는 유기체의 좋은 예이다. ② 그것은 복부에 발광 기관을 가지고 있는데, 이것은 루시페린이라고 불리는 효소가 산소와 다른 유기 화합물과 결합할 때 작동된다. ③ 빛을 낼 수 있는 또 다른 유기체는 하와이 짧은꼬리오징어인데, 이 오징어는 기능을 하기 위해 공생하는 박테리아에 의존하는 발광 기관을 가지고 있다. (④ 사실, 박테리아에서 상어와 같은 해양 척추동물에 이르기까지 대다수 유기체들의 종류 중에는 생물 발광을 할 수 있는 몇몇 종들이 있다.) ⑤ 이러한 박테리아는 오징어 아랫부분에 살며 숙주의 발광 기관과 상호작용함으로써 오징어가 밤에 사냥할 때 사용할 수 있는 빛을 만들어낸다.

(어휘) bioluminescence 생물 발광 emission 방출 firefly 반딧불이
ward off 가까이 오지 못하게 하다 predator 포식자 abdomen 복부
trigger 작동시키다, 촉발시키다 luciferin 루시페린, 발광소
compound 화합물 vertebrate 척추 동물 reside 살다, 거주하다
host 숙주

(구문분석)
> [2행] Species that exhibit this ability **either** ①[produce light on their own through a chemical reaction that takes place in their cells] **or** ②[have a symbiotic relationship with light-producing bacteria].
> → ①[produce ~ cells]와 ②[have ~ bacteria]는 상관접속사 either A or B로 연결된 병렬 구조이다.

36 글의 순서 배열하기 정답 ④

(해설) 주어진 글은 NASA와 같은 정부 기관이 화성에 사람을 보내는 일에 앞장서고 있다는 주제를 제시한다. (C)는 NASA가 유능한 인력 그리고 수십 년간 축적된 경험과 자료를 가지고 있다는 내용이고, 주어진 글의 마지막에서 NASA와 같은 정부 기관이 현재 화성에 사람을 보내는 일에 앞장서고 있다고 했으므로 그 뒤에 와야 한다. (A)의 This는 (C)의 '연방 정부의 지원이 수조 달러의 비용을 전부 충당할 수 없는' 한계를 가리키므로 (C) 바로 다음에 오는 것이 적절하다. (B)는 순접 연결어 For instance(예를 들어)를 통해 (A)의 기업의 자산과 정부의 자산의 공동 작업에 대한 부연 설명을 하고 있으므로 (A) 뒤에 오는 것이 적절하다. 따라서 글의 순서로 가장 적절한 것은 ④ (C) - (A) - (B)이다.

(해석) 인간을 화성에 보내는 것은 많은 사람들에 의해 공유되는 목표이며, NASA와 같은 정부 기관들이 현재 원정의 선두에 있다.

(C) NASA는 기술과 경험이 중요한 전문가를 고용한다. 그 기관은 또한 끌어낼 수 있는 수십 년의 경험과 자료를 가지고 있다. 하지만 더 많은 것이 필요하다. 연방 정부의 지원이 예상되는 수조 달러의 비용을 전부 충당할 것이라고 기대하기 어렵기 때문에 자금 조달은 주요 관심사이다.

(A) 바로 여기에 Elon Musk(일론 머스크)와 같은 기업가들이 참여한다. 그의 항공 우주 산업 회사인 스페이스X와 그와 같은 다른 회사들은 정부가 부족한 자금을 보유하고 있어 보다 탄탄한 연구와 자금 조달을 허용한다. 기업

들이 자신들의 자산을 정부의 자산과 결합한다면, 그 결과는 우주 비행의 발전이 된다.

(B) 예를 들어, 스페이스X는 오직 NASA의 케네디 우주 센터의 민간인들만 승무원으로 태운 최초의 우주 비행을 시작했다. 이는 화성으로의 유인 우주 비행이라는 궁극적인 목표에 첫 걸음을 제공했던 협력인, 스페이스X와 미국 정부의 공동 작업을 통해서만 가능했다.

[어휘] government agency 정부 기관 forefront 선두 quest 원정, 탐색 entrepreneur 기업가, 사업가 aerospace 항공 우주 산업 robust 탄탄한, 굳건한 asset 자산, 재산 man 승무원으로 태우다 civilian 민간인 manned 유인의 mission 우주 비행 backing 지원 projected 예상되는

[구문분석]
[5행] His aerospace company SpaceX, and others like it, possess funds the government lacks, [allowing for more robust research and financing].
→ [allowing ~ financing]은 결과를 나타내는 분사구문으로, 분사구문의 주어가 주절의 주어(His aerospace company SpaceX)와 같아서 생략되었다.

[17행] NASA employs **experts** [whose skills and experience are critical].
→ [whose ~ critical]은 선행사 experts를 수식하며, 소유격 관계대명사 whose가 이끄는 관계대명사절이다.

---

37 글의 순서 배열하기 　　정답 ③

[해설] 주어진 글은 문자 체계가 있는 고대 문명은 그들이 문서로 남긴 정보를 통해 우리가 역사를 이해할 수 있다는 주제를 제시한다. (B)는 구입 물품 목록만큼 간단한 것조차 매우 흥미로운 사실을 보여줄 수 있다는 내용이고, 주어진 글 마지막에 그들이 기록된 문서로 남긴 모든 정보 덕분에 우리가 역사를 이해할 수 있다고 했으므로 그 뒤에 와야 한다. (C)의 this kind of information은 (B)의 '일상적인 세부 사항들'을 가리키므로 (B) 뒤에 오는 것이 적절하다. (A)는 역접 연결어 However(그러나)를 통해 (C)의 내용에 대한 반전 설명을 하고 있으며 these는 (C)의 '최근 형태의 언어들'을 가리키므로 (C) 바로 다음에 오는 것이 적절하다. 따라서 글의 순서로 가장 적절한 것은 ③ (B) - (C) - (A)이다.

[해석] 문자 체계를 발달시킨 고대 문명은 그들이 기록된 문서로 남긴 모든 정보 때문에 우리가 역사를 이해하는 데 도움을 준다.
(B) 구입 물품 목록만큼 간단한 것조차도 매우 흥미로운 사실을 보여줄 수 있다. 이러한 물건들은 고대인들이 어떻게 살았는지를 보여주는데, 그저 보통의 의미에서가 아니라; 그것들은 그들이 먹던 것, 그 지역에서 구할 수 있는 음식의 종류, 그리고 물건이 얼마인지와 같은 일상적인 세부 사항들에 대한 흥미로운 통찰력을 제공할 수 있다.
(C) 물론 이런 종류의 정보를 얻는 것은 천 년 혹은 그 이상 사용되지 않았던 복잡한 문자 체계를 판독하는 능력에 달려 있을 수 있다. 이를 하기 위해 고고학자들과 언어학자들은 참고 자료로 좀 더 최근 형태의 언어들에 의존해야 할 것이다.
(A) 그러나, 이것들과 고대 방언 간에는 유사함이 거의 없어서, 이는 해독하는 것을 엄청나게 시간이 걸리고 추측에 기반하게 만들 수 있다. 기계 번역 소프트웨어와 같은 새로운 기술이 고고학자들이 추측의 일부를 줄이는 데 도움을 줄 수 있을 것이라고 기대된다.

[어휘] civilization 문명 resemblance 유사함, 비슷함 decode 해독하다 speculative 추측에 기반한 archaeologist 고고학자

---

guesswork 추측, 어림짐작 revealing 흥미로운 사실을 보여주는 insight 통찰력, 이해 linguist 언어학자 reference 참고 (자료))

[구문분석]
[1행] Ancient civilizations ①[that developed writing systems] (주어) **help** us understand history ②[because of all the information (동사) ((that/which) they left behind in written documents)].
→ ①[that ~ systems]는 선행사 ancient civilizations를 수식하는 주격 관계대명사절이다.
→ ②[because ~ documents]는 '전치사(because of) + 명사(all the information) + 목적격 관계대명사 that/which가 생략된 관계절(they ~ documents)'의 형태로 앞의 절 전체를 수식한다.

---

38 주어진 문장의 위치 찾기 　　정답 ④

[해설] 주어진 문장의 대명사 It으로 보아, 주어진 문장 앞에는 가축 수를 상당히 줄이고 천연자원에 대한 부담을 덜어줄 요인에 대한 내용이 나와야 한다는 것을 알 수 있다. 이 글에서는 ①~② 뒤 문장까지 축산업이 환경에 미치는 악영향에 대해 설명하고 있고, ③ 뒤 문장의 cellular agriculture가 주어진 문장의 It으로 이어지고 있다. 게다가 ④ 뒤 문장이 연결어 also를 통해 세포 농업의 또 다른 기대 효과를 언급하지만 ③ 뒤 문장에는 세포 농업의 첫 번째 기대 효과가 언급되지 않는다는 점을 통해 글의 흐름이 끊겼음을 알 수 있다. 따라서 주어진 문장이 들어가기에 가장 적절한 곳은 ④이다.

[오답분석] ⑤ 뒤 문장은 ④ 뒤 문장에 이어서 세포 농업을 통해 식품 안정성이 상당히 향상될 수 있다는 내용을 다루고 있다.

[해석] 고기와 우유를 얻기 위해 가축을 기르는 것이 더 이상 지속 가능하지 않다는 것이 점점 더 분명해지고 있다. (①) 축산업은 막대한 토지와 물이 필요할 뿐만 아니라 온실가스 배출량의 최대 87%를 차지한다. (②) 하지만 고기에 대한 수요와 함께 세계의 인구가 빠르게 증가함에 따라, 할 수 있는 일이 있을까? (③) 그 문제에 대한 한 가지 잠재적인 해결책은 세포 농업에 있을 수 있는데, 이는 세포들이 살아있는 동물로부터 추출되고 실험실에서 배양되어 동물성 식품이 되는 과정이다. (④) 그것은 가축의 수의 상당한 감소를 허용하고, 더 나아가 우리의 천연자원에 대한 부담을 덜어 줄 것이다.) 그것은 또한 식품 안전성을 상당히 향상시킬 수 있다. (⑤) 세포 농업을 통해 생산되는 식품은 그 과정의 모든 단계에 걸쳐 면밀하게 감시되기 때문에 식품 오염으로 인해 발생되는 질병의 위험이 크게 줄어든다.

[어휘] apparent 분명한 sustainable 지속 가능한 animal agriculture 축산업 cellular 세포의 cultivate 배양하다, 경작하다 animal product 동물성 식품 contamination 오염

[구문분석]
[15행] [**Since** food produced via cellular agriculture is closely monitored through all steps of the process], the risk of diseases caused by food contamination is greatly reduced.
→ [Since ~ process]는 since(~하기 때문에)가 이끄는 이유의 부사절이다.

---

39 주어진 문장의 위치 찾기 　　정답 ③

[해설] 주어진 문장에 명시적 단서가 없는 경우에는 글의 흐름이 끊기는 곳을 찾아야 한다. ③ 앞까지는 맥거핀의 개념과 맥거핀이 활용된 영화에 관한 내용이 이어지다가 ③ 뒤 문장에서는 맥거핀이 유용한 도구인지 지나치게 의지하게

되는 것인지 많은 논쟁이 있다는 내용이 나오고 있다. ③ 앞 문장에는 such a device가 가리키는 대상이 나오지 않고 ③ 앞뒤의 내용이 유기적으로 연결되지 않는다는 점을 통해 글의 흐름이 끊겼음을 알 수 있다. 따라서 주어진 문장이 들어가기에 가장 적절한 곳은 ③이다.

(오답분석) ① 뒤 문장은 첫 문장에 이어서 맥거핀의 기능을 설명하고, ② 뒤 문장은 ① 뒤 문장에 이어서 맥거핀이 활용된 영화의 예시를 언급하고 있으므로 주어진 문장은 이 내용이 끝난 이후에 들어가야 한다.

(해석) "맥거핀"은 영화에서 자주 사용되는 구성 장치이다. (①) 그것은 주인공들에게 동기를 부여하고 이야기를 앞으로 나아가게 하는 사물, 사건, 혹은 인물이지만, 그 자체로는 아무런 의미를 지니지 않는다. (②) 잘 알려진 예는 John Huston (존 휴스턴)의 1941년 고전 누아르 영화 <말타의 매>인데, 그 영화에서 매의 동상은 이야기의 촉매제 역할을 한다. (③ 맥거핀을 사용하는 것은 해롭지 않은 것처럼 들리지만, 많은 작가들이 플롯의 허점들이나 부족한 저술을 꾸며대기 위해 결국 그렇게 한다(맥거핀을 사용한다).) 그러한 장치가 유용한 도구인지 혹은 지나치게 의지하게 되는 것인지에 대해서는 많은 논쟁이 있지만, 아마도 그 단어의 발명자는 힌트를 제공할 수 있을 것이다. (④) 맥거핀이라는 용어는 보통 영국 시나리오 작가이자 스크립트 에디터인 Angus MacPhail(앵거스 맥파일)의 공이라고 믿어진다. (⑤) MacPhail은 자신의 성의 첫 부분을 가져다가 "허튼소리"라는 뜻의 "guff"와 결합하여, 이야기에서 "쓸모 없는" 요소를 나타내는 용어를 만들었다고 추정된다.

(어휘) explain away 꾸며대다, 잘 해명하다 plot 구성, 줄거리, 플롯
hole 허점, 구멍 falcon 매 debate 논쟁하다 credit ~의 공이라고 믿다
guff 허튼소리, 실없는 이야기 nonsense 허튼소리, 말도 안 되는 소리

(구문분석) [1행] ~ but many writers end up doing so [to explain away plot holes or poor writing].
→ [to ~ writing]은 to부정사의 부사적 용법으로, 목적을 의미한다.

---

40 요약문 완성하기 정답 ②

(해설) 글의 중반부에서 의식에 대한 전념이 경기의 중요성과 결과에 대한 불확실성이 모두 높은 상황에서 더 흔하다고 했고, 글의 후반부에서는 운동선수가 자신의 능력 밖의 변수가 결과를 초래한다는 믿음인 외적 통제 소재로 알려진 것을 가질 때 의식에 대한 전념의 가능성이 높아진다고 했다. 따라서 지문의 uncertainty를 unpredictable로, one's power를 responsible로 바꾸어 표현한 ②이 정답이다.

(오답분석) 운동선수가 자신의 능력 밖의 변수가 결과를 초래한다고 믿을 때 의식에 대한 전념의 가능성이 높아진다고 했으므로 ①, ④의 prepared와 ⑤의 eligible은 (B)에 들어갈 단어로 적절하지 않다.

(해석) 많은 사람들이 특정 옷을 입기부터 경기 직전에 특정 음악을 듣기에 이르는 의식들을 한다고 알려져 있음에 따라, 운동선수들이 왜 그렇게 미신을 믿는지에 관한 연구에서 연구원들은 여러 요인들이 작용하고 있다는 것을 알아냈다. 스포츠에서의 미신에 대한 이전의 가설과 일치하게, 그렇게 하는 것이 수행 성공을 가져올 것이라는 믿음에 근거하여 동일한 의식을 수행하는 것인 **의식에 대한 전념이 경기의 중요성과 결과에 대한 불확실성이 모두 높은 상황에서 더 흔하다는 것이 발견되었다.** 다른 말로 하자면 중대한 챔피언 결정전은 한 시즌 내 다른 경기들에서보다 선수들이 미신적 의식을 행하는 것으로 이어질 가능성이 더 높다는 것이다. 또한 **운동선수가 자신의 능력 밖의 변수가 결과를 초래한다는 믿음인 외적 통제 소재로 알려진 것을 가질 때 의식에 대한 전념의 가능성이 높아진다**는 것이 발견되었다. 그러한 사고방식을 가진 스포츠 선수들에게 의식에 대한 전념은 그들이 향후 경기에 영향을 미치는 것에 최소한 어느 정도 관계가 있는 것처럼 느낄 수 있는 방법을 제공한다.

연구는 중요한 경기의 결과가 (A) 예측할 수 없을 때 그리고 운동선수가 자신의 결과에 대해 완전히 (B) 원인이 되는 것은 아니라고 믿을 때 운동선수들 사이에서 미신적인 행동의 발생 정도가 증가한다는 것을 보여준다.

	(A)		(B)
①	전략적인	……	준비된
②	예측할 수 없는	……	원인이 되는
③	논의된	……	원인이 되는
④	무기한의	……	준비된
⑤	참을 수 없는	……	적격인

(어휘) superstitious 미신을 믿는, 미신적인 ritual 의식; 의식에 대한
at play 작용하고 있는 consistent with ~와 일치하는
commitment 전념, 약속 high-stakes 중대한, 사활을 건
external locus of control 외적 통제 소재 incidence 발생 (정도)

(구문분석) [14행] It was also found [that the likelihood of ritual

　　　　　　가주어　　　　　　　진주어(that절)
commitment increases when an athlete has what **is known as** an external locus of control — a belief that variables beyond one's power produce outcomes].
→ 해당 문장은 가주어 it이 길이가 긴 진주어 that절 [that ~ outcomes] 대신 주어 자리에 쓰인 형태이다.
→ be known as는 '~으로 알려져 있다'라는 의미로, by 이외의 전치사를 쓰는 수동태 구문이다.

41~42 장문 독해 1

(해석) 길들이기에 대한 우리의 오랜 견해인, 일반적으로 어떤 종에게도 적용할 수 없는 부자연스러운 과정이라는 것이 현재 다양한 동물 개체군의 주목할 만한 변화로 인해 이의 제기를 받고 있는데, 이는 자연에 대한 우리의 이해가 얼마나 (a)부족한지를 다시 한번 강조한다. ⁴¹**실제로는, 수많은 종의 야생 동물들이 스스로를 길들이고 두드러진 행동 변화를 나타내고 있는 것처럼 보인다.** 이 개념은 야생종 내의 "공격성을 거스르는 선택"이 전통적인 길들이기 과정과 (b)유사한 결과를 가져올 수 있다고 가정하는 자기 길들이기 가설에 따른 것이다. 이러한 발달은 보노보들의 행동에 대한 그의 관찰과 관련된 연구 보고서를 출판한 Duke 대학의 진화 인류학자 Brian Hare (브라이언 헤어)의 연구에 의해 설명된다. ⁴²보노보들은 Hare의 말로는 "다정하다"; 그들은 서로 (c)협력하고 많은 시간을 노는 데 보내며, 싸우지 않는다. 이는 보노보와 유전적으로 비슷한 침팬지들의 행동과는 현저하게 다르다. ⁴²Hare는 보노보들이 자신들의 친척들과 달리 수백만 년 전에 효과가 나타났던 경쟁의 부재로 인해 길들여졌다고 가정한다. 덜 (d)온화하게(→폭력적이게) 되면서 그 특권을 가질 수 있게 된 듯하고, Princeton 대학의 진화 인류학자 Frank Albert(프랭크 알버트)는 보노보들의 조상이 이 점에서 "진화의 혜택을 받았을 것"이라고 말한다. 이와 같은 변화는 지금도 일어나고 있을 것이며, 특히 인간 (e)가까이 그리고 인구 밀집 지역에 사는 동물들의 경우에는 더욱 그러하다. ⁴¹그들은 계속해서 진화할 것이며, 그 과정에서 "더 다정하게" 될 것이다.

(어휘) domestication 길들이기 inapplicable 적용할 수 없는
challenge 이의 제기를 하다, 도전하다 domesticate 길들이다, 사육하다
prominent 두드러진, 현저한 in accordance with ~에 따라
selection 선택, 도태 aggression 공격성 anthropologist 인류학자
strikingly 현저하게 take effect 효과가 나타나다 perk 특권, 특전

---

ancestor 조상　densely populated area 인구 밀집 지역

구문분석

[6행] In fact, numerous species of wild animals [appear to be] domesticating themselves and exhibiting prominent behavioral shifts.
→ [appear to be]는 'appear + to부정사(~처럼 보인다, ~인 것 같다)'의 형태로, to부정사가 주격 보어 역할을 한다.

[24행] Becoming less violent, [it seems], can have its perks, and Frank Albert, an evolutionary anthropologist ~
→ [it seems]는 '~인 듯하다'라는 뜻으로 '주어 + 동사'가 삽입된 형태이다.

41 제목 파악하기　정답 ⑤

(해설) 수많은 야생 동물들이 스스로를 길들이고 있으며, 보노보의 예시를 통해 동물들은 진화를 계속하며 그 과정에서 더 다정하게 될 것이라고 설명하고 있다. 따라서 글의 제목으로 가장 적절한 것은 ⑤ '자기 길들이기: 덜 폭력적인 방향으로의 진화'이다.

(오답분석) ①, ③, ④은 글의 일부만을 다루고 있는 오답이다. ②은 수많은 야생 동물들이 스스로를 길들이고 있다는 글의 내용과 반대되는 내용이기 때문에 오답이다.

(해석) ① 종들은 우리가 생각하는 것보다 더 많이 협력한다!
② 동물을 길들이는 것의 부자연스러운 과정
③ 길들여지지 않는 동물들의 행동 특성
④ 왜 어떤 종들은 다른 종들보다 더 진화했는가?
⑤ 자기 길들이기: 덜 폭력적인 방향으로의 진화

42 어휘 적절성 파악하기　정답 ④

(해설) 보노보들은 서로 협력하고 싸우지 않으며, 수백만 년 전에 효과가 나타났던 경쟁의 부재로 인해 길들여져서 덜 폭력적이게 되었다는 맥락이 되어야 하므로 ④의 gentle(온화한)은 그와 반대되는 의미의 violent(폭력적인)와 같은 단어로 바꾸어야 문맥상 적절하다.

(오답분석) ①은 길들이기가 어떤 종에게도 부자연스러운 과정이라는 오랜 견해가 야생 동물들의 주목할 만한 변화에 의해 이의 제기를 받고 있다고 했고, 이는 자연에 대한 우리의 이해가 부족했음을 보여준다는 문맥이 되어야 하므로 limited가 오는 것이 적절하다.

43~45 장문 독해 2

(해석) (A) Norma는 도로변에서 오도 가도 못하고 있었다. 그녀의 차 타이어는 펑크가 났고 그녀는 70세였기 때문에 스스로 타이어를 교체할 힘이 없었다. 그녀는 가장 가까운 마을을 향해 걸어갈까 생각했지만 날이 어두워지고 비가 내리기 시작했다. 차들이 줄지어 지나가다가 마침내 한 대가 멈췄다. 한 남자가 나와서 그가 도울 수 있을지 물었다. 그녀는 처음에는 조금 긴장했다. 그가 그녀를 강탈하려고 했을까? 하지만 그 남자는 친절하게 웃으며 "제가 펑크 난 타이어를 고치는 동안 (a)당신은 가로등 옆에서 기다리는 게 어때요?"라고 말했다.
(C) 순식간에 그 남자는 그녀의 타이어를 교체했다. "오, 정말 고마워요! 당신의 도움에 보답해드리고 싶어요"라고 (c)그녀가 말했다. 하지만 그 남자는 받으려 하지 않았다. "만약 당신이 정말로 저를 위해 무언가를 해주고 싶으시다

면, 제가 당신을 도왔던 것처럼, 다른 누군가를 우연히 마주쳤을 때, 그냥 그 사람들을 도와주세요"라고 그 남자는 말했다.
(B) Norma는 다시 그에게 감사 인사를 하고는 차를 몰고 떠났다. 얼마 후에, 그녀는 음식을 좀 먹기 위해 작은 식당에 들렀다. 그 식당은 오래되고 지저분했으며 음식도 별로였다. 그러나, ⁴⁴그 종업원은 임신 중임에도 불구하고 명랑하고 친절했다. (b)그녀는 분명히 피곤해 보였지만, 그것이 그녀의 일에 영향을 미치도록 내버려 두지 않았다. Norma는 식사를 하고, 식사비를 지불하고, 떠날 때 손을 흔들어 인사했다.
(D) ⁴⁵그 종업원이 그릇들을 치우기 시작하려던 그때 그녀는 Norma가 남긴 작은 쪽지를 보았다. 그 쪽지에는 이렇게 쓰여 있었다: "누군가가 (d)저를 돕고 나서 제게 선행을 베풀라고 한 적이 있습니다. 바라건대, 당신도 언젠가 같은 일을 할 수 있기를 바랍니다." 그 쪽지 아래에는 200달러의 팁이 있었다! 그 종업원은 그것이 믿기지 않았다. 그녀는 집에 도착해서 그녀의 남편에게 그 일에 대한 모든 것을 말했다. 그는 어떤 여분의 현금이라도 도움이 되었으므로 매우 행복해했다. "당신은 다사다난한 하루를 보낸 것 같네요."라고 그가 아내에게 말했다. "나도 그랬어요. 나는 한 (e)여성이 타이어를 교체하는 것을 도왔어요."

(어휘) be stuck on ~에서 오도 가도 못하다　rob 강탈하다, 털다　shabby 지저분한　wave goodbye 손을 흔들어 인사하다　in no time at all 순식간에, 지체 없이　eventful 다사다난한, 파란만장한

구문분석

[24행] The waitress started to clean up the dishes [when she noticed a small note Norma had left].
→ [when ~ left]는 접속사 when이 이끄는 부사절이다. Norma가 쪽지를 남긴 것이 종업원이 그것을 알아차린 것보다 더 이전에 발생한 일이므로 과거완료 had left가 쓰였다.

43 글의 순서 배열하기　정답 ②

(해설) (A)는 차 타이어가 펑크가 나서 오도 가도 못하고 있는 Norma에게 한 남성이 도움을 주기 위해 나타났다는 내용이다. (C)의 첫 문장은 그 남성이 순식간에 타이어를 교체했다는 내용이므로, (C)는 도움을 주려는 남성이 나타났다는 (A) 바로 뒤에 오는 것이 적절하다. (B)에서 Norma가 그에게 감사 인사를 하고 떠났다고 했으므로, 남성이 타이어를 교체해주고 보답보다는 선행 베풀기를 권했다는 (C) 뒤에 와야 한다. (D)에서 종업원이 그릇을 치우기 시작하는 것은 (B)에서 Norma가 식사를 마치고 떠난 이후가 되어야 하므로 (B) 다음에 오는 것이 적절하다. 따라서 글의 순서로 가장 적절한 것은 ② (C) - (B) - (D)이다.

44 지칭 대상 파악하기　정답 ②

(해설) (a), (c), (d), (e)는 모두 Norma를 가리키지만 (b)는 식당의 종업원을 가리키므로, ②이 정답이다.

45 세부 정보 파악하기　정답 ⑤

(해설) (D)의 The waitress started to ~ when she noticed a small note Norma had left를 통해 식당 종업원이 Norma가 남긴 쪽지를 발견했다는 것을 알 수 있는데, ⑤은 쪽지를 발견하지 못했다고 일부 정보를 잘못 나타냈으므로 글의 내용과 일치하지 않는 것은 ⑤이다.

문제집 p.50

정답

18	⑤	19	④	20	②	21	⑤	22	④	23	⑤	24	③	25	⑤	26	④	27	④
28	⑤	29	③	30	④	31	③	32	⑤	33	⑤	34	①	35	③	36	②	37	③
38	⑤	39	③	40	①	41	③	42	④	43	⑤	44	④	45	⑤				

18 목적 파악하기 정답 ⑤

(해설) 글의 중간 이후에서 유명한 작가에게 지역의 글쓰기 동아리 모임에 초청 연사로 와 줄 수 있는지 문의하고 있으므로 정답은 ⑤이다.

(해석) Roberts 씨께

우선, 제가 귀하의 작품의 열렬한 팬이라는 사실을 알려드리고 싶습니다. 저는 지역의 글쓰기 동아리를 운영하고 있고, 많은 저희의 회원들은 그들 스스로를 당신의 팬이라고 생각합니다. 그래서 말인데, 저희는 귀하께서 저희 동아리 모임 중 하나에 참석해 주실 수 있다면 정말 좋겠습니다. 종종, 저희는 저희와 함께 글쓰기 기술과 팁에 대해 논의하기 위해 초청 연사를 초대합니다. 저희는 귀하가 다가오는 저희의 모임 중 하나에 초청 연사로 오셔서 귀하의 경험들을 공유해 주실 수 있으면 정말 기쁠 것 같습니다. 저희 회원들은 모두 그렇게 유명한 작가님으로부터의 어떠한 조언도 고마워할 장차 작가가 되려는 사람들입니다. 비록 저희는 귀하가 매우 바쁠 것이 틀림없다는 것을 알지만, 그저 연락을 취해서 이것이 실현 가능한 것인지 알고 싶었습니다. 귀하께서 관심이 있으시다면 저희에게 알려주세요.

Julie Chang 드림

(어휘) admirer 팬 every so often 종종 upcoming 다가오는
aspiring 장차 ~가 되려는 renowned 유명한
exceptionally 매우, 예외적으로 feasible 실현 가능한

(구문분석)
[5행] That being said, we would **love** [if you could attend one of our club meetings].

→ [if ~ meetings]는 접속사 if가 이끄는 명사절로, 동사 love의 목적어 역할을 한다.

19 심경 파악하기 정답 ④

(해설) 심경은 간접적으로 표현된다. 글의 초반부의 'This is it', 'This is the moment I've been waiting for'를 통해 경주 시작 직전에는 몇 달 동안 훈련해온 경주에 대해 열망하고 있는 것을 알 수 있고, 후반부의 he started to feel stiff and tired, pushed himself too hard, fearing the miles ahead 등을 통해 완주할 수 있을지 불안함을 느끼는 것을 파악할 수 있으므로 Steve의 심경 변화로 가장 적절한 것은 ④이다.

(해석) '드디어 시작이야'라고 Steve는 생각했다. '이게 바로 내가 기다려온 순간이야.' 그는 다시 한번 그의 다리를 쭉 펴면서, 자신이 활짝 웃는 것을 느꼈다. Steve는 몇 달 동안 이 경주를 위해 훈련해왔다. 그가 조깅을 하면서 보냈던 모든 이른 아침을 돌이켜 생각하면, 그는 이제 노력을 보상받을 준비가 되어 있었다. 그는 출발선에 서서 출발 신호를 기다렸다. 출발 신호 총이 쏘아졌을 때, 모두가 달리기 시작했다. Steve는 전력 질주를 시작하고 자신을 무리 속

으로 나아가게 했다. 잠시 후에, 그는 뻐근하고 피곤함을 느끼기 시작했다. 그의 다리는 분투로 화끈거렸고, 그의 폐는 아팠다. Steve는 경주 초반에 자기 자신을 너무 심하게 몰아붙였다는 것을 깨달았다. 남은 거리에서 그의 원래 속도를 유지하기가 어려울 것 같았다. 이제 앞으로의 몇 마일이 두려워졌고, Steve는 그가 결승선에 도달할 수 있을지 확신할 수 없었다.

① 지루한 → 모험을 즐기는 ② 자랑스러운 → 깜짝 놀란
③ 긴장한 → 감동한 ④ 열망하는 → 불안한
⑤ 매우 기뻐하는 → 무관심한

(어휘) this is it 드디어 시작이다, 올 것이 왔다 grin 활짝 웃다; 활짝 웃음
hard work 노력, 근면 pay off 보상받다, 성과를 거두다
launch into ~을 시작하다, ~에 나서다 sprint 전력 질주, 단거리 경주
propel 나아가게 하다 stiff (근육이) 뻐근한, 뻣뻣한 burn 화끈거리다

(구문분석)
[2행] He felt himself grin [as he once again stretched his legs].
　　　동사　목적어　목적격 보어

→ 지각동사 felt의 목적어로 himself, 목적격 보어로 동사원형 grin이 쓰였다.

→ [as ~ legs]는 시간을 나타내는 접속사 as(~하면서)가 이끄는 부사절이다.

[6행] He stood at the starting line, [waiting for the starting signal].

→ [waiting ~ signal]은 '~하면서'라는 의미의 분사구문으로, 분사구문의 주어가 주절의 주어(He)와 같아서 생략되었다.

20 주장 파악하기 정답 ②

(해설) 글의 마지막 두 문장에서 회사의 지도자들은 어떠한 사안에 관해서라도 좋은 시기와 나쁜 시기에 모두 직원들에게 솔직해야 한다고 주장하고 있으므로 정답은 ②이다.

(오답분석) ①은 글에서 '소통'을 강조하고는 있지만 '화합'에 관한 내용은 언급되지 않았으므로 오답이다.

(해석) 열린 의사소통은 현대 사회의 모든 분야에서 중시되고, 이는 직장에서 특히 사실이다. 유감스럽게도, 많은 상사들이 "꼭 알아야 하는 것만 알려주는 방식"이라고 불리는 것을 바탕으로 일하고, 직원들에게 절대적으로 필요할 때에만 정보를 제공한다. 그보다는, 그들은 좋은 시기와 나쁜 시기에 모두 직원들에게 솔직해야 한다. 왜 이것이 매우 중요한가? 그것은 많은 사람들이 그들이 하는 업무에서 주인 의식을 느끼고 위기가 발생할 경우에 그들이 해결책의 일부가 될 수 있다고 생각하고 싶어 하기 때문이다. 그러므로 지도자들은 직원들이 그들의 동료이기도 하다는 점을 기본적으로 인정하면서, 회사나 팀이 직면하고 있을지도 모르는 어떠한 사안에 관해서라도 직원들에게 솔직해야 한다.

이는 직원들의 개입 수준을 높이는 동시에, 그들이 직원들의 신뢰와 존경을 얻는 데에 도움이 될 것이고, 그러한 것은 회사에 전체적으로 득이 된다.

어휘 clear 열린, 분명한 operate 일하다, 운영하다
transparent 솔직한, 투명한 upfront 솔직한
essentially 기본적으로, 근본적으로 acknowledge 인정하다
involvement 개입, 관여

구문분석 [3행] Unfortunately, many bosses operate **on** [what is called a "need-to-know basis,"] providing staff with information only when absolutely necessary.

→ [what ~ basis]는 관계대명사 what(~하는 것)이 이끄는 명사절로, 전치사 on의 목적어 역할을 한다.

[13행] This will <u>help</u> <u>them</u> <u>win</u> the trust and respect of their
동사 목적어 목적격 보어
employees [**while** increasing the level of staff involvement], which benefits the company as a whole.

→ 준사역동사 help의 목적어로 them, 목적격 보어로 동사원형 win이 쓰였다.

→ [while ~ involvement]는 접속사 while(~하면서)이 이끄는 시간의 부사절이다.

---

21 밑줄 의미 추론하기 정답 ⑤

해설 뇌는 사고 과정에서 사전 지식에 의존하거나 거짓 기억으로 우리를 속일 수 있다고 했다. 따라서 글의 주제를 비유적으로 표현한 they have a mind of their own(그것들이 그들만의 사고를 갖는다)이 의미하는 것은 ⑤ '뇌는 사람을 잘못된 방향으로 유도할 수 있다'이다.

오답분석 ①, ②은 글의 핵심 소재 brain을 사용하여 헷갈리게 하는 오답이다.

해석 뇌는 많은 중요한 일들을 담당하는 놀라울 정도로 복잡한 구조이다. 하지만, 그러한 중요한 기관임에도 불구하고, 그것들은 완벽하지 않다; 누구는 심지어 그것들이 그들만의 사고를 갖는다고 말할 수도 있다. 문제 해결에 관해서라면, 사람의 뇌는 해법에 이르기 위해서 지름길(휴리스틱이라고도 알려진)을 택하는 것을 선호한다. 그것은 비판적 사고를 건너뛰기 위해서 비슷한 과거의 상황을 생각나게 하거나 사전 지식에 의존할 것이고, 그 방식은 나태하다. 이는 한 사람이 다른 선택 사항들을 고려하거나 중요한 것을 충분히 오래 심사숙고하는 것을 막을 수 있다. 뇌는 또한 사람들이 이전에 실제로 한 적이 없는 경험들을 했다고 생각하게 할 수도 있다(거짓 기억). 만약 한 사람이 이야기를 듣거나 영상을 보면, 그 또는 그녀의 뇌는 그들이 듣거나 본 것을 경험했다고 생각하도록 그들을 속인다. 처리해야 할 정보가 너무 많기 때문에, 우리의 두뇌가 때때로 실수를 하는 것은 놀라운 일이 아닐 것이다.

① 뇌는 한 번에 너무 많은 일에 집중할 수 없다.
② 뇌의 여러 부분들은 서로 모순된다.
③ 인간은 결정을 하는 데 있어 어려움을 겪는다.
④ 대부분의 사람들은 매우 제한적인 주의 지속 시간을 갖고 있다.
⑤ 뇌는 사람을 잘못된 방향으로 유도할 수 있다.

어휘 an abundance of 많은, 풍부한 shortcut 지름길, 손쉬운 방법
heuristics 휴리스틱(논리적 근거가 아닌 어림짐작을 통해 답을 도출해내는 경향)
bypass 건너뛰다, 우회하다 contemplate 심사숙고하다, 고려하다
slip up 실수를 하다 [선택지] contradict 모순되다, 반박하다
mislead 잘못된 방향으로 유도하다 attention span 주의 지속 시간

구문분석 [4행] **When it comes to** problem-solving, the human brain prefers taking shortcuts ~

→ When it comes to는 '~에 관해서라면'이라는 의미의 관용 표현이다.

[16행] With so much information to process, it shouldn't be a surprise [that our minds slip up sometimes]. 가주어
진주어(that절)

→ 가주어 it이 길이가 긴 진주어 that절 [that ~ sometimes] 대신 주어 자리에 쓰인 형태이다.

---

22 요지 파악하기 정답 ④

해설 글의 마지막 두 문장에서 번역이 번역가의 언어적 능통함과 작품에 대한 이해를 필요로 하고, 비유적 표현 및 작가가 선택한 단어는 문자 그대로 정확히 번역될 수 없기 때문에 번역본에서 원작의 의미가 사라질 수 있다는 요지가 제시되어 있으므로, 이 글의 요지로 가장 적절한 것은 ④이다.

오답분석 ①은 글에서 언급된 '비유적 표현'을 사용하여 헷갈리게 하는 오답이다. ②은 이 글에서는 '언어 장벽'이 아니라 정확한 번역이 불가능해서 잘못 이해될 수 있다고 말하고 있으므로 오답이다. ③은 글에서 언급된 '고전 문학'을 사용하여 헷갈리게 하는 오답이다. ⑤은 글의 핵심 소재 '번역'을 사용하여 헷갈리게 하는 오답이다.

해석 많은 사람들이 <오디세이>와 같은 고전 문학의 번역본을 읽는다. 번역본이 편해 보일 수도 있는 반면, 모든 번역이 신뢰할 만하지는 않기 때문에 원작의 작가가 말하고자 했던 것을 우리가 완전히 이해한다고 항상 확신할 수 없다. 중요한 것은, 번역가들이 번역에 수반된 언어를 둘 다에 동등하게 능통해야 하고, 작품 자체에 대한 충분한 이해가 있어야 한다는 것이다. 비유적 표현의 사용으로 인해 정확한 번역이 불가능할 수 있고, 비유적 표현은 문자 그대로 번역될 수 없다. 게다가, 작가들이 그들 작품에 사용하는 단어들은 보통 매우 신중하게 선택된다. 예를 들어, 시인들은 운이 맞는 단어들을 선택할 수도 있고, 그 단어들은 다른 언어로 모방되기가 불가능할 수도 있다. <u>따라서 원작의 의미가 사라질 수 있다.</u> 영국 문화 번역 센터의 센터장은 "제가 번역하는 어떤 언어들에서도, 영어에 있는 단어로 완벽하게 나타낼 수 있는 말은 하나도 없습니다. 따라서 그것은 항상 해석에 의한 것이고, 대략적이고, 창조적입니다."라고 주장하며 그 사안에 대해 언급했다.

어휘 translation 번역본, 번역 fully 완전히 reliable 신뢰할 만한
the thing is 중요한 것은 ~이다, 실은 proficient 능통한, 능숙한
figurative 비유적인, 상징하는 literally 문자 그대로 rhyme 운이 맞다
duplicate 모방하다, 복제하다 map 나타내다, 지도를 만들다
interpretative 해석에 의한, 설명적인

구문분석 [3행] ~ we can't always be sure that we fully understand what the original writers <u>were trying</u> **to say** because not all translations are reliable.

→ 동사 were trying의 목적어로 to부정사가 쓰여 '~하려고 노력하다'의 의미를 갖는 구문이다. try의 목적어로 동명사가 쓰일 경우 '시험 삼아 ~해보다'라는 완전히 다른 의미로 쓰인다.

[8행] Exact translations can be impossible due to the use of **figurative language**, [which can't be translated literally].

→ [which ~ literally]는 선행사 figurative language를 수식하는 주격 관계대명사절로, 콤마 뒤에서 계속적 용법으로 쓰였다.

23   주제 파악하기   정답 ⑤

(해설) 습지대가 폭풍 해일 감소, 영양분 여과, 생태계 유지에 중요한 역할을 하며, 강 어귀의 삼각주를 형성하는 자연 발생적인 과정을 다시 만들어냄으로써 습지대의 소멸을 막을 수 있다는 내용의 글로, 루이지애나의 해안 종합 계획과 굴 껍데기의 사용을 예를 들어 설명하고 있다. 따라서 이 글의 주제로 가장 적절한 것은 ⑤ '습지대들의 중요성과 그것들의 소멸을 막기 위한 해결책들'이다.

(오답분석) ②은 글의 핵심 어구 Coastal Master Plan을 사용하여 헷갈리게 하는 오답이다. ③은 글의 일부만을 다루고 있는 오답이다. ④은 글에 언급된 flood, Louisiana를 사용하여 헷갈리게 하는 오답이다.

(해석) 1927년의 파괴적인 홍수 이후에, 의회는 미시시피 강과 지류 프로젝트를 승인했고, 이는 2만 마일의 제방과 방수로의 건설로 이어졌다. 이는 미시시피 강의 정교한 물줄기들의 균형을 무너뜨렸고, 주변의 습지대들이 가라앉기 시작했다. 지금까지, 1,800제곱마일의 루이지애나 습지대가 사라졌다. 이 재앙은 엄청난 피해를 가져왔다. 사라지는 습지들은 폭풍 해일 감소와 영양분 여과에 있어서 중요한 역할을 할 뿐만 아니라, 중요한 생태계이다. 실제로, 미국에서 멸종 위기에 직면하거나 절멸할지도 모를 종들의 거의 절반이 습지대에 의존한다. 한 가지 가능성 있는 해답은 루이지애나의 해안 종합 계획이다. 그것은 그 주의 삼각주를 형성하는 자연 발생적인 과정을 다시 만들어내는 것을 목표로 하고, 그 자연 발생적인 과정은 현존하는 습지대를 보호하고 사라졌던 지역들을 복원할 것이다. 대중들이 도울 수 있는 쉬운 방법도 있다: 굴을 먹는 것이다. 굴 껍데기는 암초를 재건하는 데에 사용될 수 있다. 루이지애나 식당들에서의 재활용 프로그램 덕분에, 약 5천 톤의 껍데기들이 이미 이를 위해 사용되어 왔다.

① 없어서는 안 될 동물 서식지들을 복원할 때 직면하는 어려움들
② 루이지애나의 해안 종합 계획의 성공의 이유들
③ 홍수로 이어지는 폭풍에 대한 습지대의 경감 효과
④ 루이지애나에서의 홍수의 위험과 예방 조치들의 필요성
⑤ 습지대들의 중요성과 그것들의 소멸을 막기 위한 해결책들

(어휘) floodway 방수로, 분수로 watercourse 물줄기, 수로 wetland 습지대
subside 가라앉다, 진정되다 take a toll 피해를 가져오다 swamp 습지
storm surge 폭풍 해일 filtration 여과 threatened 멸종 위기에 직면한
endangered 절멸할지도 모를 delta (강어귀의) 삼각주
oyster 굴, 식용 조개 [선택지] mitigate 경감시키다, 완화하다
threat 위험, 위협

(구문분석)
[8행] The vanishing swamps **not only** ①[play a vital role in storm surge reduction and nutrient filtration] **but also** ②[are a critical ecosystem].
→ ①[play ~ filtration]과 ②[are ~ ecosystem]은 상관접속사 not only A but also B로 연결된 병렬 구조이다.

24   제목 파악하기   정답 ③

(해설) 첫 두 문장과 마지막 두 문장으로 미루어 보아 인플레이션이 부정적인 암시를 지니는 경향과는 달리 실제로는 소비를 촉진시킴으로써 경제를 활성화하고 최대 고용을 유지하는 방법이 될 수 있다는 내용의 글로, 경제학자 John Maynard Keynes의 주장을 예를 들어 설명하고 있다. 따라서 글의 제목으로 가장 적절한 것은 ③ '경제 성장 수단으로서의 인플레이션'이다.

(오답분석) ①, ②은 글의 일부만을 다루고 있는 오답이다. ④은 인플레이션의 긍정적인 효과에 관한 글의 내용과 반대되는 내용이기 때문에 오답이다. ⑤은 글의 일부만을 다루고 있는 오답이다.

(해석) 인플레이션은 흔히 줄어든 구매력 및 화폐 저축과 연결되어 생각되기 때문에 부정적인 암시를 지니는 경향이 있다. 하지만, 몇몇 경제학자들은 정상적인 인플레이션은 실제로 국민에게 유리하게 작용할 수도 있다고 주장한다. 가장 두드러지게는, 저명한 경제학자 John Maynard Keynes(존 메이너드 케인스)가 적당한 인플레이션이 절약의 모순에 대응하는 데에 결정적임을 주장했는데, 절약의 모순이란 저축이 실제로는 경제 성장에 해로울 수 있음을 말한다. 만약 사람들이 돈을 쓰지 않고 있다면, 전체적인 수요가 더 적기 때문에 경제는 더 나빠진다. 인플레이션은 또한 담보 대출자와 학자금 대출이 있는 사람들과 같은 채무자들에게 재정적 부양책을 제공할 수도 있다. 대출금의 가치는 인플레이션으로 줄어들고, 이는 결국 소비를 촉진시킨다. 물가 안정 목표제, 즉 정해진 인플레이션율을 유지하기 위해 조정하는 것은 경제를 활성화하고 최대 고용을 유지하려는 목적에서 전 세계의 중앙은행에 의해 이용된다. 만약 사람들이 미래에 물가가 오를 것임을 안다면, 그것은 그들이 지금 물건과 서비스들을 구매하도록 유도한다.

① 지금 소비하고, 나중에 절약하라!
② 경제 정책들이 대출에 어떻게 영향을 미치는가?
③ 경제 성장 수단으로서의 인플레이션
④ 인플레이션: 상승하는 물가의 해로운 영향
⑤ 인플레이션과 실업률 간의 관계

(어휘) inflation 인플레이션, 물가 상승률 connotation 암시, 함축(된 의미)
monetary 화폐의, 통화의 healthy 정상적인, 건강한 favor 유리, 이익
distinguished 저명한, 뛰어난 counteract 대응하다, 반대로 작용하다
thrift 절약, 검소 suffer 더 나빠지다, 피해를 입다
student loan 학자금 대출 boost 부양책
inflation targeting 물가 안정 목표제 stimulate 활성화하다, 자극하다

(구문분석)
[9행] ①[If people are not spending their money], ②[the economy suffers] ③[because there is less overall demand].
→ ②[the economy suffers]가 전체 문장의 주절이고, ①[If ~ money]와 ③[because ~ demand]는 각각 조건을 나타내는 접속사 if(만약 ~한다면), 이유를 나타내는 접속사 because(~ 때문에)가 이끄는 부사절이다.

25   도표 정보 파악하기   정답 ⑤

(해설) 2050년에 전체 세계 인구 중 아시아의 비율은 54.2퍼센트로, 전체 세계 인구의 절반인 50퍼센트보다 많으므로 수치의 비교 표현이 잘못 반영되었다. 따라서 도표의 내용과 일치하지 않는 것은 ⑤이다.

(해석)

2017년과 2050년의 지역별 세계 인구

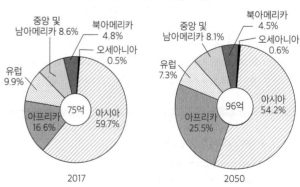

위의 두 원그래프는 2017년과 2050년의 지역별 세계 인구 분포를 보여준다. ① 전체 세계 인구는 2017년에서 2050년 사이에 20억 이상이 증가할 것으로 예상된다. ② 6개의 지역 중에서, 2017년과 2050년 사이에 전체 세계 인구 중

비율에서 증가를 보일 것으로 예상되는 유일한 두 지역은 아프리카와 오세아니아이다. ③ 유럽이 2017년에 전체 세계 인구 중 비율에서 3위를 차지했지만, 2050년에는 7.3퍼센트로 4위를 차지할 것으로 예상된다. ④ 2050년에, 전체 세계 인구 중 유럽과 북아메리카의 비율의 합이 아프리카의 비율의 절반보다 적을 것으로 예상된다. ⑤ 전체 세계 인구 중 아시아의 비율은 2017년과 비교하여 2050년에 5.5퍼센트가 감소할 것으로 예상되고, 이는 그 비율이 전체 세계 인구의 절반보다 적게 만든다.

(어휘) **distribution** 분포, 분배 **region** 지역 **percentage** 비율, 백분율 **rank** (순위를) 차지하다

(구문분석)

[7행] [While Europe ranked third in percentage of total world population in 2017], it is predicted to rank fourth in 2050 with 7.3%.

→ [While ~ 2017]은 접속사 while(~하지만)이 이끄는 양보의 부사절이다.

[11행] ~ population of Europe and Northern America is expected to be [less than] half of Africa's.

→ [less than]는 '비교급 + than'(~보다 ~한)의 형태로 비교를 나타내는 구문이다.

26 세부 정보 파악하기   정답 ④

(해설) his most notable work was the short novel *L'Étranger(The Stranger)*를 통해 Albert Camus의 가장 유명한 작품은 단편 소설이라는 것을 알 수 있는데, ④은 수필이라고 일부 정보를 잘못 나타냈으므로 글의 내용과 일치하지 않는 것은 ④이다.

(해석) 알제리로 이주한 프랑스인 가정에서 1913년 11월에 태어난 Albert Camus(알베르 카뮈)는 20세기의 가장 유명한 작가들 중의 한 명이자 노벨상 수상자가 되었다. 그의 결핵 진단과 일생 동안 앓았던 것뿐만 아니라, 어린 시절 빈곤의 경험이 그의 업적에 크게 영향을 주었다. 그는 삶의 의미가 존재하지 않기 때문에 삶의 의미를 찾으려고 노력하는 것은 무의미하다고 제시하는 철학인 부조리주의를 발전시킨 것으로 가장 유명하다. 그는 세계, 그리고 더 구체적으로는 인간 행동이 얼마나 합리성을 결여하는지를 보이기 위해, 등장인물들을 중대한 상황에 처하게 만들었다. 비록 그의 가장 유명한 작품은 단편 소설인 <이방인>이었지만, 그는 이 사상에 초점을 둔 많은 희곡, 수필, 단편 소설을 출판했다. 그는 자동차 충돌로 1960년 1월에 생을 마감했고, 그때 그는 46세였다.

(어휘) **diagnosis** 진단 **illness** 아픔, 병 **pointless** 무의미한 **rationality** 합리성 **revolve around** ~에 초점을 두다 **collision** 충돌

(구문분석)

[1행] [**Born** in November of 1913 to a French family that had relocated to Algeria], Albert Camus would become ~

→ [Born ~ Algeria]는 과거분사(Born)로 시작하는 수동형 분사구문이다.

[14행] His life ended in an automobile collision in January **1960**, [when he was 46].

→ [when ~ 46]는 선행사 1960를 수식하며, 시간을 나타내는 관계부사 when이 이끄는 관계부사절이다.

27 안내문 정보 파악하기   정답 ④

(해설) Third place will receive $2,500 (no trophy)를 통해 3등은 트로피 없이 2,500달러만 받을 것을 알 수 있으므로, 글의 내용과 일치하지 않는 것은 ④이다.

(해석)

Travel Life 사진 콘테스트

Travel Life Magazine이 사진 콘테스트를 개최합니다. 아마추어와 전문가들이 자유롭게 참가할 수 있습니다.

규정
- 참가자당 사진 3장
- 마감일은 5월 1일임.
- 모든 사진은 JPG 형식이어야 하고 photocontest@travellife.org로 이메일로 보내야 함.
  * 디지털 편집은 허용되지 않음.

상
- 1등은 10,000달러와 6월호에서의 특집 기사를 받을 것임.
- 2등은 7,000달러와 트로피를 받을 것임.
- 3등은 2,500달러를 받을 것임 (트로피는 없음).

알림
- 시상식은 5월 20일 금요일에 열릴 것입니다. 대중에게 개방됩니다.

더 많은 정보를 위해서는 저희 웹사이트를 방문하십시오.

(어휘) **entry** 참가자, 참가 **first place** 1등 **feature** 특집 기사, 특징

(구문분석)

[17행] The award ceremony [will be held] on Friday, May 20.

→ [will be held]는 조동사(will)가 있는 '조동사 + be + p.p.' 형태의 수동태이다.

28 안내문 정보 파악하기   정답 ⑤

(해설) Other Events의 Special lectures from celebrity guests를 통해 영화 상영 외에 유명 초대 손님의 특별 강연이 있다는 것을 알 수 있으므로, 글의 내용과 일치하는 것은 ⑤이다.

(해석)

Colin Springs 영화 축제

최신의 그리고 가장 훌륭한 영화적 재능을 경험하기 위해 앞줄 좌석을 원하시나요? 그렇다면 독점적인 첫 관람을 위해 제9회 연례 Colin Springs 영화 축제에 들르셔야 합니다.

언제 & 어디서
- 4월 3일-7일 오전 10시에서 오후 8시
- Colin Springs 영화의 전당

티켓
- 전체 기간 동안 모든 곳에 들어갈 수 있는 입장권은 150달러
- 일일권은 50달러

영화
- 모든 장르의 70편 이상의 영화들
- 20개 이상의 여러 국가들의 영화들
- 어린이들을 위한 프로그램들

다른 행사들
- 영화 감독 및 배우들과의 공개 토론회
- 유명 초대 손님의 특별 강연

축제에 대해 더 알아보시려면 www.colinspringsfilm.com을 방문해주십시오.

(어휘) **annual** 연례의　**panel discussion** 공개 토론회　**director** 감독, 책임자

(구문분석) [20행] Please visit www.colinspringsfilm.com [to learn more about the festival].

→ [to ~ festival]은 to부정사의 부사적 용법으로, 목적을 의미한다.

---

29 어법상 틀린 것 찾기 정답 ③

(해설) 뒤에 주어 they, 동사 contain, 목적어 the instructions for reproduction이 모두 있는 완전한 절이 왔으므로 ③의 전치사 despite을 부사절 접속사 although 또는 though로 고쳐야 한다.

(오답분석) ①은 단수 취급하는 동명사 imagining이 주어이므로 단수동사 is를 사용하여 어법상 적절하다. ②은 선행사 DNA or RNA를 수식하는 형용사절을 이끄는 관계대명사 that을 사용하여 어법상 적절하다. ④은 동명사 replicating이 나타내는 행위의 주체와 대상이 모두 The cell이고, 주체와 대상이 같은 것을 가리킬 때에는 목적어 자리에 재귀대명사가 와야 하므로 itself를 사용하여 어법상 적절하다. ⑤은 분사구문의 주어가 따로 없으므로 주절의 주어 Each new virus가 분사구문의 의미상 주어이고, Each new virus가 '반복하는' 행위의 주체이므로 현재분사 repeating을 사용하여 어법상 적절하다.

(해석) 유기적 생물의 가장 작은 구성 요소인 인간 세포들의 단순성을 볼 때, 훨씬 덜 복잡한 존재인 바이러스들이 그것들을 장악할 수 있다고 상상하는 것은 쉽지 않다. 하지만 그것들은 할 수 있고, 그렇게 한다. 가장 단순한 바이러스에는 단 두 가지 요소가 있다: 더 많은 바이러스를 만들기 위한 청사진인 DNA 혹은 RNA, 그리고 보호를 위한 단백질 막이다. 하지만, 그것들에 복제를 위한 명령이 내재되어 있더라도, 스스로 그렇게 할 수 있기 위한 고유의 화학 작용 물질인 효소가 없다. 그것들은 조금이라도 무언가를 할 수 있으려면 숙주가 필요하다. 그것들은 먼저 세포에 침투하고, 안으로 들어가면 그것들의 유전자 청사진을 넣는다. 그 세포는 차이를 인식하지 못하고 알아차리지 못한 채 그것 자체를 복제하는 대신에 더 많은 바이러스를 만들어내기 시작한다. 각각의 새로운 바이러스는 감염 주기를 반복하면서, 그 후에 다른 세포를 감염시킬 수 있다.

(어휘) **simplicity** 단순성　**building block** 구성 요소　**entity** 존재, 실체
overtake 장악하다, 추월하다　**blueprint** 청사진　**proper** 고유의, 알맞은
enzyme 효소　**host** 숙주, 진행자　**infiltrate** 침투하다, 스며들다
unknowingly 알아채지 못하고, 모르고　**replicate** 복제하다
infection 감염　**cycle** 주기

(구문분석) [1행] When looking at the simplicity of human cells, [the smallest building blocks of organic life], imagining that ~

→ [the ~ life]는 'the + 최상급 + of'('-에서 가장 ~한)의 형태로 최상급을 나타내는 구문이다.

[11행] They first infiltrate a cell, and then, [once (they are) inside], add their genetic blueprint.

→ [once inside]는 주절과 부사절의 주어가 같을 때 부사절에서 '주어 + be동사'가 생략된 형태이다.

---

30 어휘 적절성 파악하기 정답 ④

(해설) 포퓰리스트 지도자가 권력을 얻으면 현재 상태에 대한 공포감을 형성해서, 지도자의 해결책들이 실제로는 가장 이익이 되지 않을 때에도 대중들이 그 지도자를 지지하게 한다는 맥락이 되어야 하므로, ④의 withdraw(철회하다)를 그와 반대되는 의미의 offer(제시하다) 또는 give(주다)와 같은 어휘로 바꾸어 offer their support(지지하다)가 되어야 문맥상 적절하다.

(오답분석) ②은 포퓰리즘으로 전향하는 것은 사회 구성원들이 서로에게 등을 돌리게 하고 편협을 조장할 수 있어 사회 질서에 해가 된다는 문맥이 되어야 하므로 destructive가 오는 것이 적절하다.

(해석) 포퓰리즘은 한쪽에는 모든 것을 지배하는 부패한 정부의 최상위층 사람들과, 다른 쪽에는 기대치가 충족되지 않고 있는 선량하고 평범한 사람들로 세계가 ① 나누어져 있다고 보는 정치적 접근법을 가리킨다. 주류의 정치 조직이 때때로 대중의 기대치를 충족시키지 못하는 것이 사실이더라도, 대안으로써 포퓰리즘으로 전향하는 것은 사회 질서에 ② 해가 될 수 있다. 포퓰리스트 지도자가 권력을 얻으면, 그들은 보통 문제들이 ③ 시급해졌고 현재 상태를 유지하는 것은 대중에게 문제를 악화시키기만 할 것이라는 암시를 준다. 이는 공포감을 형성하고, 소위 이민이나 자유 무역과 같은 문제들에 대한 지도자의 해결책들이 실제로는 모든 대중에게 가장 이익이 되지 않을 때에도 대중이 그 지도자에 대한 지지를 ④ 철회하도록(→하도록) 한다. 그것은 "대중"이 흔히 소수 집단들과 인구 중에서 소외된 다른 이들을 ⑤ 배제하기 때문이고, 이는 포퓰리즘이 같은 사회의 구성원들이 서로에게 등을 돌리도록 하면서 편협을 조장하고 전반적으로 추가적인 문제들을 일으킬 수 있다는 것을 의미한다.

(어휘) **populism** 포퓰리즘(대중의 견해와 바람을 대변한다고 주장하는 정치적 형태)
corrupt 부패한, 부정한　**government** 정부, 정치 조직
destructive 해가 되는, 파괴적인　**rise to power** 권력을 얻다
immigration 이민　**marginalize** 사회에서 소외되다
intolerance 편협, 참을 수 없음

(구문분석) [1행] Populism refers to a political approach that views the world as divided, with corrupt government elites on one end controlling everything and **good, ordinary people** [whose expectations **are** not **being met**] on the other.

→ [whose ~ met]은 선행사 good, ordinary people을 수식하며, 소유격 관계대명사 whose가 이끄는 관계대명사절이다.

→ are being met은 'be + being + p.p.' 형태의 진행형 수동태이다.

---

31 빈칸 추론하기 정답 ③

(해설) 족제비들이 인간처럼 미래의 결과를 인지할 수 있다는 내용의 글이고, 빈칸 앞의 두 문장에서 족제비들은 익지 않은 바나나가 미래에는 익을 것임을 인지하고 있었기 때문에 익지 않은 바나나를 그대로 두었다가 익었을 때 다시 가서 먹는다고 하였다. 따라서 주제와 관련된 빈칸에는 ③ '있음 직한'이 와서 족제비들이 있음 직한 결과를 추론하고 그에 따라서 행동할 수 있다는 의미가 되어야 한다.

(오답분석) ①, ②, ④, ⑤은 익지 않은 바나나가 미래에는 익는다는 있을 법한 결과를 설명하는 단어로 적절하지 않다.

(해석) 인간은 미래를 상상할 수 있고, 충분히 흥미롭게도, 일부 동물들도 할 수 있는 것처럼 보인다. 한 연구에서, 족제비의 한 종이 익은 바나나는 바로 먹지만 그리고 나서 익지 않은 다른 것들은 익도록 하면서 나무에 비축해두는 것이 관찰되었다. 그리고 그들은 나중에 다시 와서 남겨두었던 그 과일을 먹었다. 이는 족제비들이 가까운 미래에 그 바나나가 먹기 충분하게 익을 것이라는 점을

어느 정도 인지하고 있었다는 것을 보여준다. 즉, 그들은 있음 직한 결과를 추론하고 그에 따라서 행동할 수 있었다. 미래를 대비하는 이러한 능력은 다양한 동물 종들에서 발견되어 왔다. 이는 그들이 머릿속에서의 시간 이동이 가능할 뿐만 아니라 그들은 또한 생존을 위해 취할 행동의 최선의 방향을 판단하기에 충분한 이성과 논리를 지닌다는 것을 증명한다.

① 직접적인　　　　　　② 즉각적인
③ 있음 직한　　　　　　④ 부정적인
⑤ 자발적인

(어휘) **envision** 상상하다, 계획하다　**ripe** 익은, 숙성한
deduce 추론하다, 추정하다　**outcome** 결과　**accordingly** 그에 따라서
reasoning 이성, 논리

(구문분석) [1행] Humans are able to envision the future, and interestingly enough, it seems as though some animals **can** too.

→ can 뒤에는 envision the future가 생략되어 있는데, Humans ~ future에서 이미 언급되었기 때문에 생략되었다.

[3행] In one study, a species of weasel [was observed **eating** ripe bananas immediately] but then storing ~

→ 지각동사 observe를 사용한 [was ~ immediately]는 'observe + 목적어 + 목적격 보어' 형태의 능동태를 'be observed + 목적격 보어' 형태의 수동태로 바꾼 것이다. 지각동사의 목적격 보어가 현재분사(eating)일 때에는 동작이 진행되고 있음을 강조한다.

32　빈칸 추론하기　　　　정답 ⑤

(해설) 주제문에 해당하는 빈칸 문장에서 이 기제, 즉 자가포식이 '무엇'을 통해서 세포를 재생시키는 방법이라고 하고, 글의 중반에서 제대로 기능을 하지 않는 세포들을 효과적으로 겨냥하여 그것들의 제거를 확실히 한다고 했다. 따라서 빈칸에는 ⑤ '손상된 세포 성분의 제거'가 와서 자가포식이 손상된 세포 성분의 제거를 통해 신체가 새롭고 건강한 세포를 재생시키는 방법이라는 의미가 되어야 한다.

(오답분석) ①의 건강한 장기의 보존은 글의 내용과 관련이 없다. ②은 글에 언급된 proteins를 사용하여 헷갈리게 하는 오답이다. ③의 의료 시술의 적용은 글의 내용과 관련이 없다. ④은 글에서 제대로 기능을 하지 않는 세포는 제거한다고 했으므로 이와 반대되는 내용이어서 오답이다.

(해석) 인간의 신체에서 가장 주목할 만한 측면들 중 하나는 스스로를 조절하고 최상의 기능을 유지하는 능력이다. 이를 성취하기 위해, 신체는 자가포식이라는 자기 소화 체계를 포함하는 다양한 자연적 과정들을 이용한다. 이 기제는 손상된 세포 성분의 제거를 통해서 신체가 새롭고 건강한 세포를 재생시키는 방법이다. 인간의 세포들이 스트레스를 받으면, 신체의 정상적인 작용을 확실히 하고 그것을 항상성 내에서 유지하기 위해서 자가포식이 증가한다. 그것은 흔히 손상되고 유독한 단백질의 분해를 통해서, 제대로 기능을 하지 않는 세포들을 효과적으로 겨냥하여 그것들의 제거를 확실히 한다. 다시 사용되는 세포의 성분들은 세포 내의 유동체인 세포질과 세포 기관들이고, 이것들은 특정 기능이 있는 조직들이다. 이것들은 아미노산으로 분해되는데, 신체는 이것들을 에너지와 세포 복원을 위해 이용한다. 이러한 방식으로, 자가포식은 파킨슨병이나 알츠하이머병과 같은 수많은 건강상 질환들을 예방하는 데에 도움이 되고, 감염 질환들에 대항하는 데에도 도움이 될 수 있다.

① 건강한 장기의 보존
② 섭취 가능한 특정 단백질의 섭취
③ 의료 시술의 적용
④ 제대로 기능을 하지 않는 세포의 회복
⑤ 손상된 세포 성분의 제거

(어휘) **optimal** 최상의　**mechanism** 기제, 방법　**target** 겨냥하다, 목표로 삼다
dysfunctional 제대로 기능을 하지 않는, 고장 난　**degradation** 분해, 악화
cytoplasm 세포질　**organelle** 세포 기관　**amino acid** 아미노산
[선택지] **ingestion** 섭취　**restoration** 회복, 복구

(구문분석) [1행] One of the most remarkable aspects of the human body is its ability ①[to regulate itself] **and** ②[(to) maintain optimal functioning].

→ to부정사구 ①[to regulate itself]와 ②[maintain optimal functioning]은 등위접속사 and로 연결된 병렬 구조로 두 번째 to는 생략되었다.

33　빈칸 추론하기　　　　정답 ⑤

(해설) 주제문에 해당하는 빈칸 문장에서 공유재는 대부분의 대중이 이용 가능하다고 하고, 글의 중반에서 시간이 지남에 따라 재화가 부당하게 이용될 수 있어서 의존할 수 없는 비축량으로 이어진다고 했다. 따라서 빈칸에는 ⑤ '남용에 취약한 한정된 저장물이 있다'가 와서 공유재는 남용에 취약한 한정된 저장물이 있더라도 대부분의 대중이 이용 가능한 재화라는 의미가 되어야 한다.

(오답분석) ②은 글에서 언급된 public을 사용하여 헷갈리게 하는 오답이다. ③은 자원의 이익을 부당하게 이용하면 의존할 수 없는 비축량으로 줄어든다는 글의 내용과 반대되는 내용이므로 오답이다. ④은 글에서 언급된 overconsumption을 사용하여 헷갈리게 하는 오답이다.

(해석) 공유재는 남용에 취약한 한정된 저장물이 있더라도, 대부분의 대중에게 이용 가능한 재화이다. 예를 들어, 많은 숲이 있더라도 만약 모든 사람이 이 숲에서 가능한 한 많은 나무를 가져가려고 한다면, 그것들의 감소는 불가피할 것이다. 시간이 지남에 따라 이와 같은 재화는 부당하게 이용될 수 있고, 개인들이 남에게 손해를 끼치면서 그 자원을 소비함에 따라 의존할 수 없는 비축량으로 이어진다. 부족은 사회나 공동체의 다른 구성원들뿐만 아니라 그 비축량을 찾아내서 그것을 소비할 수 있는 바로 그 사람들에게도 영향을 끼친다. 이것이 바로 "공유지의 비극"이라고 알려진 것이다. 그러한 재화의 과잉 소비 혹은 고갈을 막는 것은 정부 규제와 한때 공유재였던 자원을 사유재로 만드는 것을 포함한 많은 조치들을 통해 이루어진다. 개인들이 자원을 보존하기 위해 함께 노력하기 때문에 집단적 행동 또한 자원의 소비를 통제하는 효과적인 방법이다.

① 그것들에 대한 많은 수요가 없다
② 대중이 그것들을 이용하기가 어렵다
③ 자원은 쉽게 보충될 수 있다
④ 기업들이 재화의 과잉 소비를 통제한다
⑤ 남용에 취약한 한정된 저장물이 있다

(어휘) **common-pool resources** 공유재　**good** 재화, 상품
inevitable 불가피한　**exploit** 부당하게 이용하다, 착취하다
supply 비축량, 공급량　**detriment** 손해, 손상　**shortage** 부족
tragedy of the commons 공유지의 비극　**overconsumption** 소비 과잉
depletion 고갈, 소모　**private good** 사유재
[선택지] **renew** 보충하다, 갱신하다　**stock** 저장물, 비축
abuse 남용; 남용하다

(구문분석) [3행] For example, although there are plentiful forests, if every person [**were to collect** as much wood as possible from these forests], their decline would be inevitable.

→ [were ~ forests]는 주어를 서술하는 'be + to부정사' 구문으로, 의도의 의미를 나타낸다.

[12행] [Preventing the overconsumption or depletion of such goods] is accomplished through ~

→ [Preventing ~ goods]는 문장의 주어 역할을 하는 동명사구이다.

---

34 빈칸 추론하기 정답 ①

(해설) 주제문에 해당하는 빈칸 문장에서 현대 사회에서는 탐욕 자체는 사회에서 비난받는 반면, 탐욕과 유사한 개인의 행동은 부추겨지고, 이어서 탐욕이 개인을 이롭게 하지만 제한되지 않을 경우 문명사회가 대가를 치르게 될 수 있다고 했다. 따라서 빈칸에는 ① '탐욕은 다소 역설적이다'가 들어가야 한다.

(오답분석) ②은 글에서 언급된 impulses를 사용하여 헷갈리게 하는 오답이다. ③은 글에서 현대 사회에서도 탐욕은 여전히 억제되어야 한다고 했지만, 제어하기 어려워졌다는 내용은 언급되지 않았다. ④은 글에서 언급된 urges를 사용하여 헷갈리게 하는 오답이다. ⑤의 materialism은 글의 내용과 관련이 없다.

(해석) 탐욕은 인간 본성에 내재된 생물학적 기반의 행동이다. 욕구는 모든 살아있는 생명체의 생존에 필수적이지만, 인간은 생물학적 관점에서뿐만 아니라 사회적 관점에서의 욕구도 경험한다. 이는 인간이 갖는 충동들을, 번식하려는 본능적 욕구와 같이 동물이 느끼는 것들로부터 구별 짓는다. 사람들은 단순히 살아 있는 것 이상을 원한다; 그들은 또한 물질적 소유물과 부를 원한다. 하지만 현대 사회에서, **탐욕은 다소 역설적인데, 탐욕 자체는 사회에서 비난받는 반면, 탐욕과 유사한 개인의 행동은 당연하고 부추겨지며, 사람들이 할 수 있는 한 부와 번영을 추구하도록 권장되기 때문이다.** 이는 탐욕이 실제로 개인을 이롭게 하지만, 제한되지 않을 경우 문명사회가 대가를 치르게 될 수 있기 때문이다. 사회학자들은 사회가 억제되지 않은 탐욕을 악이라 부름으로써 여전히 제한하는 것과 동시에 탐욕을 가진 개인들에게 동기를 부여하는 균형 상태를 찾는 것을 목표로 한다고 주장한다.

① 탐욕은 다소 역설적이다
② 사람들은 그들의 충동을 자제할 수 있다
③ 욕구는 제어하기 어려워졌다
④ 동물적 욕구는 거의 사라졌다
⑤ 물질주의는 더 이상 주요한 사안이 아니다

(어휘) greed 탐욕, 욕심 intrinsic 내재하는, 고유한 urge 욕구, 충동
standpoint 관점, 견해 drive 본능적 욕구, 충동
natural 당연한, 자연 발생적인 to the best of ~하는 한
condemn 비난하다 equilibrium 균형 (상태)
label ~이라고 부르다, 꼬리표를 달다 vice 악, 악덕
[선택지] paradox 역설적인 것 all but 거의, 사실상

(구문분석)
[5행] This differentiates the impulses humans have from those felt by animals, such as the **drive** [to reproduce].

→ [to reproduce]는 to부정사의 형용사적 용법으로, 명사 drive를 수식한다.

[15행] Sociologists **assert** [that society aims to find an equilibrium of motivating individuals with greed while still limiting unrestrained greed by labeling it as a vice].

→ [that ~ vice]는 접속사 that이 이끄는 명사절로, 동사 assert의 목적어 역할을 한다.

---

35 흐름과 관계 없는 문장 찾기 정답 ③

(해설) 클라우드 컴퓨팅에 의해 기업에서의 데이터 저장 및 관리 방식이 변화한 모습을 설명하는 내용의 글이다. 그런데 ③은 원격 접속 기술을 활용할 때의 주의 사항에 대한 내용이므로 핵심 소재는 같지만 주제에서 벗어나 있어 글의 흐름과 무관하다.

(해석) 클라우드 컴퓨팅은 이미 전 세계에서 많은 기업이 운영되는 방식을 변화시켰고, 곧 사람들의 생활 방식을 구체화할 것이다. 가장 큰 변화 중 하나는 **직장에서의 증가된 유연성**이다. ① 이제 기업들이 클라우드에 모든 파일을 저장, 처리, 관리할 수 있는 능력을 갖게 되었기 때문에 직원들은 인터넷에 접속할 수만 있다면 원격으로 데이터에 접근할 수 있게 되었다. ② 그들은 더 이상 특정 정보를 얻기 위해 **물리적으로 사무실을 방문할 필요가 없고** 만나는 시간을 따로 마련하지 않고 가상으로 다른 사람들과 협업할 수 있다. (③ 기업은 원격접속 기술을 활용할 때 외부 데이터 공유에 주의해야 한다.) ④ 클라우드 저장소는 또한 사람들이 콘텐츠를 사용하거나 공유하기 위해 그만큼 **많은 기기에 의존할 필요가 없다**는 것을 의미한다. ⑤ USB 드라이브를 사용하는 과정을 거쳐야만 하는 것보다는 클라우드에 파일을 저장하고, 링크를 생성하고 다른 사람이 볼 수 있도록 초대하기만 하면 된다.

(어휘) flexibility 유연성 remotely 원격으로 virtually 가상으로
set aside 따로 마련하다 external 외부의 storage 저장소

(구문분석)
[1행] Cloud computing has already **transformed** [how many business operate around the world], and it will soon shape people's lifestyles.

→ [how ~ world]는 의문사 how가 이끄는 명사절로, 동사 transformed의 목적어 역할을 한다. many business가 명사절의 주어, operate가 동사이다.

[5행] Now that companies have the power to store, process, and manage all of their files on the cloud, employees are able to access data remotely [**as long as** they can connect to the Internet].

→ [as ~ Internet]은 접속사 as long as(~하는 한)가 이끄는 조건의 부사절이다.

---

36 글의 순서 배열하기 정답 ②

(해설) 주어진 글은 Carl Jung의 많은 개념들 중에서 치료사들에게 가장 유용한 것은 진단에 대한 그의 접근법이라는 주제를 제시한다. (B)는 "complex"에 대한 Carl Jung의 개념은 임상의들이 환자들의 상충되는 문제들이 얽혀 있는지를 확인하고 환자들의 행동을 이해하게 한다는 내용이고, 주어진 글 마지막에서 치료사들에게 가장 유용한 Carl Jung의 개념은 진단에 대한 그의 접근법이라고 했으므로 그 뒤에 와야 한다. (A)의 the complex는 (B)의 "complex"를 가리키므로 (B) 바로 다음에 오는 것이 적절하다. (C)의 these terms는 (B)의 "complex"와 (A)의 "hidden mass of memories"를 가리키므로 (A) 다음에 오는 것이 적절하다. 따라서 글의 순서로 가장 적절한 것은 ② (B) - (A) - (C)이다.

(해석) 스위스 심리학자 Carl Jung(카를 융)은 그 분야에서 가장 오래 지속되는 많은 개념들에 대한 공로를 인정받는다. 하지만 현장에서 활동하는 치료사들에게 이것들 중에서 가장 유용한 것은 **진단에 대한 그의 접근법**이다.

(B) "콤플렉스"에 대한 Jung의 개념은 임상의들이 심리적 현상들을 별개의 장애로 분류하고 환자들을 일률적인 치료법으로 실어 나르기보다, 그들의

상충되는 문제들이 어떻게 얽혀 있는지를 확인하게 한다. 이러한 접근은 콤플렉스에 따라 행동하는 특정 환자들의 행동을 이해하는 데에 매우 유용하다.

(A) Jung에게, 콤플렉스란 무의식 속에서 작용하는 서로 관련된 관념들의 집합이다. 이 "숨겨진 기억의 집합"은 우리의 어린 시절에 형성되고 긍정적이고 부정적인 방식 모두를 통해 우리의 현재나 미래에 강력한 영향력을 행사한다.

(C) 이러한 용어들로 문제를 이야기하는 것은 치료사들이 이런 종류의 기제가 전체론적 의미에서 어떻게 작용하는지를 논하게 한다. 게다가, 그것은 비현실적으로 빠른 완화를 환자들에게 주어야 한다는 압박감을 완화시킨다.

 credit 공로를 인정해주다 **enduring** 오래 지속되는, 영구적인
practicing (현재) 활동하고 있는 **wield** (힘을) 행사하다, 휘두르다
phenomena(phenomenon의 복수형) 현상, 경이로운 것
discrete 별개의, 분리된 **disorder** 장애, 이상 **shuttle** 실어 나르다, 오가다
one-size-fits-all 일률적인, 두루 적용되도록 만든 **clinician** 임상의
intertwine 얽히게 하다 **holistic** 전체론적인, 전체론의

구문분석

[10행] **Rather than** ①[classifying psychological phenomena as discrete disorders] and ②[shuttling patients into one-size-fits-all treatments], Jung's concept of the "complex" <u>allows</u> (동사) <u>clinicians</u> (목적어) to <u>identify</u> (목적격 보어(to부정사)) how their conflicting problems are intertwined.

→ ①[classifying ~ disorders]와 ②[shuttling ~ treatments]는 전치사 rather than의 목적어 역할을 하는 동명사구이다.

→ 동사 allow의 목적어로 clinicians, 목적격 보어로 to부정사 to identify가 쓰였다.

---

37 글의 순서 배열하기 정답 ③

해설 주어진 글은 대중문화의 중심이 이동하면서 돈이 이동하고 창작자 경제가 확립되었다는 주제를 제시한다. (B)의 this new ecosystem은 주어진 글의 '창작자 경제'를 가리키므로 주어진 글 바로 다음에 오는 것이 적절하다. (C)의 they는 (B)의 "Internet celebrities"를 가리키므로 (B) 바로 다음에 오는 것이 적절하다. (A)의 This는 (C) 마지막에서 인터넷 플랫폼이 급속하게 부상하고 소셜 미디어 거물들의 탄생 장소가 되었다고 언급한 것을 가리키고, 이것이 권력의 역학 관계의 변화로 이어져서 이제는 플랫폼이 인플루언서들에게 적절한 보상을 해야 한다고 부연 설명하고 있으므로 (A)는 (C) 뒤에 와야 한다. 따라서 글의 순서로 가장 적절한 것은 ③ (B) − (C) − (A)이다.

해석 대중문화가 유명인 중심에서 인플루언서 중심으로 이동함에 따라, 돈도 이에 따라 이동해왔다. 이는 창작자 경제의 확립으로 이어졌다.

(B) 소셜 미디어 스타들에 의해 추진력을 얻는 이 새로운 생태계는 빠른 성장을 하고 있다; 2021년에만, 창작자 경제는 13억 달러 이상의 자금을 끌어모았다. 하지만, 그것이 언제나 그렇게 수익성이 높은 분야는 아니었고, "인터넷 유명인들"은 전통 상업계의 오랜 수호자들에 의해 한때 업신여겨졌다.

(C) 그들이 거의 아무것도 달성하지 않았고 대중의 인식 속으로 완전히 그들의 길을 내지 못했음을 고려하면, 아주 놀라운 일이 아니다. 그 후에 갑자기, 인터넷 플랫폼이 급속한 부상을 시작하고 엄청난 추종자들을 끌어모으는 소셜 미디어 거물들의 탄생 장소가 되었다.

(A) 이는 권력의 역학 관계의 변화로 이어졌다. 플랫폼들은 이제 수백만의 이용자들을 유인하는 그들의 인플루언서들에게 보상할 수 있어야 한다. 그렇다고 하더라도 점점 더 많은 창작자들이 그들만의 방식으로 부를 축적하고 있기 때문에 그것으로 충분하지 않을지도 모른다.

---

 popular culture 대중문화 **creator economy** 창작자 경제
dynamics 역학 관계 **compensate** 보상하다
accumulate 축적하다, 모으다 **profitable** 수익성이 있는
marketplace 상업계, 시장 **penetrate** ~의 내부로 들어가다, 스며들다
meteoric 급속한, 유성의 **birthplace** 발생지, 출생지
amass 끌어모으다, 축적하다 **following** 추종자, 팬

구문분석

[13행] But it **wasn't always** such a profitable field, ~

→ not always는 '언제나 ~인 것은 아니다, 반드시 ~하는 것은 아니다'라는 의미로 부분 부정을 나타내는 구문이다.

[16행] Not much of a surprise, **considering** they barely made anything ~

→ considering은 '~을 고려하면'이라는 의미의 분사구문 관용 표현이다.

---

38 주어진 문장의 위치 찾기 정답 ⑤

해설 주어진 문장의 However, unlike science(하지만 과학과는 달리)로 보아, 주어진 문장 앞에는 과학과 철학의 유사한 점에 대한 내용이 나와야 한다는 것을 알 수 있다. 이 글에서는 ②~④ 뒤 문장까지 철학과 과학의 연관성 및 유사점에 대해 설명하고 있고, 주어진 문장의 philosophy asks why는 ⑤ 뒤 문장에서 This로 이어지고 있으므로 주어진 문장이 들어가기에 가장 적절한 곳은 ⑤이다.

오답분석 ③, ④ 뒤 문장은 ② 뒤 문장에 이어서 철학이 어떻게 과학과 연관되고 유사한지에 대해 언급하고 있다.

해석 만약 과학과 기술이 현재 궤도대로 계속된다면, 최종 결과는 종으로서 '호모 사피엔스'의, 혹은 적어도 우리가 알고 있는 문명사회의 종말일 수밖에 없다. 어느 시점에는, 인공 지능이 완성될 것이고, 이는 훨씬 더 많은 지능을 만들어 내는 등 인간성을 무의미하게 만들 것이다. (①) 따라서, 절제의 지혜를 가지고 발견에 대한 우리의 욕구를 누그러뜨리는 것은 우리의 존재를 위함이다. (②) 이와 관련하여, 철학은 과학적 탐구의 억제되지 않은 위험들에 대한 우리의 최고의 방어 수단이다. (③) 철학은 종종 대립되는 세력으로 생각되지만, 사실상 과학과 밀접하게 연관되고 위기들을 막기에 충분히 강력하다. (④) 철학은 논리와 철저한 논증의 이상을 과학과 공유한다. (⑤ 하지만, 오로지 방법만을 묻는 과학과는 달리, 철학은 이유를 묻는다.) 이는 과학에는 없지만 매우 필요한 고려 사항이다.

 end result 최종 결과 **spawn** 만들다, (알을) 낳다
irrelevant 무의미한, 무관한 **in the interest of** ~을 (도모하기) 위하여
temper 누그러뜨리다, 완화하다 **untamed** 억제되지 않은
robust 강력한, 튼튼한 **ward off** 막다, 피하다 **ideal** 이상
rigorous 철저한, 엄격한 **argumentation** 논증, 논의 **sorely** 매우, 심하게

구문분석

[8행] Therefore, <u>it</u> (가주어) is in the interest of our existence [<u>to temper our need for discovery with the wisdom of restraint</u>]. (진주어(to부정사구))

→ 가주어 it이 길이가 긴 진주어 to부정사구 [to ~ restraint] 대신 주어 자리에 쓰인 형태이다.

[13행] ~ philosophy is actually closely associated with science and [robust enough to ward off crises].

→ [robust ~ crises]는 '형용사 + enough + to부정사'의 형태로, '~하기에 충분히 ~한'이라는 의미의 to부정사 표현이다.

---

39 주어진 문장의 위치 찾기　정답 ③

(해설) 주어진 문장에 명시적 단서가 없는 경우에는 글의 흐름이 끊기는 곳을 찾아야 한다. ③ 앞까지는 심적 시연이 다양한 분야에서 유용하며 여러 이점들을 지닌다는 내용이 이어지다가 ③ 뒤 문장에서 자신이 경주에서 결승선을 지나가거나 성공적으로 맺어진 거래에 대해 고객과 악수를 하고 있는 것을 마음속으로 그려볼 수 있을 것이라는 내용이 나오고 있다. ③과 ④ 뒤 내용에서 주어진 문장의 senses(감각들)에 대한 부연 설명으로 visualize(마음속에 그리다)와 sense of hearing(청각)을 예로 들고 있고, ③ 앞뒤의 내용이 유기적으로 연결되지 않는다는 점을 통해 글의 흐름이 끊겼음을 알 수 있다. 따라서 주어진 문장이 들어가기에 가장 적절한 곳은 ③이다.

(오답 분석) ④ 뒤 문장의 Then은 ③ 뒤 문장의 마음속으로 그려보는 것 다음을 의미하며, ④ 뒤 문장은 ③ 뒤 문장과 마찬가지로 주어진 문장의 senses(감각들)의 예시로 sense of hearing(청각)을 들고 있으므로 주어진 문장은 이것보다 앞에 와야 한다. ⑤ 뒤 문장에서는 outcomes such as these를 통해 바로 앞 문장들에서 언급된 성공적으로 맺어진 거래, 동료의 축하의 말들을 지칭하고 있으므로 주어진 문장은 이것보다 앞에 와야 한다.

(해석) 심적 시연은 현실 세계에서 행동을 수행하기 전에 당신의 머릿속에서 그것을 연습하는 기술을 말한다. (①) 그것은 운동선수들에게서 흔하지만, 다른 다양한 분야와 시도들에서도 유용하다. (②) 그것의 이점은 잘 알려져 있고 향상된 자신감과 집중력, 감소된 불안감, 잠재적인 문제들의 해결책을 마음속에 그려보는 능력을 포함한다. (③ 최고의 결과를 얻기 위해, 당신이 할 수 있는 한 많은 감각들을 관여시키는 것이 도움이 된다.) 당신은 당신 자신이 경주에서 결승선을 지나가거나 성공적으로 맺어진 거래에 대해 고객과 악수를 하고 있는 것을 마음속으로 그려볼 수 있을 것이다. (④) 그리고, 당신의 청각을 이용해, 당신은 기운을 돋우는 군중의 환호성이나 당신 동료의 축하의 말을 상상해볼 수 있다. (⑤) 이와 같은 긍정적인 결과를 그려보는 것은 당신이 당신의 준비성에 대해 가질 수 있는 어떠한 걱정이라도 사라지게 하고 다가오는 일에 대해 통제력을 갖도록 도울 수 있다.

(어휘) mental rehearsal 심적 시연　endeavor 시도, 노력
envision 마음속에 그리다, 상상하다　sense of hearing 청각
roar 환호성, 고함　melt away 사라지다

(구문 분석) [1행] To get the best results, it helps to engage [as many of your senses as you can].
→ [as ~ can]은 'as + many + of + 명사 + as can'(가능한 한 많은~)의 형태로 동등 비교를 나타내는 구문이다. senses가 가산명사이므로 형용사 many가 원급으로 쓰인 형태이다.

40 요약문 완성하기　정답 ①

(해설) 글의 전반부에서 연구 참가자는 혼자 정답을 고르기보다는 틀린 다수에게 동조한다고 했고, 글의 후반부에서는 의견을 같이 하는 사람이 있다면 다수를 따르는 일이 거의 없다고 했다. 따라서 지문의 go along with를 conform으로, almost never followed를 resist로 바꾸어 표현한 ①이 정답이다.

(오답 분석) 한 명이라도 의견을 같이 하는 사람이 있다면 다수를 따르는 일이 거의 없다고 했으므로 ②의 achieve와 ③의 allow는 (B)에 들어갈 단어로 적절하지 않다.

(해석) 1950년대에 Solomon Asch(솔로몬 애쉬)는 참가자들이 그들에게 다른 것과 길이가 가장 비슷한 선을 식별하기를 요구하는 시각적 지각 테스트를 수행한 한 실험에서 동료 집단 압력의 힘을 증명했다. 실제 실험에 앞선 독립된 테스트에서는 99%의 경우 참가자들에게 정답이 명백했으므로, 이것은 간단한 과제였다. 실제 실험 중에, 한 명의 연구 참가자는 몇 명의 배우들과 함께 한 방에 배치되었다. 사전에 배우들은 질문에 틀린 답을 하라는 말을 들었고, 이것이 실제 연구 참가자들에게 미친 영향은 비웃음을 당할까 봐 두려워서 그 무리의 나머지에 동조하는 것이라는 점이 발견되었다. 실제로, 정답이 그들에게 명백함에도 불구하고, 많은 참가자들이 다수와 의견을 같이 했고 이 실험의 12회의 결정적인 시행에서 틀린 답을 내놓았다. 그러나 한 명이 아닌 두 명의 참가자가 같은 연구에 포함되고 둘 다 정답이 무엇인지 알고 있을 때, 그들이 다수를 따르는 일은 거의 없었다.

↓

위 실험은 사람들이 무리에 (A) 따르기 위해 틀린 줄 아는 일을 할 수도 있지만, 다른 누군가가 그들과 의견을 공유할 때는 이 행동에 (B) 저항할 가능성이 더 많다는 것을 시사한다.

	(A)		(B)
①	따르다	……	저항하다
②	따르다	……	달성하다
③	어울리다	……	허락하다
④	다투다	……	저항하다
⑤	다투다	……	받아들이다

(어휘) peer pressure 동료 집단 압력　perception 지각　prior to ~에 앞서
ridicule 비웃다　[선택지] conform 따르다, 순응하다　match 어울리다

(구문 분석) [11행] ~ and it was found that the effect this had on the actual study participant was [to go along with the rest of the group out of fear of being ridiculed].
동사　주격 보어
→ [to ~ ridiculed]는 to부정사의 명사적 용법으로 be동사 was의 주격 보어 역할을 한다.

41~42 장문 독해 1

(해석) 음절을 이루거나 어표를 사용했던 글자의 가장 초기 유형은 마야인과 중국인으로부터 생겨났다. 이러한 체계에서, 각 단어나 문장은 독립적인 상징이었고, 단독으로 쓰일 수 있었다. 따라서 띄어쓰기, 마침표, 쉼표, 그리고 누군가가 글을 이해하는 것을 돕는 그러한 다른 도구들이 필요하지 않았다. 하지만, [4]알파벳 글자가 생겨나기 시작하면서, 구두점의 (a)부재는 실질적인 문제가 되었다. 과장하지 않고 말하자면 글을 읽는 것이 어려워졌고, 몇 가지 형태의 체계가 필요했다.

비잔티움의 그리스 학자인 [41]Aristophanes(아리스토파네스)가 두루마리를 읽을 때 더 적은 (b)시간이 걸리게 하기 위해 특정 부호의 사용을 도입한 기원전 3세기 말쯤이 되어서야 이에 대한 해결책이 생겨났다. 그는 구절이 끝나는 곳을 나타내고 소리 내어 읽을 때에 필요한 (c)휴지의 길이를 보여주기 위해 점을 넣을 것을 제안했는데, 엘리트 계층만이 글을 읽는 방법을 알았기 때문에 소리 내어 읽는 것이 흔히 평민들에게 글이 전달되는 방법이었다. 일부, 특히 로마의 많은 유명 연설가들은 그것의 시행을 (d)칭찬했지만(→무시했지만/거부했지만), [42]그 부호는 표준화될 때까지 서서히 점점 더 사수 문서들에 등장하기 시작했다. 특히 기독교도들이 핵심 교리를 기록하는 것을 강조했기 때문에 구두법을 확립하는 데에 중요한 역할을 했다. 따라서 [4]기독교가 유럽 전역에 퍼지기 시작하면서, 구두법의 포함이 더 (e)번성했고, 결과적으로 오늘날에 우리가 그것을 사용하는 방식으로 발전했다.

(어휘) syllabic 음절을 이루는, 음절의　logographic 어표(생략 부호)를 사용하는
self-contained 독립적인, 자급자족의　on one's own 단독으로, 혼자서
absence 부재, 없음　punctuation 구두점, 구두법

scroll 두루마리(책), 족자 passage 구절, 통과
pause 휴지(멈추는 것), 중단 commoner 평민, 서민
[선택지] interpretation 해석 outdated 시대에 뒤진

구문
분석

[11행] The remedy for this [did **not** appear **until** around the end of the 3rd century BC] when Greek scholar ~

→ [did ~ BC]는 부정을 나타내는 not A until B(B가 되어서야 A하다) 구문으로, not A until B는 it is not until B that A로 바꿔 쓸 수 있다.

[15행] He suggested inserting dots to **indicate** ①[where a passage ended] and to show the length of pause needed when <u>reading aloud</u>, ②[which was how text was often conveyed to commoners] since only the elite knew how to read.

→ ①[where ~ ended]는 의문사 where가 이끄는 명사절로, 동사 indicate의 목적어 역할을 한다.

→ ②[which ~ commoners]는 관계대명사 which가 계속적 용법으로 쓰인 구문으로, 앞의 reading aloud에 대해 추가적인 설명을 하는 역할을 한다.

41　제목 파악하기　　　정답 ③

해설　초기 글자에는 띄어쓰기, 마침표, 쉼표 등의 구두법이 없었지만, 알파벳 글자가 생겨나기 시작하면서 구두법이 필요해졌고 기독교의 전파에 힘입어 오늘날의 방식으로 발전되었다는 것이 글의 주된 내용이다. 따라서 글의 제목으로 가장 적절한 것은 ③ '읽기의 필수 보조로서의 구두법의 발전'이다.

오답
분석　①은 글에서 구두법이 더 번성했다고는 했지만, 유럽을 넘어 전 세계적으로 확산되었다는 내용은 없으므로 오답이다. ⑤은 구두법이 현재도 사용된다는 글의 주제와 반대되는 내용이므로 오답이다.

해설　① 전 세계적인 구두법의 확산
② 초기 글자 체계의 현대적 매력
③ 읽기의 필수 보조로서의 구두법의 발전
④ 고대의 문자가 역사 해석에 어떻게 영향을 미쳤는가?
⑤ 구두법: 문자 체계에서 시대에 뒤진 방식

42　어휘 적절성 파악하기　　　정답 ④

해설　일부는 구두법의 시행을 반대했지만 구두법이 점점 더 자주 문서들에 등장하기 시작했다는 맥락이 되어야 하므로 ④의 praised(칭찬하다)를 그와 반대되는 의미의 dismissed(무시했다) 또는 rejected(거부했다)와 같은 어휘로 바꾸어야 문맥상 적절하다.

43~45　장문 독해 2

해석　(A) 먼 옛날에, 현명한 사제가 근처의 마을을 향해 가고 있었다. 그 사제는 왕에 의해 그를 만나러 오라고 부름을 받았다. (a)그가 마을로 가는 길을 따라 걷고 있을 때, 땅바닥에서 금화 하나를 발견했다. 그 사제는 검소한 삶을 살고 있었고 그가 부유하지는 않더라도 그가 가진 모든 것에 행복했다. 그래서, 그는 그 동전을 그보다 더 그것을 필요로 하는 누군가에게 주기로 하고 계속 길을 갔다.

(D) 사제는 마침내 마을 광장에 도착했다. 그는 많은 사람들이 바쁘게 그날 하

루를 준비하고 있는 것을 보았다. [45]상인들은 그들의 가게에서 즐겁게 외치고 있었고, 손님들은 길에서 서로에게 인사했다. 아이들은 웃으며 주위를 뛰어다녔다. '얼마나 좋은 곳인가'라고 사제는 생각했다. 그는 걸어 다니며 많은 사람들과 이야기를 나눴지만, 누구도 금화를 필요로 하지 않았다. 갑자기, (e)그는 큰 경적 소리를 들었다.

(C) 광장으로 행군하는 왕과 그의 군대였다. 그들은 이웃 나라로 갈 준비를 하고 있었다. 왕은 사제를 발견했다. "나는 내 왕국을 넓히기 위해 다른 나라를 침략할 것이기 때문에 (c)당신을 여기로 불렀소"라고 그가 말했다. "현명한 사제여, 내가 승리할 수 있도록 내 노고를 축복해 주시오!" 사제는 생각에 잠겨 [44]왕을 보고 나서, (d)그에게 금화를 주었다.

(B) "이것의 의미가 무엇이오?"라고 왕이 물었다. "나는 여기서 가장 부유한 사람이오. 내가 이 동전을 무엇에 필요로 하겠소?" 사제는 "저는 가난한 누군가에게 그것을 기부하려 했지만, (b)제가 귀하의 왕국을 거닐어보니 아무도 없었습니다. 모두가 그들이 가진 것에 만족하며 풍요롭고 행복한 삶을 살고 있습니다. 오로지 귀하께서만 더 많이 얻고자 하는 욕망을 가지고 계시고 귀하께서 가지신 것에 만족하지 않으십니다. 귀하께서는 제가 본 그 누구보다도 더 이 동전을 필요로 하십니다"라고 대답했다.

어휘　summon 부르다, 소환하다 stroll 거닐다, 산책하다 content 만족하는 invade 침략하다, 침입하다 endeavor 노고, 애씀

구문
분석

[23행] "①[Please bless my endeavors], wise priest, ②[so that I may be victorious]!"

→ ①[Please ~ endeavors]가 전체 문장의 주절이고, ②[so ~ victorious]는 so that(~하도록)이 이끄는 목적의 부사절이다. so that은 in order that으로 바꿔 쓸 수 있다.

43　글의 순서 배열하기　　　정답 ⑤

해설　(A)는 현명한 사제가 근처 마을로 가는 길에 금화를 발견했고 계속 길을 갔다는 내용이다. (D)는 사제가 마을 광장에 도착해서 마을 사람들과 이야기를 하다가 경적 소리를 들었다는 내용이므로, 마을을 향해 계속 길을 갔다고 한 (A) 뒤에 와야 한다. (C)는 왕과 그의 군대가 광장으로 행군하고 있었다고 했으므로, 사제가 마을 광장에서 경적 소리를 들었다고 한 (D) 뒤에 와야 한다. (B)의 "What is the meaning of this?"의 this는 (C)의 the gold coin을 가리키므로 (C) 다음에 와야 한다. 따라서 글의 순서로 가장 적절한 것은 ⑤ (D) - (C) - (B)이다.

44　지칭 대상 파악하기　　　정답 ④

해설　(a), (b), (c), (e)는 모두 사제를 가리키지만 (d)는 왕을 가리키므로, ④이 정답이다.

45　세부 정보 파악하기　　　정답 ⑤

해설　(D)의 Merchants shouted happily from their stores and customers greeted each other on the street. Children laughed and ran around를 통해 상인들이 가게에서 즐겁게 외치고 있었고 아이들은 웃으며 주위를 뛰어다녔다는 것을 파악할 수 있는데, ⑤은 상인들이 아이들에게 화가 나 있었다고 일부 정보를 잘못 나타냈으므로 글의 내용과 일치하지 않는 것은 ⑤이다.

05회 실전모의고사

정답

18	⑤	19	③	20	⑤	21	④	22	⑤	23	①	24	④	25	⑤	26	④	27	⑤
28	④	29	①	30	②	31	③	32	③	33	⑤	34	③	35	④	36	③	37	②
38	③	39	④	40	③	41	②	42	③	43	③	44	④	45	④				

18 목적 파악하기 정답 ⑤

해설 글의 중간 이후에서 여름 과학 캠프의 참가 지원서를 제출할 때 선생님의 추천서도 함께 보내도 되는지를 문의하고 있으므로, 정답은 ⑤이다.

해석 프로그램 진행자님께,

여름이 다가오기 때문에, 저는 여름 과학 캠프에 참가하는 것에 대한 저의 관심과 관련하여 귀하께 이 이메일을 씁니다. 저는 등록하기 위해 필요한 모든 요건들을 제가 충족하는지를 확실히 하고 싶기 때문에, 귀하께서 제게 한 가지 사항을 명확히 해주시면 감사하겠습니다. 제가 본 공고에는 지원서 제출 시에 자기소개서, 성적 증명서, 그리고 에세이만 요구된다고 나와 있었습니다. 하지만, 제 선생님의 추천서도 보내도 되는지 궁금합니다. 그것은 제가 어떤 학생인지에 대한 유익한 통찰을 포함하고 있어 추가 서류로서 도움이 될 것처럼 느껴집니다. 저는 이것이 가능한 일이기를 바라며, 귀하의 시간을 내주셔서 감사합니다.

Grace Evans 드림

어휘 coordinator 진행자, 조정자 clarify 명확히 하다, 분명히 말하다
cover letter 자기소개서 transcript 성적 증명서 forward 보내다
letter of recommendation 추천서 supplementary 추가의, 보충하는

구문분석
[2행] [**As** summer approaches], I am writing this email about my interest in participating in the summer science camp.
→ [As summer approaches]는 as(~ 때문에)가 이끄는 이유의 부사절이다.

[7행] **The advertisement** [(that/which) I saw] said that only a cover letter, a transcript, and an essay were needed for application submission.
→ [I saw]는 선행사 The advertisement를 수식하는 관계대명사절로, 목적격 관계대명사 that/which가 생략되었다.

19 심경 파악하기 정답 ③

해설 심경은 간접적으로 표현된다. 글의 초반부의 I was worn out, just wanted to lie down을 통해 'I'가 지쳐서 집에 가서 혼자 쉬고 싶어 하는 것을 알 수 있고, 후반부의 forgot my fatigue, looked forward to the fun night ahead를 통해 친구들이 집에 준비해 놓은 깜짝 생일 파티를 보고 피로를 금방 잊고 즐거운 저녁을 기대하며 신이 났다는 것을 알 수 있다. 따라서 'I'의 심경 변화로 가장 적절한 것은 ③이다.

해석 나는 어서 퇴근해서 집에 가고 싶었다. 금요일이었고, 나는 직장에서의 힘든 한 주로 인해 매우 지쳐있었다. 보통 나는 약속이 있지만, 그날 저녁은 그냥 내 침대에 눕고 싶었다. TV를 보면서 잠에 드는 것이 혼자 보내는 이상적인 저녁 시간처럼 들렸다. 나는 문을 열고 놀랐다. 모든 나의 친구들이 내 집에서 형형색색의 풍선에 둘러싸여 있었다. 그들은 내가 안으로 들어오자 "생일 축하해!"라고 외쳤다. 식탁 위에 피자 박스들과 큰 케이크가 있었다. 그들은 축하하기 위해 밤새도록 활동들을 계획해두었다. 나는 피로를 금방 잊고 다가오는 즐거운 저녁을 기대했다.

① 외로운 → 무서워하는
② 질투하는 → 기쁜
③ 지친 → 신이 난
④ 겁에 질린 → 자신 있는
⑤ 걱정스러운 → 힘을 얻은

어휘 impatient 어서 ~하고 싶어 하는 worn out 매우 지친
gasp (숨이 막힐 정도로) 놀라다 fatigue 피로 [선택지] jealous 질투하는
thrilled 신이 난

구문분석
[4행] **Falling asleep** [**while** I was watching television] sounded like the ideal night alone.
→ Falling asleep은 문장의 주어 역할을 하는 동명사구이다.
→ [while ~ television]은 부사절 접속사 while(~하면서)이 이끄는 시간 부사절이다.

20 주장 파악하기 정답 ⑤

해설 상처받지 않기 위해서 약한 모습을 보이지 않으려고 마음을 닫고 혼자 지내면 다른 사람들과의 진정한 관계를 형성하지 못한다고 주장하고 있으므로 정답은 ⑤이다.

해석 많은 사람들에게, 약한 모습을 보이는 것은 위험이 따르기 때문에 무섭다. 당신의 두려움에 대해서 마음을 열고 다른 사람들과 당신의 비밀을 공유함으로써 당신은 평가받거나 혹은 더 심하게는 거부당할 가능성이 항상 있다. 이는 매우 고통스럽고, 상처받는 것으로부터 자신을 보호하기 위해서 당신은 더 이상 스스로를 약해 보이게 하지 않으려 할 것이다. 표면적으로 당신은 다른 사람들로부터의 비난의 가능성을 피하는 것이 당신의 고통을 없애줄 것이라고 생각하기 때문에 마음을 닫고 혼자 지내는 것이 좋은 것이라고 생각할지도 모른다. 실제로는 이러한 접근은 그저 당신이 다른 사람들과의 진정한 관계를 형성하는 것을 막을 뿐이다. 저명한 전문가 Brené Brown(브레네 브라운) 박사에 따르면, "취약성은 의미 있는 인간 경험의 중심이자 핵심이다." 그것 없이는, 당신은 다른 사람들로부터 공감을 얻을 가능성이 적고, 고립감과 외로움에 이르게 된다.

어휘 vulnerable 약한 데가 있는, 상처받기 쉬운 reject 거부하다
keep to oneself 혼자 지내다 genuine 진정한 vulnerability 취약성
empathy 공감 isolation 고립

05회 실전모의고사 43

[구문분석] **[6행]** On the surface, you might think shutting down and keeping to yourself is a good thing [**because** you **feel** (that avoiding the possibility of criticism from others will eliminate your pain)].

→ [because ~ pain]은 접속사 because(~ 때문에)가 이끄는 이유의 부사절이며, 동사 feel의 목적어 역할을 하는 that절 (that ~ pain)을 포함하고 있다.

21 밑줄 의미 추론하기 정답 ④

[해설] ESG 기준이 생기기 전에 투자자들은 금전적 수익만을 보고 기업에 투자했지만, 이후에 환경적, 사회적 문제들이 더 중요해짐에 따라 ESG 기준은 투자자들에게 판단의 기준을 만들어주었다고 설명하고 있다. 따라서 글의 주제를 비유적으로 표현한 blazed a new trail(새로운 길을 냈다)이 의미하는 것은 ④ '기업이 어떻게 성공하게 되는지를 재정립했다'이다.

[오답분석] ①은 ESG 기준이 대두됨에 따라 기업이 투자받기 위해서는 이윤뿐만 아니라 윤리적 문제들까지 고려해야 하게 되었다는 글의 내용과 반대되는 내용을 다루고 있으므로 오답이다. ②은 글에서 전문적으로 관리되는 자산의 3분의 1이 ESG 기준을 적용한다고는 했지만, 관리 방법에 대해 의문을 가졌다는 내용은 언급되지 않았다. ⑤은 투자할 기업을 평가하는 기준이 생겼다고 하는 글의 내용과 관련이 없으므로 오답이다.

[해석] 환경, 사회, 지배구조(ESG)의 기준이 생기기 전에, 기업에 투자하는 주요 기준은 금전적 수익이었다. 기업이 얼마나 지속 가능한지 혹은 사업을 어떻게 했는지와 상관없이 기업을 통해 이윤이 추구되었다. 하지만, 시간이 지나면서 특히 밀레니얼 세대와 Z세대 구성원들에게 환경적 그리고 사회적 문제들이 더 중요해짐에 따라, 책임감 있게 돈을 투자하는 것도 중요해졌다. ESG 기준은 윤리적 관행을 따르는 기업들에 자금을 제공하길 원하는 투자자들에게 판단의 기준을 만들어준다. 그들은 기업이 얼마나 생태 친화적인지, 그들의 직원들과 고객들에게 어떤 영향을 주는지, 그리고 그 회사의 장기적인 전략들이 성취되고 있는지와 같은 요인들을 고려한다. 전문적으로 관리되는 모든 자산의 3분의 1이 이러한 기준의 적용을 받는 것과 더불어 ESG 기준의 영향력은 깊어졌다. 그것들은 새로운 길을 냈고, 기업들뿐만 아니라 사람들이 주목하고 있다.

① 투자받는 것을 더 쉽게 만들었다
② 투자가 어떻게 관리되는지 의문을 가졌다
③ 정책들을 집행하는 새로운 방식을 고안했다
④ 기업이 어떻게 성공하게 되는지를 재정립했다
⑤ 기업에 부과된 제약들을 바꾸었다

[어휘] **governance** 지배구조 **criteria**(criterion의 복수형) 기준, 표준 **return** 수익 **sustainable** 지속 가능한 **a point of reference** 판단의 기준 **ethical** 윤리적인 **practice** 관행 **ecologically friendly** 생태 친화적인 **profound** 깊은, 심오한 **asset** 자산 **blaze** 길을 내다 [선택지] **enforce** 집행하다, 강행하다 **redefine** 재정립하다 **impose** 부과하다

[구문분석] **[3행]** Profits were sought through companies [**no matter how** sustainable they were or how they did business].

→ [no ~ business]는 no matter how(얼마나 ~하는지 상관없이, ~하더라도)가 이끄는 양보의 부사절이다.

[구문분석] **[5행]** However, as environmental and social issues became more important over time, especially to Millennials and members of Generation Z, **so** <u>did</u> <u>investing money</u> responsibly.
동사 주어

→ so(~ 역시 그렇다)가 절 앞에 와서 동사(did)와 주어(investing money)가 도치된 구조로 쓰였다.

22 요지 파악하기 정답 ⑤

[해설] 글의 마지막 문장에서 마음이 모든 감각과 감정들을 자유롭게 경험하는 "마음 챙김"이라는 명상법을 통해 감정적인 반응들을 객관적으로 받아들여 걱정을 줄일 수 있다는 요지가 제시되어 있으므로, 이 글의 요지로 가장 적절한 것은 ⑤이다.

[오답분석] ②은 글의 핵심 소재인 "마음 챙김" 명상법이 아닌 흔한 형태의 명상에 대해 설명한 글의 일부에 대한 내용이므로 오답이다. ③은 "마음 챙김" 명상법은 모든 감각과 감정을 비판 없이 경험하게 하는 것이라고 설명한 글의 내용과 반대이므로 오답이다.

[해석] 명상에 대한 흔한 오해는 마음을 비우기 위해 하나의 생각이나 동작에 완전한 집중이 필요하다는 것인데 이는 매우 어려워 보이기 때문에 몇몇 사람들이 이 실천을 포기하게 만들었다. 그들이 모를 수도 있는 것은 "마음 챙김"이라고 불리는 명상의 형태가 있다는 것이다. 그러한 기법은 어떻게 작용하는가? 그것은 마음이 모든 감각과 감정들을 강렬하게 의식할 것을 요구한다; 이것들을 억압하거나 무시하려고 애쓰기보다, 우리는 우리 스스로가 그것들을 자유롭고 판단 없이 경험하게 해야 한다. 따라서, 명상하는 동안 개인적 문제 혹은 끝나지 않은 일에 대한 생각이 당신의 머릿속에 들어오는 것을 발견하면, 그저 그것을 인정하고 그것들이 당신이 어떻게 느끼게 만들었는지 주목해라. 이 접근법은 당신이 객관적인 태도로 당신의 감정적인 반응들을 처리하게 하는데, 이는 당신의 전반적인 걱정을 줄여줄 수 있다.

[어휘] **misconception** 오해 **meditation** 명상 **sensation** 감각 **suppress** 억압하다 **judgment** 판단, 비판 **objective** 객관적인

[구문분석] **[10행]** So, if you <u>find</u> <u>thoughts about personal problems or</u>
동사 목적어
<u>unfinished tasks</u> <u>entering your head</u> while meditating, simply
목적격 보어
acknowledge them and take note of how they make you feel.

→ 동사 find의 목적어로 명사구 thoughts ~ tasks가, 목적격 보어로 현재분사구 entering your head가 쓰여 진행의 의미를 강조하고 있다.

23 주제 파악하기 정답 ①

[해설] 아이러니의 정의는 단순해 보이지만 사실 아이러니는 쉽사리 분명하게 규정될 수 없다는 내용의 글로, 아이러니의 정의인 표면상으로 보이는 것과 실제의 차이가 너무나 미묘하고, 하나로 분류될 수 없는 특성들을 근거로 들어 설명하고 있다. 따라서 이 글의 주제로 가장 적절한 것은 ① '아이러니 이면에 있는 추론의 애매모호성'이다.

[오답분석] ②은 글에서 언급되고 있지 않다. ③, ④은 글의 일부만을 다루고 있는 오답이다. ⑤은 글에서 아이러니의 정의에 대해서는 설명하고 있지만, 시간에 따른 아이러니 정의 방식의 발전에 대해서는 언급되고 있지 않다.

[해석] 정의에 있어서, 아이러니는 다소 단순한 것을 갖는다: 어떤 것들이 표면상으로 어떻게 보이는지가 그것들이 실제로 무엇인지와 대립한다. 그것은 이해하

기 충분히 쉬운 개념처럼 보이지만, 그것은 너무나 포착하기 어렵고 미묘한 차이를 가져서 아이러니가 어떻게 이해되는지를 연구하는 데 전념하는 신경 과학자들과 심리학자들이 있다. 대부분의 사람들이 눈보라로 인해 눈싸움 축제가 취소되는 것의 아이러니를 알아차리는 것이 가능하지만, 아이러니가 쉽사리 분명하게 규정되지 못하는 이유는 모든 우연, 역설 또는 뜻밖의 이상함이 하나로 분류되지 못하기 때문이다. 더 나아가 아이러니는 다음 세 개의 범주: 상황적, 언어적 그리고 극적 아이러니 중 하나로 분류될 수 있기 때문에 상황은 더욱 불분명해진다. 심지어 더 복잡하게 만들도록, 언어적 아이러니와 그것의 형제뻘인 풍자는 많은 경우 구분이 되지 않는다.

① 아이러니 이면에 있는 추론의 애매모호성
② 아이러니가 어떤 상황의 원동력에 미치는 영향
③ 아이러니를 밝히는 일과 연관된 직업들
④ 다양한 종류의 아이러니들의 특성들
⑤ 시간에 따른 아이러니 정의 방식의 발전들

 어휘 irony 아이러니, 역설 oppose 대립하다, 반대하다
subtle 포착하기 어려운, 미묘한 nuance 미묘한 차이를 주다; 뉘앙스
blizzard 눈보라 pin down 분명하게 규정하다, 속박하다
coincidence 우연 oddity 이상함 categorize 분류하다 verbal 언어적
muddy the waters (이야기·상황 등을) 복잡하게 만들다
cousin 형제뻘인 것 sarcasm 풍자 [선택지] ambiguous 애매모호한
reasoning 추론 dynamics 원동력, 역학

구문분석 [4행] ~ grasp, yet it is [so subtle and nuanced that there are neuroscientists and psychologists dedicated to studying how irony is understood].
→ [so ~ understood]는 '너무 ~해서 -하다'라는 의미의 'so + 형용사 + that -' 구문으로, that절(that ~ understood)은 결과를 나타낸다.

[8행] ~ blizzard, yet the reason ①[(why) irony cannot be pinned down so easily] is because not every coincidence, paradox, or unexpected oddity can be categorized as one.
→ ①[irony ~ easily]는 선행사 the reason을 수식하는 관계부사절로, 선행사가 이유를 나타내는 일반적인 명사(reason)일 때 관계부사 why가 생략된 형태이다.
→ not every는 '모두 ~인 것은 아니다'라는 의미로 부분 부정을 나타내는 구문이다.

24 제목 파악하기 정답 ④

해설 어린 시절 학대를 당했던 사람들에게 식이 장애는 통제력을 줄 수도 있고, 음식은 주의를 돌리거나 위안을 주는 역할을 할 수도 있기 때문에 폭식과 같은 식이 장애를 겪게 될 수 있다는 내용의 글로, 한 연구 결과를 예를 들어 설명하고 있다. 따라서 글의 제목으로 가장 적절한 것은 ④ '아동기 트라우마: 식이 장애의 원인'이다.

오답분석 ①은 스트레스의 결과로 식습관에 문제가 생겼다는 글의 내용과 반대이므로 오답이다. ⑤은 글에서 음식이 위안이 될 수 있다고는 했지만, 건강한 식사에 대한 내용은 없으므로 오답이다.

해석 유니버시티 칼리지 런던의 연구에 따르면, 식이 장애는 대응 수단일 수도 있다. 어린 나이에 학대를 경험했던 사람들에게, 식이 장애는 그들이 아무것도 없다고 느낄 때 그들에게 어느 정도의 통제력을 제공해줄지도 모른다. 만약 어떤 사람이 자라면서 지속적으로 비난받았다면, 그 이후 그들 스스로를 가치 없다고 여기기 시작할 수 있다는 건 자연스러울 뿐이다. 피해자들은 그들이 충분히 훌륭하다는 것을 받아들이지 못하기 때문에, 이 사고방식은 장애를 생기게

할 수 있다. 또한 음식은 주의를 돌리거나 위안을 주는 역할을 할 수 있다. 그 연구에서, 스트레스를 받는 상황에 놓였던 몇몇 아이들은 전혀 먹지 못한 반면, 다른 아이들은 대처하기 위해 간식에 의존했다. 과거의 충격적인 사건들에 사로잡히는 것은 부정적인 감정을 쉽게 느끼는 사람이 되게 만들 수 있다. 그 결과, 그들은 고통스러운 기억들을 감당하기 위해 자주 폭식을 하면서 음식을 통해 위안을 찾는지도 모른다.

① 식습관이 어떻게 스트레스의 원인이 되는가
② 식이 장애에 대처하는 방법들
③ 아이들 사이의 식이 장애 증가
④ 아동기 트라우마: 식이 장애의 원인
⑤ 건강한 식사: 당신의 기분을 개선하는 해결책

 어휘 eating disorder 식이 장애 cope 대응하다, 대처하다
distraction 주의를 돌리는 것 comfort 위안을 주는 것
traumatic 충격적인 binge eating 폭식 distressing 고통스러운

구문분석 [5행] If a person is continuously criticized when growing up, it is only natural [that they might then begin to view themselves as unworthy].
가주어   진주어(that절)
→ 가주어 it이 길이가 긴 진주어 that절 [that ~ unworthy] 대신 주어 자리에 쓰인 형태이다.

[15행] As a result, they might seek relief through food, [frequently partaking in binge eating to deal with distressing memories].
→ [frequently ~ memories]는 '~하면서'라는 의미의 분사구문으로, 분사구문의 주어가 주절의 주어(they)와 같아서 생략되었다.

25 도표 정보 파악하기 정답 ⑤

해설 2015년에 기타 곡물류의 식품으로 소비된 비율과 사료로 소비된 비율의 차이는 34%이고 2025년에는 28%이므로 수치의 비교 표현이 잘못 반영되었다. 따라서 도표의 내용과 일치하지 않는 것은 ⑤이다.

해석

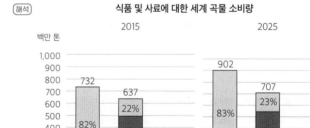

식품 및 사료에 대한 세계 곡물 소비량

위 그래프는 2015년과 2025년 식품과 사료에 대한 세계 곡물 소비량을 보여준다. ① 2015년에서 2025년 사이에 식품과 사료에 대한 옥수수 소비량을 합친 것은 1억 7천만 톤만큼 증가할 것으로 예상되고, 식품과 사료에 대한 밀 소비량을 합친 것은 7천만 톤만큼 증가할 것으로 예상된다. ② 2015년처럼, 2025년에 옥수수의 80퍼센트 이상이 사료에 사용될 것으로 예상되는 반면 밀은 80퍼센트 미만이 식품으로 소비될 것으로 예상된다. ③ 한편 식품으로 소비되는 옥수수의 비율은 2015년과 2025년 사이에 1퍼센트만큼 감소할 것으로 예상된다. ④ 2025년에, 사료로 사용된 옥수수와 밀 소비량의 비

율은 둘 다 각 1퍼센트씩 증가할 것으로 추정된다. ⑤ 두 해 모두, 식품으로 소비된 기타 곡물류의 비율과 사료로 소비된 그것(기타 곡물류)의 비율 간 차이는 30퍼센트보다 더 크다.

(어휘) grain 곡물 consumption 소비량 respectively 각각

(구문분석)
> [10행] In 2025, the percentage of **both** ① [corn] **and** ②[wheat consumption] of feed is projected to increase by 1%, respectively.
>
> → ①[corn]과 ②[wheat consumption]은 상관접속사 both A and B 로 연결된 병렬 구조이다.

26 세부 정보 파악하기 　　　　정답 ④

(해설) his final show was in New York later that year를 통해 Alfred Brendel은 마지막 공연을 뉴욕에서 했다는 것을 알 수 있는데, ④은 Vienna에서 마지막 공연을 했다고 일부 정보를 잘못 나타냈으므로, 글의 내용과 일치하지 않는 것은 ④이다.

(해석) 유명한 작곡가이자 피아니스트인 Alfred Brendel(알프레드 브렌델)은 1931년 1월 5일에 체코슬로바키아에서 태어났다. 그는 6살이라는 어린 나이부터 피아노 레슨을 받았지만, 기관에서 정식으로 음악을 공부한 적은 없었다. 그럼에도 불구하고 그는 10대 때, 그 자신의 곡들 중 하나와 Bach(바흐)와 Brahms(브람스)의 곡들을 연주하며 공개 발표회를 했다. 1952년에 그는 첫 번째 녹음을 한 후 계속해서 다른 음반 회사 세 곳과 많은 앨범을 발표했다. 그의 작품은 그에게 세계적 명성을 얻게 했고 그는 비엔나 교향악단의 객원이 되었다. 2008년에 Brendel은 비엔나에서 공연을 하는 중에 은퇴를 선언했고 그의 마지막 공연은 그 해 말에 뉴욕에서 했다. 그 이래로 그는 상을 받은 다큐멘터리에서 모습을 드러냈고, 시집도 출간했다.

(어휘) recital 발표회 garner 얻다, 모으다 honorary member 객원, 명예 회원 retirement 은퇴

(구문분석)
> [2행] [**Although** he took piano lessons as a child], beginning at the age of six, he never studied music formally at an institute.
>
> → [Although ~ child]는 although(비록 ~지만)가 이끄는 양보의 부사절이다.

27 안내문 정보 파악하기 　　　　정답 ⑤

(해설) 예외 조항과 관련된 부분인 This tour is available for members only를 통해 투어는 회원만 이용 가능한 것을 알 수 있으므로, 글의 내용과 일치하지 않는 것은 ⑤이다.

(해석)
Ocean Voyage 수족관 투어

Ocean Voyage 수족관에서 가장 인기 있는 전시의 투어를 즐기세요. 이 특별한 투어는 여러분이 바로 가까이에서 동물들을 볼 수 있게 해줍니다.

세부내용:
- 매주 화요일과 금요일에 이용 가능함
- 투어 시간: 오전 9시, 오전 11시, 오후 3시, 오후 5시
- 투어는 90분간 진행됩니다.

- 투어당 최대 10명 (아이들 포함)
- 이용 금액: 성인 10달러, 12세 미만 어린이 5달러

투어 활동:
- 여러분은 바다사자에게 먹이를 줄 기회를 가질 것입니다.
- 펭귄 섬을 방문해서 지느러미 발과 악수를 해 보세요!
- 아기 동물들이 있는 놀이방을 방문합니다.

> 이 투어는 회원들만 이용 가능합니다.

(어휘) up-close 바로 가까이의 flipper (펭귄·거북·고래 등의) 지느러미 발 nursery 놀이방, 유아원

(구문분석)
> [13행] You will get **a chance** [to feed the sea lions].
>
> → [to ~ lions]는 to부정사의 형용사적 용법으로 앞의 명사 a chance 를 수식한다.

28 안내문 정보 파악하기 　　　　정답 ④

(해설) 추가 정보와 관련된 부분인 Tickets can be booked by phone or online을 통해 전화나 온라인으로 입장권 예매가 가능한 것을 알 수 있으므로, 글의 내용과 일치하는 것은 ④이다.

(해석)
'Nature and Nurture' 미술 전시

국립 현대 미술관은 다음 달에 가장 새로운 전시 'Nature and Nurture'를 선보입니다.
- 8월 11일부터 12월 15일까지
- 화요일부터 토요일까지, 오전 9시-오후 5시까지 개장
- 입장료 30달러 (6세 미만 어린이는 무료)

내용
- 60점 이상 전시
- 25명의 유명한 예술가들의 작품
- 육아, 어린이, 청소년에 대해 다룬 주제와 그림들

추가 정보
입장권은 전화나 온라인으로 예약 가능합니다. 가이드 투어는 예약을 통해서만 이용 가능합니다.

전시 미리 보기를 위해서는, 저희 웹사이트 www.NMCA.com을 방문해 주세요.

(어휘) debut 선보이다 touch on 다루다 parenting 육아 preview 미리 보기

(구문분석)
> [11행] **Themes and images** [that touch on parenting, childhood, and adolescence]
>
> → [that ~ adolescence]는 선행사 Themes and images를 수식하며, 주격 관계대명사 that이 이끄는 관계대명사절이다.

29 어법상 틀린 것 찾기 　　　　정답 ①

(해설) 뒤에 명사구(those of the United States and Germany)가 왔으므로, 형용사 또는 부사로만 쓰이는 ①의 alike를 전치사 like로 고쳐야 한다.

(오답분석) ②은 선행사 없이 동사 do의 목적어가 없는 불완전한 절을 이끌고 있으므로 선행사 the thing을 포함하는 목적격 관계대명사 what을 사용한 것은 어법

상 적절하다. ③은 who가 이끄는 주격 관계대명사절의 선행사 people이 복수명사이므로 복수동사 see를 사용한 것은 어법상 적절하다. ④은 앞에 비교급 higher가 있으므로 비교 대상 앞에 than을 사용한 것은 어법상 적절하다. ⑤의 재귀대명사 itself는 전치사 to의 목적어 the meeting을 바로 뒤에서 강조하기 위해 쓰였으므로 어법상 적절하다.

(해석) 시간에 대한 인식은 문화마다 다른데, 이는 국제적으로 사업을 할 때 어려움을 야기할 수 있다. 미국과 독일 문화권처럼 선형적인 시간 감각을 가진 문화권에서는, 과거는 어떤 것과도 관련이 없는 채로, 시간은 일직선으로 미래를 향해 빠르게 나아가는 것으로 인식된다. 과거는 되찾을 수 없기 때문에, 그러한 문화권의 사람들은 그들이 시간을 들여서 하는 일이 그들에게 어떤 식으로든 이득이 되길 바란다. 그렇지 않으면 그것은 낭비된 것으로 간주된다. 따라서 그러한 방식으로 시간을 인식하는 사람들에게는 시간 엄수가 중요하다는 것은 놀랍지 않다. 그러나 스페인과 이탈리아 같은 나라에서는 회의의 질이나 중대성이 정확한 일정을 고집하는 것보다 중요성에서 더 높은 순위를 차지함에 따라, 초점이 현재에 더 맞춰져 있다. 이러한 문화권의 사람들은 회의 자체에 비해서 회의 시간을 무의미하게 여기고 약속에 늦을 수 있어, 어쩌면 다른 문화권의 고객이나 동업자에게 불쾌감을 줄 수 있다.

(어휘) linear 선형의 bearing 영향, 관련 reclaim 되찾다
punctuality 시간 엄수 irrelevant 무의미한

(구문분석)
[4행] ~, time is perceived as moving quickly into the future in a straight line, [with the past having little bearing on anything].
명사 / 현재분사
→ [with ~ anything]은 'with + 명사 + 분사' 형태의 분사구문으로, '~한 채로'라는 의미로 해석한다.

30 어휘 적절성 파악하기   정답 ②

(해설) 사실 고용주들은 이민자들에게 미국인 근로자와 동일한 임금을 지불한다고 했으므로, 미국인들은 이민자들은 더 적은 돈을 받고 기꺼이 일하려고 해서 그들의 일자리를 빼앗는다고 생각한다는 맥락이 되어야 한다. 따라서 ②의 more(더 많은)를 그와 반대되는 의미의 less(더 적은)로 바꾸어야 문맥상 적절하다.

(해석) 많은 미국인들은 이민자 수를 줄이는 것이 미국에 ① 이익이 될 것이라고 믿으면서, 자국의 경제적 문제들을 이민자의 탓으로 돌린다. 하지만 실제로, 통계는 이민자들의 기여가 중요하고 미국의 계속된 성공은 그것들에 의지한다는 것을 보여준다. 한 가지 일반적인 믿음은 이민자들은 ② 더 많은(→ 더 적은) 돈을 받고 기꺼이 일하려고 하기 때문에 미국인들에게서 일자리를 빼앗는다는 것이다. 사실은 고용주들은 그렇게 하지 않으면 불법이기 때문에 이민자들에게 미국인 근로자와 동일한 임금을 지불한다. 또한 만약 이민자들이 없었다면 몇몇 고용주들은 미국 경제를 움직이는 농업과 제조업의 ③ 필수적인 일자리를 채우기 위해 애썼을 것이다. 이러한 산업의 일자리들은 미국인들에게는 점점 더 ④ 달갑지 않은 것으로 비춰진다. 더욱이, 이민자들은 일자리를 빼앗기보다 그들 스스로를 위해서든 새로운 직원들을 위해서든 실제로 일자리를 창출할 가능성이 더 높다. 미국으로 이민 간 사람들은 날 때부터 미국 시민인 사람들이 두 배 비율로 새로운 사업을 ⑤ 시작한다.

(어휘) cut back on ~을 줄이다 contribution 기여, 공헌 reliant 의지하는
struggle ~하려고 애쓰다 drive ~을 움직이다, 추진하다

(구문분석)
[6행] One common belief is [that immigrants take jobs away from Americans because they're willing to work for less money].

→ [that ~ money]는 접속사 that이 이끄는 명사절로, be동사 is의 주격 보어 역할을 한다.

31 빈칸 추론하기   정답 ③

(해설) 주제문에 해당하는 빈칸 문장에서 우리가 '무엇'의 동물이라는 점이 우리가 가장 좋아하는 영화와 TV쇼를 반복해서 보는 이유를 설명할 수 있을지도 모른다고 했다. 글의 중반에서 예측 가능한 콘텐츠는 우리가 갈망하는 질서와 안전성을 제공하며 우리는 전에 본 적 있는 콘텐츠에 감정적으로 어떻게 반응할지 알고 있으므로, 이는 불안감을 없애주는 경험이 될 수 있다고 했다. 따라서 빈칸에는 ③ '확실성'이 와서 우리가 확실성의 동물이라는 의미가 되어야 한다.

(오답분석) ①, ②, ④, ⑤은 지문에서 설명하는 불안감을 없애주는 경험을 반복하는 인간의 특징을 설명하는 단어로 적절하지 않다.

(해석) 인간은 확실성의 동물인데, 이는 우리가 왜 가장 좋아하는 영화와 TV쇼를 몇 번이고 반복해서 보는 경향이 있는지를 설명할 수 있을지도 모른다. 온라인 스트리밍 서비스는 새로운 콘텐츠에 접근하는 것을 쉽게 만들었지만, 많은 사람들은 여전히 오래된 영화와 TV쇼에 끌리는 그들 자신을 발견한다. 하지만 우리는 왜 시작부터 끝까지 이미 알고 있는 작품들을 보는 것을 좋아할까? 조사는 실제로 이것이 불안감을 없애주는 경험이 될 수 있음을 보여준다. 우리는 질서와 안전성을 갈망하며, 예측 가능한 콘텐츠는 이러한 특징들을 제공한다. 잘 알고 있는 과거의 영화나 시리즈에는 정신적으로 처리해야 할 새로운 것이 없고, 우리는 전에 본 적이 있는 것에 우리가 어떻게 감정적으로 반응할지 알고 있다. 우리의 뇌는 모르는 것을 피하도록 설정되어 있어서, 우리는 우리에게 익숙한 것을 고집한다. 이것은 또한 사람들이 오래된 영화와 프로그램을 좋아하는 기억과 연관시키기 때문에 우리에게 향수를 불러일으킬 수도 있다. 고전적인 크리스마스 영화를 보는 것은 당신이 가족들과 있는 것을 생각나게 할 수도 있고, 한 시트콤은 당신을 당신의 어린 시절로 데려갈 수도 있다. 그 과정은 위로가 되고 당신이 계속해서 또 다른 것을 위해 돌아오게 한다.

① 유머   ② 지능
③ 확실성   ④ 상상
⑤ 관계

(어휘) reassuring 불안감을 없애주는, 안심시키는 crave 갈망하다
programme 설정하다, 프로그램을 짜다 nostalgic 향수를 불러일으키는
fond 좋아하는 comforting 위로가 되는

(구문분석)
[4행] Online streaming services have made it easy [to access new content], and yet many people still find themselves drawn to older films and shows.
가목적어 / 진주어(to부정사구)

→ 가목적어 it이 길이가 긴 진목적어 to부정사구 [to ~ content] 대신에 목적어 자리에 쓰인 형태이다.

[19행] The routine of it is comforting and keeps you coming back for more.
동사 / 목적어 / 목적격 보어

→ 동사 keep의 목적어로 you, 목적격 보어로 현재분사 coming이 쓰였다. 동사 keep의 목적격 보어로 현재분사가 쓰일 경우 '(목적어가) 계속 ~하게 하다'라는 의미로 해석한다.

32 빈칸 추론하기
정답 ③

(해설) 주제문에 해당하는 빈칸 문장에서 자폐증을 가진 사람들은 한 연구에서 심적 이미지를 만들고 통제하는 더 발달된 능력을 '무엇한다'는 것을 증명했다고 하고, 글의 후반에 실험에서 자폐 스펙트럼 장애가 있는 사람들은 그렇지 않은 사람들보다 더 빠르고 정확하게 심적 이미지를 인지하고, 살피고, 판단했다고 했다. 따라서 빈칸에는 ③ '갖고 있을지도 모른다'는 내용이 오는 것이 적절하다.

(오답 분석) ①, ④, ⑤은 지문에서 설명하는 자폐 스펙트럼 장애를 가진 사람들의 시각적 능력에 대해 설명하는 표현으로 적절하지 않다. ②은 글의 내용과 관련이 없다.

(해석) 비록 부족한 언어 능력이 자폐 스펙트럼 장애 (ASD)의 징후이지만, 한 연구는 자폐증을 가진 사람들이 심적 이미지를 만들고 통제하는 더 발달된 능력을 갖고 있을지도 모른다는 것을 증명했다. 이 능력은 시각적 패턴과 이미지를 분석하고 다루는 데에 핵심적이며, 공간 시각에 관한 테스트의 완료를 통해 평가될 수 있다. 연구 참가자들에게 그러한 과제 한 가지가 주어졌는데, 그들이 원 안에 있는 하나의 글자를 상상하게 했다. 그리고 나서 원의 부분들이 강조 표시되었고, 피실험자들은 어느 부분이 그 글자를 가장 많이 포함하고 있는지 질문을 받았다. 그 연구는 또한 참가자들이 3D 물체들을 비교해서 만약 그것들이 회전되면 어떻게 보일지 시각화해야 하는 실험도 포함했다. 두 실험 모두에서, 자폐 스펙트럼 장애가 있는 사람들은 자폐증이 없는 사람들을 능가했다. 그들은 더 빠르고 정확하게 심적 이미지들을 인지하고, 살피고 그리고 판단할 수 있었다. 이것은 자폐 스펙트럼 장애가 인상적인 시각 기억뿐만 아니라 우수한 시각적 탐지 능력도 야기할 수 있다고 보여준 이전의 연구와 일직선에 있다.

① 서서히 잃는다
② 식별할 수 있다
③ 갖고 있을지도 모른다
④ 필요로 한다
⑤ 완전히 감춘다

(어휘) autism 자폐증 manipulate 다루다, 조작하다 assess 평가하다
completion 완료 visuospatial 공간 시각에 관한 rotate 회전시키다
outperform 능가하다 align with ~와 일직선에 있다
detection 탐지, 발견 [선택지] conceal 감추다, 숨기다

(구문 분석) [11행] The study also included **a test** [in which participants had to compare 3D objects and **visualize** (what they would look like if they were rotated)].
→ [in ~ rotated]는 선행사 a test를 수식하며 '전치사 + 관계대명사' in which가 이끄는 관계대명사절이다.
→ (what ~ rotated)는 의문사 what(무엇)이 이끄는 명사절로, 동사 visualize의 목적어 역할을 한다.

33 빈칸 추론하기
정답 ⑤

(해설) 주제문에 해당하는 빈칸 문장에서 새로운 증거가 '무엇한다'는 것을 시사한다고 하고, 빈칸 앞 문장에서 천문학자들은 처음에 별들의 수가 은하의 블랙홀 크기를 결정한다고 추정했다고 했다. 글의 후반에서는 새로운 증거를 통해 밝혀진 바, 각 은하 내의 암흑 물질이 합쳐져 거대한 블랙홀을 만들어내므로 과학자들은 이것이 은하의 모양을 결정하고, 블랙홀의 성장을 이끄는 것이라 생각한다고 했다. 따라서 빈칸에는 ⑤ '암흑 물질이 더 큰 역할을 한다'가 와서 새로운 증거가 암흑 물질이 더 큰 역할을 한다는 것을 시사했다는 의미가 되어야 한다.

(오답 분석) ①, ③은 글에서 언급되지 않았다. ②은 글에서 암흑물질이 중력에 발휘하는 힘으로 인해 탐지할 수 있다고는 했지만 블랙홀이 눈에 보이게 된다는 내용은 언급되고 있지 않다. ④은 글에서 은하의 모양에 대해서는 설명했지만 암흑 물질이 다양한 모양을 띤다는 내용은 언급되고 있지 않다.

(해석) 관측된 거의 모든 은하의 중심에는 블랙홀이 있는데, 결과적으로 이것은 우리가 보는 천체들 측면에 위치되어 있다. 이 모든 것을 둘러싸고 있는 것은, 관측 불가능함에도 불구하고 그것이 중력에 발휘하는 힘으로 인해 탐지할 수 있는 암흑 물질인 "헤일로"이다. 처음에 천문학자들은 은하의 블랙홀 크기를 결정하는 것은 바로 별들의 수라고 추정했다; 별이 많을수록, 블랙홀 크기가 더 큰 것이다. 그러나, 새로운 증거는 암흑 물질이 더 큰 역할을 한다는 것을 시사한다. 그 연관성은 타원형 은하가 진화한 방식을 분석함으로써 발견되었다. 더 작은 은하 두 개가 합쳐져서 타원형이 되었을 때, 각 은하 내의 암흑 물질이 합쳐져 거대한 블랙홀을 만들어낸다. 과학자들은 이것이 궁극적으로 새로운 은하의 모양을 결정하고 그것의 블랙홀의 성장을 이끄는 것이라고 생각한다. 이는 암흑 물질이 그 과정에 있는 어떤 것보다도 무게가 많이 나간다는 사실 때문이고, 이에 따라 다른 요소들에 미치는 그것의 영향이 두드러진다.

① 몇몇 별들이 더 큰 중력을 가한다
② 블랙홀은 눈에 보이게 될 수 있다
③ 중력이 암흑 물질의 성장에 영향을 미친다
④ 암흑 물질은 다양한 모양을 띤다
⑤ 암흑 물질이 더 큰 역할을 한다

(어휘) galaxy 은하 flank ~의 측면에 위치하다, 측면에 배치하다
celestial body 천체
halo 헤일로(은하의 중심부 밖에 있는 넓은 공 모양의 영역)
dark matter 암흑 물질 unobservable 관측 불가능한
detectable 탐지할 수 있는 exertion (힘의) 발휘
merge 합치다, 융합시키다 dictate 결정하다, 명령하다
[선택지] exert (압력 등을) 가하다, 발휘하다 assume (성질·양상을) 띠다

(구문 분석) [1행] [**At the center of nearly every observed galaxy** lies a black hole], which in turn is flanked by the celestial bodies we see.
(동사: lies / 주어: black hole)
→ [At ~ hole]은 장소를 나타내는 부사구 At ~ galaxy가 강조되어 문장 맨 앞에 나왔기 때문에, 주어와 동사가 도치되어 '동사(lies) + 주어(a black hole)'의 어순으로 쓰였다.

[5행] Initially, astronomers presumed **it was** the number of stars **that** determined the size of a galaxy's black hole; ~
→ the number of stars를 강조하는 it is(was) ~ that 강조구문이 쓰였다.

[15행] This is due to **the fact** [that dark matter weighs more than anything else in the process], and ~
→ [that ~ process]는 the fact와 동격을 이루는 명사절이다.

34 빈칸 추론하기
정답 ③

(해설) 정치적 발언 중에 고의로 동음이의어를 사용하여 화자는 말하고자 하는 바를 불분명하게 만들 수 있다는 내용의 글이다. 글의 중반에서 화자가 한 문장에서 right을 '권리'와 '정당한'의 의미로 반복해 사용하는 것을 예로 들어 동음이의어를 사용하면 청자가 뜻을 혼동할 수 있다고 설명했다. 따라서 빈칸에는 ③ '말한 것의 의미가 잘못 해석될 수 있다'는 내용이 오는 것이 적절하다.

①의 청자들의 이념적 믿음에 관한 내용은 글에서 언급되고 있지 않다. ②, ⑤은 글의 내용과 관련이 없다. ④은 명백한 거짓말을 피하기 위해 동음이의어를 사용할 수 있다는 글의 내용과 반대되는 내용이므로 오답이다.

(해석) "동음이의어 사용"은 두 개의 동일한 음성들을 가리키며, 그것이 정치적 발언 중에 나오면, 말한 것의 의미가 잘못 해석될 수 있다. 이러한 화법은 화자가 어떤 질문에 직접적인 답변을 제공하는 것을 피하고 싶지만 명백한 거짓말은 하길 원치 않을 때 자주 쓰인다. 이를 위해, 화자는 고의로 그들이 진짜 말하고자 하는 바를 불분명하게 만든다. 예를 들어, 그들이 "저는 제가 원하는 것을 말할 '권리'가 있으므로, 제가 그렇게 하는 것은 '정당할' 뿐입니다"라고 말한다면, 그것은 청자로 하여금 자신의 견해를 표명할 화자의 법적 자유가 그들이 도덕적으로 훌륭하다는 것과 같은 뜻이라고 생각하도록 혼란스럽게 만들 수도 있다. 명시적 의미의 변화는 면밀히 정밀 조사하지 않으면 많은 경우 간과되고, 우리 마음속에서 우리는 두 개의 서로 전혀 다른 개념들을 잘못 합치거나 연결한다. 만일 나중에 화자가 부도덕한 일을 한다면, 우리는 그 발언을 다시 들먹이며 그들에게 유죄 판결을 내릴 수 없다. 화자는 "저는 거짓말하지 않았습니다"라고 사실대로 주장할 수 있으므로, 잘못은 청자에게 있게 된다.

① 그것은 청자들의 이념적 믿음을 반영한다
② 그 의도는 청자들의 마음을 안심시키려는 것이다
③ 말한 것의 의미가 잘못 해석될 수 있다
④ 그것은 화자의 이전 발언들과 직접적으로 모순될 수 있다
⑤ 상대에 대한 허위 진술은 한 명의 화자에 의해 생긴다

(어휘) equivocation 동음이의어 사용   purposely 고의로, 일부러
equivalent 같은 뜻의, 동등한   denotation 명시적 의미
scrutiny 정밀 조사   conflate 합치다, 융합하다
disparate 서로 전혀 다른   statement 발언, 말한 것, 진술
fall on ~에 있다   [선택지] ideological 이념적인
misinterpret 잘못 해석하다   contradict 모순되다

(구문 분석)
[6행] To this end, the speaker purposely makes what they are really saying unclear.
동사 / 목적어 / 목적격 보어

→ 동사 makes의 목적어로 명사절 [what ~ saying]이, 목적격 보어로 형용사 unclear가 쓰였다. 동사 make의 목적격 보어로 형용사가 쓰일 경우 '(목적어를) ~하게 만들다'라는 의미로 해석한다.

35 흐름과 관계 없는 문장 찾기   정답 ④

(해설) 안내견들이 임무에서 배제되는 이유는 흔히 행동상의 문제들이며, 개의 나이에 따라 발생하는 문제점이 다르고 이를 예측할 수 있는 것은 임무에서 물러나는 것의 발생을 줄이는 훈련 프로그램 개발에 도움이 된다는 내용의 글이다. 그런데 ④은 은퇴한 안내견을 계속 보살피는 것이 주인에게 쉽지 않다는 내용이므로 핵심 소재는 같지만 주제에서 벗어나 있어 글의 흐름과 무관하다.

(오답 분석) ⑤의 Studies like this의 this는 ①의 a study를 가리키고 있으므로, 조사 결과와 개의 나이별 문제를 언급하는 ①, ②, ③ 뒤에 이어지는 것이 적절하다.

(해석) 시각 장애가 있는 사람들과 활동하는 안내견들은 광범위한 훈련을 받고 가장 최고의 개들만 임무에 투입되더라도, 일부는 은퇴 외의 이유들로 임무에서 물러난다. ① 한 연구에 따르면 일찍 물러나는 가장 흔한 이유들은 두려움이나 공격성과 같은 행동상의 문제들이다. ② 이것들은 3.5세 이하의 수컷 개들에게서 가장 흔하게 발생한다. ③ 6세 이상의 개들과 흔히 관련된 문제인 개의 활동 의지는 또한 임무에서의 배제를 정당화할 수 있다. (④ 주인들은 보통 은퇴 후에도 그들의 안내견을 계속 둘 것인지에 대한 선택이 주어지지만, 대부분의 주인들은 새로운 개와 훈련하면서 그들을 보살필 수가 없다.) ⑤ 다양한 연령대에서 개들의 행동상 변화를 예측할 수 있는 것은 임무에서 물러나는 일의

발생을 줄일 수 있는 훈련 프로그램의 개발에 도움이 될 수도 있기 때문에 이와 같은 연구들은 가치가 있다.

(어휘) guide dog 안내견   impaired ~에 장애가 있는, 약화된
withdraw 물러나게 하다   willingness 의지, 기꺼이 ~하려는 마음
warrant 정당화하다   removal 배제, 제거   occurrence 발생

(구문 분석)
[12행] ~, but most owners are unable to care for them [while training with a new dog].

→ [while ~ dog]은 분사구문의 의미를 분명하게 하기 위해 부사절 접속사(while)가 분사구문 앞에 온 형태이다.

[14행] Studies like this are valuable **because** [being able to predict behavioral changes in dogs at different ages] may help in the development of training programs that can reduce the occurrence of service withdrawal.

→ 동명사구 [being ~ ages]는 전치사구(in dogs, at different ages)를 포함하며, 전체가 접속사 because(~ 때문에)가 이끄는 부사절의 주어이다.

36 글의 순서 배열하기   정답 ③

(해설) 주어진 글은 젠트리피케이션이 저소득층 가정에 반드시 나쁜 것은 아니라는 주제를 제시한다. (B)는 부유한 사람들이 가난한 동네로 이사하면서 이전 거주자들을 강제로 내쫓는 등의 부정적인 영향에 대해 설명하는 내용이고, (C)는 역접 연결어 Yet을 통해 계속 머무르는 사람들에게는 일자리, 낮은 범죄율 등의 분명한 이점이 있다고 하며 (B)의 내용에 대한 반전 설명을 하고 있다. (A)의 less poverty and safer streets(줄어든 가난과 더 안전한 거리)는 (C)의 '일자리를 구할 수 있고 범죄율이 낮다'는 것의 결과 이므로 (C) 뒤에 (A)가 이어지는 것이 자연스럽다. 따라서 글의 순서로 가장 적절한 것은 ③ (B) - (C) - (A)이다.

(해석) 젠트리피케이션은 흔히 연상되는 부정적인 함의에도 불구하고, 그것은 저소득층 가정에 반드시 나쁜 것은 아니다.

(B) 부유한 사람들이 가난한 동네로 이사할 때, 그들은 변화를 만들고 사업 발전을 촉진하기 위해 그들의 돈을 사용한다고 보통 추정된다. 이것의 결과는 부동산 가치의 증가이며, 이것은 임대료를 빠르게 끌어올리고 이전 거주자들을 강제로 내쫓는다.

(C) 그러나 계속 머무르는 사람들에게는 분명한 이점이 있다. 근처로의 자금의 유입은 덜 부유한 가구가 일자리를 구할 수 있고 범죄율이 낮은 활력 있는 도시 지역에서 살 수 있는 더 많은 기회로 필연적으로 이어진다.

(A) 전반적으로 줄어든 가난과 더 안전한 거리로 인해, 이전 거주자들, 특히 아이들에게 미치는 영향은 크다. 주변에서 그들이 보는 사람과 보는 것들에 영향을 받아, 젠트리피케이션화 되고 있는 지역의 아이들은 다양한 사회적 네트워크를 만들고 대학 교육을 계속할 가능성이 더 높은데, 이는 그들에게 사회적 계층의 상향 이동을 성취할 기회를 제공한다.

(어휘) implication 함의, 암시
gentrification 젠트리피케이션(주택가의 고급 주택화)   upward 상향의
social mobility 사회적 계층 이동   impoverished 가난한
drive up 빠르게 끌어올리다   influx 유입   well-off 부유한

(구문 분석)
[6행] [**Influenced** by who and what they see around them], children in gentrifying areas are more likely to develop diverse social networks ~

→ [Influenced ~ them]은 과거분사(Influenced)로 시작하는 수동형 분사구문이다.

[14행] The consequence of this is **an increase** in property values, [which drives up the cost of rent and forces former residents out].

→ [which ~ out]은 선행사 an increase를 수식하는 주격 관계대명사절로, 콤마 뒤에서 계속적 용법으로 쓰였다.

37 글의 순서 배열하기 정답 ②

(해설) 주어진 글은 지구의 대기가 약화되는 것을 막는 자기권의 역할에 관한 내용이다. (B)는 In this regard를 통해 자기권의 역할에 대한 부연 설명을 하고 있으므로, 주어진 글 바로 다음에 오는 것이 적절하다. (A)는 태양풍이 자기권을 파열시켜 지자기 폭풍을 일으킬 수 있으며 행성의 자극이 뒤집혔을 때 자기권이 약화된다는 내용이고, (B)의 마지막에서 그것이 많은 요인들에 영향을 받을 수 있다고 했으므로 그 뒤에 와야 한다. (C)는 자기권 약화로 인해 발생할 수 있는 기술적 문제와 건강상 문제 등 약간의 장애를 언급하고 있고, (A)의 마지막에 자기권 약화가 많은 영향을 야기할 수 있다고 했으므로 그 뒤에 와야 한다. 따라서 글의 순서로 가장 적절한 것은 ② (B) - (A) - (C)이다.

(해석) 태양계의 내행성들 중에서, 지구만이 자기권이라 불리는 자기장을 자랑한다. 그것은 태양의 하전 입자로 인해 발생하는 대기의 약화로부터 우리를 보호하기 때문에 우리의 생존에 아주 중대하다.

(B) 이 점에서, 그것은 또한 우주 방사선과 생명에 해로운 다른 불필요한 에너지를 저지함에 따라, 방패막과 아주 유사하게 작용한다. 그것이 효과적인 문지기라고 할지라도, 그것은 많은 요인들에 영향을 받을 수 있다.

(A) 태양풍이 그것을 파열시켜, 대기를 관통하여 우리의 인공위성을 방해하는 지자기 폭풍으로 이어질 수 있다. 게다가 그것은 행성의 자극이 점차 위치를 바꾸어 확 뒤집혔을 때 상당히 약화되는데, 이는 많은 영향을 야기할 수 있다.

(C) 최소의 자기장으로, 나침반은 작동하지 않을 것이고 인공위성에 관한 기술적 문제가 발생할 것이다. 오존은 파괴될 가능성이 높고 자외선 노출이 증가할 것이다. 이러한 영향 중 되돌릴 수 없고 즉각적인 재난을 불러일으키는 것은 없지만, 그 결과가 약간의 장애를 일으키기 충분할 것이라고 말해도 무방하다.

(어휘) **inner planet** 내행성(소행성대 안쪽에 위치한 수성, 금성, 지구, 화성의 총칭)
boast 자랑하다, 뽐내다 **magnetic field** 자기장 **magnetosphere** 자기권 **atmospheric** 대기의 **erosion** 약화, 침식 **charged particles** 하전 입자 **geomagnetic** 지자기의 **obstruct** 방해하다 **satellite** (인공)위성 **flip** 확 뒤집히다 **repercussion** 영향 **cosmic radiation** 우주 방사선 **gatekeeper** 문지기 **compass** 나침반 **ultraviolet radiation** 자외선 **irreversible** 되돌릴 수 없는

(구문분석)
[6행] Solar winds can disrupt it, [leading to geomagnetic storms that penetrate the atmosphere and obstruct our satellites].

→ [leading ~ satellites]는 결과를 나타내는 분사구문으로, 분사구문의 주어가 주절의 주어(Solar winds)와 같아서 생략되었다.

[20행] ~ disaster, it's safe to say that the consequences would be **enough to cause** some disorder.

→ 'enough + to부정사'는 '~하기에 충분히'라는 의미를 나타내는 to부정사 표현이다.

38 주어진 문장의 위치 찾기 정답 ③

(해설) 주어진 문장의 though(그러나)로 보아, 주어진 문장 앞에는 독점에 대한 긍정적인 내용이 나와야 한다는 것을 알 수 있다. 이 글에서 ①~② 뒤 문장까지는 주로 독점 기업에게 있어서 독점의 긍정적인 영향에 대해서 설명하고 있고, ③~⑤ 뒤 문장은 독점이 소비자에게 미치는 부정적인 영향에 대해서 이야기하고 있다. 또한, 주어진 문장의 regarded by most consumers as a negative는 ③ 뒤 문장의 For one thing(우선)으로 이어지고 있으므로, 주어진 문장이 들어가기에 가장 적절한 곳은 ③이다.

(해석) 독점 기업은 한 산업에서 사실상 시장 점유율의 전부 혹은 대부분을 지배하는 기업이다. 독점력을 가진 기업에게, 시장에서 발생된 수입이 전적으로 그들에 의해 모인다는 점에서 이것은 분명 긍정적인 상황이다. (①) 독점 기업은 "규모의 경제"를 더 쉽게 달성할 수 있고 다른 기업에 맞서 그들을 광고하는 데에 거액을 지출하지 않아도 되기 때문에, 더 많이 벌 뿐만 아니라 더 적게 쓴다. (②) 독점 기업들은 가격 안정성을 제공하고 그들이 아낀 돈을 더 나은 제품을 개발하는 데에 투자할 수 있기 때문에, 소비자에게도 이익을 줄 수 있다. (③ 그러나 일반적으로 독점 기업들은 대부분의 소비자들에게 부정적인 것으로 여겨진다.) 우선, 독점 기업은 경쟁의 위협을 거의 직면하지 않는데, 이는 소비자들은 그들(독점 기업)이 제공하는 것을 살 수밖에 없음을 의미한다. (④) 그러면 그들은 소비자들이 다른 이를 찾을까 봐 걱정하지 않고 가격을 거의 모든 수준으로 설정할 수 있다. (⑤) 그리고 독점 기업은 그들이 제공하는 것을 개선할 의무가 없어서, 이는 혁신을 저지하고 더 낮은 품질의 제품과 서비스로 이어질 수 있다.

(어휘) **monopoly** 독점 기업, 독점 **effectively** 사실상, 실질적으로 **revenue** 수익 **sum** 액수, 총액 **confer** 주다 **stability** 안정성 **obligation** 의무 **restrain** 제지하다, 억제하다

(구문분석)
[15행] ~ competition, meaning that consumers **have no choice but to** buy [what they offer].

→ 'have no choice but + to부정사'는 '~할 수 밖에 없다'라는 의미를 나타내는 관용 표현이고, 'cannot (help) but + 동사원형'의 형태로 바꾸어 쓸 수 있다.

→ [what they offer]는 관계대명사 what(~하는 것)이 이끄는 명사절로, 동사 buy의 목적어 역할을 한다.

39 주어진 문장의 위치 찾기 정답 ④

(해설) 주어진 문장의 this로 보아, 주어진 문장 앞에는 이상적이게 들리는 미래의 모습에 대한 내용이 나와야 하고, 주어진 문장의 cause for concern을 통해 다음 문장에서는 우려하는 것에 대한 내용이 나와야 한다는 것을 알 수 있다. ④ 앞 문장에서 "최초의 초지능적인 기계는 인간이 결코 다시 만들어낼 필요가 없을 것 같은 발명품이다"라고 했고, ④ 뒤 문장에서 인공 지능으로 인한 우려에 대해서 설명하고 있으므로 주어진 문장이 들어가기에 가장 적절한 곳은 ④이다.

(오답분석) ③ 뒤 문장은 전문가의 말을 이용해 앞 문장의 인공지능의 특징에 대한 내용을 다루고 있으므로 주어진 문장이 들어가기에 적절하지 않다.

(해석) 1997년에 인공 지능 컴퓨터 Deep Blue(딥 블루)가 체스 챔피언 Gary Kasparov(가리 카스파로프)를 이겼을 때, 그것은 많은 사람들에게 종말의 시작이었다. (①) 인공 지능 혁명의 다음 단계는 그러한 좁은 인공 지능(ANI)의 한계를 넘어 범용 인공 지능(AGI)을 만드는 것이었다. (②) ANI와 달리, AGI는 컴퓨터가 스스로를 가르치는 능력을 갖게 될 것이라는 것을 의미한다;

그것들은 진화하고, 학습하고, 그들 자신의 더 나은 버전을 "재생산"할 것이다. (③) Irving Good(어빙 굿)은 "최초의 초지능적인 기계는 인간이 결코 다시 만들어낼 필요가 없을 것 같은 발명품이다."라고 말했다. (④ 이것이 그리는 미래는 일부에게는 이상적이게 들릴지도 모르지만, 그것은 우려의 중요한 원인을 제공한다.) 결국 우월한 지능을 가진 존재가 그것을 발명한 것에 대해 인간들에게 감사함을 느끼고 우리의 최고의 이익을 위해 일할 것이라고 추정할 근거가 없다. (⑤) 초지능적인 기계는 대신에 인간이 모든 면에서 열등하다는 것을 깨닫고 인류가 쓸모 없다는 결론을 내리고 우리를 몰아낼 수 있다.

(어휘) **parameter** 한계, 한도 **presume** 추정하다, 간주하다 **obsolete** 쓸모 없는 **eradicate** 몰아내다, 박멸하다

(구문분석)

[5행] The next step in AI evolution was ①[to go beyond the parameters of such artificial narrow intelligence (ANI)] **and** ②[(to) create artificial general intelligence (AGI)].

주어 / 동사 / 주격 보어

→ be동사 was의 주격 보어로 쓰인 to부정사구 ①[to ~ (ANI)]와 ②[create ~ (AGI)]는 등위접속사 and로 연결된 병렬 구조로 두 번째 to는 생략되었다.

	(A)	(B)
①	창조자 ……	빠른
②	수령인 ……	강한
③	매개체 ……	약화된
④	창조자 ……	느린
⑤	매개체 ……	높아진

(어휘) **facilitate** 용이하게 하다 **colony** 군집 **bear** 견뎌내다 **encounter** 만나다 **counterintuitive** 직관에 어긋나는 **underactive** 비정상적으로 활발하지 못한 **counteract** 중화시키다, 대응하다

(구문분석)

[2행] [**Not only** does their tendency to live in groups facilitate] the transfer of pathogens among colony members, but their ability to fly enables these pathogens to be spread fast and efficiently elsewhere.

조동사 / 주어 / 동사

→ [Not ~ facilitate]는 부정어 not only가 강조되어 문장 맨 앞에 나왔기 때문에, 주어와 조동사가 도치되어 '조동사(does) + 주어(their ~ groups) + 동사(facilitate)'의 어순으로 쓰였다.

---

40 요약문 완성하기   정답 ③

(해설) 글의 전반부에서 인간에게 질병을 옮기는 동물인 박쥐는 무리 생활과 날 수 있는 능력으로 인해 병원균들을 다른 곳으로 빠르게 전파할 수 있다고 했고, 글의 후반부에서는 박쥐의 면역 체계는 바이러스에 강하게 반응하는 것을 막도록 즉, 면역 체계가 활발하지 않게 되도록 진화했으므로 어떤 질병에도 영향을 받지 않고 바이러스의 숙주가 될 수 있다고 설명한다. 따라서 spread fast and efficiently elsewhere를 carriers로, underactive를 reduced로 바꾸어 표현한 ③이 정답이다.

(오답분석) 박쥐는 인간에게 질병을 옮기는 동물이며, 병원균들이 다른 곳으로 전파될 수 있게 한다고 했으므로 ①, ④의 creators는 (A)에 들어갈 단어로 적절하지 않다. 박쥐는 그들의 면역 체계를 활발하지 못하게 만들어서 바이러스에 강하게 반응하는 것을 막도록 진화했다고 했으므로 ②의 strong과 ⑤의 raised는 (B)에 들어갈 단어로 적절하지 않다.

(해석) 인간에게 질병을 옮기는 동물에 있어서, 박쥐는 특히 우려된다. 무리 지어 생활하는 그들의 경향은 군집 구성원들 사이에서 병원균의 이동을 용이하게 할 뿐만 아니라, 날 수 있는 능력도 이 병원균들이 다른 곳으로 빠르고 효과적으로 전파될 수 있게 한다. 오랫동안, 박쥐들이 그들 자신은 영향을 받지 않고 어떻게 그렇게 많은 치명적인 바이러스들의 숙주가 될 수 있는지는 알려지지 않았다. 최근의 연구는 그렇게 하는 그들의 능력이 바이러스에 대한 그들의 독특한 반응과 관련이 있다는 것을 발견했다. 기본적으로, 박쥐는 대부분의 육상 포유 동물들의 면역 체계가 질병을 만났을 때 그러하듯이, 그들의 면역 체계가 그것들이 견뎌내는 바이러스에 강하게 반응하는 것을 막도록 진화했다. 이것은 그들이 겪는 어떤 질병의 영향도 제한한다. 비정상적으로 활발하지 못한 면역 체계로부터 유기체가 이익을 본다는 것이 직관에 어긋나는 것처럼 보일 수 있지만, 이것은 염증 수준과 관련이 있다. 질병에 대응하는 적당한 양의 염증은 그것을 중화시킬 수 있지만, 과도한 염증은 유기체에 광범위하고 심지어 평생에 걸친 손상을 일으킬 수 있고, 이는 인간에게 흔히 있는 일이다.

↓

박쥐는 인간에게 해로운 다양한 질병의 (A) 매개체이지만 (B) 약화된 면역 반응으로 인해 그들 스스로는 병에 걸리지 않는다.

41~42 장문 독해 1

(해석) 진화가 연속적이고 때로는 엄청나게 빠른 과정이지만, 장기간에 걸친 진화적 변화는 실제로 꽤 오랜 시간이 걸린다. 정확히 말해, 약 백만 년 정도다. 과학자들이 10년에서 100년의 짧은 기간의 진화적 변화에 관한 데이터를 화석 기록으로 증명된 것처럼 훨씬 더 긴 기간에 걸쳐 발생한 것(진화적 변화)들과 비교했을 때, [41, 42]그들은 급격한 변화는 많은 경우 (a) 영구적인 것이 될 수 없다는 것을 발견했다. 게다가 이러한 발달은 더 적은 개체군들에 국한되어 있을지도 모른다. 반면 장기간에 걸친 변화는 연구자들이 말하는 "놀라울 정도로 일관된 패턴"이라는 것에 따라 상당히 (b) 천천히 일어난다. 그것들은 시간의 흐름에도 지속되고 더 큰 규모의 개체군들에 영향을 미치는 힘에 의해 자극을 받는다. 이 가설은 1970년대에 대두된 단속 평형설을 (c) 뒷받침하는데(→반박하는데), 단속 평형설은 진화적 변화가 "정체기"라 일컬어지는, 변화가 거의 없는 상태를 지나고 나서 "단속적 변화"가 오는 패턴을 따른다고 제시한다. 동물학자 Josef Uyeda(요제프 우예다)가 말하길, "진화적 적응은 환경 변화, 포식 혹은 인위적 교란과 같은 자연 선택의 일부 영향력에 의해 일어나고, 이러한 영향력은 그 변화가 지속되고 축적되도록 (d) 계속해서 널리 퍼져야 한다." 계산 생물학자 Michael Palmer(마이클 팔머)에 따르면, 이러한 변화는 또한 정확히 이해될 수도 있는데, "어느 시점에나 소수의 생존 가능한 돌연변이가 있으며, 이는 심지어 더 긴 기간에 걸쳐 그 역학을 (e) 예측 가능하고 반복 가능하게 만들기" 때문이다. 장기간에 걸친 변화들은 영속하지만 느리고, 대부분의 종들은 멸종하거나 완전히 새로운 종이 되기까지 백만 년에서 천만 년보다 짧게 생존할 뿐이다.

(어휘) **evolutionary** 진화의 **permanent** 영구적인 **population** 개체군, 인구 **punctuated equilibrium** 단속 평형설 **stasis** 정체기, 정지 상태 **punctuational change** 단속적 변화 **zoologist** 동물학자 **natural selection** 자연 선택 **predation** 포식 **disturbance** 교란, 방해 **computation** 계산 **viable** 생존 가능한, 실행 가능한 **mutation** 돌연변이 **persistent** 영속하는

(구문분석)

[10행] In addition, these developments [might be restricted] to smaller populations.

→ [might be restricted]는 조동사(might)가 있는 '조동사 + be + p.p.' 형태의 수동태이다.

[28행] ~ "there are only a few viable mutations at any point, [which makes the dynamics predictable and repeatable, even over the long term]."

→ [which ~ term]은 선행사 앞 문장 전체를 선행사로 수식하는 주격 관계대명사절로 콤마 뒤에서 계속적 용법으로 쓰였다.

41 제목 파악하기 정답 ②

해설 급격한 진화는 많은 경우 영구적인 것이 될 수 없는 반면, 장기간에 걸친 진화적 변화는 일관된 패턴에 따라 상당히 천천히 일어난다는 내용의 글로, 그 가설을 반박하는 동물학자 Josef Uyeda의 주장과 계산 생물학자 Michael Palmer의 말을 인용하여 설명하고 있다. 따라서 이 글의 제목으로 가장 적절한 것은 ② '장기간에 걸친 진화적 변화는 어떻게 일어나는가?'이다.

오답분석 ①은 글에서 진화적 적응은 자연 선택의 영향력에 의해 일어난다고는 했지만 그것의 미래 적응 형태를 예상하는 것에 대해서는 언급되지 않았다. ④은 글에서 적응의 패턴이 동물들에게 이득이 되었는지는 언급되지 않았다. ③, ⑤은 글의 일부만을 다루고 있는 오답이다.

해석 ① 현재의 종의 미래 적응 형태를 예측하라!
② 장기간에 걸친 진화적 변화는 어떻게 일어나는가?
③ 자연 선택: 살아남기 위해 변하는 종
④ 동물들에게 이득이 되었던 적응의 패턴
⑤ 개체군의 크기와 진화의 속도 간 관계

42 어휘 적절성 파악하기 정답 ③

해설 This hypothesis(이 가설)는 장기간에 걸친 변화는 일관된 패턴으로 천천히 일어난다는 입장이지만, 단속 평형설은 거의 변화가 없는 "정체기" 이후에 "단속적 변화"가 오는 패턴을 따른다는 이론이다. 따라서 '이 가설'이 단속 평형설을 반박한다는 맥락이 되어야 하므로, ③의 supports(뒷받침한다)를 그와 반대되는 의미의 counters(반박한다)와 같은 어휘로 바꾸어야 문맥상 적절하다.

43~45 장문 독해 2

해석 (A) Ellie Strickland는 자라서 많은 중요한 발견을 한 유명한 과학자가 되었다. 그녀는 다른 연구원들과는 다른 창의적인 방법으로 문제에 대해 생각함으로써 이것을 할 수 있었다 한 기자가 그녀에게 어떻게 (a) 그녀가 그렇게 혁신적이고 고정관념에서 벗어나 생각할 수 있었는지 물었다. Ellie는 그 기자에게 어린 시절 이야기를 들려주는 것으로 답했다.

(C) 그녀는 5살 때 냉장고에서 우유 한 병을 혼자 힘으로 가져오려고 했다고 말했다. 유감스럽게도, 그 병은 너무 무거웠고 그녀는 잘못해서 그것을 바닥에 떨어뜨려서 우유를 사방에 쏟았다. ⁴⁴그녀의 어머니가 걸어 들어와서 엉망진창인 것을 보았다. ⁴⁵하지만 그녀를 꾸짖거나 벌을 주는 대신, (d) 그녀는 "참 지저분하구나! 음, 이미 일은 일어났어. 그것을 치우기 전에 그 안에서 좀 놀아볼까?"라고 말했다.

(D) 그래서 두 사람은 그녀의 어머니가 "우리가 어질러 놓을 때마다, 우리는 결국 그것을 치우고 다시 올바르게 만들어야 해. 하지만 우리가 그걸 어떻게

할지는 정해지지 않았어. 그럼 (e) 너는 이것을 어떻게 치우고 싶니? 우리는 스펀지, 걸레, 또는 수건을 사용할 수 있어."라고 말하기 전까지 한동안 웅덩이에서 놀았다.

(B) Ellie는 스펀지를 골랐다. 마침내, 그들이 끝낸 후, 그녀의 어머니는 (b) 그녀를 위해 한 가지 가르침을 더 주었다. "이번은 작은 손으로 큰 병을 옮기는 방법에 대한 실패한 실험이었어. 이제, 병에 물을 채우고 네가 어떻게 떨어뜨리지 않고 그것을 옮길 수 있는지 알아보기 위해 다른 방법을 시도해보는 것은 어떨까." 이 경험은 그녀에게 실수하는 것을 두려워하지 않아도 된다는 것을 가르쳐 주었다. 그것이 그녀가 지금 (c) 그녀의 실수를 새로운 것들을 시도하고 발견하기 위한 기회로 사용하는 이유이다.

어휘 think outside the box 고정관념을 깨다 spill 쏟다 scold 꾸짖다 puddle 웅덩이 mop 걸레

구문분석 [10행] "This was a failed experiment on [how to carry a big bottle with small hands].

→ [how ~ hands]는 '~하는 방법'이라는 의미의 'how + to부정사' 구문이다.

[18행] She said that when she was 5 years old, she tried to get a bottle of milk from the fridge by herself.

→ 동사 tried의 목적어로 to부정사 to get이 쓰여 '~하려고 노력하다'의 의미를 갖는 구문이다. try의 목적어로 동명사가 쓰일 경우 '시험 삼아 ~하다'라는 다른 의미로 쓰인다.

43 글의 순서 배열하기 정답 ③

해설 (A)는 유명한 과학자가 된 Ellie가 기자에게 그녀의 어린 시절 일화를 소개해준다고 말하는 내용이고, (C)에서 She said that when she was 5 years old라며 Ellie의 어린 시절 이야기를 시작하고 있으므로 (C)는 (A) 바로 뒤에 오는 것이 적절하다. (D)의 So the two of them played around in the puddle은 (C)에서 Ellie의 엄마가 Should we play in it a bit이라고 한 부분과 이어지므로 (C) 다음에 오는 것이 적절하다. (B)의 Ellie chose the sponge의 the sponge는 (D) 마지막에 Ellie의 어머니가 제시한 세 가지 선택지 중 하나이므로 (D) 다음에 오는 것이 적절하다. 따라서 글의 순서로 가장 적절한 것은 ③ (C) - (D) - (B)이다.

44 지칭 대상 파악하기 정답 ④

해설 (a), (b), (c), (e)는 모두 Ellie를 가리키지만 (d)는 Ellie의 어머니를 가리키므로, ④이 정답이다.

45 세부 정보 파악하기 정답 ④

해설 (C)의 But instead of scolding her or punishing her, she said, "What a big mess! ~ before we clean it up?"을 통해 그녀의 어머니가 그녀를 혼내지 않고 치우기 전에 함께 놀자고 말했다는 것을 알 수 있는데, ④은 어머니가 Ellie를 혼냈다고 일부 정보를 잘못 나타냈으므로, 글의 내용과 일치하지 않는 것은 ④이다.

정답

문제집 p. 74

18	②	19	⑤	20	⑤	21	④	22	⑤	23	③	24	④	25	③	26	④	27	④
28	⑤	29	⑤	30	①	31	②	32	②	33	④	34	⑤	35	④	36	③	37	②
38	⑤	39	④	40	⑤	41	①	42	④	43	②	44	④	45	④				

18 목적 파악하기
정답 ②

(해설) 글의 중간 이후에서 Could I(~할 수 있을까요)를 이용해 별을 관찰하는 탐험대 프로그램을 예약할 수 있을지 문의하고 있으므로, 정답은 ②이다.

(해석) Harlow 교수님께,

저희 가족은 휴가를 위해 다음 달에 Cape City를 방문할 예정입니다. 최근에, 저는 온라인에서 아이들을 위한 당신의 별을 관찰하는 탐험대에 관해 읽었고, 그것이 굉장한 경험이 될 것 같다고 생각했습니다. 제 남편과 저는 6살과 8살인 남자 아이 둘이 있습니다. 그들은 우주에 매우 관심이 있고, 제 생각에 그들은 당신의 프로그램을 좋아할 것 같습니다. 그것은 훌륭한 가족 활동이 될 것 같습니다. 저는 사전에 예약이 반드시 이루어져야 한다는 것을 당신의 웹사이트에서 확인했습니다. 8월 13일에 4명 예약을 할 수 있을까요? 아직 저희가 참여할 수 있는 자리가 남아있길 바랍니다. 시간 내주셔서 감사합니다.

Eleanor Small 드림

(어휘) stargaze 별을 관찰하다 expedition 탐험대

(구문분석) [7행] ~ I **think** [(that) they would love your program].
→ [they ~ program]은 동사 think의 목적어 역할을 하는 명사절로, 접속사 that이 생략되었다.

19 분위기 파악하기
정답 ⑤

(해설) 분위기는 간접적으로 표현된다. 글의 초반부의 shouting and yelling in panic, bumping into each other and knocking things over를 통해 불이 붙은 배에 타고 있는 사람들의 긴급한 상황을, 마지막 문장인 They went as fast as they could, as the fire was making its way up to where they were를 통해 배를 탈출해야 하는 상황의 필사적인 분위기를 느낄 수 있으므로, 글의 분위기로 가장 적절한 것은 ⑤이다.

(해석) 선원들이 당황하여 소리를 지르고 고함을 치며 뛰어다녔다. 짙은 연기는 무슨 일이 일어나고 있는 건지 보기 어렵게 만들었고, 사람들은 서로 부딪치고 물건들을 무너뜨리고 있었다. 아무도 정말 어떻게 불이 시작되었는지 몰랐지만, 불은 오래된 선박을 빠르게 가로지르며 퍼졌다. 선장은 밤하늘을 올려다보았지만, 하늘은 맑고 별들로 차 있었다; 비구름의 조짐조차 없었다. "배를 버리고 떠나라!"라고 그가 외쳤다. 그의 명령이 아래층 갑판으로 울려 퍼지자, 선원들은 불길을 꺼보려는 시도를 멈추고 구명 뗏목을 내리기 시작했다. 불길이 그들이 있는 곳까지 올라오고 있었으므로, 그들은 그들이 할 수 있는 한 빠르게 갔다.

① 지루하고 단조로운
② 열렬하고 열광적인
③ 희망차고 위안이 되는
④ 엄숙하고 신성한
⑤ 긴급하고 필사적인

(어휘) heavy 짙은, 무거운 bump into ~에 부딪치다 knock over ~를 무너뜨리다 vessel 선박 command 명령 life raft 구명 뗏목
[선택지] monotonous 단조로운 comfort 위안하다 solemn 엄숙한 desperate 필사적인

(구문분석) [1행] The sailors rushed around, [shouting and yelling in panic].
→ [shouting ~ panic]은 '~하면서'라는 의미의 동시 동작을 나타내는 분사구문으로, 분사구문의 주어가 주절의 주어(The sailors)와 같아서 생략되었다.

20 주장 파악하기
정답 ⑤

(해설) 글의 첫 부분에서 내담자가 상담사에게 치료를 받을 때 치료를 통해 무엇을 이루고 싶은지를 표현해야 하고, 자신이 극복하고자 하는 문제가 무엇인지 말해야 한다고 주장하고 있으므로 정답은 ⑤이다.

(오답분석) ①, ④은 내담자가 특정 치료 방식을 요청해야 하거나 상담사에게 어떤 형태의 도움을 제공해 달라고 명시해야 하는 건 아니라고 한 글의 내용과 반대되므로 오답이다. ②은 이 글에서는 상담사가 아니라 내담자가 가져야 할 자세를 말하고 있으므로 오답이다.

(해석) 심리 치료에 관해서, 내담자는 그저 상담사의 지도를 따르면 된다는 널리 퍼져 있는 오해가 있다. 사실은, 도움을 구하는 사람이 첫 상담 시작에서 그가 치료를 받으면서 이루고 싶은 것을 표현하는 것이 매우 중요하다. 이것은 내담자가 특정 치료 방법을 요청해야 한다거나 상담사가 어떤 형태의 도움을 제공해야 하는지를 명시해야 한다는 의미로 해석되어서는 안 된다; 그보다는 내담자는 이루길 원하는 것뿐만 아니라 극복되어야 할 문제를 명확히 말해야 한다. 사회 불안을 겪고 있는 사람은 "저는 방금 만난 사람들과 소통하는 것에 어려움을 느끼는데, 새로운 친구들을 더 쉽게 사귀고 싶어요"라고 말할 수 있을 것이다. 이런 식으로 목표를 설정함으로써, 그 내담자는 상담사가 효과적인 치료 과정을 계획할 수 있을 가능성을 높이는 것이다.

(어휘) misperception 오해 counselor 상담사 onset 시작 therapeutic 치료의 specify 명시하다 likelihood 가능성

[구문분석] **[9행]** Rather, the client must clearly state ①[the problem that needs to be overcome] **as well as** ②[what he or she hopes to accomplish].

→ ①[the ~ overcome]과 ②[what ~ accomplish]는 A as well as B (B뿐만 아니라 A도) 형태로 연결된 병렬 구조이며, 상관접속사 not only B but (also) A로 바꿔 쓸 수 있다.

[11행] A person who is experiencing social anxiety might say, "I find **it** difficult [to interact with **people** ((that/whom) I have
가목적어   진목적어(to부정사)
just met)], ~

→ 가목적어 it이 길이가 긴 진목적어 to부정사구 [to ~ met] 대신 동사 find의 목적어 자리에 쓰인 형태이다.

→ (I ~ met)은 선행사 people을 수식하는 관계대명사절로, 목적격 관계대명사 that/whom이 생략되었다.

21 밑줄 의미 추론하기   정답 ④

[해설] 세상이 과거보다 더 세계화되었고 다양한 인종의 반 친구가 있을 가능성이 높다는 점에서, 다양성이 찬미되어야 한다는 가르침을 주기 위해 학교 교과 과정에 다문화주의를 장려하는 책들을 추가하는 것이 바람직하다고 말하고 있다. 따라서 글의 주제를 상징적으로 표현한 what they see should be what they get(그들이 보는 것이 그들이 얻을 수 있는 것이어야 한다)이 의미하는 것은 ④ '학생들은 교실의 다양성을 반영한 책들을 접할 수 있어야 한다'이다.

[오답분석] ①, ②, ⑤은 글에서 언급된 내용이 아니다. ③은 글의 일부만을 다루고 있는 오답이다.

[해석] 과거에, 학생 세대들은 민족적으로 다양한 등장인물들을 주연으로 하는 극히 일부의 책들과 함께 자랐고, 그들 중 다수가 인종적인 감수성 없이 묘사되었다. 오늘날에는, 학교들이 학생들에게 다른 문화들에 대한 지식을 전달할 필요성을 점점 더 인식하고 있으며, 그 결과 다문화주의를 장려하는 책들을 교과 과정에 추가하고 있다. 한 예로, Mem Fox(멤 폭스)의 <네가 누구이더라도>는 비록 전 세계 아이들이 매우 달라 보일 수 있는 삶을 살지라도, 그들이 모두 같은 감정을 가진다는 사실을 설명한다. 이와 같은 책들은 아이들에게 다양성이 우려되기보다는 찬미되어야 한다는 것을 가르치는데, 이는 세상이 과거 어느 때보다 더 세계화되었고 다양한 배경을 가진 반 친구가 있을 가능성이 높은 점을 고려한다면 귀중한 교훈이다. 이런 측면에서, 현대의 학생들이 이용할 수 있는 문학에 관한 한, 그들이 보는 것이 그들이 얻을 수 있는 것이어야 한다.

① 아이들은 다양한 문화들에 의해 쉽게 혼란을 겪는다.
② 학교들은 현대 작가들의 작품을 구입해야 한다.
③ 다문화주의를 장려하는 문학은 현재 학교에서 흔하다.
④ 학생들은 교실의 다양성을 반영한 책들을 접할 수 있어야 한다.
⑤ 학급은 다양한 민족적 배경을 가진 학생들을 항상 포함해야 한다.

[어휘] fraction 일부, 부분 feature 주연으로 하다 ethnically 민족적으로 racially 인종적으로 insensitive 감수성이 없는, 둔감한 impart 전달하다 multiculturalism 다문화주의 [선택지] have access to ~을 접할 수 있다

[구문분석] **[8행]** As one example, *Whoever You Are* by Mem Fox illustrates **the fact** [that (**although** children around the world lead lives that may seem very different), they all have the same emotions].

→ [that ~ emotions]는 the fact와 동격을 이루는 명사절이다.

→ (although ~ different)는 접속사 although(비록 ~일지라도)가 이끄는 양보의 부사절이다.

22 요지 파악하기   정답 ⑤

[해설] 글의 첫 문장과 마지막 문장에서 자기 사업을 하려는 사람이 스스로를 파악하지 못하고 있으면 상당한 어려움을 겪을 것이므로 자기 인식의 정확성을 높이는 것이 중요하다는 요지가 제시되어 있고, 화자가 진행하는 워크숍을 예로 들어 설명하고 있다. 따라서 이 글의 요지로 가장 적절한 것은 ⑤이다.

[오답분석] ①의 정기적인 사업과 훈련은 글에서 언급된 내용이 아니다. ②의 사업 운영에 유리한 특정한 성격의 특징은 글에서 언급된 내용이 아니다.

[해석] 사업을 시작하려고 계획 중인 사람들을 위해 내가 진행하는 워크숍에서, 나는 그들이 그들 자신을 정확히 인지하게 하는 활동을 진행하는 것이 유용하다고 생각한다. 나는 각각의 사람에게 다양한 성격 특성을 묘사하는 형용사 목록을 백지 몇 장과 함께 나눠준다. 종이 한 장에, 나는 그들 자신에게 적용될 것 같은 몇몇 형용사들을 적을 것을 요청한다. 그 후, 그들은 집단 내 다른 구성원들에 대해 같은 것을 해야 한다. 이 단계가 끝나면, 나는 각각의 사람에게 다음 순서로: "공개된", "숨겨진", 그리고 "맹점"의 세 개의 범주들이 있는 목록을 만들게 한다. 각각의 참여자들에게 있어서, 첫 번째 범주는 본인의 목록과 또 다른 집단 구성원의 그것(목록)에 포함되어 있던 특징들이다; 두 번째 것은 참여자들이 스스로를 묘사하기 위해 사용했지만 다른 사람들은 사용하지 않았던 단어들을 포함한다; 그리고 세 번째 것은 그들을 묘사하기 위해 집단의 다른 구성원들에 의해 선정된 형용사들만 있다. 이렇게 하는 것은 집단 구성원들의 그들 스스로에 대한 인식의 정확도에 통찰력을 제공한다. 만약 당신이 스스로에 대해 잘 모른다면, 당신이 당신의 사업을 하려 할 때 상당한 어려움을 겪을 가능성이 있다.

[어휘] adjective 형용사 character 성격 trait 특성 blind spot 맹점 accuracy 정확도 be one's own boss 본인의 사업을 하다

[구문분석] **[18행]** ①[**If** you do not know yourself], ②[you are likely to experience significant difficulties] ③[**when** you try to be your own boss].

→ ②[you ~ difficulties]가 문장의 주절이고, ①[If ~ yourself]는 접속사 if(만약 ~한다면)가 이끄는 조건의 부사절, ③[when ~ boss]는 접속사 when(~할 때)이 이끄는 시간의 부사절이다.

23 주제 파악하기   정답 ③

[해설] 어떤 상황을 충분히 다루지 못하거나 모호한 표현이 있는 법을 이해하기 위해 입법자의 근본적인 목적을 확인해야 하는데, 이 과정에는 법안 통과와 관련된 문서들에 대한 분석을 필요로 한다는 내용의 글이다. 남성 시민들만 투표권을 가졌던 시기에 만들어진 법률의 "모든 남성"이라는 표현은, 입법 취지를 고려했을 때 현대의 판사들은 여성을 포함한 "모든 유권자"를 의미하는 것으로 이해할 것이라는 예시를 통해 내용을 뒷받침하고 있다. 따라서 이 글의 주제로 가장 적절한 것은 ③ '판사에 의해 법이 이해되는 방식'이다.

[오답분석] ①은 글의 일부만을 다루고 있는 오답이다. ②의 명확한 법률 제정의 중요성은 글에서 언급된 내용이 아니다. ④의 새로운 법안은 글에서 언급된 내용이 아니다. ⑤의 현실적인 목표는 글에서 언급되고 있지 않다.

[해석] 어떤 상황을 충분히 다루지 못하거나 모호한 표현이 있는 법을 이해하려고 시도할 때 판사들은 보통 입법 취지를 고려할 것이 요구된다. 이것은 법원에 의

해 처리되고 있는 문제에 대한 법의 적용을 결정하기 위해 법을 만든 사람들의 근본적인 목적을 확인하는 것을 수반한다. 대부분의 경우, 그 과정은 논의 기록, 처음의 초안과 같은 법안 통과와 관련된 문서들에 대한 분석을 필요로 한다. 그 정보는 그 후 그 법과 그 법이 명확하게 중점을 두지 않은 문제 간의 관계를 이해하는 데 이용될 것이다. 예를 들어, 오직 남성 시민들만 투표할 자격이 있었던 시기에 만들어진 법안에는 선거 참여에 관한 특정한 권리를 부여할 때 "모든 남성"이라는 표현을 포함했을 수 있다. 관련 문서를 검토하고 그것이 투표할 권리가 있는 누구에게나 적용하도록 의도되었던 것을 발견한 현대의 판사는 그 표현을 여성들을 포함한 "모든 유권자"를 의미하는 것으로 이해할 것이다.

① 모호하게 표현된 법률과 관련된 문제들
② 명확한 법률 제정의 중요성
③ 판사에 의해 법이 이해되는 방식
④ 새로운 법안을 만드는 데 있어서 판사의 역할
⑤ 입법자들이 현실적인 목표를 가져야 하는 이유

 address 다루다 ambiguous 모호한 legislative intent 입법 취지
underlying 근본적인 passage 통과 legislation 법안, 법률
explicitly 명확하게 eligible 자격이 있는 relevant 관련된
cast a ballot 투표하다 [선택지] legislator 입법자

구문분석
[1행] [**When** attempting to understand a law that does not fully address a situation or that has ambiguous language], judges are often required to consider legislative intent.

→ [When ~ language]는 분사구문의 의미를 분명하게 하기 위해 부사절 접속사(when)가 분사 앞에 온 형태이다.

---

24 제목 파악하기 정답 ④

해설 첫 두 문장과 마지막 문장으로 미루어 보아 과도한 위생이 사람의 면역 체계를 오히려 약화시킬 수 있으며, 미생물에 건강한 방식으로 노출되는 것이 면역 체계에 좋다는 내용의 글이다. 미생물이 부족한 환경에서 자란 사람들이 알레르기와 천식과 같은 병에 걸릴 가능성이 더 높다는 위생 가설을 예로 들어 설명하고 있다. 따라서 글의 제목으로 가장 적절한 것은 ④ '강한 면역력을 위한 미생물 받아들이기'이다.

오답분석 ②은 글에서 언급되고 있지 않다. ③, ⑤는 미생물에 노출되는 것이 더 회복력 있는 면역 체계를 가질 수 있게 해준다는 글의 내용과 반대되는 내용이므로 오답이다.

해석 위생은 하수 시스템의 발달 이후로 상당히 개선되었다. 그럼에도 불구하고, 일부 연구는 아이들은 박테리아, 곰팡이, 바이러스에 대한 건강한 노출로부터 이익을 얻을 수 있음에 따라 과도한 위생이 실제로는 사람들의 면역 체계를 약화시킬 수 있다고 시사한다. 이러한 개념을 뒷받침하는 위생 가설은 이러한 미생물이 부족한 환경에서 자라는 사람들이 알레르기와 천식과 같은 병에 걸릴 가능성이 더 높다고 제시한다. 그들의 면역 체계는 다양한 미생물과 접촉하지 않았기 때문에 자연이 의도한 대로 길들여지지 않았다. 이 과정은 한 사람의 건강과 전염병과 싸우는 그들의 신체의 능력에 도움이 된다. 반대로, 만약 아이들이 다양한 미생물을 접하게 하는 방식으로 자란다면, 즉 그들이 밖에서 놀고 조금 더러워지는 것이 허락된다면, 그들의 면역 체계는 더 회복력을 가질 수 있다.

① 무균 환경이 존재할 수 있을까?
② 강한 면역 체계가 작용하는 방식
③ 미생물을 제거하는 방법
④ 강한 면역력을 위한 미생물 받아들이기
⑤ 청결 유지: 건강의 비결

---

 hygiene 위생 sewage system 하수 시스템 impair 약화시키다
immune system 면역 체계 fungi 곰팡이 contract ~에 걸리다
asthma 천식 condition 길들이다, 조절하다 microorganism 미생물
instrumental 도움이 되는, 중요한 infection 전염병, 감염
microscopic organism 미생물 resilient 회복력 있는
[선택지] germ-free 무균의 embrace 받아들이다

구문분석
[4행] ~ impair people's immune systems, [with children
(명사)
possibly benefiting from a healthy exposure to bacteria,
(현재분사)
fungi, and viruses].

→ [with ~ viruses]는 'with + 명사(구) + 분사' 형태의 분사구문으로, '~함에 따라'라는 의미로 해석한다.

---

25 도표 정보 파악하기 정답 ③

해설 종이 제품과 금속의 제조에서 발생하는 오수를 합한 비율은 37퍼센트로, 화학 제품 및 석유 제조에서 발생하는 오수 비율인 36퍼센트보다 높으므로 수치의 비교 표현이 잘못 반영되었다. 따라서 도표의 내용과 일치하지 않는 것은 ③이다.

해석

스페인에서의 점오염원별 오수 발생 분석

점오염원별 오수 발생   제조업에서의 오수 발생

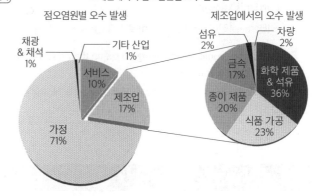

위의 원그래프들은 스페인에서의 점오염원별 오수 발생의 분석을 보여주는데, 특히 제조업에 중점을 두고 있다. ① 점오염원별 오수 발생의 경우, 가정이 다른 모든 부문을 합친 것보다 더 많은 오수 비율을 차지한다. ② 제조업에서 나온 오수 중 종이 제품 제조에서 발생된 비율이 차량 제조에서 발생된 비율의 10배에 이른다. ③ 종이 제품과 금속의 제조에서 발생된 오수 비율을 합한 것은 화학 제품 및 석유 제조에서 발생된 그것(오수 비율)보다 여전히 낮다. ④ 제조업에서의 2위와 3위의 오수 발생원 간 격차는 3퍼센트에 불과하지만 1위와 2위 간 차이는 10퍼센트 이상이다. ⑤ 섬유와 차량 제조 둘 다에서 발생된 오수의 비율은 각각 2퍼센트에 불과하다.

 breakdown 분석, 분류 wastewater 오수 generation 발생
point source 점오염원(특정한 지점에서 발생하는 오염원) petroleum 석유
account for (부분·비율을) 차지하다 proportion 비율

구문분석
[11행] ~ is [**still** lower than] that generated in chemical and petroleum manufacturing.

→ [still lower than]은 '비교급 + than'(~보다 -한)의 형태로 비교를 나타내는 구문으로, still는 비교급을 강조한다.

26 세부 정보 파악하기 정답 ④

해설 in 1914, Carrier and several of his coworkers quit their positions at the manufacturer를 통해 Willis Carrier가 사직한 것임을 알 수 있는데, ④은 해고되었다고 일부 정보를 잘못 나타냈으므로, 글의 내용과 일치하지 않는 것은 ④이다.

해석 1876년 뉴욕 Angola에서 태어난 엔지니어 Willis Carrier(윌리스 캐리어)는 현대식 에어컨 시스템의 발명가로 알려져 있다. Carrier는 1901년 Cornell 대학교에서 공학 석사 학위를 받고 졸업했다. 1902년, 그는 습한 날씨 동안 출판사가 겪는 문제들을 해결하기 위해 공기의 수분 함량을 줄일 수 있는 장치를 만들었다. 그리고 나서 그는 그것을 개선하는 데 몇 년을 보냈다. Carrier는 1906년에 습도를 낮추면서 동시에 공기를 차갑게 할 수 있는 시스템에 대한 특허를 받았다. 이 기간 동안, 그는 Buffalo Forge Company라는 회사에 엔지니어로 고용되었다. 그러나 1914년 Carrier와 그의 동료 몇몇은 그 제조 회사에서 사직했다. 그들은 에어컨을 생산하는 그들만의 사업체를 차리기 위해 그들이 저축한 돈을 모았다. Carrier Corporation은 나아가 뉴욕에서 가장 큰 기업 중 하나가 되었고, 지금은 다국적 기업이다.

어휘 master's degree 석사 학위 address 해결하다 humid 습한 patent 특허 humidity 습도 quit one's position 사직하다 pool 모으다 multinational 다국적의

구문분석
[1행] [Born in Angola, New York in 1876], engineer Willis Carrier is known ~
→ [Born ~ 1876]는 과거분사(Born)로 시작하는 수동형 분사구문이다.

[14행] They pooled their saving [to set up their own business producing air conditioners].
→ [to ~ conditioners]는 to부정사의 부사적 용법으로, 목적을 의미한다.

27 안내문 정보 파악하기 정답 ④

해설 추가 정보와 관련된 부분인 The top 10 entrants will also receive thorough feedback from our renowned editors를 통해 상위 10명의 참가자들 모두 편집자의 피드백을 받을 수 있음을 알 수 있으므로, 글의 내용과 일치하지 않는 것은 ④이다.

해석
공상 과학 단편 소설 공모전
모든 공상 과학 소설 작가 분들께 알립니다! 여러분의 창의력을 뽐내고, 출판되고 상을 탈 수 있는 기회를 얻기 위해 공상 과학 단편 소설을 <Future Worlds Literary Magazine>에 제출하세요!

마감일: 11월 22일 오전 10시

응모작
· 2,000단어 이상일 수 없음
· 참가자당 한 개의 제출물
· 이전에 출판된 적이 없어야 함

심사 기준
· 줄거리
· 배경과 분위기
· 주제

상품
· 1위: 잡지에 소설 게재, 100달러

· 2위: 무료 연간 잡지 구독권, 50달러
(상위 10명의 참가자들은 저희의 유명 편집자로부터 꼼꼼한 피드백을 받을 것입니다.)
* 제출은 www.futureworldslitmag.com에서 온라인상으로 이루어져야 합니다.

어휘 show off 뽐내다, 과시하다 submission 응모작, 제출(물) entrant 참가자 theme 주제 thorough 꼼꼼한, 철저한

구문분석
[4행] ~ for a chance ①[to be published] and ②[(to) win a prize]!
→ 앞의 명사 a chance를 수식하는 형용사적 용법(~할)으로 쓰인 to부정사구 [to be published]와 ②[win a prize]는 등위접속사 and로 연결된 병렬 구조로, 두 번째 to는 생략되었다.

28 안내문 정보 파악하기 정답 ⑤

해설 추가 정보와 관련된 부분인 New parts or accessories can be purchased at any Sense One store or online ~을 통해 새 부품 또는 부속품을 모든 Sense One 매장 또는 온라인에서 구입할 수 있음을 알 수 있으므로, 글의 내용과 일치하는 것은 ⑤이다.

해석
Sense One 가상 현실 헤드셋
사용 방법:
1. 기기를 머리에 씁니다.
2. 수동 조작기를 사용하여 Sense One을 켭니다.
3. 화면의 설치 안내에 따릅니다.
4. 게임 스테이션에 연결합니다.

주의:
- 어지러움을 느끼시면 사용하지 마십시오.
- 기기를 고온이나 습기에 노출하지 마십시오.
- 물이나 세정제로 기기를 청소하지 마십시오; 마른 천으로 닦으십시오.
- Sense One은 12세 미만의 어린이에 의해 사용될 수 없습니다.

새 부품 또는 부속품은 모든 Sense One 매장 또는 www.sense1vr.com에서 온라인으로 구입하실 수 있습니다.
헤드셋에 문제가 있으면 수신자 부담 번호 1-800-439-9900으로 전화 주십시오.

어휘 virtual 가상의 cleaning agent 세정제 accessory 부속품 toll-free number 수신자 부담 번호

구문분석
[14행] New parts or accessories [can be purchased] at any Sense One store or online at www.sense1vr.com.
→ [can be purchased]는 조동사(can)가 있는 '조동사 + be + p.p.' 형태의 수동태이다.

29 어법상 틀린 것 찾기 정답 ⑤

해설 what 뒤에는 완전한 절이 올 수 없고 what은 앞에 있는 명사를 수식할 수 없다. 완전한 절을 이끌면서 an understanding과 동격을 나타내는 접속사는 명사절 접속사 that이므로, ⑤의 what을 that으로 고쳐야 한다.

(오답분석) ①은 선행사 the skill을 수식하는 형용사절을 이끄는 주격 관계대명사 that을 사용한 것은 어법상 적절하다. ②은 동사 became의 주격 보어 자리이므로 형용사 역할을 하는 분사 associated를 사용한 것은 어법상 적절하다. ③은 동명사의 의미상 주어 Crafts와 동명사가 '공예품들에 꼬리표가 붙여지다'라는 의미의 수동 관계이므로, 동명사의 수동형 being labeled를 사용한 것은 어법상 적절하다. ④은 주어 자리에 복수명사 these works가 왔으므로 복수동사 have를 사용한 것은 어법상 적절하다.

(해석) 서양 문화권에서는 몇몇 공예품들의 아름다움과 그것들을 만드는 데 쓰인 기술에도 불구하고, 공예품들이 회화 작품이나 조각품보다는 덜 세련된 것으로 묘사되어 왔다. 르네상스 이전에, 예술과 공예는 작은 공장에서 일하며 예술적 창의력보다는 그들의 손재주의 우수성에 중점을 두었던, 제작자들의 더 규모가 큰 산업의 별개의 부분으로 여겨졌다. 이는 르네상스와 함께 변했는데, 이 시기에 예술가들은 각각의 예술 작품이 그 예술가 개인의 천재성의 발산물로 여겨지면서, 그들의 작품과 더 많이 결부되었다. 공예품들은 여성들의 작품 혹은 민속 문화라는 꼬리표가 붙여짐으로써 더욱 평가 절하되었고, 대량 생산은 많은 장인들을 생산 과정에서 완전히 배제시켰다. 보다 최근에는, 이러한 예술 작품들과 공예품들이 전체로서 재평가되고 있다. 이는 그것들(공예품들)의 미적 우수성과 제작자들의 기술에 대한 재평가 때문만이 아니라, 이러한 공예품들이 주류 예술에서 배제된 소외 집단들에게 발언권을 준다는 것에 대한 이해 때문이기도 하다.

(어휘) craft 공예 sophisticated 세련된, 정교한 emanation 발산물, 분출 devalue 평가 절하하다 mass 대량의 artisan 장인 reappraisal 재평가 marginalized 소외된 mainstream 주류

(구문분석) [16행] This is due **not only** ①[to a reappraisal of their aesthetic qualities and the skill of the makers], **but** ②[to an understanding that these crafts give a voice to marginalized groups that were excluded from mainstream art].
→ ①[to ~ makers]와 ②[to ~ art]는 상관접속사 not only A but (also) B로 연결된 병렬 구조이다.

---

30 어휘 적절성 파악하기 정답 ①

(해석) (A) 나무늘보는 색맹을 야기하는 유전 질환과 느린 소화 속도로 인해 움직임이 느릴 수밖에 없다고 설명하고 있다. 따라서 '그들이 보다 더 활동적이게 되는 것을 싫어한다는 생각은 근거 없는 통념'이라는 의미가 되어야 하므로 reluctant(싫어하는)가 문맥상 적절하다.

(B) 나무늘보들의 신체적 특성을 고려할 때, 조금이라도 다른 수가 있을지 의심스럽다는 의미가 되어야 하므로 doubtful(의심스러운)이 문맥상 적절하다.

(C) 나무늘보들은 많이 먹을 수 없어서 쓸 수 있는 에너지가 제한되어 있기 때문에 그들이 하는 모든 것은 에너지를 되도록 많이 비축하는 것에 초점을 맞추게 만든다는 의미가 되어야 하므로 saving(비축하는 것)이 문맥상 적절하다.

따라서 정답으로 가장 적절한 것은 ①이다.

(오답분석) (A)의 willing, (B)의 apparent, (C)의 wasting은 모두 정답 어휘와 문맥상 반대되는 의미이므로 오답이다.

(해석) 영장류나 유대류로의 잘못된 분류에서부터 지능에 대한 근거 없는 의견까지 나무늘보들에 대한 많은 오해가 있지만, 그것들이 보다 더 활동적이게 되는 것을 (A) 싫어한다는, 즉 단지 게으르다는 생각은 가장 큰 근거 없는 통념이다. 사실, 그들의 신체적 특성을 고려할 때, 그것들이 조금이라도 다른 수가 있을지 (B) 의심스럽다. 우선, 나무늘보는 "간상체 단색형 색각"이라고 불리는 희귀한 유전 질환으로 인해 색맹인데, 이는 나무 꼭대기를 빠른 속도로 돌아다니는 것을, 심지어 그렇게 할 수 있는 생명체들에게 있어서도 어렵게 만들고,

나무늘보는 그럴 수 없다. 이는 대부분 그것들의 느린 소화 속도 때문이다 (나무늘보는 빠르게 가득 차고 배부른 상태를 지속적으로 유지하는 네 개의 위가 있는데, 전문가들은 잎 한 장이 소화되는 데 한 달까지 걸릴 수 있다고 말한다). 그들은 그다지 많이 먹을 수 없기 때문에, 그것들이 쓸 수 있는 에너지의 양은 대단히 제한되어 있고, 이는 그들이 하는 모든 것은 그것(에너지)을 가능한 한 많이 (C) 비축하는 것에 맞춰진다.

	(A)		(B)		(C)
①	싫어하는	……	의심스러운	……	비축하는 것
②	싫어하는	……	분명한	……	비축하는 것
③	싫어하는	……	분명한	……	낭비하는 것
④	기꺼이 하는	……	의심스러운	……	낭비하는 것
⑤	기꺼이 하는	……	분명한	……	낭비하는 것

(어휘) misconception 오해 sloth 나무늘보 abound 많이 있다 misclassification 잘못된 분류 primate 영장류 unfounded 근거 없는 myth 근거 없는 통념, 신화 condition 질환 rod 간상체(눈의 망막에 있는 막대 모양의 세포) monochromacy 단색형 색각 navigate 돌아다니다 gear toward ~에 맞추다

(구문분석) [16행] ~ is seriously limited, making everything they do

사역동사 ━━━ 목적어
geared toward saving as much of it as possible.
목적격 보어
→ 분사 자리에 온 사역동사 making의 목적어로 everything they do, 목적격 보어로 과거분사 geared가 쓰였다. 사역동사는 목적어와 목적격 보어가 수동 관계일 때, 목적격 보어로 과거분사를 취한다.

---

31 빈칸 추론하기 정답 ②

(해설) 주제문을 재진술하는 빈칸 문장에서 권리가 헌법에 확립된 경우에도, 구체적인 조치가 취해지지 않는 한 일부 사람들에게는 '무엇'할 수도 있다고 했다. 글의 초반에서 권리는 행사되기 전까지 개념일 뿐이라 하고, 빈칸 앞 문장에서 정부가 장애를 가진 학생들을 위한 특별 시설들을 설치하지 않으면 의무인 학교 교육을 제공받지 못한다는 예시를 들고 있다. 따라서 빈칸에는 ② '실현되지 않은'이 와서 일부 사람들에게는 권리가 실현되지 않을 수도 있다는 의미가 되어야 한다.

(오답분석) ③은 헌법상으로 권리가 보장되었다는 글의 내용과 반대되는 내용이므로 오답이다.

(해석) 헌법상의 권리는 모든 국민에게 적용되는 권리이다. 그러나 권리는 그것이 실제로 행사될 때까지 종이 위에 고이 간직된 개념으로 남는다. 그러므로, 정부는 모든 사람들이 그들의 권리에 대해 알고 있고 모두가 그것을 이용할 동등한 능력을 가지고 있다는 것을 확실히 하는 것이 중요하다. 교육받을 권리를 예로 들어보자. 많은 나라에서, 모든 아이들에게 학교 교육에 접근할 권리를 제공하는 것은 의무이다. 대부분의 경우, 이것은 무상 공립 학교 체제를 구축함으로써 이루어진다. 하지만 장애를 가진 사람들은 수업에 참여하는 것이 불가능할 수도 있다. 만약 정부가 이러한 학생들의 필요를 충족시키는 특별 시설을 설립하지 않는다면, 그들은 법에 따라 권리로 부여받은 교육을 받을 수 없을 것이다. 다시 말해, 권리가 헌법에 굳건히 확립된 경우조차도, 구체적인 조치가 취해지지 않는 한 일부 사람들에게는 실현되지 않은 채로 남아 있을 수 있다는 것이다.

① 제정된	② 실현되지 않은
③ 금지된	④ 지정된
⑤ 관련된	

어휘 **constitutional** 헌법상의 **applicable to** ~에 적용되는
enshrine 고이 간직하다 **requirement** 의무, 필수 조건
entitle to ~에게 권리를 부여하다 **entrench** 굳건히 확립하다
[선택지] **institute** 제정하다 **designate** 지정하다

구문분석

[15행] ~ it can remain unrealized for some people [**unless** specific actions are taken].

→ [unless ~ taken]은 접속사 unless(~하지 않는 한)가 이끄는 조건의 부사절이다.

---

32 빈칸 추론하기 정답 ②

해설 주제문에 해당하는 빈칸 문장에서 '무엇'이 위협받고 있다는 것이 최근 몇십 년 사이에 과학계에 분명해졌다고 하고, 이어서 과학자의 연구가 특정 의제에 따르지 않는 경우 그 과학자가 처벌을 받고 있다고 했다. 글의 후반에서는 한 과학자가 투명하고, 종합적이고, 편파적이지 않은 연구를 추구했다는 이유로 해고되는 현실에 직면해 있다고 했다. 따라서 빈칸에는 ② '과학 연구의 독립'이 와서 과학 연구의 독립이 위협받고 있다는 것이 분명해졌다는 의미가 되어야 한다.

오답분석 ①은 브라질 대통령의 의견에 모순되는 연구 결과를 발표했다는 이유로 한 과학자가 이사직에서 해임되었다는 글의 내용과 반대되는 내용이므로 오답이다. ③의 정확한 증거의 고려, ⑤의 과학적 지식을 재구성하려는 시도는 글의 내용과 관련이 없다. ④의 정부의 무조건적인 지원은 글에서 언급되고 있지 않다.

해석 그리스 철학자 Aristotle(아리스토텔레스)의 사상에서 유래된 과학적 탐구 모델은 진정한 지식을 얻는 것을 기준으로 만들었다. 그러나 최근 몇십 년 사이에 과학 연구의 독립이 위협받고 있다는 것이 과학계에 분명해졌다. 브라질의 한 과학 기관의 이사직에서 해임된 일류 과학자의 경우가 그러했듯이, 과학자들은 그들의 연구가 특정 의제에 따르지 않으면 그로 인해 처벌을 받고 있다. 그 과학자는 공개적으로 대통령의 의견에 동의하지 않았고 아마존이 늘어난 삼림 벌채로 인해 불타고 있었다는 증거를 제시하는 데 도움을 주었는데, 그것은 화재 건수가 역사적 평균 범위 내에 있다는 정부의 주장에 모순되었다. 이 생태계 문제에 대한 연구를 발표하는 것을 도왔던 생태학 전문가 Erika Berenguer(에리카 베렝게르)는 그녀와 다른 연구진들이 그 해고에 충격을 받았으며 향후 응징이 두려웠다고 말했다. 전 세계의 다른 과학자들처럼, 그녀는 투명하고, 종합적이고, 편파적이지 않은 연구를 추구했다는 이유로 해고되는 현실에 직면해 있다.

① 전통적 권력자의 지침
② 과학 연구의 독립
③ 정확한 증거의 고려
④ 정부의 무조건적인 지원
⑤ 과학 지식을 재구성하려는 시도

어휘 **inquiry** 탐구, 연구 **derive from** ~에서 유래하다 **directorship** 이사직
deforestation 삼림 벌채 **contradict** ~에 모순되다 **ecological** 생태계의
dismissal 해고 **transparent** 투명한 **unbiased** 편파적이지 않은, 공정한
[선택지] **authority figure** 권력자 **unconditional** 무조건적인

구문분석

[6행] ~ if it does not conform to certain agendas, [**as** was the case] with a top scientist ~
　　　　　　　　　　　　　　　　　　　　　　　동사 주어

→ [as ~ case]는 as(~하듯이) 뒤에서 주어와 동사가 도치되어 '동사(was) + 주어(the case)'의 어순으로 쓰인 구조이다.

---

33 빈칸 추론하기 정답 ④

해설 글의 중반에서 인간은 최고의 결정을 내리기 위한 모든 논리적 사실들과 잠재적인 오류에 대해 아는 것이 현실적으로 불가능하다고 했고, 글의 후반에서는 인간은 몇 가지 중요한 요구들만을 충족시키는 선택을 내리는 것이 더 현명할 것이라고 했다. 따라서 주제문에 해당하는 빈칸에는 ④ '특정 기준을 충족하는 결정을 내린다'가 와서 우리는 최적의 선택을 하지 않고도 특정 기준을 충족하는 결정을 내릴지도 모른다는 의미가 되어야 한다.

오답분석 ①은 인간이 시간 제약, 불완전한 정보, 또는 부족한 정신적 능력과 같은 한계로 인해 제한된 합리성을 가지고 판단을 한다는 글의 내용과 반대되는 내용이므로 오답이다.

해석 우리는 최선의 선택을 하지 않고도 특정 기준을 충족하는 결정을 내릴지도 모른다. 경제학에서는, 우리가 "그런대로 괜찮은" 것을 받아들인다는 생각이 제한된 합리성 이론으로 설명되는데, 이는 인간은 가능한 최선의 선택을 내리는 것이 그들에게 이익이 되므로 그렇게 하는 합리적인 존재라는 믿음과 모순된다. 완전히 합리적이기 위해서, 그 믿음은 인간은 어떤 상황에 대한 모든 논리적 사실들을 알고 그것들을 의사 결정 과정에 적용해야 한다고 주장한다. 그들은 또한 그들의 논리에서의 실수를 바로잡기 위해 모든 잠재적인 오류에 대해 알아야 할 것이다. 이것은 현실적이지 않기 때문에, 제한된 합리성 이론은 시간 제약, 불완전한 정보, 또는 부족한 정신적 능력과 같은 요소들을 지적한다. 우리 대부분은 매일 고려해야 할 것들이 많지만, 이러한 한계들은 그렇게 하는 것을 불가능하게 만든다. 그저 몇 가지 중요한 요구들을 충족시키는 데 실패하지 않는 웬만한 선택을 하는 것이 더 현명할 것이다.

① 자료 부족 때문에 판단을 미룬다
② 불가능한 결과를 선호한다
③ 결과에 상관없이 선택을 거부한다
④ 특정 기준을 충족하는 결정을 내린다
⑤ 기존 계획의 대안을 찾는다

어휘 **optimal** 최선의, 최적의 **bounded rationality** 제한된 합리성
contradict 모순되다, 반박하다 **fallacy** 오류 **constraint** 제약
insufficient 부족한 **sensible** 현명한 **tolerable** 웬만한, 꽤 괜찮은
[선택지] **criteria** 기준 **arrangement** 계획, 배열

구문분석

[4행] ~ which contradicts **the belief** [that humans are **logical beings** (who make the best possible decisions because it is in their self-interest to do **so**)].

→ [that ~ so]는 the belief와 동격을 이루는 명사절이다.

→ (who ~ so)는 선행사 logical beings를 수식하며, 주격 관계대명사 who가 이끄는 관계대명사절이다.

→ so는 앞의 make the best possible decisions를 가리킨다.

[16행] **It** would be more sensible [**to make** tolerable choices
　　　　가주어　　　　　　　　　　　　　　　　진주어(to부정사구)
that just don't fail to meet some important needs].

→ 가주어 it이 길이가 긴 진주어 to부정사구 [to ~ needs] 대신 주어 자리에 쓰인 형태이다.

---

34 빈칸 추론하기 정답 ⑤

해설 철학자 Karl Popper가 과학적 이론에 관찰에 근거한 귀납주의가 아닌 과학자들의 예측 후에 관찰을 통해 이를 반박하는 연역적 접근법을 선택해야 한다고 주장하는 내용의 글이다. 빈칸 앞에서 과거에 관찰에 의해 모든 백조는 흰색이라고 내려졌던 결론은 호주에서 흑조류가 발견되면서 거짓으로 밝혀졌다

고 하며 귀납주의의 반증가능성에 대해 설명하고 있다. 따라서 주제문을 재진술하는 빈칸에는 ⑤ '관찰에 근거한 이론들은 나중에 반증될 위험이 있다'가 와서 관찰에 근거한 이론들이 이후 반증될 위험이 있어, 이는 그것들을 실제 과학보다는 사이비 과학 수준에 두게 된다는 의미가 되어야 한다.

[오답분석] ①, ③, ④은 글에서 언급되고 있지 않다. ②은 흑조류의 발견이라는 경험적 증거로 인해 모든 백조가 흰색이라는 이론이 거짓으로 밝혀졌다는 글의 내용과 반대되는 내용이므로 오답이다.

[해석] <과학적 발견의 논리>에서, 철학자 Karl Popper(칼 포퍼)는 귀납주의에 비판적이었는데, 이것은 가설을 입증하고 이론을 발전시키기 위해 관찰이나 경험적 증거를 사용하는 것을 수반한다. 그는 이 접근법이 효과적이지 않고 비과학적이라고 주장했는데, 언제 어디서나 이용할 수 있는 증거가 제한적이고 모든 관찰이 우리의 기존 이해에 의해 영향을 받을 것이기 때문이다. 그는 과학자들이 먼저 예측을 한 다음 관찰을 통해 반박을 시도하는 연역적 접근법의 채택을 통해 과학이 더 잘 실현될 것이라고 믿었다. 이런 식으로, 낡은 이론들은 폐기되고 최신 이론들이 도입될 수 있어, 과학을 진보하게 한다. 그는 반증가능성이라고 알려진 이 원리를, 과거에 유럽 과학자들에 의해 모든 백조는 흰색이라는 결론이 내려졌다고 지적함으로써 설명했다. 그 후 호주에서 흑조류가 발견되면서 그 이론은 거짓으로 밝혀졌기 때문에 Popper가 느끼기에 관찰에 근거한 이론들은 나중에 반증될 위험이 있어, 이는 그것들을 실제 과학보다는 사이비 과학 수준에 두게 된다.

① 이론들은 과학자들이 다뤄야 할 새로운 문제들을 만들었다
② 이론들은 경험적 증거를 사용하여 그것들의 진실성을 평가받았다
③ 연역적 추론을 사용하여 나타낸 이론들은 결론에 이르지 못했다
④ 이론들은 단순히 사건을 묘사하거나 예측하는 것 이상을 했다
⑤ 관찰에 근거한 이론들은 나중에 반증될 위험이 있다

[어휘] inductivism 귀납주의 empirical 경험적인 verify 입증하다
hypothesis 가설 deductive 연역적인 refute 반박하다
discard 폐기하다 [선택지] tackle 다루다 integrity 진실성
inconclusive 결론에 이르지 못하는 disprove 반증하다

[구문분석] [9행] ~ through the adoption of **a deductive approach**, [in which scientists made predictions first and then attempted to refute them through observation].
→ [in ~ observation]은 선행사 a deductive approach를 수식하며, '전치사 + 관계대명사' in which가 이끄는 관계대명사절이다.

35 흐름과 관계 없는 문장 찾기 정답 ④

[해설] 장애인들의 스포츠 참여가 사회 전반에 장애인들이 사실 많은 역량을 가졌다는 것을 가르칠 수 있고, 이를 통해 장애인들에 대한 인식이 개선되고 장애인들이 차별 없이 주류 사회에 통합될 수 있다는 내용의 글이다. 그런데 ④은 휠체어 농구 선수들이 견고하면서도 가벼운 소재로 제작된 특수 휠체어를 사용한다는 내용이므로 주제에서 벗어나 있어 글의 흐름과 무관하다.

[오답분석] ②의 This stigma는 '장애인들이 다른 사람들에게 의존하거나 거동이 매우 제한적이라는 생각'을 가리키고 있으므로 ① 뒤에 오는 것이 자연스럽다. ③은 However를 통해 ②의 내용에 대한 반전 설명을 하고 있으므로 ② 뒤에 오는 것이 적절하다. ⑤의 this knowledge는 '장애인들이 사실 많은 역량을 가졌다'는 것을 가리키고 있으므로 ③ 뒤에 오는 것이 자연스럽다.

[해석] 스포츠에의 참여는 장애인의 삶에 큰 영향을 미칠 수 있는데, 단지 운동과 관련된 신체적 이익 때문만은 아니다. ① 신체가 건강한 사회 구성원들은 장애에 대한 한정된 지식을 가지고 있을 수 있는데, 이는 그들이 장애를 가진 모든 사람들이 다른 사람들에게 의존하거나 그들의 거동에 있어서 매우 제한적이

라고 생각하게 할 수 있다. ② 이러한 오명은 공동체 생활의 많은 측면에서 장애인의 미포함으로 이어져서 장애인들에게서 기회를 박탈할 수 있다. ③ 하지만, 휠체어 농구와 같은 스포츠는 장애가 있는 사람들이 사실 많은 역량을 가졌다는 것을 사회 전반에 가르치는 데 도움을 줄 수 있다. (④ 이러한 형태의 농구를 하는 선수들은 견고하면서도 가벼운 소재로 제작된 특수 휠체어를 사용한다.) ⑤ 이러한 지식을 통해, 신체 건강한 사람들은 한 사람의 장애를 대수롭지 않게 여길 수 있게 되어, 장애인들이 차별받지 않고 주류 사회에 통합될 수 있게 해줄 것이다.

[어휘] able-bodied 신체가 건강한 mobility 거동, 이동성 stigma 오명, 낙인
deprive A of B A에게서 B를 박탈하다 capable 역량이 있는
see past 대수롭지 않게 여기다, 무시하다 integrate 통합하다
discriminate 차별하다

[구문분석] [7행] This stigma can lead to the non-inclusion of disabled people in many aspects of community life, [depriving them of opportunities].
→ [depriving ~ opportunities]는 앞의 절에 대한 결과를 나타내는 분사구문으로, 분사구문의 주어가 주절의 주어(This stigma)와 같아서 생략되었다.

36 글의 순서 배열하기 정답 ③

[해설] 주어진 글은 감정이 종종 압도적으로 느껴지는 경우가 있으며, 그 이유에 대한 과학적 설명이 있다는 주제를 제시한다. (B)는 감정이 체내의 감각과 반응을 촉발시킨다는 내용이고 주어진 글의 마지막에서 감정이 종종 압도적으로 느껴지는 이유에 대한 과학적 설명이 있다고 했으므로 그 뒤에 와야 한다. (C)의 These collections of reactions(이러한 반응들의 집합)는 (B)의 '그것만의 뚜렷한 변화들의 집합'을 가리키므로 (B) 바로 다음에 오는 것이 적절하다. (A)의 The person은 (C)의 화를 낸다고 가정한 '어떤 사람'을 가리키므로 (C) 바로 다음에 오는 것이 적절하다. 따라서 글의 순서로 가장 적절한 것은 ③ (B) - (C) - (A)이다.

[해석] 감정은 종종 압도적으로 느껴질 수 있는데, 이것이 왜 그러한지에 대한 과학적인 설명이 있다.
(B) 감정은 신체적인 수준에서 사람들에게 영향을 미칠 수 있으며, 체내의 감각과 반응을 촉발시킨다. 사람이 행복할 때 미소를 짓듯이, 각각의 감정은 그것만의 뚜렷한 변화들의 집합을 야기한다.
(C) 이러한 반응들의 집합은 연구자들에 의해 "정서 프로그램"으로 불리고, 각각은 감정들에 의해 야기되는 다양한 골격계 및 신경계 반응, 발성, 그리고 얼굴 표정으로 이루어져 있다. 그래서, 예를 들어 만약 어떤 사람이 화가 나면, 그들은 주먹을 꽉 쥐고, 이를 갈고, 껄끄러운 감각을 경험하고, 노려봄을 보여줄지도 모른다.
(A) 그 사람은 또한 아드레날린과 노르아드레날린과 같은 화학 물질이 밀려드는데, 그들이 부당함을 당했다고 느껴 그들의 신체가 싸움을 준비하기 때문이다. 비슷하지만 유일무이한 과정은 다른 감정들에서도 일어날 수 있으며, 사람에 따라 정도가 다를 수 있다.

[어휘] overwhelming 압도적인, 저항하기 어려운 surge 밀려듦, 치밀어 오름
injustice 부당함 trigger 촉발시키다 sensation 감각, 느낌
affect 정서, 감정 skeletal 골격의 clench 꽉 쥐다 prickly 껄끄러운
glare 노려봄

[1행] Emotions can often feel overwhelming, and there's a scientific explanation **for** [why this is the case].

→ [why ~ case]는 의문사 why가 이끄는 명사절로, 전치사 for의 목적어 역할을 한다.

---

37 글의 순서 배열하기 정답 ②

(해설) 주어진 글은 호기심이 뇌의 작용이기도 하다는 주제를 제시한다. (B)는 익숙하지 않거나 예상치 못한 것을 맞닥뜨렸을 때, 뇌는 그 상황을 더 잘 다루기 위해 정보를 수집하려 한다는 내용이고, 주어진 글 마지막에 호기심은 뇌의 작용이라고 했으므로 그 뒤에 와야 한다. (A)의 this state(이 상태)는 (B)의 '호기심 상태'를 가리키므로 (B) 바로 다음에 오는 것이 적절하다. (C)의 도파민이 분비되면 사람은 무언가를 알아낸 후에 기쁨을 느끼게 된다는 내용은 (A)의 마지막에서 정보를 수집하고 지능을 높이는 것이 뇌의 보상 체계를 활성화한다는 내용과 관련이 있으므로 (A) 뒤에 와야 한다. 따라서 글의 순서로 가장 적절한 것은 ② (B) - (A) - (C)이다.

(해석) 호기심은 사람을 혁신하게 하고, 새로운 지식을 흡수하게 하며, 문제들에 대한 해결책을 찾도록 할 뿐만 아니라 뇌의 작용이기도 하다.
(B) 익숙하지 않거나 예상치 못한 것을 맞닥뜨렸을 때, 뇌는 그 상황을 더 잘 다루기 위해 정보를 수집하려고 한다. 그것은(뇌) 불편한 환경에 반응하는 뇌 영역이 활성화되는 상태인 "호기심 상태"에 들어가는데, 그것이 지식 부족을 인식하기 때문이다.
(A) 이 상태에서, 뇌가 최적의 수준으로 기능하기 때문에, 사람은 감각 기관을 이용해 조사하고 답을 찾을 준비가 되어 있다. 이러한 정보를 수집하고 지능을 높이는 것은 매우 만족을 준다. 실제로, 그것은 뇌의 보상 체계를 활성화시킨다.
(C) 도파민이 분비되면, 그 결과 사람은 무언가를 알아낸 후에 기쁨을 느끼게 된다. 이 생물학적 과정은 초기 인류가 그들의 목적을 달성하기 위한 새로운 방법을 발견했던 것처럼 그들의 생존에 필수적이었고, 그래서 이 특성은 오늘날 사람들에게 유전되어 우리가 이 호기심의 전통을 계속하게 해주었다.

(어휘) apart from ~뿐만 아니라 mechanism 작용, 기제 sensory 감각의
boost 높이다, 증진시키다 gratifying 만족을 주는 navigate 다루다
figure out ~을 알아내다 integral 필수적인 inherit 유전하다
inquisitiveness 호기심 많음

 [7행] [Gathering this information and boosting intelligence] is highly gratifying.

→ [Gathering ~ intelligence]는 문장의 주어 역할을 하는 동명사구이다.

---

38 주어진 문장의 위치 찾기 정답 ⑤

(해설) 주어진 문장에 명시적 단서가 없는 경우에는 글의 흐름이 끊기는 곳을 찾아야 한다. ⑤ 앞까지는 비타민 C가 각종 질병을 막는다는 Linus Pauling의 주장이 근거가 없음에도 불구하고 사람들이 받아들이고 있다는 내용이 이어지다가 ⑤ 뒤 문장에서 신체는 어쨌든 비타민 C를 필요로 한다는 내용이 나오고 있다. ⑤ 뒤 문장의 After all(어쨌든)이 무엇에 대한 부연 설명을 의도한 것인지 ⑤ 앞 문장에서는 나오지 않고 ⑤ 앞뒤의 내용이 유기적으로 연결되지 않는다는 점을 통해 글의 흐름이 끊겼음을 알 수 있다. 따라서 주어진 문장이 들어가기에 가장 적절한 곳은 ⑤이다.

(오답분석) ①~③은 비타민 C에 대한 Linus Pauling의 주장과 그의 태도에 대한 내용이므로 주어진 문장보다 앞에 와야 한다. ④ 뒤 문장은 As a result를 통해 ③ 뒤 문장의 결과를 나타내므로, 사이에 다른 문장이 들어올 수 없다.

(해석) 노벨상 2회 수상자인 Linus Pauling(라이너스 폴링) 덕분에 비타민 C가 감기를 예방하는 데 도움을 줄 수 있다는 생각이 지속되고 있다. (①) 그의 1970년 저서 <비타민 C와 감기>에서 그는 감기부터 암에 이르기까지 모든 것을 막기 위해 매일 3천 밀리그램의 매우 많은 용량의 비타민 C를 섭취할 것을 권고했다. (②) 말할 필요도 없이, 당시 많은 의학 전문가들은 알려진 과학적 사실에 근거하지 않은 Pauling의 주장을 무시했다. (③) 어떤 비판을 받든, Pauling은 그의 주장을 고수했고, 많은 사람들에게 그것의 신빙성을 납득시켰다. (④) 그 결과, 비록 오늘날 대다수의 연구자들은 더 이상 비타민 C가 심각한 질병에 대해 어떠한 효능도 가지고 있지 않다고 생각하지만 비타민의 효능을 둘러싼 믿음은 완전히 사라지지 않았다. (⑤ 대부분의 사람들은 감기와 독감의 유행 시기에 비타민 C 보충제를 섭취하는 것이 우리의 면역력을 증진시키고 증상들을 완화하는 데 도움이 된다고 여전히 믿는다.) 어쨌든, 비록 대부분의 사람들이 단순히 그들이 먹는 음식으로부터 비타민 C를 충분히 섭취하기는 하지만 신체는 건강을 유지하기 위해 비타민 C를 필요로 한다.

(어휘) supplement 보충제 boost 증진시키다 immunity 면역력
alleviate 완화하다 persist 지속되다 common cold (보통) 감기
ward off 막다 dismissive 무시하는 credibility 신빙성

 [12행] [**No matter what** criticism he received], Pauling maintained his claim, ~

→ [No ~ received]는 no matter what(=whatever)이 이끄는 양보의 부사절이다.

---

39 주어진 문장의 위치 찾기 정답 ④

(해설) 주어진 문장의 Blockchain transactions take place automatically, however(그러나 블록체인 거래는 자동으로 이뤄진다)로 보아, 주어진 문장 앞에는 블록체인을 통하지 않은 거래에 대한 내용이 나와야 한다는 것을 알 수 있다. 이 글에서는 ①~② 뒤 문장까지 블록체인의 문제점에 대해서 소개하다가 ③ 뒤 문장에서는 블록체인을 통하지 않는 전통적인 은행 업무의 예시를 언급하고 있다. 게다가 ④ 앞뒤 문장이 유기적으로 연결되지 않는다는 점을 통해 글의 흐름이 끊겼음을 알 수 있다. 따라서 주어진 문장이 들어가기에 가장 적절한 곳은 ④이다.

(오답분석) ④ 뒤 문장의 a decentralized financial system은 주어진 문장의 '전 세계의 수많은 네트워크에 그 정보가 기록되고 저장되는 것'을 가리키므로 주어진 문장보다 뒤에 있어야 한다. ⑤ 뒤 문장의 This(이것는)는 ④ 뒤 문장의 '어떠한 문제에 대해서든 아무도 책임을 질 수 없는 것'을 가리키므로 주어진 문장이 들어가기에 적절하지 않다.

(해석) 블록체인 또는 분산원장기술(DLT)은 비트코인과 같은 암호화폐에 사용되는 기본적인 소프트웨어이다. (①) 블록체인의 광범위한 시행이 이뤄질 수 있기 전에 해결되어야 할 다양한 법적 문제들이 있는데, 이 중 거의 대부분이 DLT가 분산되어 있다는 사실과 관련이 있다. (②) 이는 금융 기관이나 정부와 같은 특별히 지정된 기관에 대한 필요성 없이 거래가 발생하고 기록될 수 있다는 의미이다. (③) 전통적인 은행 업무에서는, 예를 들어, 어떤 사람이 미국에서 헝가리로 전자 송금을 하려는 경우, 미국에 있는 은행은 그 거래를 처리할 때 모든 법적 규정들이 준수되었는지 확실히 할 책임이 있을 것이다. (④ 그러나 블록체인 거래는 그 정보들이 전 세계의 수많은 네트워크에 디지털 방식으로 기록되고 저장되면서, 자동으로 이루어진다.) 무엇보다도 분산된 금융시스템으로는 발생할 수 있는 어떠한 문제에 대해서든 아무도 책임을 질 수 없다. (⑤)

이는 어떤 거래에나 일반적으로 적용되었을 법과 규제들을 근본적으로 무효화하여 법적 우려를 야기한다.

 blockchain 블록체인, 공공 거래 장부 **transaction** 거래 **distributed ledger technology** 분산원장기술(데이터 블록들을 체인처럼 연결하는 기술) **underlying** 기본적인 **wide-scale** 광범위한 **decentralize** 분산시키다 **designated** 지정된 **authority** 기관, 당국 **wire transfer** 전자 송금 **invalidate** 무효화하다

구문분석

[19행] This essentially invalidates **the laws and regulations** [that would typically apply to any given transaction], creating legal concerns.

→ [that ~ transaction]은 선행사 the laws and regulations를 수식하며, 주격 관계대명사 that이 이끄는 관계대명사절이다.

---

40 요약문 완성하기   정답 ⑤

해설 글의 중반부에서 회의주의는 사람이 어떤 것에 확신할 때까지 열린 마음을 갖도록 하는 특성이라고 했고, 글의 후반부에서는 냉소주의를 보이는 사람들은 모든 증거를 거부하고 그들만의 견해를 고집하는 경향이 있다고 했다. 따라서 to stay open minded를 possibility로, to reject ~ views를 unwilling으로 바꾸어 표현한 ⑤이 정답이다.

오답분석 회의주의는 사람이 어떤 것에 확신할 때까지 열린 마음을 갖도록 하는 특성이라고 했으므로 ①, ②의 certainty는 (A)에 들어갈 단어로 적절하지 않다. 냉소주의를 보이는 사람들은 모든 증거를 거부하고 그들만의 견해를 고집하는 경향이 있다고 했으므로 ④의 eager는 (B)에 들어갈 단어로 적절하지 않다.

해석 비록 회의주의와 냉소주의가 모두 사람의 태도와 관련이 있지만, 그것들은 여러모로 서로 다른 별개의 개념이다. 회의주의는 어떤 것이 사실인지 혹은 유용한지 의심하거나 의문을 제기하는 것을 포함한다. 예를 들어, 어떤 사람은 특정한 주장에 대해 회의감을 표현할 수 있다; 따라서 그들은 그것을 정확한 것으로 받아들이기를 주저한다. 그들은 발언의 결정에 초점을 맞춰서 특정한 가정에 이의를 제기할 수 있다. 회의적이라는 것은 사람이 설득력 있는 증거와 주장에 흔들릴 수 없다는 것을 의미하지는 않는다. 오히려, 회의주의는 한 사람이 어떤 것에 대해 확신할 때까지 열린 마음을 갖도록 하는 특성이다. 반면, 냉소주의는 부정적으로 여겨지는데, 이러한 태도를 보이는 사람들은 모든 증거를 거부하고 그들의 견해를 고집하는 경향이 있기 때문이다. 냉소적인 사람은 이기심이 사람들의 행동 이면에 있는 주요 동기라고 믿는다. 따라서, 그들은 다른 사람들에 의해 만들어진 것들을 성공할 수 없거나 잘못된 이유로 만들어진 것으로 보는 경향이 있다.

↓

회의주의는 사상과 이론들을 신뢰할 (A) 가능성을 가지고 그것들에 이의를 제기하는 것이 특징인 반면, 냉소주의는 어떤 사람이 타인에게 믿음을 갖기를 (B) 꺼릴 때 나타난다.

	(A)	(B)
①	확실성	할 것 같지 않은
②	확실성	저항하는
③	책임감	절박한
④	가능성	열심인
⑤	가능성	꺼리는

어휘 **skepticism** 회의주의 **cynicism** 냉소주의 **pertain to** ~와 관련이 있다 **hesitant** 주저하는 **dispute** 이의를 제기하다, 반박하다 **assumption** 가정 **sway** 흔들다 **compelling** 설득력 있는 **motivator** 동기

구문분석

[13행] On the other hand, cynicism is regarded negatively [**since** people (who demonstrate this attitude) tend to reject all evidence and remain stubborn in their views].

→ [since ~ views]는 접속사 since(~ 때문에)가 이끄는 이유의 부사절이다. 주격 관계대명사절 (who ~ attitude)는 선행사 people을 수식한다.

41~42 장문 독해 1

해석 행동주의라는 개념은 개들에 대한 연구를 통해 그의 실험 대상의 행동이 (a) 조건화될 수 있다는 것을 알게 되었던 Ivan Pavlov(이반 파블로프)와 함께 시작되었다; 종소리를 음식과 관련지어 생각하게 한 뒤에, 그 개들은 음식 그 자체보다는 종소리에 반응하여 침을 흘리곤 했고, 이는 기대가 결과를 낳을 수 있음을 암시했다. 오래 지나지 않아, 20세기 초에 심리학자 John Watson(존 왓슨)과 B. F. Skinner(B. F. 스키너)가 처벌과 보상이 인간의 행동에 어떻게 영향을 미칠 수 있는지를 보여주면서 그 개념을 확장했다. [41]그들은 우리가 우리의 환경에서 무엇을 경험하는지가 우리가 어떻게 행동할지를 결정한다고 주장했다. 그 이후로, 그 이론은 교육자들이 학생들을 학업적으로 성과를 거두게 하고 올바르게 행동하도록 (b) 장려하는 방법을 이해하게끔 돕는 데 있어 필수적이게 되었다.

[41]교실 환경에서, 좋은 성적이나 적절한 행동에 대해 긍정적 강화를 반복적으로 받는 학생들은 선생님의 반응이 그들이 한 행동의 결과라는 것을 이해하게 된다. 긍정적 강화는, 예를 들자면 칭찬이나 작은 간식과 같이, 학생이 (c) 탐난다고 여기며 다시 받고 싶어 하는 어떤 형태의 것으로든 나타날 수 있다. 그러나 교사는 긍정적 강화에 있어 (d) 자주 변하는(→일관성을 갖는) 것이 필요한데, [42]교사가 기대했던 보상을 주지 않을 때 학생은 수행할 동기가 있다고 느끼지 못할 수 있기 때문이다. 또한, 높은 점수나 긍정적인 행동에 반응하지 못하는 것은 그 학생에게 그들의 성과의 우수성이 (e) 가치가 없다는 걸 의미할 수 있음에 따라 부정적인 강화의 한 형태로 이해될 수 있어서, 그들이 탁월함에 대한 추구를 그만두게 만들 수 있다.

어휘 **behaviorism** 행동주의 **subject** 실험 대상 **condition** 조건화하다, 길들이다 **reinforcement** 강화 **inconsistent** 자주 변하는 **withhold** 주지 않다, 보류하다 **signify** 의미하다 **abandon** 그만두다 **pursuit** 추구 [선택지] **by design** 의도적으로, 고의로 **intrinsic** 내재적인 **relevant** 유의미한, 적절한

구문분석

[11행] They argued that [what we experience in our environment] determines how we act.

→ [what ~ environment]는 의문사 what(무엇)이 이끄는 명사절로, that절의 주어 역할을 한다.

---

41 제목 파악하기   정답 ①

해설 Ivan Pavlov의 행동주의를 바탕으로 우리가 어떤 환경에서 무엇을 경험하는지가 이렇게 행동할지를 결정한다고 밝힌 John Watson과 B. F. Skinner의 이론을 다룬 글로, 학생의 좋은 성적이나 적절한 행동에 대해 긍정적 강화를 반복하면 학생은 긍정적인 행동을 계속할 동기를 얻을 것이라는 점을 예로 들어 설명하고 있다. 따라서 글의 제목으로 가장 적절한 것은 ① '의도적으로 교육하기: 학생들에게 동기 부여하기 위해 보상을 사용하기'이다.

오답분석 ②은 긍정적 강화가 제때 이루어지지 않을 경우 학생이 긍정적 행동을 계속할 동기를 느끼지 못할 수 있다고 한 글의 내용과 반대되는 내용이므로 오답이다. ③, ④은 글의 핵심 소재 Behaviorism을 사용하여 헷갈리게 하는 오답이다.

⑤은 글에서 언급되고 있지 않다.

(해석) ① 의도적으로 교육하기: 학생들에게 동기 부여하기 위해 보상을 사용하기
② 보상 체계가 내재적 동기를 어떻게 해치는가
③ 행동주의: 구식인가 아니면 여전히 유의미한가?
④ 학교 내 행동주의의 기원 추적
⑤ 교실에서 부정적 강화가 사용되어야 하는가?

42 어휘 적절성 파악하기 정답 ④

(해설) 교사가 기대했던 보상을 주지 않을 때 학생은 수행할 동기가 있다고 느끼지 못할 수 있기 때문에, 교사가 긍정적 강화에 있어 일관성을 갖는 것이 필요하다는 맥락이 되어야 하므로 ④의 inconsistent(자주 변하는)를 그와 반대되는 의미의 consistent(일관성을 갖는)와 같은 어휘로 바꾸어야 문맥상 적절하다.

(오답분석) ①은 개들이 음식 그 자체보다는 종소리에 반응하여 침을 흘리곤 했던 실험을 통해 실험 대상의 행동이 조건화될 수 있다는 것을 알았다는 문맥이 되어야 하므로 conditioned가 오는 것이 적절하다.

43~45 장문 독해 2

(해석) (A) 그날은 대학교 연기 수업의 첫날이었고, 나는 매우 자신감이 넘쳤다. 교실을 둘러보면서, 나는 다른 학생들 중 누구도 나만큼 많은 경험을 가진 학생은 없을 것이라고 생각했다. 나는 고등학교 때 이미 여러 작품에 참여했기 때문에 이 수업이 쉬울 것이며 거의 노력하지 않고 교수님에게 깊은 인상을 줄 것이라고 확신했다. 그는 매우 성공한 배우였기 때문에 나는 (a)그에게 내 실력을 보여줄 생각에 들떴다.

(C) 교수님께서 우리가 무엇을 배울지에 대해 말씀하셨을 때, 나는 수업이 주로 다양한 연기 기법을 소개하는 데 중점을 둘 것이라는 말을 듣고 짜증이 났다. 연기할 기회가 많지 않을 것이다. [45]나는 강의가 나에게 어떻게 도움을 줄지 모르겠어서 교수님 말씀에 거의 귀 기울이지 않았다. 내가 우리들은 우리의 기술을 쓸 기회가 절대 없을 것이라고 생각했던 바로 그때, (c)그가 우리의 첫 번째 연기 과제를 발표했고 우리에게 연습할 장면을 주었다.

(B) 나는 무척 많이 준비해야 할 이유를 알지 못했다. (b)그가 대략적으로 설명했던 장면들은 쉬웠고, 나는 이미 그 장면들에 익숙했다. 기회가 주어졌을 때, 나는 내 능력이 얼마나 뛰어난지 증명해 보일 것이라고 알고 있었다. 수업 당일, 교수님은 연기할 학생들 그룹을 부르기 시작했다. 나는 그들 중 많은 이들이 대사를 완벽하게 외웠다는 데 깜짝 놀랐고, 그 장면이 그런 식으로 연기되는 걸 본 적이 없었다. 나는 초조해지기 시작했다.

(D) 교수님께서 나를 부르셨고, [44]같은 반 다른 학생과 함께 한 장면을 읽으라고 말씀하셨다. 나는 내 심장이 더 빨리 뛰기 시작하고 머리가 하얘지는 것을 느낄 수 있었다. [44]내 파트너는 (d)그의 대사를 다 외웠는데, 나는 내 대사를 잊어버렸다. 우리가 끝마쳤을 때, 나는 아마 틀림없이 내가 학급에서 누구보다도 가장 못했다는 것을 알고 있었다. 비록 내가 선생님께 큰 인상을 남길 것을 당연하다고 여겼지만, 나는 (e)그가 실망했음을 알 수 있었다.

(어휘) **assume** 당연하다고 여기다, 추정하다 **positive** 확신하는, 긍정적인
outline 대략적으로 설명하다 **advanced** 뛰어난, 상급의
be blown away 깜짝 놀라다 **line** 대사
go blank 머리가 하얘지다, 아무 생각이 안 나다 **easily** 아마 틀림없이

(구문분석) [2행] [Looking around the room], I assumed that none of the other students had as much experience as I did.

→ [Looking ~ room]은 '~하면서'라는 의미의 분사구문으로, 분사구문의 주어가 주절의 주어(I)와 같아서 생략되었다.

43 글의 순서 배열하기 정답 ②

(해설) (A)는 화자가 대학교 첫 연기 수업에 참여하며, 고등학생 때 많은 연기를 했던 자기 자신에 대해 자만하는 내용이다. (C)는 화자가 교수님이 연기 수업에서 주로 여러 연기 기법을 소개하는 데 중점을 두어 짜증이 났고 수업에 집중하지 않는 모습을 보여주는 내용이므로, 자신의 연기 능력에 자만하고 교수님께 연기를 보여줄 생각에 들떠 하는 (A) 뒤에 와야 한다. (B)는 화자가 연기 과제를 많이 준비할 필요성을 못 느껴, 제대로 준비하지 않은 채 연기 수업에 참여했다고 했으므로, 교수님이 첫 번째 연기 과제를 발표하고 연습할 장면을 주었다는 (C) 뒤에 와야 한다. (D)에서 교수님이 화자를 불러 다른 학생과 함께 장면을 읽으라고 한 것은 (B)에서 교수님이 연기할 여러 학생들을 부르기 시작하고 그들이 너무 잘해 화자가 초조해진 이후의 일이므로, (B) 다음에 오는 것이 적절하다. 따라서 글의 순서로 가장 적절한 것은 ② (C) - (B) - (D)이다.

44 지칭 대상 파악하기 정답 ④

(해설) (a), (b), (c), (e)는 모두 교수를 가리키지만 (d)는 화자와 함께 연기했던 파트너인 다른 학생을 가리키므로, ④이 정답이다.

45 세부 정보 파악하기 정답 ④

(해설) (C)의 I didn't see how the lectures would help me, so I rarely listened to my professor를 통해 강의가 도움이 될 것 같지 않아 교수의 말에 화자가 귀 기울이지 않았음을 알 수 있는데, ④은 연기 수업을 열심히 들었다고 정보를 잘못 나타냈으므로 글의 내용과 일치하지 않는 것은 ④이다.

문제집 p.86

18 목적 파악하기   정답 ②

(해설) 글의 중간 이후에서 ask(문의하다)를 이용해 신제품 사진 촬영을 위해 커피숍을 하루 종일 빌릴 수 있는지 문의하고 있으므로 정답은 ②이다.

(해석) Pearson 씨께,

제 이름은 Henry Lowell입니다. 저는 TM Media에서 일하고 있으며 제 고객 중 하나는 Topper Coffee Beans입니다. 그것은 인기를 얻고 있는 새로운 지역 사업체입니다. 그 회사는 신제품 사진 촬영을 하고 싶어서, 저에게 장소를 찾는 것을 도와달라고 부탁했습니다. 저는 당신의 아름다운 커피숍이 완벽할 것이라고 생각합니다. 촬영을 위해 저희가 당신의 매장을 하루 종일 빌릴 수 있을지 문의드리고자 합니다. 당신은 충분한 보상을 받을 것이고, 게다가 그것은 당신의 매장을 위한 무료 광고가 될 수 있을 것입니다. 당신의 답변을 기다리겠습니다. 당신의 배려에 감사드립니다.

Henry Lowell 드림

(어휘) ample 충분한   compensation 보상

(구문분석)
[5행] The company would like a photo shoot for their newest product and <u>asked</u> <u>me</u> <u>to help</u> them find a location.
                                      동사   목적어   목적격 보어

→ 동사 asked의 목적어로 me, 목적격 보어로 to부정사 to help가 쓰였다.

19 심경 파악하기   정답 ③

(해설) 심경은 간접적으로 표현된다. 글의 첫 문장의 I thought the rainy weather reflected my mood perfectly를 통해 'I'가 시험 성적으로 인해 우울해하는 것을 알 수 있고, 마지막 문장의 She always knew exactly how to brighten my day를 통해 Jenny의 따뜻함에 위로를 받았다는 것을 알 수 있으므로, 'I'의 심경 변화로 가장 적절한 것은 ③이다.

(해석) 비 오는 날씨가 내 기분을 완벽히 반영했다는 생각이 들었다. 나는 학교에서 집으로 천천히 걸어가면서 심지어 비가 쏟아지는 것을 신경 쓰지도 않았다. 그것은 내가 받아본 최악의 시험 성적이었고, 나는 그것에 지나치게 집착하는 것을 멈출 수 없었다. 내가 길모퉁이를 돌았을 때, 나는 "Sarah!"라고 외치는 목소리를 들었다. 내 이웃인 Jonny가 현관에 서서 니에게 손을 흔들고 있었디. "오늘 하루는 어땠어?"라고 그녀가 물었다. "수업 시간에 좀 속상해 보이더라. 들어올래?" 나는 고개를 끄덕이고 그녀를 따라 안으로 들어갔고, Jenny는 김이 나는 핫초콜릿 한 잔과 함께 내게 몸을 녹일 수 있는 부드러운 담요를 건네주었다. 나는 Jenny에게 따뜻하게 미소를 지어 보였다. 그녀는 항상 내 하루를 밝혀줄 방법을 정확히 알고 있었다.

① 겁먹은 → 활기 넘치는
② 짜증이 난 → 의기양양한
③ 우울한 → 위로를 받은
④ 흥미 있어 하는 → 무관심한
⑤ 부러워하는 → 즐거워하는

(어휘) reflect 반영하다   obsess over ~에 지나치게 집착하다   porch 현관   brighten 밝히다   [선택지] triumphant 의기양양한   indifferent 무관심한

(구문분석)
[6행] My neighbor Jenny was standing on her porch, [waving me over].

→ [waving me over]는 '~하면서'라는 의미의 분사구문으로, 분사구문의 주어가 주절의 주어(My neighbor Jenny)와 같아서 생략되었다.

20 주장 파악하기   정답 ⑤

(해설) 글의 첫 세 문장에서 경외심을 불러일으키는 사건이 일어났을 때 사람들과 공유하기 위해 그 순간 감상하기를 포기하고 소셜 네트워크에 자신의 삶을 전시하고 사교적으로 관련된 상태를 유지하려 한다면, 주변에서 일어나는 일을 완전하게 받아들일 수 없다고 주장하고 있으므로 정답은 ⑤이다.

(오답분석) ②, ③은 소셜 미디어에서 자신의 삶을 전시하고 사교적으로 관련된 상태를 유지하는 데 시간을 쓰지 말아야 한다는 글의 내용과 반대되는 내용을 다루고 있으므로 오답이다.

(해석) 때때로, 당신은 무언가를 카메라에 담을지 아니면 화면의 방해 없이 그것을 볼지 선택해야 하는 딜레마에 직면할 수 있다. 아마 당신은 사람들과 공유하기 위해 경외심을 불러일으키는 어떤 사건을 영상으로 기록한 후 그 순간을 감상하는 것을 넘어가기로 결정한 것에 대해 가벼운 후회를 느낀 적이 있을 것이다. 마치 역할을 맡은 듯, 당신은 친구들을 즐겁게 하는 데 집중하지만, 당신의 삶을 전시하고 사교적으로 관련된 상태를 유지하려는 욕구를 충족시키면서, 당신의 주변에서 일어나는 일을 완전히 "받아들일" 수는 없다. 너무 자주, 개인의 대중적 이미지를 통제하고 계속 관계를 맺고 있으려는 끌림은 사람들이 소셜 네트워크를 통해 프로필과 게시물을 신중하게 엄선하는 데 시간을 쓰게 한다. 이는 개개인이 그들의 실제 현실을 거의 반영하지 못하는 장밋빛 필터를 통해 자신의 삶을 알리는 데 가치를 둠에 따라 그들이 느끼는 어떠한 만족감도 피상적이게 한다.

(어휘) distraction 방해, 산만함   mild 가벼운   pass on 넘어가다, 지나가다   savor 감상하다, 만끽하다   awe-inspiring 경외심을 불러일으키는   showcase 전시하다   draw 끌림   involved 관계를 맺고 있는   prompt ~하게 하다   curate (작품 등을) 엄선하다   contentment 만족   shallow 피상적인, 얕은   rose-tinted 장밋빛의

구문분석

[1행] From time to time, you may face the dilemma of choosing **whether** ① [to capture something on camera] or ② [(to) witness it without the distraction of a screen].

→ to부정사구 ①[to ~ camera]와 ②[witness ~ screen]은 명사절 접속사 whether A or B(A인지 B인지)로 연결된 구조로 두 번째 to는 생략되었다.

[10행] All too often, ①[the draw to control one's public image and remain involved] prompts people to ②[spend their time carefully curating their profiles and posts via social networks].

→ ①[the ~ involved]는 to부정사구(to control ~ image, (to) remain involved)를 포함하며, 전체가 이 문장의 주어인 명사구이다.

→ ②[spend ~ networks]는 spend A (on) v-ing의 형태로, '~하는 데 A(시간)를 쓰다'라는 의미의 동명사 관용 표현이다.

21　밑줄 의미 추론하기　정답 ③

해설 빠르게 성공하기 위해서 에너지가 소진될 정도로 바쁜 생활을 하기보다는 느린 삶을 살며 관계와 건강, 그리고 현재를 살아가는 데 집중하는 것이 오히려 행복이나 성취로 이어질 가능성이 더 크다고 말하고 있다. 따라서 글의 주제를 비유적으로 표현한 move heaven and earth(천지를 움직이다)가 의미하는 것은 ③ '스스로를 지나치게 몰아붙이려고 하다'이다.

오답분석 ①은 글의 핵심 내용이지만 밑줄 친 어구 앞에 don't need to가 있으므로 정답이 될 수 없다.

해석 사람들이 빠른 성공, 더 빠른 기술 그리고 동시에 여러 가지 일을 처리하는 더 효율적인 방법을 원함에 따라, 현대 문화는 속도가 전부다. 사람들이 하나의 업무나 회의에서 그 다음 것으로 끊임없이 서두르기 때문에, 에너지 소진의 위험이 불안하게 다가온다. 무리한 노력을 방지하려면 한 걸음 물러서는 것이 중요하다. 바로 이 시점에 느린 삶이 필요하게 된다. 이 마음가짐의 핵심은 잠시 멈춰서 숨을 고르는 것이 이로운 것이 언제인지를 인지하는 일에 관한 것이다. 그것은 하루 중 모든 시간을 업무로 채우려 항상 노력하지 않는 것을 포함한다. 2천 년보다 더 이전에 Socrates(소크라테스)가 "바쁜 삶의 황량함을 조심하라"라고 현명하게 말하며 깨달았듯이, 더 많은 일을 하는 것이 항상 행복이나 성취로 이어지지는 않지만, 관계, 건강, 현재를 살아가는 것에 집중하는 것은 그럴지도 모른다. 사람들은 성공하기 위해 천지를 움직일 필요는 없다.

① 성공에 대한 새로운 관점을 얻다
② 마지못해 일을 떠맡다
③ 스스로를 지나치게 몰아붙이려고 하다
④ 성취에 방해가 되는 것들을 제거하다
⑤ 누군가를 기쁘게 하기 위해 일하다

어휘 burnout 에너지 소진, 극도의 피로　loom 불안하게 다가오다
overexertion 무리한 노력　catch one's breath 숨을 고르다
engagement 업무, 약속　barrenness 황량함　fulfillment 성취, 이행
move heaven and earth 천지를 움직이다, 백방으로 노력하다
prosper 성공하다　[선택지] with reluctance 마지못해
push oneself too far 스스로를 지나치게 몰아붙이다
for the sake of ~을 위하여　gratify 기쁘게 하다

구문분석

[1행] Modern culture is all about speed, [with people wanting
　　　　　　　　　　　　　　　　　　　　　　명사　　　현재분사
quick success, faster technology, and more effective ways to multitask].

→ [with ~ multitask]는 'with + 명사(구) + 분사' 형태의 분사구문으로, '~하면서'라는 의미로 해석한다.

[12행] ~ doing more does **not always** lead to happiness or fulfillment, but focusing on relationships, health, and living in the present just **might**.

→ not always는 '항상 ~인 것은 아니다'라는 의미로 부분 부정을 나타내는 구문이다.

→ 조동사 might 뒤에는 동사구 lead to happiness or fulfillment가 생략되어 있는데, 앞서 doing ~ fulfillment에서 이미 언급되었기 때문이다.

22　요지 파악하기　정답 ②

해설 글의 첫 두 문장에서 미래 세대에게 현대 기술 활용 능력이 더욱 중요해짐에 따라 기술이 기본 교육의 일부가 되어야 한다고 하고, 이어서 기술이 교육에 통합되면 학습에 많은 도움을 줄 수 있다는 요지가 제시되어 있으므로, 이 글의 요지로 가장 적절한 것은 ②이다.

오답분석 ①은 개인화 교육에 대해서는 글에서 언급하고 있지만 수준별 개인화 교육에 대해서는 언급되고 있지 않다. ③, ④은 글의 일부만을 다루고 있는 오답이다. ⑤의 교사가 수업 방식을 바꿀 필요가 있다는 내용은 글에서 언급되고 있지 않다.

해석 4차 산업혁명의 도래와 함께, 현대 기술을 활용하는 능력이 의사소통이나 비판적 사고와 마찬가지로 필수적인 삶의 기술이 되고 있다. 따라서 기술은 기본 교육의 일부가 되어야 하는데, 특히 미래 세대들은 점점 더 기술에 의존할 것이기 때문이다. 기술을 학습 과정에 통합시키는 것은 학생들에게 사물 인터넷, 증강 현실, 인공 지능과 같은 혁신적인 것들에 의해 규정된 세계에서 그들이 성공할 수 있게 해줄 지식을 제공한다. 게다가 이러한 통합은 교육을 더욱 개인화되고 매력적인 형태로 만들 수 있다. 새로운 기술을 알아보는 것에 바탕을 둔 수업은 참여와 협동에 유익하며, 멀티미디어 학습 환경은 수많은 학습 방식에 부응한다. 예를 들어, 동영상과 이미지는 시각형 학습자의 관심을 끌 수 있는 한편, 스마트 보드와 팟캐스트는 각각 운동 감각형 학습자와 청각형 학습자의 관심을 끌 수 있다.

어휘 advent 도래　incorporate 통합시키다　pupil 학생
Internet of Things 사물 인터넷　integration 통합
personalized 개인화된　engaging 매력적인
cater to ~에 부응하다, ~의 구미에 맞추다　engage 관심을 끌다
kinesthetic 운동 감각의

구문분석

[12행] **A lesson** [that's based on investigating new technologies] is beneficial for participation and cooperation, and ~

→ [that's ~ technologies]는 선행사 A lesson을 수식하며, 주격 관계대명사 that이 이끄는 관계대명사절이다.

23　주제 파악하기　정답 ④

해설 첫 문장으로 미루어 보아 예술 작품의 구성 요소는 창작 당시 사회에 대한 많은 것을 반영할 수 있다는 내용의 글로, 고전주의 예술가들의 작품과 현대 예술가들의 작품들의 주제를 예를 들어 설명하고 있다. 따라서 글의 제목으로 가장 적절한 것은 ④ '문화와 문명이 그 시대의 예술에 미친 영향'이다.

①, ②, ⑤은 글에서 언급되고 있지 않다. ③은 글의 핵심 소재 art와 글에서 언급된 history를 사용했지만, 역사적 흐름에 따라 예술 작품의 주제가 달라졌다는 글의 내용과 관련이 없으므로 오답이다.

(해석) 예술 작품의 구성 요소는 그것의 창작 당시의 사회에 대한 많은 것을 반영할 수 있다. 역사적으로 말하자면, 기원전 5세기부터 기원전 4세기 첫 3분기까지 이르는 고대 그리스 미술사의 한 시기에 해당하는 고전주의 시대의 예술가들은 사람들 그리고 신과 우상에 대한 그들의 헌신을 묘사한 작품을 제작했다. 그 예술적 제작 활동은 보통 그 시기 동안 높이 평가된 신화나 종교에서 유래한 이야기들을 들려주었고, 질서와 문명의 업적에 대한 경외심을 전달했다. 19세기 후반에 주목을 받게 된 현대 예술가들은 이러한 제한된 주제들을 거부하고 대신 사회의 결함에 초점을 맞추고 그들의 가장 내밀한 감정들을 표현했다. 세계대전, 정부 개혁 그리고 기술적 진보와 더불어 시간이 지나면서, 이러한 작품들은 변화와 야만성으로 가득 찬 세상을 더욱더 강조했다.

① 현대 미술에서의 고전주의의 부활
② 급격하게 변화하는 세상 속 시각 예술의 목적
③ 우리의 역사 이해를 변화시키는 예술의 능력
④ 문화와 문명이 그 시대의 예술에 미친 영향
⑤ 고전주의 미술과 현대 미술의 차이점

(어휘) composition 구성 요소   devotion 헌신   idol 우상
be derived from ~에서 유래하다   mythology 신화
hold in high regard 높이 평가하다   reverence 경외심
come to the fore 주목을 받게 되다   innermost 가장 내밀한
fraught ~로 가득 찬   brutality 야만성   [선택지] revival 부활

(구문분석)
[14행] As time progressed, [bringing the World Wars, government reformations, and technological advancements], these pieces increasingly emphasized ~

→ [bringing ~ advancements]는 앞의 부사절과 뒤의 주절 사이에 삽입된 수식어구로, bringing A, B, and C의 구조로 이루어져 있다.

24 제목 파악하기   정답 ⑤

(해설) 반이상향 소설은 장래에 재앙을 조장할 수 있는 문제들에 관해 우리에게 경고하기 위해 쓰였을 뿐 아니라, 마지막 세 문장으로 미루어 보아 독자들이 현실 세계의 문제에 관심을 갖게 만들고, 사회가 강요하는 생각들을 검토하고, 기존의 믿음에 의문을 제기하게 한다는 내용의 글이다. 따라서 제목으로 가장 적절한 것은 ⑤ '어떻게 반이상향 소설이 우리에게 거울을 비추는가'이다.

(오답분석) ①은 글의 소재인 반이상향 소설이 아닌 보통의 문학에 대해 언급하고 있으므로 오답이다. ③은 글에서 반이상향 문학이 다루는 주제를 언급하고는 있지만 그것들이 인기 주제인지는 파악할 수 없으므로 오답이다.

(해석) 가장 주목할 만한 문학 고전들 중 다수는 무서운 미래 세계를 그린다. 이러한 반이상향 소설에서, 사회는 많은 경우 현저한 정치적, 종교적, 또는 생태학적 문제 때문에 붕괴되고 있다. 장래에 재앙을 조장할 수 있는 문제들에 관해 우리에게 경고하기 위해 이러한 작품들이 쓰였다는 것이 널리 인정되고 있다. 그것들은 우리가 조심하지 않으면, 우리의 미래가 마찬가지일 수 있다고 말한다. 그러나 반이상향 소설의 주제는 또한 현재에 대해서도 논평하며, 독자들의 관심을 현실 세계의 문제로 인도하고 개혁이나 어느 정도의 변화를 촉구한다. 그것들은 또한 독자들이 사회가 사람들에게 강요하는 생각들을 검토하고 그들이 이전에 의문을 제기하지 않았을지도 모르는 믿음에 의문을 제기하도록 고무한다. 도덕과 윤리와 같은 주제는 반이상향 소설을 통해 면밀히 조사되고 탐구되어 깊은 생각과 성찰을 불러일으킨다.

① 우리가 읽는 문학이 현대 사회에 영향을 미치는가?
② 미래의 위기: 사회 붕괴를 피하는 방법
③ 문학적 반이상향의 인기 있는 주제
④ 반이상향 문학: 한 장르의 부상
⑤ 어떻게 반이상향 소설이 우리에게 거울을 비추는가

(어휘) prominent 현저한   incite 조장하다, 자극하다   construct 생각, 구성 개념
impose 강요하다   scrutinize 면밀히 조사하다
give rise to ~을 불러일으키다

(구문분석)
[4행] It's widely acknowledged [that pieces such as these are
<small>가주어</small>　　　　　　　　　　　　　　　<small>진주어(that절)</small>
written to warn us about problems that could incite disaster in the time to come].

→ 가주어 it이 길이가 긴 진주어 that절 [that ~ come] 대신 주어 자리에 쓰인 형태이다.

25 도표 정보 파악하기   정답 ④

(해설) 1990년도에 비만으로 분류된 2세에서 5세 유소년의 비율은 11퍼센트로 8퍼센트 미만에 해당하지 않으므로, 수치가 잘못 반영되었다. 따라서 도표의 내용과 일치하지 않는 것은 ④이다.

(해석)
세 연령대별 비만으로 분류되는 미국 유소년

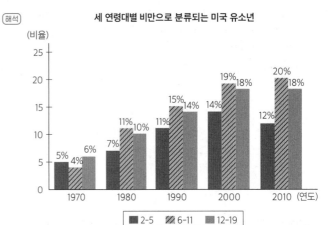

위 그래프는 서로 다른 5개 연도의 세 연령대별 미국 유소년의 비만율을 보여준다. ① 1990년에는, 2세에서 5세 사이 미국 유소년의 비만율은 1970년의 그것(2세에서 5세 사이 미국 유소년의 비만율)보다 두 배 더 높았다. ② 1970년을 제외한 모든 해에, 12세에서 19세 사이 유소년의 비만율은 전 연령대에서 두 번째로 높았다. ③ 6세에서 11세 미국 유소년의 비만율은 1980년, 1990년, 2000년, 그리고 2010년에 세 개 연령대 중 가장 높았고, 2세에서 5세 유소년은 같은 연도에 가장 낮은 비만율을 유지했다. ④ 2000년 이전 연도들에서는, 비만으로 분류된 2세에서 5세 유소년의 비율은 8퍼센트 미만에 머물렀다. ⑤ 한편, 6세에서 11세, 12세에서 19세의 유소년 집단은 1970년부터 2000년까지 매년 증가하는 비율을 보였다.

(어휘) classify 분류하다   obesity 비만   retain 유지하다   categorize 분류하다

(구문분석)
[3행] In 1990, the obesity percentage of American youth aged 2 to 5 was more than [twice as high as] the percentage in 1970.

→ [twice ~ as]는 '배수사 + as + 원급 + as'(~보다 몇 배 더 -한)의 형태로 비교를 나타내는 구문이다.

26 세부 정보 파악하기
정답 ③

(해설) For his final project prior to graduation, he wrote his first screenplay for a film called *The Steamroller and the Violin*을 통해 졸업 전 최종 프로젝트를 위해 그의 첫 영화 대본을 썼음을 알 수 있는데, ③은 졸업 후 첫 영화 대본을 썼다고 일부 정보를 잘못 나타냈으므로 글의 내용과 일치하지 않는 것은 ③이다.

(해석) Andrei Tarkovsky(안드레이 타르코프스키)는 혁신적인 영화 제작 방식으로 전 세계 비평가들로부터 찬사를 받은 유명한 러시아 감독이다. 1932년 자브라이예 마을에서 태어난 Tarkovsky는 1954년 소비에트 영화 학교 VGIK에 입학했다. 졸업 전 마지막 프로젝트를 위해, 그는 <증기기관차와 바이올린>이라는 영화를 위한 그의 첫 영화 대본을 썼는데, 이 영화는 대형 영화사에 의해 매입되었다. 그의 긴 경력 동안, 그는 칸 영화제와 같은 유명한 국제 행사에서 수상했던 많은 장편 영화를 제작했다. 하지만, 종종 공공연히 종교적인 주제를 다룬 그의 작품들은 소련 당국에 의해 심하게 검열되었다. 그 결과, 그는 1980년에 소련을 떠났고, 4년 후, 그는 다시는 돌아가지 않겠다고 공식적으로 선언했다. 이 사건 직후, 그는 폐암 진단을 받았고, 그의 마지막 영화 <희생>이 개봉되었던 해와 같은 해인 1986년에 세상을 떠났다.

(어휘) renowned 유명한   praise 찬사   screenplay 영화 대본, 시나리오
feature-length 장편의   prestigious 유명한   overtly 공공연히
censor 검열하다   diagnose 진단하다

(구문분석)
[6행] ~, he wrote his first screenplay for a film called *The Steamroller and the Violin*, [which was purchased by a major studio].
→ [which ~ studio]는 선행사 *The Steamroller and the Violin*을 수식하는 주격 관계대명사절로, 콤마 뒤에서 계속적 용법으로 쓰였다.

[16행] ~, and he passed away in 1986 — the same **year** [that his final film, *The Sacrifice*, was released].
→ [that ~ released]는 시간을 나타내는 선행사 year를 수식하며, 관계부사 when 대신 that이 쓰인 관계부사절이다.

27 안내문 정보 파악하기
정답 ⑤

(해설) Staff will explain how to report a fire를 통해 직원이 화재 신고 방법을 설명해줄 것임을 알 수 있으므로, 글의 내용과 일치하지 않는 것은 ⑤이다.

(해석)
Stonybrook 캠퍼스 기숙사 소방 훈련
소방 훈련은 미래에 여러분의 생명을 구하는 데 도움을 줄 수 있는 중요한 훈련입니다. 캠퍼스 기숙사에 사는 모든 학생들의 안전을 위해 매우 중요합니다.

일자: 3월 3일(봄 학기), 9월 20일(가을 학기)
시간: 오후 2시

훈련 중
- 기숙사에 있는 모든 학생들은 참여해야 합니다.
  *참여할 수 없다면, 사전에 직원에게 알려주십시오.
- 층별로 부착된 대피 안내도에 따라주십시오.
- 비상계단만 이용하십시오.

훈련 후
- 소방관들이 소화기를 올바르게 사용하는 방법을 설명해줄 것입니다.
- 직원이 화재 신고 방법을 설명해줄 것입니다.

문의 사항이 있으면, 982-1100으로 연락 주십시오.

(어휘) dormitory 기숙사   drill 훈련   in advance 사전에
evacuation plan 대피 안내도   fire extinguisher 소화기

(구문분석)
[15행] Firefighters will explain [how to properly use fire extinguishers].
→ [how ~ extinguishers]는 '~하는 방법'이라는 의미의 'how + to부정사' 구문이다.

28 안내문 정보 파악하기
정답 ④

(해설) All funds will be donated to underprivileged patients of Central Hospital을 통해 모든 기금이 병원의 소외 계층 환자들에게 기부된다는 것을 알 수 있으므로, 글의 내용과 일치하는 것은 ④이다.

(해석)
Central Hospital 자선 경주
Central Hospital은 저희의 첫 번째 연례 자선 경주 계획을 발표하게 되어 기쁩니다. 오셔서 좋은 일을 위해 저희와 함께 운동을 즐기세요!

언제 & 어디서
- 5월 19일 오전 9시
- Carter 근린공원

경주 세부 사항
- 5km 참가비: 25달러
- 10km 참가비: 35달러
- 각 주자들은 무료 티셔츠를 받을 것입니다.
- 각 경주의 1위, 2위, 3위 주자에게는 상이 주어질 것입니다.

기부
- 모든 기금은 Central Hospital의 소외 계층 환자들에게 기부될 것입니다.
- 추가 기부는 경주 현장이나 병원 웹사이트 www.centralhospital.org에서 가능합니다.

참가하시려면 오늘 저희 웹사이트에서 신청하세요!

(어휘) good cause 좋은 일, 대의   underprivileged 소외 계층의, 불우한

(구문분석)
[12행] Prizes [will be given] to the first, second, and third place runners of each race.
→ [will be given]은 조동사 will이 있는 '조동사 + be + p.p.' 형태의 수동태이다.

[20행] Register on our website today [to participate]!
→ [to participate]은 to부정사의 부사적 용법으로, 목적을 나타낸다.

29 어법상 틀린 것 찾기
정답 ③

(해설) be동사는 주격 보어를 취하고 somewhat effectively가 주격 보어 자리에 쓰였는데, 부사는 주격 보어 자리에 올 수 없으므로 ③의 부사 effectively를 형용사 effective로 고쳐야 한다. 참고로, somewhat(어느 정도)은 앞에서 형용사를 수식하는 부사이다.

오답분석 ①은 선행사 processes가 복수명사이므로, 주격 관계대명사 that 뒤에 복수동사 break가 쓰인 것은 어법상 적절하다. ②은 전치사 from 뒤에는 명사 역할을 하는 명사(구)/동명사(구)/대명사 등이 올 수 있으며, 동명사 accumulating을 사용해 동명사 관용 표현 prevent A from v-ing(A가 ~하는 것을 막다)의 형태를 쓴 것은 어법상 적절하다. ④은 문맥상 their가 지칭하는 것이 복수명사 Plastics이므로, 복수대명사 their가 쓰인 것은 어법상 적절하다. ⑤은 조동사 뒤에는 동사원형이 와야 하므로, must 뒤에 동사원형 take가 쓰인 것은 어법상 적절하다.

해석 플라스틱은 자연 분해되지 않는다. 즉, 다른 물질을 분해하는 자연 분해 과정에 굉장히 잘 견딘다. 결과적으로, 플라스틱 용기와 포장재가 쓰레기 매립지와 황무지 지역에 축적되는 것을 막기 위한 방법으로 재활용에 주목하고 있다. 이러한 접근법은 어느 정도 효과가 있는 것으로 입증되었지만, 플라스틱이 무기한으로 재사용될 수 없기 때문에 이상적이지 않다; 겨우 몇 번 재활용된 후에 대부분의 플라스틱은 폐기되어야 할 정도로 질이 저하된다. 플라스틱은 매 차례의 재활용 후에 점점 더 짧아지는 고분자라고 불리는 긴 가닥의 분자로 구성되어 있어서 그것들의 전반적인 질을 떨어뜨린다. 이러한 결점이 바로 대부분의 전문가들이 가까운 미래에 전 세계 정부들이 플라스틱 사용을 줄이거나 심지어 없애기 위한 조치를 취해야 한다는 데 동의하는 이유이다.

어휘 biodegradable 자연 분해되는 resistant to ~에 잘 견디는
decomposition 분해 packaging 포장재 accumulate 축적되다
landfill 쓰레기 매립지 indefinitely 무기한으로 degrade 질이 저하되다
discard 폐기하다 strand 가닥 molecule 분자 polymer 고분자
shortcoming 결점 curtail 줄이다 eliminate 없애다

구문분석
[14행] This shortcoming is [why most experts agree (that governments around the world must take action to curtail or even eliminate the use of plastics in the near future)].
→ [why ~ future]는 의문사 why가 이끄는 명사절로, be동사 is의 주격 보어 역할을 한다.
→ (that ~ future)는 접속사 that이 이끄는 명사절로, 동사 agree의 목적어 역할을 한다.

30 어휘 적절성 파악하기 정답 ④

해설 일반적인 가정에 따르면 어둠은 신체에 잠을 자라는 신호를 보내는데, 연구에서 세 집단은 모두 보름달이 뜨기 직전 날에 잠을 적게 자는 경향을 보였다고 했다. 따라서 보름달이 뜨기 직전이 이른 밤 시간 동안 가장 많은 양의 빛이 지구로 반사되는 날이라는 맥락이 되어야 하므로, ④의 smallest(가장 적은)를 그와 반대되는 의미의 largest(가장 많은)와 같은 단어로 바꾸어야 문맥상 적절하다.

해석 대부분의 기록된 역사 내내 신화와 민속은 인간 경험과 천체 활동 사이의 연관성을 이끌어냈지만, 새로운 연구는 어느 때보다도 더 구체적으로 그 ① 관계를 증명한다. 미국과 아르헨티나의 서로 다른 세 대학의 연구원들은 달의 주기가 토착민들의 휴식 능력에 주목할 만한 영향을 미칠지 알아내기 위해 거의 100명에 가까운 토착민들의 수면 패턴을 ② 추적하려고 팀을 이루었다. 참여자들은 세 개의 통제 집단으로 ③ 무리 지어졌다: 전기가 없는 시골 지역에 사는 사람들, 전기가 있는 시골 지역에 사는 사람들, 그리고 전기가 있는 도시 환경에서 사는 사람들. 이 세 집단 모두 보름달이 뜨기 직전 날들에 잠을 적게 자는 동일한 보편적 경향을 경험했는데, 그때가 이른 밤 시간 동안 ④ 가장 적은 (→가장 많은) 양의 빛이 지구로 반사되는 시기이기 때문이다. 그 결과 어둠이 신체에 잠을 자라는 신호를 보낸다는 일반적인 가정을 따른다. 사실, 인간 생명 작용에서 어느 정도의 보편성을 시사하는 연구 결과들에서, 매우 ⑤ 비슷한 결과들이 마찬가지로 참여했던 워싱턴 주립 대학생 집단에서도 기록되

었다.

어휘 myth 신화 folklore 민속 celestial 천체의 concretely 구체적으로
separate 서로 다른, 별개의 indigenous 토착의 lunar 달의
cluster 무리 짓다 universality 보편성 biology 생명 작용

구문분석
[4행] ①[Researchers (from three separate colleges) (in the
　　　　　　　　　　　주어
US and Argentina)] teamed up to track the sleep patterns of
　　　　　　　　　　　　동사
nearly 100 indigenous people to determine ②[whether lunar cycles have any notable effect on their ability to rest].
→ ①[Researchers ~ Argentina]는 전치사구(from ~ colleges)와 (in ~ Argentina)를 포함하며, 전체가 해당 문장의 주어인 명사구이다.
→ ②[whether ~ rest]는 접속사 whether가 이끄는 명사절로, 동사 determine의 목적어 역할을 한다.

31 빈칸 추론하기 정답 ⑤

해설 주제문에 해당하는 빈칸 문장에서 성격은 우리가 생각하는 것만큼 '어떠하지' 않다고 하고, 글의 후반에서 노화의 영향에 대한 연구는 우리가 더 친절해지고, 젊었던 시절보다 더 이타적인 사람으로 발전하는 경향이 있다는 것을 암시한다고 했다. 따라서 빈칸에는 ⑤ '일관적인'이 와서 성격은 우리가 생각하는 것만큼 일관적이지 않을 수 있다는 의미가 되어야 한다.

오답분석 ①, ②, ③, ④은 우리의 생각과 달리 성격은 나이가 들어감에 따라 변한다는 것을 설명하는 단어로 적절하지 않다.

해석 성격은 우리가 생각하는 것만큼 일관적이지 않을 수 있다. 우리 모두는 대부분이 자기 자신을 찾기 위해 새로운 경험을 추구하고 흥미를 개발하는 시기인, 10대에 시작되는 점진적인 성숙의 과정을 겪는다. 여러 해 동안, 심리학자들은 이 과정이 성인기까지 계속되어 30세쯤에 끝난다고 여겼는데, 대인 관계, 학교와 직장에서의 성과, 그리고 신체적 건강과 같은 요소들이 우리가 궁극적으로 되는 사람을 형성하는 데 일조하기 때문이다. 이러한 요소들이 각 개인 특유의 성격의 기반을 형성하는 것은 사실이지만, 노화의 영향에 대한 연구는 기록에 의해 충분히 입증된 신체적 변화에 더하여, 우리는 더 친절하고, 우리가 더 젊었던 시절에 그랬던 것보다 우리의 감정에 대한 더 많은 통제력을 가진 이타적인 사람으로 발전하는 경향이 있다는 것을 이제 암시한다. 이러한 경향은 모든 인간 문화에서 관찰되어 왔으며, 이는 나이가 들어감에 따라 적응하는 우리의 성향이 보편적이라는 것을 시사한다.

① 독특한　　　　　　② 무작위의
③ 복잡한　　　　　　④ 중요한
⑤ 일관적인

어휘 personality 성격 maturation 성숙 play a part in ~에 일조하다
distinctive 특유의 well-documented 기록에 의해 충분히 입증된
altruistic 이타적인 universal 보편적인, 만국의

구문분석
[10행] ①[While it is true that these elements form the basis of each person's distinctive personality], research into the effects of aging now suggest that, ②[in addition to the well-documented physical transformation], we tend to ~
→ ①[While ~ personality]는 접속사 while(~하지만)이 이끄는 양보의 부사절이다.
→ ②[in ~ transformation]은 전치사구가 삽입된 형태이다.

32　빈칸 추론하기　　정답 ③

[해설] 수학이 전 세계 사람들에게 알려진 언어이며, 일정한 규칙을 갖췄다는 내용의 글이다. 빈칸 앞에서 수학은 번역될 필요가 없다고 했고, 빈칸 뒤 문장에서 수학의 규칙은 변함이 없고 의사소통의 장벽을 극복하도록 도와, 결국 수학을 세계에서 가장 유용한 언어 중 하나로 만든다고 하였다. 따라서 주제와 관련된 빈칸에는 수학이 ③ '보편적인 언어'라는 내용이 오는 것이 적절하다.

[오답분석] ①, ②, ④은 수학이 보편적인 언어라는 것을 설명하는 글의 내용과 관련이 없다. ⑤는 글에서 언급된 communication을 사용하여 헷갈리게 하는 오답이다.

[해석] 수학은 국적과 배경에 상관없이 전 세계 사람들에게 알려진 언어이다. 그것은 데이터를 전달하고, 예측을 하고, 우리 주변의 세상을 이해하는 데 사용된다. 천문학자 Galileo Galilei(갈릴레오 갈릴레이)는 심지어 "수학은 신이 우주를 쓴 언어이다"라고 말하기까지 했다. 그리고 비록 그것이 전통적인 의미로는 언어로 인식되지 않을 수 있지만, 수학은 어휘, 문법, 그리고 구문론이 사용되는 방식과 유사한 방식으로 의미를 전달하기 위해 숫자들과 기호들을 활용하는, 문자 형태의 소통 수단이다. 예를 들어, 숫자는 명사와 같은 기능을 하고 뺄셈 기호와 곱셈 기호 같은 기호들은 동사로서의 역할을 한다. 수학 방정식은 스페인어나 중국어 문장이 그래야만 하는 것처럼 이해할 수 있도록 일정한 방식으로 배열되어야 한다. 유일한 큰 차이점은 수학은 번역될 필요가 없다는 것이다: 그것은 보편적인 언어이고 그것의 규칙은 변함이 없다. 이런 식으로, 수학은 사람들이 그 밖의 의사소통의 장벽을 극복하도록 도와, 결국 수학을 세계에서 가장 유용한 언어 중 하나로 만든다.

① 타고난 기술
② 독점 분야
③ 보편적인 언어
④ 과학의 기반
⑤ 의사소통의 기원

[어휘] nationality 국적　go as far as to ~하기까지 하다　syntax 구문론
function 기능을 하다　subtraction 뺄셈　multiplication 곱셈
comprehensible 이해할 수 있는　unvarying 변함이 없는, 일정한
[선택지] innate 타고난　exclusive 독점적인　universal 보편적인

[구문분석]
> [18행] In this way, math helps people overcome other barriers
> 　　　　　　　　 동사　목적어　목적격 보어
> of communication, ~
> → 준사역동사 helps의 목적어로 people, 목적격 보어로 동사원형 overcome이 쓰였다. help는 목적격 보어로 동사원형 또는 to부정사를 취할 수 있으므로, overcome 대신 to overcome도 쓸 수 있다.

33　빈칸 추론하기　　정답 ②

[해설] 모든 사람은 의지를 가지고 있으며, 의지란 사람들이 어떤 행동을 선택하도록 이끄는 힘이라는 Otto Rank의 주장에 관한 글이다. 주제문에 해당하는 빈칸 문장에서 인간의 행동은 의지에 의해 통제된다는 이유로, Otto Rank는 의지는 '무엇한다'는 것을 의미한다고 주장했다고 하고, 글의 후반에서 Otto Rank의 관점에 따르면 사람들은 그들 스스로 선택을 하고, 따라서 선택에 대한 책임을 져야 한다고 했다. 따라서 빈칸에는 ② '사람들은 그들 자신의 행동에 책임을 져야 한다'는 내용이 오는 것이 적절하다.

[오답분석] ①은 인간이 가진 의지가 인간의 행동을 좌우한다고 한 글의 내용과 반대되는 내용이므로 오답이다. ③은 글에서 언급되고 있지 않다. ④은 글에서 의지가 충동과 억제 사이 어딘가에 있는 것이라고는 했지만 훌륭한 균형에 대해서는 언급되지 않았다. ⑤은 의지가 인간이 행동을 선택하도록 이끄는 힘이라고 밝

힌 글의 내용과 반대되는 내용이므로 오답이다.

[해석] 오스트리아의 정신 분석학자 Otto Rank(오토 랑크)는 <의지 요법>에서 모든 사람들은 의지를 가지고 있으며, 의지는 사람들이 그것(행동)이 긍정적이든 부정적이든 그들의 행동을 선택하도록 이끄는 힘이라고 기술했다. 그는 의지가 서로 끊임없는 투쟁 상태에 있는 두 개의 대립하는 인간의 본능적 욕구인 충동과 억제 사이 그 중간 어딘가에 있고, 이 두 힘의 관리 능력이 그 자체로 뚜렷한 의지를 가진 한 인격의 발달로 이어진다고 주장했다. 각 인간은 유일무이하고 그들의 행동은 그들의 의지에 의해 통제된다는 이유로, 그는 이것이 사람들은 그들 자신의 행동에 책임을 져야 한다는 것을 의미한다고 주장했다. 이 주장은 인간은 그들이 하는 대로 행동하지 않을 수 없다는 것을 사실로 상정하며 인간은 그들의 사고에 있어서 결정론적이라고 주장하는 그의 동료이자 친구 Sigmund Freud(지그문트 프로이트)의 이론들을 포함해 당시의 많은 지배적인 이론들을 반박했다. 그러나 Rank의 관점에서 사람들은 그들 스스로 선택을 하고, 따라서 그것들에 대한 책임을 져야 한다.

① 심리 치료는 사람들이 그들 스스로를 더 잘 이해하도록 돕는다
② 사람들은 그들 자신의 행동에 책임을 져야 한다
③ 내적인 힘과 외적인 힘 모두 우리의 행동을 결정한다
④ 충동과 억제 사이에는 아주 훌륭한 균형이 있다
⑤ 우리의 선택하는 능력은 우리 자신 안에서 알아보기 어렵다

[어휘] will 의지　psychoanalyst 정신 분석학자　faculty 힘, 능력
assert 주장하다　impulse 충동　inhibition 억제　opposing 대립하는
drive 본능적 욕구, 동기　dynamic 힘, 동력　distinct 뚜렷한
prevailing 지배적인　deterministic 결정론적인　posit 사실로 상정하다
liable 책임을 져야 할

[구문분석]
> [13행] This assertion contradicted ~ thinking, [positing that humans **cannot help but act** as they do].
> → 'cannot help but + 동사원형'은 '~하지 않을 수 없다'라는 의미의 구문이며, 'have no choice but + to부정사'로 바꿔 쓸 수 있다.
> → [positing ~ do]는 이유를 나타내는 분사구문으로, 분사구문의 주어가 주절의 주어(This assertion)와 같아서 생략되었다.

34　빈칸 추론하기　　정답 ③

[해설] 디지털 시대에는 기업들이 자사의 웹사이트를 검색 엔진에 최적화해야만 더 많은 사람들에게 그 기업을 노출시킬 수 있다는 내용의 글이다. 주제문에 해당하는 빈칸 문장에서 '무엇'하기 때문에 단순히 웹사이트가 있는 것만으로는 충분하지 않다고 하고, 글의 후반에서 웹사이트에서 사용되는 핵심어나 질문들이 사람들의 검색과 더 관련 있을수록 순위가 상승하고, 어쩌면 사람들이 그 웹사이트를 우연히 접해 잠재적으로 고객이 될 가능성을 높인다고 설명하고 있다. 따라서 빈칸에는 ③ '누구나 그것을 찾을 수 있다는 보장은 없다'는 내용이 오는 것이 적절하다.

[오답분석] ①의 전통적인 광고, ④의 소셜 미디어, ⑤의 개인 차원의 연결에 대한 내용은 글에서 언급되고 있지 않다. ②은 글의 일부만을 다루고 있는 오답이다.

[해석] 디지털 시대에는 기업이 단순히 웹사이트를 갖는 것만으로는 충분하지 않은데, 누구나 그것을 찾을 수 있다는 보장이 없기 때문이다. 그것이 바로, 이용하기 가장 효과적인 디지털 마케팅 전략들 중 하나가 검색 엔진 최적화, 즉 SEO인 이유이다. 검색 엔진이 어떻게 작동하는지 아는 것은 SEO를 이해하는 데 있어서 필수적이다: 검색 엔진은 내용을 찾기 위해 인터넷을 살피고, 그들이 찾은 정보를 색인에 정리한 다음, 결과를 생성하기 위해 그 색인을 사용한다. 검색 엔진에 의해 생성된 결과들은 가장 관련 있는 페이지가 먼저 나타나면서 순위가 매겨지기 때문에 기업은 핵심어를 사용하거나 잠재 고객들이 문의할

수 있는 질문에 대한 답변을 제공함으로써 기업 웹사이트의 순위를 높이려고 시도할 수 있다. 웹사이트의 언어가 사람들의 검색과 더 관련 있을수록, 그 웹사이트는 순위가 상승하고, 어쩌면 검색 결과의 첫 페이지에 오를지도 모른다. 이는 사람들이 그 기업의 웹사이트를 우연히 접하고 잠재적으로 고객이 될 가능성을 높인다.

① 전통적인 광고가 다시 인기를 얻고 있다
② 웹사이트들은 새로운 고객을 직접 겨냥하지 못한다
③ 누구나 그것을 찾을 수 있다는 보장이 없다
④ 대부분의 사람들은 소셜 미디어를 통해 새로운 기업들을 발견한다
⑤ 웹사이트들은 종종 개인 차원에서 고객들과 연결되는 것에 실패한다

 어휘 era 시대 search engine 검색 엔진 optimization 최적화 vital 필수적인 index 색인 [선택지] make a comeback 다시 인기를 얻다 target 겨냥하다

구문분석

[11행] ~ a business can attempt to improve its website's ranking by using keywords or providing answers to **questions** [(that/which) potential customers might ask].

→ [potential ~ ask]는 앞의 선행사 questions를 수식하는 관계대명사 절로, 목적격 관계대명사 that/which가 생략되었다.

35 흐름과 관계 없는 문장 찾기 정답 ③

해설 인문학 학습이 사람들에게 제공하는 이점이 많기 때문에, 과학을 전공하는 사람들도 인문학을 학습하는 것이 유익하다는 내용의 글이다. 그런데 ③은 인문학을 연구하는 사람들도 과학자들과 마찬가지로 세상에 많은 기여를 한다는 내용이므로 핵심 소재는 같지만 주제에서 벗어나 있어 글의 흐름과 무관하다.

오답분석 ①, ②은 과학을 전공하는 사람들이 인문학과 관련된 학과 과목들을 경시하면 안 된다는 두 번째 문장에 이어, 인문학 공부의 이점을 설명하고 있으므로, 두 번째 문장과 연결된다. ④은 과학자들이 인문학 강의를 들어야 하는 이유를 설명하고 있으므로 ②과 자연스럽게 이어진다. ⑤의 It은 ④의 to take humanities courses를 가리키므로, ④과 자연스럽게 이어진다.

해석 인문학과 과학은 보통 정반대인 것으로 여겨지는데, 많은 사람들이 과학은 미래 발전을 위해 매우 중요하다고 여기고 인문학은 시간과 자금 낭비로 여기기 때문이다. 그러나 과학을 전공하는 사람들은 인문학과 관련된 학문 주제들을 그렇게 성급하게 경시해서는 안 된다. ① 인문학을 공부하는 것은 학생들에게 다양한 주제에 대한 방대한 지식을 제공할 뿐만 아니라 그들이 윤리적이고 인정이 많으며 창의적이게 되도록 장려한다. ② 이러한 특성들은 그것들이 우리에게 인간이 되는 것이 무엇을 의미하는지에 대한 보다 완전한 시각을 제공해주는 데에 도움을 주기 때문에 모두에게 유익하다. (③ 비록 과학자들이 세상에 많은 기여를 하긴 하지만, 인문학을 연구하는 사람들도 마찬가지이다.) ④ 과학자들은 냉정하고 그 밖의 사회와는 동떨어져 있다고 종종 여겨지기 때문에, 그들이 인문학 강의를 듣는 것도 도움이 될 수 있다. ⑤ 이는 그들이 자신들의 지식을 이용하여 해결해야 하는 문제들에 대한 더 나은 이해를 제공할 수 있고, 그들이 발견한 것들을 다른 세상에 전달하는 방식을 개선시킬 수 있다.

어휘 humanities 인문학 polar opposite 정반대인 것 disregard 경시하다 vast 방대한 compassionate 인정 많은, 동정적인 clinical 냉정한, 냉담한 out of touch with ~와 동떨어진, ~을 잘 모르는

구문분석

[7행] Studying the humanities **not only** ①[provides students with vast knowledge on various topics] **but also** ② [encourages them to be ethical, compassionate, and creative].

→ 동사구 ①[provides ~ topics]와 ②[encourages ~ creative]는 상관접속사 not only A but also B로 연결된 병렬 구조이다.

[10행] These qualities benefit everyone since they help give us a more complete view **of** [what it means to be human].

→ [what ~ human]은 의문사 what(무엇)이 이끄는 명사절로, 전치사 of의 목적어 역할을 한다.

36 글의 순서 배열하기 정답 ②

해설 주어진 글은 같은 종의 개체들이 짝짓기를 해 자식을 낳을 경우, 어미와 아비가 동일한 수의 염색체 반쌍을 자식에게 물려주며, 이에 따라 자식은 정상적으로 활동하고 번식할 수 있다는 통념을 제시한다. (B)는 서로 다른 두 종이 자식을 낳을 경우 그 자식은 일반적으로 번식을 할 수 없다는 내용으로, 역접 연결어 however를 통해 주어진 글에 대한 반전 설명을 하고 있으므로 주어진 글 뒤에 오는 것이 적절하다. (A)는 노새가 번식하지 못하는 이유에 관한 내용이고, (B)의 마지막에서 서로 다른 두 종의 자식의 예시로 노새를 언급했으므로 그 뒤에 와야 한다. (C)는 2007년에 노새가 자식을 낳은 사례에 관한 내용이고, 이는 (A)의 이등분될 수 없는 염색체 수 때문에 노새는 번식하지 못한다는 논리를 따르지 않은 경우에 해당하므로 (A) 바로 다음에 오는 것이 적절하다. 따라서 글의 순서로 가장 적절한 것은 ② (B) - (A) - (C)이다.

해석 같은 종의 개체들이 성공적으로 짝짓기를 하면, 어미와 아비 모두 자식에게 동일한 수의 염색체 반쌍을 준다. 이는 그들의 자식이 정상적으로 활동하게 하고, 후에 그들의 자식을 낳을 수 있게 한다.

(B) 하지만, 서로 다른 두 종이 새끼를 낳을 때에는, 그 자식은 일반적으로 번식할 수 없다. 이는 그 자식이 서로 다른 부모로부터 동등하지 않은 수의 염색체를 물려받기 때문이다. 이것의 일반적인 예는 말과 당나귀의 자식인 노새이다.

(A) 말은 64개의 염색체를 가지고 있고, 당나귀는 62개의 염색체를 가지고 있기 때문에, 노새는 63개의 염색체를 물려받는다. 63개의 염색체는 균등하게 이등분될 수 없기 때문에, 노새들은 번식할 수 없어야 한다. 그러나, 이 논리를 따르지 않는 경우들이 있다.

(C) 2007년에, 한 노새는 생물학자들이 그것(노새)의 자식이라고 유전적으로 확인한 망아지를 낳았다. 그 노새는 정확히 63개의 염색체를 가지고 있는 것으로 검사되고 확인되었기 때문에, 그 노새가 번식할 수 있었던 이유는 여전히 수수께끼이다.

 어휘 mate 짝짓기를 하다 offspring 자식, 자손 function 활동하다, 기능하다 donkey 당나귀 inherit 물려받다 evenly 균등하게, 반반으로 halve 이등분하다 defy 따르지 않다 breed 새끼를 낳다 dissimilar 서로 다른 foal 망아지

구문분석

[4행] This <u>allows</u> <u>their young</u> <u>to function</u> normally and, later,
　　　　동사　　　목적어　　　목적격 보어 1
(to) <u>produce</u> offspring of their own.
　　목적격 보어 2

→ 동사 allows의 목적어로 their young, 목적격 보어로 to부정사 to function과 (to) produce가 쓰였다. and로 연결된 두 번째 to부정사구에서는 to가 생략되었다.

37 글의 순서 배열하기
정답 ⑤

(해설) 주어진 글은 기억과 사고방식이 사회적 맥락에서 형성된다는 집단 기억이라는 주제를 제시한다. (C)는 우리가 어려서부터 배운 인물과 역사는 조작된 개념이라는 내용으로, 의식을 구성하기 위해 사건을 직접 경험할 필요가 없다는 집단 기억 이론에 따른 예시이므로 주어진 글 다음에 와야 한다. (B)의 These representations of the past는 (C)의 우리가 특정 방식으로 느끼도록 조작된 개념들인 국가의 역사를 가리키므로 (C) 바로 다음에 오는 것이 적절하다. (A)의 someone ~ elected는 (B)의 정치인이나 의제를 가진 누군가를 가리키며, 순접 연결어 Thus를 통해 (B)의 내용에 대한 부연 설명을 하고 있으므로 (B) 바로 다음에 오는 것이 적절하다. 따라서 글의 순서로 가장 적절한 것은 ⑤ (C) - (B) - (A)이다.

(해석) 집단 기억은 기억과 사고방식이 사회적 맥락에서 형성된다는, 즉 사회 구성원들은 한 사건이 그들의 의식의 일부를 구성하기 위해 그것을 직접 경험할 필요는 없다는 개념이다.

(C) 우리가 어려서부터 중시하도록 배운 인물들과 역사적 사건들은, 집단 기억에 관한 이론에 따르면, 권력을 가진 사람들에 의해 선정된다. 다시 말해, 국가의 역사는 우리가 특정 방식으로 느끼도록 의도된, 조작된 개념들이다.

(B) 이러한 과거 묘사들은 반드시 정확할 필요는 없으며, 대신 집단 내 단결을 유지하는 방식으로 해석되어야 한다. 대중이 그들의 믿음을 통해 하나가 되어 있을 때, 정치인들이나 의제를 가진 누군가가 그들에게 호소하기 쉬워진다.

(A) 따라서, 누군가가 메시지를 퍼뜨리길 원하든 당선되기를 원하든 간에, 집단 기억을 떠올리게 하는 것은 그 일을 해내도록 도울 수 있다. 가장 중요한 것은 그것이 지배적인 사고방식을 상기시켜야 한다는 것이다.

(어휘) collective 집단의 attitude 사고방식, 태도 consciousness 의식 evoke 떠올리게 하다 resonate 상기시키다 prevailing 지배적인 cohesion 단결 unify 하나로 하다 agenda 의제 manipulate 조작하다 construct 개념

(구문분석)

[1행] Collective memory is **the idea** ①[that memories and attitudes are formed through a social context] — that it is not necessary for members of a society ②[to have (가주어) (의미상 주어) personally experienced an event for it to form part of their (진주어(to부정사구)) consciousness].

→ ①[that ~ context]는 the idea와 동격을 이루는 명사절이다.

→ 가주어 it이 길이가 긴 진주어 to부정사구 ②[to ~ consciousness] 대신 주어 자리에 쓰인 구조이며, to부정사구의 의미상 주어가 'for + 명사(구)'의 형태로 쓰였다.

[6행] Thus, [**whether** someone wants to spread a message **or** (get elected)], evoking a collective memory can help get the job done.

→ [whether ~ elected]는 부사절 접속사 whether A or B(A이든 B이든)가 이끄는 양보의 부사절이다.

→ (get elected)는 get을 이용한 수동태 'get + p.p.' 형태로, 행위의 발생이나 동작에 초점을 둔 표현이다.

38 주어진 문장의 위치 찾기
정답 ③

(해설) ③ 앞까지는 공감과 투영의 차이점에 대한 내용이 이어지다가 ③ 뒤 문장에서 그들은 그들이 교류하는 사람의 실제 어려움을 진정으로 이해하지 못하며 오히려 자신의 편견과 의견에 근거하여 대응한다는 내용이 나오고 있다. ③ 앞뒤의 내용이 유기적으로 연결되지 않는다는 점을 통해 글의 흐름이 끊겼음을 알 수 있다. 또한 주어진 문장의 사람들이 투영할 때 고군분투하는 사람의 감정과 경험을 잘 반영한다고 여긴다고 한 내용은 ③ 뒤 문장에서 투영하는 사람들에 대해 설명으로 이어지고 있으므로 주어진 문장이 들어가기에 가장 적절한 곳은 ③이다.

(오답분석) ② 뒤 문장의 It은 다른 사람의 경험에 대한 자신의 생각을 다른 사람에게 옮길 때 발생한다는 ① 뒤 문장의 투영(Projection)을 가리키므로 주어진 문장이 사이에 들어갈 수 없다.

(해석) 비록 공감과 투영이 감정적 혼란에 대한 두 개의 서로 다른 반응이지만, 그 둘은 또한 구별하기 어려울 수 있다. 공감은 연습을 필요로 한다; 사람들은 고군분투하는 사람들에게 귀 기울이고 주의를 기울이려는 의식적인 노력을 반드시 해야만 하고 그들을 이해하기 위해 최선을 다해야 한다. (①) 투영은 특히 개인주의의 출현과 함께 대부분의 사람들에게 더 자연스러운 반응이다. (②) 이는 누군가가 다른 사람의 경험에 대한 자신의 생각을 다른 사람에게 옮길 때 발생한다. (③ 사람들은 공감하기보다는 투영할 때, 그들의 감정과 경험이 고군분투하는 그 사람의 그것들(감정과 경험)을 잘 반영한다고 여긴다.) 근본적으로, 그들은 그들이 교류하는 사람의 실제 어려움을 진정으로 이해하지 못하며, 오히려 그 상황에 대한 그들 자신의 편견과 의견에 근거하여 대응한다. (④) 현대 사회는 공감을 불어넣어야 하는 필요를 간과함으로써 본의 아니게 투영하는 경향이 더 많은 시민들을 길러냈다. (⑤) 공감이 없다면, 인간은 진정한 유대감을 상실하고 그들 자신의 걱정거리에만 신경 쓸 것이다.

(어휘) project 투영하다 empathize 공감하다 mirror 반영하다 empathy 공감 projection 투영 manage to 본의 아니게 ~하다 foster 기르다, 육성하다 instill 불어넣다

(구문분석)

[13행] Essentially, they <u>fail</u> to really see [the actual struggles (동사) (목적어) of the person they are interacting with] and instead react ~

→ 동사 fail의 목적어로 to부정사 to really see가 쓰였고, [the ~ with] 전체가 동사 see의 목적어이다.

39 주어진 문장의 위치 찾기
정답 ④

(해설) 주어진 문장의 In such a case(그러한 경우에)로 보아, 주어진 문장 앞에는 공정이 보호되어야 하는 특허에 대한 내용이 나와야 한다는 것을 알 수 있다. ④ 앞 문장은 디자인 특허가 거부되는 방식으로 제작되는 디자인에 대해 설명하고 있고, 주어진 문장의 the process는 ③ 뒤 문장의 a method unable to guarantee the uniformity of the design each and every time을 가리키므로 주어진 문장이 들어가기에 가장 적절한 곳은 ④이다.

(오답분석) ② 뒤 문장은 ① 뒤 문장에 이어서 디자인 특허의 또 다른 승인 요건(Another requirement)에 대해 언급하고 있다.

(해석) 제품, 공정, 또는 기계의 창작이나 개량을 보호하는 실용 특허와 달리, 디자인 특허는 물품의 장식적인 특징들을 보호한다. (①) 그러한 특허의 승인을 받으려면, 그 디자인은 독창적이어야 하고, 만약 기존 디자인과의 유사점이 있다면 그것들은 두드러지지 않아야 한다. (②) 또 다른 요건은 그 디자인이 복제 가능해야 한다는 것이다. (③) 누군가가 어느 때나 디자인의 균일성을 보장할 수 없는 방식을 통해 제작되는 디자인의 특허를 받기 원한다면, 디자인 특허는 거부될 것이다. (④ 그러한 경우에, 그 공정 자체가 보호되어야 할 것이므로, 실용 특허가 필수적이게 한다.) 물건의 디자인과 기능성 둘 다 보호되어야 하는 상황에서는, 창안자가 실용 특허와 디자인 특허 둘 다를 신청해야 할 것이다. (⑤) 두 가지 적용 범위 모두에 해당되는 창작물들은 모방되는 것으로부터 더 강하게 보호되기 때문에 일반적으로 더 높은 가치를 지니는 것

로 여겨진다.

 어휘 utility patent 실용 특허 ornamental 장식의, 장식용의
uniformity 균일성 each and every 어느 ~이나
functionality 기능성 coverage 적용 범위, 보상 (범위)

구문분석

[6행] To get approval for such a patent, the design must be original, and [**if** there are similarities to an existing design], they must be unobvious.

→ [if ~ design]은 접속사 if(만약 ~라면)가 이끄는 조건의 부사절이다.

[13행] In **situations** [where both the design and the functionality of an object need to be protected], an inventor would have to apply for both utility and design patents.

→ [where ~ protected]는 선행사 situations를 수식하며, 관계부사 where가 이끄는 관계부사절이다. 관계부사 where는 물리적 장소가 아닌 situation, point, case, circumstance 등의 추상적 의미의 장소가 선행사인 경우에도 사용된다.

---

40 요약문 완성하기 정답 ②

해설 Stanley Milgram은 독일인들이 미국인들보다 문화적으로 더 순종하는 성향이 있다는 가설을 세웠고, 이를 확인하기 위해 미국인들을 대상으로 실험을 진행했다. 글의 후반부에서 심지어 전기 충격이 엄청난 고통을 야기하는 것처럼 보이는 순간에도, "선생님들" 중 65퍼센트가 그 시험이 끝날 때까지 계속했고, 이는 그 실험의 끝에 이르기 전에 99.9퍼센트 이상이 이탈할 것이라는 Stanley Milgram의 추측이 틀렸음을 입증했다고 했다. 따라서 지문의 obedience를 compliance로, disproved를 refuting으로 바꾸어 표현한 ②이 정답이다.

해석 Stanley Milgram(스탠리 밀그램)의 획기적인 연구는 독일인들과 미국인들 간의 문화적 차이를 조사했다. 그는 다수가 홀로코스트 기간 동안 "단지 명령에 따르는 것"이라고 주장했던 독일인들이 문화적으로 더 순종하는 성향이 있다는 가설을 세웠다. 그래서 Milgram은 어느 범위까지 미국인들이 명령을 기꺼이 따를 것인지를 확인하기 위한 실험을 고안했다. 그 연구 중에, 각 피실험자는 "선생님"으로 배정되어 한 "학생"에게 단어들의 쌍을 읽도록 지시받았는데, 그 학생은 나중에 얼마나 많은 쌍을 기억하는지 시험을 볼 예정이었다. 각 오답마다 그 "선생님"은 그 "학생"에게 전기 충격을 가할 수 있는 버튼을 누르도록 지시받았고, 그 다음 오답들은 더 높은 전압의 충격으로 이어졌다. 실제로는, 그 버튼은 전류를 보내지 않았고, 그 "학생들"은 Milgram과 함께 일하는 배우들이었다. 그러나, 심지어 그 충격이 엄청난 고통을 야기하는 것처럼 보이는 순간에도, "선생님들" 중 65퍼센트가 그 시험이 끝날 때까지 계속했다. 이는 그 실험의 끝에 이르기 전에 99.9퍼센트 이상이 이탈할 것이라는 Milgram의 추측이 틀렸음을 입증했다.

↓

Stanley Milgram의 연구는 미국인들이 과업들을 이행하도록 지시받았을 때 독일인들만큼의 (A) 순종을 보인다는 것을 증명했고, 이는 그들이 지향하려는 경향이 더 강하다는 그의 추측을 (D) 반박하는 것이었다.

	(A)	(B)
①	순종 ……	지지하는 것
②	순종 ……	반박하는 것
③	순응 ……	장려하는 것
④	저항 ……	이의를 제기하는 것
⑤	저항 ……	입증하는 것

 어휘 landmark 획기적인, 매우 중요한 hypothesize 가설을 세우다
Holocaust 홀로코스트, 유대인 대학살 predisposed to ~하는 성향이 있는
subject 피실험자 quiz 시험하다 subsequent 그 다음의
disprove 틀렸음을 입증하다 defect 이탈하다
be prone to ~하는 경향이 있다 rebel 저항하다
[선택지] compliance 순종 refute 반박하다 conformity 순응
challenge 이의를 제기하다

구문분석

[17행] But even as the shocks [appeared to cause] a great deal of pain, 65 percent ~

→ [appeared to cause]는 'appear + to부정사'의 형태로, '~처럼 보이다'라는 의미를 나타내는 to부정사 표현이다.

41~42 장문 독해 1

해석 [41]George Orwell(조지 오웰)의 혁명적인 소설 <1984>에서 등장인물들은 정부의 지속적인 감시와 "빅 브라더가 당신을 지켜보고 있다"는 신호에 위협을 받는다. 물론 Orwell의 걸작은 사생활이 존재하지 않는 세상을 묘사한 소설 작품이다. 그러나 비평가들은 "빅 브라더"라는 관념이 현대 사회에서 사람들이 (a)겪는 것과 그렇게 다르지 않다고 주장한다. [41]근본적으로 우리 또한 항상 감시받고 있으며, 우리들 대부분은 어떤 (b)알려진 위법 행위가 처벌로 이어질 수 있다는 것을 알고 있다. 하지만 제재의 수단으로서의 감시는 새로운 개념이 아니며, George Orwell에 의해 발명된 것도 아니다. 사실, 최초의 감시 시스템 중 하나는 18세기에 발명되었다. 판옵티콘은 감독관이 간수들의 존재를 (c)드러내면서(→숨기면서) 죄수들을 감시할 수 있게 해주는 원형 구조물로, Samuel Bentham(사무엘 벤담)에 의해 만들어졌다. [42]이 고안물은 감독관이 눈에 띄는 일 없이 죄수에게 그들이 항상 면밀히 감시당하고 있다는 것을 상기시켜 줌으로써 죄수들을 통제하기 위해 만들어졌다.

200년이 빠르게 지나 인터넷상 개인들의 활동에서 수집된 자료들과 더불어, 감시는 컴퓨터 심리학자 Andrew Kosinski(앤드류 코진스키)가 "사생활 이후의 세계"라고 부르는 것의 도래를 알렸다. 현대의 기관들은 그럼에도 불구하고 카메라, 렌즈, 그리고 심지어 사람들을 이용하여 Bentham이 이행했던 관행의 형태를 지금까지도 (d)많이 활용하고 있다. 물리적인 그리고 온라인상의 우리의 모든 활동은, 감시되고 추적될 수 있다. [41]그러한 세계의 (e)이점은 강화된 공공 안전, 풍부한 증거 자료, 그리고 줄어든 범죄를 포함한다. 하지만, 많은 사람들은 여전히 이런 종류의 시스템과 지속적인 감시가 어떻게 악용될 수 있는지에 대해 걱정하고 있다. 사람들의 행동을 바꾸기 위해 사생활을 침해하는 것은 결국 Orwell이 글로 쓴 것과 정확히 일치한다.

 어휘 character 등장인물 surveillance 감시 reminder 신호, 암시
masterpiece 걸작 illustrate 묘사하다 subject 겪게 하다
misconduct 위법 행위 panopticon 판옵티콘, 원형 감옥
overseer 감독관 advent 도래 computational 컴퓨터의, 계산의
easy 풍부한 abuse 악용하다

구문분석

[6행] Yet critics argue that the idea of "Big Brother" is not really so different **from** [what people are subjected to in modern society].

→ [what ~ society]는 관계대명사 what(~하는 것)이 이끄는 명사절로, 전치사 from의 목적어 역할을 한다.

41 제목 파악하기 정답 ④

해설 George Orwell의 소설 <1984>의 사생활이 존재하지 않는 세상과 유사하게, 현대 사회는 감시가 만연한 세상이고, "사생활 이후의 세계"는 감시를 통해 강화된 공공 안전, 풍부한 증거 자료, 줄어든 범죄 등의 이점도 있지만, 감시가 악용될 여지가 있다는 것이 이 글의 주된 내용이다. 따라서 글의 제목으로 가장 적절한 것은 ④ '감시의 끝없는 증가: 좋은 것인가 나쁜 것인가?'이다.

오답분석 ①은 감시와 처벌에 대해서는 글에서 언급되었지만, 어떤 것이 더 효과적인지에 대해서는 언급되지 않았다. ②, ③은 글에서 언급되고 있지 않다. ⑤은 면밀한 감시를 통해 죄수들을 통제했다는 글의 내용과 반대되는 내용이므로 오답이다.

해석 ① 처벌 또는 감시: 어떤 것이 더 효과적인가?
② 노동자들의 안전을 위한 빅 브라더 활용 방법
③ 사생활을 되찾기 위해 궐기하는 법을 배워라!
④ 감시의 끝없는 증가: 좋은 것인가 나쁜 것인가?
⑤ 감시 없이 죄수들을 통제하는 방법

42 어휘 적절성 파악하기 정답 ③

해설 판옵티콘은 감독관이 눈에 띄지 않으면서, 죄수들에게 그들이 항상 면밀히 감시당하고 있다는 것을 상기시켜 주는 것이라고 했으므로, 판옵티콘은 감독관이 간수들의 존재를 숨기면서 죄수들을 감시할 수 있게 해주는 원형 구조물이라는 맥락이 되어야 하므로 ③의 revealing(드러내면서)은 그와 반대되는 의미의 concealing(숨기면서)과 같은 단어로 바꾸어야 문맥상 적절하다.

43~45 장문 독해 2

해석 (A) 결승전 축구 경기까지 2주가 남아서 Becky와 Hannah는 팀과 함께 평소보다 더 많은 연습을 해야 했다. 연습이 끝난 어느 날, 그들의 코치가 Becky를 그녀의 사무실로 불렀다. 그녀는 결승전 경기에서 뛰기 위해서는 선수들이 성적을 올려야 한다는 것을 (a)그녀에게 상기시켰다. 불행하게도, Becky의 수학 성적이 떨어졌기 때문에, Becky는 다음 큰 시험에서 잘 하지 않으면 경기를 뛸 수 없을 것이다. Becky가 무엇을 해야 하는지 물었고 그녀의 코치는 "나는 네가 개인 교사를 구해야 할 것 같구나"라고 대답했다.

(C) Becky는 자신의 안 좋은 성적이 창피했기 때문에 누군가에게 도움을 청하는 것이 겁났다. 그녀는 Hannah에게 (c)그녀의 문제에 대해 이야기하기로 했다. "누가 나의 개인 교사가 되어줄 수 있을까?" Becky가 물었다. "내가 해줄 수 있어!" Hannah가 대답했다. "나는 수학을 잘 하고 너와 함께 시험 공부를 할 수 있어!" Becky는 Hannah가 그녀를 기꺼이 도우려 한다는 사실에 놀랐다. 그들은 연습 후에 매일 만나서 공부하기로 계획했다. 시험이 일주일밖에 남지 않았었다.

(B) Becky는 Hannah가 훌륭한 개인 교사라고 생각했다. 그녀는 모든 것을 아주 명쾌하게 설명했다. 45큰 시험이 있던 날, Hannah는 Becky에게 준비가 되었는지 물었다. "그런 것 같아!" Becky가 말했다. (b)그녀는 긴장했지만 자신이 열심히 공부했다는 것을 알고 있었다. Becky가 마침내 시험을 보았을 때, 그녀는 자신이 모든 문제의 답을 안다는 것을 깨닫고 안도했다. 그녀는 Hannah가 가르쳐준 모든 것을 기억했고 시간이 끝나기 전에 시험을 마쳤다.

(D) 다음 수업에서 선생님은 Becky에게 그녀의 시험지를 건네주었고 그녀는 자신이 만점을 받은 것을 보고 놀랐다. 그녀는 Hannah를 안아주러 갔다. "정말 고마워! (d)네가 없었다면 나는 해내지 못했을 거야."라고 그녀는 44Hannah에게 말했다. 그녀의 친구는 그녀를 향해 미소 지으며 "그게 친구

좋다는 거지!"라고 말했다. Becky는 (e)그녀가 결승전 축구 경기를 뛸 수 있게 되어서 너무 행복했다. 하지만 그녀를 더욱 행복하게 만든 것은 그녀가 그렇게 좋은 친구를 두었다는 것이다.

어휘 championship 결승전 tutor 개인 교사 embarrassed 창피한

구문분석
> [15행] She felt nervous, but she **knew** [(that) she had studied hard].
> → 명사절 [she ~ hard]는 동사 knew의 목적어이며, 명사절 접속사 that이 생략되었다.
>
> [37행] But <u>what made her even happier</u> <u>was</u> that she had made such a good friend.
>   주어   동사
> → [what ~ happier]는 관계대명사 what(~하는 것)이 이끄는 명사절로, 문장의 주어 역할을 한다.

43 글의 순서 배열하기 정답 ②

해설 (A)는 Becky가 결승전 경기를 뛰기 위해서는 수학 성적을 올려야 했고, 팀 코치가 Becky에게 개인 교사를 구할 것을 제안했다는 내용이다. (C)는 Becky가 개인 교사를 구해야 하는 문제에 대해 Hannah에게 이야기하자 Hannah가 기꺼이 개인 교사가 되어 주기로 했다는 내용이므로 (A) 뒤에 와야 한다. (B)는 Becky가 Hannah에게 수학을 배웠고 시험을 잘 마쳤다는 내용이므로, 시험이 일주일밖에 남지 않았다고 한 (C) 뒤에 와야 한다. (D)는 Becky가 수학 시험에서 만점을 받아 자신을 도와줬던 Hannah에게 고마움을 느끼는 내용이며, (D)의 her test는 (B)에서 Becky가 시험 날 풀었던 수학 시험지를 가리키므로 (B) 다음에 오는 것이 적절하다. 따라서 글의 순서로 가장 적절한 것은 ② (C) - (B) - (D)이다.

44 지칭 대상 파악하기 정답 ④

해설 (a), (b), (c), (e)는 모두 Becky를 가리키지만 (d)는 Becky에게 수학을 가르쳐주었던 Hannah를 가리키므로, ④이 정답이다.

45 세부 정보 파악하기 정답 ②

해설 (B)의 On the day of the big test, Hannah asked Becky if she was ready를 통해 시험 당일 Hannah가 Becky에게 준비가 되었는지 물었다는 것을 알 수 있는데, ②은 Becky가 Hannah에게 물었다고 일부 정보를 잘못 나타냈으므로 글의 내용과 일치하지 않는 것은 ②이다.

문제집 p. 98

정답

18	④	19	②	20	④	21	②	22	②	23	⑤	24	③	25	④	26	④	27	③
28	④	29	④	30	③	31	⑤	32	④	33	③	34	⑤	35	②	36	③	37	⑤
38	③	39	③	40	②	41	④	42	①	43	②	44	④	45	④				

---

18 목적 파악하기 정답 ④

[해설] 글의 중간 이후에서 suggest(제안하다)를 이용해 카페가 더 환경친화적인 곳이 될 수 있는 방법 중 하나로 일회용 컵을 제공하지 않을 것을 제안하고 있으므로, 정답은 ④이다.

[해석] Stacy Greenwood씨께,

제가 지금까지 몇 년간 고객으로 지내온 당신의 카페에 관하여 당신께 이메일을 보냅니다. Stacy's는 훌륭한 한 잔의 커피를 즐길 수 있는 제가 가장 좋아하는 장소 중 한 곳입니다. 저는 수년에 걸쳐 당신이 만든 변화들이 모두 카페를 개선해왔다고 생각하고, 더욱 지속 가능한 방식으로 사업을 운영하려는 당신의 노력에 감사를 표합니다. 그 점을 염두에 두고, 저는 카페가 더욱 환경친화적이 될 수 있는 또 하나의 방법을 제안드리고 싶습니다. 저는 Stacy's가 더 이상 일회용 컵을 제공하지 않는 것으로부터 정말 이익을 얻을 것이라고 믿습니다. 저는 최근에 몇몇 카페들이 이 방안을 채택하는 것을 보았고, 당신이 Stacy's가 친환경 사업이 되기를 바라는 것을 알고 있으므로, 저는 그것이 당신의 관심을 끌 수도 있겠다고 생각했습니다. 당신이 이것을 고려해보기를 바라며, 당신 카페에 제 다음 방문을 기대하겠습니다.

Ken Rogers 드림

[어휘] regarding ~에 관하여   run business 사업을 운영하다
sustainable 지속 가능한   environmentally friendly 환경친화적인
single-use 일회용의   green business 친환경 사업

[구문분석]
[8행] ~ I want to suggest **another way** [(how) the café could become more environmentally friendly].

→ [the ~ friendly]는 선행사 another way를 수식하는 관계부사절로, 선행사가 방법을 나타내는 일반적인 명사(way)일 때 관계부사 how가 생략된 형태이다.

[12행] ~ and [**since** I know you want Stacy's to be a green business], I thought it might interest you, too.

→ [since ~ business]는 접속사 since(~ 때문에)가 이끄는 이유의 부사절이다.

---

19 심경 파악하기 정답 ②

[해설] 심경은 간접적으로 표현된다. 글의 중반부의 she couldn't stop yawning과 kept checking what time it was, ~ still had a long day ahead of her에서 Amy가 스키를 타지 못해 혼자서 시간을 보내며 시간이 안 가 지루해하는 것을 알 수 있고, 마지막 문장의 Soon her heart was racing as she flew down the snow-covered slopes를 통해 썰매를 타며 즐거워하는 것을 알 수 있으므로, Amy의 심경 변화로 가장 적절한 것은 ②이다.

[해석] Amy는 창밖을 내다보았고 모두가 스키를 타며 즐거워하는 것을 보았다. 그녀는 그녀의 친구들과 함께 산악 휴양지로 여행을 왔지만, 그녀는 스키 타는 법을 몰랐다! 그녀는 혼자 보내야 할 시간이 많았기에, TV를 보기로 했다. 하지만 재미있는 것이 아무것도 없어서, 그녀는 하품하는 것을 멈출 수가 없었다. 그래서 그녀는 휴대폰을 가지고 놀았지만, 그것도 빠르게 싫증이 났다. 그녀는 계속해서 몇 시인지 확인했고, 그 결과는 그녀 앞에 여전히 긴 하루가 남았다는 것을 확인할 뿐이었다. Keith가 방으로 걸어 들어왔을 때 그녀는 천장을 바라보고 있었다. 그는 그녀에게 썰매를 타러 가고 싶은지를 물었다. "응!," 의자에서 뛰쳐나와 겉옷과 목도리를 집으면서 그녀가 대답했다. 그 둘은 신선한 공기가 있는 밖으로 뛰쳐나갔다. 그녀가 눈 덮인 비탈을 나는 듯이 내려가면서 머지않아 그녀의 심장은 뛰었다.

① 외로운 → 궁금한   ② 지루한 → 신이 난
③ 우울한 → 침착한   ④ 기쁜 → 놀란
⑤ 부러워하는 → 실망한

[어휘] yawn 하품하다   only to do 그 결과는 ~할 뿐이다   sledding 썰매 타기
slope 비탈

[구문분석]
[10행] He asked her [if she wanted to go sledding].
　　　　　동사 간접 목적어　　직접 목적어

→ [if ~ sledding]은 접속사 if가 이끄는 명사절로, 동사 asked의 직접 목적어 역할을 한다.

---

20 주장 파악하기 정답 ④

[해설] 불필요한 배경의 상세한 설명들이나 일에 대한 개인적인 의견은 직원이 목표나 구체적인 요구 사항을 알아듣는 것에 방해가 되고 혼란으로 이어진다고 했다. 마지막 두 문장에서 따라서 관리자는 항상 핵심 정보만을 정확하고 간결하게 전달하려고 노력해야 한다고 주장하고 있으므로 정답은 ④이다.

[오답분석] ①, ②, ③은 글에서 언급된 내용이 아니다. ⑤은 원활한 의사소통을 위해 관리자의 명확한 정보 전달을 강조하는 글의 주장을 관리자는 직원의 의견을 경청해야 한다고 잘못 표현한 오답이다.

[해석] 최근의 조사에 따르면, 80퍼센트가 넘는 경영진이 원활한 의사소통이 성공적인 사업의 비결이라고 생각한다. 안타깝게도, 많은 수의 관리자들이 이것(과도하게 실명하는 것)이 철저하게 하는 것이라는 잘못된 믿음으로 과노하게 설명하는 경향을 보이며, 부하 직원들과 소통할 때 이 능력(원활한 의사소통)을 보이는 데 실패한다. 예를 들어, 새로운 프로젝트에 대한 지시를 내리는 사람이 불필요한 배경의 상세한 설명들과 그 일에 관한 개인적인 의견도 제공할지도 모른다. 그렇게 하는 것은 목표나 어떤 구체적인 요구 사항들을 알아듣는 것을 어렵게 하기 때문에 종종 청자 입장에서 혼란으로 이어진다. 이런 상황을 피하기 위해서, 관리자는 항상 간결하고 정확하려고 노력해야 한다. 직원과

의 회의 이전에, 그들은 그들 자신에게 "만약 팀원이 이 대화에서 한 가지를 이해하고 떠난다면, 나는 그것이 무엇이길 바라는가?"라는 질문을 해야 하고, 이 질문에 대한 답이 그들이 전달하는 데에 집중해야 하는 것이다.

(어휘) executive 경영진, 임원 management 관리, 경영 exhibit 보이다
subordinate 부하 직원 thorough 철저한 undertaking 일, 사업
objective 목표 requirement 요구 사항 strive 노력하다
concise 간결한 convey 전달하다

(구문분석) [8행] ~ also ①[provide unnecessary background details and personal opinions about the undertaking]. **Doing so** often leads to confusion on the part of the listener as it is difficult ②[to identify the objective and any specific requirements].
가주어
진주어(to부정사구)

→ Doing so는 앞 문장에서 이미 언급된 ①[provide ~ undertaking]을 가리키며, 주어 역할을 하는 동명사구이다.

→ 두 번째 문장은 가주어 it이 길이가 긴 진주어 to부정사구 ②[to ~ requirements] 대신 접속사 as가 이끄는 부사절의 주어 자리에 쓰인 형태이다.

21 밑줄 의미 추론하기   정답 ②

(해설) 인간에게는 자신이 위험을 피해갈 것이라 과도하게 확신하는 경향이 있는데, 이는 위험을 평가할 능력에 부정적인 영향을 미쳐서 해로운 행동들로 이어질 수 있다고 말하고 있다. 따라서 글의 주제를 비유적으로 표현한 see yourself through others' eyes(다른 사람의 눈을 통해 자신을 보다)가 의미하는 것은 ② '당신이 마주한 위험을 현실적으로 평가하라'이다.

(오답분석) ①은 상황에 대한 객관적인 판단을 통해 자신은 위험을 피할 것이라는 과도한 자신감을 경계해야 한다는 글의 내용과 반대되는 내용을 다루고 있으므로 오답이다. ③, ④, ⑤은 글에서 언급된 내용이 아니다.

(해석) 대부분의 사람들은 그들이 그들의 또래보다 불행한 사건들을 덜 겪을 것이라고 잘못 믿는다. 이 인지 편향의 근본적인 원인은 다른 사람의 능력과 비교하여 우리 자신의 능력을 정확하게 평가하지 못하는 능력이다. 우리는 우리의 능력을 과대평가하는 타고난 성향이 있어서, 이는 우리가 다른 사람들이 겪는 어려움을 피하는 데에 비현실적으로 자신 있다고 느끼도록 만든다. 지나치게 낙관적인 사고방식은 높은 자존감을 야기한다는 점에서 이로울 수 있지만, 그것은 위험을 평가하는 능력에 부정적으로 영향을 미칠 수도 있어서, 이는 해로운 행동들로 이어질 수 있다. 만약 당신이 미래에 성공적인 직업을 가지고 엄청난 부를 얻으리라는 것을 확신한다면, 당신은 불필요한 사치품들을 사면서 신용카드 빚을 잔뜩 지는 것에 대해 걱정하지 않을지도 모른다. 그러므로, 다른 사람의 눈을 통해 자신을 보는 것을 시도해라. 그것은 당신을 더 주저하게 만들지도 모르지만, 장기적으로는 당신을 보호해줄 수도 있다.

① 객관적이게 되어 자신감을 키워라.
② 당신이 마주한 위험을 현실적으로 평가하라.
③ 죄책감 없이 자신의 행동을 반성할 수 있는 방법을 찾아라.
④ 또래와 자신을 부정적으로 비교하는 것을 피하라.
⑤ 당신의 요구를 이해하는 사람들과 교류하라.

(어휘) underlying 근본적인 cognitive bias 인지 편향 inclination 성향
overestimate 과대평가하다 overly 지나치게, 몹시
optimistic 낙관적인, 낙천적인 self-esteem 자존감
run up a debt 빚을 잔뜩 지다 hesitant 주저하는
[선택지] reflect on ~을 반성하다

(구문분석) [8행] [**While** an overly optimistic mindset can be beneficial in that it results in greater self-esteem], it can also negatively affect your ability to assess risk, ~

→ [While ~ self-esteem]은 접속사 while(~하지만)이 이끄는 양보의 부사절이다.

22 요지 파악하기   정답 ②

(해설) 글의 마지막 두 문장에서 집단의 규모가 작으면 개인의 노력이 집단의 성공을 위해 필수적이라는 것을 느껴 추가적인 동기를 느끼지만, 큰 집단에 소속되어 있는 사람들의 경우 한 사람의 영향력이 작기 때문에 참여할 유인의 부족을 초래한다는 요지가 제시되어 있으므로, 이 글의 요지로 가장 적절한 것은 ②이다.

(오답분석) ①은 글의 일부만을 다루고 있는 오답이다.

(해석) 사람들이 집단행동을 하기 위해 함께 모일 때, 작은 집단이 큰 집단보다 공동의 목표를 더 잘 성공시킬 수 있다. 이것은 공유된 이익과 개인의 이익 사이의 근원적인 갈등에서 비롯된다. 한 요인은 무임승차 문제이다: 이는 집단 활동에 기여하지 않고 그것으로부터 이익을 얻는 것이다. 더 많은 수는 더 큰 익명성을 제공하기 때문에 이 현상은 많은 사람이 관여되었을 때 더욱 확연하다. 그렇지만, 작은 집단에서는 각각의 사람이 다른 사람에 의한 기여를 의식하고 있어서, 아무도 집단의 나머지 사람들에게 부정적인 인상의 대상이 되고 싶어 하지 않기 때문에 누군가 자신의 역할을 다하지 않을 가능성은 줄어든다. 동시에, 모든 구성원은 그들 개인의 노력이 성공을 위해 필요하다는 것을 느껴, 이는 추가적인 동기 부여를 제공한다. 큰 집단에 소속되어 있는 사람들에게는 그 반대가 진실이다; 한 사람이 기여하는 데 실패하는 것은 눈에 띄는 영향이 없을 가능성이 높으며, 이는 참여할 유인의 부족을 초래한다.

(어휘) collective action 집단행동 further 성공시키다; 더 나아가
tension 갈등, 긴장 pronounced 확연한 anonymity 익명성
likelihood 가능성 pull one's weight 자기의 역할을 다하다
incentive 유인, 장려책

(구문분석) [13행] At the same time, all members sense that their individual efforts are necessary for success, [which provides additional motivation].

→ 앞에 나온 절 전체를 받는 [which ~ motivation]은 주격 관계대명사 which가 이끄는 관계대명사절로, 콤마 뒤에서 계속적 용법으로 쓰였다.

23 주제 파악하기   정답 ⑤

(해설) 첫 두 문장으로 미루어 보아 태양 에너지가 상당한 환경적 악영향을 끼친다는 내용의 글로, 태양열 발전소와 태양광 전지가 환경에 미치는 영향을 예를 들어 설명하고 있다. 따라서 이 글의 주제로 가장 적절한 것은 ⑤ '태양 에너지가 환경에 미치는 영향에 대한 우려'이다.

(오답분석) ②은 글의 일부만을 다루고 있는 오답이다. ③은 글에서 언급된 solar cell을 사용하여 헷갈리게 하고 있지만 태양광 전지의 약점을 해결하는 방안은 글에서 언급되고 있지 않다.

(해석) 태양 에너지가 세계의 에너지 문제를 해결하는 데에 필수적일 수 있다는 것에는 의심의 여지가 없지만, 그것은 마법의 알약이 아니다. 태양 에너지는 사실 상당한 환경적 악영향을 끼친다. 대규모의 태양열 발전소는 방대한 양의 땅에

걸쳐 있어서 귀중한 서식지 구역을 차지함으로써 지역 야생 생물에 영향을 미칠 수 있다. 그러한 발전소의 배치와 설계 때문에 그것들이 차지하는 부지는 동시에 농업적 목적으로 사용될 수 없고, 이러한 시설의 설치는 환경의 질적 저하로 이어질 수 있다. 또한 태양광 전지를 제조하는 과정이 물의 사용을 필요로 하는 것을 아는 것이 중요한데, 이는 잠재적으로 그 지역의 현지 공급을 위협할 수 있다. 황산과 아세톤 같은 유독 화학물질도 이 과정에서 쓰이고, 적절히 처리되지 않는다면 사람들에게 해를 끼칠 수도 있다.

① 청정 에너지를 제조하는 과정
② 태양 에너지 발전소를 위한 토지 이용의 필요조건
③ 태양광 전지 설계의 약점을 처리하는 방안
④ 현대 농경법에 의해 야기되는 토지 오염
⑤ 태양 에너지가 환경에 미치는 영향에 대한 우려

[어휘] integral 필수적인 considerable 상당한 ramification (악)영향
simultaneously 동시에 agricultural 농업의 installation 설치
degradation 질적 저하 manufacture 제조하다 sulfuric acid 황산

[구문분석] [13행] Toxic chemicals such as sulfuric acid and acetone are also utilized during this process and could harm people [if (toxic chemicals are) not handled properly].
→ [if ~ properly]는 주절과 부사절의 주어가 같을 때 부사절에서 '주어 (toxic chemicals) + be동사(are)'가 생략된 형태이다.

24 제목 파악하기 정답 ③

[해설] 마지막 문장으로 미루어 보아 우리의 시간과 에너지를 쓸 가치가 있는 사람이 누구인지 생각해보아야 한다는 내용의 글로, 우리는 어려서부터 우리를 거절하는 집단에 소속되고 싶어 애를 쓰지만 그럴 만한 가치가 있지 않다는 것을 명심해야 한다고 설명하고 있다. 따라서 글의 제목으로 가장 적절한 것은 ③ '당신을 가치 있게 여기는 사람들과 관계를 형성하라'이다.

[오답분석] ①의 지위의 지표에 관한 내용은 글에서 언급되고 있지 않다. ②은 글의 일부만을 다루고 있는 오답이다.

[해석] 코미디언 Groucho Marx(그루초 막스)는 언젠가 그는 그를 구성원으로 받아주는 어떤 동호회에도 속하고 싶지 않을 것이라는 농담을 한 적이 있다; 이 농담의 이면은 그는 그를 받아줄 것 같지 않은 동호회에 오히려 가입하고 싶을 것이라는 것이다. 이 소속되고 싶은 이상한 갈망은 어렸을 때 시작된다. 대부분의 십 대들은 한 작은 또래들의 무리; "잘 나가는 아이들"의 일부가 되기만을 바란다. 그들은 주목받거나 인정받기 위해 애를 쓰고, 그 무리로부터 거절당하는 것은 단지 그들이 더 열심히 노력하도록 동기를 부여한다. 물론, 어른으로서 우리는 더욱더 복잡한 세상에 살고, 더 많은 사회적 집단들의 일부이다. 그러나, 흥미롭게도, 우리를 무시하는 사람들로부터의 인정에 대한 욕구가 종종 남아 있다. 어떤 것을 얻기 위해 필요한 대가가 그것의 가치와 같지는 않다는 것을 명심하는 것이 중요하므로, 우리의 시간과 에너지를 쓸 가치가 있는 사람은 누구인지 신중히 생각해보아야 한다.

① 지위의 지표인 사회적 관계
② 또래 수용: 어린 시절의 중요한 측면
③ 당신을 가치 있게 여기는 사람들과 관계를 형성하라
④ 특권 집단에 소속되는 것의 장점
⑤ 어떻게 우리의 친구가 인정받는다는 기분을 느끼게 해줄 수 있을까?

[어휘] flip side 이면 longing 갈망 recognition 인정 disregard 무시하다
linger 남다 merit 가치 [선택지] indicator 지표 exclusive 특권층의
appreciate (진가를) 인정하다

[구문분석] [7행] They go out of their way to **get noticed** or **approved** of, and ~
→ 동사 get을 이용한 수동태 'get + p.p'는 행위의 발생이나 동작에 초점을 둔 표현으로, 이 문장에서는 동작에 초점을 두고 있다.

25 도표 정보 파악하기 정답 ④

[해설] 2019년도에 미국의 1천 명당 승용차 대수는 4백 대가 안 되는 395.9대로 4백 대를 넘지 않으므로, 수치가 잘못 표현되었다. 따라서 도표의 내용과 일치하지 않는 것은 ④이다.

[해석]

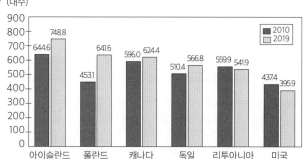

2010년과 2019년의 주민 1천 명 당 승용차 수

위의 그래프는 2010년과 2019년 선정된 국가들의 주민 1천 명당 승용차 대수를 보여준다. ① 6개 국가들 중, 리투아니아와 미국은 2010년에서 2019년까지 승용차 대수의 감소를 겪은 유일한 두 국가였다. ② 아이슬란드와 폴란드는 모두 그 기간 동안 주민 1천 명당 승용차 대수가 1백 대 이상 증가했다. ③ 독일에서는 승용차가 주민 1천 명당 6백 대를 절대 넘지 않았고, 독일은 2010년과 2019년에 모두 상위 4위를 기록했다. ④ 미국의 승용차는 2019년 주민 1천 명당 겨우 4백 대를 넘었지만 두 해 모두 5백 대 아래로 머물렀다. ⑤ 아이슬란드는 두 해 모두 주민 1천 명당 가장 많은 수의 승용차 수를 기록했고, 그것의 2019년 수치(주민 1천 명당 승용차 대수)는 두 연도의 어느 나라의 그것(주민 1천 명당 승용차 대수)도 뛰어넘었다.

[어휘] passenger car 승용차 inhabitant 주민 surpass 뛰어넘다

[구문분석] [13행] Iceland had the highest number of passenger cars per 1,000 inhabitants both years and its <u>number</u> in 2019 surpassed **that** of any other country in either year.
→ 지시대명사 that은 앞의 단수 취급하는 (the) number를 가리키며, 동일한 명사가 반복되는 것을 피하기 위해 사용되었다.

26 세부 정보 파악하기 정답 ④

[해설] Her first novel, *The Benefactor*, was released in 1963를 통해 Susan Sontag의 첫 번째 소설이 1963년에 출간되었다는 것을 알 수 있는데, ④은 마지막 소설이라고 일부 정보를 잘못 나타냈으므로 글의 내용과 일치하지 않는 것은 ④이다.

[해석] 1933년 뉴욕에서 태어난 미국 작가 Susan Sontag(수전 손택)은 현대 문화의 많은 측면을 다루는 수필과 소설을 썼다. 그녀는 하버드 대학교에서 두 개의 석사 학위를 취득했다. 첫 번째 석사 학위는 영문학이었다; 두 번째는 철학이었다. 1951년, 아직 학생일 때, 그녀는 유명 학술지인 <시카고 리뷰>에 게재되었던 글을 썼고, 그녀의 글이 발표된 처음을 기록했다. 졸업 이후, 그녀는 몇

개월간 유럽을 여행했고 뉴욕으로 다시 돌아와 몇몇 대학에서 가르쳤다. 그녀의 첫 소설 <은인>은 1963년에 출간되었고, 그 다음의 소설 작품들은 비평가들의 극찬을 받았다. Sontag은 정치적으로 활발히 활동했는데, 베트남 전쟁에 반대하는 시위에 참여하고, 그에 반대하는 수필을 썼다. 2004년 백혈병으로 인한 그녀의 죽음 이후, 그녀는 그녀 세대의 가장 영향력 있는 미국의 지식인 중 한 명으로 널리 칭송받았다.

 어휘 prominent 유명한 in print 발표된 release 출간하다
subsequent 그 다음의 be critically acclaimed 비평가들의 극찬을 받다
protest 시위 intellectual 지식인

구문분석 [16행] ~ she was widely praised as being [one of the most influential American intellectuals] of her generation.
→ [one ~ intellectuals]는 'one of the + 최상급 + 복수명사' (가장 ~한 것 중 하나)의 형태로 최상급을 나타내는 구문이다.

---

27 안내문 정보 파악하기 정답 ③

해설 Taste-test new products를 통해 신제품을 맛볼 수 있다는 것을 알 수 있으므로, 글의 내용과 일치하지 않는 것은 ③이다.

해석

Arrow 초콜릿 공장 견학

저희만큼 초콜릿을 사랑하신다면, 우리 공장 견학을 놓칠 수 없습니다. 당신이 가장 좋아하는 모든 간식이 어떻게 만들어지는지 바로 눈앞에서 확인해보십시오!

견학 일정:
- 월요일부터 금요일까지, 오전 10시-오후 3시
- 매주 토요일, 오전 10시-오후 12시
- 견학은 매시 정각에 시작되며 45분간, 진행됩니다.
* 공휴일에는 견학이 진행되지 않습니다.

입장료:
- 10달러 (10세 이상의 경우)
- 5달러 (10세 미만 어린이의 경우)

공장에서:
- 공장 전체 견학
- 신제품 시식
- 당신만의 초콜릿을 만들어보세요.

전체 규칙:
- 저희가 제공해드릴 마스크를 착용해주세요.
- 견학 인솔자를 항상 따라다니십시오.
더 많은 정보를 위해서는 1-800-233-6789로 전화하십시오.

어휘 treat 간식 at the top of every hour 매시 정각에 taste-test 시식하다

구문분석 [2행] If you love chocolate **as much as** we do, you can't miss out on our factory tour.
→ 'as + 원급 + as'는 원급을 이용한 비교구문으로 '…만큼 ~한/하게'라는 의미이다.

---

28 안내문 정보 파악하기 정답 ④

해설 First-time users must enter their credit card number into the app before use를 통해 최초 이용자는 이용 전 신용카드 번호를 입력해야 한다는 것을 알 수 있으므로, 글의 내용과 일치하는 것은 ④이다.

 해석

Jumper 전동 킥보드 대여

만약 당신이 돌아다니기에 환경적이고 편리한 방법을 찾고 있다면, 더 이상 찾지 마십시오. 도시 주변을 이동하는 것이 이보다 더 쉬웠던 적은 없었습니다!

대여하는 방법:
1. Jumper 앱을 다운로드한다.
2. 앱을 열고 회원이 된다.
3. 가장 가까운 킥보드를 찾아 QR 코드를 스캔한다.
4. 타기 시작한다!

요금:
- 첫 5분간 2달러, 이후 1분당 15센트
- 최초 이용자는 이용 전 앱에 신용카드 번호를 입력해야만 합니다.
- 이용한 분 단위로만 청구될 것입니다.

이용 종료하기:
- 킥보드 이용을 마쳤으면 앱의 "도착" 버튼을 눌러주세요.
- 반드시 킥보드를 안전한 장소에 주차하세요.

어휘 get around 돌아다니다 charge (요금을) 청구하다

구문분석 [15행] You will only **be charged for** the minutes used.
→ be charged for은 '요금이 청구되다'라는 의미로, by 이외의 전치사를 쓰는 수동태 구문이다.

---

29 어법상 틀린 것 찾기 정답 ④

해설 수식받는 명사 a bird가 flap이 나타내는 '퍼덕거리는' 행위의 주체이므로 ④의 과거분사 flapped를 현재분사 flapping으로 고쳐야 한다.

오답분석 ①은 to부정사 to record의 의미상 주어를 나타내기 위해 'for + 명사' 형태를 사용하였으므로 어법상 적절하다. ②은 help가 목적어로 동사원형과 to부정사를 모두 취할 수 있는 준사역동사이므로 동사원형 bring을 사용한 것은 어법상 적절하다. ③은 두 개의 절 Being ~ creativity와 many sounds ~ ways를 연결하는 자리에 접속사 because가 쓰여 어법상 적절하다. 참고로, despite ~ authentic은 삽입구(전치사구)이다. ⑤은 주어가 없는 불완전한 절을 이끌며 사물인 선행사 films를 받는 주격 관계대명사 that을 사용한 것은 어법상 적절하다.

해석 영화가 촬영될 때, 많은 소리들이 너무 조용하거나 불분명해서 촬영장에서 발생하고 있을 때 장비가 정확하게 녹음할 수 없다. 이 문제에 대처하기 위해, 특수 음향 효과 아티스트가 필요하다. 폴리(효과음 녹음) 아티스트라고 알려진 이러한 사람들은 카메라 영상을 주의 깊게 보고 그것과 맞는 소리를 만들 수 있는 물품들을 찾음으로써 영화에 생기를 불어넣는다. 진짜 소리인 것처럼 보임에도 불구하고, 많은 소리가 생소한 방식으로 복제되기 때문에 폴리 아티스트가 되는 것은 많은 창의력을 요구한다. 예를 들어, 새가 날개를 퍼덕거리는 소리는 가죽 지갑으로 만들어질 수가 있다. 궁극적으로, 폴리 아티스트의 작업은 그렇지 않으면 거의 시각 정보에만 의존해야 했을 영화에 진짜 같은 느낌과 분위기를 더해주기 때문에 매우 귀중하다.

어휘 footage 영상, 장면　authentic 진짜인　replicate 복제하다
flap (새가 날개를) 퍼덕거리다　ultimately 궁극적으로
invaluable 아주 귀한　authenticity 진짜임

구문분석

[11행] Ultimately, the work of a Foley artist is invaluable [as it adds a sense of authenticity and mood to films that would otherwise have to rely mostly on their visuals].

→ [as ~ visuals]는 접속사 as(~ 때문에)가 이끄는 이유의 부사절이다.

---

30 어휘 적절성 파악하기　정답 ③

해설 뉴턴의 운동 제3법칙은 모든 작용에는 크기는 같고 방향은 반대인 반작용이 있고, 모든 힘은 짝을 이룬다고 설명하고 있다. 또한 사람이 걷는 것에 대한 예시를 통해 신체가 지면에 아래로 힘을 가하는 것과 같은 힘을 지면은 위로 밀어낸다고 했다. 따라서 작용-반작용 쌍은 자연의 대칭을 나타낸다는 맥락이 되어야 하므로 ③의 asymmetry(비대칭)를 그와 반대되는 의미의 symmetry(대칭)와 같은 단어로 바꾸어야 문맥상 적절하다.

오답분석 ①은 작용-반작용이 우리가 경험하지만 거의 의식하지 못하고 있다는 문맥이 되어야 하므로 rarely가 오는 것이 적절하다. ②은 사람이 걸을 때 신체가 지면에 아래로 힘을 가한다는 문맥이 되어야 하므로 downwards가 오는 것이 적절하다. ④은 two such forces를 묶어서 두 힘이 모두 같은 물체에 작용하고 있다는 문맥이 되어야 하므로 both가 오는 것이 적절하다. ⑤은 사람이 베개에 올라서면 베개라는 동일한 물체에 사람과 지면이 힘을 가해 두 힘이 상쇄될 것이라는 문맥이 되어야 하므로 cancelling이 오는 것이 적절하다.

해석 뉴턴의 세 가지 운동 법칙은 물리학의 기반이다. 세 가지 중, 제3법칙은 모든 작용에 크기는 같고 방향은 반대인 반작용이 있다고 말한다. 이것은 우리가 경험하지만 ① 드물게 의식하는 것이다; 모든 힘은 짝을 이룬다는 것이다. 만약 사람이 걷고 있다면, 신체는 지면에 ② 아래로 힘을 가한다. 이것은 우리가 걸을 때 보고 느끼는 것이기 때문에 우리가 인식하는 것이다. 그동안에, 지면도 위로 향하는 같은 힘을 밀어낸다. 작용-반작용 쌍은 자연의 ③ 비대칭(→대칭)을 나타낸다. 그리고 누군가는 이 두 힘이 서로를 상쇄시킬 것이라고 생각할지도 모르지만, 흥미롭게도, 이것은 ④ 두 힘이 같은 물체에 작용하고 있을 때에만 일어난다. 위의 예시에서, 땅의 힘이 사람에 작용하는 동안 사람의 힘은 땅에 작용한다. 그러나, 만약 그 사람이 베개에 올라선다면, 사람과 땅은 그들의 힘을 베개에 가할 것이고, 이는 그 힘을 ⑤ 상쇄시킨다.

어휘 bedrock 기반　action 작용, 행위　reaction 반작용, 반응　exert 가하다
asymmetry 비대칭, 불균형　offset 상쇄하다　meanwhile 그동안에, 한편
cancel 상쇄하다, 무효로 하다

구문분석

[2행] Among the three, the third **states** [that for every action there is an equal and opposite reaction].

→ [that ~ reaction]은 접속사 that이 이끄는 명사절로, 동사 states의 목적어 역할을 한다.

---

31 빈칸 추론하기　정답 ⑤

해설 선택 교배의 한계를 극복하기 위해 유전자 변형 농산물을 이용해 원하는 형질만 가진 새로운 생물을 만들어낼 수 있다는 내용의 글이고, 글의 후반부에서 농작물이 더 탄력 있고 영양가가 높게 변형되어 소비자가 더 저렴하고 좋은 음식을 접하게 된다고 하였다. 따라서 주제와 관련된 빈칸에는 ⑤ '개량된'이 와서 유전자 변형 기술이 모든 종에 걸쳐 실행되어 개량된 생물의 개발을 가속

화할 수 있다는 의미가 되어야 한다.

해석 선택 교배를 통해 증가한 크기나 질병에 대한 저항력을 포함하여 원하는 속성을 더 많이 가진 자손이 만들어질 수 있다. 그러나 이 방법의 부작용은 이 방식으로 만들어진 일부 식물이나 동물이 원치 않는 특질도 물려받는다는 것이고, 따라서 이 기술은 완벽하지 못하다. 바로 그 지점에 유전자 변형 생물(GMOs)이 들어온다. 특정한 특징을 보이는 자손을 희망하며 생물의 모체를 인위적으로 고르는 대신, 유전자 변형은 공학자들이 한 생물로부터 특정한 형질을 가진 유전자를 분리한 다음, 그 같은 유전자를 다른 생물의 세포에 삽입하는 것을 가능하게 한다. 이것은 모든 종에 걸쳐 실행되어 개량된 생물의 개발을 가속화할 수 있다. 농업은 이 기술이 일반적으로 사용되는 한 산업이다. 농작물들은 더 탄력 있고 영양가가 높게 변형되어 소비자가 더 저렴하고 좋은 음식을 접하게 한다.

① 드문　　　　　　　　② 단단한
③ 이상한　　　　　　　④ 소형의
⑤ 개량된

어휘 selective breeding 선택 교배　desired 원하는, 훌륭한　offspring 자손
attribute 속성　resistance 저항력　side effect 부작용　inherit 물려받다
artificially 인위적으로　modification 변형, 조작　trait 형질
accelerate 가속화하다　resilient 탄력 있는, 회복력이 있는

구문분석

[8행] ~ selecting the parents of an organism [with the hope of offspring exhibiting certain characteristics], ~

　　　　　　　　명사　　　현재분사

→ 수식 받는 명사 offspring이 특정한 특징을 '보이는' 주체이므로 현재분사 exhibiting을 썼다.

[15행] Agriculture is one **industry** [in which this technique is commonly used].

→ [in ~ used]는 선행사 industry를 수식하며, '전치사 + 관계대명사' in which가 이끄는 관계대명사절이다.

---

32 빈칸 추론하기　정답 ④

해설 주제문에 해당하는 빈칸 문장에서 자기 도취증이 실제로는 사람들이 '무엇'하기 위한 내적 기제라고 하고, 이어서 자기 도취자들은 내면의 취약성을 드러내고 싶지 않아서 강하고 당당해 보이기 위해 뭐든지 한다고 했다. 따라서 빈칸에는 ④ '자신감과 관련된 문제에서 생겨나는 수치심을 다루다'가 와서 자기 도취증이란 자신감과 관련된 문제에서 생겨나는 수치심을 다루기 위한 내적 기제라는 의미가 되어야 한다.

오답분석 ①은 자기 도취자들의 무정한 행동이 사람들을 떠나게 만든다는 글의 내용과 반대되므로 오답이다. ②은 자기 도취자들은 자신의 취약성을 들키기 싫어서 다른 사람들과 가까워지기를 꺼린다는 글의 내용과 반대되는 내용이므로 오답이다. ③의 약점을 극복한다는 것은 글의 내용과 관련이 없다. ⑤은 자기 도취자들은 공감을 발달시킬 기회였을 수도 있는 진정한 관계 형성을 피한다는 글의 내용과 반대되는 내용이므로 오답이다.

해석 자기 도취증은 단순히 자만심이 강하거나 부당한 권리 의식을 가지고 있는 것보다 훨씬 더 복잡하다. 이것들이 확실히 증상이긴 하지만, 자기 도취증이 실제로는 사람들이 자신감과 관련된 문제에서 생겨나는 수치심을 다루기 위한 내부적 기제라는 것을 믿을 만한 이유가 있다. 몇몇 이론가들은 많은 자기 도취자의 강경한 태도 투영은 그들의 자존감이 실은 보여지는 방식과는 정반대라는 사실을 감추는 가장이라고 주장한다. 이 내면의 연약함을 드러내고 싶지 않기 때문에, 그들은 강한 척과 그들의 행동이 완전히 정당한 척을 하기 위해 할 수 있는 모든 것을 한다. 자기 도취자는 다른 사람들과 너무 가까워져서 동

료들이 자신의 약점을 알게 되는 것으로부터 자신을 보호하는 것에 열심이고, 그래서 실제로 공감 능력을 발달시킬 기회였을 수도 있는 어떤 진실한 관계들도 형성하는 것을 피한다. 비록 그들이 처음에는 다른 사람들을 능숙하게 조종하는 것처럼 보여도, 그들의 무정한 행동은 결국 사람들을 떠나게 한다.

① 다른 사람들을 염려하는 것처럼 보이기 위해 그들의 행동을 바꾸다
② 그들의 동료들과 친하게 지냄으로써 자존감을 높이다
③ 그들의 태도를 개선함으로써 자신의 약점을 극복하다
④ 자신감과 관련된 문제에서 생겨나는 수치심을 다루다
⑤ 관계를 형성하기 위해 다른 사람들에 대한 그들의 공감을 보여주다

 어휘 narcissism 자기 도취증, 자기애 　vain 자만심이 강한 　unwarranted 부당한
entitlement 권리, 자격 　projection 투영 　fragility 연약함, 취약성
justified 당당한, 정당한 　empathy 공감
manipulate 조종하다 　uncaring 무정한, 무신경한
[선택지] stem from ~에서 생기다

구문분석

[1행] Narcissism is [**far** more complicated than] simply being vain or having an unwarranted sense of entitlement.

→ [far ~ than]은 '비교급 + than'(~보다 -한)의 형태로 비교를 나타내는 구문으로, far는 비교급을 강조한다.

[9행] [**Not** wanting to reveal this inner fragility], they do everything they can to pretend to be ~

→ [Not ~ fragility]는 분사구문의 부정형으로, 분사 앞에 not을 붙여 만든다.

---

33 빈칸 추론하기 　　　정답 ③

해설 주제문에 해당하는 빈칸 문장에서 모든 사람이 자신이 원하는 모든 것을 말하는 것이 아니라 '무엇'하는 것이 중요하다고 하고, 글의 후반에서 혐오 수사법은 취약한 집단들을 심리적으로 조종하는 식으로 비방하고 다른 사람을 승격시키기 때문에 모든 생각이 발언될 필요가 없다는 걸 보여준다고 했다. 따라서 빈칸에는 ③ '말할 가치가 있는 모든 것이 말해지다'가 와서 중요한 것은 모든 사람이 자신이 원하는 모든 것을 말하는 것이 아니라 말할 가치가 있는 모든 것이 말해지는 것이라는 의미가 되어야 한다.

오답분석 ①의 말하는 것 이면의 좋은 의도에 대한 내용은 글에서 언급되고 있지 않다. ②은 말은 위험한 도구로 사용될 가능성이 있다는 글의 내용과 반대되는 내용이므로 오답이다. ④은 글의 내용과 관련이 없다. ⑤의 생각이 정직하게 전달된다는 것에 대한 내용은 글에서 언급되고 있지 않다.

해석 표현의 자유는 건전한 민주주의 사회의 특징이다. 그것은 특히 아무리 평판이 나쁘더라도 자신이 하는 말을 정당화하고 싶어 하는 사람들에 의해 옹호된다. 이것은 모든 시민의 권리이지만, 말은 위험한 도구로 사용될 가능성이 있다. 혐오 발언은 폭력 행위로 이어지는 불관용과 적개심의 씨앗을 심는 힘이 있다. 많은 사람들은 표현의 자유가 어떤 종류의 자기 표현도 정당화한다는 관념을 지지하지만, 이는 솔직하게 말하는 것이 무엇을 의미하는지의 중요성을 약화시킨다; 즉, 중요한 것은 모든 사람이 자신이 원하는 모든 것을 말하는 것이 아니라 말할 가치가 있는 모든 것이 말해지는 것이다. 표현의 자유가 결과가 따르지 않는 발언으로 대치되면, 우리는 우리의 도덕성을 포기하게 된다. 혐오 수사법은 교묘하고, 취약한 집단들을 심리적으로 조종하여 그들이 덜 가치 있는 것처럼 느끼게 만든다. 그것이 어떤 사람들을 비방하고 다른 사람들을 승격시키는 방식은 모든 생각이 발언될 필요는 없다는 충분한 증거이다.

① 그들이 말하는 것의 이면에는 좋은 의도가 있다
② 사용되는 언어는 본질적으로 중립적이다
③ 말할 가치가 있는 모든 것이 말해지다

---

④ 표현된 것이 청자들에게 명확하다
⑤ 그들의 생각이 정직하게 전달되다

 어휘 hallmark 특징 　democratic 민주주의의 　champion 옹호하다
intolerance 불관용 　hostility 적개심 　advocate 지지하다
undermine 약화시키다 　significance 중요성
substitute 대치되다, 대신하다 　surrender 포기하다 　morality 도덕성
gaslight 심리적으로 조종하다 　vulnerable 취약한 　tear down 비방하다
utter 발언하다 　[선택지] intention 의도 　neutral 중립적인
convey 전달하다

구문분석

[2행] It is particularly championed by those who wish to justify what they say, [**no matter how** unpopular].

→ [no ~ unpopular]는 no matter how(아무리 ~하더라도)가 이끄는 양보의 부사절이다.

[16행] The way it tears down some people and elevates others is proof enough that **not every** thought needs to be uttered.

→ not every는 '모두 ~인 것은 아니다'라는 의미로 부분 부정을 나타내는 구문이다.

---

34 빈칸 추론하기 　　　정답 ⑤

해설 빈칸 문장에서 it(그것)이 너무 빠르게 발전하는 것처럼 보이기 때문에 '무엇'은 놀랍지 않은 일이라고 했다. 이어서 생명 윤리는 건강과 생물학에 연관된 윤리적인 문제들을 포함한다고 했고, 글의 후반에서 생명 윤리는 소득에 따른 건강 격차를 줄이고 많은 사람들이 의료비 문제를 겪지 않도록 보장하는 것을 도울 최선의 방법을 검토한다고 했다. 따라서 주제문에 해당하는 빈칸에는 ⑤ '의학 분야가 윤리적인 감독을 필요로 한다'가 와서 의학 분야가 너무 빠르게 발전하는 것처럼 보이기 때문에 의학 분야가 윤리적인 감독을 필요로 한다는 것은 놀랍지 않은 일이라는 의미가 되어야 한다.

오답분석 ①의 도덕성 개념에 대한 내용은 글에서 언급되고 있지 않다. ②의 과학적 절차에 대한 내용은 글에서 언급되고 있지 않다. ③은 글의 내용과 관련이 없다.

해석 윤리학은 인간의 행동이나 활동에 관해 무엇이 옳고 그른지, 또는 무엇이 도덕적이고 비도덕적인지를 고찰한다. 이 철학의 분야는 모든 상황들의 방식에 적용될 수 있고 공동의 이익을 위해 문제들이 어떻게 다뤄져야 하는지 질문한다. 그렇다면 의학 분야가 너무나도 빠르게 발전하는 것처럼 보이기 때문에 의학 분야가 윤리적인 감독을 필요로 하는 것은 놀랍지 않은 일이다. 생명 윤리는 이 역할을 수행하고 과학 실험을 평가하는 것부터 의사-환자 관계를 평가하는 것까지 건강과 생물학에 연관된 윤리적 문제들을 아우른다. 유전자 실험, 장기 이식, 혼수상태의 환자를 치료하는 것과 같은 논란이 많은 문제는 모두 숙고를 요구하는 윤리적 함의가 있고, 그것들이 유발하는 질문들은 종종 완전한 확실성을 갖고 대답하기 어렵다. 예를 들어, 심지어 보다 발전된 치료 선택지들이 시장에 진입하면서 저소득층과 고소득층의 건강 격차가 커지고 있기 때문에 의료비는 중요한 논의 대상이다. 생명 윤리는 이러한 차이를 줄이고 그저 부유층만이 아닌 다른 많은 사람들이 적당한 가격의 효과적인 의료 서비스를 이용할 수 있도록 보장하는 것을 도울 최선의 방법을 검토한다.

① 도덕성의 개념은 시간이 지나면서 변동을 거듭해왔다
② 과학적 절차들이 윤리학과 관련 있게 되었다
③ 의료계가 인기 있는 직업 분야가 되고 있다
④ 치료가 더욱 환자 중심이 되었다
⑤ 의학 분야가 윤리적인 감독을 필요로 한다

어휘 ethics 윤리학 　branch 분야 　bioethics 생명 윤리
fulfill 수행하다, 충족시키다 　encompass 아우르다

controversial 논란이 많은 organ transplantation 장기 이식
implication 함의, 영향 deliberation 숙고 evoke 유발하다, 불러일으키다
certainty 확실성 affordable 적당한 가격의, 감당할 수 있는
[선택지] fluctuate 변동을 거듭하다 oversight 감독, 감시

 [구문분석]
[4행] ~ and questions [how matters should be dealt with for the common good].
→ [how ~ good]은 의문사 how가 이끄는 명사절로, 동사 questions 의 목적어 역할을 한다.

35 흐름과 관계 없는 문장 찾기 정답 ②

[해설] 동물의 삶이 개선되었으면 하는 바람에서 사용하는 인간의 디지털 기술은 동물들이 기술에 의존하게 하거나 자연과의 관련성을 약화시킬 수도 있다는 우려를 나타내는 내용의 글이다. 그런데 ②은 자연 보호의 모습이 기술 덕분에 엄청나게 변화하고 있다는 내용이므로 주제에서 벗어나 있어 글의 흐름과 무관하다.

[오답분석] ④의 such innovations는 ③의 pet products와 interactive touchscreens 를 가리키고 있으므로, ③ 뒤에 이어지는 것이 적절하다.

[해석] 동물은 인간이 만든 기술과 수십 년간 상호 작용해왔는데, 가장 일반적으로는 그들의 인지에 대한 우리의 이해를 발전시키기 위해 고안된 행동 실험과 생산을 최대한 효과적으로 하기 위한 농업의 환경에서이다. ① 그러나 디지털 기술이 점점 더 흔해지면서, 우리는 그것을 사용해서 그들의 삶을 개선하고자 하는 희망을 가지고 기술의 범위를 넓히고 있다. (② 자연 보호의 모습은 디지털 기술 덕분에 앱과 도구들이 우리의 습관을 점진적으로 형성하면서 엄청나게 변화하고 있다.) ③ 요즘, 시장은 사람들이 자신의 고양이와 강아지를 원격으로도 관찰하고 같이 놀 수 있도록 해주는 반려동물 제품으로 넘쳐나고, 동물원은 영장류에 그들이 필요로 하는 정신적 자극을 제공할 수 있는 상호작용이 가능한 터치스크린을 쓰고 있다. ④ 그러한 혁신들이 무해한 것처럼 보일 수 있지만, 몇몇 사람들은 인간이 만든 기술을 다른 종에게 접하게 하는 것이 동물들을 기술에 의존하게 하거나 자연 세계에 대한 관련성을 약화시킬 것이라고 걱정한다. ⑤ 본질적으로, 우리가 기술로부터 혜택을 입지 않을지도 모를 생물체에 기술을 강요하고 있을 수 있다는 인식이 있다.

[어휘] cognition 인지 optimize 최대한 효과적으로 하다 ubiquitous 아주 흔한
conservation 보호, 보전 profound 엄청난, 심오한
progressively 점진적으로 remotely 원격으로 stimulation 자극
reliant 의존하는 relevance 관련성, 적합성

 [구문분석]
[10행] These days, the market is flooded with pet products that allow people to monitor and play with their cats and
　　　　　　　　동사　목적어　　목적격 보어
dogs remotely, ~
→ 동사 allow의 목적어로 people, 목적격 보어로 to부정사 to monitor 가 쓰였다.

36 글의 순서 배열하기 정답 ③

[해설] 주어진 글은 프랑스 혁명 이전 프랑스의 측정 단위는 약 1천 년 간 바뀌지 않았으며 지역마다 달랐다는 내용이다. (B)의 up to 800 different names for units of measurement(최대 800개의 다른 측정 단위의 명칭)는 주어진 글의 '측정 단위가 지역마다 달랐다'는 내용을 가리키므로 주어진 글 바로 다음

에 오는 것이 적절하다. (C)의 the confusion and lack of unity는 (B)의 '분쟁과 사기 혐의'와 '최대 800개의 다른 측정 단위'를 의미하므로 그 뒤에 와야 한다. (A)의 this는 (C)에서 설명하는 주된 측정 단위가 미터인 Charles Maurice de Talleyrand가 제안했던 새로운 체계를 가리키므로 (C) 뒤에 오는 것이 자연스럽다. 따라서 글의 순서로 가장 적절한 것은 ③ (B) - (C) - (A) 이다.

[해석] 프랑스 혁명 이전에, 프랑스의 측정 단위는 약 1천 년 간 바뀌지 않았을 뿐만 아니라 지역마다 크게 달랐다.

(B) 최대 800개의 다른 측정 단위의 명칭이 있었기 때문에, 많은 상인은 그들만의 측정 장치를 사용했다. 그러나, 이것은 자주 분쟁과 사기 혐의의 원인이 되었다.

(C) 낡은 제도가 야기한 그 혼란과 통일성 부족을 끝내기 위해, Charles Maurice de Talleyrand(샤를 모리스 드 탈레랑)은 1790년대에 그것을 자연의 특성에 기반을 둔 새로운 체계로 대체할 것을 제안했다. 그가 제안한 체계에서 주된 측정 단위는 미터였는데, 그것은 적도에서 북극까지의 거리의 천만 분의 1로 기록되었다.

(A) 현재 미터법으로 알려진 이것은 더 간단한 측정법이었고 다른 유럽 국가들의 전문가와의 회의를 통해 더욱 발전되었다. 비록 프랑스가 이것의 사용을 의무적으로 만드는 데에는 대략 50년 정도가 걸렸지만, 오늘날 세계의 대부분에서 두루 쓰이기 때문에 이것의 영향은 부인하기 어렵다.

[어휘] measurement 측정 metric system 미터법 mandatory 의무적인
undeniable 부인하기 어려운, 명백한 accusation 혐의 fraud 사기
unity 통일성 equator 적도

[구문분석]
[1행] Prior to the French Revolution, French units of measurement had **not only** ①[gone unchanged for about 1,000 years] **but also** ②[varied widely from region to region].
→ ①[gone ~ years]와 ②[varied ~ region]은 상관접속사 not only A but also B로 연결된 병렬 구조이다.

[5행] [Now **known** as the metric system], this was a simpler system of measurement ~
→ [Now ~ system]은 과거분사(known)로 시작하는 수동형 분사구문이다. 부사 now가 과거분사 known을 수식하고 있다.

37 글의 순서 배열하기 정답 ⑤

[해설] 주어진 글은 과일의 숙성에 대해 설명하면서, 에틸렌 가스가 전반적인 과정을 가속화한다는 주제를 제시한다. (C)의 how much ethylene은 주어진 글의 마지막 부분에서 언급된 '전반적인 과정을 가속화하는 에틸렌 가스'와 이어지므로 주어진 글 바로 다음에 오는 것이 적절하다. (B)의 The burst of ethylene은 (C)의 '갑작스러운 그 가스의 증가'를 가리키므로 (C) 바로 다음에 오는 것이 적절하다. (A)의 Non-climacteric fruit(후숙되지 않는 과일)은 (B)의 후숙 과일에 대한 설명과 반대되는 새로운 내용이므로 가장 마지막에 오는 것이 적절하다. 따라서 글의 순서로 가장 적절한 것은 ⑤ (C) - (B) - (A) 이다.

[해석] 과일은 숙성하면서 더 달아지는 것부터 새로운 색깔을 띠는 것까지 외부적인 변화와 내부적인 변화를 모두 겪는다. 이러한 변화들은 에틸렌 가스를 포함한 다양한 호르몬과 신호에 의해 이뤄지는데, 이는 전반적인 과정을 가속화한다.

(C) 각 과일은 생명 주기 동안 얼마나 많은 양의 에틸렌이 존재하는지는 다르지만, 보통 성장하는 동안 두 가지 패턴을 따른다. 사과, 바나나, 그리고 배와 같은 후숙 과일은 전반적으로 더 많은 에틸렌을 만들어 내고, 익는 기간 동안

갑작스러운 그 가스의 증가를 경험한다.

(B) 에틸렌의 폭증은 늘어난 호흡률을 동반한다. 이 과일들은 수확이 된 후에도 익을 수 있고, 외부의 에틸렌에 영향을 받을 수 있으므로, 만약 낮은 농도의 그 가스를 가진 후숙 과일이 더 높은 농도의 가스를 가지고 있는 것 옆에 놓인다면, 그것의 숙성은 더 빨라질 것이다.

(A) 후숙되지 않는 과일은 에틸렌이나 호흡의 급증이 없고, 식물에 의존해 숙성하여 일단 수확되면 익지 않는다. 딸기, 체리, 그리고 포도가 이런 방식으로 익는 과일의 예시이다.

어휘 **mature** 숙성하다 **undergo** 겪다 **alteration** 변화 **ethylene** 에틸렌 **hasten** 가속화하다, 앞당기다 **surge** 급증 **ripen** 익다, 숙성하다 **respiration** 호흡 **accompany** 수반하다 **lifecycle** 생명 주기

구문분석 [1행] As a fruit matures, it undergoes **both** ①[external (changes)] **and** ②[internal changes], from acquiring ~
→ ①[external (changes)]과 ②[internal changes]는 상관접속사 both A and B(A와 B 모두)로 연결된 병렬 구조이다.

38 주어진 문장의 위치 찾기
정답 ③

해설 주어진 문장의 It also(그것은 또한)로 보아, 주어진 문장 앞에는 It이 가리키는 대상과 그 대상의 한계점에 대한 내용이 나와야 한다는 것을 알 수 있다. 이 글에서는 ② 뒤 문장에서 비평가들의 패션에 대한 평가가 예술성의 영역을 좁히는 한계를 가지고 있다고 설명하고 있고, 주어진 문장의 '예술이 전달될 수 있는 방식'의 구체적인 내용으로 ③ 뒤 문장에서 사회와 시대의 표현으로서 패션을 언급하고 있다. 따라서, 주어진 문장이 들어가기에 가장 적절한 곳은 ③이다.

오답분석 ② 뒤 문장의 This assessment는 ① 뒤 문장의 '비평가들이 옷은 순수 예술로 분류되어서는 안 된다고 느낀 것'을 가리키므로 주어진 문장이 들어가기에 적절하지 않다. ④, ⑤ 뒤 문장은 ③ 뒤 문장에 이어서 패션이 예술로 인정되어야 하는 이유를 설명하고 있다.

해석 역사적으로, 패션은 예술계에서 회화, 음악, 또는 문학과 같은 지위로 승격된 적이 단 한 번도 없었다. 이 격차는 1983년 메트로폴리탄 미술관의 한 전시에서 드러났다. (①) Rembrandt(렘브란트)와 Picasso(피카소)의 걸작과 같은 방식으로 특정한 상징적인 옷들을 전시한 것은 옷이 순수 예술로 분류되어서는 안 된다고 느꼈던 많은 비평가를 화나게 했다. (②) 이 평가는 예술성의 영역을 시대에 뒤처지고 제한적인 상자 하나로 좁힌다. (③ 그것은 또한 예술이 전달될 수 있는 무수히 많은 방식을 고려하지 못한다.) 모든 예술처럼, 패션은 우리가 사는 사회를 명시하는 것이고 우리가 한 부분인 시대의 표현이다. (④) 우리가 감탄하는 그림들이 우리가 무엇을 아름답고, 감동적이라고 여기는지 보여주는 것과 같은 방식으로 그것(패션)은 한 사람으로서 우리가 누구인지를 나타낼 수 있다. (⑤) 패션은 틀림없이 하나의 산업이지만, 다른 어떤 예술적 노력만큼 많은 헌신과 솜씨를 필요로 하는 창조적인 것(산업)이다.

어휘 **myriad** 무수히 많은 **elevate** 승격시키다 **disparity** 격차 **bring to light** 드러내다, 밝히다 **iconic** 상징적인 **masterpiece** 걸작 **outdated** 시대에 뒤처진 **restrictive** 제한적인 **manifestation** 명시하는 것, 표명 **dedication** 헌신 **craftsmanship** 솜씨, 숙련

구문분석 [7행] The display of ~ angered **many critics** [who did not feel clothes should be categorized as fine art].
→ [who ~ art]는 선행사 many critics를 수식하며, 주격 사람 관계대명사 who가 이끄는 관계대명사절이다.

39 주어진 문장의 위치 찾기
정답 ③

해설 주어진 문장의 Meanwhile(한편)로 보아, 주어진 문장 앞에는 민간 보험에 의존하지 않는 시민들에 대한 내용이 나와야 한다는 것을 알 수 있다. 이 글에서는 ② 뒤 문장에서 의료비의 일부 혹은 전체를 정부 제도를 통해 지원받고 있는 가난하거나, 장애가 있거나, 나이 든 시민들에 대해 설명하고 있다. 또한 주어진 문장의 68% of citizens는 ③ 뒤 문장에서 언급된 those enrolled in private insurance policies(민간 보험 정책에 가입된 사람들)로 이어지고 있으므로, 주어진 문장이 들어가기에 가장 적절한 곳은 ③이다.

오답분석 ② 뒤 문장의 this system은 ① 뒤 문장의 private system을 가리키므로 주어진 문장이 들어가기에 적절하지 않다. ④ 뒤 문장은 ③ 뒤 문장에 이어서 deductibles에 대해 구체적인 예시를 통해 부연설명하고 있다.

해석 다른 경제 선진국에서 미국으로 이주한 사람들은 의심의 여지없이 미국의 의료 보험 제도의 이상한 작동 방식에 당황했다. (①) 세계의 거의 모든 다른 산업화된 국가들과 달리, 미국 정부는 공적으로 운영되는 전 국민 의료 보험 형식을 제공하지 않고, 대신 대부분 민간 제도를 운용한다. (②) 이 제도 아래에서, 가난하고, 장애가 있고, 그리고 나이 든 시민들은 그들의 의료비의 일부 혹은 전부가 정부 지원의 제도를 통해 충당될 수 있는 자격을 가진다. (③ 한편, 시민의 68퍼센트는 보험 회사를 통한 민간 보험에 의존하고, 다른 8퍼센트는 보험이 아예 없다.) 게다가, 보험 혜택이 발효되기 전에 다달이 내는 비싼 보험료 외에 납입되어야 하는 자기 부담 비용인 높은 공제액은 민간 보험 정책에 가입된 사람들 중 대부분이 의료 서비스를 확실히 이용할 수 있는 것을 방해한다. (④) 한 분석에 따르면, 미국인 개인 공제액의 평균은 5,940달러인데, 많은 사람의 경제력을 넘어서는 금액이다. (⑤) 이러한 이유로, 비평가들은 입법 기관이 도입하는 것을 고려할 수 있도록 많은 다른 모델들을 제안해 왔다.

어휘 **coverage** 보험, 보장 **healthcare system** 의료 보험 제도 **industrialized** 산업화된 **predominately** 대부분 **impoverished** 가난한 **deductible** 공제 금액 **out-of-pocket** 자기 부담의, 일시불의 **legislature** 입법 기관

구문분석 [14행] Moreover, high deductibles ~ [**prevent** many of those enrolled in private insurance policies **from** being able to reliably access medical services].
→ [prevent ~ services]는 prevent A from v-ing의 형태로 'A가 ~하는 것을 방해하다'라는 의미를 나타내는 동명사 관용 표현이다.

40 요약문 완성하기
정답 ②

해설 글의 전반부에서 공간 학습에서 수면의 역할을 밝혀내기 위해 3차원 가상 미로를 빠져나가는 실험을 했다고 했고, 글의 후반부에서는 훈련 후에 잠을 잤던 집단의 구성원들이 그들의 움직임에 관해 내린 결정들이 더 자주 정확했다고 했다. 따라서 지문의 get through를 navigate로, correct를 accurate으로 바꾸어 표현한 ②이 정답이다.

(오답분석) 미로를 빠져나가는 실험이라고 했으므로 ①과 ④의 design은 (A)에 들어갈 단어로 적절하지 않다. 참가자들이 자신들의 움직임에 대해 내린 결정이 더 자주 정확했다고 했으므로 ③의 communicative와 ⑤의 observant는 (B)에 들어갈 단어로 적절하지 않다.

(해석) 뇌의 해마에 의존하는 능력인 공간 학습에서 수면의 역할을 밝혀내기 위해 연구자들은 3차원 가상 미로를 얼마나 잘 빠져나갈 수 있는지를 시험하는 학술적 수면 실험에 지원자들을 모집했다. 참가자들은 두 집단으로 나뉘었고, 그 두 집단 모두 어떻게 미로를 끝마치는지에 대한 훈련을 받았다; 첫 번째 집단의 교육은 오전 10시에 이루어졌고, 두 번째 집단의 교육은 오후 10시에 이뤄졌다. 두 집단 모두 훈련 11시간 이후 그들이 배운 것에 대해 시험을 치렀는데, 두 번째 집단은 하룻밤을 잔 후에 다음 날 그들이 배운 것을 보여주었다. 평가되기 전 잠을 잤던 집단이 첫 번째 집단을 능가한다는 것이 밝혀졌다. 비록 이 집단의 구성원들이 과제를 끝마치는 데에 더 빠르지는 않았지만, 그들이 미로에서 그들의 움직임과 관련하여 내리는 결정은 더 자주 정확했다. 이 실험 결과는 궁극적으로 수면이 해마에서의 공간 정보 처리를 강화한다는 것을 시사한다.

↓

가상의 미로에서 (A) 길을 찾는 그들의 능력에 대한 시험에서, 훈련 후에 잠을 잔 참가자들이 잠을 자지 않은 참가자들보다 더 (B) 정확했다.

	(A)		(B)
①	설계하다	……	전념하는
②	길을 찾다	……	정확한
③	끝내다	……	말을 잘하는
④	설계하다	……	정밀한
⑤	길을 찾다	……	관찰력 있는

(어휘) determine 밝히다　spatial 공간의　dimensional 차원의
virtual 가상의　maze 미로　demonstrate 보여주다
outperform 능가하다　enhance 강화하다

(구문분석) [23행] ~ participants who slept following their training were more accurate than **those** who **did not**.
→ 대명사 those는 앞의 participants를 가리키며, 비교구문에서 동일한 명사가 반복되는 것을 피하기 위해 사용되었다.
→ did not 뒤에는 sleep following their training이 생략되어 있는데 who ~ training에서 이미 언급되었기 때문이다.

41~42 장문 독해 1

(해석) 오늘날 성공적인 기업이 되는 것은 그저 고품질의 상품을 제공하는 것 이상이다. 기업은 이익을 창출하는 조직으로서뿐만 아니라 공익을 위해 일하는 기관으로서도 기능할 것으로 기대된다. 사회가 많은 경제적, 사회적, 환경적 문제에 직면하면서, 기업은 자신이 어디에서 소비하는지에 신중한 소비자들에 의해 더 면밀히 분석되고 있다; 다시 말해서, ⁴²환경친화적이라는 평판을 지닌 기업이 환경 오염으로 악명 높은 기업보다 소비자를 끌어들일 가능성이 더 높다는 것이다. 기업의 사회적 책임(CSR)에 따라 운영되는 사업은 이를 염두에 둔다.
그런 단체 중 하나가 Lego인데, 그것은 지난 몇 년간 많은 지속 가능성 목표를 세워왔다. 그것은 세계 자연 기금(WWF) 기후 살리기 프로그램 파트너로 명명된 유일한 장난감 기업이고, 그들은 2030년까지 모든 주요 상품과 포장에 환경친화적인 소재들을 쓰겠다고 서약했다. CSR은 시간이 지남에 따라 Lego에 이익이 되었는데, 그 기업은 2021년 상반기에만 순이익이 140퍼센트 증가했다고 발표하였다. 그러므로, ⁴¹·⁴²그들은 지속 가능성과 교육에 투자

하는 것으로 눈부신 평판을 구축했을 뿐만 아니라, 이익도 증가시켰다. 이것은 CSR이 어떻게 기업에 이익이 되는 사업 모델인지 보여준다. 사람들과 서식지를 착취하기보다, 그들을 육성하고 돌보기 위해 행동하는 기업들이 미래에 번창할 것이다.

(어휘) common good 공익　an abundance of 많은　wary 신중한, 경계하는
reputation 평판　notorious 악명 높은　sustainability 지속 가능성
pledge 서약하다　net profit 순이익　cultivate 구축하다
foster 육성하다, 조성하다　[선택지] prosper 번창하다
mend 개선하다, 고치다

(구문분석) [2행] Companies are expected to not only function ~ as institutions [(that/which are) working for the common good].
→ [working ~ good]은 선행사 institutions를 꾸며주는 관계절로, '주격 관계대명사(that/which) + be동사(are)'가 생략된 형태이다.

41 제목 파악하기　　　정답 ④

(해설) 마지막 부분으로 미루어 보아 CSR(기업의 사회적 책임)이 어떻게 기업에 이익이 되는 사업 모델인지 설명하는 내용의 글로, 기업 Lego를 예를 들어 설명하고 있다. 따라서 글의 제목으로 가장 적절한 것은 ④ '사회적으로 책임감이 있는 기업이 오늘날 번창하는 이유들'이다.

(오답분석) ①, ③, ⑤은 글의 일부만을 다루고 있는 오답이다. ②은 글에서 언급되고 있지 않다.

(해석) ① 환경친화적 기업이 되기 위한 팁
② 기업의 사회적 책임에 숨겨진 비용
③ 지속 가능성: 평판을 개선하기 위한 해결책
④ 사회적으로 책임감이 있는 기업이 오늘날 번창하는 이유들
⑤ 이익을 극대화하는 데에 가장 중요한 요소는 무엇인가?

42 빈칸 추론하기　　　정답 ①

(해설) 빈칸 문장은 사람들과 서식지를 '무엇'하기보다, 그들을 육성하고 돌보기 위해 행동하는 기업들이 미래에 번창할 것이라고 했다. 글의 중반에서 환경친화적이라는 평판을 가진 기업이 환경 오염으로 악명 높은 기업보다 소비자를 끌어들일 가능성이 더 높다고 했고, 빈칸 앞 문장에서는 CSR 모델을 따르는 기업인 Lego가 지속 가능성과 교육에 투자하는 것에 대한 눈부신 평판을 구축해서 이익을 증가시켰다고 했다. 따라서 빈칸에는 ① '착취하기'가 와서 사람들과 서식지를 착취하는 것보다 그들을 육성하고 돌보기 위해 행동하는 기업들이 미래에 번창한다는 의미가 되어야 한다.

(오답분석) ②, ③, ④, ⑤은 사람들과 서식지를 부정적으로 이용한다는 의미를 설명하는 단어로 적절하지 않다.

(해석) ① 착취하기　　　② 전복시키기
③ 대체하기　　　④ 충족시키기
⑤ 보호하기

(어휘) exploit 착취하다　indulge 충족시키다, 채우다

43~45 장문 독해 2

(해석) (A) Anay의 생일이었고 그는 그의 가족과 친구들로부터 많은 선물들을 받았다. 그러나 그가 받은 가장 좋은 선물은 그의 형으로부터 받은 것: 빛나는 새 자동차였다! (a)그는 그것이 매우 자랑스러웠고 매일 자신의 직장에 타고 갔다. 그는 종종 행인들이 그의 소중한 소유물을 부러운 듯 바라보는 것을 보았다.

(C) 어느 날, Anay가 그의 사무실을 나와서 그의 차를 향해 갔을 때, 그의 차를 보고 있는 사람 중 한 명이 어린 소년인 것을 보았다. 그는 찢어진 옷을 입은 채 조금 지저분해서 Anay는 그가 형편이 좋지 않다는 것을 알 수 있었다. 친절한 사람인 Anay는 ⁴⁴그 소년에게 가서 (d)그에게 집까지 차를 타고 가고 싶은지 물어보았다.

(B) 어린 소년의 눈이 빛났다! 그는 자동차를 타본 적이 없어서 신이 났다. Anay와 그 소년이 동네를 차로 지나갈 때, 소년은 (b)그에게 차를 어디서 얻었냐고 물어보았다. Anay는 그의 형이 그것을 생일 선물로 주었다고 대답했다. "그래서 당신은 한 푼도 내지 않아도 됐다는 말이에요?" 그 소년이 놀라며 물었다. "맞아," Anay가 대답했다. "와… 저도…," 그 소년이 말하기 시작했지만 Anay는 그가 뭐라고 말할지 알고 있었다. "너도 내 형과 같은 형이 있었으면 좋겠구나, 그렇지?" (c)그가 말했다.

(D) 그 소년은 고개를 저었다. ⁴⁵"저도 그런 형이 될 수 있으면 좋겠어요"라고 그가 말했다. Anay는 그의 대답에 놀랐다. 그러나, Anay가 소년의 집에 그를 내려 주었을 때, 그는 그가 왜 그렇게 얘기했는지 이해할 수 있었다. "제 남동생을 데리고 와도 될까요? 저는 걔가 (e)당신의 멋진 차를 보았으면 좋겠어요." 곧 그는 다리가 마비된 작은 소년을 데리고 다시 나타났다. "저 빛나는 차 보여? 나는 너에게 차를 사줄 수 있을 만큼 충분한 돈을 벌 거고, 넌 단 한 푼도 내지 않아도 될 거야."

(어휘) **automobile** 자동차 **passersby** 행인 **prized** 소중한 **torn** 찢어진 **well-off** 형편이 좋은 **magnificent** 멋진, 장엄한 **paralyze** 마비시키다

(구문분석) [5행] He often <u>saw</u> <u>passersby</u> <u>looking</u> at his prized possession with envy.
동사　　목적어　　목적격 보어

→ 지각동사 saw의 목적어로 passersby, 목적격 보어로 현재분사 looking이 쓰였다. 참고로, 지각동사는 목적격 보어로 동사원형도 쓰일 수 있는데, 현재분사가 쓰이면 동작이 진행 중인 것이 강조된다.

43 글의 순서 배열하기　　정답 ②

(해설) (A)는 Anay가 생일 선물로 자동차를 받아 타고 다녔고, 행인들이 종종 부러운 듯이 봤다는 내용이다. (C)는 Anay가 그의 차를 보고 있는 사람들 가운데 어린 소년을 보았다는 내용이므로, 종종 사람들이 그의 차를 쳐다봤다고 한 (A) 뒤에 와야 한다. (B)는 그 소년이 차에 타서 Anay와 나눈 대화이므로, Anay가 그 소년에게 차를 타고 싶냐고 물어본 (C) 다음에 오는 것이 적절하다. (D)의 The boy shook his head. "I hope that I can be a brother like that"은 (B)의 "You wish you had an older brother like mine, don't you?"에 대한 대답이므로 (B) 뒤에 와야 한다. 따라서 글의 순서로 가장 적절한 것은 ② (C) - (B) - (D)이다.

44 지칭 대상 파악하기　　정답 ④

(해설) (a), (b), (c), (e)는 모두 Anay를 가리키지만 (d)는 그의 차를 보고 있던 한 소년을 가리키므로, ④이 정답이다.

45 세부 정보 파악하기　　정답 ④

(해설) (D)의 "I hope that I can be a brother like that,"을 통해 소년은 Anay와 같은 형이 되고 싶다고 말한 것이 아니라 자동차를 사준 Anay의 형과 같은 형이 될 수 있으면 좋겠다고 말한 것을 알 수 있다. 따라서 글의 내용과 일치하지 않는 것은 ④이다.

정답

문제집 p. 110

18	⑤	19	③	20	②	21	⑤	22	⑤	23	④	24	②	25	④	26	④	27	⑤
28	④	29	⑤	30	④	31	④	32	⑤	33	③	34	①	35	④	36	②	37	④
38	④	39	③	40	②	41	③	42	②	43	④	44	③	45	④				

18 목적 파악하기

정답 ⑤

해설 글의 중간 이후에서 아이들을 위한 놀이터를 만들어 달라고 제안하고 있으므로, 정답은 ⑤이다.

해석 관계자분께:

제 이름은 Winnie Anderson입니다. 저는 최근에 이 동네로 이사 왔고 얼마나 많은 아름다운 공원들이 있는지에 놀랐습니다. 제 가족과 함께 자연을 즐길 수 있어서 매우 좋았습니다. 저는 대부분의 공원들에 어른을 위한 많은 운동 기구와 활동들이 있지만 아이들을 위한 것은 그렇게 많지 않다는 점을 알게 되었습니다. 저는 아이들이 항상 주위를 뛰어다니는 것을 보며 그들이 놀기에 안전한 공간이 필요하다고 생각했습니다. 그게 바로 제가 이 편지를 보내는 이유입니다. 저는 시 웹사이트에서 주민들의 제안을 환영한다는 것을 보았고, 아이들을 위해 몇 개의 놀이터가 만들어진다면 좋을 것이라고 생각합니다. 고려해주셔서 감사합니다.

Winnie Anderson 드림

어휘 as many 같은 수만큼의 (것) welcome 환영하다, 기꺼이 받아들이다

구문 분석

[10행] I saw ①[that the city website welcomes suggestions from residents], and I **think** ②[(that) it would be great if a few playgrounds could be built for the children].

→ 명사절 ①[that ~ residents]와 ②[it ~ children]은 각각 동사 saw와 think의 목적어 역할을 하며, ②[it ~ children]에는 명사절 접속사 that이 생략되었다.

19 심경 파악하기

정답 ③

해설 심경은 간접적으로 표현된다. 글의 초반부의 I always thought I'd be an ideal candidate for the university를 통해 'I'가 대학 입학에 대해 자신감 있어 한 것을 알 수 있고, 마지막 문장의 I sighed and threw the letter away in frustration을 통해 불합격하여 실망감을 느꼈다는 것을 알 수 있으므로, 'I'의 심경 변화로 가장 적절한 것은 ③이다.

해석 나는 편지를 뜯어서 열었다. 나는 그것을 읽고 싶어서 기다릴 수가 없었다. 나는 내가 지원했던 대학에 이상적인 지원자일 거라고 항상 생각했었다. 나는 엄마에게 큰 소리로 편지를 읽어주었다. "Summers 양께, Crimson University에 대한 귀하의 지원서가 접수되었고, 귀하의 입학을 위한 모든 자격들을 충족시킵니다." 나는 "그래! 합격이야!"라고 생각하면서 미소를 지었다. 하지만 곧이어 나는 다음 줄을 읽었다. "그러나, 저희는 이미 입학할 신입생들의 최대 인원에게 입학을 제안했습니다. 따라서, 귀하는 저희의 대기 명단에 올라 있습니다." 엄마가 나를 위로하려고 애쓰셨지만, 나는 내가 불합격했다는 것을 믿을 수가 없었다. 이것은 아주 많은 노력과 헌신 후의 정말 큰 실패 같

이 느껴졌다. 나는 한숨을 쉬었고 좌절해서 편지를 버렸다.

① 충격을 받은 → 자랑스러운
② 걱정하는 → 안도하는
③ 자신감 있는 → 실망한
④ 감동한 → 자포자기한
⑤ 침착한 → 부러워하는

어휘 rip open 뜯어서 열다, 찢어서 열다 qualification 자격 admission 입학

구문 분석

[6행] I smiled, [thinking "That's it! I'm in!"]

→ [thinking ~ in]은 '~하면서'라는 의미의 분사구문으로, 분사구문의 주어가 주절의 주어(I)와 같아서 생략되었다.

20 주장 파악하기

정답 ②

해설 글의 마지막 세 문장에서 미래의 잠재적인 부정적 결과에 대해 미리 걱정하는 것보다 더 나은 내일을 추구하며 현재에 몰입하는 것이 중요하다고 주장하고 있으므로 정답은 ②이다.

오답 분석 ①은 미래에 대해 미리 불안해하지 말고 오늘을 최대한 활용하는 것이 중요하다는 글의 내용과 다르므로 오답이다. ③은 불안감의 근본적인 원인에 대해서는 글에서 언급되고 있지 않다.

해석 불안감은 원치 않는 시간 여행의 한 형태이다. 그것은 한 사람을 소중히 여겨질 수 있는 현재에서 벗어나 몹시 싫은 미래로 이동시킨다. 영국의 철학자 John Locke(존 로크)는 "당신을 불안하게 하는 것이 당신을 지배한다"고 했다. 만약 당신이 오로지 잠재적인 부정적 결과들에만 집중한다면, 당신은 사실상 미리 실패를 겪고 있는 것이다. 이는 당신이 계획한 어떤 시도에서든 성공하지 못할 가능성을 크게 높인다. 사실상 당신은 부정적인 피드백의 고리에 갇혀서, 당신의 걱정이 당신을 실패로 이끌고, 이는 미래에 당신을 더 불안하게 만든다. 이러한 덫을 피하기 위해, 결국에는 현재가 정말로 존재하는 유일한 시간이기 때문에 현재에 온전히 몰입해 있는 것이 중요하다. 미래는 환상이고, 과거는 환영이다. 요령은 오늘이 어제의 우리의 기대에 부응하든 말든 더 나은 내일을 추구하며 오늘을 최대한 활용하는 것이다.

어휘 cherish 소중히 여기다 detest 몹시 싫어하다 master 지배하다, 숙달하다
odds 가능성, 확률 loop 고리 whereby 그래서 trick 요령, 비결
make the most of ~을 최대한으로 활용하다 live up to ~에 부응하다

구문 분석

[1행] It transports one out of **a present** ①[that could be cherished] into **a future** ②[that is detested].

→ ①[that ~ cherished]와 ②[that is detested]는 각각 선행사 a present와 a future를 수식하며 주격 관계대명사 that이 이끄는 관계대명사절이다.

[6행] This greatly increases your odds of not succeeding in [whatever endeavor you have planned].

→ [whatever ~ planned]는 '복합관계형용사(whatever) + 명사 + 주어 + 동사'의 구조이며, whatever가 뒤의 명사 endeavor를 수식하여 '어떤 시도에서든'의 의미로 해석한다.

21 밑줄 의미 추론하기   정답 ⑤

(해설) 과거에 어떤 데이터나 자료를 되는 대로 보여주던 것과 달리, 최근에는 특정한 대상들에게 특별히 맞춰진 정보를 전달하는 방법론인 데이터 스토리텔링을 사용해 정보를 전달함으로써 훨씬 더 마음을 끌고 더 강한 효과가 있음을 보여준다고 말하고 있다. 따라서 글의 주제를 비유적으로 표현한 a story without a voice(의견이 없는 이야기)가 의미하는 것은 ⑤ '의미나 관련성이 부족한 것'이다.

(오답분석) ①은 정보나 데이터를 보여주는 방식에 대한 글의 내용과 관련이 없으므로 오답이다. ③은 글에서 헷갈리는 정보에 대해서 다루고 있지 않으므로 오답이다.

(해석) 과거에는, 데이터와 통계 자료를 도표와 다른 시각화 형태로 이용하는 것은 되는 대로 하는 것이었고, 일부 발표 자료는 <u>의견이 없는 이야기</u>와 마찬가지였다. 하지만, 지난 10년 동안, 점점 더 많은 조직들이 특정한 대상들에게 특별히 맞춰진 정보를 전달하는 방법론인 데이터 스토리텔링에 의지함으로써 이 문제를 해결하려고 시도해왔다. 회사나 제품에 대한 어떤 정보를 단순히 보여 주는 것 대신에, 데이터 스토리텔링은 기술 덕분에 기업이 현재 이용 가능한 풍부한 정보를 활용해서 이를 맥락화한다. 예를 들어, 승차 공유 애플리케이션인 Uber는 이용자가 1년 동안 이동한 마일수와 같은 정보를 공유하기 위해서 데이터 스토리텔링을 이용해서 Uber가 그 이용자의 삶에 얼마나 많은 가치를 더해주는지를 보여주기 위해 그것(정보)을 넓게 본다. 단순히 당신이 돈을 얼마나 썼는지를 듣는 것보다, 당신이 그 서비스를 이용해서 지구를 두 바퀴 도는 거리와 맞먹는 거리를 주행했다고 듣는 것이 훨씬 더 마음을 끌고 더 강한 효과가 있다.

① 설득력이 없는 주장을 제시하는 것
② 기술을 통합하는 것에 실패하는 것
③ 헷갈리는 정보를 특징으로 삼는 것
④ 이미 알려진 세부 사항들을 공유하는 것
⑤ 의미나 관련성이 부족한 것

(어휘) hit or miss 되는 대로 하는   little more than ~과 마찬가지 methodology 방법론, 절차   tailor 맞추다, (옷을) 맞추어 짓다 contextualize 맥락화하다   put A into perspective A를 넓게 보다 compelling 마음을 끄는   [선택지] unconvincing 설득력 없는 feature ~을 특징으로 삼다   relevance 관련성

(구문분석)
[16행] [**Being told** that you've used the service to drive the equivalent of two journeys around Earth] is far more compelling and ~

→ [Being ~ Earth]는 that절을 포함한 동명사의 수동태 형태(being + p.p.)로, 전체 문장의 주어 역할을 한다.

22 요지 파악하기   정답 ⑤

(해설) 글의 마지막 문장에서 문학은 궁극적으로 우리가 얼마나 잘 살아가는지에 영향을 미치기 때문에 실용적 용도가 없는 시대에 뒤떨어진 과목으로 보는 것은 매우 근시안적이라는 요지가 제시되어 있으므로, 이 글의 요지로 가장 적절한

것은 ⑤이다.

(오답분석) ①, ②은 글의 일부만을 다루고 있는 오답이다. ③은 글에서 과학이 중요하지 않다고 한 것은 아니므로 오답이다.

(해석) 과학, 수학, 컴퓨터 프로그래밍 등과 같은 더 "고용 조건에 맞는" 것을 전공하는 것이 문학을 공부하는 것보다 훨씬 더 매력적이다. 전국 대학교들의 통계 자료가 이 주장을 뒷받침하는데, 문학 학위가 있는 학생들의 수가 지난 10년 동안 25퍼센트 감소했으며 이러한 하향 추세는 계속될 것으로 보이기 때문이다. 하지만, 문학은 단지 책을 읽는 것 이상이라는 점에 주목하는 것이 중요하다. 그것은 창의성을 자극하고 비판적 사고를 장려한다. 그것은 의사소통을 향상시키고 공감을 형성한다. 전부 오늘날 성공하는 데에 필수적인 능력들이다. 캐나다 총리인 Justin Trudeau(쥐스탱 트뤼도)는 분명 그의 영문학 학위를 적절하게 이용했고, 우주에 간 최초의 미국 여성이 물리학과 더불어 문학을 공부했던 타당한 이유가 틀림없이 있을 것이다. 문학은 궁극적으로 우리가 얼마나 잘 살아가는지에 영향을 미치기 때문에, 그것을 오로지 오락의 한 형태이자 실용적 용도가 없는 시대에 뒤떨어진 과목으로만 보는 것은 너무 근시안적이다.

(어휘) employable 고용 조건에 맞는   downward 하향의, 하락의 fuel 자극하다, 연료를 채우다   short-sighted 근시안적인, 근시의 inform 영향을 미치다, 알리다

(구문분석)
[1행] Majoring in something more "employable" — science, math, computer programming, etc. — is [**much** more attractive than] studying literature.

→ [much ~ than]은 '비교급 + than'(~보다 -한)의 형태로 비교를 나타내는 구문으로, much는 비교급을 강조한다.

[13행] ~ and there must be **a good reason** [that the first American woman in space studied literature alongside physics].

→ [that ~ physics]는 이유를 나타내는 선행사 a good reason을 수식하며, 관계부사 why 대신 that이 쓰인 관계부사절이다.

23 주제 파악하기   정답 ④

(해설) 첫 두 문장으로 미루어 보아 큰 두뇌를 가진 '호모 사피엔스'는 빙하기의 혹독한 환경을 견디기에 충분히 영리했다는 내용의 글로, 언어 사용, 도구 만들기, 효과적인 주거지 조성 등이 가능했다고 설명하고 있다. 따라서 이 글의 주제로 가장 적절한 것은 ④ '초기 인간 생존에 지능이 한 역할'이다.

(오답분석) ①, ⑤은 글에서 언급되고 있지 않다. ②은 글에서 '호모 사피엔스'가 이용한 사냥용 도구에 대해서는 언급되었지만 사냥 기술에 대해서는 언급되지 않았으므로 오답이다. ③은 글의 일부만을 다루고 있는 오답이다.

(해석) 가장 최근 빙하기는 약 2만 1천년 전에 절정에 이르러서, 그 결과 북반구 대부분이 두꺼운 얼음판으로 뒤덮였다. 이는 '호모 사피엔스'에게 도전이 되었지만, 그들의 큰 두뇌는 그들을 혹독한 환경을 견디기에 충분히 영리하게 했다. 중요한 하나의 이점은 언어 사용으로, 그것은 초기 인간이 서로 정보를 공유할 수 있게 했다. 저명한 인류학자 Brian Fagan(브라이언 페이건)에 따르면, 이는 또한 그들에게 "개념화하고 미리 계획하는 능력"을 주었다. 그 결과, 그들은 거의 항상 충분한 음식을 확보할 수 있는 매우 능숙한 사냥꾼으로 성장했다. 인간은 다양한 쓸모 있는 도구들을 만들 수 있었기에 도구 만들기도 중요한 요인이었다. 사냥용 창과 같은 무기 외에도, 그들에게는 극심한 추위로부터 보호해주는 몸에 딱 맞는 옷을 만드는 바늘도 있었다. 또 다른 중요한 요인은 효과적인 주거지 조성이었다. '호모 사피엔스'는 동굴과 다른 자연적인 구조를 비바

람에 잘 견디게 만들기 위해 대대적으로 개조했다.

① 추운 기후가 인간 진화에 미친 영향
② '호모 사피엔스'에 의해 이용된 사냥 기술들
③ '호모 사피엔스'가 마주한 환경적 도전들
④ 초기 인간 생존에 지능이 한 역할
⑤ 마지막 빙하기 동안 인간 뇌에 생긴 변화들

 ice age 빙하기 reach its peak 절정에 이르다
northern hemisphere 북반구 endure 견디다 harsh 혹독한
conceptualize 개념화하다 adept 능숙한 secure 확보하다
implement 도구 spear 창 contributor 요인, 기여자
extensively 대대적으로 modify 개조하다 formation 구조
weatherproof 비바람에 잘 견디는 [선택지] employ 이용하다

> [1행] The most recent ice age reached its peak nearly 21,000 years ago, [resulting in much of the northern hemisphere being covered by thick sheets of ice].
>
> → [resulting ~ ice]는 결과를 나타내는 분사구문으로, 분사구문의 주어가 주절의 주어(The most recent ice age)와 같아서 생략되었다.
>
> [5행] One significant advantage was the use of language, [which enabled early humans to share information with each other].
>
> → 앞에 나온 절 전체를 수식하는 [which ~ other]는 주격 관계대명사 which가 이끄는 관계대명사절로, 콤마 뒤에서 계속적 용법으로 쓰였다.

24 제목 파악하기
정답 ②

해설 첫 세 문장으로 미루어 보아 지리 정보 시스템은 일기 예보부터 범죄 활동이 활발한 지역의 조사까지 많은 용도로 이용되는데, 질병의 전파를 예측할 수도 있다는 내용의 글이다. 이어서 태국의 연구자들은 조류 독감의 위험에 처한 지역을 예측하는 데에 이 시스템을 이용했다는 것을 예시로 들어 설명하고 있다. 따라서 제목으로 가장 적절한 것은 ② '질병 지도 만들기: GIS의 바이러스의 경로를 예측하는 능력'이다.

오답 분석 ①, ⑤은 글의 핵심 소재인 GIS를 사용하여 헷갈리게 하는 오답이다. ③은 글에서 언급되고 있지 않다. ④은 글의 핵심 소재인 Avian Flu를 사용하여 헷갈리게 하는 오답이다.

해석 지리 정보 시스템(GIS)은 지구 표면의 위치와 관련된 동향과 패턴을 조사하기 위해 고안되었다. 그것은 일기 예보부터 범죄 활동이 많은 지역의 조사까지 다양한 목적에 이용될 수 있다. 그러나 GIS의 가장 유익한 점들 중 하나는 넓은 지역에 걸쳐 질병의 전파를 예측하는 능력이다. 태국의 연구자들은 2004년 발발 이후 조류 독감의 위험에 처한 지역을 예측하는 데에 이 시스템을 이용했다. 그 바이러스는 매우 전염성이 강해 양계장에 심각한 영향을 미쳤는데, 바이러스의 직접적인 결과로써 또는 강제적 도살을 통해 6천 2백만 마리가 넘는 조류의 죽음과 지역 및 국가 경제에 광범위한 피해를 야기했다. 그 지역, 그곳의 공동체와 사례들에 관한 중요한 정보를 입력함으로써 과학자들은 예방 조치가 시행될 수 있도록 질병의 잠재적인 확산 패턴을 보다 잘 이해할 수 있었다.

① GIS 기술: 그것의 미래는 무엇을 준비해 두었는가?
② 질병 지도 만들기: GIS의 바이러스의 경로를 예측하는 능력
③ 지도 제작 소프트웨어가 태국 경제에 미치는 영향
④ 태국의 양계업은 조류 독감 이후로 회복할 수 있을까?
⑤ GIS 세계 시장의 떠오르는 경향과 예측들

 design 고안하다 spread 전파 anticipate 예측하다 outbreak 발발
contagious 전염성이 있는 poultry farm 양계장 slaughter 도살
extensive 광범위한 diffusion 확산 preventive measures 예방 조치
put in place 시행하다 [선택지] in store 준비하여 map 지도를 만들다
poultry industry 양계업

> [9행] The virus is highly contagious and severely impacted poultry farms, **causing** ①[the deaths of more than 62 million birds] — either as a direct result of the virus or through forced slaughter — **and** ②[extensive damage to the local and national economies].
>
> → 현재분사 causing의 목적어 역할을 하는 명사구 ①[the ~ birds]와 ②[extensive ~ economies]는 등위접속사 and로 연결된 병렬 구조이다.
>
> [15행] ~ scientists were able to gain a better understanding of the disease's potential diffusion patterns [**so that** preventive measures could be put in place].
>
> → [so ~ place]는 접속사 so that이 이끄는 목적의 부사절이다. 이때 so that은 in order that으로 바꿔 쓸 수 있다.

25 도표 정보 파악하기
정답 ④

해설 말리의 남성 청소년 식자율은 57.8퍼센트이고 중앙아프리카 공화국의 남성 청소년 식자율은 47.8퍼센트이므로, 말리가 10퍼센트 더 높으므로 수치의 비교 표현이 잘못 반영되었다. 따라서 도표의 내용과 일치하지 않는 것은 ④이다.

해석

아프리카 국가에서의 청소년 식자율

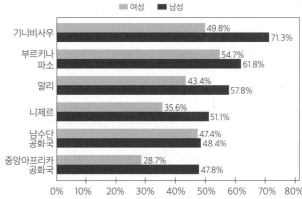

위 도표는 6개의 아프리카 국가들에서 남성과 여성의 청소년 식자율을 보여준다. ① 6개 국가들 중에서, 부르키나파소에서의 여성 청소년 식자율이 50퍼센트 이상으로 가장 높다. ② 중앙아프리카 공화국과 니제르에서의 여성 청소년 식자율은 모두 40퍼센트 미만이다. ③ 6개 국가들 중 남성 청소년 식자율이 50퍼센트를 넘지 못하는 유일한 두 국가는 남수단 공화국과 중앙아프리카 공화국이다. ④ 말리에서, 남성 청소년 식자율은 중앙아프리카 공화국의 그 비율보다 10퍼센트 더 낮다. ⑤ 남수단 공화국의 남성과 여성 청소년 식자율 간의 차이는 단 1퍼센트인 반면, 기니비사우의 그것(남성과 여성 청소년 식자율 간 차이)은 20퍼센트 이상이다.

[4행] The rates [of youth literacy for females in the Central African Republic and Niger] are both under 40%.

→ [of ~ Niger]는 주어 The rates를 수식하는 전치사구이다.

[6행] **The only two countries** among the six countries [in which the male youth literacy rate does not exceed 50%] are the Republic of South Sudan and Central African Republic.

→ [in ~ 50%]는 선행사 The only two countries를 수식하며, '전치사 + 관계대명사' in which가 이끄는 관계대명사절이다.

26 세부 정보 파악하기 정답 ④

(해설) When he returned to England in 1805, he had a collection of over 3,900 plants를 통해 Robert Brown이 식물 채집 후 1805년에 영국으로 돌아왔다는 것을 알 수 있는데, ④은 1801년이라고 일부 정보를 잘못 나타냈으므로, 글의 내용과 일치하지 않는 것은 ④이다.

(해석) 세계에서 가장 유명한 식물학자들 중 한 명인 Robert Brown(로버트 브라운)은 1772년에 스코틀랜드의 몬트로즈에서 태어났다. 그는 특히 호주 토착 식물들의 형태학과 지리학적 분포에 대한 그의 연구로 잘 알려져 있다. 그는 Edinburgh 대학에서 의학을 공부했고 영국군에서 외과의로 복무하면서 5년을 보냈지만, 식물학에 큰 관심이 있었다. 군에서의 시간 동안, 그는 많은 식물 표본들을 수집했고, 학술 논문들을 썼으며, 저명한 식물학자들과 서신을 주고받았다. 1801년에, 그는 호주 해안을 탐사하는 조사 선박인 'Investigator'에서 동식물 연구가 직책을 맡았다. 그가 1805년에 영국으로 돌아왔을 때, 그는 3천 9백가지 이상의 식물을 채집해있었고, 그 중 대부분은 이전에 발견되지 않았던 종이었다. 난초의 수정 과정에 대한 그의 이후 연구에서, 그는 세포핵에 대한 상세한 정보를 제공했고 그것에 오늘날에 여전히 사용되는 이름을 부여했다.

(어휘) **serve** 복무하다, 봉사하다 **specimen** 표본, 견본
correspond 서신을 주고 받다 **naturalist** 동식물 연구가, 박물학자
fertilization 수정, 비옥화 **orchid** 난초
observation (관찰 등을 통한) 정보, 관찰 **nucleus** 핵, 핵심

[4행] ~ geographic distribution of plants, particularly **those** native to Australia.

→ 지시대명사 those는 앞의 명사 plants를 가리킨다.

27 안내문 정보 파악하기 정답 ⑤

(해설) 예외 조항과 관련된 부분인 Overnight guests can use all facilities free of charge를 통해 투숙객들은 모든 시설을 무료로 이용 가능하다는 것을 알 수 있으므로, 글의 내용과 일치하지 않는 것은 ⑤이다.

(해석)
Sun 온천
저희의 천연 지열 온천에 오셔서 휴식을 취하세요. 여러분의 모든 걱정이 사라질 것입니다.

입장료:
- 1일 이용권 45달러
- 2시간 이용권 20달러

야외 입욕:
- 오전 5시에서 오후 10시
- 라운지 침대는 대여 가능함.
- 모든 음식 및 음료는 지정된 구역에서 섭취되어야 함.

실내 입욕/스파:
- 오전 5시에서 오후 8시
- 사우나에서 시끄러운 대화 금지
- 다양한 마사지 테라피 이용 가능함 (예약 필수)

* 일박 투숙객들은 모든 시설을 무료로 이용하실 수 있습니다.

더 많은 정보를 원하시면 www.sunhotsprings.com을 방문해주세요.

(어휘) **hot spring** 온천 **geothermal** 지열의 **melt** 사라지다, 녹다
bathing 입욕, 목욕 **overnight** 일박의

 [10행] All food and drink [must be consumed] at the designated area.

→ [must be consumed]는 조동사(must)가 있는 '조동사 + be + p.p.' 형태의 수동태이다.

28 안내문 정보 파악하기 정답 ④

(해설) Requirements: First Aid Certification을 통해 요건으로 응급 처치 자격증이 있어야 한다는 것을 알 수 있으므로, 글의 내용과 일치하는 것은 ④이다.

(해석)
아이스 스케이트 강사 구함
The Fargo 아이스 링크는 전임으로 지도할 아이스 스케이트 강사를 구하고 있습니다.

직무:
- 5세에서 13세의 어린이 지도
- 고급반 배치를 위한 기량 평가
- 각 수업의 과정 구성
- 빙상 상태 및 스케이팅 장비 관리

요건:
- 우수한 의사소통 기술 및 지도력
- 이전의 강사 경력
- 응급 처치 자격증
- 최소 25세

지원자들은 www.ficerink.com에서 온라인 지원서를 작성해야 합니다. 이력서를 첨부해 주십시오. 문의 사항은, 저희 웹사이트에서 질의응답 코너를 확인하십시오.

(어휘) **full time** 전임으로 **placement** 배치, 분반 **First Aid** 응급 처치, 응급 치료

 [2행] The Fargo Ice Rink is looking for **an ice skating instructor** [to teach full time].

→ [to ~ time]은 to부정사의 형용사적 용법(~할)으로, 앞의 명사 an ice skating instructor를 수식한다.

29 어법상 틀린 것 찾기 　　　정답 ⑤

(해설) attribute는 목적어를 취하는 타동사인데 밑줄 뒤에 목적어가 없고, '직장 내 괴롭힘의 많은 경우들이 이러한 심리적 현상에서 기인될 수 있다'라는 수동의 의미가 되어야 하므로, ⑤의 attribute를 be attributed로 고쳐야 한다.

(오답분석) ①은 과거분사 used의 목적을 나타내기 위해 부사적 용법의 to부정사 to reduce를 사용한 것은 어법상 적절하다. ②은 '~할 때'라는 의미로 시간을 나타내는 종속절을 이끄는 부사절 접속사 when을 사용한 것은 어법상 적절하다. ③은 동사 triggered를 앞에서 수식하는 부사 initially를 사용한 것은 어법상 적절하다. ④은 주어 they와 전치사 of의 목적어가 동일한 대상 (individuals with a narcissistic personality)을 가리키므로 목적어 자리에 재귀대명사 themselves를 사용한 것은 어법상 적절하다.

(해석) 방어 기제는 불편한 상황에 의해 야기되는 불안을 줄이기 위해 사용되는 무의식적인 대처 기술이다. 이것의 한 가지 예는 전위된 공격성인데, 이는 한 사람이 누군가에게 화가 나지만 적대적인 행동을 할 다른 대상을 선택할 때 발생한다. 가장 흔하게, 처음에 분노를 유발한 사람은 권력이 있는 자리에 있고, 따라서 보복의 영향을 받지 않는다. 전위된 공격성은 흔히 자기애적인 성격을 지닌 사람들에게서 나타난다; 그들은 그들 자신을 높이 평가하고 타인들에 대한 공감이 부족하기 때문에, 감지되는 모욕으로부터 나아가는 능력이 떨어지고 그들의 분노를 무고한 사람에게 푸는 것에 더 개의치 않는다. 유감스럽게도, 전위된 공격성의 피해자들은 한 집단에서 공격받기 쉬운 구성원들인 경향이 있다. 직장 내 괴롭힘의 많은 경우들이 이러한 심리적 현상에서 기인될 수 있고, 분노를 표출하고픈 욕망을 느끼는 관리자는 상사보다 하급자를 겨냥할 가능성이 더 높다.

(어휘) defense mechanism 방어 기제　displaced aggression 전위된 공격(성)
immune to ~에 영향을 받지 않는　retaliation 보복, 앙갚음
have a high opinion of ~을 높이 평가하다　slight 모욕, 경멸
innocent 무고한 사람　subordinate 하급자　superior 상사

(구문분석) [17행] ~ phenomenon — **a manager** [feeling the urge to express anger] is more likely to target a subordinate than a superior.
→ 현재분사구 [feeling ~ anger]는 명사 a manager를 수식한다.

30 어휘 적절성 파악하기 　　　정답 ④

(해설) 시각적 입력 정보가 부족해도 뇌의 시각 중추에서의 활동이 활발하다는 것은 뇌가 기억에서 이미지를 만들어내려는 시도에서 기인하는 것이라는 맥락이 되어야 하므로, ④의 delete(없애다)를 그와 반대되는 의미의 generate(만들어내다)와 같은 어휘로 바꾸어야 문맥상 적절하다.

(오답분석) ⑤은 환자들이 보는 이미지들이 정적이거나 단순하지 않고 윤곽이 분명하고 색깔이 있다는 문맥이 되어야 하므로 well-defined가 오는 것이 적절하다.

(해석) 실명은 환각의 이미지를 보는 ① 예상치 않은 증상을 야기할 수 있다. 알츠하이머병과 같은 정신적 문제와 달리, 이 현상은 인지 불안정의 징후가 아니다. 대신에, 그것은 뇌가 받아들이는 데 익숙해진 감각 정보의 일반적인 양의 ② 감소로 인해 발생한다. 눈이 더 적게 감지함에 따라, 뇌세포는 빠진 세부 정보를 채우기 위해 과민해진다. 더 알아보기 위해, 신경 과학자들이 이러한 이상이 있는 많은 사람들의 뇌를 정밀 검사했고, 시각적 입력 정보의 부족에도 불구하고 그들의 뇌의 시각 중추에서의 활동이 활발하게 유지되었다는 것을 발견했다. 일부 경우들에서는, ③ 정상적인 시력을 가진 사람들보다 더 많은 움직임이 있었다. 과학자들은 이 결과가 뇌가 원래 하는 대로 수동적으로 정보를 받아들이기보다는 기억에서 이미지를 ④ 없애려는(→만들어내려는) 뇌

의 시도에서 기인한다고 생각했다. 게다가, 그 이미지들은 정적이거나 단순하지 않았다. 환자들은 항상 ⑤ 윤곽이 분명하고 총천연색의 움직이는 부분들, 사람들, 기하학적 모양들, 동물들을 보았다고 말했다.

(어휘) hallucinatory 환각의, 망상의　indication 징후, 암시　instability 불안정
sensory 감각의　overactive 과민성의, 과도한
neuroscientist 신경 과학자　scan 정밀 검사하다, 훑어보다
condition (건강상의) 이상, 상태　input 입력 정보　visual center 시각 중추
static 정적인, 정지된　geometric 기하학적인, 기하학의
well-defined 윤곽이 분명한, 명확한

(구문분석) [4행] Instead, it occurs because of a decline in the typical load of **sensory information** [(that/which) the brain is used to receiving].
→ [the ~ receiving]은 선행사 sensory information을 수식하는 관계대명사절이며, 목적격 관계대명사 that/which가 생략되었다.

[6행] As the eyes perceive less, the brain cells become overactive **in order** [to fill in missing details].
→ 목적의 뜻을 분명히 하기 위해 to부정사구 [to ~ details] 앞에 in order를 쓴 형태이다.

31 빈칸 추론하기 　　　정답 ④

(해설) 주제문에 해당하는 빈칸 문장에서 진정으로 지속 가능한 건축은 '무엇'이라고 생각된다고 하고, 이어서 우리는 건설업의 부정적인 영향들을 줄이려면 갈 길이 멀지도 모른다고 했다. 따라서 빈칸에는 ④ '규칙이라기보다는 예외'가 와서 친환경적이라고 광고되는 건물들이 실제로 더 적은 환경상 흔적을 남길 수도 있지만 진정으로 지속 가능한 건축은 규칙이라기보다는 예외라고 생각된다는 의미가 되어야 한다.

(오답분석) ⑤은 환경친화적인 실천들이 아직은 현재의 건축물들에 잘 반영되지 않는다는 글의 내용과 반대되는 내용이므로 오답이다.

(해석) 건설업은 그것이 얼마나 필수적인지 때문에 많은 경우 간과되는 엄청난 환경적 영향을 지닌다; 세계 인구가 계속 증가하는 상황에서, 새로운 건설에 대한 수요에 맞추는 것 그 자체만으로도 도전이다. 건설로 인해 야기되는 피해를 방지하려는 노력의 일환으로, 건설 관행에서의 지속 가능성에 대한 요구가 더 컸던 적이 없고, "환경친화적인"과 "친환경의"와 같은 용어들이 그 업계 내에서 아주 흔해지고 있다. 하지만, 많은 사람들은 이러한 용어들이 과장된 유행어라고 생각한다. 이러한 방식으로 광고되고 있는 건물들은 실제로 과거의 건물들보다 더 적은 환경상 발자국을 남길 수도 있지만, 진정으로 지속 가능한 건축은 규칙이라기보다는 예외라고 생각된다. 더 많은 건축가와 건설업자들이 설계와 건설 과정의 마지막 한 측면까지 환경친화적인 실천들을 포함하려고 신경 쓸 때까지, 우리는 건설업이 지구에 미치는 부정적인 영향들을 줄이기까지 갈 길이 멀지도 모른다.

① 미래 세대들이 생존하기 위한 비결
② 실현하기에 비용이 엄청나게 비싼
③ 성의를 내리기가 점점 어려운
④ 규칙이라기보다는 예외
⑤ 우리의 현대 건축물들에 반영된

(어휘) overlook 간과하다　combat 방지하다, 싸우다　buzzword 유행어
sustainable 지속 가능한　every last 마지막 한 ~까지
[선택지] prohibitive 엄청나게 비싼

구문
분석

[13행] ~ past, [it is believed that truly sustainable architecture
　　　　　　　　가주어　　　　　　　진주어(that절)
is the exception rather than the rule].

→ 동사 believe의 목적어가 that절인 경우, [it ~ rule]과 같이 가주어 it을
사용하여 'it is p.p. that' 형태의 수동태 구문으로 쓸 수 있다.

32 빈칸 추론하기 　　　　　　　　　　정답 ⑤

(해설) 로마 제국의 복지 시스템이 오히려 현대보다 더 진보적이었을 수 있다는 내용의 글이고, 빈칸 뒤 문장에서 우리가 특권을 누려온 과학적, 문화적 토대는 로마 시스템을 넘어서는 진보를 야기시키기는커녕 변변찮은 발전을 이뤘고 어쩌면 퇴보했을 수도 있다고 하였다. 따라서 빈칸에는 ⑤ '그것들에서 얼마나 조금 향상되었는지는 실망스럽다'는 내용이 오는 것이 적절하다.

(오답 분석) ②은 글에서 현재 복지 시스템의 자금 부족에 대해서는 언급되지 않았으므로 오답이다. ③, ④은 현대 복지 시스템이 로마 제국 때와 비교해서 크게 발전하지 못했다는 글의 내용과 반대되는 내용이므로 오답이다.

(해석) 노예 제도와 같은 관행의 부도덕성에도 불구하고, 로마 제국은 오늘날 우리보다 복지에 관해서는 거의 틀림없이 훨씬 더 진보적이었다. 로마 제국은 전체 인구에게 혜택을 주기 위한 사회 프로그램을 체계화할 능력이 있었다. 제국은 가난한 사람들을 위한 공동 주택 단지인 인술라 4만 4천 8백 5십 채를 가지고 있었는데, 이것은 위에는 개인 주택과 함께 1층에는 상점과 가게가 있었다. 다른 프로그램에는 일주일에 한 번 곡물과 돼지고기 나눠주기, 무료 목욕탕과 식수 제공하기, 그리고 심지어 보조금이 지급되는 방식의 의료 서비스 실시하기가 포함되었다. 현대 사회가 그러한 정책들로부터 계승한 것들이 현재 자리한 시스템 내에 분명히 있긴 하지만, 그것들에서 얼마나 조금 향상되었는지는 실망스럽다. 우리가 수 세기 넘게 특권을 누려온 과학적 및 문화적 토대는 천년이 지난 로마 시스템을 훨씬 넘어서는 진보를 야기했어야 한다; 그 대신 우리는 변변찮은 발전을 이루었고 심지어 어쩌면 퇴보했을 수도 있다.

① 생활비가 얼마나 많이 올랐는지가 걱정스럽다
② 사람들이 기초 의료 서비스를 감당할 자금이 부족한 것이 절망스럽다
③ 복지가 다수의 사람들에게 이용 가능하다는 것이 고무적이다
④ 사회 프로그램이 그렇게 빨리 발달했다는 것이 놀랍다
⑤ 그것들에서 얼마나 조금 향상되었는지는 실망스럽다

(어휘) **notwithstanding** ~에도 불구하고 **immorality** 부도덕성
slavery 노예 제도 **progressive** 진보적인 **block** 단지, 건물
insula 인술라(고대 로마의 집합주택) **communal** 공동의
subsidized 보조금이 지급되는 **inherit** 계승하다 **privilege** 특권
meager 변변찮은, 빈약한 **stride** 발전 **regress** 퇴보하다
[선택지] **alarming** 걱정스러운

구문
분석

[12행] Although ①[what modern society has inherited from
such policies] is evident in the systems now in place, it is
　　　　　　　　　　　　　　　　　　　　　　　　　　가주어
disappointing ②[how little has been improved upon them].
　　　　　　　　진주어(명사절)

→ 부사절의 주어 ①[what ~ policies]는 관계대명사 what(~하는 것)이
이끄는 명사절이다.

→ 주절은 가주어 it이 길이가 긴 진주어 명사절 ②[how ~ them] 대신 주어 자리에 쓰인 형태이다.

33 빈칸 추론하기 　　　　　　　　　　정답 ③

(해설) 주제문에 해당하는 빈칸 문장에서 뇌가 '어떠하다'고 하고, 글의 후반에서 뇌가 신체에 대한 이미지를 휠체어를 포함하도록 조정해서 기구를 이용해야만 하는 사람들이 자연스럽고 반사적인 방식으로 활동을 할 수 있게 한다고 했다. 따라서 빈칸에는 ③ '신체적 변화들이 발생할 때 그것들을 상쇄하도록 작용한다'는 내용이 오는 것이 적절하다.

(오답 분석) ①의 신체에 의해 발생한 자극에 대한 내용은 글에서 언급되고 있지 않다. ②은 뇌가 장애에 의해 영구적으로 손상된다는 내용은 글의 내용과 관련이 없다. ④, ⑤은 기구를 사용하는 사람들은 그것을 신체의 일부로 여긴다는, 즉 뇌가 신체에 대한 이미지를 휠체어를 포함하도록 조정한다는 글의 내용과 관련이 없으므로 오답이다.

(해석) 뇌는 신체적 변화들이 발생할 때 그것들을 상쇄하도록 작용한다. 신경 과학자들은 뇌에서 정보를 처리하는 새로운 신경 세포들을 생성하는 능력인 신경 발생이 성장 중에만 일어난다고 생각하곤 했지만, 이제는 우리의 뇌가 우리의 일생 동안 다양한 상황과 문제들에 대응하기에 충분히 탄력적이고 회복력이 있다고 이해된다. 이는 사고나 장애로 인해 기능하지 않는 사지를 보철 기구나 휠체어와 같은 도구로 대체해야 하는 것을 포함한다. 쇠약성 척수 부상으로 휠체어에 의지하는 참가자들에게 연구를 위해서 설문했을 때, 그들이 이동을 돕는 데에 사용되는 기구들을 외적인 도구들로 보기보다는 그들 자신들의 일부로 그것들을 본다는 것을 발견했다. 이것이 의미하는 것은 뇌가 신체에 대한 뇌의 이미지를 휠체어를 포함하도록 조정해서, 그것들을 이용해야만 하는 사람들이 자연스럽고 반사적인 방식으로 활동을 할 수 있게 한다는 것이다.

① 신체에 의해 발생한 자극과 조화를 이룬다
② 장애에 의해 영구적으로 손상될 수 있다
③ 신체적 변화들이 발생할 때 그것들을 상쇄하도록 작용한다
④ 도구들을 이용하는 방법을 배우는 무의식적인 능력을 지닌다
⑤ 시간이 갈수록 근육의 움직임을 통제할 능력을 잃는다

(어휘) **neuroscientist** 신경 과학자 **neurogenesis** 신경 발생
resilient 회복력 있는, 탄력 있는 **limb** 사지, 돌출부
wheelchair-bound 휠체어에 의지하는 **debilitating** 쇠약하게 하는
spinal cord 척수, 등골 **automatic** 반사적인
[선택지] **stimuli**(stimulus의 복수형) 자극 **offset** 상쇄하다, 벌충하다

구문
분석

[7행] This **includes** [having to **replace** non-functioning
limbs that result from accidents or disabilities **with** a tool
such as a prosthetic device or a wheelchair].

→ [having ~ wheelchair]는 동사 includes의 목적어 역할을 하는 동명사구이다.

→ replace A with B는 'A를 B로 대체하다'라는 의미의 구문이다.

[16행] ~, allowing those [who must use them] to carry out
　　　　　　　동사　　　　목적어　　　　　　목적격 보어
activities in natural, automatic ways.

→ 분사 자리에 온 동사 allowing의 목적어로 명사구 those ~ them, 목적격 보어로 to부정사 to carry out이 쓰였다.

→ [who ~ them]은 선행사 those를 수식하며 주격 관계대명사 who가
이끄는 관계대명사절이다.

34 빈칸 추론하기 　　　　　　　　　　정답 ①

(해설) 매너리즘은 조화와 균형을 특징으로 했던 자연주의와 고전주의로부터 이탈한 부자연스러움과 세련미를 특징으로 하는 예술 양식이라는 내용의 글이고,

빈칸 뒤 문장에서 이런 작품들에서 신체들은 더 긴 사지, S자 형상, 작은 머리를 가진 "뱀 같은 형상"으로 묘사되었다고 하였다. 따라서 빈칸에는 ① '왜곡된 대상과 불균형으로 두드러졌다'는 내용이 오는 것이 적절하다.

 ②은 매너리즘 양식의 작품은 실감 나는 장면을 포착하기보다는 부자연스러움을 특징으로 하는 요소들을 포함한다는 글의 내용과 반대되는 내용이므로 오답이다. ③은 매너리즘 작품은 비정상적인 배경에서 무작위한 요소들에 둘러싸인 부자연스러운 신체를 보였다고 하는 글의 내용과 반대되는 내용이므로 오답이다. ④은 글에서 이미지가 비난받고 있는지는 언급되고 있지 않다. ⑤은 매너리즘은 르네상스의 자연주의로부터의 이탈을 나타냈다는 글의 내용과 반대되는 내용이므로 오답이다.

(해석) 16세기 이탈리아에서 출현한 예술 양식인 매너리즘은 르네상스의 자연주의로부터의 이탈을 나타냈고 작품들에 대한 좀 더 철학적인 접근법으로의 전환을 포괄했다. 사람들을 중심으로 등장시키는 실감 나는 장면을 포착하기보다, 매너리즘 작품은 왜곡된 대상과 불균형으로 두드러졌다. 이런 작품들에서 신체들은 보통 '세르펜티나타 양식' 혹은 "뱀 같은 형상"으로 더 긴 사지, S자 형상 그리고 작은 머리를 가진 것으로 묘사되었다. 또한 그것들은 보통 비정상적인 배경에서 무작위한 요소들에 둘러싸인 채 이상하고 부자연스러운 자세로 보여진다. 부자연스러움과 세련미를 특징으로 하는 이러한 디테일과 요소들은 관람객에게 지적 경험을 선사하도록 의도되었는데, 예술가들은 그때까지는 주로 기술자로 여겨졌기에 이로써 그들을 시인과 학자와 동등한 위치에 두었다. 조화와 균형을 도모했던 자연주의와 고전주의의 기본 원칙으로부터의 이 이탈은 이 시대 동안 일어났던 종교적 그리고 사회적 격변을 반영한 것으로 해석될 수 있다.

① 왜곡된 대상과 불균형으로 두드러졌다
② 그것의 불완전한 묘사로 더 현실적이라 여겨진다
③ 구도의 간결한 점유로 유명하다
④ 도달하기 어려운 인간 신체의 이미지를 조장하므로 비난받는다
⑤ 그것에 앞선 양식의 핵심 원리에 대한 헌신으로 유명하다

(어휘) naturalism 자연주의 life-like 실감 나는, 실물과 똑같은
focal point 중심, 초점 serpentine 뱀 같은, 구불구불한
artificiality 부자연스러움, 인위성 sophistication 세련미
on par with ~과 동등한 craftsman 기술자, 장인 classicism 고전주의
[선택지] asymmetry 불균형, 비대칭 occupation 점유
composition 구도, 구성 unattainable 도달하기 어려운 tenet 원리, 교리

(구문분석) [17행] [This break (from the basic principles of naturalism and classicism), (which promoted harmony and balance)], could be interpreted as a reflection of the religious and social upheaval that occurred during this era.
→ [This ~ balance]는 명사 break를 수식하는 전치사구(from ~ classicism)와 This ~ classicism을 수식하는 관계대명사절(which ~ balance)을 포함하며, 전체가 문장의 주어이다.

35 흐름과 관계 없는 문장 찾기 정답 ④

(해설) 프로 선수가 되는 것은 확률상 매우 어려운 일이므로 청소년 운동선수들은 프로 스포츠에 진출하지 못할 경우를 대비해 자신의 전망을 다각화해서 어떤 대안이 되는 기회가 와도 잘 적응할 수 있도록 해야 한다는 내용의 글이다. 그런데 ④은 시간을 들여 전문으로 삼을 분야를 찾아야 한다는 내용으로 핵심 소재는 같지만 주제에서 벗어나 있어 글의 흐름과 무관하다.

(오답분석) ①은 첫 문장에 이어서 프로 스포츠의 제약에 대한 내용을 다루고 있으므로 첫 문장과 자연스럽게 이어진다. ②은 As such를 통해 ①의 내용에 대한 부

연 설명을 하고 있으므로 ① 뒤에 오는 것이 적절하다. ③은 청소년 운동선수들이 한 가지 일에 모든 것을 걸지 말아야 한다는 내용으로 이 글의 주제문에 해당하는 문장이다. ⑤의 Doing so는 ③의 to diversify their prospects를 가리키고 있으므로 ③ 뒤에 이어지는 것이 적절하다.

(해석) 프로 스포츠의 경제적 전망과 과잉 경쟁은 열정을 가지고 경력을 쌓아나가길 바라는 청소년 운동선수들에게 극심한 제약을 가한다. ① 대학 팀에 자리를 확보하는 것이 이미 도전이지만, 프로 리그는 기하급수적으로 더 선별적이다. ② 이런 이유로, 대학 수준에서 경쟁할 정도로 충분히 운이 좋은 아주 적은 비율의 사람들이 계속해서 그들의 각 경기에서 최상위에 오를 수 있는 능력을 지니고, 대다수는 학교 교육이 끝나면 다른 직업들로 어쩔 수 없이 옮겨가게 한다. ③ 청소년 운동선수들은 그들의 야망이 결실을 맺지 못할 경우에는 기꺼이 그들의 전망을 다각화해야 해야 하기 때문에, 한 가지 일에 모든 것을 걸지 말아야 한다는 격언은 따라서 청소년 운동 선수들에게 특히 중요한 교훈이다. (④ 그들은 일자리 확보를 위해 전문으로 삼을 전도유망한 분야를 찾는 데 시간을 들여야 하는데, 이것이 그들의 미래에 아주 중요한 요소이기 때문이다.) ⑤ 그렇게 하는 것은 개인들이 적응할 수 있도록, 즉 그들에게 올 수 있는 어떤 대안이 되는 기회들에도 대응하고 성공할 수 있도록 보장할 것이다.

(어휘) constraint 제약, 제한 exponentially 기하급수적으로
collegiate 대학의, 대학생의
Don't put all your eggs in one basket 한 바구니에 네 모든 달걀을 넣지 마라(한 가지 일에 네 모든 것을 걸지 마라)
fruition 결실 adaptable 적응할 수 있는, 융통성 있는
present oneself (기회 등이) 오다

(구문분석) [11행] **The saying ①[that you shouldn't put all your eggs in one basket] is thus a particularly valuable lesson for youth athletes, as they must be willing to diversify their prospects ②[in the event that] their ambitions do not come to fruition.**
→ ①[that ~ basket]은 The saying과 동격을 이루는 명사절이다.
→ ②[in ~ fruition]은 접속사 in the event that(~하는 경우에)이 이끄는 조건의 부사절이다.

36 글의 순서 배열하기 정답 ②

(해설) 주어진 글은 인터넷 접속 가능 기기들의 네트워크인 사물 인터넷(IoT)이 농업에도 적용될 수 있다는 주제를 제시한다. (B)는 인구 증가로 더 많은 식량을 생산할 필요성이 있다는 내용이고, 주어진 글의 마지막에서 농업에서도 IoT를 이용할 수 있다고 했으므로 그 뒤에 와야 한다. (A)는 순접 연결어 As a result(결과적으로)를 통해 (B)에서 언급한 농업의 어려움에 대한 대책으로 농부들이 IoT에 관심을 둔다고 부연 설명하고 있으므로 (B) 뒤에 오는 것이 적절하다. (C)의 This information(이 정보)은 (A)의 '거대한 양의 정보'를 가리키므로 (A) 바로 다음에 오는 것이 적절하다. 따라서 글의 순서로 가장 적절한 것은 ② (B) - (A) - (C)이다.

(해석) 원격으로 사물들을 제어하는 인터넷 접속 가능 기기들의 네트워크라는 개념은 사물 인터넷(IoT)으로 알려져 있다. IoT의 적용은 기술 주도 부문들에서 더 명백해 보일 수 있지만, 농업에서도 잠재적인 쓰임이 있다.

(B) 인구가 증가함에 따라 우리가 직면하는 중대한 문제는 더 많은 식량을 생산해야 하는 우리의 필요성이다. 도시의 확장으로 인해 농지가 줄어들고 있고 환경적 손상이 천연자원의 가용성을 줄였기 때문에 이는 쉽지 않다.

(A) 결과적으로, 농부들은 토지의 생산성을 극대화하길 원한다. 따라서, 그들은 IoT와 같은 기술들로 관심이 향하고 있다. IoT가 아직 새로운 개념이기 때문에, 지금까지의 이익들의 대부분은 농장 도처에 놓인 센서들이 수집할 수

있는 거대한 양의 정보에서 온다.

(C) 이 정보는 토양의 질, 온도나 습도의 측정값, 심지어 해충의 위치를 포함할 수 있다. 실시간으로 그리고 최소한의 노력으로 그들에게 제공되는 이러한 세부 정보들 때문에, 농부들은 그들의 농장에 필요한 것들을 가늠하고 그에 맞춰서 대응하는 것을 더 잘 할 수 있다.

 어휘 Internet-enabled 인터넷 접속이 가능한   availability 가용성
measurement 측정값   pest 해충   in real time 실시간으로

구문분석 [1행] The concept of a network of Internet-enabled devices that controls things remotely **is known as** the Internet of Things (IoT).
→ be known as는 '~으로 알려져 있다'라는 의미로, by 이외의 전치사를 쓰는 수동태 구문이다.

---

37   글의 순서 배열하기   정답 ④

해설 주어진 글은 화산 폭발 시 가장 심각한 위험 중 하나는 화산 이류라는 주제를 제시한다. (C)는 화산 이류의 위험성에 대해 말하고 있으므로 주어진 글 바로 다음에 오는 것이 적절하다. (A)의 such places(그러한 곳들)는 (C)의 '화산에서 몇 마일 떨어져 있는 지역 사회들'을 가리키므로 (C) 바로 다음에 오는 것이 적절하다. (B)는 순접 연결어 also(또한)를 통해 (A)에서 언급한 화산 이류의 위험 신호 이외에 추가적으로 화산 이류의 위험성이 높은 곳에 대해 언급하고 있으므로 (A) 뒤에 오는 것이 적절하다. 따라서 글의 순서로 가장 적절한 것은 ④ (C) - (A) - (B)이다.

해석 화산 폭발은 가장 일반적으로 용암과 화산재 퇴적물이 연상되지만, 사실 가장 심각한 위험들 중의 하나는 많은 양의 바위 부스러기들과 섞여 흐르는 물의 범람인 화산 이류에서 비롯된다.
(C) 빠른 속도로 커다란 바위들을 주변 계곡들로 휩쓸어 가기에 충분한 힘과 그것이 여러 차례 연달아 일어날 가능성으로 인해, 화산 이류는 화산 폭발 시 주요 사망의 원인이다. 게다가 그것들은 먼 거리를 이동할 수 있기 때문에, 화산에서 몇 마일 떨어져 있는 지역 사회들도 위험에 처한다.
(A) 대피가 그러한 곳들에서 유일한 선택지인데, 다행히도 때때로 위험 경고 신호들이 있다. 집중 강우는 단단하지 않은 퇴적물을 쉽게 침식시키고 거주 지역을 향해 아래로 폭포처럼 흐르면서 그것을 옮기기 때문에, 만약 큰 비가 예상된다면 화산 이류가 발생할 가능성이 증가한다.
(B) 일반적으로 얼음과 눈으로 덮인 화산에서도 폭발의 열기가 그것을 녹일 수 있기 때문에 화산 이류의 가능성이 높다. 그리고 폭염에 의해 초목과 토양이 파괴되면서, 물이 흐르는 길에 있는 모든 것을 집어삼키기 때문에 아무것도 물의 속도를 늦출 수 없다.

어휘 lava 용암   ash fall 화산재 퇴적물   debris 바위 부스러기, 잔해
evacuation 대피, 피난   erode 침식시키다, 약화시키다   sediment 퇴적물
cascade 폭포처럼 흐르다; 작은 폭포   vegetation 초목   engulf 집어삼키다
boulder 바위   in quick succession 연달아

구문분석 [13행] And [with <u>any vegetation and soil</u> <u>being destroyed</u> by the intense heat] ~
(명사구 / 과거분사 수동형)
→ [with ~ heat]은 'with + 명사(구) + 분사' 형태의 분사구문으로, '~하면서'라는 의미로 해석한다.

---

38   주어진 문장의 위치 찾기   정답 ④

해설 주어진 문장에 명시적 단서가 없는 경우에는 글의 흐름이 끊기는 곳을 찾아야 한다. ④ 앞까지는 바로크 시대와 비교해서 고전주의 시대 음악이 갖는 특징들인 "노래하기 쉬운" 멜로디와 느린 화성 리듬에 관한 내용이 이어지다가, ④ 뒤 문장에서 거의 모든 박자마다 바뀌는 화음에 관한 내용이 나오고 있다. ④ 앞뒤의 내용이 유기적으로 연결되지 않는다는 점을 통해 글의 흐름이 끊겼음을 알 수 있다. 또한, 주어진 문장에서는 화성 리듬이 빨랐다는 내용이고 ④ 뒤 문장은 화음이 거의 모든 박자마다 바뀐다는 내용을 다루고 있으므로 주어진 문장과 자연스럽게 이어진다. 따라서 주어진 문장이 들어가기에 가장 적절한 곳은 ④이다.

오답분석 ③ 뒤 문장은 "노래하기 쉬운" 멜로디에 대해 언급하는 ①, ② 뒤 문장에 이어서 고전주의 시대 음악의 단순성을 보여주는 또 다른 예시로 느려진 화성 리듬에 대해 언급하고 있다. ⑤ 뒤 문장의 on the other hand는 앞 문장의 거의 모든 박자마다 바뀌는 화음과의 대조를 나타내므로 주어진 문장이 들어가기에 적절하지 않다.

해석 바로크 시대가 정교하고 복잡한 작품들로 특징지어지는 반면, 고전주의 시대는 단순성으로의 전환을 나타냈다. 층층이 쌓아올린 다성 음악을 만들기보다, 고전주의 시대 작곡가들은 단순하고, 기억할 만하며, "노래하기 쉬운" 멜로디를 공들여 만들었다. (①) 그 멜로디는 보통 악보의 가장 윗줄에서 전달되었다: 화음에서 소프라노 목소리 혹은 오케스트라에서 바이올린처럼 말이다. (②) 그 멜로디 아래에는, 뒷받침하는 악기들이 화음을 부연했다. (③) 단순성을 향한 움직임의 일환으로, <u>화음이 한 작품 내에서 바뀌는 속도인 화성 리듬이 상대적으로 느려졌고, 이는 이전 시대로부터의 뚜렷한 이탈이었다.</u> (④ 바로크 시대에 화성 리듬은 꽤 빨랐다.) <u>보통, 화음은 거의 모든 박자마다 바뀌곤 했다.</u> (⑤) 반면에, 고전주의 시대에서는 소절당 겨우 한 번이나 두 번의 화음 변화를 포함하며 화성 리듬이 더 느슨했다.

어휘 harmonic rhythm 화성 리듬   composition 작품, 작곡
layer upon layer 층층이   singable 노래하기 쉬운   music 악보
expand on ~을 부연하다   departure 이탈, 변경   relaxed 느슨한, 느긋한
measure (노래 등에서의) 소절

구문분석 [12행] As part of the movement towards simplicity, there was **a relative slowing of harmonic rhythm — the pace** ①[at which chords changed within a piece] — ②[which was a marked departure from the prior period].
→ ①[at ~ piece]는 선행사 the pace를 수식하며, '전치사 + 관계대명사' at which가 이끄는 관계대명사절이다.
→ ②[which ~ period]은 선행사 a relative slowing of harmonic rhythm을 수식하며 주격 관계대명사 which가 이끄는 관계대명사절이다.

[18행] ~ relaxed, including a chord change **no more than** once or twice per measure.
→ 부정어가 쓰인 비교구문 no more than은 '~일 뿐, 단지 ~에 지나지 않다'라는 의미로, only로 바꿔 쓸 수 있다.

---

39   주어진 문장의 위치 찾기   정답 ③

해설 주어진 문장의 informal agreements dealing with other issues(그 밖의 문제들을 다루는 비공식적인 합의 사항들)로 보아, 주어진 문장 앞에는 공식적인 합의 사항이 나와야 한다는 것을 알 수 있다. 이 글에서는 ③ 앞까지는 계

약법의 기원과, 계약법은 서면 합의 하에 약속된 돈을 되찾도록 돕는 것이라고 설명하고 있다. 그러다가 ③ 뒤 문장에서는 약속의 태만한 이행에도 조치가 취해졌고, 이것이 적용되는 범위를 제한할 필요성이 있다는 내용이 나와 ③ 앞뒤의 내용이 유기적으로 연결되지 않는다는 점을 통해 글의 흐름이 끊겼음을 알 수 있다. 따라서 주어진 문장이 들어가기에 가장 적절한 곳은 ③이다.

[오답분석] ①, ② 뒤 문장은 계약법의 기원과 초기 목적에 대한 내용이므로 주어진 문장보다 앞에 와야 한다. ④ 뒤 문장의 this는 ③ 뒤 문장의 an action을 가리키며, ④ 뒤 문장은 ③ 뒤 문장에 대한 보충 설명이므로 주어진 문장이 들어가기에 적절하지 않다. ⑤ 뒤 문장은 ④ 뒤 문장에 따른 결과이므로, 주어진 문장은 이러한 내용보다 앞에 와야 한다.

[해석] 가장 기본적으로, 계약은 두 당사자 간의 법적 구속력이 있는 합의이다. (①) 비록 오늘날 우리가 이해하고 있는 계약법의 진정한 발전은 상인들 간의 분쟁을 해결하기 위한 방법으로 서유럽에서 발달했지만, 계약법은 라틴 원칙 'pacta sunt servanda'("모든 합의는 준수되어야 한다")까지 그 기원이 거슬러 올라갈 수 있다. (②) 이는 초기에 그것이 명시된, 즉 서면 합의 하에 약속된 돈을 당사자들이 되찾도록 돕기 위해 만들어졌음을 의미한다. (③ 그 밖의 문제들을 다루는 비공식적 합의 사항들에 대한 위반을 구제하기 위한 조치들은 15세기가 되어서야 발달하기 시작했다.) 마침내, 약속의 태만한 이행이 있는 경우, 'assumpsit'("그가 약속했다")로 알려진 조치가 회수의 형태로 취해졌다. (④) 이것이 많은 상황들을 아우를 수 있는 가능성이 있기 때문에, 법원은 그 범위를 제한할 필요성을 인지했다. (⑤) 따라서 그들은 "약인"의 원칙을 고안해냈는데, 이는 교환이 이루어졌거나 약속되었을 경우에만 계약이 법적 구속력을 지닐 수 있음을 명시했다.

[어휘] remedy 구제하다, 바로잡다 violation 위반 binding 법적 구속력이 있는 party 당사자 be traced back to 기원이 ~까지 거슬러 올라가다 dispute 분쟁 express 명시된, 분명한 negligent 태만한 undertaking 약속 encompass 아우르다 scope 범위 devise 고안하다

[구문분석]
[16행] Because this had **the potential** [to encompass many situations], the courts found the need to limit its scope.
→ [to ~ situations]는 to부정사의 형용사적 용법(~할)으로, 명사 the potential을 수식한다.

---

40 요약문 완성하기 정답 ②

[해설] 글의 전반부에서 한 남자가 아이스크림을 주문하는 상황이 제시되는 연구에서는 그 남자가 선호하는 맛이 없이 무작위로 주문했을 때 가장 로봇 같고 가장 적게 호감이 가는 것으로 여겨졌다고 했고, 글의 후반부에서는 Woolley의 연구는 전반적으로 흐름에 맡기는 사람은 덜 유능한 것으로 여겨진다는 것을 보여주었다고 했다. 따라서 지문의 preference를 opinions로, less capable을 incompetent로 바꾸어 표현한 ②이 정답이다.

[해석] 많은 사람들은 문제를 일으키는 사람이라거나 너무 독단적이라는 꼬리표가 붙기를 원하지 않기 때문에, 일상적인 소통에서 수동적인 역할을 맡는다. 그러한 사람이 다른 사람들에게 어떻게 인식되는지를 알아내기 위해, Kaitlin Woolley(케이틀린 울리) 교수는 300명의 참가자들에게 하나의 상황이 제시되는 연구를 진행했다: 한 남자가 아이스크림을 주문하는 상황이다. 그들은 세 가지 선택지의 순위를 매기도록 요구되었는데, 선택지는 그가 초콜릿 맛을 별로 선호하지 않는 것, 그가 메이플 베이컨 맛을 많이 선호하는 것, 그리고 그가 선호 사항이 없고 무작위로 맛을 선택하는 것이었다. 흥미롭게도, 그 남자가 무작위로 주문했을 때, 그는 참가자들에게 가장 로봇 같고 가장 적게 호감이 가는 것으로 여겨졌다. 추가적인 연구는 선호 사항이 없는 것이 직업적 생

활에서 한 사람이 어떻게 여겨지는지에 악영향을 미친다는 것을 보여주었다. 피실험자들은 업무의 질에는 차이가 없었다는 사실에도 불구하고, 좋아하는 음식이나 음악이 있다고 한 사람에 반하여 없다고 한 지원자들을 고용하는 데에 관심을 덜 보였다. Woolley의 연구는 전반적으로 그저 "흐름에 맡기는" 사람은 덜 호감이 가고 덜 유능한 것으로 여겨진다는 것을 보여준다.

특정한 (A) 의견이 없는 사람들은 덜 호의적으로 여겨지고 그것들을 가진 사람들보다 더 (B) 무능하다고 생각된다.

	(A)		(B)
①	생각	……	무식한
②	의견	……	무능한
③	이유	……	순응하는
④	계획	……	특별한
⑤	방안	……	제멋대로인

[어휘] label 꼬리표를 붙이다 assertive 독단적인, 단정적인 likeable 호감이 가는 go with the flow (자연스러운) 흐름에 맡기다 favorably 호의적으로, 유리하게

[구문분석]
[1행] [Not wanting **to be labeled** a troublemaker or too assertive], many take a passive role in their daily interactions.
→ [Not ~ assertive]는 'not + 분사' 형태로, 분사구문의 부정형이다.
→ 현재분사 wanting의 목적어 to be labeled는 to부정사의 수동형(to be + p.p.)으로 쓰였다.

41~42 장문 독해 1

[해석] 만약 과학 지식 중 단 하나만 미래 세대들에게 전해질 수 있다면, 미국의 물리학자 Richard Feynman(리처드 파인만)은 그것이 "모든 것은 원자로 이루어져 있다"여야 한다고 주장했다. 이 지식으로부터 아주 많은 과학적 진보와 발견이 전개되었고, 이 지식은 [41]그리스의 철학자 Leucippus(레우키포스)와 그의 제자인 Democritus(데모크리토스)에 의해 고대 원자론이 제시되었던 기원전 5세기에 기원을 둔다. 실제로, Democritus는 "나눌 수 없는"으로 번역되는 'atomos'라는 용어를 만들었다. [42]그의 이론은 원자가 구성 요소에 있어서 불변하고 균일한 물질의 나눌 수 없는 입자라는 것이다. 그 주제에 대한 Aristotle(아리스토텔레스)과 시인 Lucretius(루크레티우스) 같은 유명한 사상가들의 추가적인 의견과 더불어, 이 관념은 모두 (A) 실험과 [42]사실적 과학보다는 철학과 사색에 토대를 둔다.

[41]약 2천 년 이후 유명한 화학자인 John Dalton(존 돌턴)의 시도에 이르러서야 이러한 가설들이 과학적으로 다듬어졌다. Dalton은 실증적 증거에 근거하여 이러한 철학적 관념들을 과학 이론들로 전환시킬 수 있었고, 원자 화학의 토대를 제공했다. 게다가, Dalton의 연구 결과는 고대 원자론의 핵심적인 관념들 중의 일부가 (B) 틀렸음을 입증했다. [42]그는 서로 다른 요소들의 원자들이 실제로 크기나 질량에 있어서 다르다는 것을 알아냈다. 그의 연구로부터 더 많은 실험과 이론들이 많이 있었고, 마침내 우리가 오늘날에 가지고 있는 과학 지식의 본체를 이루었다.

[어휘] atom 원자 atomic theory 원자론 uncuttable 나눌 수 없는 indivisible 나눌 수 없는 particle 입자, 미립자 uniform 균일한 composition 구성 요소 reflection 의견, 생각 speculation 사색, 추측 endeavor 시도, 노력 refine 다듬다, 정제하다 empirical 실증적인 abound 많이 있다 body 본체 [선택지] empiricism 경험주의

<table>
<tr><td>

구문 분석

[6행] ~ finds its origins in **the 5th century BC** [when ancient atomic theory was proposed by Greek philosopher Leucippus and his student Democritus].

→ [when ~ Democritus]는 선행사 the 5th century BC를 수식하며, 시간을 나타내는 관계부사 when이 이끄는 관계부사절이다.

[18행] **It wasn't until** the endeavors of famous chemist John Dalton some 2,000 years later **that** these assumptions would be scientifically refined.

→ 부정을 나타내는 it is not until A that B(A가 되어서야 B하다) 구문으로, it is not until A that B는 not B until A로 바꿔 쓸 수 있다.

</td></tr>
</table>

41 제목 파악하기 정답 ③

해설 Leucippus와 Democritus가 기원전 5세기에 철학과 사색에 토대를 두고 제시한 원자론을 약 2천 년 이후에 John Dalton이 실증적 증거에 근거해 과학적 이론으로 전환시켰다는 내용의 글이다. 따라서 글의 제목으로 가장 적절한 것은 ③ '원자론의 과학적 전환'이다.

오답 분석 ②, ⑤은 글의 일부만을 다루고 있는 오답이다. ④은 글에서 언급된 Philosophy를 사용하여 헷갈리게 하는 오답이다.

해석 ① 원자론: 경험주의의 토대
② 물질의 나눌 수 없는 입자의 구조
③ 원자론의 과학적 전환
④ 현대 과학자들이 철학에 뿌리를 두는 이유
⑤ 현대 과학: 과거에 기원을 두는 지식

42 빈칸 추론하기 정답 ②

해설 (A) 고대의 원자론은 사실적 과학보다는 철학과 사색에 토대를 둔다고 했으므로 '사실적 과학'과 동일한 문맥을 이루는 experimentation이 문맥상 적절하다.
(B) 빈칸 다음 문장에서 Dalton은 서로 다른 요소들의 원자들이 실제로 크기나 질량에 있어서 다르다는 것을 알아냈다고 했으므로 고대의 원자론에서 원자가 변하지 않고 균일한 입자라고 했던 것과 대조되는 내용임을 알 수 있다. 따라서 disproved가 문맥상 적절하다.
따라서 정답으로 가장 적절한 것은 ②이다.

해석 　(A)　　　　　(B)
① 비유 …… 비난했다
② 실험 …… 틀렸음을 입증했다
③ 실험 …… 칭찬했다
④ 가설 …… 평가했다
⑤ 가설 …… 무시했다

43~45 장문 독해 2

해석 (A) Erica는 병원에서 긴 하루 동안 일한 후에 피곤했다. 그녀는 간호조무사였고, 쉽지 않았지만 사람들을 돕는 것을 좋아했다. 그녀가 퇴근할 준비를 하고 있었을 때, 수간호사인 Jill이 (a)그녀가 얼마나 피곤해 보이는지를 알아차렸다. "잠깐만요, Erica. 커피 한 잔 하시겠어요?" Erica는 기꺼이 응했다.
(D) 그들이 같이 앉아 있었을 때, 45Jill은 (d)그녀가 특히 조용하다는 것을 알

아차렸다. "무슨 문제가 있어요?"라며 그녀가 물었다. Erica는 결국 그녀에게 문제를 이야기했다. "제가 더 이상 병원에서 계속해서 근무할 수 있을 것 같지가 않아요. 저는 정말로 금전적으로 허덕이고 있거든요. 제가 일하는 동안 제 부모님이 제 아이들을 돌봐주시지만, 그들은 나이가 들어가고 있어요." Jill은 Erica가 환자들과 함께 하는 것을 얼마나 좋아하는지 알았고 제안을 했다. "(e)당신이 간호 학교에 가는 건 어때요? 병원에는 아주 훌륭한 재정 지원 프로그램이 있어요. 저는 당신이 학위를 따는 동안에 부모님께서 도와주실 거라고 확신해요."
(B) "저는 그러기에 나이가 너무 많아요"라고 그녀가 답했다. "저는 이미 38살이에요." Jill은 웃으며 "나이가 많은 게 전혀 아니에요. 제가 어떻게 아는지를 (b)당신에게 말해줄게요"라고 말했다. 그리고, Jill은 자신이 어떻게 간호사가 되었는지에 대해 Erica에게 이야기해주었다. 그녀의 아버지가 직장을 잃고 그녀가 가족을 도와야 했기 때문에 그녀는 대학을 중퇴해야 했다. 그녀는 경력이나 학위가 없었기 때문에 종업원으로 일하기 시작했다. 그녀는 지배인이 될 때까지 계속해서 열심히 일했다.
(C) "저는 급료를 받을 때마다 계속해서 약간의 돈을 모았어요. 그게 많지는 않았어요. 하지만, 어느 날 저는 마침내 학교로 돌아갈 만큼 충분히 돈을 모았어요"라며 Jill이 웃었다. "저는 41살이었을 때 졸업장을 받았어요." Erica는 깜짝 놀랐다. "저는 (c)당신이 그렇게 힘들었는지 몰랐어요." "맞아요, 힘들었어요. 하지만 저는 제 인생에서의 어려움을 감사히 생각하게 되었어요"라고 44Jill이 대답했다. "만약 제 경험이 다른 사람들이 길을 찾는 데에 도움이 될 수 있다면, 그러면 저는 하나도 잃은 것이 없어요."

어휘 nurse's aide 간호조무사 head nurse 수간호사 gratefully 기꺼이
drop out 중퇴하다 paycheck 급료 diploma 졸업장, 수료증

<table>
<tr><td>

구문 분석

[15행] I kept saving a little money [**every time** I got a paycheck].

→ [every ~ paycheck]은 접속사 every time(~할 때마다)이 이끄는 시간의 부사절이다.

</td></tr>
</table>

43 글의 순서 배열하기 정답 ④

해설 (A)는 수간호사인 Jill이 피곤해 보이는 간호조무사인 Erica에게 커피를 마시자고 했다는 내용이다. (D)는 Erica와 Jill이 같이 앉아서 Erica의 문제에 대해 이야기했다는 내용이므로 Erica가 Jill과 커피를 마시기로 했다고 한 (A) 뒤에 와야 한다. (B)의 I'm too old for that에서 that은 (D)의 go to nursing school을 가리키므로 (D) 다음에 오는 것이 적절하다. (C)는 Jill이 학교로 돌아가기 위해 급료를 조금씩 모았고 41살에 졸업장을 받았다고 하는 내용이므로 Jill이 자신이 어떻게 간호사가 되었는지에 대해 이야기하겠다고 한 (B) 뒤에 와야 한다. 따라서 글의 순서로 가장 적절한 것은 ④ (D) - (B) - (C)이다.

44 지칭 대상 파악하기 정답 ③

해설 (a), (b), (d), (e)는 모두 Erica를 가리키지만 (c)는 Jill을 가리키므로, ③이 정답이다.

45 세부 정보 파악하기 정답 ④

해설 (D)의 I don't think I can keep working at the hospital anymore. I'm really struggling financially를 통해 Erica가 병원에서 간호조무사로 일하며 금전적인 문제를 겪고 있는 것을 알 수 있는데, ④은 많은 돈을 벌었다고 일부 정보를 잘못 나타냈으므로 글의 내용과 일치하지 않는 것은 ④이다.

18 목적 파악하기 정답 ④

해설 글의 중간 이후에서 notify(알리다)를 이용해 아파트 관리인이 시의 새로운 법안에 따라 다세대 주거용 건물에 휠체어 경사로를 설치하는 작업의 일정에 대해 알리고 있으므로 정답은 ④이다.

해석 주민분들께,

지난주에, 시는 신체적으로 장애가 있는 사람들이 그들의 집에 출입하는 것을 더 용이하게 만들기 위한 새로운 법안을 통과시켰습니다. 그것은 모든 다세대 주거용 건물들이 정문에 휠체어 경사로를 포함할 것을 요구합니다. 이 규정을 준수하는 데에는 6개월의 기간이 있지만, 저희는 장애가 있는 주민들과 방문객들이 저희 건물을 이용하는 데에 마주하는 어떠한 어려움이라도 가능한 한 빨리 줄이기 위해 즉시 필요한 조치를 취하기로 결정했습니다. 따라서, 저희는 5월 15일에서 17일까지 작업자들이 건물 정문으로 이어지는 휠체어 경사로를 설치할 것임을 모두에게 알려드리려고 합니다. 이것이 초래할 수 있는 불편에 대해 사과드리며 여러분의 인내심에 감사드립니다.

Greenwoods 아파트 관리인 David Greer 드림

어휘 mandate 요구하다, 명령하다   ramp 경사로   comply 준수하다, 따르다

구문분석 [7행] ~ we have decided to take the necessary steps immediately in order to reduce any **difficulties** [faced in accessing our property] for disabled residents and guests as early as possible.

→ [faced ~ property]는 명사 difficulties를 수식하는 과거분사구이다.

19 심경 파악하기 정답 ①

해설 심경은 간접적으로 표현된다. 글의 초반부의 But as her body settled into a slower rhythm, so did her mind and soul을 통해 느긋한 Melanie의 모습을, 후반부의 All her senses were in tune with nature, and she felt a peace of mind she hadn't ever felt before를 통해 자연에서 느끼는 평화로움에 만족하는 Melanie의 심경을 파악할 수 있으므로, 정답은 ①이다.

해석 Melanie는 깊게 숨을 쉬며 나무의 신선한 향을 들이마셨다. 오두막에서의 처음 며칠 동안에는, 그녀는 무엇을 해야 할지 몰랐다. 그녀는 20년 넘게 쉬지 않고 일했었고, 갑자기 할 일이 없는 것은 이상한 경험이었다. 하지만, 그녀의 몸이 더 느긋한 리듬에 적응함에 따라, 그녀의 마음과 영혼도 그러했다. 그녀는 숲 사이로 천천히 걸었고 그녀가 가장 좋아하는 독서 장소인 아름다운 잔디밭에 도착했다. 그녀는 누워서 위의 나뭇잎들 사이를 통과하는 따뜻한 햇빛을 만끽했다. 그녀는 근처 시냇물 소리와 그녀 주변의 작은 생물들의 바스락거리는 소리를 들었다. 그녀의 모든 감각은 자연과 조화되었고, 그녀는 이전에 느껴보지 못했던 마음의 평안을 느꼈다.

① 느긋하고 만족하는
② 무관심하고 지루한
③ 슬프고 우울한
④ 혼란스럽고 어리둥절한
⑤ 자랑스럽고 기쁜

어휘 inhale 들이마시다, 빨아들이다   settle into 적응하다   patch 밭, 좁은 땅
rustling 바스락거리는 소리, 살랑거리는 소리
in tune with ~과 조화되어, 장단이 맞아서
[선택지] content 만족하는   puzzled 어리둥절한, 얼떨떨한

구문분석
[12행] All her senses were in tune with nature, and she felt **a peace of mind** [(that/which) she hadn't ever felt before].

→ [she ~ before]는 선행사 a peace of mind를 수식하는 관계대명사 절이며, 목적격 관계대명사 that/which가 생략되었다.

20 주장 파악하기 정답 ③

해설 글의 마지막 문장에서 익숙한 것을 선호하는 것이 당신의 삶을 향상시키는 것을 막게 하지 말라고 주장하고 있으므로 정답은 ③이다.

해석 변화를 주는 것과 상황을 그대로 유지하는 것 간의 선택권을 마주할 때, "왜 평온을 깨뜨리는가?"를 묻는 자연스러운 경향이 있다. 하지만 현상 유지 편향이라고 알려진 이 경향은 놓친 기회들을 야기할 수 있고, 이것이 바로 족쇄에서 벗어나는 것이 중요한 이유이다. 당신이 몇 년 동안 같은 자리에서 일해왔다고 상상해보아라; 그것이 당신의 꿈의 직업이 아니더라도, 당신은 아마 꽤 편해졌을 것이다. 만약 당신의 친한 친구들 중의 한 명이 갑자기 당신에게 그 또는 그녀의 회사에서의 중요한 역할을 제안한다면, 당신은 스스로에게 "상황들이 지금 괜찮은데 왜 잘 알지 못하는 것의 위험을 무릅쓰는가?"라고 물을지도 모른다. 아무것도 하지 않는 것이 사실상 가장 안전한 행동 방침일 수도 있지만, 그것은 또한 당신이 더 나은 상황에 놓일 가능성을 막는다. 신중한 것은 중요하지만, 익숙한 것에 대한 선호가 당신이 삶을 향상시키는 것을 막게 하지 말아라.

어휘 rock the boat 평온을 깨뜨리다, 평지풍파를 일으키다
predisposition 경향, 성향   status quo bias 현상 유지 편향
course of action 행동 방침   preclude 막다, 불가능하게 하다

구문분석
[13행] ~ it also precludes the possibility of <u>you</u> <u>ending up</u> in a better situation.
    의미상 주어 동명사구

→ 목적격 대명사 you가 전치사 of의 목적어 역할을 하는 동명사구 ending up의 의미상 주어로 쓰였다. 참고로, 일상적으로 말하는 상황에서는 동명사의 의미상 주어로 소유격 대신 목적격을 쓸 수도 있다.

21 밑줄 의미 추론하기 정답 ②

[해설] 학위를 따는 것이 성공과 재정적 안정을 얻기 위한 전제 조건으로 여겨지게 된 상황을 비판하는 내용의 글이다. 대학들은 학생들이 적은 비용으로 최대의 경제적 가치를 가져다주는 학위를 따는 것을 목표로 삼게 하기보다는 그들에게 새로운 방향을 제시하고 스스로 목표를 발견하고 그것을 성취할 수 있도록 자극해야 한다고 말하고 있다. 따라서 글의 주제를 비유적으로 표현한 providing a ticket to the ball(무도회의 티켓을 제공하는 것)이 의미하는 것은 ② '수익성 있는 직업을 얻는 수단으로서 역할을 하는 것'이다.

[오답분석] ①은 글의 일부만을 다루고 있는 오답이다. ③은 학위를 경제적 상품으로만 여기는 상황을 대학이 두고 보아서는 안 된다고 한 글의 내용과 반대되는 내용을 다루고 있으므로 오답이다. ④, ⑤은 글에서 언급된 내용이 아니다.

[해석] 학사 학위나 석사 학위를 따는 것은 직업상의 성공과 그것으로 인해서 재정적 안정을 얻기 위한 전제 조건으로 여겨지게 되었다. 이를 고려하여, 많은 학생들은 당연한 반응을 보인다: 그들은 인지도가 가장 높은 대학들에 지원하고, 미래의 소득을 극대화하게 해줄 학과들을 전공하며, 높은 학점을 받을 수 있는 용이함을 근거로 수업들을 선택한다. 실제로, 학위는 상품으로 여겨지며, 학생의 목표는 가장 적은 비용으로 최대의 가치를 얻는 것이다. 유명한 경제학자인 Eamon O'Shea(이몬 오셰)에 따르면 이는 중대한 문제를 제기하는데, 그는 "교육에 대한 시장 기반의 경제적 수익에만 집중함으로써" 중요한 것을 놓치고 있다고 주장한다. 그저 무도회의 티켓을 제공하는 것보다는, 대학들은 그들 스스로에게 도전으로의 새로운 방향을 제시하고 젊은이들이 삶에서 그들의 목표를 발견하고 그것을 성취하기를 시도할 수 있도록 젊은이들에게 지적인 자극을 주어야 한다; 다시 말해서, 학생들은 진정한 행복을 추구하도록 장려되어야 한다.

① 특정 분야의 학문을 전문으로 하는 것
② 수익성 있는 직업을 얻는 수단으로서 역할을 하는 것
③ 학생들이 교육적 목표를 추구하도록 동기를 부여하는 것
④ 부유해지는 방법에 관해 조언을 제공하는 것
⑤ 학문적으로 재능이 있는 사람들에게 직접적인 지원을 제공하는 것

[어휘] **bachelor's degree** 학사 학위 **master's degree** 석사 학위
prerequisite 전제 조건 **name recognition** 인지도
commodity 상품, 필수품 **ball** 무도회 **reorient** 새로운 방향을 제시하다

[구문분석]
[1행] ①[Obtaining a bachelor's or master's degree] has come to be seen as a prerequisite **for** ②[achieving professional success and, thereby, financial stability].
→ ①[Obtaining ~ degree]는 문장의 주어 역할을 하는 명사구이고, ②[achieving ~ stability]는 전치사 for의 목적어 역할을 하는 명사구이다.

[18행] ~ in other words, students **need** to be encouraged to pursue real happiness.
→ 동사 need의 목적어로 to부정사의 수동형인 to be encouraged가 쓰였다.
→ 동사 encourage가 수동태(be encouraged)로 쓰이면서 바로 뒤에 목적어 없이 목적격 보어로 to부정사 to pursue가 쓰였다.

22 요지 파악하기 정답 ③

[해설] 글의 첫 두 문장에서 유머(코미디)는 틀에 박히지 않은 방법으로 사회적 문제들을 탐구하고 종종 그 과정에서 새로운 통찰력을 제시하는 수단이 된다는 요지가 제시되어 있으므로, 이 글의 요지로 가장 적절한 것은 ③이다.

[오답분석] ①은 글에서 언급된 '농담'을 사용하여 헷갈리게 하는 오답이다. ⑤은 유머가 사회적으로 소외되는 집단의 입장을 긍정적으로 보여주는 것에 집중한다는 글의 내용과 반대되는 내용이므로 오답이다.

[해석] 유머가 사람들이 그들의 삶에 직접적인 영향을 미치는 현실의 문제들을 가볍게 여기게 함으로써 스트레스를 덜어 준다는 점에서 본래 현실 도피의 한 형태라는 널리 확산된 믿음이 있다. 이것이 코미디의 기능이지만, 그것은 또한 훨씬 더 중요한 역할을 할 수 있는데, 그것은 틀에 박히지 않은 방법으로 사회적 문제들을 탐구하고 종종 그 과정에서 새로운 통찰력을 제시하는 수단이라는 것이다. 유머는 소수 집단에 속하는 특정 집단의 사람들에 대한 유해한 고정 관념들에 이의를 제기하는 데에 이용될 수 있다. 이는 농담에 반응하는 것이 사회적 유대의 한 방식이기 때문이고, 유머가 사회적으로 소외되는 집단의 입장을 긍정적인 방식으로 보여주는 것에 집중할 때, 그것은 그렇지 않으면 무시되거나 심지어 폄하될지도 모르는 사람들에 대한 공감을 조성한다. 이런 식으로, 코미디는 논란이 많은 문제들을 공유된 경험으로서 보여주는 구조화 장치로서 작용하여, 사람들이 자기 자신의 편견 너머로 보게 한다.

[어휘] **escapism** 현실 도피 **make light of** ~을 가볍게 여기다, 경시하다
bonding 유대, 결합 **marginalize** 사회적으로 소외하다
disparage 폄하하다, 얕보다 **framing** 구조화, 틀 짜기

[구문분석]
[1행] There is **a widely held belief** [that humor is primarily a form of escapism] **in that** it relieves stress by ~
→ [that ~ escapism]은 a widely held belief와 동격을 이루는 명사절이다.
→ in that은 '~라는 점에서, ~이므로'라는 의미의 부사절 접속사이다.

23 주제 파악하기 정답 ③

[해설] 첫 문장과 마지막 두 문장으로 미루어 보아 인터넷의 영향으로 누구나 예술을 접할 수 있게 되고 예술품의 수가 급증했으며, 이러한 변화와 더불어 예술계는 수익을 바라고 더 많은 원본 작품을 만들어내는 일종의 공장이 되었고 예술품은 그저 구매되고 팔리는 것이라는 내용의 글이다. 따라서 이 글의 주제로 가장 적절한 것은 ③ '예술의 대중화와 상품화 간의 연관 관계'이다.

[오답분석] ①, ②, ④은 글의 일부만을 다루고 있는 오답이다. ⑤은 글에서 언급되지 않았다.

[해석] 인터넷은 예술을 더 다가가기 쉽게 만들었다; 그것은 더 이상 단지 매우 부유한 수집가들의 영역이 아니다. 인터넷이 제공하는 노출은 당연히 예술가들에게 유익한데, 중개인이 먼저 화랑에 작품을 전시해주기를 기대할 필요 없이 그들(예술가들)에게 작품을 소개할 기회를 주기 때문이다. 하지만 그들의 작품이 엄밀히 말해 모두가 볼 수 있도록 온라인에 공개되어 있지만, 온라인 작품 큐레이팅은 너무 많은 작품들로 압도되어 좋은 예술품과 나쁜 예술품 사이의 경계가 불분명해졌다; 모든 게 그저 누구나 이용 가능한 예술일 뿐이다. 게다가, 점점 더 많은 원본 작품이 만들어질수록 수익의 가능성이 더 높아지면서, 예술계 자체는 일종의 공장이 되었다. 오늘날, 예술 작품은 미적인 또는 탁월한 특성으로 인해 소중히 여겨지는 "값을 매길 수 없는" 것이 아니라 이제는 그저 구매되고 팔리는 것이기 때문에 예술가들은 1년에 신경 써서 만든 한 점의 작품보다는 매달 30점의 그저 그런 작품들을 만들어낼 때 훨씬 더 상업적으로 성공할 수 있다.

① 대량 생산된 예술 작품에 대한 높아지는 선호도의 이유
② 예술 작품의 우수함이 평가되는 방법에 대한 인터넷의 영향
③ 예술의 대중화와 상품화 간의 연관 관계
④ 예술가들의 수익에 미치는 예술의 상업화의 영향

⑤ 현대 예술 작품에 값을 정하는 것의 어려움

[어휘] **priceless** 값을 매길 수 없는, 아주 귀중한
treasure 소중히 여기다; 대단히 귀중한 것 **aesthetic** 미적인
transcendent 탁월한, 초월한 [선택지] **democratization** 대중화, 민주화
commodification 상품화, 상업화

[구문분석] [7행] ~ online art curating is overwhelmed with [**so much** content **that** the lines between good and bad art have been blurred]; it's all just art, available to anyone.

→ [so ~ blurred]는 '너무 ~해서 -하다'라는 의미를 나타내는 'so + 형용사 + a(n) + 명사 + that -'으로, that절(that ~ blurred)은 결과를 나타낸다. 이 문장에서는 명사 content가 불가산 명사로 쓰여서 관사(a) 없이 쓰였다.

[11행] ~ with ①[the more original art] being produced, ②[the higher] the potential for profit.

→ ①[the ~ art]와 ②[the higher]는 '~할수록 점점 더 -하다'라는 의미의 비교급 구문 'the + 비교급 ~, the + 비교급 -'을 만든다. ②[the higher] 뒤의 절에는 be동사가 생략되었다.

24 　제목 파악하기　　　　　　　　정답 ④

[해설] 첫 두 문장과 마지막 세 문장으로 미루어 보아 많은 사람들이 여가 시간을 부업을 하는 데에 이용하고 있으며 단기 계약 근무의 유행을 나타내는 용어인 "긱 경제"에서 많은 기술이 계약 고용을 가능하게 하기 위해 개발되었다는 내용의 글로, Uber를 예를 들어 설명하고 있다. 따라서 글의 제목으로 가장 적절한 것은 ④ '긱 경제에서의 부업의 부상'이다.

[오답분석] ②은 글의 핵심 소재 Gig Economy를 사용하여 헷갈리게 하는 오답이다. ③은 글에서 유연성을 부업의 핵심 요소라고 한 것이지, 증가된 고용의 비결이라고 한 것이 아니므로 오답이다. ⑤의 부업을 얻는 비결에 대해서는 글에서 언급되고 있지 않다.

[해석] 임금의 구매력이 지난 40년 동안 상대적으로 변동 없이 유지되면서, 더 많은 사람들이 수입과 지출의 균형을 맞추기 위해 애쓰고 있다. 근로자들은 청구서를 지불할 방안으로써 그들의 여가 시간을 부업을 하는 데에 이용하고 있다. 이러한 사람들에게, 부업이 원래의 직업에 지장을 주지 않도록 유연성이 부업의 핵심 요소이다. 기술은 이를 가능하게 만드는 것을 도왔고, 사람들이 자신이 선택한 시간 동안 많은 회사들의 단기적 필요를 충족시키는 독립적인 계약자로 근무하는 것을 가능하게 했다. '긱 경제'는 단기 계약 근무의 유행을 설명하는 상대적으로 새로운 용어이다. Uber와 같은 새로운 플랫폼들이 계약 고용을 가능하게 하도록 개발되었고, Uber는 사람들이 돈을 받고 다른 사람들을 태워주는 것을 가능하게 한다. 생각할 수 있는 모든 분야에서 단기 업무에 사람들을 연결시켜주기 위해 수많은 웹사이트들이 존재하고, 그것들 중 다수는 원격으로 고정된 일정 없이 이루어질 수 있다.

① 전문 직업의 몰락
② 긱 경제에서 성공하기 위한 기술
③ 유연성: 증가된 고용의 비결
④ 긱 경제에서의 부업의 부상
⑤ 근면이 부업을 얻는 비결이다!

[어휘] **purchasing power** 구매력(어떤 재화나 용역을 할 수 있는 재력)
make ends meet 수입과 지출의 균형을 맞추다, 겨우 먹고 살 만큼 벌다
second job 부업 **flexibility** 유연성, 탄력성
gig economy 긱 경제(임시직 선호 경제) **prevalence** 유행, 보급
[선택지] **downfall** 몰락, 낙하

[구문분석] [14행] Numerous websites exist to connect people with short-term jobs in every area imaginable, **many of which** can be done remotely and without a fixed schedule.

→ 선행사 short-term jobs가 사물이고, many of 뒤에서 전치사 of의 목적어 역할을 하므로 목적격 관계대명사 which가 쓰였다.

25 　도표 정보 파악하기　　　　　　　정답 ⑤

[해설] 2018년에 숙박 서비스 부문의 취업 인구수는 21,380이고 문화 산업은 27,320으로, 숙박 서비스 부문이 문화 산업 부문의 절반보다 더 많으므로 수치의 비교 표현이 잘못 반영되었다. 따라서 도표의 내용과 일치하지 않는 것은 ⑤이다.

[해석]
덴마크의 관광업 분야 취업 인구 수치

2008년		2018년	
부문	취업 인구(수)	부문	취업 인구(수)
식음료	83,830	식음료	119,600
승객 수송	57,810	스포츠 산업	63,250
스포츠 산업	28,060	승객 수송	55,720
문화 산업	25,850	문화 산업	27,320
숙박 서비스	21,020	숙박 서비스	21,380
여행 중개업	6,820	여행 중개업	6,740
합계	223,400	합계	294,020

* 참고: 반올림으로 인해 세부 항목들이 합계와 맞지 않을 수도 있음

위의 표들은 2008년과 2018년의 덴마크의 관광업 분야 취업 인구수를 보여준다. ① 덴마크 관광업의 총 취업 인구수는 2008년부터 2018년까지 7만 명 이상 증가했다. ② 식음료 부문에 관해서는, 같은 기간에 취업 인구수가 3만 5천 명 이상 증가했다. ③ 2008년과 2018년 두 해 모두, 취업 인구가 1만 명 미만이었던 유일한 부문은 여행 중개업이었다. ④ 승객 수송과 스포츠 산업 부문은 2008년에 각각 두 번째 및 세 번째로 높은 순위를 차지한 반면에, 2018년에는 그 순위들이 서로 위치를 바꾸었다. ⑤ 2018년에, 숙박 서비스 부문에서의 취업 인구수는 문화 산업의 그것(취업 인구수)의 절반보다 더 적었다.

[어휘] **employment** 취업 인구, 고용 **with regard to** ~에 관해서는

[구문분석] [6행] In both 2008 and 2018, [**the only division** in which employment was less than 10,000] was travel agencies.

→ [the ~ 10,000]는 선행사 the only division을 수식하는 '전치사 + 관계대명사' in which가 이끄는 관계대명사절(in ~ 10,000)을 포함하며, 전체가 문장의 주어이다.

26 　세부 정보 파악하기　　　　　　　정답 ⑤

[해설] Adult antlions range in size from one-and-a-half to three inches long을 통해 성충 개미귀신은 크기가 1.5인치에서 3인치에 이른다는 것을 알 수 있는데, ⑤은 대략 0.5인치 정도라고 일부 정보를 잘못 나타냈으므로 글의 내용과 일치하지 않는 것은 ⑤이다.

[해석] 개미귀신은 명주잠자리과에 속하는 곤충이다. 그 이름은 그것들의 유충에서 기인하는데, 그 유충들은 선천적으로 포식성이다. 개미귀신은 생애 주기를 알로 시작하고, 그 이후에 유충의 형태로 부화한다. 개미귀신 유충은 납작하고 날개가 없으며 타원형의 몸통이 있고, 갈색이다. 그것은 6개의 다리와, 한 쌍의 거대한 집게발이 달린 머리를 가지고 있다. 유충이 최대 크기에 이르면(거의

0.5인치 길이), 그것은 고치를 만들고 변태를 거치며, 성충으로 모습을 드러낸다. 성충 개미귀신은 길고 가늘며 날개가 있어 잠자리와 거의 비슷하다. 성충 개미귀신은 크기에 있어서 1.5인치에서 3인치에 이른다. 그것들은 4개의 길고 얇으며 맥이 있는 날개가 있고, 머리 위에는 2개의 구부러진 더듬이가 놓여져 있다.

(어휘) antlion 개미귀신, 명주잠자리 larva 유충, 애벌레
predatory 포식성의, 육식의 hatch 부화하다 pincer 집게발
cocoon (곤충의) 고치, 보호막 slender 가는 veined 맥이 있는
antenna 더듬이

(구문
분석)
[7행] ①[**Once** the larva reaches its maximum size (roughly half an inch long)], ②[it forms a cocoon and undergoes metamorphosis], ③[emerging as an adult].

→ ②[it ~ metamorphosis]가 전체 문장의 주절이다. ①[Once ~ long]은 접속사 once(일단 ~하면)가 이끄는 조건의 부사절이고, ③[emerging ~ adult]는 '(그 결과) ~하다'라는 의미의 분사구문으로, 분사구문의 주어가 주절의 주어(it)와 같아서 생략되었다.

---

27 안내문 정보 파악하기   정답 ④

(해설) 수치가 포함된 부분인 Books can be renewed 3 times를 통해 도서는 3번 대출 연장될 수 있다는 것을 알 수 있으므로, 글의 내용과 일치하지 않는 것은 ④이다.

(해석)
**Parson 시립 도서관의
대출 및 연장 규정**

Parson 시립 도서관은 저희의 대출 및 연장 규정의 변경 사항을 알려 드리고자 합니다.

대출:
◆ 도서
- 한번에 최대 7권까지 대출하실 수 있습니다.
- 각 도서는 14일 이내에 반납되어야 합니다.

◆ 디지털 미디어
- DVD, CD, 오디오북을 포함합니다.
- 한번에 최대 5개까지 대출하실 수 있습니다.
- 각 품목은 30일까지 대출될 수 있습니다(DVD 제외, DVD는 20일까지 대출됩니다).

연장:
- 도서는 3번 연장될 수 있습니다.
- 디지털 미디어는 2번 연장될 수 있습니다.
- 각 연장은 추가 10일입니다.
- 연장은 반납일 전에 되어야 합니다.

(어휘) renewal 연장, 갱신 due date 반납일

(구문
분석)
[12행] Each item can be kept up to 30 days (except for **DVDs**, [which can be kept for up to 20 days]).

→ [which ~ days]는 선행사 DVDs를 수식하는 주격 관계대명사절로, 콤마 뒤에서 계속적 용법으로 쓰였다.

---

28 안내문 정보 파악하기   정답 ⑤

(해설) advance registration is required를 통해 캠프에 참가하려면 사전 등록이 요구된다는 것을 알 수 있으므로, 글의 내용과 일치하는 것은 ⑤이다.

(해석)
Little Chefs 요리 캠프

만약 당신의 자녀가 즐거운 시간을 보내면서 삶의 중요한 기술을 배우기를 원한다면, 오늘 그들을 Little Chefs 요리 캠프에 등록시키세요!
• 그들은 전 세계의 요리들에 대해 알게 될 것입니다.
• 그들은 다양하고 신선한 재료들로 요리할 것입니다.
• 그들은 중요한 주방 안전과 장비에 대해 배울 것입니다.

강사: The Dinner Table 레스토랑의 주방장 Tim Roberts
연령: 8세-12세의 아이들을 환영합니다.
기간: 6월 10일부터 6월 14일까지
비용: 100달러 (무료 앞치마 포함)

자리가 한정되어 있으니, 사전 등록이 요구됩니다.
메뉴와 활동에 대한 더 많은 정보는 www.littlechefs.com을 방문하시기 바랍니다.

(어휘) equipment 장비 apron 앞치마

(구문
분석)
[2행] If you <u>want</u> <u>your child</u> <u>to learn</u> important life skills
　　　　동사　　목적어　　목적격 보어
[while still having fun], then sign them up for Little Chefs Cooking Camp today!

→ 동사 want의 목적어로 your child, 목적격 보어로 to부정사 to learn이 쓰였다.
→ [while ~ fun]은 분사구문의 의미를 분명하게 하기 위해 부사절 접속사(while)가 분사 앞에 온 형태이다.

---

29 어법상 틀린 것 찾기   정답 ①

(해설) 동사 allow는 목적격 보어로 to부정사를 취하므로 ①의 create을 to create으로 고쳐야 한다.

(오답
분석)
②은 단수명사 awareness가 주어이므로 단수동사 is를 사용한 것은 어법상 적절하다. ③은 선행사 Individuals를 수식하는 형용사절을 이끄는 주격 관계대명사 who를 사용하여 어법상 적절하다. ④은 수식 받는 명사 complaints가 '높아지는' 행위의 주체이므로 현재분사 Rising을 사용한 것은 어법상 적절하다. ⑤은 to부정사 to provide의 동사 provide를 수식하기 위해 동사원형 앞에 부사 voluntarily를 사용한 것은 어법상 적절하다.

(해석) 사람들이 인터넷을 사용할 때 그들을 추적하는 기술의 발전은 온라인으로 제품들을 홍보하는 회사들에게 이익이 된다고 증명되었다. 그것은 그들이 연령에서부터 관계 상태, 순자산에 이르는 특정한 데이터 포인트를 기반으로 잠재적인 고객들을 대상으로 하는 개인화된 광고를 만드는 것을 가능하게 한다. 하지만 이것이 사생활에 가하는 위협에 대한 높아진 소비자 인식이 광고업에서의 중요한 변화로 이어지고 있다. 특히 주목할 것은 옵트아웃 방식의 정보 수집에서 옵트인 방식으로의 점진적인 변화이다. 대부분의 소셜 미디어 사이트와 검색 엔진들은 자동으로 광범위한 이용자 정보를 수집한다. 이를 피하고 싶은 사람들은 변경하려는 적절한 설정을 찾기 위해 복잡한 메뉴들 전체를 스크롤해야 한다. 이러한 관행에 대해 높아지는 불만은 일부 회사들이 조치를 취하도록 했다. 그들은 이제 고객들이 자발적으로 개인 정보를 제공하도록 권장하는 홍보 콘텐츠를 만든다. 특히, 잘 설계된 테스트는 높은 수준의 고객 참여를 수반하고 그 결과 광고에 매우 유용한 정보를 수집하게 된다.

어휘 **boon** 이익, 요긴한 것　**net worth** 순자산
opt-out 옵트아웃(당사자가 거부 의사를 밝히기 전까지 데이터 수집을 할 수 있는 방식)　**opt-in** 옵트인(당사자가 동의한 경우에만 데이터를 수집할 수 있는 방식)　**by default** 자동으로, 자연스럽게

구문분석
[12행] Individuals who **want** ①[to avoid this] must scroll through complicated menus ②[to find **the appropriate setting**] ③[to change].
→ ①[to avoid this]는 동사 want의 목적어 역할을 하고, ②[to ~ setting]은 to부정사의 부사적 용법으로 목적을 의미한다. ③[to change]는 to부정사의 형용사적 용법(~할)으로, 앞의 명사 the appropriate setting을 수식한다.

30 어휘 적절성 파악하기 정답 ④

해설 울프톤을 줄이기 위한 방법들도 악기의 전반적인 소리에 영향을 미치기 때문에 최소한의 간섭으로 울프톤을 억제해야 한다는 맥락이 되어야 하므로, ④의 maximally(최대한으로)를 그와 반대되는 의미의 minimally(최소한으로)와 같은 어휘로 바꾸어야 문맥상 적절하다.

오답분석 ①은 저품질의 악기들이 울프톤을 만들어낼 가능성이 더 적다고 했으므로, 울프톤이 나는 악기가 사실 고품질의 악기들이라는 문맥이 되어야 하므로 high-quality가 오는 것이 적절하다. ⑤는 추의 배치와 질량이 정확하게 조정된다면 울프톤이 억제될 수 있다는 문맥이 되어야 하므로 adjusted가 오는 것이 적절하다.

해석 울프톤은 현악기 상판의 자연 발생적인 울림 진동수가 연주되는 음과 일치할 때 발생되는 원치 않는 둥둥 울리거나 윙윙거리는 소리이다. 어떤 사람은 울프톤이 나는 악기는 품질이 의심스럽다고 생각할 수도 있지만, 그것을 겪는 것은 사실 ① 고품질의 악기들이다. 그 이유는 아주 단순하다: 더 저품질의 악기들은 ② 덜 울리는 재료들로 만들어진다. 따라서, 그것들은 울프톤을 만들어낼 가능성이 더 적고, 만약 만들어낸다 하더라도, 그 진폭은 보통 거의 들리지 않을 정도로 작다. 반대로, 더 고품질의 악기들은 매우 깊이 울리고 ③ 알아차릴 수 있을 정도로 충분히 증폭되는 울프톤을 발생시키기 더 쉽다. 그 현상을 줄이기 위한 방법들도 악기의 전반적인 소리에 영향을 미치기 때문에 균형적인 방법이 필요하다. 목표는 ④ 최대한으로(→최소한으로) 간섭하는 해결책으로 울프톤을 억제하는 것이다. 이는 일반적으로 악기의 줄받침 아래에 있는 현에 추를 달아서 이루어진다. 추의 배치와 질량은 적절한 조합을 찾기 위해서 ⑤ 조정되어야 하지만, 만약 정확하게 된다면 울프톤의 윙윙거리는 소리는 억제될 수 있다.

어휘 **beat** (북이) 둥둥 울리다　**howl** 윙윙거리다; 윙윙거리는 소리
resonate (소리가 깊이) 울리다, 공명하다　**frequency** 진동수, 빈도
top plate 상판　**resonant** (소리가 깊이) 울리는　**apt** ~하기 쉬운
amplify 증폭시키다　**invasive** 간섭하는, 침략하는　**weight** 추, 무게
bridge (현악기의) 줄받침　**tame** 억제하다, 길들이다

구문분석
[5행] ~ **it's** actually the high-quality instruments **that** suffer from it.
→ 명사구 the high-quality instruments를 강조하는 it is(it's) ~ that 강조 구문이 쓰였다.

31 빈칸 추론하기 정답 ④

해설 개발 도상국과 같은 신흥 시장에서 전자 상거래가 엄청난 성장 가능성을 가지고 있다는 내용의 글이고, 빈칸 앞 문장에서 신흥 시장에의 전자 상거래 보급은 미국과 같은 주요 시장들에의 보급보다 늦어졌다고 하였다. 따라서 주제와 관련된 빈칸에는 ④ '미개발의'가 와서 아직 많은 부분이 미개발 상태인 개발 도상국 신흥 시장에서 전자 상거래의 성장 잠재력이 높다는 의미가 되어야 한다.

오답분석 ①, ③은 전자 상거래 보급이 늦어진 신흥 시장의 상태를 설명하는 단어로 적절하지 않다. ②, ⑤은 신흥 시장에서의 전자 상거래는 이제 막 기회가 열렸고 많은 잠재력을 갖고 있다는 글의 내용과 반대되는 내용이므로 오답이다.

해석 편리함에 대한 우리의 계속 늘어나는 요구에 의해 주로 주도되는 전자 상거래의 인기는 앞으로의 몇 년 내에 세계적인 규모로 성장할 것으로만 예상된다. 이것에는 자동화와 오프라인 거래 감소를 포함한 많은 요인들이 작용하지만, 신흥 시장들의 성장도 온라인 거래의 미래에 주목할 만한 영향을 미칠 것으로 예상된다. 이전에는, 신흥 시장에의 전자 상거래 보급은 미국과 같은 주요 시장들에의 보급보다 뒤처졌지만, 최근의 경제 성장으로 인해, 개발 도상국들의 30억 명이 2022년까지 인터넷 접속이 가능할 것이라고 예상된다. 전통적인 소매상들이 오랫동안 상업 활동들을 지배해왔으므로 이러한 시장들의 대부분이 현재 미개발 상태라는 점을 고려하면, 이 지역들에서의 전자 상거래는 당연히 많은 잠재력이 있다. 아주 많은 기회들이 이제 열리면서, 새로운 전자 상거래 브랜드가 등장할 것이 예상되고, 인터넷을 통해 소비하는 소비자들의 성장이 증대됨에 따라 전통적인 브랜드들은 적절한 상태를 유지하기 위해서 온라인 역량을 개발할 것이다.

① 자율의　　　　　　② 경쟁적인
③ 혁신적인　　　　　④ 미개발의
⑤ 포화된

어휘 **e-commerce** 전자 상거래　**ever-increasing** 계속 늘어나는
brick-and-mortar 오프라인 거래의, 소매의　**emerging market** 신흥 시장
penetration 보급, 진입　**lag behind** ~보다 뒤처지다
emerging nation 개발 도상국

구문분석
[3행] While **a number of factors** play into this, [including automation and the decline of brick-and-mortar businesses], the growth of emerging markets is ~
→ [including ~ businesses]는 a number of factors를 부연 설명하는 전치사구가 삽입된 형태이다.

[10행] ~ but due to recent economic growth, [it is expected
　　　　　　　　　　　　　　　　　　　　가주어
that three billion people from emerging nations will have
　　　　　　　　　　　진주어(that절)
access to the Internet by 2022].
→ 동사 expect의 목적어가 that절인 경우, [it ~ 2022]와 같이 가주어 it을 사용하여 'it is p.p. that' 형태의 수동태 구문으로 쓸 수 있다.

32 빈칸 추론하기 정답 ⑤

해설 주제문에 해당하는 빈칸 문장에서 결속이 '무엇'에서 주요한 역할을 하는 행동이라고 언급하고, 이웃들에게 호의를 베풀 때, 직장에서 동료들과 협력하고 서로 도울 때, 정치나 사회 운동을 할 때 등의 사회 전반의 여러 영역에서의 결속의 예시를 설명하며, 결속이 공동체에서 삶의 근본적인 기둥이 된다고 이야기하고 있다. 따라서 빈칸에는 ⑤ '건전한 사회 구조를 유지하는 것'이 와서 건전한 사회 구조를 유지하는 데에 주요한 역할을 하는 행동들 중에 결속이 가

장 널리 경험되는 것들 중에 하나라는 의미가 되어야 한다.

(오답분석) ①은 결속이 집단 내 상호 지지 과정이며 단체 행동을 위해 사람들이 협력하는 방식으로 드러난다는 글의 내용과 반대되는 내용이므로 오답이다. ②, ④은 글의 내용과 관련이 없다. ③은 글에서 언급된 community를 사용하여 헷갈리게 하는 오답이다.

(해석) 건전한 사회 구조를 유지하는 것에서 주요한 역할을 하는 행동들 가운데, 집단 내의 상호 지지 과정인 결속은 가장 널리 감지되는 것들 중 하나이다. 이웃들이 보통 옆집에 사는 사람들을 돕기 위해 호의를 베풀 때 사소한 방식으로 이런 행동을 보인다. 직장에서는, 동료들이 협력과 상호 간의 지원을 받아들이지 않는 한 사실상 어떤 계획이나 업무도 성취되지 않을 것이다; 실제로, 건설 노동자들이 단결하여 벽을 세워야 할 때처럼, 많은 육체 노동 직업은 물리적으로 협력을 필요로 한다. 정치와 사회 운동의 영역은 지금까지의 결속에 대한 요구와 이행의 아마도 가장 명백한 예시들 중 하나를 보여준다. 대중적인 사회 정의 운동은 이런 행동의 완벽한 발현인데, 그것은 사람들이 압제적인 정부에 항의하기 위해 모이거나 경제 불황의 시기 동안 동료 시민들에게 음식과 거처를 제공하는 방식으로 드러난다. 이 모든 경우들이 결속이 어떻게 공동체 내 삶의 근본적인 기둥이 되는지를 보여준다.

① 사회 구성원들 간의 분열을 강화하는 것
② 사람들이 개인적 성공을 추구하도록 동기를 부여하는 것
③ 문제들에 대한 공동체의 인식을 높이는 것
④ 대규모의 공공 재앙들을 막는 것
⑤ 건전한 사회 구조를 유지하는 것

(어휘) **solidarity** 결속, 유대 **embrace** 받아들이다, 수용하다 **reciprocal** 상호 간의 **manual labor** 육체노동 **realm** 영역, 범위 **explicit** 명백한 **manifestation** 발현, 표명 **fellow** 같은 처지에 있는 **pillar** 기둥 [선택지] **division** 분열, 분할 **healthy** 건전한

(구문분석)
[6행] In work settings, virtually no projects or tasks stand to be accomplished [**unless** colleagues embrace collaboration and reciprocal assistance]; indeed, ~

→ [unless ~ assistance]는 접속사 unless(~하지 않는 한)가 이끄는 조건의 부사절이다.

---

33 빈칸 추론하기 정답 ②

(해석) 주제문에 해당하는 빈칸 문장에서 리튬 이온 배터리가 더 지속 가능한 미래를 위한 길을 닦는 데에 도움이 될 수 있지만, '무엇하다'고 하고, 글의 중반에서 리튬 이온 배터리를 처리하는 것은 중금속과 다른 환경 오염 물질들을 방출하고, 만드는 것도 많은 물을 필요로 해서 초목의 감소, 가뭄, 기온의 상승 등을 야기할 수 있다고 했다. 따라서 빈칸에는 ② '그것들이 제기하는 환경적 문제들이 상쇄되어야 한다'는 내용이 오는 것이 적절하다.

(오답분석) ①의 비용이 더 적게 드는 EV 대체재는 글에서 언급되고 있지 않다. ③의 리튬 이온 배터리에 대한 높은 수요가 낮아질 것이라는 내용은 글에서 언급되고 있지 않다. ④의 그것들의 수명이 늘리는 것의 가능성은 글에서 언급되고 있지 않다. ⑤의 다른 설계와 소재들을 사용하는 것은 글에서 언급되고 있지 않다.

(해석) 전기 자동차(EV)로의 이행이 현재 진행 중임에 따라, EV의 전력원인 리튬 이온 배터리의 수요가 치솟고 있어 새로운 우려를 불러일으킨다: 그것들이 수명 주기의 끝에 이르면 우리는 그것들로 무엇을 할 것인가? 가루로 분쇄된 후에 재활용 과정에서 녹거나 용해되는 다른 종류의 배터리들과는 달리, 리튬 이온 배터리는 처리하기가 더 어렵다. 그것들은 중금속과 다른 환경 오염 물질들을 방출하기 때문에 그것들을 처리하는 것은 해롭다. 그것들에 대한 현재의 재활용 과정은 비용이 많이 들고 그 결과 낮은 가치의 상품이 되기 때문에, 리튬을

재활용하려고 애쓰는 것보다 더 많은 리튬을 채굴하는 것이 더 저렴하다. 하지만, 이러한 배터리들을 만들기 위해 필요한 금속을 채굴하는 것은 막대한 양의 물을 필요로 하고, 물의 이용은 줄어드는 초목, 가뭄, 그리고 더 높은 기온과 관련되어 왔다. 리튬 이온 배터리가 더 지속 가능한 미래를 위한 길을 닦는 데에 결국에는 도움이 될 수 있지만, 더 효율적인 재활용 과정을 통해 그것들이 제기하는 환경적 문제들이 상쇄되어야 한다는 것은 분명하다.

① 비용이 더 적게 드는 EV 대체재의 개발이 달성될 수 있다
② 그것들이 제기하는 환경적 문제들이 상쇄되어야 한다
③ EV 제조업체들 사이의 그것들에 대한 높은 수요는 낮아질 것이다
④ 그것들의 수명을 늘리는 것은 가까운 미래에 가능할 수도 있다
⑤ 다른 설계와 소재들이 사용되어야 할 수도 있다

(어휘) **underway** 진행 중인 **lithium-ion** 리튬 이온 **skyrocket** 치솟다, 급등하다 **shred** 분쇄하다, 절단하다 **dissolve** 용해시키다 **heavy metal** 중금속 **contaminant** 오염 물질 [선택지] **neutralize** 상쇄하다, 중립화하다

(구문분석)
[11행] ~ and results in low-value products, making it cheaper [to mine more lithium] than to try to reuse it.
　　　　　　　　　　　　　　　　　　　　　　　　　　가목적어
　　　　진목적어(to부정사구)

→ 가목적어 it이 진목적어 to부정사구 [to ~ lithium] 대신 현재분사 making의 목적어 자리에 쓰인 형태이다.

---

34 빈칸 추론하기 정답 ⑤

(해석) '파울러자유아메바' 감염은 치명적이고 기후 변화로 인해 '파울러자유아메바'가 북쪽으로 퍼져서 사람들의 우려를 낳고 있다는 내용의 글이다. 빈칸 뒤 문장에서 '파울러자유아메바'는 코를 통해서 뇌로 들어가서 조직을 먹을 수 있으므로 코마개 착용이 사람들을 보호해줄 수 있다고 했다. 따라서 주제와 관련된 빈칸에는 ⑤ '사람들이 경계를 늦추지 않아야 한다'가 와서 감염 사례가 매우 드물긴 해도, 사람들이 경계를 늦추지 않고 예방 조치를 취해야 한다는 의미가 되어야 한다.

(오답분석) ①의 새로운 종류의 '파울러자유아메바'에 대해서는 글에서 언급되고 있지 않다. ②의 담수에서의 활동을 피하라는 내용은 글에서 언급되고 있지 않다. ③은 지난 10년 동안 34건이 '파울러자유아메바' 감염으로 기록되었다는 글의 내용과 반대되는 내용이므로 오답이다. ④의 치료법에 대한 내용은 글에서 언급되고 있지 않다.

(해석) 담수에서 발견되는 대부분의 다른 미생물들과는 달리, '파울러자유아메바'는 그것이 감염시키는 거의 모두에게 치명적인데, 이는 주로 감염이 빠르게 진행되고 두통, 열, 그리고 구토 같은 초기 증상이 많은 다른 질병들과 유사해서 그것을 오진하기가 쉽게 만들기 때문이다. '파울러자유아메바'는 따뜻한 물에서 번식하고, 이는 그것이 한때는 남쪽 지역에서만 발견되었다는 뜻이지만 기후 변화와 뒤이은 수온의 상승이 그 미생물을 최근 몇 년 동안 북쪽으로 퍼지게 하여, 호수와 강에서 오락 활동을 즐기는 사람들 사이에서 우려를 높이고 있다. 좋은 소식은 '파울러자유아메바'의 사례가 아직은 매우 드물다는 것이다; 질병통제예방센터는 지난 10년 동안 단 34건을 기록했다. 그럼에도 불구하고, 전문가들은 사람들이 경계를 늦추지 않아야 한다고 말한다. 그 미생물은 물이 코를 통해 흡입될 때에만 전염성이 있고, 그때 그것은 비강을 따라서 그 미생물이 조직을 먹기 시작하는 뇌 속으로 이동하기 때문에, 코마개를 착용할 것을 기억하는 것이 효과적으로 보호해줄 수 있다.

① 새로운 종류의 '파울러자유아메바'들이 발견되고 있다
② 담수에서의 활동들은 무슨 수를 써서라도 피해야 한다
③ 이러한 사례들은 결코 제대로 진단되지 않았다
④ 감염에 대해 알려진 치료법이 없다
⑤ 사람들이 경계를 늦추지 않아야 한다

[어휘] **microorganism** 미생물 **freshwater** 담수, 민물 **misdiagnose** 오진하다
ensuing 뒤이은, 다음의 **bug** 미생물, 병원균
transmissible 전염성의, 보낼 수 있는 **inhale** 흡입하다
nasal cavity 비강 [선택지] **strain** 종류, 긴장
let one's guard down 경계를 늦추다

[구문분석] [18행] ~ into **the brain** [where it begins to feed on the tissue], remembering **to wear** a nose clip can provide effective protection.

→ [where ~ tissue]는 선행사 the brain을 수식하며, 장소를 나타내는 관계부사 where가 이끄는 관계부사절이다.

→ 동명사 remembering의 목적어로 to부정사 to wear가 쓰여 '(미래에) ~할 것을 기억하다'의 의미로 해석한다.

35 흐름과 관계 없는 문장 찾기 정답 ④

[해설] 복잡한 현대 사회에서 많은 조치들이 가동되고 있지만, 위기들이 주관적이기 때문에 관리하기가 어렵다는 내용의 글이다. 그런데 ④은 지도자들에게 대중들이 그들의 관점을 전달하는 것이 도움이 될 수 있다는 내용이므로 주제에서 벗어나 있어 글의 흐름과 무관하다.

[오답분석] ①은 However를 통해 첫 번째 문장의 내용에 대한 반전 설명을 하고 있으므로 첫 번째 문장 뒤에 오는 것이 적절하다. ②의 This는 ①의 that we live in a "culture of fear"를 가리키고 있으므로 ① 뒤에 이어지는 게 적절하다. ③의 such crises는 ②의 full-blown crises를 가리키고 있으므로 ② 뒤에 이어지는 게 적절하다. ⑤은 위기가 주관적이라고 한 ③에 이어서 위기가 사람마다 다르게 판단될 수 있다는 내용을 다루고 있으므로 ③과 연결된다.

[해석] 현대 사회는 점점 더 복잡해져 왔고, 시민들의 복지를 최우선으로 하고 진전을 촉진하기 위해 많은 조치들이 가동 중이다. ① 하지만, 그러한 보호 장치들, 즉 우리가 모든 잠재적인 위험들로부터 당국에 의해 보호받을 것이라는 기대의 결과로, 우리가 "공포 문화"에서 살고 있다고 주장될 수 있다. ② 이는 실제 위험의 수준이 강해지지 않았음에도 불구하고 위험에 대한 우리의 인식이 강해졌다는 것을 의미하며, 이는 왜 사회의 많은 문제들이 정책 입안자들의 통제하는 능력에 제한될 수 있는 본격적인 위기로 발전하는지에 대한 설명을 제공한다. ③ 그러한 위기들을 관리하는 데에 있어서 어려움 중 일부는 그것들이 흔히 주관적이라는 사실과 관련이 있다. (④ 지도자들에게, 대중의 구성원들이 그 상황에 대한 그들의 개념을 받아들이게 하는 것은 불확실함을 줄이고 정보를 전파하는 데에 도움이 될 수 있다.) ⑤ 사회의 일부 구성원들에게는 전적으로 무해하다고 보여질 수 있는 것이 다른 사람들에게는 옳지 않다고 판단될 수 있어서, 감당할 수 없는 상황으로 이어진다.

[어휘] **in place** 가동 중인 **safeguard** 보호 장치 **authorities** 당국, 관계자
full-blown 본격적인, 완전히 진행된 **get out of hand** 감당할 수 없게 되다

[구문분석] [7행] This means that our perception of danger **has increased**, even if the actual level of risk ①[**has not**], providing an explanation **for** ②[why many problems in society develop into full-blown **crises** (that policy makers may be limited in their ability to get under control)].

→ ①[has not] 뒤에는 동사 increased가 생략되었는데 앞의 has increased에서 이미 언급되었기 때문이다.

→ ②[why ~ control]은 전치사 for의 목적어 역할을 하는 명사절이며 그 안의 (that ~ control)은 목적격 관계대명사 that이 이끄는 관계절이다.

36 글의 순서 배열하기 정답 ⑤

[해설] 주어진 글은 어떤 부모들은 아이의 정서적 요구를 상대해야 하는 상황에 불안해진다는 주제를 제시한다. (C)의 their nervousness(그들의 불안)는 주어진 글의 '어떤 부모들은 불안해진다'는 내용을 가리키므로 주어진 글 바로 다음에 오는 것이 적절하다. (B)는 감정적인 것이 나쁘게 받아들여질 것이라는 걸 알 때 아이들이 감정을 억제하는 법을 배운다는 내용이고, (C)의 마지막에서 아이들이 부모의 부정적인 반응으로부터 부모에게 정서적으로 의지할 수 없다는 것을 깨닫는다고 했으므로 그 뒤에 와야 한다. (A)의 This tendency to self-soothe(스스로 달래는 이러한 성향)는 (B)의 부모 없이 '스스로를 위로하는 방법'을 가리키므로 (B) 바로 다음에 오는 것이 적절하다. 따라서 글의 순서로 가장 적절한 것은 ⑤ (C) - (B) - (A)이다.

[해석] 어떤 부모들은 아이의 정서적 요구를 상대해야 하는 상황에 직면했을 때 불안해진다.

(C) 그들의 불안 때문에, 그들은 편안하게 해주는 방식으로 아이들에게 반응해주기가 불가능하거나 그러기를 꺼릴 수 있는데, 이는 그들이 아이들을 외면하게 하거나, 화를 내게 하거나, 어떠한 감정 표현을 했다고 그들에게 창피를 주게 만들 수도 있다. 이러한 반응은 아이가 부모에게 정서적인 지지를 바라고 의지할 수 없다는 것을 깨닫게 하고, 그들은 회피성 애착을 형성한다.

(B) 감정적인 것이 나쁘게 받아들여질 것임을 알 때, 아이는 그들의 감정을 억제하는 법을 배운다. 그들이 계속해서 슬픔과 다른 감정들을 경험하더라도, 그들은 이러한 감정들이 중요하지 않다는 것을 스스로가 깨닫고 그들의 부모에게 의지하는 것을 수반하지 않는 스스로를 위로하는 방법을 찾는다.

(A) 스스로 달래는 이러한 성향은 성인기까지 이어진다. 회피성 애착을 지닌 사람들은 자기 자신에게 의지하는 법을 배웠기 때문에, 다른 사람들로부터 정신적인 지지를 받거나 그들의 어려움을 이야기하는 것에 불편함을 느낄 수 있어서, 이는 그들이 친밀한 관계를 형성하는 것을 어렵게 만들 수 있다.

[어휘] **soothe** 달래다, 위로하다 **carry over** 이어지다 **avoidant** 회피성의
attachment 애착, 믿음 **hold back** 억제하다, 참다
comfort 위로하다 **go to** ~에게 의지하다 **nervousness** 불안, 긴장

[구문분석] [10행] [Knowing that being emotional will be poorly received], the child learns to hold their feelings back.

→ [Knowing ~ received]는 '~할 때'라는 의미의 분사구문으로, 분사구문의 주어가 주절의 주어(the child)와 같아서 생략되었다.

[17행] ~ in a comforting way, which may **cause** them ①[to ignore their child], ②[(to) become angry], **or** ③[(to) shame them for any emotional displays].

→ 동사 cause의 목적격 보어로 쓰인 to부정사구 ①[to ~ child]와 ②[become angry], ③[shame ~ displays]는 등위접속사 or로 연결된 병렬 구조로 두 번째와 세 번째 to는 생략되었다.

37 글의 순서 배열하기 정답 ③

[해설] 주어진 글은 보도 사진가 Kevin Carter의 사진 "독수리와 소녀"에 대한 설명이다. (B)의 The photo(그 사진)는 주어진 글의 "독수리와 소녀"를 가리키고, (B)는 그 사진이 <뉴욕타임즈>에 실렸을 때 사람들이 Kevin Carter가 소녀를 돕지 않았다는 사실에 분노했다는 내용인데, 주어진 글 마지막에 독수리 앞에 소녀가 쓰러져 있었다고 했으므로 그 뒤에 와야 한다. (C)는 Kevin Carter가 사진을 찍은 후에 독수리를 쫓아냈음에도 불구하고 반발이 계속되었다는 내용이고, (B)의 마지막에서 많은 사람들이 그가 돕지 않은 것이 비정하다고

생각했다고 했으므로 그 뒤에 와야 한다. (A)의 This(이것)는 (C)의 'Carter에게 질문들이 쏟아지고 반발이 계속된 상황'을 가리키므로 (C) 바로 다음에 오는 것이 적절하다. 따라서 글의 순서로 가장 적절한 것은 ③ (B) - (C) - (A)이다.

[해석] 1993년 퓰리처 상을 수상한 사진인 "독수리와 소녀"는 수단에서 보도 사진가 Kevin Carter(케빈 카터)에 의해 촬영되었다. 그 유명한 사진은 독수리 한 마리가 뒤에서 지켜보는데 기아에 시달리는 한 아이가 땅바닥에 쓰러져 있는 것을 보여준다.

(B) 그 사진은 <뉴욕타임스>에 실렸을 때 많은 원초적 감정을 이끌어냈다. 물론, 굶주리는 아이에 대한 걱정도 있지만, Carter를 향한 분노도 있었는데, 많은 사람들은 그가 돕지 않은 것이 비정하다고 생각했다.

(C) Carter는 그 사진을 찍은 후에 그 독수리를 쫓아냈고, UN 급식 센터로 기어가고 있었던 그 아이는 보도에 따르면 결국 그곳에 도착했다. 그럼에도 불구하고, Carter에게 "왜 당신은 더 도와주지 않았습니까?"와 같은 질문들이 쏟아졌다. 반발은 끊임없었다.

(A) 이것은 보도 사진가로서의 큰 정신적 대가의 아주 좋은 예시이다. 많은 보도 사진가들이 무모하게 전쟁이나 자연재해 속으로 들어가므로 그 직업은 위험할 뿐만 아니라, 대중으로부터 끊임없는 비난도 있는데, 그들은 객관성보다는 카메라 뒤의 사람에게 훨씬 더 많은 것을 기대한다.

[어휘] vulture 독수리 stricken 시달리는, 고통받는 collapse 쓰러지다, 무너지다
look on 지켜보다, 구경하다 toll 대가, 희생 headfirst 무모하게, 황급히
reproach 비난 elicit 이끌어내다, 도출하다 raw 원초적인, 날것의
shoo away 쫓아내다, 쉬이하고 쫓다 crawl 기어가다
feeding 급식의, 먹이를 주는 bombard 쏟아붓다, 퍼붓다
backlash 반발 incessant 끊임없는

[구문분석]
[7행] **Not only** ①[is the occupation dangerous] — with
동사 주어
many photojournalists going headfirst into wars and natural disasters — **but** ②[there is constant reproach from the public, who expect much more from the person behind the camera than objectivity].

→ ①[is ~ dangerous]와 ②[there ~ objectivity]는 상관접속사 not only A but (also) B로 연결된 구조이다. 부정어 not only가 강조되어 문장 맨 앞에 나왔기 때문에 '동사(is) + 주어(the occupation)'의 어순으로 쓰였다.

38 주어진 문장의 위치 찾기   정답 ③

[해설] 주어진 문장의 a number of challenges emerged(많은 문제들이 일어났다)로 보아, 주어진 문장 뒤에는 그 법의 문제점에 대해 나와야 하는 것을 알 수 있다. 이 글에서는 ①, ② 뒤 문장까지는 NCLB의 시행 배경 및 목표에 대해 설명하고 있고, 주어진 문장의 '많은 문제들'은 ③ 뒤 문장에서 Among these were difficulties(이러한 어려움 중에서는)로 이어지고 있으므로 주어진 문장이 들어가기에 가장 적절한 곳은 ③이다.

[오답분석] ② 뒤 문장의 this way는 ① 뒤 문장의 to improve standards and hold schools accountable for underperforming students(수준을 향상시키고 평균 이하의 학생들에 대한 책임을 학교에 묻는 것)를 가리키므로 주어진 문장이 들어가기에 적절하지 않다. ④ 뒤 문장은 ③ 뒤 문장에 이어서 NCLB의 시행 결과에 대한 내용을 다루고 있다.

[해석] 한때 세계 상위권을 차지했던 미국 교육 시스템이 2000년부터 다른 국가들보다 뒤처지기 시작했다. 순위를 높이고 학생들을 보다 경쟁력 있게 만들기 위

해, 2001년에 낙제학생방지법(NCLB)과 같은 교육 개혁이 도입되었다. (①) 그 법률의 목적은 수준을 향상시키고 평균 이하의 학생들에 대한 책임을 학교에 묻기 위함이었다. (②) 이러한 방식으로, 모든 인종, 배경, 경제적 지위의 학생들이 대학과 직장을 위해 충분히 준비될 것이었다. (③ 하지만, 그 법이 시행되었을 때 많은 문제들이 일어났다.) 이러한 어려움 중에는 기준의 일관적인 적용과 여러 주들의 준수를 확실히 하는 것이 있었다. (④) 결국, NCLB는 2015년에 모든학생성공법(ESSA)으로 대체되었다. (⑤) 그것의 시행에 있어서 여전히 불완전하지만, ESSA는 학교들에 그들이 활용하는 기준과 그들이 성적을 평가하는 방법 둘 다에서 더 많은 융통성을 제공했다.

[어휘] legislation 법률, 입법 hold A accountable for A에게 ~의 책임을 묻다
implementation 시행, 이행

[구문분석]
[3행] [**Once** ranked among the top in the world], the US educational system had, by the year 2000, begun to fall behind other nations.

→ [Once ~ world]는 과거분사(ranked)로 시작하는 수동형 분사구문이고, 분사구문의 의미를 분명하게 하기 위해 부사절 접속사(Once)가 분사 앞에 온 형태이다.

[13행] [**Among these** were difficulties] ensuring a consistent
동사   주어
application of standards and compliance from different states.

→ [Among ~ difficulties]는 부사구 Among these가 강조되어 문장 맨 앞에 나왔기 때문에, 주어와 동사가 도치되어 '동사(were) + 주어(difficulties)'의 어순으로 쓰였다.

[17행] [Though (ESSA is) still imperfect in its implementation], ESSA has provided schools with more flexibility ~

→ [Though ~ implementation]은 주절과 부사절의 주어가 같을 때 부사절에서 '주어(ESSA) + be동사(is)'가 생략된 형태이다.

39 주어진 문장의 위치 찾기   정답 ②

[해설] 주어진 문장의 It으로 보아, 주어진 문장 앞에는 "기술적 솔루셔니즘"의 예시가 되는 내용이 나와야 한다는 것을 알 수 있다. 이 글에서는 ① 뒤 문장까지 급속히 발전하는 의료용 소프트웨어 사업과 의료 기술의 장려에 대해 설명하고 있고, 주어진 문장의 "technological solutionism"은 ② 뒤 문장에서 this approach로 이어지고 있으므로 주어진 문장이 들어가기에 가장 적절한 곳은 ②이다.

[오답분석] ① 뒤 문장의 this promotion of medical technology는 ① 앞 문장의 AI programs that can carry out a range of diagnostic tasks(다양한 진단 업무를 수행할 수 있는 AI 프로그램)를 가리키므로 주어진 문장이 들어가기에 적절하지 않다. ③ 뒤 문장은 This issue also를 통해 ② 뒤 문장에서 언급한 프로그램의 문제에 대해 이어서 설명하고 있으므로 주어진 문장이 들어가기에 적절하지 않다. ④ 뒤 문장은 ③ 뒤 문장에 이어서 프로그램의 내부 처리 과정들을 알 수 없다는 내용을 다루고 있다.

[해석] 의료 기술 회사들이 다양한 진단 업무를 수행할 수 있는 AI 프로그램을 병원과 의사들에게 서둘러 제공하면서, 의료용 소프트웨어는 급속히 발전하는 사업이다. (①) 부분적으로, 의료 기술의 이러한 장려는 의료 종사자들과 서비스 기관들의 부담을 일부 덜어주려는 시도이다. (② 그것은 또한 모든 사회의 문제들이 새로운 형태의 기술의 발명으로 해결될 수 있다는 널리 퍼진 관념인

"기술적 솔루셔니즘"의 한 예시이다.) 그러나 이러한 프로그램들이 절대 오류가 없지 않고 종종 그것을 개발한 사람들의 편향을 반영한다는 것을 포함해서 이러한 접근에는 다양한 문제들이 있는데, 이는 특정 부류의 환자들을 위험에 처하게 한다. (③) 이 문제는 또한 이러한 프로그램들의 내부 처리 과정이 프로그래머들을 제외한 모두에게 숨겨져 있다는 사실로 인해 악화된다. (④) 알고리즘의 평가 프로그램을 이용하는 많은 보험사들은 프로그램이 어떻게 결론에 이르는지를 확인할 방법이 없다는 것을 인정하지만, 그들은 그럼에도 불구하고 그것을 따를 의무가 지워진다. (⑤) 책임의 부재와 그것이 전파할 수 있는 편향은 이러한 프로그램들이 더 널리 이용되기 전에 해결되어야 한다.

(어휘) **booming** 급속히 발전하는 **diagnostic** 진단의 **infallible** 절대 오류가 없는
exacerbate 악화시키다 **obligate** 의무를 지게 하다, 강요하다
accountability 책임 **propagate** 전파하다, 늘리다

(구문분석) [17행] **Many insurance firms** ①[that utilize algorithmic assessment programs] **admit** ②[that there is no way to find out how a program reached a conclusion], but they are nonetheless obligated to follow it.

→ ①[that ~ programs]는 선행사 Many insurance firms를 수식하며 주격 관계대명사 that이 이끄는 관계대명사절이다.

→ ②[that ~ conclusion]은 접속사 that이 이끄는 명사절로, 동사 admit의 목적어 역할을 한다.

40 요약문 완성하기   정답 ⑤

(해설) 글의 전반부에서 찌르레기들이 날면서 어떻게 응집력 있는 통일체를 구성할 수 있는지가 오랫동안 과학자들에게 관심의 대상이었다고 했고, 글의 후반부에서는 George F. Young과 그의 팀이 찌르레기가 주변의 7마리의 새들에 주의를 기울여 움직임을 예상한다는 것을 발견했다고 했다. 따라서 a cohesive whole을 unity로, predict를 anticipating으로 바꾸어 표현한 ⑤가 정답이다.

(오답분석) 찌르레기가 찌르레기 떼라고 불리는 조직화된 패턴으로 날면서 응집력 있는 통일체를 구성한다고 했으므로 ①의 disadvantage와 ④의 certainty는 (A)에 들어갈 단어로 적절하지 않다. 찌르레기가 날면서 주변 새들에게 집중하고 움직임을 예상한다고 했으므로 ②의 disregarding과 ③의 comparing은 (B)에 들어갈 단어로 적절하지 않다.

(해석) 겨울에 찌르레기들은 찌르레기 떼라고 불리는 조직화된 패턴으로 날기 때문에 수백 혹은 수천 마리의 찌르레기가 급강하하거나 빙빙 도는 것을 보는 것이 흔하지 않은 광경은 아니다. 어떻게 그 새들이 그렇게 많은 개별적 구성원으로 이루어진 하나의 무리로서 그러한 응집력 있는 통일체를 형성할 수 있는지는 오랫동안 과학자들에게 관심의 대상이었지만, George F. Young(조지 F. 영)과 그의 팀의 연구가 마침내 설명을 제시할지도 모른다. 비디오 영상을 주의 깊게 관찰함으로써, 그들은 각각의 찌르레기들이 믿을 수 없는 속도와 정확성으로 반응하면서, 그것들의 움직임을 예측하고 그것들 스스로 실행할 수 있도록 일정한 숫자, 정확히는 7마리의 옆에서 비행하고 있는 새들에게 주의를 기울인다는 것을 발견했다. Young에 따르면, 이러한 다른 새들에게만 집중하는 것은 찌르레기가 어디로 또는 어떻게 그 무리가 날아갈 것인지 알지 못하는 것과, 다른 새들과 충돌하거나 무리 밖으로 날아가지 않고 그 무리와 함께 이동하는 것 사이의 정교한 균형을 유지할 수 있게 한다. 이 7의 규칙 내에서, 작은 무리들이 더 대규모의 체계인 찌르레기 떼를 구성하기 위해서 합쳐진다.

↓

찌르레기 떼 안에서 찌르레기의 (A) 통일성은 무리의 각 구성원들이 그것들과 가장 가까이 있는 새들의 움직임을 (B) 예상하는 것의 결과이다.

(A)   (B)
① 약점 …… 모방하는
② 조화 …… 무시하는
③ 정밀함 …… 비교하는
④ 확실성 …… 통제하는
⑤ 통일성 …… 예상하는

(어휘) **swoop** 급강하하다, 급습하다 **swirl** 빙빙 돌다, 소용돌이치다
cohesive 응집력 있는 **whole** 통일체, 전체 **delicate** 정교한
flock 무리, 떼

(구문분석) [1행] In winter, it is not an uncommon sight [to see hundreds
(가주어)
or thousands of starlings swooping and swirling] as they fly
(진주어(to부정사구))
in a coordinated pattern called a murmuration.

→ 해당 문장은 가주어 it이 길이가 긴 진주어 to부정사구 [to ~ swirling] 대신 주어 자리에 쓰인 형태이다.

[4행] [How the birds are able to form such a cohesive whole as a group composed of so many individual members] has
(주어)   (동사)
long been a subject of interest for scientists, but ~

→ [How ~ members]는 의문사 how가 이끄는 명사절로, 첫 번째 절 How ~ scientists의 주어 역할을 한다.

41~42 장문 독해 1

(해석) 영어 단어 dialogue는 'dia'는 "통해서"(또는 "사이의")로, 'logos'는 "말"로 번역되는 그리스어 용어 'dialogos'에서 유래되었다. 오늘날, 사람들은 이 단어를 (a)단순히 여러 당사자들 간의 대화를 의미하는 것으로 정의한다. 하지만, 다른 사람들은 이 용어에 더 많은 미묘한 차이가 있어서 이해와 통찰의 추구를 암시한다고 말했다. 미국의 물리학자이자 철학자인 David Bohm(데이비드 봄)이 그러한 한 명이다; 그는 그 단어의 철학적 측면들을 연구하기 시작했다. 마침내, 이러한 노력들을 통해, 그는 현재 Bohm Dialogue라고 알려진 것을 제시했고, 그것은 경청과 관찰을 통해 사람들 간에 (b)이해에 이르는 것을 목표로 하는 일종의 집단 상호 작용이다.
Bohm의 대화는 수단으로 여겨질 수 있다; 사전의 가정이나 판단에 의해 (c)방해받지 않는 ⁴¹건설적인 논의를 하기 위한 방법이다. 개인은 열린 사고방식과 방어적이지 않은 태도를 가지고 이러한 유형의 대화에 접근해야 한다. ⁴²그들은 대화 중에 이야기되는 것에 대해 주의하여 생각하고, 그들이 특정 방식으로 자라고 특정 상황들에 있음으로써 길들여진 사고를 경험하는 때를 인지할 수 있어야 한다. ⁴¹그것을 인지함으로써, 그들은 그것에 의문을 제기할 수 있고, 그래서 진정으로 새로운 사상과 사고방식들을 경험할 수 있다. 이렇게, 정보, 견해, 감정들이 좀 더 자유롭게 교환됨에 따라 창의성이 집단 내에서 (d)번성할 수 있다. 이러한 유형의 대화를 통해, 더 많은 이해와 통찰이 얻어지고 이것은 적절한 상황 내에서 그 단어에 더 깊은 의미가 있다는 것을 (e)반증한다(→증명한다).

(어휘) **derive** 유래하다, 끌어내다 **nuance** 미묘한 차이를 주다 **disrupt** 방해하다
assumption 가정, 추정 **mindfully** 주의하여, 마음에 두고
condition 길들이다, 조건 지우다 **authentically** 진정으로, 확실히
flourish 번성하다

(구문분석) [21행] ~ and **recognize** [when they experience **thinking** (that they've been conditioned to by growing up a certain way and being in particular situations)].

→ [when ~ situations]는 의문사 when이 이끄는 명사절이며 동사 recognize의 목적어 역할을 한다.

→ (that ~ situations)는 선행사 thinking을 수식하며, 목적격 관계대명사 that이 이끄는 관계대명사절이다.

---

41 제목 파악하기 정답 ③

(해설) 마지막 부분으로 미루어 보아 David Bohm에 따르면 대화란 가정과 판단으로부터 자유로운 건설적인 논의를 하기 위한 방법으로, Bohm Dialogue를 통해 새로운 사상과 사고방식을 경험할 수 있고 창의성을 번성시킬 수 있다고 설명하고 있다. 따라서 글의 제목으로 가장 적절한 것은 ③ '의미 있는 대화의 잠재력'이다.

(오답분석) ①은 글의 핵심 소재 Dialogue를 사용하여 헷갈리게 하는 오답이다. ②의 말하기 보다 듣는 법을 배우라는 내용은 글에서 언급되고 있지 않다. ④은 대화가 가정이나 판단에 의해 방해받지 않아야 한다는 글의 주제와 반대되는 내용이기 때문에 오답이다. ⑤은 글에서 언급된 Interaction, Conditioned, Thinking을 사용하여 헷갈리게 하는 오답이다.

(해석) ① 대화를 시작하는 방법
② 말하기보다 듣는 법을 배우라!
③ 의미 있는 대화의 잠재력
④ 어떻게 대화가 판단으로 이어질 수 있는가
⑤ 상호 작용: 길들여진 사고의 토대

---

42 어휘 적절성 파악하기 정답 ⑤

(해설) 대화 중에 이야기되는 것에 대해 주의하여 생각하고, 그들이 특정 방식으로 자라고, 특정한 상황에 있음으로써 길들여졌던 생각을 경험한 때를 알아볼 수 있어야 한다고 설명하고 있다. 따라서, 적절한 상황 내에서 그 단어에 더 깊은 의미가 있다는 것을 증명한다는 맥락이 되어야 하므로, ⑤의 disproving(반증한다)을 그와 반대되는 의미의 proving(증명한다)과 같은 어휘로 바꾸어야 문맥상 적절하다.

(오답분석) ②은 Bohm Dialogue가 경청과 관찰을 통해 사람들 간에 이해에 이르는 것을 목표로 하는 일종의 집단 상호 작용이라는 문맥이 되어야 하므로 understanding이 오는 것이 적절하다. ③은 Bohm Dialogue는 사전의 가정이나 판단에 의해 방해받지 않는 건설적인 논의를 하기 위한 방법이라는 문맥이 되어야 하므로 disrupted가 오는 것이 적절하다.

43~45 장문 독해 2

(해석) (A) 나는 퇴근하고 집으로 운전해서 가고 있었고 라디오의 음악을 듣고 있었다. 비슷하고 따분한 팝 히트곡들이 지겨워서, 나는 다른 채널들을 살펴보기로 했다. 나는 어떻게 하다가 클래식 채널로 돌리게 되었고, 내가 한 대의 피아노에서 나오는 장엄한 선율을 들은 것이 바로 그때였다. 매우 아름다운 그 멜로디는 내가 어렸을 때 할머니가 연주하는 것을 봤던 것을 생각나게 했다. 그녀는 음악에 대단히 재능이 있었고, 나는 (a) 그녀가 이 곡을 좋아했으리라는 걸 알았다.

(B) 나는 집에 도착했고, 약간의 검색을 한 후에 그 곡이 Franz Liszt(프란츠 리스트)의 <탄식>이었음을 알아냈다. 나는 어릴 때 이후로 피아노를 만져본 적이 없음에도 불구하고 그것을 연주하는 법을 배우기로 결심했다. 할머니께서 내게 조금 가르쳐주셨지만, (b) 그녀는 그렇게 어려운 무언가를 연주

하는 법을 보여주신 적은 없었다. 그래도 나는 그것을 배우기로 마음먹었다.

(D) 첫 번째로 내가 해야 했던 일은 할머니의 오래된 피아노를 조율하는 것이었다. 그녀는 몇 년 동안 그것을 연주하지 않았었지만, 그것은 훌륭한 악기였다. 내가 연주하려고 시도한다는 생각에 그녀가 (d) 그녀의 얼굴에 미소를 띄었을 것이라고 확신했다. 나는 또한 그 곡의 악보를 주문했다. 그 곡을 훑어봤을 때, 나는 혼자서는 그것을 익힐 수 없을 것임을 깨달았고 그래서 나를 도와줄 ⁴⁴피아노 선생님을 고용하기로 했다. (e) 그녀는 그 일이 어렵겠지만 우리가 함께 그것을 해낼 것이라고 내게 알려주었다. 우리는 곧 첫 번째 만남을 가질 계획을 세웠다.

(C) 내 첫 번째 레슨 날에, 나는 음표들의 어지러운 배열을 보고 다시 한번 숨이 막혔다. ⁴⁵나는 할머니와, 내 어린 시절 동안 우리가 같이 곡들을 배웠을 때에 그녀가 내게 얼마나 인내심이 있었는지에 대해 생각했다. (c) 그녀는 내가 노력을 들이는 한, 내가 원하는 무엇이든 이룰 수 있다고 항상 말했었다. 내 피아노 선생님은 나에게 시작하라고 지시했고, 나는 신이 나서 그녀에게 고개를 끄덕였다. 사람들은 모든 여정이 단 한 걸음으로 시작한다고 말한다; 자, 이제 첫 걸음을 내딛는다.

(어휘) **station** 채널, 전파 주파수 **heavenly** 장엄한
stunning 매우 아름다운, 굉장히 멋진 **determined** 단단히 결심한
array 배열, 배치 **sheet music** 악보, 악보로 발행되는 음악

(구문분석) [12행] I decided to learn how to play it despite not [having touched a piano] since childhood.

→ [having ~ piano]는 'having + p.p.' 형태로, 동명사의 완료형이다.

[21행] She always said that [**as long as** I put in the effort], I could achieve whatever I wanted.

→ [as ~ effort]는 접속사 as long as(~하는 한)가 이끄는 조건의 부사절이다.

---

43 글의 순서 배열하기 정답 ①

(해설) (A)는 'I'가 집에 가면서 라디오에서 아름다운 피아노 선율을 듣게 되었고 할머니께서 피아노를 연주하시던 것을 생각했다는 내용이다. (B)는 'I'가 집에 와서 피아노곡을 찾아보았고 그 곡을 연주하는 법을 배우기로 마음먹었다는 내용이므로 (A) 뒤에 와야 한다. (D)는 피아노곡을 익히기 위해 악보를 주문하고 피아노 선생님을 고용했다는 내용이므로 연주하는 법을 배우기로 했다고 한 (B) 뒤에 와야 한다. (C)는 피아노곡을 배우기 위한 첫 번째 레슨을 시작했다는 내용이므로 피아노 선생님과의 첫 번째 만남의 약속을 잡았다고 한 (D) 뒤에 와야 한다. 따라서 글의 순서로 가장 적절한 것은 ① (B) - (D) - (C)이다.

---

44 지칭 대상 파악하기 정답 ⑤

(해설) (a), (b), (c), (d)는 모두 'I'의 할머니를 가리키지만 (e)는 'I'의 피아노 선생님을 가리키므로, ⑤이 정답이다.

---

45 세부 정보 파악하기 정답 ③

(해설) (C)의 I thought of my grandmother and how patient she was with me when we learned pieces together during my youth를 통해 어린 시절 동안 할머니와 같이 곡을 배웠을 때에 할머니가 자신에게 얼마나 인내심이 있었는지를 생각했다는 것을 알 수 있는데, ③는 혼났다고 하여 일부 정보를 잘못 나타냈으므로 'I'에 관한 내용과 일치하지 않는 것은 ③이다.

18　목적 파악하기　정답 ④

해설 글의 중간 이후에서 퇴직할 미술관 수석 큐레이터의 후임자 자리에 대한 채용을 공지하고 있으므로, 정답은 ④이다.

해석 Tallinn 미술관은 수석 큐레이터인 Erin Lowe가 5월 15일에 퇴직할 것이라고 금요일에 발표했습니다. Lowe 씨가 그 기관에서 20년 이상 동안 근무했고 미술관의 가장 성공적인 전시들의 대부분을 기획했다는 것을 고려할 때, 그녀가 없어서 매우 아쉬울 것입니다. 미술관은 자격을 갖춘 그녀의 후임자를 찾고 있습니다. 직무는 소장품을 감독하고 미술관의 목표를 규정하는 것뿐만 아니라, 미술관의 다양한 전시들을 운영하고 감독하는 것을 포함합니다. 지원자들은 유사한 분야에서의 이전 경력이 있어야 합니다. 이 직책에 관심 있는 분들은 humanresources@tallinnmuseum.org로 이력서와 추천서를 보내야 합니다.

어휘 replacement 후임자, 대체　duty 직무, 의무　oversee 감독하다
collection 소장품, 수집품　define 규정하다, 분명히 하다

구문분석
[7행] Duties include ①[managing and directing the museum's various exhibitions], **as well as** ②[overseeing collections and defining the museum's objectives].
→ ①[managing ~ exhibitions]와 ②[overseeing ~ objectives]는 A as well as B(B뿐만 아니라 A도) 형태로 연결된 병렬 구조이며, 상관접속사 not only B but (also) A로 바꿔 쓸 수 있다.

19　심경 파악하기　정답 ④

해설 심경은 간접적으로 표현된다. 글의 초반부의 Mia was incredibly weary와 She breathed heavily ~ the other를 통해 Mia가 등산 중에 매우 지친 것을 알 수 있고, 글의 후반부에서 She was so happy와 she felt a weight drop off her shoulders를 통해 정상이 얼마 남지 않았다는 것을 알고 안도감을 느꼈음을 알 수 있다. 따라서 Mia의 심경 변화로 가장 적절한 것은 ④이다.

해석 5시간의 등산 후에, Mia는 매우 지쳤고 그녀가 산의 정상에 오를 수 있을지에 대해 확신이 없었다. 그녀는 산길이 이렇게 가파를 것이라고 예상하지 못했다. 그녀는 거칠게 숨을 쉬었고 그녀의 무거운 다리가 한 발 앞에 또 한 발 계속해서 움직이게 하려고 애를 썼다. 그녀는 포기하고 다시 아래로 내려가려던 참이었는데 그때 모퉁이를 돌아서 그녀에게 희망을 주는 무언가를 발견했다: 정상이 단 150미터 앞에 있음을 보여주는 표지판이었다. 그녀는 그것을 보고 너무 기뻐서 거의 눈물이 나왔다. 그녀는 어깨가 가벼워지는 것을 느끼며 크게 숨을 내쉬었다. Mia는 미소 지었고 산꼭대기에 설 때까지 계속해서 올라가서, 마침내 주위의 풍경을 감상할 수 있었다.

① 침착한 → 슬픈
② 기쁜 → 불안한
③ 실망한 → 화난
④ 지친 → 안도하는
⑤ 신이 난 → 낙담한

어휘 weary 지친, 피곤한　trail 산길, 자국　will 애를 쓰다; 의지
tears come to one's eyes 눈물이 나오다
exhale (숨·연기 등을) 내쉬다　[선택지] discouraged 낙담한

구문분석
[8행] She was [**so** happy to see it **that** tears almost came to her eyes].
→ [so ~ eyes]는 '너무 ~해서 -하다'라는 결과를 나타내는 부사절 접속사 so ~ that이 'so + 형용사 + (that) -' 형태로 쓰였다.

20　주장 파악하기　정답 ②

해설 글의 마지막 세 문장에서 그룹 프로젝트의 성공은 팀원들이 성공에 대한 공통된 정의를 가지고 있는지에 달려 있다고 주장하고 있으므로 정답은 ②이다.

오답분석 ④은 글의 일부만을 다루고 있는 오답이다. ⑤은 팀원들이 개별적인 목표를 추구하는 경향을 극복해야 한다는 글의 내용과 반대되는 내용이므로 오답이다.

해석 그룹 프로젝트 중에 흔히 맞닥뜨리는 문제는 관련된 모두가 다른 방향으로 가서 여러 가지의 그리고 많은 경우 상충하는 목표들을 실현시키려고 노력한다는 것이다. 이것은 엄청난 수준의 비효율로 이어질 수 있어서, 이는 시간과 자원이 낭비되는 것을 야기한다. 만약 당신이 팀 리더라면, 당신의 부하 직원들이 개별적인 목표를 추구하는 성향을 극복하는 것이 당신이 직면할 가장 큰 문제들 중의 하나일 것이다. 결국은, 당신의 팀원들이 성공에 대한 공통된 정의를 가지는지 가지지 않는지에 프로젝트의 성공이나 실패가 달려 있을 것이다. 당신 팀의 각 개인은 궁극적인 목표와, 무엇이 그것(목표)의 성취를 구성하는지를 분명하게 이해해야 한다. 이는 당신이 이루고자 하는 것에 대한 솔직한 의사 전달과 당신의 팀원들 모두가 합류해 있는지를 확인하는 정기적인 사후 점검을 필요로 한다.

어휘 competing 상충하는, 모순된　subordinate 부하 직원, 하급자
at the end of the day 결국은　rest on ~에 달려 있다
constitute 구성하다　necessitate 필요로 하다
straightforward 솔직한, 직접의　follow-up 사후 점검, 후속 조치
on board 합류한, 승선한

구문분석
[6행] If you are a team leader, ①[overcoming the tendency of your subordinates to pursue individual goals] will likely be one of **the greatest challenges** ②[(that/which) you will face].
→ ①[overcoming ~ goals]는 전치사구(of your subordinates)와 to 부정사구(to pursue individual goals)를 포함하며, 전체가 주절의 주어인 동명사구이다.

→ ②[you will face]는 선행사 the greatest challenges를 수식하는 관계대명사절로, 목적격 관계대명사 that/which가 생략되었다.

---

21 밑줄 의미 추론하기   정답 ⑤

[해설] Sergei Eisenstein이 "지적 몽타주"의 사용을 통해 생각과 감정을 이끌어내려고 노력했다고 말하며, 서로 다른 장면의 병치를 통해 지배적인 사상을 전달하려고 한 영화 <파업>의 예시를 들어 설명하고 있다. 따라서 글의 주제를 상징적으로 표현한 the very grammar of the film(영화의 진짜 원리)이 의미하는 것은 ⑤ '관객들의 반응을 불러일으키기 위해 기법을 사용하는 것'이다.

[오답분석] ②, ④은 글의 일부만을 다루고 있는 오답이다.

[해석] 소련의 영화 제작자이자 이론가인 Sergei Eisenstein(세르게이 에이젠슈타인)의 작품에서, 편집은 이야기가 앞으로 나아가게 하는 것보다 훨씬 더 많은 것을 하는데, 그것(편집)이 영화의 진짜 원리이다. Eisenstein은 연속적인 장면을 만들기 위해 일련의 이미지나 장면을 이어 붙이는 것을 수반하는 기법인 몽타주의 선구자였다. 가장 흔히, 몽타주 기법은 시간의 경과나 주인공의 진행을 묘사하기 위해 영화에서 사용된다. 하지만, "지적 몽타주"라고 알려진 다른 유형의 몽타주의 사용을 통해, Eisenstein은 생각과 감정을 끌어내려고 했다; 다시 말해서 예술 작품을 만들려고 노력했다. 예를 들어, 1925년 영화 <파업>의 마지막에서, 그 영화는 도살되고 있는 황소와, 혁명 이전의 러시아에서 공장 노동자들의 파업의 폭력적인 진압 장면들 사이를 왔다 갔다 전환했다. 이렇게 서로 전혀 다른 이미지들의 병치는 노동자들이 소처럼 없어도 되는 존재라는 지배적인 사상을 표현하기 위해 의도되었다.

① 영화 제작의 사회적 역할을 설명하는 이론을 입증하는 것
② 연결이 잘 안 되는 이미지들을 사용함으로써 주인공을 소개하는 것
③ 많은 관객들의 흥미를 끄는 이야기를 만드는 것
④ 시간의 경과를 나타내기 위해 몽타주 기법을 보여주는 것
⑤ 관객들의 반응을 불러일으키기 위해 기법을 사용하는 것

[어휘] grammar (기본) 원리, 기초   piece together 이어 붙이다, 짜 맞추다
footage 장면, 화면   sequence 장면, 순서   passage 경과, 통로
protagonist 주인공   elicit 끌어내다   slaughter 도살하다
suppression 진압, 억압   disparate 서로 전혀 다른, 이질적인
overarching 지배적인, 무엇보다 중요한
dispensable 없어도 되는, 불필요한   [선택지] validate 입증하다, 인증하다
convey 나타내다, 전달하다   evoke 불러일으키다, 일깨우다

[구문분석]
[6행] Most frequently, montages are used in films [to depict the passage of time or the progress of the protagonist].
→ [to ~ protagonist]는 to부정사의 부사적 용법으로, 목적을 의미한다.

---

22 요지 파악하기   정답 ②

[해설] 글의 첫 세 문장과 마지막 문장에서 신조어의 발생과 사용이 대중매체와 인터넷의 번영으로 인해 상당히 빨라졌고 이러한 추세가 미래에 더 확연해질 것이라는 요지가 제시되어 있으므로, 이 글의 요지로 가장 적절한 것은 ②이다.

[오답분석] ①, ④은 글의 일부만을 다루고 있는 오답이다. ③의 언어 습관에 관한 내용은 글에서 언급되고 있지 않다. ⑤의 사전에 등재되지 못한 일부 어휘는 글에서 언급되고 있지 않다.

[해석] 영어는 매년 수천 개의 어휘들이 만들어지면서 끊임없이 발달하고 있다. 새로

추가된 것들의 다수가 다른 언어들에서 유래하거나 기존 단어들의 조합인 반면, 일부는 사실상 무(無)에서 만들어진다. 흥미로운 것은 이것이 발생하는 속도가 대중매체와 인터넷의 번영으로 인해 최근 몇 년 동안 상당히 빨라졌다는 점이다. William Shakespeare(윌리엄 셰익스피어)와 John Milton(존 밀턴)과 같은 작가들은 'lonely(외로운)'와 'fragrance(향기)'처럼 오늘날에도 여전히 사용되고 있는 수백 개의 어휘들을 만든 공을 인정받는다. 그러한 경우들에서, 신조어들이 널리 사용되는 데에 수십 년, 혹은 심지어 수 세기가 걸렸다. 하지만, 매우 열성적인 팬이 되는 것을 의미하는 'stan'이라는 어휘는 2000년에 랩 노래에서 처음 등장했고 2017년에 옥스퍼드 영어 사전에 등재되었다. 이러한 추세는 미래에 훨씬 더 확연해질 것이고, 변화의 속도가 계속해서 가속화될 것임을 의미한다.

[어휘] evolve 발달하다, 진화하다   from scratch 무(無)에서, 아예 처음부터
rise 번영, 증대   credit A with B A에게 B의 공이 있다고 인정하다
pronounced 확연한, 단호한   accelerate 가속화되다

[구문분석]
[5행] ①[What's interesting] is that **the speed** ②[at which this happens] has increased significantly ~
→ ①[What's interesting]은 관계대명사 what(~하는 것)이 이끄는 명사절로, 문장의 주어 역할을 한다.
→ ②[at ~ happens]는 선행사 the speed를 수식하며, '전치사 + 관계대명사' at which가 이끄는 관계대명사절이다.

[10행] In those cases, it took many decades, or even centuries, for the new words [to be widely used].
                                의미상 주어   to부정사구
→ for ~ words는 'for + 명사' 형태로, 수동형 to부정사구 [to ~ used]의 의미상 주어이다.

---

23 주제 파악하기   정답 ③

[해설] 마지막 세 문장으로 미루어 보아 실패를 경험할 때 불운으로 비난을 모면하거나 자신에게 너무 엄한 것보다는 자기 연민을 실천하는 것이 미래의 문제 영역들을 공략하는 데에 도움이 된다는 내용의 글이다. 따라서 이 글의 주제로 가장 적절한 것은 ③ '성장을 이루는 데에 있어서 자기 연민의 이점'이다.

[오답분석] ②은 글의 일부만을 다루고 있는 오답이다. ④, ⑤은 글에서 언급되고 있지 않다.

[해석] 당신이 실패를 경험할 때, 당신은 두 가지 방법 중 하나로 대응하는 경향이 있을지도 모른다: 당신의 불운으로 비난을 모면하거나 당신 자신에게 너무 엄하게 한다. 두 대응 방법들 모두 자연스러울지 모르지만, 그것들은 실수로부터 배우거나 미래의 시도를 위한 개인적인 성장을 추구하는 것에 거의 도움이 되지 않는다. 불운을 방패로 이용하는 것은 당신이 당신 자신을 성장시키는 것을 막는 반면, 과도하게 자기 비판적인 것은 당신이 패배주의를 겪게 한다. 실패 후에 실제로 성과를 향상시키기 위해서, 연구는 당신이 그 대신에 자기 연민을 실천해야 한다고 시사한다. 이는 반성을 통해서 당신의 태도와 행동에 대한 더 현실적인 평가로 이어지고, 따라서 당신이 미래의 문제 영역들을 공략하는 데에 도움이 된다. 여전히 당신의 강점과 한계 둘 다를 인식하면서도 당신 자신에게 친절함으로써, 당신은 능력을 발전시키고 행복을 증진시킬 가능성이 더 높다. 이러한 마음가짐을 통해, 당신은 실패에 얽매이게 되지 않고 당신의 목표들을 달성하기 위해 노력할 수 있다.

① 동료들에게 동기를 부여하기 위해 비판을 효과적으로 이용하는 방법
② 실패를 회피하는 마음가짐을 갖는 것의 결과
③ 성장을 이루는 데에 있어서 자기 연민의 이점
④ 성공하는 데에 있어서 자기 계발의 중요성
⑤ 목표를 향해 노력하면서 친절함을 베푸는 것의 문제점

어휘 endeavor 시도, 노력 shield 방패 defeatism 패배주의, 패배주의적 행동
setback 실패, 좌절 compassion 연민, 동정 reflection 반성, 성찰
mindset 마음가짐, 사고방식 [선택지] criticism 비판, 비난
drawback 문제점, 결점

구문 분석 [3행] Both responses may be natural, but [they're **hardly** helpful] for learning from mistakes ~

→ [they're hardly helpful]은 '거의 ~ 않다'라는 의미의 부정어 hardly 가 쓰인 부정 구문이다.

[13행] **By** ①[being kind to yourself] **while** still ②[being aware of both your strengths and limitations], you are more likely to develop your skills and improve well-being.

→ ①[being ~ yourself]는 전치사 by의 목적어 역할을 하는 동명사구 이고, ②[being ~ limitations]는 부사절 접속사 while 뒤에 온 분사구 문이다.

24 제목 파악하기 정답 ⑤

해설 과학자들도 사람이기에 확증 편향 등에 영향을 받는 것이 자연스럽지만, 실험 중에는 편향의 영향을 방지해야 한다는 내용의 글이다. 따라서 글의 제목으로 가장 적절한 것은 ⑤ '객관성: 과학자들의 지속적인 난제'이다.

오답 분석 ①은 글의 핵심 소재 confirmation bias를 사용하여 헷갈리게 하는 오답이다. ②은 글의 일부만을 다루고 있는 오답이다.

해석 과학자들은 사람이므로, 다른 누구나처럼 다양한 종류의 편향에 취약하다. 이러한 경향은 그들의 실험에 영향을 끼칠 수 있다. 정보 수집에서부터 연구 결과의 발표에 이르기까지, 사람들이 자신들의 기존 생각이나 가설을 입증하는 정보를 선호하는 성향인 확증 편향은 과학적 과정의 어느 단계에서든 역할을 할 수 있다. 물론, 자신을 속이는 것이 자연스러운 충동이라 하더라도, 이것은 실험 중에 무슨 수를 써서라도 방지되어야 할 결점이다. 하지만, 어떻게 하면 사람이 제2의 천성인 습성을 버리는가? 한 가지 방법은 다른 사람들이 그 과정을 쉽게 감시할 수 있는 방식으로 연구를 수행하는 것이다. 반대 입장의 추측을 검토하고 고려하는 것뿐만 아니라, 연구에 더 많은 사람들을 관여시키는 것은 더 적은 편향을 보장할 것이다. 실험을 설계하고 어떤 결과들이 실제로 가설을 강화하거나 반증하는지에 대한 기준을 세울 때 세심한 숙고도 이루어져야 한다.

① 확증 편향: 연구할 가치가 있는 주제
② 기준의 중요성을 명심하라!
③ 과학적 방법에서의 결점을 처리해야 할 때
④ 실험에서 추론 오류를 확인하는 것
⑤ 객관성: 과학자들의 지속적인 난제

어휘 inclination 경향, 성향 confirmation bias 확증 편향
at all costs 무슨 수를 써서라도 urge 충동, 욕구
second nature 제2의 천성 conjecture 추측, 해독
benchmark 기준, 벤치마크 disprove 반증하다, 반박하다
[선택지] reasoning 추론, 이성 objectivity 객관성

구문 분석 [7행] ~ this is a flaw that should be avoided at all costs during experimentation, [**even if** misleading oneself is a natural urge].

→ [even ~ urge]는 접속사 even if(비록 ~일지라도)가 이끄는 양보의 부사절이다.

[15행] Careful consideration should also be given when designing the experiment and setting the benchmarks **for** [what results actually reinforce or disprove a hypothesis].

→ [what ~ hypothesis]는 전치사 for의 목적어 역할을 하는 명사절로, 의문형용사 what이 명사 results를 수식하여 '어떤 결과'의 의미가 되고, 그 뒤에 불완전한 절이 오는 구조이다.

25 도표 정보 파악하기 정답 ④

해설 칠레의 자격 미달의 비율은 16.5%로, 자격 초과의 비율인 30.5%의 절반보다 많으므로, 수치의 비교 표현이 잘못 반영되었다. 따라서 도표의 내용과 일치하지 않는 것은 ④이다.

해석

아메리카 국가들에서의 업무 자격 불일치

자격 미달 자격 초과

	자격 미달	자격 초과
미국	17.7%	15.6%
캐나다	21.7%	16.2%
페루	9.3%	26.2%
아르헨티나	21.2%	27.2%
브라질	9.4%	28.2%
칠레	16.5%	30.5%
멕시코	12.6%	37.7%

(전국 취업 인구 대비 비율)

위의 도표는 북아메리카와 남아메리카에서 선정된 국가들에서의 업무 자격 불일치, 즉 자격 미달 또는 자격 초과를 백분율로 보여준다. ① 7개의 국가들 중에서, 미국과 캐나다가 자격 초과의 비율이 20퍼센트를 넘지 않는 유일한 두 국가이다. ② 페루와 브라질에서의 자격 미달의 비율이 10퍼센트 미만인 반면, 캐나다와 아르헨티나의 그것(자격 미달의 비율)은 20퍼센트 이상이다. ③ 자격 미달과 자격 초과의 합계 비율이 전국 취업 인구의 절반이 넘는 유일한 국가는 멕시코이다. ④ 칠레의 경우, 자격 미달의 비율은 자격 초과의 그것(비율)의 절반보다 더 적다. ⑤ 자격 미달의 비율과 자격 초과의 비율 간의 차이에 관해 말하자면, 미국이 가장 적은 차이를 나타냈다.

어휘 qualification 자격, 능력 mismatch 불일치, 부조화
employment 취업 인구 as for ~에 관해 말하면

구문 분석 [6행] While the percentages of underqualification in Peru and Brazil are below 10%, **those** in Canada and Argentina are over 20%.

→ 지시대명사 those는 앞의 복수명사 the percentages of underqualification을 가리키며, 동일한 명사가 반복되는 것을 피하기 위해 사용되었다.

26 세부 정보 파악하기 정답 ③

해설 His first job ~ *The Wall Street Journal*, where his interest in economics began을 통해 Henry Hazlitt이 경제에 대한 관심을 갖기 시작한 것은 <월 스트리트저널>에서 일할 때였다는 것을 알 수 있는데, ③은 대학에 다니는 동안이라고 일부 정보를 잘못 나타냈으므로 글의 내용과 일치하지 않는 것은 ③이다.

(해석) 1894년에 태어난 Henry Hazlitt(헨리 해즐릿)은 미국 역사상 가장 중요한 경제 기자 중 한 명이었다. 비록 그는 상대적 빈곤 속에서 자랐지만, Hazlitt은 뉴욕의 시립 대학에 다닐 수 있었다. 안타깝게도, 그는 어머니를 돌보기 위해 중퇴해야 했다. 그럼에도 불구하고, 그가 대학에 있었던 짧은 기간은 그에게 배우고자 하는 큰 갈망을 주었고, 그는 혼자서 모든 종류의 대학교 교과서들을 읽기 시작했다. 그의 첫 번째 직업은 <월스트리트저널>이라고 불리는 당시에 새롭게 설립된 신문사에서였고, 그곳에서 경제에 대한 그의 관심이 시작되었다. 그는 계속해서 수많은 간행물에 경제 사설을 썼는데, 그것은 정식 교육을 받지 않은 사람에게는 상당한 성과였다. 그는 경력 동안 총 15권의 책을 썼고, 그가 겨우 21살이었을 때 그의 첫 번째 책이 출간되었다. 그의 저작물들은 그에게 명성을 얻게 해 주었고, 그는 1993년에 98세의 나이로 사망할 때까지 계속해서 경제사상에 대해 글을 쓰고 경제사상에 기여했다.

(어휘) journalist 기자, 저널리스트 relative 상대적인 poverty 빈곤
drop out 중퇴하다, 탈퇴하다 editorial 사설; 편집의 renown 명성

(구문분석) [6행] Still, **the short time** [(when) he was at university] gave him a great desire to learn, and ~
→ [he ~ university]는 선행사 the short time을 수식하는 관계부사절로, 선행사가 때를 나타내는 일반적인 명사(time)일 때 관계부사 when이 생략된 형태이다.

27 안내문 정보 파악하기 정답 ③

(해설) Requirements: Have taken at least one Spanish class를 통해 참가 요건이 최소 1개의 스페인어 수업을 들은 적이 있어야 하는 것임을 알 수 있으므로, 글의 내용과 일치하지 않는 것은 ③이다.

(해석)
스페인어 교환 프로그램

스페인에 가는 것을 항상 꿈꿔 오셨나요? 이제 스페인어 교환 프로그램(SEP)과 함께 당신은 갈 수 있습니다. 언어와 문화를 배워보세요! 일생의 한 번뿐인 이 기회를 놓치지 마세요.

대상: 고등학생 (10, 11, 12학년)
시간: 6월 19일 - 6월 28일 (10일)
요건:
• 최소 평점 3.0
• 최소 1개의 스페인어 수업을 들은 적이 있음

스페인에 있는 동안, 학생들은 다음을 포함하는 다양한 활동들에 참여할 것입니다:
• 박물관 탐방
• 문화 축제 참가
• 스페인 식품 시장 방문
• 스페인 학생들과 언어 교환
* 학생들은 또한 매일 도시를 탐방할 2시간의 자유 시간을 가질 것입니다.

지원서는 4월 20일까지 제출되어야 합니다. 더 많은 정보를 위해서는 www.sep.edu를 방문해주세요.

(어휘) GPA(grade point average) 평점 turn in 제출하다, 반납하다

(구문분석) [13행] [While (students are) in Spain], students will take part in a variety of activities including:
→ [While in Spain]은 주절과 부사절의 주어가 같을 때 부사절에서 '주어 + be동사'가 생략된 형태이다.

28 안내문 정보 파악하기 정답 ⑤

(해설) 추가 정보와 관련된 부분인 Refreshments will be for sale을 통해 간단한 음식물이 판매될 것임을 알 수 있으므로, 글의 내용과 일치하는 것은 ⑤이다.

(해석)
핼러윈 거리 퍼레이드

Lawson City는 연례 핼러윈 거리 퍼레이드를 개최할 것입니다. 50개 회사들로부터 후원받은 다양한 무서운 퍼레이드 풍선들이 있을 것입니다.

날짜: 10월 31일, 일요일
시간: 오후 4시에서 오후 6시
장소: Main Street (퍼레이드는 City Hall에서 시작해서 Mason Park에서 끝날 것입니다.)
행사:
• 호박 조각하기   • 라이브 음악
• 의상 경연대회   • 자선 경매

아이들을 위한 활동 (모두 무료):
• 페이스 페인팅   • 사탕 만들기
• 장애물 경기장   • 유령의 집
* 간단한 음식물이 판매될 것입니다.

더 많은 정보를 원하시면, www.lawsonparade.com을 방문하십시오.

(어휘) haunted 유령이 나오는, 겁에 질린 for sale 판매하는

(구문분석) [7행] The parade will begin at City Hall and [end at Mason Park].
→ [end ~ Park] 앞에는 '주어 + 조동사' the parade will이 생략되어 있는데, The parade ~ City Hall에서 이미 언급되었기 때문이다.

29 어법상 틀린 것 찾기 정답 ④

(해설) 밑줄 친 What 뒤에 주어 the caterpillar와 동사 does not rely가 모두 있는 완전한 절이 있고, 문장 전체의 동사인 was determined의 주어 역할을 하는 명사절을 이끄는 명사절 접속사가 와야 하므로, ④의 What을 That으로 고쳐야 한다.

(오답분석) ①은 '너무 ~해서 -하다'라는 의미를 나타내는 'so + 형용사/부사 + that -' 형태로 쓰였는데 동사 camouflage를 수식하고 있으므로 부사 effectively를 사용한 것은 어법상 적절하다. ②은 뒤에 있는 비교급 more complex를 강조하는 부사 far를 사용한 것은 어법상 적절하다. ③은 Other creatures ~ fish에서 that ~ fish는 수 일치에 영향을 미치지 않는 수식어이고 복수명사 Other creatures가 주어이므로 복수동사 have를 사용한 것은 어법상 적절하다. ⑤은 명사구 this impediment 앞에 전치사 Despite를 사용한 것은 어법상 적절하다.

(해석) 회색가지나방('Biston betularia')의 애벌레는 자기 자신을 매우 효과적으로 위장할 수 있어서 잔가지와 구분되지 않아 보인다. 과거의 과학자들은 정확히 어떻게 애벌레가 이렇게 할 수 있는지를 알지 못했지만, 그 과정은 그 곤충이 자신이 본 것에 자신의 겉모습을 맞출 것을 필요로 했다고 추정되었다. 하지만, 이제 이 애벌레는 훨씬 더 복잡한 방식의 의태를 이용한다고 알려져 있는데, 그것은 피부에 있는 감각 기관을 관여시킨다. 카멜레온이나 어류의 일부 종들처럼 위장을 이용하는 다른 생물들도 유사한 체계를 지닌다. 회색가지나방의 애벌레가 시각에 의존하지 않는다는 것은 애벌레들의 눈이 이용되지 못하도록 검은색 물감으로 덮여 있었던 한 실험에 의해 밝혀졌다. 이러한 방해에도 불구하고, 애벌레들은 그들의 겉모습을 그들이 놓인 다양한 형태의 잔가

지들에 맞출 수 있었고, 이는 이 곤충의 의태 방식이 시각적 지각에 근거하는 것이 아님을 나타낸다.

(어휘) **caterpillar** 애벌레 **peppered moth** 회색가지나방
camouflage 위장하다; 위장 **indistinguishable** 구분이 안 되는
twig (나무의) 잔가지 **sensor** 감각 기관, 감지 장치 **impediment** 방해, 장애
perception 지각, 인지 **appearance** 겉모습, 외모

(구문 분석) [7행] However, [it is now **known that** this caterpillar utilizes a far more complex form of mimicry], which involves ~
→ 동사 know의 목적어가 that절인 경우, [it ~ mimicry]와 같이 가주어 it을 사용하여 'it is p.p. that' 형태의 수동태 구문으로 쓸 수 있다.

30 어휘 적절성 파악하기 정답 ④

(해설) 모든 것을 아는 존재라고 했으므로 불분명한 것은 아무것도 없다는 맥락이 되어야 한다. 따라서 ④의 definite(분명한)을 그와 반대되는 의미의 uncertain (불분명한)과 같은 어휘로 바꾸어야 문맥상 적절하다.

(오답 분석) ①은 사람들은 자연을 기계로 여기고 모든 것이 계산될 수 있다고 생각했다고 했으므로, 자연을 분류될 수 있는 것으로 여겼다는 문맥이 되어야 하므로 broken down이 오는 것이 적절하다. ③은 모든 것을 아는 존재를 상상했다고 했으므로 precise가 오는 것이 적절하다. ⑤은 뒤에서 우리의 행동에서 우리는 선택권이 없다고 했으므로 predetermined가 오는 것이 적절하다.

(해석) 과학 혁명 동안, 사람들은 자연을 일종의 기계, 즉 ① 분류될 수 있으며 수학과 물리학의 적용을 통해서 이해할 수 있는 무언가로 여기기 시작했다. 모든 것이 계산될 수 있다는 발상은 생명과 우주의 수수께끼를 ② 풀기 위해 노력하는 과학자들과 철학자들에게 매우 흥미로웠고, 프랑스 물리학자 Pierre-Simon Laplace(피에르 시몽 라플라스)도 예외는 아니었다. 1814년에, 그는 "라플라스의 악마"라고 흔히 일컬어지는 사고 실험을 진행했다. 그 안에서, 그는 실재하는 모든 원자의 ③ 정확한 위치와 운동량, 그리고 더 나아가 그것의 과거와 미래에 대한 모든 것을 아는 존재를 상상했다. 이 가상의 모든 것을 아는 존재에게, ④ 분명한(→불분명한) 것은 아무것도 없었다. 근본적으로, Laplace는 세상의 어느 것에 대해서든 충분한 정보를 모으고 그것을 분석함으로써, 누구나 그것의 과거를 이해하고 미래를 예측할 수 있음을 뜻하고 있었다. 이는 또한 우주 안의 모든 것의 미래가 ⑤ 미리 결정되어 있고, 자유 의지는 없으며, 우리의 행동에서 우리는 선택권이 없다는 것을 의미할 것이다.

(어휘) **break down** 분류하다, 분해하다 **application** 적용, 응용
figure out 계산하다 **entity** 존재, 독립체 **momentum** 운동량, 가속도
atom 원자 **by extension** 더 나아가 **hypothetical** 가상의 **will** 의지

(구문 분석) [10행] In it, he imagined an entity that **knew** ①[the precise location and momentum of every atom in existence] **and**, by
목적어 1
extension, ②[everything about its past and future].
목적어 2
→ 동사 knew의 목적어로 명사구 ①[the ~ existence]와 ②[everything ~ future]가 and로 연결된 구조이다.

31 빈칸 추론하기 정답 ②

(해설) 주제문에 해당하는 빈칸 문장에서 대부분의 이론들은 혹등고래가 물 위로 뛰어오르는 이유가 '무엇하기' 위해서라는 견해를 중심으로 다룬다고 하고, 이어

서 고래가 떨어질 때에 만들어내는 엄청난 충격이 다른 고래들에게 포식자, 근처의 먹이, 또는 짝짓기에 대한 욕구를 알린다고 했다. 따라서 빈칸에는 ② '의사소통하다'가 와야 한다.

(오답 분석) ①, ③, ④, ⑤은 혹등고래가 물 위로 뛰어오르는 이유가 다른 고래들에게 포식자, 근처의 먹이, 또는 짝짓기에 대한 욕구를 알리는 의사소통을 하기 위해서라는 것을 설명하는 단어로 적절하지 않다.

(해석) 혹등고래들 사이에서 물 위로 뛰어오르는 것은 고래가 속도를 올려 거의 완전히 물 밖으로 뛰어오르고 나서 공중에서 빙그르르 돌 때 일어나고, 등이나 옆으로 떨어질 때 엄청난 물보라를 일으키면서 일어난다. 자연 다큐멘터리들이 종종 이러한 장엄한 행동의 장면을 보여주지만, 일반적으로 무게가 30톤이 나가는 동물에게 그것을 하는 것은 많은 양의 에너지가 든다는 점을 고려하면 혹등고래가 물 위로 뛰어오르는 것은 사실 매우 희귀하다. 이 거대한 해양 포유동물들이 물 위로 뛰어오르는 이유는 완전히 이해되지 않지만, 몇 가지의 다양한 이론들이 있고, 그것들의 대부분은 혹등고래가 의사소통하기 위해 물 위로 뛰어오른다는 견해를 중심으로 다룬다. 소리는 땅 위나 공기를 통해서보다 물속에서 더 빠르고 멀리 이동하기 때문에, 고래가 떨어질 때에 만들어내는 엄청난 충격이 바다를 통해 먼 거리로 울려 퍼지고, 그렇게 함으로써 다른 고래들에게 포식자, 근처의 먹이, 또는 짝짓기에 대한 욕구를 알린다고 생각된다.

① 속이다 ② 의사소통하다
③ 가속하다 ④ 항해하다
⑤ 탈출하다

(어휘) **humpback whale** 혹등고래 **pick up speed** 속도를 올리다
whirl 빙그르르 돌다 **awe-inspiring** 장엄한, 경외심을 불러일으키는
revolve around ~을 중심으로 다루다 **tremendous** 엄청난, 굉장한
reverberate 울려 퍼지다, 반향하다 **thereby** 그렇게 함으로써, 그것에 의해

(구문 분석) [1행] Breaching among humpback whales occurs when ~ in the air, [creating a great splash upon landing on its back or side].
→ [creating ~ side]는 '~하면서'라는 의미의 분사구문으로, 분사구문의 주어가 주절의 주어(Breaching)와 같아서 생략되었다.

[9행] **The reasons** [(why) these giant marine mammals breach] are not fully understood, but ~
→ [these ~ breach]는 선행사 The reasons를 수식하는 관계부사절로, 선행사가 이유를 나타내는 일반적인 명사(reason)일 때 관계부사 why가 생략된 형태이다.

32 빈칸 추론하기 정답 ④

(해설) 언어뿐만 아니라 문화가 의사소통 실패의 원인이 되기 때문에 다른 문화와 관습에 대해 알아야 한다는 내용의 글이고, 빈칸 앞의 두 문장에서 서로에 의해 당황하거나 모욕을 당하게 된 사람들은 의사소통에 실패할 수 있는데, 미국인은 대화 중에 시선을 맞추려 하는 반면 일본인은 시선을 적극적으로 피한다고 하였다. 따라서 주제와 관련된 빈칸에는 ④ '어떠한 불쾌감도 주는 것을 방지한다'가 와서 이러한 차이는 두 나라 출신 사람들이 의사소통할 때에 어떠한 불쾌감도 주는 것을 방지하기 위해 명심할 사항일 수 있다는 의미가 되어야 한다.

(오답 분석) ①, ③, ⑤은 글의 내용과 관련이 없다. ②은 마지막 문장에서 의사소통의 장벽을 피하기 위해 다른 문화와 관습을 아는 것이 필수적이라고 했으므로 다른 사람을 화나게 하기 위해 명심해야 할 사항이라는 것은 글의 내용과 반대되는 오답이다.

[해석] 효과적인 의사소통을 막는 장벽은 언어를 넘어선다. 사실, 문화는 당신이 생각할 수 있는 것보다 더 자주 의사소통 오류의 원인이 된다. 다른 나라 출신의 사람들이 만나면, 신체 언어, 몸짓, 가치관, 심리 상태를 포함하되 그에 국한되지 않는 다수의 요인들이 그들의 상호 작용의 성공에 영향을 미칠 수 있다. 이것들은 중요하지 않아 보일 수도 있지만, 서로에 의해 당황하거나 모욕을 당하게 된 사람들로 인해 그것들이 의사소통에서의 실패의 이유가 될 수 있다. 예를 들어, 미국인들은 대화 중에 강력한 시선 맞추기를 하는 경향이 있는 반면, 일본인들은 그것이 그들을 불편하다고 느끼게 만들기 때문에 그것을 적극적으로 피한다. 만약 이 두 나라 출신의 사람들이 의사소통하려고 한다면, 이는 어떠한 불쾌감도 주는 것을 방지하기 위해 명심할 사항일 수 있다. 다른 문화와 그것의 관습을 알고 있는 것은 의사소통에 대한 모든 종류의 장벽을 피하기 위해 필수적이다.

① 합의에 이르다
② 다른 사람을 화나게 하다
③ 논의를 빨리 끝내다
④ 어떠한 불쾌감도 주는 것을 방지하다
⑤ 대화를 유익하게 만들다

[어휘] a multitude of 다수의 psychology 심리 (상태)
insignificant 중요하지 않은 account for ~의 이유가 되다, ~을 설명하다
breakdown 실패, 고장 actively 적극적으로, 활발히
evade 피하다, 모면하다 [선택지] irritate 화나게 하다

[구문분석]
> [11행] ~ while the Japanese actively avoid it since it makes
> them feel uncomfortable.
> 목적어 목적격 보어   동사
> → 사역동사 makes의 목적어로 them, 목적격 보어로 동사원형 feel이 쓰였다.

---

33 빈칸 추론하기   정답 ⑤

[해설] 개인들의 머리에서 창의성이 나온다는 가정과 달리 사실 창의성은 사회문화적 현상일 수 있다는 내용의 글이다. 빈칸 앞 문장에서 동시에 다수의 사람들로부터 독립적으로 획기적인 발전과 발명이 이루어지는 사건, 즉 다중 발견에 대한 개념을 예시로 들어 사회학자들과 인류학자들은 창의성이 사회문화적 현상이라고 주장했다고 하였다. 따라서 주제와 관련된 빈칸에는 ⑤ '공통적인 의식을 형성하다'라는 내용이 오는 것이 적절하다.

[오답분석] ①, ②, ④은 글의 내용과 관련이 없다. ③은 혁신은 특정 개인들의 머리에서 나온다는 건 가정일 뿐이라는 글의 내용과 반대되는 내용이므로 오답이다.

[해석] 창의성이 다양한 형태를 취할 수 있고, 세상은 그것에서 비롯되는 발명, 발견, 예술로부터 엄청나게 이익을 얻는다는 것은 잘 알려져 있다. 하지만, 창의성이 독특한 사고방식의 산물에 지나지 않는가? 수년 동안, 창의성은 주로 심리학과 교육에 관심이 있는 사람들에 의해 연구되었고, 그 주제에 대해 더 많이 배우면 특정 사람들을 더 잘 이해하게 될 것이라는 생각이 바탕이었는데, 왜냐하면 혁신은 개인들의 머리에서 나오기 때문이다. 적어도, 그것이 가정이었다. 그 이후로, 사회학자들과 인류학자들은 사실상 창의성이 사회문화적 현상임을 주장하며 다중 발견에 대한 개념과 같은 예시들을 들어왔다: 이는 획기적 발전과 발명이 동시에 다수의 사람에 의해 독립적으로 이루어지는 사건이다. 그들이 말하기를, 그러한 사건들은 역사의 모든 시기 동안 공통적인 의식을 형성하는 본질적 의미를 규정하는 정신 즉 "시대 정신"이 있기 때문에 일어나고, 발생하는 창의성의 양과 그것이 취하는 형태에 영향을 미친다.

① 일부 사람들이 그들의 개인적 가치들을 재고하게 이끌다
② 개인들이 변화를 지지하도록 하다
③ 독특한 사고방식의 발상들에 의존하다

④ 사람들이 사회에 대해 더 비판적이게 만들다
⑤ 공통적인 의식을 형성하다

[어휘] immensely 엄청나게, 대단히 nothing more than ~에 지나지 않는
cite (이유·예를) 들다 occurrence 사건, 발생
breakthrough 획기적 발전, 돌파구 defining 본질적 의미를 규정하는
zeitgeist 시대 정신, 시대 사조 [선택지] distinctive 독특한
collective 공통의, 집단의 consciousness 의식, 생각

[구문분석]
> [1행] It is well established ①[that creativity can take many
> 가주어   진주어 1
> forms] and ②[that the world benefits immensely from the
>   진주어 2
> inventions, discoveries, and art that result from it].
> → 가주어 It이 접속사(and)로 연결된 진주어 that절 ①[that ~ forms]와 ②[that ~ it] 대신 주어 자리에 쓰인 형태이다.

---

34 빈칸 추론하기   정답 ③

[해설] 타자성은 자신들을 구별 짓고 정체성을 확고히 하게 해줄 뿐만 아니라 그 핵심에는 타자가 자신보다 열등하다는 생각이 있다는 내용의 글이다. 빈칸 앞 문장에서 그리스인들의 야만인 관점을 받아들인 로마인들이 제국을 확장하며 정복한 종족과 사람들을 열등하게 보았다고 하였다. 따라서 주제와 관련된 빈칸에는 ③ '그들이 그들과 다른 사람들의 가치를 낮춰 볼 수 있다'라는 내용이 오는 것이 적절하다.

[오답분석] ①은 로마인들이 제국을 확장하며 정복한 종족과 사람들을 열등하게 여겼다는 글의 내용과 반대되는 내용이므로 오답이다. ②, ④은 글의 내용과 관련이 없다. ⑤은 글에서 언급된 civilizations를 사용하여 헷갈리게 하는 오답이다.

[해석] 타자성이라는 개념은 어떻게 사회에 뿌리를 내렸는가? 사람들은 항상 그들의 것과 다르게 기능하는 문명과 사람들을 경계해 왔다. 그러나 기원과 관련해서 아마 이 개념을 대중화한 것은 고대 그리스인들이었을 것인데, Hippocrates (히포크라테스)와 같은 역사적 인물들은 일부 국가는 본래 다르고 열등하다고 주장했다. 그리스인들은 여러 국가 출신의 외국인들을 "야만인"이라 일컬었는데, 이는 그들 자신을 구별 짓고 공유된 그리스인의 정체성을 확고히 하게 해주었다. 그러나 타자화의 과정은 정체성을 확립하는 데에만 유용한 것이 아니다. 타자성의 핵심에는 타자가 자기보다 열등하다는 생각이 있다. 지배 집단은 이 정체성들을 발전시켜 그 결과 타자를 차별할 수단을 합리화할 수 있다. 예를 들어 고대 로마인들은 그리스인들로부터 야만인 관점을 받아들여, 그들의 제국이 확장하는 동안 정복한 종족과 사람들을 열등하고 따라서 정당한 이유가 있어서 지배를 받는다고 보았다. 그들이 그들과 다른 사람들의 가치를 낮춰 보고 그들을 지배하는 힘을 유지할 수 있도록 그들은 스스로를 구분 지었다.

① 그들이 다른 문화에 대해 더 많이 배울 수 있다
② 그들이 사회 내 다양성을 장려할 수 있다
③ 그들이 그들과 다른 사람들의 가치를 낮춰 볼 수 있다
④ 그들이 사람들 사이에 관용을 장려할 수 있다
⑤ 그들이 다른 문명에 그들의 가치를 전파할 수 있다

[어휘] otherness 타자성, 다름 take root 뿌리를 내리다 wary 경계하는
civilization 문명 popularize 대중화하다 notion 개념, 관념
by nature 본래 barbarian 야만인, 이방인 distinguish 구별 짓다
solidify 확고히 하다 othering 타자화 second-class 열등한, 이류의
the Self 자기(自己) formulate 발전시키다 rationalize 합리화하다
discriminate 차별하다 conquer 정복하다 spread 확장, 전파
justifiably 정당한 이유가 있어 retain 유지하다
[선택지] devalue 가치를 낮춰 보다 tolerance 관용

구문분석

[4행] With reference to origin, however, perhaps **it was** the ancient Greeks **who** popularized this notion, ~

→ the ancient Greeks를 강조하는 it is(was) ~ who 강조구문이 쓰였다.

[12행] [**At the core of otherness** is the suggestion] that the Other is second-class to the Self.
　　　　　　　　　　　　　　　동사　　주어

→ 장소를 나타내는 부사구 At the core of otherness가 문장 앞에 와서, 동사(is)와 주어(the suggestion)가 도치된 구조로 쓰였다.

---

35 흐름과 관계 없는 문장 찾기　　정답 ③

(해설) 인공 감미료가 뇌와 신체에 초래하는 부정적인 반응에 대해 설명하는 내용의 글이다. 그런데 ③은 균형 잡힌 영양분 섭취를 필요로 하는 과정에 대해 이야기하고 있으므로 주제에서 벗어나 있어 글의 흐름과 무관하다.

(오답분석) ① 앞 문장은 뇌와 신체가 인공 감미료에 부정적인 반응을 보인다는 내용이고, ①, ②은 신체에서 나타나는 인공 감미료의 부정적인 반응과 이에 따른 영향을 설명하고 있으므로 자연스럽게 연결된다. 이어서, ④, ⑤는 뇌에서 나타나는 인공 감미료의 부정적인 반응과 이로 인한 결과를 이야기하고 있으므로 글의 흐름과 자연스럽게 연결된다.

(해석) 인공 감미료는 칼로리를 포함하고 있지 않기 때문에 진짜 설탕의 놀라운 대체물인 것처럼 보일 수도 있다. 유감스럽게도, 뇌와 신체 모두 이 합성 물질에 부정적인 반응을 보인다는 강력한 증거가 있고, 많은 의학 전문가들은 그것들을 피해야 한다고 권고한다. ① 위는 음식을 소화시키는 많은 유익한 박테리아를 함유하고 있고, 한 연구는 이 미생물들이 인공 감미료와 상호 작용한 후에 효율이 감소한다는 것을 보여주었다. ② 이 물질을 대량으로 섭취하는 사람은 그 또는 그녀가 먹는 다른 음식에서 충분한 영양분을 얻지 못할 수도 있다. (③ 성장, 에너지, 세포 재생은 모두 균형 잡힌 영양분 섭취를 필요로 하는 과정들이다.) ④ 인공 감미료는 또한 거짓 만족감을 초래하는데, 이는 과식으로 이어질 뿐이다. ⑤ 강한 단맛과 칼로리가 없는 것의 조합은 뇌에서 결핍 반응을 유발하고, 그 사람이 매우 배고프다고 느끼게 만든다.

(어휘) artificial 인공의　sweetener 감미료　substitute 대체물　synthetic 합성한, 인조의　microorganism 미생물　intake 섭취　hollow 거짓의, 헛된　starvation 결핍, 기아

구문분석

[10행] **A person** [who consumes these substances in large amounts] may not be able to get sufficient nutrients from ~

→ [who ~ amounts]는 선행사 A person을 수식하며, 주격 관계대명사 who가 이끄는 관계대명사절이다.

[14행] Artificial sweeteners also bring about **hollow satisfaction**, [which only leads to overeating].

→ [which ~ overeating]은 선행사 hollow satisfaction을 수식하는 주격 관계대명사절로, 콤마 뒤에서 계속적 용법으로 쓰였다.

---

36 글의 순서 배열하기　　정답 ④

(해설) 주어진 글은 서양 세계는 19세기에 오래된 양식과 전통이 약화되고, 모더니즘이라는 새로운 시기에 진입했다는 주제를 제시한다. (C)의 this time(이 시기)은 주어진 글의 '모더니즘이라고 알려진 새로운 시기'를 가리키므로 주어진 글

바로 다음에 오는 것이 적절하다. (A)의 this new concept of art(예술의 이러한 새로운 개념)는 (C)의 '예술이 더 개인적인 표현의 수단이 되는 것'을 가리키므로 (C) 바로 다음에 오는 것이 적절하다. (B)는 추상 미술의 한 가지 측면이 형식주의라는 내용이므로, 추상 미술이 부상했다고 한 (A) 뒤에 와야 한다. 따라서 글의 순서로 가장 적절한 것은 ④ (C)-(A)-(B)이다.

(해석) 19세기 후반, 오래된 양식들과 전통들이 약화되기 시작하고 새로운 사상들과 표현 방식들이 장악하기 시작함에 따라, 서양 세계는 모더니즘이라고 알려진 새로운 시기에 진입했다.

(C) 이 시기 이전에는, 예술의 가치는 그것이 얼마나 세계를 그대로 잘 보여줬는지에 있었다; 자연과 인간 문명을 재현하는 능력이 그것의 우수성의 중요한 척도였다. 하지만, 사실주의에 대한 평가의 약화는 예술이 더 개인적인 표현의 수단이 되는 것에 이르게 했다.

(A) 예술의 이러한 새로운 개념이 인기를 얻으면서, 추상 미술이 부상했다. 그것은 형식 자체가 감정을 불어넣을 수 있으며, 색채, 선, 명암, 질감이 감정을 자아내기에 충분하다는 것을 시사했다. 작품의 배경이나 예술가의 의도를 포함한 다른 모든 것들은 비교적 중요하지 않았다.

(B) 추상 미술의 한 가지 측면은 형식주의였는데, 그것은 "예술을 위한 예술"이라는 표어에 의해 가장 전형적으로 드러난다. 이는 예술이 내용에서 분리될 수 있고 물감이 실제로 캔버스 위에 어떻게 배치되었는지가 그것의 진정한 가치가 있는 부분이라는 관념이었다.

(어휘) take hold 장악하다　tone 명암, 색조　of secondary importance 비교적 중요하지 않은　abstract 추상적인　formalism 형식주의　notion 관념, 개념　subject matter 내용, 주제　reside in ~에 있다　hold a mirror up to ~을 그대로 보여주다　reproduce 재현하다, 모사하다　indicator 척도　quality 우수성, 질　appreciation 평가, 감상

구문분석

[5행] [With this new concept of art gaining popularity], abstract art emerged.
　　　　　　　　　명사구　　　　　　현재분사

→ [With ~ popularity]는 'with + 명사(구) + 분사' 형태의 분사구문으로, '~하면서'라는 의미로 해석한다.

[6행] It **suggested** [(that) form itself could inspire feeling — color, line, tone, and texture were enough to evoke emotion].

→ [form ~ emotion]은 동사 suggested의 목적어 역할을 하는 명사절로, 접속사 that이 생략되었다.

[13행] This was **the notion** ①[that art could be separated from its subject matter] and ②[that how paint was actually
　　　　　　　　　　　　　　　　　　　　　　　주어
arranged on a canvas was where its true value was].
　　　　　　　　　　동사　　　　보어

→ ①[that ~ matter]와 ②[that ~ was]는 모두 the notion과 동격을 이루는 명사절이다.

---

37 글의 순서 배열하기　　정답 ⑤

(해설) 주어진 글은 사람들이 사회주의와 공산주의를 동일한 이념으로 여겨 두 용어를 때때로 혼용하는데, 어쨌든 사회주의와 공산주의가 생겨난 목표는 같다는 통념을 제시한다. (C)는 역접 연결어 though를 통해 공산주의와 사회주의의 차이점에 대해 이야기하며, 두 이념의 공통점을 언급한 주어진 글의 내용에 대한 반전 설명을 하고 있으므로 주어진 글 바로 뒤에 오는 것이 적절하다. (B)

는 역접 연결어 In contrast를 통해 사회주의의 핵심 원칙에 대해 이야기하며, 공산주의의 핵심 원칙을 언급한 (C)의 내용에 대한 반전 설명을 하고 있으므로 (C) 바로 뒤에 오는 것이 적절하다. (A)는 also를 통해 (C), (B)에서 언급한 핵심 원칙 이외의 추가적인 차이점인 수립 방식에 대해 언급하고 있으므로 그 뒤에 와야 한다. 따라서 글의 순서로 가장 적절한 것은 ⑤ (C)-(B)-(A)이다.

(해석) 사람들은 사회주의와 공산주의를 동일한 이념으로 여기기 때문에, 때때로 사회주의와 공산주의라는 용어들을 서로 바꿔서 사용한다. 어쨌든, 이 정치적 이념들 둘 다 소득 격차가 많이 크지 않은 좀 더 평등한 사회를 만드는 것을 목표로 생겨났다.

(C) 그렇지만, 공산주의와 사회주의는 사실상 몇 가지 핵심 원칙에 있어서 나뉜다. 공산주의 하에서, 모든 경제적 자원은 국가에 의해 소유되고 사람들은 중앙 집권화된 정부에 의해 그들이 필요한 것을 배분받는다. 개인들은 사유 재산이나 자산을 보유할 수 없다.

(B) 그에 반해서, 사회주의는 사유 재산을 허용하고 정부는 단지 재화의 생산을 감독하고 지휘하기를 요구한다. 이것의 목적은 더 적절한 가격과 생산량을 보장해서 상위 계층뿐만 아니라 전체 인구가 이익을 얻을 수 있게 하는 것이다.

(A) 이 두 체제들은 또한 다른 방식으로 수립된다. 공산주의는 혁명과 중간 및 상위 계층의 타도를 통해 행해지는 반면, 사회주의는 정책 수정을 통해 민주적으로 주입된다.

(어휘) socialism 사회주의   communism 공산주의   overthrow 타도, 추방
democratically 민주적으로   amendment 수정, 개정
call for ~을 요구하다   output 생산량   diverge 나뉘다, 갈라지다
publicly 국가에 의해, 공적으로   centralized 중앙 집권화된, 집중화된

(구문분석)
[1행] Individuals sometimes use the terms socialism and communism interchangeably, [considering them identical philosophies].
→ [considering ~ philosophies]는 '~ 때문에'라는 의미의 분사구문으로, 분사구문의 주어가 주절의 주어(Individuals)와 같아서 생략되었다.

[14행] The purpose of this **is** [to guarantee fairer prices and output] so the entire population ~
→ [to ~ output]은 to부정사의 명사적 용법(~하는 것)으로, be동사 is의 주격 보어 역할을 한다.

38 주어진 문장의 위치 찾기   정답 ②

(해설) 주어진 문장의 Rather(오히려)로 보아, 주어진 문장 앞에는 화성으로의 우주 비행이 주는 다른 도전에 대한 내용이 나와야 한다는 것을 알 수 있다. 이 글에서는 ① 뒤 문장까지 유인 우주 비행을 보내기 전에 화성에 사람이 살기 적합한 기지를 만드는 도전 과제가 있다는 내용이 이어지다가 ② 뒤 문장에서 방사선의 위험성에 대한 내용이 나오고 있다. ② 뒤 문장의 That이 가리키는 내용이 ① 뒤 문장에 없고 ② 앞뒤 내용이 유기적으로 연결되지 않는다는 점을 통해 글의 흐름이 끊겼음을 알 수 있다. 따라서 주어진 문장이 들어가기에 적절한 곳은 ②이다.

(오답분석) ③, ④, ⑤ 뒤 문장은 ② 뒤 문장에서 언급한 방사선의 위험성에 대해 보충 설명하고 있으므로 주어진 문장은 이것보다 앞에 와야 한다.

(해석) 2030년까지, 지속적인 우주 탐사 계획의 일부로, NASA는 화성으로의 유인 우주 비행을 실행하기를 희망한다. 어떠한 유인 우주 비행이 그 붉은 행성에 착륙할 수 있기 전에, 로봇에 의한 지하 거주지의 건설을 포함한 준비들이 이루어져야 한다. (①) 하지만, 살기에 적합한 기지를 화성에 만드는 것에 대한

가능성은 그 여정에서 가장 결정적인 난관이 아니다. (② 오히려, 우주 비행사의 최우선의 도전은 단지 화성으로의 이동에서 살아남는 것이 될 것이다.) 그것은 우리의 대기권의 보호막 외부에 존재하는 방사선으로 인해 우주 여행이 인간에게 매우 위험하기 때문이다. (③) 여기 지구에서, 우리는 지구의 핵에서 액체 상태의 철의 흐름에 의해 생성되는 강한 자기장에 의해 보호되지만, 우리가 우리의 행성에서 더 멀리 이동할수록, 자기장은 더 약해진다. (④) 지구의 자기장이 거의 4만 마일까지 뻗어 나가고 화성은 1억 4천만 마일 떨어져 있음을 고려하면, 방사선에의 노출은 불가피하다. (⑤) 결과적으로, 방사선이 중추 신경계에 심각한 영향을 미치고 암 발생의 가능성을 급격하게 증가시킬 수 있기 때문에, 이는 도전을 제기한다.

(어휘) foremost 최우선의, 가장 중요한   mission 우주 비행, 임무
prospect 가능성, 기대   radiation 방사선, 방사   cocoon 보호막
magnetic field 자기장   inevitable 불가피한
central nervous system 중추 신경계

(구문분석)
[1행] Rather, the astronauts' foremost challenge would **be** simply [surviving the trip to Mars].
→ [surviving ~ Mars]는 be동사의 주격 보어 역할을 하는 동명사구이다.

[13행] Here on Earth, we are shielded by a strong magnetic field produced by the flow of liquid iron in the Earth's core, but ①[the further] we move away from our planet, ②[the weaker] the magnetic field gets.
→ ①[the further]와 ②[the weaker]는 '~할수록 점점 더 -하다'라는 의미의 비교급 구문 'the + 비교급 ~, the + 비교급 -'을 만든다.

39 주어진 문장의 위치 찾기   정답 ③

(해설) 주어진 문장의 Compounding the problem(그 문제를 악화시키는 것)으로 보아, 주어진 문장 앞에는 문제가 무엇인지에 대한 내용이 나와야 한다는 것을 알 수 있다. 이 글에서는 ② 뒤 문장까지 야구의 지루함과 그 이유 중 하나인 구단주들이 최대한 적은 위험을 감수하는 승리 방법에 초점을 두는 것에 대해 설명하고 있고, 주어진 문장의 today's players는 ③ 뒤 문장에서 pitchers와 hitters로 이어지고 있으므로 주어진 문장이 들어가기에 가장 적절한 곳은 ③이다.

(오답분석) ⑤ 뒤 문장의 This absurd state of affairs는 ④ 뒤 문장의 an endless parade of strikeouts and walks punctuated by occasional homeruns (이따금 홈런이 간간이 끼어드는, 스트라이크와 포볼에 의한 출루의 끊임없는 행렬)를 가리키므로 주어진 문장이 들어가기에 적절하지 않다.

(해석) 사소한 성취들이 따르는 헛된 볼과 스트라이크의 긴 간격들로 인한 야구의 느긋한 흐름이 향수를 불러일으키는 19세기적 매력의 일부이긴 하지만, 일부 사람들은 그 경기가 지루하고 축구와 농구의 기운 나게 하는 활기가 없다고 불평한다. (①) 하지만, 최근에는 경기의 혹평가들이 아니라 가장 열광적인 팬들에게서 지루함에 대한 비난이 나오고 있다. (②) 구단주들은 한때 야구에서 가장 짜릿한 사건 중 하나였던 도루의 경우를 줄이면서, 가능한 한 적은 위험을 감수하는 것을 포함하는 승리를 향한 통계학적 경로들에 더 초점을 두게 되었다. (③ 그 문제를 악화시키는 것은 어린 나이부터 스카우트되고 수년에 걸쳐 점점 더 전문화된 트레이닝을 받는 오늘날의 선수들의 향상된 조건 형성이다.) 근육이 발달한 투수는 늘 하는 시속 100마일의 속구를 던지는데, 타자는 그 결과로서 공을 칠 가능성이 거의 없다. (④) 그 결과는 이따금 홈런이 간간이 끼어드는, 스트라이크와 포볼에 의한 출루의 끊임없는 행렬이다. (⑤) 이 터무니없는 문제들의 사태는 메이저리그 야구가 규정들을 변경해서, 경기의

핵심적인 특징을 유지하면서도 그 방식들을 더 재미있게 만들려고 노력하는 것으로 이어졌다.

어휘 **compound** 악화시키다 **leisurely** 느긋한, 여유로운
nostalgic 향수를 불러일으키는, 향수의 **invigorating** 기운 나게 하는, 상쾌한
action 활기, 활동 **electrifying** 짜릿한, 열광시키는 **pitcher** 투수
steady diet 늘 하던 것 **fastball** 속구 **hitter** 타자 **strikeout** 삼진
punctuate 간간이 끼어들다 **absurd** 터무니없는, 황당한
enliven 더 재미있게 만들다 **proceeding** 방식, 진행

구문분석 [10행] Recently, however, charges of boredom are emerging **not** ①[from the game's critics] **but** ②[from its most passionate fans].

→ ①[from ~ critics]와 ②[from ~ fans]는 상관접속사 not A but B로 연결된 병렬 구조이다.

40 요약문 완성하기 정답 ③

해설 한 사람을 묘사하는 단어들의 같은 목록을 읽고 응답하는 연구에서, 첫 번째 집단과 두 번째 집단에게 제공하는 목록의 순서만 반대로 제공했는데, 두 집단 모두 목록의 첫 번째 단어들로 같은 사람을 다르게 묘사했다는 내용의 글이다. 따라서 impressions를 perceptions로, from the first words를 initially로 바꾸어 표현한 ③이 정답이다.

오답분석 어휘가 나열된 순서가 달라지자 동일한 질문에 대한 사람들의 응답이 달라졌다고 했으므로 ②의 simultaneously는 (B)에 들어갈 단어로 적절하지 않다.

해석 한 연구에서, 참가자들은 그들이 한 번도 만난 적이 없는 한 사람에 대해 묘사하는 단어들의 목록을 읽도록 요구되었다. 한 목록은 다음을 포함했다: '똑똑한', '부지런한', '충동적인', '비판적인', '완고한', '질투하는'. 응답자들에게 이 형용사들이 완전히 같은 순서로 주어졌다. 목록에 있는 단어들을 읽는 것 외에는 그들에게 지시도 주어지지 않았다. 이후에, 그 사람을 묘사하도록 요구되었을 때, 그들 모두는 목록에 있는 처음 두 단어인 '똑똑한'과 '부지런한'을 선택했다. 그 다음에, 다른 집단에게 같은 목록이 주어졌지만, '질투하는'과 '완강한'이 목록의 맨 위에 나오도록 단어들이 반대 순서로 나열되었다. 놀랍게도, 같은 사람을 묘사하도록 요구되었을 때, 이 집단은 그 사람을 '질투하는'과 '완강한'으로 묘사했다. 종합해 보면, 각 집단은 그들이 목록에서 읽은 첫 번째 단어들로 그들이 만든 인상을 바탕으로 같은 사람을 다르게 묘사했다.

↓

한 연구의 결과는 타인들에 대한 사람들의 평가가 그들에게 (B) 처음에 주어진 정보를 바탕으로 그들이 형성하는 (A) 인식에 의해 영향받을 수 있음을 시사했다.

	(A)		(B)
①	갈등	……	즉각적으로
②	인식	……	동시에
③	인식	……	처음에
④	개념	……	공식적으로
⑤	갈등	……	자연스럽게

어휘 **descriptive** 묘사하는, 서술하는 **industrious** 부지런한
impulsive 충동적인 **stubborn** 완고한 **envious** 질투하는
reverse 반대의, 거꾸로의

구문분석 [8행] At a later time, [**when** asked to describe the individual], all of them chose the first two words ~

→ [when ~ individual]은 분사구문의 의미를 분명하게 하기 위해 부사절 접속사(when)가 분사 앞에 온 형태이다.

41~42 장문 독해 1

해석 1990년대 후반 이후로, 경제 발전에서 제도들의 역할은 ⁴¹제도의 질이 한 국가의 번영 수준과 (a) 직접적인 상관관계가 있다는 의견 일치와 함께 경제학 영역에서 매우 인기 있는 주제였다. 이러한 맥락에서, 제도는 인간의 상호 작용을 좌우하는 모든 제약이다. 그것들은 규정과 법과 같은 공식적 제약과, 사회적 관습과 행동 규범과 같은 비공식적 제약 둘 다로 이루어진다. 경제학에서의 지배적인 관점은 ⁴¹자유 경제, 재산권, 보편적인 수준의 신뢰와 같은 개념들을 장려하는 것들인 질 높은 제도가 적절한 유인을 만들어내기 때문에 (b) 번영으로 이어진다는 것이다. 예를 들어, 자본주의 경제에서 사람들은 이익에 의해 장려된다. 자본주의 경제에서의 규칙과 규제들은 기업가들이 수익을 올리는 것을 가능하게 하고 그들이 제품과 서비스를 팔아서 그들이 얻는 것을 차지할 수 있음을 보장하기 때문에, 사람들은 혁신적이고 번창하도록 (c) 동기가 부여된다. 더 많은 기업가들이 성공할 때 경제가 성장하고, 협력과 정직과 같이 제일 먼저 그들의 성공을 가능하게 했던 핵심적인 비즈니스 가치들이 사회적 (d) 기준들이 된다. 반면에, 경제가 중앙 정부의 주도하에 계획되는 전체주의 국가와 같이, ⁴²열등한 제도가 있는 국가의 시민들은 그들 자신만의 사업체를 시작하거나 앞으로의 수익을 차지할 자유가 없다. 그 국민들은 이익을 내기 위해 현재의 상황을 (e) 유지할(→도전할) 확실한 동기를 찾지 못할 수 있다.

어휘 **institution** 제도, 기관 **consensus** 의견 일치, 합의
correlation 상관관계, 연관성 **constraint** 제약 **convention** 관습
norm 규범, 기준 **prevailing** 지배적인, 만연한
capitalist 자본주의의 **incentivize** 장려하다
prosperous 번창하는, 번영하는 **totalitarian** 전체주의의
viable 확실한, 실행 가능한 **status quo** 현재의 상황, 현상
[선택지] **driving force** 원동력, 추진력 **bridge** 극복하다, 메우다
strained 부자연스러운, 팽팽한

구문분석 [7행] They consist of **both** ①[formal constraints, like regulations and laws], **and** ②[informal constraints, like societal conventions and behavioral norms].

→ ①[formal ~ laws]와 ②[informal ~ norms]는 상관접속사 both A and B로 연결된 병렬 구조이다.

[16행] Because the rules and regulations in capitalist 주어
economies ①[enable entrepreneurs to make profits] **and** 동사 1   목적어   목적격 보어
②[ensure that they can keep (what they gain from selling 동사 2
goods and services)], ~

→ and로 연결된 ①[enable ~ profits]와 ②[ensure ~ services]는 because가 이끄는 부사절의 동사에 해당한다.

→ ② 안의 (what ~ services)는 관계대명사 what(~하는 것)이 이끄는 명사절로 앞의 동사 keep의 목적어 역할을 한다.

41 제목 파악하기 정답 ②

해설 경제 발전에 있어서 제도의 질은 한 국가의 번영 수준과 직접적인 상관관계에 있다는 내용의 글로, 질 좋은 제도가 있는 자본주의 경제와 열등한 제도가 있는 전체주의 국가를 비교해서 설명하고 있다. 따라서 글의 제목으로 가장 적절한 것은 ② '제도들: 경제 성장 이면의 원동력'이다.

오답분석 ①은 글에서 언급된 Incentives를 사용하여 헷갈리게 하는 오답이다. ④의 지배적 이론들의 재고에 관한 내용은 글에서 언급되고 있지 않다. ⑤은 경제 발전에 있어서 제도들이 국가의 번영 수준과 직접적인 상관관계에 있다는 글의 주제와 반대되는 내용이기 때문에 오답이다.

해석 ① 다음 단계: 장려책들이 실패하면 무슨 일이 생기는가?
② 제도들: 경제 성장 이면의 원동력
③ 선진국과 개발도상국 간의 격차 극복하기
④ 경제 발전을 돕기 위한 지배적인 이론들 재고하기
⑤ 제도와 경제 발전: 부자연스러운 관계

42 어휘 적절성 파악하기 정답 ⑤

해설 자신만의 사업체를 시작하거나 앞으로의 수익을 차지할 자유가 없으면 국민들은 이익을 내기 위해 현재의 상황에 도전할 확실한 동기를 찾지 못할 수 있다는 맥락이 되어야 하므로 ⑤의 preserve(유지하다)를 그와 반대되는 의미의 challenge(도전하다)와 같은 어휘로 바꾸어야 문맥상 적절하다.

오답분석 ②은 자본주의 경제에서 이익으로 사람들이 장려되듯이 질 좋은 제도는 적절한 유인을 만들어서 번영으로 이어진다는 문맥이 되어야 하므로 prosperity가 오는 것이 적절하다. ③은 자본주의 경제에서 기업가들이 판매 활동에서 얻은 수익을 차지할 수 있게 하기 때문에 혁신적이고 번창하도록 동기가 부여된다는 문맥이 되어야 하므로 motivated가 오는 것이 적절하다.

43~45 장문 독해 2

해석 (A) Raju와 Vinod가 사무실 건물 밖으로 걸어 나와서 인도에 올라섰을 때 도시는 활기로 소란스러웠다. 이 시간에, 그들은 보통 집에 곧장 가곤 했다. 하지만, 오늘 그들은 일자리를 잃었고 (a) 그들의 가족들에게 이야기하기가 두려웠다. "강가에서 산책이나 하자"라고 Vinod가 말했다.

(D) 그들이 강둑을 따라 걷고 있을 때, Raju와 Vinod는 한 무리의 아이들이 주위를 뛰어다니는 것을 보았다. "내가 보기에 저들은 게임을 하고 있는 것 같아"라고 Raju가 말했다. "구경해보자." (e) 그들은 각각의 아이들이 상자를 가지고 있는 것과 물가에서 찾은 재료들로 상자를 채우려고 하는 것을 보았다. 그들은 누가 가장 빨리 상자를 채울 수 있는지를 보고 싶었다. ⁴⁵이긴 아이는 그의 상자를 돌멩이들로 채웠다. 두 번째 아이는 자갈과 다른 약간의 작은 쓰레기를 이용하려고 했고, 마지막 아이는 그의 손가락 사이로 계속 빠져나가는 흙을 이용했다.

(B) Raju가 한 교수님이 그와 Vinod에게 가르치려고 했던 예전의 교훈을 기억해낸 것은 바로 그때였다. 그 교수님은 (b) 그들에게 돌멩이들로 채워진 용기를 보여주었고, 그들은 그것이 꽉 찼다는 것에 동의했다. 그리고 나서, 그는 돌멩이 사이로 빠지는 자갈들을 더 넣었고, 용기를 그 이상으로 채웠다. 마지막으로, 그는 모래를 더 넣었고 그것은 남아 있는 모든 공간을 채웠다. "돌멩이들은 가족과 같이 ⁴⁴가치 있는 것들을 나타낸단다. 다른 무언가가 없이도, (c) 그것들은 우리가 완전한 삶을 살도록 도와준단다"라고 그가 말했다.

(C) 그 후에 교수님은 자갈들을 가리키며 그것들은 직업이나 돈과 같이 가치가 더 적은 것들을 나타낸다고 말했다. 그것들은 중요하지만 사람들은 그

것들 없이도 살 수 있다. 마지막으로, 그는 모래가 의미하는 것을 설명했다. "이것은 물질적 소유물이나 우리가 걱정하느라 시간을 허비하는 사소한 걱정들과 같이, 모든 것들 중에서 가장 가치가 적은 것들을 나타낸단다. 중요하지 않은 일들에 너희의 시간을 쏟는 것은 중요한 것을 위한 여유를 남기지 않는단다." Raju는 마침내 그 교훈을 이해하고는 Vinod와 공유했고, 그 후에 (d) 그들은 각자 집에 있는 가족들에게 돌아갔다.

어휘 buzz 소란스럽다, 윙윙거리다 activity 활기, 활동 pebble 자갈, 조약돌 room 여유, 공간 stand for ~을 의미하다 trivial 사소한 riverbank 강둑, 강기슭 shore 물가, 해안 slip 빠져나가다, 미끄러지다

구문분석 [7행] **It was** then **that** Raju recalled an old lesson that a professor had tried to teach him and Vinod.
→ then을 강조하는 it is(was) ~ that 강조구문이 쓰였다.

[12행] Lastly, he added sand, which **took up** [whatever room remained].
→ [whatever room remained]는 복합관계형용사 whatever가 이끄는 명사절로, 동사 took up의 목적어 역할을 한다. whatever가 뒤의 명사 room을 수식하므로 '모든 공간, 어떤 공간이든'의 의미로 해석한다.

43 글의 순서 배열하기 정답 ④

해설 (A)는 일자리를 잃은 Raju와 Vinod가 집에 가기 전에 강가로 산책을 가기로 했다는 내용이다. (D)는 강둑을 따라 걸으면서 Raju와 Vinod가 게임을 하고 있는 한 무리의 아이들을 보았다는 내용이므로 Raju와 Vinod가 강가로 산책을 가기로 한 (A) 뒤에 와야 한다. (B)의 It was then에서 then은 아이들이 각각 돌멩이, 자갈, 흙으로 상자를 채우는 것을 본 시점을 가리키므로 (D) 다음에 오는 것이 적절하다. (C)의 The professor는 (B)의 a professor에 해당하므로 (B) 다음에 오는 것이 적절하다. 따라서 글의 순서로 가장 적절한 것은 ④ (D) - (B) - (C)이다.

44 지칭 대상 파악하기 정답 ③

해설 (a), (b), (d), (e)는 모두 Raju와 Vinod를 가리키지만 (c)는 '가치 있는 것들'을 가리키므로, ③이 정답이다.

45 세부 정보 파악하기 정답 ⑤

해설 (D)의 The child who won ~ and the last one had used dirt를 통해 이긴 아이는 상자를 돌멩이로 채우고 두 번째와 마지막 아이는 각각 자갈과 쓰레기, 흙으로 상자를 채웠다는 것을 알 수 있는데, ⑤은 아이들 모두 돌멩이로 채웠다고 일부 정보를 잘못 나타냈으므로 글의 내용과 일치하지 않는 것은 ⑤이다.

문제집 p.146

18 목적 파악하기   정답 ③

해설 글의 중간 이후에서 쓰레기를 버릴 곳이 없는 거리에 쓰레기통을 설치해 줄 것을 요청하고 있으므로, 정답은 ③이다.

해석 관계자분께

제 남편과 저는 Strickland 지역의 새로운 주민들입니다. 저희는 이 동네와 여기서 이용 가능한 편의 시설들을 좋아하지만, Seymour 가에는 쓰레기를 버릴 데가 없다는 것을 알게 되었습니다. 이로 인해 비닐 봉지와 오래된 음식물 용기와 같은 물품들이 거리를 따라 정원을 어지럽히고 있습니다. 저는 이것이 우리 지역을 방문하는 사람들에게 잘못된 메시지를 전달하고 저희의 수준을 반영하지 못하는 것 같습니다. 다른 거리들에는 쓰레기를 처리할 방법이 있는데, 이는 동네 전체에서 일관적이어야 한다고 생각합니다. 저희는 다른 주민들과 이것을 논의했고 그들은 Seymour 가에 쓰레기통을 설치하는 것이 좋은 생각이라는 점에 동의합니다. 저희는 당신이 이 요청을 고려해주시기를 바라고 당신에게서 빠른 시일 내에 소식을 받기를 바랍니다.

Davies 부부 드림

어휘 neighborhood 동네, 이웃 facility 편의 시설 dispose of ~을 버리다 litter 어지럽히다 disposal 처리 consistent 일관적인

구문분석
[6행] This **leads to** items like plastic bags and old food
    명사구
containers littering the gardens all along the street.
    현재분사

→ 'lead to + 명사구 + 현재분사'의 구조로, '이로 인해 명사구가 ~하고 있다'의 의미로 해석한다.

19 심경 파악하기   정답 ①

해설 심경은 간접적으로 표현된다. 글의 초반부의 Lisa frowned ~ so she was reluctant to go를 통해 Lisa가 연극이 재미없을 것이라고 의심하는 것을 알 수 있고, 후반부의 The actors were incredibly ~ was dramatic과 At the end of the performance ~ and clapping을 통해 예상과 달리 훌륭한 연극에 놀라워하는 것을 알 수 있으므로, Lisa의 심경 변화로 가장 적절한 것은 ①이다.

해석 룸메이트가 신나는 모습으로 들어왔을 때 Lisa는 집에서 저녁을 먹고 있었다. "오늘밤 우리에게 연극 티켓이 생겼어!" 그녀는 유쾌하게 소리쳤다. 그녀는 연극 제목은 <고요한 밤>이고 전쟁 영웅에 대한 내용이라고 설명했다. Lisa는 그것이 그녀가 재미있게 볼 만한 것 같지 않아서 싫은 내색을 보였고, 그래서 그녀는 가기를 주저했다. 그러나 긴 애원 끝에, 룸메이트는 그녀가 가도록 설득했다. 그날 밤 그들이 자리에 앉으면서, Lisa는 한숨을 쉬었고 연극이 시작

하기를 기다렸다. 그녀는 연극이 시작했을 때는 집중하려고 하지 않았으나, 그녀는 곧 무대에서 일어나는 일에 완전히 빠져들었다. 배우들은 놀라울 정도로 재능이 있었고 이야기는 극적이었다. 공연이 끝날 때, Lisa는 일어나서 박수를 치고 있는 자신을 발견했다. 그 경험은 잊을 수 없었다.

① 의심하는 → 놀란   ② 기쁜 → 짜증 난
③ 편안한 → 불안한   ④ 흥분한 → 화가 난
⑤ 스트레스 받는 → 느긋한

어휘 exclaim 소리치다 frown 싫은 내색을 보이다 convince 설득하다 immerse 빠져들게 하다 clap 박수를 치다

구문분석
[3행] She explained ①[that the play was called *Silent Night*]
        동사   목적어 1
and ②[that it was about a war hero].
        목적어 2

→ 동사 explained의 목적어에 해당하는 that절 ①[that ~ *Night*]와 ②[that ~ hero]는 등위접속사 and로 연결된 병렬 구조이다.

[13행] ~ Lisa found herself standing up and clapping.
        동사 목적어   목적격 보어

→ 동사 found의 목적어로 재귀대명사 herself가, 목적격 보어로 현재분사구 standing up and clapping이 쓰였다. 목적어로 재귀대명사가 쓰였으므로 '~하고 있는 자신을 발견하다'의 의미로 해석한다.

20 주장 파악하기   정답 ⑤

해설 글의 마지막 두 문장에서 개인의 도덕적 평가는 우리의 선입견 때문에 본래 편향되어 있으므로 다른 사람들의 관점을 고려하여 상황을 판단해야 한다고 주장하고 있다. 따라서 정답은 ⑤이다.

오답분석 ①, ④은 글에서 언급된 내용이 아니다. ③은 선입견에 기반해 단정적인 판단을 내리는 것을 피하라고 한 글의 내용과 반대되는 내용이므로 오답이다.

해석 우리는 어느 정도의 확신과 단호함을 가지고 복잡한 시나리오를 평가하기 위해 우리 자신의 개인적인 도덕의 잣대를 이용함으로써, 어떤 주어진 상황의 윤리를 종종 성급하게 평가한다. 대부분의 사람들에게 이러한 판단은 의심할 여지가 없고 확실해 보인다; 다르게 생각하는 사람이 틀린 것이다. 이런 식의 접근이 종종 강점으로 여겨지지만, 우리의 기준만이 타당하다고 믿는 것은 딜레마를 야기할 수 있다 우리의 개인적 기준을 근거에 두는 것의 핵심적인 문제는 모든 개인의 도덕적 평가는 본래 편향되어 있다는 점이다. 다시 말해, 우리의 평가는 세상에 대한 우리의 선입견에 기반하고 있어 마찬가지로 타당할 수도 있는 다른 관점을 고려하지 못한다. 이것이 우리가 불공평하거나 부당하게 되는 심각한 실수를 저지르지 않기 위해 단정적인 판단을 내리는 것은 피하고 대신 다른 사람들의 관점에서 상황을 보아야 하는 이유이다.

어휘 moral compass 도덕의 잣대 appraise 평가하다, 값을 매기다

finality 단호함, 결정적임 unquestionable 의심할 여지가 없는
valid 타당한, 정당한 by nature 본래, 천성적으로 biased 편향된
preconceived notion 선입견 conclusive 단정적인, 결정적인
unjust 부당한, 불공평한

구문분석

[13행] This is [why we must avoid making conclusive judgments but instead view a situation from the perspective of others **in order not to make** the serious mistake of being unfair or unjust].

→ [why ~ unjust]는 의문사 why가 이끄는 명사절로 be동사 is의 주격 보어 역할을 한다.

→ to부정사의 부정형은 to 앞에 not을 붙이며, 목적의 뜻을 분명히 하기 위해 not to make 앞에 in order가 쓰인 형태이다.

21 밑줄 의미 추론하기 정답 ④

해설 시각화할 때 신중하지 않으면, 그저 다른 현실을 상상하는 것인 백일몽에 빠질 위험이 있는데, 진정한 시각화는 일어났으면 하는 시나리오와 그것을 현실화하기 위해 해야 하는 구체적인 일을 모두 시각화하는 것이며, 이에 더해 그 일을 실제로 수행해야 한다고 말하고 있다. 따라서 글의 주제를 비유적으로 표현한 planting seeds that never grow(절대 자라지 않을 씨앗을 심고 있는)가 의미하는 것은 ④ '그들의 목표를 달성하기 위해 행동에 옮기지 못하는 것'이다.

오답분석 ①, ⑤은 글에서 언급된 내용이 아니다. ②은 일어났으면 하는 시나리오와 그것을 실현하기 위해 해야 하는 구체적인 일들을 모두 시각화해야 한다는 글의 내용과 반대되는 내용을 다루고 있으므로 오답이다. ③의 현실적인 목표 설정은 글에서 언급된 내용이 아니다.

해석 많은 경우, 자신이 시각화를 연습하고 있다고 생각하는 사람들은 사실 절대 자라지 않을 씨앗을 심고 있다. 미래에 당신이 이루고 싶은 것을 상상하는 일은 성공의 중요한 요소이다. 작가 Napoleon Hill(나폴레온 힐)이 말했듯, 이 기법은 "뇌를 한 사람의 지배적인 생각, 목표 그리고 목적에 대응하는 것들을 끌어당기는 전자석과 같은 것으로 전환시킨다." 그러나 당신이 신중하지 않으면, 백일몽이라고 알려진 활동에 끌려들 위험이 있는데, 이는 그저 다른 현실을 상상하는 것이다. 당신이 달성하고 싶은 것에 탐내듯이 열광하는 것은 생산적이지 않을뿐더러, 당신이 당신의 목표를 이행할 가능성을 낮게 만든다. 대신 당신은 일어났으면 하는 시나리오와 그것이 일어나기 위해 당신이 해야 하는 구체적인 일들을 모두 시각화하도록 확실하게 할 필요가 있다. 그리고 당신의 꿈이 현실이 되도록 이 일들을 실제로 수행하도록 하라.

① 그들의 생각을 지배하는 부정적인 생각을 하는 것
② 자신들의 상상을 이용하는 것을 멈추는 것
③ 현실적인 목표를 세울 가능성 줄이는 것
④ 그들의 목표를 달성하기 위해 행동에 옮기지 못하는 것
⑤ 그들 자신을 시시한 환상으로 제한하는 것

어휘 visualization 시각화 convert 전환시키다
equivalent ~와 같은 것, 등가물 electromagnet 전자석
counterpart 대응하는 것 dominating 지배적인
run the risk of ~할 위험이 있다 daydreaming 백일몽
wistfully 탐내듯이, 아쉬운 듯이 fanaticize 열광하다 carry out 이행하다
[선택지] take action 행동에 옮기다 uninspiring 시시한

구문분석

[13행] Instead, you need to ensure that you visualize **both** ①[the scenario that you want to occur] **and** ②[the specific things you must do for it to happen].

→ ①[the ~ occur]와 ②[the ~ happen]은 상관접속사 both A and B로 연결된 병렬 구조이다.

22 요지 파악하기 정답 ⑤

해설 글의 후반부에 부모가 아이에게 짜증을 느끼는 것은 아이 자체를 싫어하는 게 아니라 아이의 행동을 싫어하는 자연스러운 반응이니 죄책감을 가지지 않아도 된다는 요지가 제시되어 있으므로, 이 글의 요지로 가장 적절한 것은 ⑤이다.

해석 자신의 아이들을 아무리 많이 사랑하더라도, 어떤 부모든 아이들이 정말 짜증나는 순간들이 있다는 사실을 증언할 수 있다. 아마 그것은 그날에만 다섯 번째 짜증을 내는 3살짜리이거나, 그들의 집안일을 하기를 거부하는 10대일 수 있다. 이유가 무엇이든, 부모들은 너무 화가 나서 그들이 자신의 아이들을 실제로 싫어하는 건 아닌지 의심하기 시작해서 엄청난 죄책감으로 이어지게 된다. 그들은 이러한 감정이 무조건적으로 그들의 아이들을 사랑하는 그들의 당연한 의무와 모순된다고 여긴다. 그럼에도 불구하고 이는 지극히 자연스러운 반응이다. 부끄러워하는 대신에, 정신과 의사들은 부모가 그런 감정은 아이들 자체보다는 특정 행동에 대한 반응일 뿐이라는 것을 알아야 한다고 충고한다. 즉, 그 감정은 "내 아이가 싫다"가 아니라 "내 아이가 하는 행동이 싫다"를 의미한다. 이에 유념하는 것은 부모들이 진정하고 그런 감정은 행동만큼이나 일시적일 것이라는 걸 받아들이게 해줄 것이다.

어휘 attest 증언하다, 입증하다 infuriating 짜증 나는
exasperated 몹시 화가 난 tremendous 엄청난
contradict 모순되다 natural 당연한, 자연스러운
unconditionally 무조건적으로, 절대적으로 psychiatrist 정신과 의사

구문분석

[1행] [**No matter how** much someone loves their children], any parent can attest to the fact that ~

→ [No ~ children]은 no matter how(아무리 ~하더라도)가 이끄는 양보의 부사절이다.

[18행] ~ accept that such emotions will be **as temporary as** the behavior.

→ 'as + 원급 + as'는 원급을 이용한 비교구문으로 '···만큼 ~한/하게'라는 의미이다.

23 주제 파악하기 정답 ③

해설 첫 두 문장과 마지막 문장으로 미루어 보아 공간적 사고 능력은 진정한 이해를 돕는 지적 작용을 수반하기 때문에 학생들이 연습을 통해 공간적 사고 능력을 발달시키는 것이 필요하다는 내용의 글이다. 따라서 이 글의 주제로 가장 적절한 것은 ③ '학생들의 공간적 사고 능력을 발달시키는 것의 중요성'이다.

오답분석 ①은 글의 핵심 소재 spatial thinking을 사용하여 헷갈리게 하는 오답이다. ④, ⑤은 글의 일부만을 다루고 있는 오답이다.

해석 GPS 기반의 도구들이 더 널리 보급됨에 따라, 공간적 사고 능력이 저하되고 있음을 보여주는 증거가 증가하고 있다. 단순히 모르는 장소의 길을 찾는 능력을 제공하는 것 이상으로, 공간적 사고는 진정한 이해를 돕는 지적 작용을 수반한다; 그것은 물리적 환경을 우리가 실제로 경험하는 것과 연결하는, 즉 새로운 각도와 관점에서 세상을 시각화하는 방법이다. 오늘날의 학생들 사이에서 공간적 사고 능력을 함양하는 것은 교육자들이 단순히 그들에게 장소가 어디에 있는지에 대한 느슨한 이해를 제공하는 것을 넘어설 것을 요구한다. 대신

에, 학생들은 지리학적 표현들(지도, 지구본, 도표)을 이해하고 그들이 찾은 정보를 수집하고 정리하여, 그것을 지도 내에서나 기술의 이용을 통해 재해석해야 한다. 연습을 통해, 그들은 지리학 분야에서 문제들을 해결하고 결정을 내리는 데에 필수적인 중요한 기술들을 습득하는 동시에, 위치 간의 관계를 더잘 이해하고 공간적 패턴의 심상을 형성하는 수단을 갖게 될 것이다.

① 다양한 학문 분야에서의 공간적 사고의 응용
② 새로운 기술들의 지리학 수업으로의 통합
③ 학생들의 공간적 사고 능력을 발달시키는 것의 중요성
④ GPS 기반 장치가 학생들의 지적 능력에 미치는 영향
⑤ 학생들의 공간적 추리력 저하의 원인들

 어휘 mounting 증가하는 spatial thinking 공간적 사고 navigate 길을 찾다
representation 표현 [선택지] discipline 학문 분야
deterioration 저하, 하락 reasoning 추리력, 추론

구문분석
[9행] ~ educators go beyond just giving them a loose understanding **of** [where places are].

→ [where ~ are]는 의문사 where가 이끄는 명사절로 전치사 of의 목적어 역할을 한다.

[14행] With practice, they will acquire the tools to better understand relationships between locations and form mental images of spatial patterns [**while** gaining vital skills necessary for solving problems and making decisions in the field of geography].

→ [while ~ geography]는 분사구문의 의미를 분명하게 하기 위해 부사절 접속사(while)가 분사 앞에 온 형태이다.

24 제목 파악하기   정답 ②

해설 글의 도입부에서 나트륨이 부족하면 "나트륨 식욕" 신경 세포를 자극하여 우리가 음식에서 나트륨을 찾게 만든다고 했다. 또한, 글의 마지막 세 문장으로 미루어 보아 소금의 맛을 감각하는 것이 나트륨 식욕 신경 세포의 억제에 필수적인 역할을 한다는 내용의 글로, 염분을 핥아서 맛보았을 때는 나트륨 식욕 신경 세포가 둔화되었지만 다른 방식으로 나트륨을 주입했을 때는 신경 억제가 일어나지 않았다고 설명하고 있다. 따라서 글의 제목으로 가장 적절한 것은 ② '신경 세포들과 소금 간의 관계'이다.

오답분석 ①, ④은 글의 일부만을 다루고 있는 오답이다. ③은 글에서 음식을 갈망하는 것이 아니라 소금을 갈망하는것과 신경 세포들 간의 관계에 대해 말하고 있으므로 오답이다. ⑤의 나트륨 식욕 신경 세포를 조작하는 것의 이점은 글에서 언급되고 있지 않다.

해석 나트륨을 과다 섭취하는 것의 위험들은 잘 알려져 있지만, 이 이온은 중대한 목표에 기여한다: 우리가 살아 있게 하는 것이다. 우리는 근육과 신경 기능을 유지하고 체액의 농도를 조절하기 위해 그것을 필요로 하기 때문에, 그것이 부족한 것은 "나트륨 식욕" 신경 세포들을 자극하여 우리가 음식에서 그것을 찾게 만든다. 무엇이 소금에 대한 우리의 욕구를 몰아붙이는지 더 알아보기 위해, Caltech 연구원들이 쥐의 뇌에 있는 나트륨 식욕 신경 세포를 조작했는데, 그것은 그 동물들이 만족할 때까지 암염을 핥게 했다. 연구원들은 쥐의 나트륨 식욕 신경 세포들의 활동이 그들의 혀에 나트륨이 닿은 몇 초 내에 둔화되었음을 발견했다. 그들이 이후에 나트륨을 쥐의 위에 직접적으로 주입하거나 혀에 있는 짠맛 수용기를 억제하는 약물을 사용했을 때, 그들은 신경 억제가 일어나지 않았음을 발견했다. 이는 소금을 맛볼 수 있다는 것은 나트륨 식욕 신경 세포의 억제에 필수적인 역할을 한다는 것을 나타낸다.

① 우리가 생각하는 것만큼 소금이 정말로 건강에 해로운가?

② 신경 세포들과 소금 간의 관계
③ 과도한 음식에 대한 갈망 이면의 주요한 원인
④ 미각: 그것을 억제하는 것이 어떻게 나트륨에 대한 갈망을 높이는가
⑤ 나트륨 식욕 신경 세포들을 조작하는 것이 어떻게 우리에게 도움이 될 수 있는가

 어휘 sodium 나트륨 fluid 체액, 유동체 level (체액의) 농도, 수준
be low on ~이 부족하다, 얼마 안 남다 appetite 식욕, 욕구
neuron 신경 세포, 뉴런 lick 핥다 rock salt 암염 infuse 주입하다
receptor 수용기, 감각 기관 integral 필수적인, 완전한

구문분석
[3행] Because we require it ①[to maintain muscle and nerve function and regulate fluid levels], being low on it triggers "sodium-appetite" neurons, ②[compelling us to seek it out from food].

→ ①[to ~ levels]는 to부정사의 부사적 용법으로 목적을 의미한다.

→ ②[compelling ~ food]는 연속동작을 나타내는 분사구문으로, 분사구문의 주어가 주절의 주어(being low on it)와 같아서 생략되었다.

[7행] ~ Caltech researchers manipulated the sodium-appetite neurons in the brains of mice, [which prompted the animals to lick rock salt until they were satisfied].

→ 앞에 나온 절 전체를 받는 [which ~ satisfied]는 주격 관계대명사 which가 이끄는 관계대명사절로, 콤마 뒤에서 계속적 용법으로 쓰였다.

25 도표 정보 파악하기   정답 ④

해설 2019년 북아메리카의 목화 생산량의 비율은 16.7퍼센트로, 아프리카, 유럽, 오세아니아의 비율을 합친 9퍼센트의 두 배인 18퍼센트보다 작으므로 수치의 비교 표현이 잘못 반영되었다. 따라서 도표의 내용과 일치하지 않는 것은 ④이다.

해석
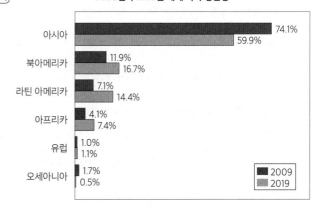

2009년과 2019년 세계 목화 생산량

위의 그래프는 2009년과 2019년 지역별 세계 목화 생산량을 보여준다. ① 2009년에서 2019년 사이에 목화 생산량의 비율이 감소한 유일한 두 지역은 아시아와 오세아니아였다. ② 아시아는 2009년에서 2019년 사이에 세계 목화 생산량의 비율에서 가장 큰 감소를 보였지만, 2019년 목화 생산량에서 1위에 머물렀다. ③ 라틴 아메리카는 2009년과 2019년 모두 세 번째로 목화 생산량이 많은 지역이었고, 2019년 목화 생산량의 비율은 2009년의 그것(목화 생산량의 비율)의 두 배 이상이었다. ④ 2019년, 북아메리카의 목화 생산량의 비율은 아프리카, 유럽 그리고 오세아니아의 비율을 합친 것의 두 배만큼 높았다. ⑤ 모든 지역 가운데 유럽은 2009년 목화 생산량의 비율과 2019년의 그것(목화 생산량의 비율) 사이에 가장 작은 차이가 있었다.

어휘 cotton 목화, 면 region 지역

구문분석
[5행] [**Even though** Asia showed the biggest decrease in the percentage of global cotton production from 2009 to 2019], it remained in first place in ~

→ [Even ~ 2019]은 even though(비록 ~하지만)가 이끄는 양보의 부사절이다.

[11행] In 2019, the percentage of cotton production in North America was [twice as high as] the combined percentage of Africa, Europe, and Oceania.

→ [twice ~ as]는 '배수사 + as + 원급 + as'(~보다 몇 배 더 -한)의 형태로 비교를 나타내는 구문이다.

26 세부 정보 파악하기 정답 ④

해설 Sapir accepted a position at the Canadian National Museum as the head anthropologist를 통해 Edward Sapir가 수석 인류학자 자리를 받아들였음을 알 수 있는데, ④은 그 자리를 거절했다고 일부 정보를 잘못 나타냈으므로 글의 내용과 일치하지 않는 것은 ④이다.

해석 Edward Sapir(에드워드 사피어)는 가장 권위 있는 미국 언어학자 중 한 명으로 널리 알려져 있다. 독일에서 태어나, Sapir는 1890년 미국으로 이전하기 전에 그의 가족과 함께 1888년에 영국으로 이주했다. Sapir는 컬럼비아 대학교에 다녔고 마침내 박사 학위를 취득했다. 이 기관에서 언어학과 인류학을 연구하는 동안, Sapir는 그 대륙 토착민들의 언어에 대한 그의 흥미를 자극한 한 세미나에 참여했다. 졸업 후 몇 년 동안 그는 컬럼비아 대학교와 펜실베이니아 대학교의 아메리카 원주민 언어에 관한 연구 프로젝트에 참여했다. 1910년에 Sapir는 캐나다 국립 박물관의 수석 인류학자 자리를 받아들였다. 그가 현대 연구자들에게 계속해서 영향을 미치는 언어와 문화의 관계에 초점을 맞춘 학제간 접근법을 개발함에 따라, 언어학과 인류학 둘 다에서의 그의 경험이 그의 유산을 형성했다.

어휘 relocate 이전하다 linguistics 언어학 anthropology 인류학
indigenous 토착의 head 수석의 legacy 유산
interdisciplinary 학제간의(여러 학문 분야가 관련된)

구문분석
[15행] ~ as he developed **an interdisciplinary approach** ①[that focused on the **relationship between language and culture**] ②[that continues to influence modern researchers].

→ ①[that ~ culture]는 선행사 an interdisciplinary approach를 수식하는 관계대명사절이고, ②[that ~ researchers]는 선행사 relationship between language and culture를 수식하는 관계대명사절이다.

27 안내문 정보 파악하기 정답 ⑤

해설 The winner will be awarded a trophy at the ribbon-cutting ceremony를 통해 우승자는 트로피를 받는다는 것을 알 수 있으므로, 글의 내용과 일치하지 않는 것은 ⑤이다.

해석
도시공원 이름 짓기 공모전
새로운 도시공원이 막 공사를 마쳤고 5월 15일에 모든 사람들에게 공개될 예정입니다. 개장을 기념하여 이름 짓기 공모전을 엽니다. Fairfield 주민들이 우리의 아름다운 새 공원에 무슨 이름을 붙일지를 결정할 것입니다!

응모작 제출:
• 한 명당 응모작 한 개
• 기호를 포함해서는 안 됨
• 우리 웹사이트(www.cparkname.com)에서 3월 1일부터 3월 31일까지

투표:
이름 짓기 위원회가 최상위 응모작 5개를 골라 투표를 위해 웹사이트에 게시할 것입니다. 투표는 4월 20일부터 5월 5일까지 실시될 것입니다.

우승자:
• 한 명의 우승자만 있을 것입니다.
• 우승자는 개장식에서 트로피를 받을 것입니다.

어휘 construction 공사 in honor of ~을 기념하여 entry 응모작
submission 제출 ribbon-cutting ceremony 개장식, 개관식

구문분석
[4행] The residents of Fairfield **will decide** [what to name our beautiful new park]!
　　　　　　　　　　　　　　　　　　　　　　의문사 to부정사

→ 명사절 [what ~ park]는 동사 will decide의 목적어 역할을 하며, '무엇(동사) 할지'라는 의미의 'what + to부정사' 구문이다.

28 안내문 정보 파악하기 정답 ③

해설 수치가 포함된 부분인 5 hours of playback time on a full charge를 통해 완충 시 5시간 동안 사용할 수 있음을 알 수 있으므로, 글의 내용과 일치하는 것은 ③이다.

해석
Arrow Pro 무선 블루투스 스피커
사용 방법:
1. 스피커를 완전히 충전한다.
2. 전원 버튼을 한 번 눌러서 켠다.
3. 파란색 블루투스 버튼을 누른다.
4. 당신의 기기에 Arrow Pro 앱을 다운로드한다.
5. 앱을 열어서 Arrow Pro와 동기화한다.

특징:
- 스마트폰 및 태블릿과 호환 가능
- 완충 시 5시간의 재생 시간
- 스피커는 20분 뒤에 대기 모드에 들어감

주의 사항:
- 방수가 되지 않습니다. 액체류를 멀리하세요.
- 제품에서 불꽃이 일어난다면 즉시 사용을 멈추세요.

* 품질 보증 기간은 1년입니다. 이 기간 이후에는 수리 비용이 청구될 것입니다.

어휘 sync with ~와 동기화하다 compatible 호환 가능한 playback 재생
standby mode 대기 모드 warranty period 품질 보증 기간

구문분석
[16행] After this period, you [will be charged] for repairs.

→ [will ~ charged]는 조동사(will)가 있는 '조동사 + be + p.p.' 형태의 수동태이다.

29 어법상 틀린 것 찾기 정답 ⑤

[해설] 주어 They(Plaintiffs)가 order가 나타내는 수임료 지불을 '명령하는' 행위의 주체가 아닌 명령받는 대상이므로 ⑤의 order를 수동태 be ordered로 고쳐야 한다.

[오답 분석] ①은 조건을 나타내는 부사절의 동사 자리이므로 미래의 의미를 나타내기 위해 미래시제 대신에 현재시제 fails를 사용한 것은 어법상 적절하다. ②은 뒤에 완전한 절이 이어지고 있고 의미상 '~ 때문에'라는 의미가 되는 것이 자연스러우므로, 부사절 접속사 as를 사용한 것은 어법상 적절하다. ③은 주절에 충고의 의미를 가진 형용사 necessary가 쓰여 '~해야 한다'는 당위성의 의미를 나타낼 때 뒤에 이어지는 that절의 동사는 '(should) + 동사원형'의 형태로 쓰이므로 should를 생략한 동사원형 begin을 사용한 것은 어법상 적절하다. ④은 뒤에 주어 없이 동사가 바로 왔고, 관계절이 수식하는 선행사 Plaintiffs가 사람을 가리키는 명사이므로, 주격 관계대명사 who가 온 것이 적절하다.

[해석] 1980년 제한법에 따르면, 분쟁 해결을 모색하는 원고는 알맞은 공소 시효 내에 소송을 제기해야 한다. 원고가 공소 시효 내에 법원 소송 절차를 개시하지 못하면, 원고는 재정적인 결과를 마주할 것이다. 신체적 상해는 공소 시효가 3년인 반면 임대료 회수는 6년인 등 소송 제기의 각 유형에 따라 다른 공소 시효가 있으므로, 특정 사건의 공소 시효를 명확히 하는 것이 중요한데, 특히 공소 시효는 변경될 수 있기 때문이다. 이 때문에 모든 공소 시효는 분쟁을 야기한 행위가 발생한 시점으로부터 시작한다는 점을 명심해야 한다. 사건의 공소 시효가 만료되고 소송을 제기한 원고는 그렇게 하는 것이 자동적으로 피고에 유리한 판결로 이어질 것이므로 자신이 실수를 했다는 걸 알게 될 것이다. 그들은 또한 자신의 수임료를 이미 지불한 것에 더해 피고의 수임료를 지불할 것을 명령받을 수도 있다.

[어휘] act 법령 plaintiff 원고, 고소인 resolution 해결 dispute 분쟁 file a claim 소송을 제기하다 limitation period 공소 시효 initiate 개시하다 proceeding 소송 절차 complaint 소송 제기 personal injury 신체적 상해 rent recovery 임대료 회수 ruling 판결 in one's favor ~에 유리하게 legal fee 수임료, 변호사 비용

[구문 분석]
[11행] To this end, it is necessary [to keep in mind that all
　　　　　　　　　　　　가주어
limitation periods begin from the time ((when) the action that
　　　　　　　　　　　　　　진주어(to부정사구)
caused the dispute arises)].

→ 가주어 it이 길이가 긴 진주어 to부정사구 [to ~ arises] 대신에 주어 자리에 쓰인 형태이다.

→ (the ~ arises)는 관계부사 when이 생략된 관계부사절로, 선행사 the time을 수식한다.

30 어휘 적절성 파악하기 정답 ③

[해설] (A) 시간 압박을 받아 급하게 결정을 내려야 한다고 느끼는 사람은 쉽게 영향을 받고 덜 엄격하다는 의미가 되어야 하므로 rigid(엄격한)가 문맥상 적절하다

(B) 빨리 자동차를 사야 하는 상황을 판매원이 알아차린다면 적게 할인을 받고 그 좋지 않은 거래를 받아들이게 될 가능성이 높다는 의미가 되어야 하므로 accepting(받아들이는)이 문맥상 적절하다.

(C) 시간 압박을 받는 것은 불리한 조건이기 때문에 유리한 입장에서 협상을 하려면 이 정보는 감추는 것이 가장 좋다는 의미가 되어야 하므로 conceal(감추다)이 문맥상 적절하다.

따라서 정답으로 가장 적절한 것은 ③이다.

[오답 분석] (A)의 flexible, (B)의 rejecting, (C)의 disclose는 모두 정답 어휘와 문맥상 반대되는 의미이므로 오답이다.

[해석] 현명한 협상가들이 우위를 차지하기 위해 이용하는 한 방법은 시간 압박을 가하는 것이다. 사람들이 급하게 결정을 내려야 한다고 느낄 때 더 쉽게 영향을 받고 덜 (A) 엄격하다는 것이 드러났다. 가능한 한 빨리 새로운 자동차를 구입해야 하는 것을 생각해 보자. 만약 판매원이 이를 알아차린다면, 큰 할인을 받는 대신 적은 할인을 받을 가능성이 높고, 마찬가지로 좋지 못한 거래를 강제로 (B) 받아들이게 될 가능성도 높다. 시간 압박을 받는 것은 불리하므로, 당신이 유리한 입장에서 협상을 할 수 있도록 이 정보는 (C) 감추는 것이 가장 좋다. 만약 반대편도 어떤 시간 제약을 받고 있다고 확신한다면, 당신은 이를 이용해야 한다. 어느 협상에서든 시간 압박의 요인을 알아봄으로써, 당신은 더 나은 거래를 달성하거나 교착 상태가 발생했을 때 극복하기 위해 그것을 성공적으로 이용할 수 있을 것이다.

	(A)	(B)	(C)
①	엄격한	거부하는	밝히다
②	융통성 있는	받아들이는	감추다
③	엄격한	받아들이는	감추다
④	융통성 있는	거부하는	감추다
⑤	엄격한	받아들이는	밝히다

[어휘] negotiator 협상가, 교섭가 rigid 엄격한, 완고한 flexible 융통성 있는 inferior 좋지 못한, 열등한 disadvantage 불리, 약점 disclose 밝히다, 드러내다 conceal 감추다 position of strength 유리한 입장 time constraint 시간 제약 take advantage of ~을 이용하다

[구문 분석]
[1행] One method that smart negotiators use to gain an advantage **is** [to apply time pressure].

→ [to ~ pressure]는 to부정사의 명사적 용법(~하는 것)으로, be동사 is의 주격 보어 역할(~하는 것)을 한다.

[10행] ~ it's best to conceal this information [**so** (that) you can negotiate from a position of strength].

→ [so ~ strength]는 목적을 나타내는 부사절로, 접속사 so that(~하기 위해서)에서 that이 생략된 형태로 쓰였다.

[15행] ~, you may be able to employ it successfully to reach a better deal or overcome an impasse [should one arise].

→ [should one arise]는 if를 생략하고 주어와 조동사가 도치되어 '조동사(should) + 주어(one) + 동사(arise)'의 어순으로 쓰인 조건의 부사절이다.

31 빈칸 추론하기 정답 ③

[해설] 신비평은 글과 외부 요인의 관계를 중시하는 문학의 전통적 해석에 반대하여, 문학 작품의 가치는 글 그 자체에 담겨 있다고 본다는 내용의 글이다. 주제와 관련된 빈칸 문장에서 작가에게 '무엇'을 직접 물어보지 않는 한 밝혀질 수 없다고 하고 있고, 빈칸 뒤 문장에서 작가에게 그들이 쓴 것을 왜 썼는지를 직접 물어볼 수 있다고 해도 그 글은 그 자체로 가치를 지니기 때문에 중요하지 않다고 하였다. 따라서 빈칸에는 ③ '의도'가 와서 작가의 의도는 직접 물어보지 않는 한 밝혀질 수 없다는 의미가 되어야 한다.

[해석] 신비평 선구자 John Crowe Ransom(존 크로 랜섬)과 Cleanth Brooks(크린스 브룩스)는 그들이 느끼기에 그 글의 역사, 그리고 작가의 배경, 비교 자료 또는 역사적 맥락 등의 외부 요인과의 관계에 지나치게 초점이 맞춰져 있는 문

학의 전통적 해석에 기꺼이 맞서고자 했다. 대신, 그들은 "자세히 읽기"를 옹호했는데, 그것에서 작품은 그 자체로 성립되므로 작품에 대한 분석이 행해졌다. 신비평가들은 작가의 <u>의도</u>는 그나 그녀에게 그것이 무엇인지 직접 물어보지 않는 한 밝혀질 수 없다고 생각했고, 이는 어떤 작품을 해석할 때 그것(작가의 의도)을 고려하는 것을 무의미하게 만든다. 비록 그들(신비평가들)이 작가에게 그들이 쓴 것을 왜 썼는지 물어볼 수 있다고 하더라도, 그 글은 그 자체의 가치를 지니기 때문에 그것은 중요하지 않다. 그것은 작가가 원래 의도한 것과 별개로 다른 의미 혹은 의의를 가질 수도 있다. 달리 말해, 신비평가들에게 문학 작품의 가치는 전적으로 그 글 그 자체 안에 담겨 있는 것으로 여겨져야 한다.

① 재능
② 태도
③ 의도
④ 전문성
⑤ 신뢰성

[어휘] New Criticism 신(新)비평 pioneer 선구자 go up against ~에 맞서다 reading 해석, 읽기 comparative 비교의 champion 옹호하다 determine 밝히다, 알아내다 piece 작품 merit 가치, 훌륭함 conceive 여기다, 생각하다 [선택지] expertise 전문성 credibility 신뢰성, 믿을 수 있음

[구문분석]
[2행] ~ go up against **traditional readings of literature** [that (they felt) focused too heavily on the history of the text and its relation to external factors — the author's background, comparative sources, or historical context].

→ [that ~ context]는 선행사 traditional readings of literature를 수식하며 주격 관계대명사 that이 이끄는 관계대명사절이다.

→ (they felt)는 관계대명사 that 바로 뒤에 '주어 + 동사'가 삽입된 형태이다.

[12행] Even if they were able to <u>ask</u> <u>the author</u> [<u>why they wrote what they wrote</u>], it should not matter because ~
(동사 / 간접 목적어 / 직접 목적어)

→ [why ~ wrote]은 의문사 why가 이끄는 명사절로, 동사 ask의 직접 목적어 역할을 한다.

32 빈칸 추론하기   정답 ④

[해설] Frida Kahlo가 환상적 사실주의를 통해 자신의 삶에서 겪은 신체적·정신적 고통을 그녀의 예술 작품에 고스란히 담았다는 내용의 글이고, 빈칸 앞 부분에서 그녀의 그림에 드러난 고통이 사람들에게 깊은 반향을 불러일으키고, 그녀의 사생활은 작품과 뗄 수 없으며, 작품 속 상상력과 더불어 그녀의 작품들은 단지 기억으로만 증류될 수 없다고 하였다. 따라서 주제와 관련된 빈칸에는 ④ '비극적 현실과 환상을 하나로 엮어 낼'이 와야 한다.

[오답분석] ①은 그림 속에 Frida Kahlo의 신체적·정신적 고통이 표현되어 있다는 글의 내용과 반대되는 내용이므로 오답이다. ②은 Frida Kahlo의 그림이 고통을 겪은 이들에게 깊은 반향을 불러일으켰다고 했을 뿐 다른 사람들의 고통을 덜어준다는 내용은 언급되고 있지 않으므로 오답이다. ③, ⑤은 글의 내용과 관련이 없다.

[해석] 정식 교육을 받은 적이 없는 Frida Kahlo(프리다 칼로)의 예술은 그녀가 개척한 일종의 원시적인 환상적 사실주의를 이용한다. 이 독창적인 표현법은 그녀의 가장 잊히지 않는 작품들 중 일부에서 드러나 있는데, 그 중에서 그녀는 소아마비와 버스 사고로 인해 그녀가 겪은 만성적인 고통을 표현한 그녀 몸의 자화상을 가장 많이 그렸다. Kahlo의 작품들은 또한 정신적 고통에서 유래했다. 멕시코의 정치적 혼란, 남편과의 결별 그리고 그녀 삶의 다른 주요 사건들

이 그녀의 손을 캔버스로 이끌었다. 이와 같이 그녀의 예술 작품은 고통받는 이들에게 너무 잘 전해져서, 그녀의 조국인 멕시코에서 그녀는 "고통의 영웅"으로 일컬어진다. 그녀의 그림에 분명히 드러난 고통은 자신의 삶에서 고난을 겪었던 사람들에게 깊은 반향을 불러일으킨다. 이는 그녀의 사생활을 그녀의 작품과 뗄 수 없게 만들었다. 그러나 그녀의 작품들에게 불어넣어졌던 상상력 때문에, Kahlo의 작품들은 단지 기억으로만 전락해 증류될 수 없다. 그녀의 유산은 그녀가 얼마나 아름답게 비극적 현실과 환상을 하나로 엮어 낼 수 있었는지를 보여주는 증거이다.

① 예술을 창조하기 위해 고통을 억누를
② 다른 사람들의 고통을 덜어 줄
③ 전통적인 회화 스타일을 재정립할
④ 비극적 현실과 환상을 하나로 엮어 낼
⑤ 그녀 주변 사람들을 현실적으로 묘사할

[어휘] naïve 원시적인, 순진한 magical realism 환상적 사실주의 pioneer 개척하다 haunting 잊히지 않는 self-portrait 자화상 chronic 만성적인 speak (감정·의견 등을) 전하다 torment 고통, 괴로움 inextricable 뗄 수 없는 imbue with ~에게 불어넣다 distill 증류하다 testament 증거 [선택지] suppress 억누르다 suffering 고통 redefine 재정립하다 weave 엮다 tragic 비극적인 depict 묘사하다

[구문분석]
[10행] As such, in her native land of Mexico, she is referred to as "the heroine of pain," [**so well** <u>does</u> <u>her artwork</u> <u>speak</u>] to others who suffer.
(조동사 / 주어 / 동사)

→ 부사구 so well이 강조되어 절의 맨 앞에 나왔기 때문에, 주어와 조동사가 도치되어 '조동사(does) + 주어(her artwork) + 동사(speak)'의 어순으로 쓰였다.

33 빈칸 추론하기   정답 ②

[해설] 지구에서는 대부분의 생명체가 산소에 의존하며 살아가지만 이와 달리 다른 행성에서는 산소가 아닌 기체, 예를 들면 수소로 구성된 대기에서도 생명체가 살 수 있는 가능성이 있다는 내용의 글이다. 주제문에 해당하는 빈칸 문장에서 다른 행성의 생명체가 산소 대기에 의존하는 지구의 생물 형태 대부분과 '어떨' 가능성이 있다고 하고, 글의 후반부에서 산소가 없는 수소로 구성된 대기에서 살아남은 박테리아를 예로 들고 있다. 따라서 빈칸에는 ② '~과 다른 화학적 성질을 가질'이라는 내용이 오는 것이 적절하다.

[오답분석] ①, ⑤은 글의 내용과 관련이 없다. ③은 수소 등 다른 기체에 의존하는 생물 형태의 예시를 들고 있는 글의 내용에 부합하지 않는 내용이므로 오답이다. ④은 지구와 달리 산소가 없는 수소 대기에서 살아남는 생물 형태의 가능성을 말하는 글의 내용과 반대되는 내용이므로 오답이다.

[해석] 태양계외 행성이라 알려진, 다른 항성 주위를 궤도를 그리며 도는 행성에서의 생명체 발견은 그 대기의 분석을 통해 일어날 가능성이 가장 크다. 행성을 둘러싼 기체는 그것이 지구에 사는 생명체와 비슷한 생명체를 지속시킬 수 있는지 여부를 보여 줄 수 있다. 그러나, 다른 행성의 생명체가 지구의 산소 대기에 의존하는 지구의 생물 형태 대부분과 다른 화학적 성질을 가질 가능성이 항상 있다. 예를 들어 수소로 구성된 대기도 상상컨대 생명체를 지속시킬 수 있다. 우리의 행성에 있는 박테리아(여러 가지 '대장균')는 산소가 없는 수소 대기에서 살아남아 번식할 수 있는 능력을 보여주었고, 이 박테리아의 산물은 이 환경에서 생명체 흔적 혹은 생명체에 대한 증거의 역할을 할 수 있는 여러 기체를 만들어 낸다. 수소는 또한 액체를 특징으로 할 만큼 충분히 행성을 따뜻하게 유지할 가능성이 있으므로 생명체도 그렇다. 이는 다른 행성에서 생명체를 찾는 일의 범위를 넓힌다.

① ~에 동일한 특성을 적용시킬

② ~과 다른 화학적 성질을 가질
③ ~과 달리 기체에 의존하지 않을
④ ~과 같은 환경에 살고 있을
⑤ ~에 의해 진전된 연구의 혜택을 받을

[어휘] **orbit** ~ 주위를 궤도를 그리며 돌다 **exoplanet** 태양계외 행성
atmosphere 대기 **gas** 기체 **support** 지속시키다, 유지하다
organism 생명체 **conceivably** 상상컨대
bacterium 박테리아(**bacteria**의 단수형)
E. coli 대장균(Escherichia coli) **multiply** 번식하다
devoid of ~이 없는 **biosignature** 생명체 흔적
[선택지] **chemistry** 화학적 성질 **inhabit** 살다, 서식하다

[구문분석]
[3행] The gases that surround the planet can **indicate** [if it is able to support life similar to that on Earth].
→ [if ~ Earth]는 접속사 if가 이끄는 명사절로, 동사 indicate의 목적어 역할을 한다.

[10행] A bacterium on our own planet (a variety of *E. coli*) has demonstrated **the capability** [of surviving and multiplying in a hydrogen atmosphere devoid of oxygen], ~
→ [of ~ oxygen]은 the capability와 동격을 이루는 명사구이다.

34 빈칸 추론하기   정답 ⑤

[해설] 얼굴 표정은 다른 사람들을 관찰하고 습득하는 것이 아니라 주어진 상황에 반응하는 자연스러운 방법이라는 내용의 글이고, 글의 후반에서 올림픽 메달 수여식에서 눈이 보이지 않는 선수들이 앞을 볼 수 있는 선수들과 똑같이 미소를 보였다는 것을 예시로 들고 있다. 따라서, 빈칸에는 ⑤ '그들에게 아마도 선천적인 능력이 있었을 것이다'가 와서 눈이 보이지 않는 선수들에게 보고 배우지 않아도 미소를 보일 수 있는 선천적인 능력이 있었을 것이라는 의미가 되어야 한다.

[오답분석] ①은 글의 내용과 관련이 없다. ②은 글의 핵심 소재 facial expressions를 사용하여 헷갈리게 하는 오답이다. ③, ④은 얼굴 표정은 배우는 것이 아니라 선천적인 것이라는 글의 내용과 반대되는 내용이므로 오답이다.

[해석] 놀람을 나타내는 올라간 눈썹에서부터 만족을 드러내는 환한 미소까지 얼굴 표정은 감정을 전달한다. 이는 사회적으로 적절한 감정을 드러내기 위해 사람들이 다른 사람들에 대한 주의 깊은 관찰을 통해 습득하는 행동인 것처럼 보일 수도 있지만, 얼굴 표정은 사실상 주어진 상황에 반응하는 자연스러운 방법이다. 우리의 유전자는 우리가 어떻게 느끼는지나 어떤 종류의 상황에 있는지에 따라 우리가 특정한 방식으로 얼굴 근육을 배치하게 한다. 메달 수여식 동안 올림픽 대회 출전 선수들의 얼굴의 모습을 비교한 한 연구는 눈이 보이지 않는 선수들과 앞을 볼 수 있는 선수들의 표정이 같은 사회적 상황에서 다르지 않음을 알아냈다. 은메달을 받는 눈이 보이지 않는 사람들과 앞을 볼 수 있는 사람들 모두 그들의 입 근육만 사용하는 예의 바른 미소를 보였다. 눈이 보이지 않는 선수들은 처음에 다른 사람들에게서 그 표정을 보고 배우지 않았을 것이며, 이는 그들에게 아마도 신천적인 능력이 있었을 것임을 보여준다.

① 의사소통이 언제나 구두로 되는 것은 아니다
② 얼굴 표정은 쉽게 바뀔 수 있다
③ 그들은 이 능력을 숙달하는 데에 큰 어려움에 직면했다
④ 그들이 다른 방법으로 그것을 익혀야 했을 것이다
⑤ 그들에게 아마도 선천적인 능력이 있었을 것이다

[어휘] **expression** 표정, 표현 **means** 방법, 수단 **arrange** 배치하다, 배열하다
sighted 앞을 볼 수 있는, 시력이 정상인 **context** 상황, 맥락

[선택지] **with ease** 쉽게, 용이하게 **innate** 선천적인, 타고난

[구문분석]
[13행] **Both blind and sighted individuals** [receiving silver medals] exhibited polite smiles that ~
→ 주어 Both ~ individuals는 현재분사구 [receiving silver medals] 의 수식을 받고 있다.

35 흐름과 관계 없는 문장 찾기   정답 ③

[해설] 같은 팀의 팬들이 함께 어울리고 다른 팀의 팬들보다 같은 팀의 팬들을 더 긍정적으로 평가하는 등 사람들이 내집단 편애 현상의 영향을 받는다는 내용의 글이다. 그런데 ③은 문화나 삶의 방식을 통해 사람들이 다른 사람들을 더 넓은 관점에서 인식하게 된다는 내용이므로 주제에서 벗어나 있어 글의 흐름과 무관하다.

[오답분석] ④의 They는 ②의 people을 가리키며, ②에 이어서 스포츠 팀에 대한 애정을 통해 집단 정체성을 부여받는다는 내용을 다루고 있으므로 ②과 연결된다. ⑤은 Therefore를 통해 ④의 내용에 대한 결과를 나타내고 있으므로 ④ 뒤에 이어지는 것이 적절하다.

[해석] 사회 심리학자들에 따르면, 사람들은 내집단 편애라고 알려진 현상에 영향을 받기 쉬운데, 이는 사람들이 그들 자신이 받아들인 정체성 관념을 더 잘 나타내는 다른 사람들을 편애한다는 것을 의미한다. ① 이것의 실제 예시는 스포츠 행사에서 같은 팀의 팬들은 다른 팀의 팬들과 어울리기보다는 모여 앉는 것과 같이 스포츠 팬들이 서로 잘 어울리는 방식에서 볼 수 있다. ② 개인적인 관계가 없음에도, 사람들은 그들이 선호하는 팀과 관련된 사람들을 그들이 동일한 문화 집단에 있기 때문에 더 긍정적으로 평가한다. (③ 문화 혹은 한 사회의 삶의 방식은 사람들이 더 넓은 관점에서 다른 사람을 인식하게 한다.) ④ 그들은 스포츠 팀에 대한 애정을 통해 집단 정체성을 부여받고, 이는 그들이 다른 팬들과 그들을 구분 짓는 것을 쉽게 만든다. ⑤ 따라서 이것은 또한 그들이 자신과 더 비슷하다고 여기는 특정 사람들을 향한 편애를 드러내는 것을 더 쉽게 만든다.

[어휘] **in-group favoritism** 내집단 편애 **reflect** 나타내다, 반영하다
practical 실제의 **consort** 어울리다 **evaluate** 평가하다
affiliate 관련되다 **perceive** 인식하다 **separate** 구분 짓다

[구문분석]
[15행] ~ and this has made it easy for them [to separate themselves from other fans].
가목적어 의미상 주어 진목적어(to부정사구)
→ 등위접속사 and 뒤에 나오는 절은 가목적어 it이 진목적어 to부정사구 [to ~ fans] 대신 동사(has made)의 목적어 자리에 쓰인 구조이며, to부정사의 의미상 주어가 'for + 목적격'의 형태로 쓰였다.

36 글의 순서 배열하기   정답 ③

[해설] 주어신 글은 게임 이론이 사회석 상황에서 경기사를의 의사 결정과 선탁을 이해하기 위한 이론적 틀이라는 주제를 제시한다. (B)의 Players ~ situations는 주어진 글의 competing parties ~ social situations를 의미하며, 이러한 상황에 있는 경기자들이 어떻게 해야 가장 유익한 결과를 얻는지 등 게임 이론에 대해 추가 설명하고 있으므로 주어진 글 바로 다음에 오는 것이 적절하다. (C)는 순접 연결어 for example을 통해 집을 사고 파는 상황에서 구매자와 현재 소유주에게 가장 유익한 결과가 무엇인지를 예시를 들어 설명하고 있으므로 the most beneficial outcome for themselves를 언급한 (B) 뒤에

오는 것이 적절하다. (A)의 Both players (the buyer and seller)는 (C)에서 예로 든 집 구매자와 현재 소유주를 가리키므로 (C) 뒤에 오는 것이 적절하다. 따라서 글의 순서로 가장 적절한 것은 ③ (B) - (C) - (A)이다.

(해석) 게임 이론은 사회적 상황에서 경기자라고 불리는 경쟁자들의 의사 결정과 전략을 이해하기 위한 이론적 틀이다.

(B) 그러한 상호작용 상황에 있는 경기자들은 서로의 장래의 결정을 고려하도록 유도되는데, 그들의 선택이 상호 의존적이기 때문이다. 게임 이론은 합리적인 경기자가 그들의 상대방이 무엇을 할 것인지에 대한 신중한 숙고와 효과적인 전략의 활용을 통해서 자신들에게 가장 유익한 결과를 생기게 할 수 있을 거라고 시사한다.

(C) 예를 들어, 집을 사는 데에 관심이 있는 사람에게 가장 이로운 결과는 가능한 한 가장 낮은 가격에 그것을 구입하는 것일 것이다. 반면에, 현재 소유주는 수익을 내기 위해 어느 정도의 금액에 집을 팔아야 할 것이다.

(A) 두 경기자(구매자와 판매자)는 서로에 대해 알고 있는 것을 기반으로 협상하고, 유리한 결론을 전략적으로 유도하기 위해 이 정보를 이용한다. 그들이 사용하는 논리는 게임 이론과 그것의 규칙에 관련이 있다. 이것은 금전적 거래에만 적용되는 것이 아니라 상호 작용과 관련된 거의 모든 결정에 적용된다.

(어휘) theoretical 이론적인 strategically 전략적으로 induce 유도하다 prospective 장래의, 다가오는 interdependent 상호 의존적인 deliberation 숙고 utilization 활용, 이용 turn a profit 수익을 내다

(구문분석)
[1행] Game theory is a theoretical framework **for** [understanding the decision-making and strategies of competing parties, referred to as players, in social situations].
→ [understanding ~ situations]는 전치사 for의 목적어 역할을 하는 동명사구이다.

37 글의 순서 배열하기   정답 ②

(해설) 주어진 글은 역사적 특수주의가 진화론에 반대된다는 주제를 제시한다. (B)의 it은 주어진 글의 historical particularism을 가리키며, 진화론에 대비되는 역사적 특수주의를 소개하는 주어진 글에 대한 부연 설명을 하고 있으므로 주어진 글 뒤에 오는 것이 적절하다. (A)의 this logic(이 논리)은 (B)의 '문화적 특성이 독립적으로 전개된다'는 내용을 가리키므로 (B) 바로 다음에 오는 것이 적절하다. (C)의 This는 (A)의 가장 진보된 사회와 덜 발전된 사회가 앞서거나 뒤처진 것이 아니라는, 진화론과 반대되는 역사적 특수주의의 내용을 가리키므로 (A) 바로 다음에 오는 것이 적절하다. 따라서 글의 순서로 가장 적절한 것은 ② (B) - (A) - (C)이다.

(해석) 인류학자 Franz Boas(프란츠 보아스)에 의해 대중화된 역사적 특수주의는 진화론에 반대하는 입장에 있다.

(B) 모든 인류 문화가 야만에서 문명으로 가는 길에서 일련의 미리 정해진 단계를 거친다고 암시하는 대신, 그것은 역사적인 사건들을 바탕으로 문화적 특성이 독립적으로 전개된다고 가정한다. 기본적으로, 각 사회의 과거는 그것이 각각의 문화적 궤적에서 어디에 있고 언젠가 어디에 있을 것인지에 영향을 끼친다.

(A) 이 논리에 따르면, 가장 진보된 사회가 가장 멀리 나아갔다고 볼 수 없다; 그것들은 결코 우월하지 않으며 문화가 어떠해야 하는지에 대한 본보기가 되어서는 안 된다. 마찬가지로, 덜 발전된 사회는 같은 길에 있지 않거나 아예 경주를 하지 않고 있기 때문에 더디게 움직이거나 따라잡아야 하는 것으로 볼 수 없다.

(C) 이것은 중요한 차이인데 왜냐하면 사회 진화에 대한 이전의 이론들은 사

람들을 다양한 발달 수준으로 분류하는 것을 정당화하기 위해 사용되었기 때문이다. 모든 문화가 다르다는 관념은 또한 문화를 직접 경험하는 것이 그것에 대해 배우는 가장 효과적인 방법이라는 이해로 이어졌다.

(어휘) particularism 특수주의 in opposition to ~에 반대하여 superior 우월한 savagery 야만(성) posit 가정하다, 단정하다 unfold 전개되다, 진행되다 dictate 영향을 끼치다, 지시하다 distinction 차이, 구별

(구문분석)
[7행] Likewise, less developed societies cannot be seen ①[**as** slow-moving or **as** needing to catch up] ②[**as** they are not on the same path or running a race at all].
→ ①[as ~ up]의 as는 전치사로, '~으로, ~이라고'의 의미로 해석한다.
→ ②[as ~ all]의 as는 이유를 나타내는 부사절 접속사로, '~때문에'로 해석한다.

[21행] **The notion** [that all cultures are different] also led to **the understanding** [that engaging with a culture directly is the most effective way to learn about it].
→ [that ~ different]는 The notion과 동격을 이루고, [that ~ it]은 the understanding과 동격을 이루는 명사절이다.

38 주어진 문장의 위치 찾기   정답 ④

(해설) 주어진 문장의 Another possibility(또 다른 가능성)로 보아, 주어진 문장 앞에는 소빙하기의 기원에 대한 다른 학설이 나와야 한다는 것을 알 수 있다. 이 글에서는 ②~③ 뒤 문장까지는 소빙하기의 기원과 관련된 학설 중 하나인 열대 지방의 화산 폭발에 대한 내용이 나오고 있다. 또한 ④ 뒤 문장에 '유럽인들이 15세기에 아메리카 대륙에 도달한 것'은 주어진 문장의 colonialism(식민주의)과 관련이 있으므로 주어진 문장이 들어가기에 가장 적절한 곳은 ④이다.

(해석) 대부분의 사람들은 수백만 년 전에 발생했던 빙하기에 대해서는 알지만, 서기 1300년에서 1850년 사이에 일어난 일인 소빙하기를 아는 사람은 거의 없다. (①) 이 기간 동안, 온도가 상당히 떨어졌는데, 발트해가 얼어붙고 북극으로부터의 총빙이 남쪽으로 멀리 대서양까지 이어졌다. (②) 소빙하기의 기원과 관련한 학설들이 많은데, 한 흥미로운 도전자는 열대 지방의 화산들의 폭발이다. (③) 이 지질학적 사건은 에어로졸을 대기로 내뿜어서 태양으로부터 빛을 굴절시키고 지구를 더 춥게 만들었을 것이다. (④ 우리가 고려할 수 있는 또 다른 가능성은 소빙하기가 식민주의와 동시에 일어났다는 것이다.) 유럽인들이 15세기에 아메리카 대륙에 도착한 것은 그 대륙 전역에 수많은 질병을 퍼지게 했고 결과적으로 원주민 약 5천 6백만 명의 사망을 야기했다. (⑤) 너무 많은 사람들이 갑자기 사라지면서, 경작지의 대규모 산림녹화가 발생했을 것이고, 이는 이산화탄소 수치가 내려가게 하여 지구를 차가워지게 했을 것이다.

(어휘) coincide with ~과 동시에 일어나다 colonialism 식민주의 pack ice 총빙(바다 위에 떠다니는 얼음이 모여서 언덕처럼 얼어붙은 것) abound 많다, 풍부하다 contender 도전자, 경쟁자 eruption 폭발 geological 지질학의 spew 내뿜다, 분출하다 aerosol 에어로졸, 연기 deflect 굴절시키다, 빗나가게 하다 reforestation 산림녹화, 재식림(숲 다시 만들기)

(구문분석)
[18행] [With so many people suddenly gone], mass
       (명사구)   (과거분사)
reforestation of cultivated land would ~
→ [With ~ gone]은 'with + 명사(구) + 분사' 형태의 분사구문으로, '~하면서'라는 의미로 해석한다.

39 주어진 문장의 위치 찾기 정답 ③

(해설) 주어진 문장에 명시적 단서가 없는 경우에는 글의 흐름이 끊기는 곳을 찾아야 한다. ③ 앞까지는 인터넷 언어의 확산이 오히려 환상적인 오픈 소스 프로젝트가 되었다는 내용이 이어지다가, ③ 뒤 문장에서 형편없는 문법의 확산이 구문 규칙의 학습을 초래하는 식의 새로운 방식으로 언어가 보강되었다는 내용이 나오고 있다. ③ 앞뒤의 내용이 유기적으로 연결되지 않는다는 점을 통해 글의 흐름이 끊겼음을 알 수 있고, 주어진 문장은 ③ 앞 문장에서 언급된 오픈 소스 프로젝트의 비유에 대한 부연 설명에 해당한다. 따라서 주어진 문장이 들어가기에 가장 적절한 곳은 ③이다.

(오답분석) ④~⑤ 뒤 문장은 ③ 뒤 문장에 이어서 언어가 새롭고 예상치 못한 방식으로 보강되는 사례를 보이고 있으므로 주어진 문장이 들어가기에 적절하지 않다.

(해석) 오늘날 디지털 원주민들은 모두 어느 정도는 두 개의 언어를 할 줄 아는데, 그들은 그들의 모국어와 인터넷 언어를 둘 다 알기 때문이다. (①) 사실, 매일매일, 특히 젊은 세대에게 채팅 언어는 보조적인 것이기보다는 그들의 의사소통의 주요 수단일 것이다. (②) 한때는 이러한 경향이 말하기를 이모티콘이나 말도 안 되는 소리에 지나지 않는 것으로 바꿔 놓을 것이라고 생각되었지만, 언어는 오히려 가장 환상적인 오픈 소스 프로젝트가 되었는데, 이는 무료로 이용 가능하고 재배포되거나 수정될 수 있는 프로젝트이다. (③ 언어적으로 창의적인 전 세계 인터넷 이용자들의 무수한 방언과 지역 은어 덕분에 수천 개의 새로운 단어가 어휘 목록에 추가되었다.) 언어는 또한 새롭고 예상치 못한 방식으로 보강되었다; 심지어 형편없는 문법의 확산은 구문 규칙이 학습되고 공유되는 것을 초래했고, 사람들은 어느 때보다도 더 정확하게 말하고 있다. (④) 재미 삼아 일부러 문법에 맞지 않는 댓글을 쓰거나 자기 자신을 GIF 형식으로 표현하는 것은 언어 그 자체가 이미 이용자들에 의해 충분히 잘 이해되고 있음을 의미한다. (⑤) 이 경우, 변화는 쇠퇴가 아닌 진화와 같다.

(어휘) myriad 무수한, 막대한 inventive 창의적인
bilingual 두 개의 언어를 할 줄 아는 on a day-to-day basis 매일매일
supplementary 보조적인 syntactical 구문의, 문장의
purposely 일부러, 고의로 for a laugh 재미 삼아, 농담으로
equate to ~과 같다, 동일시하다 decay 쇠퇴

(구문분석) [18행] [To write purposely ungrammatical comments for a laugh or express oneself through GIFs] means language itself is already understood well enough by the user.
→ [To ~ GIFs]는 to부정사의 명사적 용법(~하는 것)으로, 문장의 주어 역할을 한다.

40 요약문 완성하기 정답 ③

(해설) 글의 전반부에서 공리주의는 어떤 상황에서든 가장 도덕적인 것은 최대 다수의 사람들에게 최소한의 고통과 최대한의 기쁨을 가져다 주는 방식으로 행동하는 것이라고 간주한다고 했고, 글의 후반부에서는 공리주의는 또한 도덕적으로 얼마나 의문스러운 행동인지와는 상관없이 결국 가장 좋은 결과를 낳는다면 어떠한 행동이든 허용한다고 했다. 따라서 the most를 maximize로, questionable을 controversial로 바꾸어 표현한 ③이 정답이다.

(오답분석) 공리주의는 가장 최대 다수에게 최대한의 기쁨을 가져다 주는 방식으로 행동하는 것을 가장 도덕적인 것으로 간주한다고 했으므로 ①, ⑤의 exploit과 ②의 measure는 (A)에 들어갈 단어로 적절하지 않다. 또한 공리주의가 거짓말, 도둑질, 살인 등과 같이 도덕적으로 의문스러운 행동이라도 좋은 결과를 낳는다면 어떠한 행동도 할 수 있게 한다고 했으므로 ④의 justifiable은 (B)에 들어갈 단어로 적절하지 않다.

(해석) 공리주의는 결과에 초점을 맞춤으로써 옳고 그름을 밝히는 윤리 이론이다. 이는 어떤 상황에서든 가장 도덕적인 것은 최대 다수의 사람들에게 최소한의 고통과 최대한의 기쁨을 가져다주는 방식으로 행동하는 것이라고 간주한다. 사실상, 그것은 이기주의의 개념을 거부하고, 사람은 자기 자신뿐만 아니라 자신의 행동으로 영향을 받을 수 있는 모든 사람들에게, 그것이 다른 한 명의 사람이든 나라 전체이든, 무엇이 최선인지를 판단해야 한다고 가정한다. 공리주의의 비판자들은 그것이 비현실적이라고 생각하는데, 빠른 선택을 해야 할 때 한 사람의 행동의 모든 가능한 결과를 가늠하는 것이 불가능하지는 않지만 어렵기 때문이다. 또한 그것은 거짓말, 도둑질, 살인 등 도덕적으로 얼마나 의문스러운 행동인지와는 상관없이 결국 가장 좋은 결과를 낳는다면 어떠한 행동이든 허용한다. 게다가, 그 이론은 다수에게 이익이 되기 때문에 소수를 위한 정의라는 개념을 무의미하게 만든다.

> 비록 공리주의가 세상의 행복을 (A) 최대화하려고 하기는 하지만, 윤리적으로 (B) 논란의 여지가 있는 행동에 제한을 두지는 않는다.

(A) (B)
① 이용하다 …… 안내된
② 측정하다 …… 편파적인
③ 최대화하다 …… 논란의 여지가 있는
④ 최대화하다 …… 정당한
⑤ 이용하다 …… 불확실한

(어휘) utilitarianism 공리주의 hold 간주하다, 생각하다
egoism 이기주의, 자기중심주의 postulate 가정하다
impractical 비현실적인 weigh up 가늠하다 in the end 결국
doctrine 이론, 교리 irrelevant 무의미한, 무관한
[선택지] exploit (부당하게) 이용하다, 착취하다 partial 편파적인

(구문분석) [6행] In effect, it rejects the notion of egoism and postulates that one must judge what is best **not only** ①[for oneself] **but** ②[for everyone who might be affected by one's actions], ③[**whether** that's a single other person **or** an entire country].
→ 전치사구 ①[for oneself]와 ②[for ~ actions]는 상관접속사 not only A but (also) B로 연결된 병렬 구조이다.
→ ③[whether ~ country]는 whether A or B(A이든 B이든)가 이끄는 양보의 부사절이다.

[10행] Critics of utilitarianism believe it is impractical, as [weighing up all the possible outcomes of one's actions] is difficult, if not impossible, to do when ~
→ [weighing ~ actions]는 부사절의 주어 역할을 하는 동명사구이다.

41~42 장문 독해 1

(해석) "불규칙한 모양의 진주"를 의미하는 포르투갈어 용어 "barroco"에서 유래된 "baroque"라는 단어는 처음에는 (a) 일관된 멜로디가 없어 보이고 음정과 박자가 계속 바뀌는 음악을 비판하기 위해 사용된 비난의 뜻을 내포한 용어였다. 그러나 오늘날, "baroque"는 대략 1600년에서 1750년 사이에 작곡된 다채롭고 화려한 음악 양식을 묘사하기 위해 사용된다.
서양 세계가 르네상스 시대에서 벗어나 현재 "이성의 시대"로 알려진 시대에 접어들면서 ⁴¹새로운 사상이 모든 영역에 퍼지기 시작한 것은 바로 이 시기 동안이었다. 음악에서, 그러한 사상 중 하나는 적절한 소리가 만들어진다면 음악이 청자에게 감정을 (b) 불러일으키는 수단인 의사소통의 더 고도로 발달

한 형태가 될 수 있다는 것이었다. ⁴¹,⁴²이전에는, 음악이 하나의 멜로디로 구성되는 경향이 있었지만, 음악이 줄 수 있는 가능성에 대한 새로운 관심은 지금까지 들어온 것의 경계를 확장했다. 오늘날 우리에게 익숙한 음악의 조성 즉 장조와 단조의 사용은, 모티프를 특징으로 하는 멜로디와 짧은 악구의 사용이 그러했듯이 바로크 음악의 (c) 사소한(→두드러진) 특징이 되었다. 작곡가들은 트릴(빠르게 음을 교대하는 것)로 정교하게 (d) 꾸미면서 모티프를 반복하고 발전시켰다. 멜로디 또한 작곡가들이 대위법이라고 불리는 기법을 통해 그것들을 엮으면서 길어졌다. 이것은 소리의 층을 쌓기 위해 중첩 효과로 다양한 악기들이 연주되고 서로 다른 목소리들이 (e) 동시에 노래를 부르는 것을 포함했다. Johann Sebastian Bach(요한 제바스티안 바흐)와 George Frideric Handel(게오르크 프리드리히 헨델)과 같은 작곡가들은 그러한 기법들이 그 시대의 음악적 특징으로 확립되게 했다.

어휘 irregular 불규칙한 coherent 일관된 key 음정, 조 meter 박자
extravagant 화려한, 사치스러운 emerge from ~에서 벗어나다
realm 영역 arouse 불러일으키다 afford 주다, 제공하다
tonality 조성(調聲) motif 모티프(주제를 전개시킬 수 있는 2음 이상의 선율)
phrase 악구(樂句), 구절 trill 트릴, 떨리는 소리 knit together 엮다
counterpoint 대위법 overlapping 중첩되는
[선택지] replicate 복제하다, 모사하다
revolutionize 변혁을 일으키다, 혁명화하다

구문분석

[1행] [Taken from the Portuguese term "barroco," which means "a pearl of irregular shape,"] the word "baroque" was initially a pejorative term used to ~

→ [Taken ~ shape"]은 과거분사(Taken)로 시작하는 수동형 분사구문으로, 분사구문의 주어가 주절의 주어(the word "baroque")와 같아서 생략되었다.

[9행] It was during this period, [as the Western world emerged from the Renaissance and entered what is now known as the "Age of Reason,"] that new ideas began to spread across all realms.

→ [as ~ Reason"]은 접속사 as(~하면서)가 이끄는 시간의 부사절이 삽입된 형태이다.

→ during this period를 강조하는 it is(was) ~ that 강조구문이 쓰였다.

[19행] The tonality in music that we are familiar with today — the use of major and minor keys — became a major characteristic of baroque music, [as did the use of melodies that featured motifs, or short musical phrases].
(동사 / 주어)

→ [as ~ phrases]는 as(~처럼 역시)가 절 앞에 와서 동사(did)와 주어(the ~ phrases)가 도치된 구조로 쓰였다. 여기서 as did는 앞서 언급된 became a major characteristic of baroque music을 뜻한다.

41 제목 파악하기
정답 ⑤

해설 바로크 음악의 특징을 설명하는 내용의 글로, 새로운 사상이 모든 영역에 퍼지기 시작하면서, 음악의 경계가 확장되어 새로운 특징을 가지게 되었다고 설명하고 있다. 따라서 글의 제목으로 가장 적절한 것은 ⑤ '새 것과 함께: 바로크 시대가 음악에 변혁을 일으킨 방법'이다.

오답분석 ①은 글의 일부만을 다루고 있는 오답이다. ②은 글에서 언급된 Age of Reason과 Renaissance를 사용하여 헷갈리게 하는 오답이다.

해석 ① 바로크 시대의 음악적 기법의 원동력
② 이성의 시대: 르네상스 음악을 탐험하다
③ 바로크 시대의 중복되는 시기들
④ 바로크 소리: 그것은 오늘날 정말로 복제될 수 있는가?
⑤ 새 것과 함께: 바로크 시대가 음악에 변혁을 일으킨 방법

42 어휘 적절성 파악하기
정답 ③

해설 바로크 음악은 새로운 기법들을 사용했다고 했고, 이전에는 음악이 하나의 멜로디로 구성되는 경향이 있었지만 음악의 가능성에 대한 새로운 관심은 이때까지 들어왔던 것의 경계를 확장했다고 했다. 글의 후반부에서는 바로크 음악의 주요 특징들을 설명하고 있으므로 ③의 trivial(사소한)을 그와 반대되는 의미의 outstanding(두드러진)과 같은 단어로 바꾸어야 문맥상 적절하다.

43~45 장문 독해 2

해석 (A) Jenny는 한 번도 미국을 벗어나 여행한 적이 없었다. 그렇게 해서(미국을 떠나서) 그녀가 항상 가장 관심을 가졌던 곳: 프랑스를 방문하는 것이 그녀의 꿈이었다. Jenny는 끊임없이 그곳에 있는 멋진 지역 명소와 박물관을 방문하는 (a) 그녀 자신을 상상했다. 하지만 그녀는 그러한 여행을 위한 비용을 어떻게 지불할 수 있을지 몰랐다. 그녀는 그저 그만한 돈을 가지고 있지 않았다.

(C) 어느 날 직장에서, Jenny의 동료는 (c) 그녀가 에펠 탑 사진을 쳐다보고 있는 것을 발견했다. 그녀는 Jenny에게 왜 그녀가 그것을 직접 보기 위해 여행을 예약하지 않았는지 물었다. "저는 그것을 지불할 수가 없어요. 그 여행은 비용이 너무 많이 들어요."라고 Jenny가 슬프게 대답했다. Jenny의 동료는 (d) 그녀에게 미소를 지으며 말했다. "아니에요, 아직 할 수 있어요. 그저 잔돈을 모으기 시작하면 되고, 그것이 결국엔 충분해질 거예요. 아무리 적은 양도 중요하니까요."

(D) Jenny는 그것에 대해 생각했고 시도해서 나쁠 것이 없다고 판단했다. 그래서 다음 몇 달 동안, (e) 그녀는 가능한 모든 잔돈을 모았다. 그녀는 커피를 사고 식당에 가는 것을 줄였다. 무언가 새로운 것을 사고 싶을 때마다, 그녀는 저장해두었던 프랑스의 사진들을 보았고 그녀의 목표를 마음에 새겼다. ⁴⁵그녀는 항공편, 호텔, 그리고 관광을 찾아보기 시작했다. 오래지 않아 Jenny에게는 충분한 돈이 있었고 그녀는 마침내 꿈의 여행을 떠날 수 있었다.

(B) Jenny는 프랑스에 도착했을 때 믿을 수가 없었다. 그녀는 그것을 이루어낸 그녀 자신이 자랑스러웠다. 그녀는 결코 올 수 없을 것이라고 생각했지만, 충분한 노력과 결단력으로 해낼 수 있었다. 그녀는 ⁴⁴그녀의 동료에게 (b) 그녀의 격려와 Jenny에게 정말 마음을 먹으면 무엇이든 할 수 있다는 것을 보여준 것에 감사하며 엽서를 보내기로 결심했다.

어휘 landmark 지역 명소, 랜드마크 determination 결단력, 투지
in person 직접 put away 모으다 penny 잔돈, 약간의 돈
cut back on ~을 줄이다

구문분석

[5행] But she didn't **know** [how she would ever be able to pay for such a trip].

→ [how ~ trip]은 의문사 how가 이끄는 명사절로 동사 know의 목적어 역할을 한다.

43 글의 순서 배열하기 정답 ③

(해설) (A)는 Jenny가 프랑스 여행을 매우 가고 싶어 했지만 충분한 돈이 없었다는 내용이다. (C)는 Jenny의 직장 동료가 에펠 탑 사진을 보고 있던 Jenny에게 여행 경비를 모으는 방법을 제안하는 내용이므로 그녀가 어떻게 여행 경비를 지불할지 몰랐다는 (A) 바로 뒤에 오는 것이 적절하다. (D)는 Jenny가 동료의 조언에 따라 잔돈을 아껴서 돈을 모아 마침내 꿈꾸던 여행을 떠날 수 있었다는 내용이므로 (C) 뒤에 와야 한다. (B)에서 Jenny가 프랑스에 도착해서 스스로를 자랑스러워하는 것은 경비를 다 모았다는 (D) 다음에 오는 것이 적절하다. 따라서 글의 순서로 가장 적절한 것은 ③ (C) - (D) - (B)이다.

44 지칭 대상 파악하기 정답 ②

(해설) (a), (c), (d), (e)는 모두 Jenny를 가리키지만 (b)는 Jenny의 동료를 가리키므로 ②이 정답이다.

45 세부 정보 파악하기 정답 ⑤

(해설) (D)의 She started to search for flights, hotels, and tours를 통해 Jenny가 항공편 등을 찾아본 것을 알 수 있는데, ⑤은 Jenny의 동료가 했다고 일부 정보를 잘못 나타냈으므로 글의 내용과 일치하지 않는 것은 ⑤이다.

정답

문제집 p. 158

18	③	19	①	20	③	21	⑤	22	③	23	②	24	②	25	④	26	⑤	27	④
28	⑤	29	②	30	③	31	⑤	32	①	33	③	34	①	35	④	36	③	37	②
38	⑤	39	④	40	②	41	④	42	⑤	43	②	44	④	45	②				

18 목적 파악하기 정답 ③

(해설) 글의 중간 이후에서 인터넷 공급업체의 직원이 고객인 Levi 씨에게 미납된 세 달 치 대금을 납부해줄 것을 요청하고 있으므로 정답은 ③이다.

(해석) Levi 씨께,

제 이름은 Donald Miller이고, 저는 Cast Internet의 직원입니다. 귀하께서는 저희의 오랜 고객이시며, 귀하의 인터넷 공급업체로 저희를 이용해주셔서 감사드리고 싶습니다. 유감스럽게도, 저희의 기록은 귀하께서 지난 세 달 치 청구서에 대한 대금을 내지 않으셨음을 보여줍니다. 이 문제를 처리하기 위해 저희가 전화로 여러 차례 귀하께 연락을 시도했지만, 귀하께서는 저희의 전화를 받으시지도 메시지에 답을 하지도 않으셨습니다. 이것이 최종 경고임을 감안해주시기 바랍니다. 귀하께서는 이번 달 말까지 귀하의 계정에 대한 미지불된 잔액을 다 갚으셔야 합니다. 만약 귀하께서 그렇게 하지 못하실 경우, 저희는 귀하의 인터넷 서비스의 공급을 끊을 수밖에 없습니다. 귀하께서는 온라인에서나 저희 지사 중 어디에서든 지불하실 수 있습니다. 만약 문의 사항이 있으시다면, 555-0393으로 제게 연락 주십시오.

Donald Miller 드림

(어휘) **pay off** 다 갚다, 청산하다 **outstanding** 미지불된 **balance** 잔액, 균형 **branch office** 지사

(구문분석)
[13행] If you do fail to do so, we will **have no choice but to disconnect** your Internet service.

→ 'have no choice but + to부정사'는 '~할 수밖에 없다'라는 의미의 구문이며, 'cannot (help) but + 동사원형'으로 바꿔 쓸 수 있다.

[14행] You can pay online or [at any of our branch offices].

→ [at ~ offices] 앞에는 '주어 + 동사' you can pay가 생략되어 있는데, 앞의 You can pay online에서 이미 언급되었기 때문에 생략되었다.

19 심경 파악하기 정답 ①

(해설) 심경은 간접적으로 표현된다. 글의 초반부의 he was shaking like a leaf 를 통해 Noah가 심사위원인 그의 우상 앞에서 연주하게 되어 떨리고 긴장한 것을 알 수 있고, 후반부의 took a bow with the biggest grin, his smile grew wider, floated off the stage in elation 등을 통해 연주를 잘 마치고 사람들과 그의 우상에게 박수를 받으며 기쁨을 느꼈다는 것을 알 수 있으므로, Noah의 심경 변화로 가장 적절한 것은 ①이다.

(해석) 마침내 Noah의 차례였고, 그는 벌벌 떨고 있었다. 그것은 단지 그가 수백 명의 사람들이 그를 쳐다보는 가운데 무대 위에 있기 때문이 아니었다. 그것은 단지 오디션에서 우승하는 것이 그에게 엄청난 기회를 줄 수도 있어서가 아니었다.

그는 심사위원인 자신의 우상 앞에서 피아노를 연주할 것이다! 그는 앉아서 떨리는 손가락을 건반 위에 올려놓았다. 그가 연주를 시작했을 때, 그의 가슴에서는 그의 심장이 크게 두근거렸지만, 그의 아름다운 음악이 콘서트장을 채웠다. 그가 마치기도 전에 박수갈채가 시작되었고, 그는 일어서서 가장 크게 활짝 웃으며 인사했다. 그리고, 그의 음악 영웅이 그에게 기립 박수를 보내고 있는 것을 보았을 때 그의 미소는 더 커졌다! "브라보!" Noah는 크게 기뻐하며 무대에서 미끄러지듯 걸어 내려가면서 그가 첫 번째 줄에서 외치는 것을 들었다.

① 긴장한 → 기쁜
② 짜증 난 → 만족한
③ 슬픈 → 침착한
④ 무관심한 → 안도한
⑤ 당황한 → 어리둥절한

(어휘) **shake like a leaf** 벌벌 떨다 **break** 기회, 휴식 **thump** 두근거리다 **grin** 활짝 웃음; 활짝 웃다 **ovation** 박수 **float** 미끄러지듯 걷다 **elation** 크게 기뻐함, 들뜸

(구문분석)
[5행] He would be playing the piano in front of **his idol** [who was the judge]!

→ [who ~ judge]는 선행사 his idol을 수식하며 주격 관계대명사 who 가 이끄는 관계대명사절이다.

20 주장 파악하기 정답 ③

(해설) 글의 첫 두 문장에서 오늘날 브랜드의 성공은 진정성과 관련이 있고, 현대의 소비자들은 진정성과 정직함이 있는 곳에서 나오는 일관된 이야기에 반응한다고 주장하고 있으므로 정답은 ③이다.

(오답분석) ①, ②은 글의 일부만을 다루고 있는 오답이다. ④은 오늘날 브랜드의 성공이 가능한 한 눈에 띄는 것과 별로 관련이 없다고 한 글의 내용과 반대되는 내용을 다루고 있으므로 오답이다. ⑤은 글의 핵심 어구 '진정성'을 사용하여 헷갈리게 하는 오답이다.

(해석) 오늘날 브랜드의 성공은 가능한 한 눈에 띄는 것과는 별로 관련이 없고, 진정성 있는 것과 더 관련이 있다. 요즘, 소비자들은 전형적인 메시지 전달이나 마케팅 술책들이 아니라 진정성과 정직함이 있는 곳에서 나오는 일관된 이야기에 반응한다. 브랜드들이 그들이 누구인지와 그들이 지지하는 가치에 대해 이야기할 때, 사람들은 기업 전문 용어('벤처 자금', '시장 점유율' 등)가 아니라 그들이 대화의 일원인 것처럼 느끼게 만드는 것, 즉 그들이 신뢰할 수 있는 친구에게 이야기하고 있는 것처럼 느껴지게 하는 것을 듣고 싶어 한다. 브랜드가 한때 얼마나 도처에 존재했는지는 중요하지 않다; 그들(소비자들)이 지지하는 브랜드가 사명을 지니고 그들(브랜드)이 말하는 것이 진심이기를 기대하는 현대의 소비자들과 브랜드가 연결되지 못한다면, 그렇게 할 수 있는 전도유망한 브랜드에 밀려날 것이다.

authentic 진정성 있는, 진짜의 gimmick 술책, 장치
sincerity 진정성 terminology 전문 용어
ubiquitous 도처에 존재하는, 어디에나 있는 crowd out 밀어내다
up-and-coming 전도유망한, 떠오르는

[구문분석]
[1행] The success of brands today has less to do with being [as visible as possible] and more to do with being authentic.
→ [as ~ possible]은 'as + 원급 + as possible'(가능한 한 ~한)의 형태로 비교를 나타내는 구문이다.

 [구문분석]
[20행] Shakespeare's tragedy influenced future generations of dramatists **for whom** personality is the horse that drives the cart of fate.
→ 이 문장은 각각의 문장인 Shakespeare's tragedy influenced future generations of dramatists. And for dramatists, personality is the horse that drives the cart of fate.을 한 문장으로 합치면서 접속사 and와 중복되는 단어인 dramatists가 하나로 묶여 목적격 관계대명사 whom이 되었고, for는 whom 앞으로 가서 '전치사 + 관계대명사' 형태인 for whom으로 쓰였다.

---

21 밑줄 의미 추론하기   정답 ⑤

[해설] 밑줄 친 어구가 포함된 문장은 셰익스피어의 비극 속 성격에 관한 내용이다. 이 글에서는 Aristotle은 비극이 구조와 행동으로 이루어졌다고 본 반면, William Shakespeare의 비극은 사건들이 등장인물들의 결점에 의해 촉발되는 것과 같이 상세하고 면밀한 캐릭터의 구축으로 특징지어진다고 말하고 있다. 따라서 글의 주제인 William Shakespeare의 비극 속 성격의 역할을 비유적으로 표현한 horse that drives the cart of fate(운명의 수레를 모는 말)가 의미하는 것은 ⑤ '비극에서 본질적 의미를 규정하는 사건들의 원인'이다.

[오답분석] ①은 William Shakespeare의 비극에서 주인공의 성격적 결함이 비극적 사건들을 촉발하는 원인이라고 한 글의 내용과 반대되는 내용을 다루고 있으므로 오답이다. ②, ③은 글에서 언급된 내용이 아니다. ④은 글에서 언급된 tragic events를 사용하여 헷갈리게 하는 오답이다.

[해석] 비극이라는 장르에서, 가장 중요한 고려 사항은 어느 것인가: 줄거리인가 등장인물인가? 달리 말하면, 우리의 삶은 주로 우리가 맞닥뜨리는 사건들을 통해서 정해지는가, 아니면 우리 성격들의 조합을 통해 정해지는가? Aristotle(아리스토텔레스)에게, 비극은 주로 구조를 통해 표현되었다. 그는 "비극이란 인간에 대한 모방이 아닌 행동에 대한 모방이고, 삶은 행동에 있다"라고 저술했다. Oedipus(오이디푸스)의 운명이 그의 아버지의 죽음에 대한 자신도 모르는 개입에 의해 바뀌었을 때처럼, 인간의 삶은 운명의 변덕에 의해 정해졌다. 수 세기 후에, William Shakespeare(윌리엄 셰익스피어)는 그의 등장인물인 Cassius(카시우스)가 "Brutus(브루투스), 잘못은 우리의 별들에 있는 것이 아니라, 우리 자신에게 있네"라고 말했을 때, 반대 입장을 지지하는 것으로 보였다. 그리스 극작가들과 대조적으로, Shakespeare의 작품은 그의 상세하고 면밀한 캐릭터 구축으로 특징지어진다; 그는 대개 다른 데서 그의 줄거리를 따왔다. 리어왕이 그의 자존심과 오만함 때문에 모든 것을 잃은 때처럼 그의 주인공들 머리 위로 무너져 내린 비극적인 사건들은 그들 자신의 결점들에 의해 촉발된다. Shakespeare의 비극은 미래 세대 극작가들에게 영향을 주었는데, 그들에게 성격이란 운명의 수레를 모는 말이다.
① 행동들의 결과를 묘사하는 방법
② 일부 캐릭터들이 맞닥뜨리는 문제에 대한 해결책
③ 인간이 자신의 존재에 의문을 제기하게 만드는 힘
④ 일련의 매우 비극적인 사건들의 피해자
⑤ 비극에서 본질적 의미를 규정하는 사건들의 원인

[어휘] put another way 달리 말하면 shape 정하다, 구체화하다
consist in ~에 있다 whim 변덕, 일시적 기분 unwitting 자신도 모르는
define 특징 짓다, 규정하다 construction 구축, 건설
playwright 극작가, 각본가 arrogance 오만함
[선택지] compel ~하게 만들다 defining 본질적 의미를 규정하는

---

22 요지 파악하기   정답 ③

[해설] 사람들이 충격적이고 선정적인 나쁜 소식들에 끊임없이 노출되면서 그러한 소식들에 무감각해진다는 내용의 글이므로, 이 글의 요지로 가장 적절한 것은 ③이다.

[오답분석] ②의 감정 훈련에 대해서는 글에서 언급되지 않았다. ⑤은 글의 일부만을 다루고 있는 오답이다.

[해석] 24시간 뉴스의 반복은 대단히 충격적인 이미지와 선정주의적인 이야기들 형태로 끝없는 나쁜 소식들의 연속에 사람들을 노출시킨다. 기술의 침투하는 성질로 인해, 이러한 유형의 보도는 사람들이 멀리하기 어렵다: 부정적인 주요 뉴스들은 소셜 미디어 플랫폼의 피드를 어수선하게 만들고 끊임없는 업데이트를 허용한다. 그러한 내용에 대해 기대되는 반응은 공감과 연민이지만, 오늘날 많은 사람들은 그것에 대한 반응으로 어떤 유형의 감정도 전혀 느끼지 못함을 겪는다. 사람들은 더 이상 뉴스 소식들로 인해 놀라거나 충격을 받지 않고, 대신에 날마다 비극과 폭력에 대해 읽는 것에 무감각해졌다. 오랜 시간 동안, 미디어는 독자층을 얻기 위해 점점 더 충격적인 소식들을 보도하려고 해왔다. 그 결과는 사람들이 동정 피로를 겪고 있고 이제는 보통은 반응을 자아냈을 이야기들에 반응하지 못한다. 나쁜 뉴스의 끊임 없는 맹공격으로 인해 사람들의 감정이 매우 지쳤기 때문에 그것은 만연한 현상이고, 각각의 새로운 불행이 그저 이전 것에 뒤섞이게 놓아둔다.

[어휘] stream 연속, 흐름 traumatic 대단히 충격적인 coverage 보도, 보상
distance 멀리하다 pervasive 침투하는 headline 주요 뉴스, 표제
litter 어수선하게 하다, 버리다 numb 무감각한, 마비된 readership 독자층
compassion fatigue 동정 피로 onslaught 맹공격, 맹습

 [구문분석]
[3행] This kind of coverage is hard <u>for people</u> [to distance <u>themselves from</u>] because of the pervasive nature of technology: ~
（의미상 주어 / to부정사구）
→ for people은 'for + 명사' 형태로, to부정사구 [to ~ from]의 의미상 주어로 쓰였다.

[17행] It's a widespread phenomenon ①[**as** people's emotions are worn out by the constant onslaught of bad news], ②[leaving each new disaster to simply blend into the last one].
→ as는 시간, 이유 등을 나타내는 접속사로, ①[as ~ news]는 as(~ 때문에)가 이끄는 이유의 부사절이다.
→ ②[leaving ~ one]은 결과를 나타내는 분사구문으로, 분사구문의 주어가 주절의 주어(It)와 같아서 생략되었다.

23 주제 파악하기   정답 ②

(해설) 첫 문장과 마지막 문장으로 미루어 보아 Gottlob Frege의 언어 철학에 따르면 의미는 표현 방식인 뜻과 실제 대상인 지시체로 이루어지고, 하나의 표현이 다른 것으로 대체될 수 있다면 논리는 두 표현들이 같은 의미를 지닌다고 할 것이라는 내용의 글이다. 따라서 이 글의 주제로 가장 적절한 것은 ② '언어에서 의미를 추론하는 논리적 접근법'이다.

(오답분석) ①은 글의 핵심 소재 sense, reference를 사용하여 헷갈리게 하는 오답이다. ③은 글이 Frege의 언어 철학에 대해 설명하고 있을 뿐, 오늘날 언어가 이해되는 방식에 대한 Frege의 영향력에 관해서는 다루고 있지 않으므로 오답이다. ④은 글의 일부만을 다루고 있는 오답이다. ⑤은 글에서 Frege가 수학적 용어들로 진술을 표현하는 체계를 발전시켰다고 했으나 글의 일부 내용이므로 오답이다.

(해석) <뜻과 지시체에 관하여>에서, Gottlob Frege(고트로프 프레게)는 의미가 두 부분: 뜻과 지시체로 이루어져 있음을 설명하고자 했던 언어 철학을 전개했다. 그는 두 단어나 문장이 동일한 지시체(Bedeutung)를 갖지만 다른 뜻(Sinn)을 지닐 수도 있음을 제시했다. "뜻"은 명제나 대상이 표현되는 방식이고, "지시체"는 논해지고 있는 실제 대상이다. "저녁별"과 "샛별"이라는 용어를 예로 들어보자. 둘 다 금성을 지칭하기 위해 흔히 사용된다. 두 표현이 동일한 지시체를 갖지만 다른 뜻을 지니기 때문에, Frege는 그 표현들의 의미가 다르게 이해될 수 있다고 생각했다. 그는 진술들을 본질적으로 수량화할 수 있는 수학적 용어들로 표현하는 체계를 발전시켰다. 만약 하나의 별개의 표현이 다른 것으로 대체될 수 있다면(a=b), 그때 논리는 두 표현들이 같은 의미를 지닌다고 결정할 것이다.

① 뜻과 지시체를 구별하는 것의 어려움
② 언어에서 의미를 추론하는 논리적 접근법
③ 언어가 오늘날에 어떻게 이해되는지에 대한 Frege의 영향력
④ 몇몇 용어들이 서로 진정한 동의어가 되지 못하는 이유
⑤ 언어에 수학을 적용할 때 Frege가 얻은 영감

(어휘) develop 전개하다, 발전시키다   meaning 의미   sense 뜻, 감각
reference 지시체, 참고   proposition 명제   Venus 금성
quantifiable 수량화할 수 있는   dictate 결정하다, 지시하다
[선택지] derive 추론하다, 끌어내다   synonymous 동의어의

(구문분석) [4행] He proposed that two words or sentences may have ①[the same reference (Bedeutung)] **but** ②[a different sense (Sinn)].
→ 명사구 ①[the ~ (Bedeutung)]과 ②[a ~ (Sinn)]은 등위접속사 but으로 연결된 병렬 구조이다.

[6행] The "sense" is **the manner** ①[in which propositions or objects are expressed], and the "reference" is the actual object ②[(which is) being discussed].
→ ①[in ~ expressed]는 선행사 the manner를 수식하며 '전치사 + 관계대명사' in which 이 이끄는 관계대명사절이다.
→ ②[being discussed]는 the actual object를 설명하는 관계절로, 앞에 '주격 관계대명사(which) + be동사(is)'가 생략되었다.

24 제목 파악하기   정답 ②

(해설) 첫 세 문장으로 미루어 보아 고통스러운 경험을 겪은 모든 사람이 외상 후 스트레스 장애(PTSD)를 겪지 않는 것은 PTSD가 다른 정신 장애나 혈통을 통해 유전되는 특성들처럼 다원유전자적이고, 유전 가능성의 확률이 다르기 때문이라는 내용의 글이다. California 대학의 연구팀의 PTSD 관련 연구를 예로 들어 설명하고 있다. 따라서 글의 제목으로 가장 적절한 것은 ② '혈통을 통하여: PTSD의 위험 이해하기'이다.

(오답분석) ①은 글의 핵심 소재인 PTSD와 Psychological Condition을 사용하여 헷갈리게 하는 오답이다. ③, ④은 글에서 언급된 내용이 아니다. ⑤은 글이 PTSD가 유전될 수 있다는 내용이지, 유전되는 가족 트라우마에 관한 내용이 아니므로 오답이다.

(해석) 일부 연구원들이 외상 후 스트레스 장애(PTSD)가 사회적 개념이라고, 즉 나쁜 일들이 일어날 때 우리는 마땅히 엄청난 충격을 받을 것이라고 우리가 집단적으로 받아들여 왔기 때문에 존재할 뿐인 것이라고 주장하긴 했지만, 전쟁, 자연재해, 그 외의 다른 고통스러운 경험을 겪고 사는 모든 사람들이 그것을 일으키는 것은 아니다. 최근의 한 연구는 이것이 PTSD에 대한 생물학적 근거가 있기 때문일 수 있음을 시사한다. 지금까지 PTSD에 대한 가장 대규모인 연구에서, California 대학의 연구팀은 PTSD가 다른 정신 질환 장애나 사람의 혈통을 통해 유전되는 특성들처럼 다원유전자적이고 그 장애의 유전 가능성이 5퍼센트에서 20퍼센트 사이임을 알아냈다. 그 연구는 정신 질환의 발생과 사람의 유전적 구성 간의 연관성의 존재를 보여주는 이전의 쌍둥이 관련 연구들을 유의미하게 뒷받침한다. 궁극적으로, 그 연구 결과들은 PTSD를 일으킬 위험이 더 높은 환자들을 식별하는 것을 더 쉽게 만들어 그들이 이 쇠약성 질환에 대한 도움을 얻기 더 쉽게 만든다.

① PTSD는 실재하는 정신 질환인가 아니면 상상된 정신 질환인가?
② 혈통을 통하여: PTSD의 위험 이해하기
③ 정신적 외상이 어떻게 DNA에 주목할 만한 변화들을 일으키는가?
④ PTSD가 가족 관계에 영향을 미쳐야 하는가?
⑤ 그것은 당신으로 끝나지 않을 것이다: 유전되는 가족 트라우마

(어휘) post-traumatic stress disorder 외상 후 스트레스 장애
construct 개념, 구조물   rightfully 마땅히, 옳게
traumatize 엄청난 충격을 주다, 정신적 외상을 초래하다   to date 지금까지
psychiatric 정신 질환의   lineage 혈통   heritability 유전 가능성
lend weight to ~을 뒷받침하다   hereditary 유전적인, 세습되는
debilitating 쇠약하게 하는   [선택지] bloodline 혈통, 혈족
measurable 주목할 만한

(구문분석) [5행] ~ we will rightfully be traumatized — **not everyone** who lives through a war, a natural disaster, or any other distressing experience develops it.
→ not everyone은 '모두 ~인 것은 아니다'라는 의미로 부분 부정을 나타내는 구문이다.

[9행] In the largest study of PTSD to date, a research team at the University of California **found** ①[that PTSD is polygenic, just like other psychiatric disorders and **traits** (that are passed on via one's lineage)], **and** ②[that the heritability of the disorder is between five and 20 percent].
→ 동사 found의 목적어 역할을 하는 ①[that ~ lineage]와 ②[that ~ percent]는 접속사 that이 이끄는 명사절로 등위접속사 and로 연결된 병렬 구조이다.
→ (that ~ lineage)는 선행사 traits를 수식하며 주격 관계대명사 that이 이끄는 관계대명사절이다.

25 도표 정보 파악하기 정답 ④

[해설] 통합적 위험 관리와 애플리케이션 보안 부분에 쓰인 금액은 각각 46억 달러, 31억 달러로, 그 합계인 77억은 소프트웨어 부문의 85억 달러보다 더 적으므로 수치의 비교 표현이 잘못 반영되었다. 따라서 표의 내용과 일치하지 않는 것은 ④이다.

[해석]

2019년 정보 보호에 대한 전 세계의 부문별 지출

부문	미국 달러 (10억)	전체 대비 비율
보안 서비스	62.0	51.28%
사회 기반 시설 보호	16.5	13.65%
네트워크 보안 장비	13.4	11.08%
계정 접근 관리	9.8	8.11%
소프트웨어	8.5	7.03%
통합적 위험 관리	4.6	3.80%
애플리케이션 보안	3.1	2.56%
데이터 보안	2.7	2.23%
클라우드 보안	0.4	0.33%
합계	120.9	100%

* 참고: 반올림으로 인해 세부 항목들이 제시된 합계로 더해지지 않을 수 있음

위의 표는 2019년의 정보 보호에 대한 전 세계의 부문별 지출을 보여준다. ① 가장 많은 금액이 쓰인 부문은 51.28퍼센트의 비율로 보안 서비스였다. ② 지출에 있어서 상위 두 개 부문 간에 450억 달러 이상의 차이가 있었던 반면, 두 번째와 세 번째 간의 차이는 31억 달러였다. ③ 계정 접근 관리 부문에 대한 지출의 비율은 8.11퍼센트였고, 그것은 통합적 위험 관리의 그것(지출의 비율)의 두 배 이상이었다. ④ 통합적 위험 관리와 애플리케이션 보안 부문에 쓰인 합계 금액은 소프트웨어 부문의 그것(금액)보다 더 많았다. ⑤ 애플리케이션 보안, 데이터 보안, 클라우드 보안은 지출이 가장 적은 세 개의 부문들이었고, 각각 전체 대비 3퍼센트보다 더 적게 차지했다.

[어휘] information security 정보 보호 infrastructure 사회 기반 시설
identity 계정, 신원 account for 차지하다, 설명하다

[구문분석] [8행] The proportion of the expenditure for the identity access management segment was 8.11%, which was over twice **that** of integrated risk management.

→ 지시대명사 that은 앞의 단수명사 The proportion of the expenditure를 가리키며, 동일한 명사가 반복되는 것을 피하기 위해 사용되었다.

26 세부 정보 파악하기 정답 ⑤

[해설] These birds are considered endangered, primarily due to changes in habitat을 통해 인간 활동 등으로 인한 서식지의 변화들로 인해 피리 물떼새가 멸종 위기에 있다는 것을 알 수 있는데, ⑤은 무분별한 포획 때문이라고 일부 정보를 잘못 나타냈으므로 글의 내용과 일치하지 않는 것은 ⑤이다.

[해석] 피리 물떼새는 북아메리카 토착의 바닷가에 사는 새이다. 바닷가에 사는 다른 새들처럼, 그것은 큰 수역 근처의 모래로 덮인 지역에 집을 짓는다. 그것은 작고, 황갈색, 흰색, 회색 깃털들로 옅은 색이다. 그 색깔들은 그것이 둥지를 트는 지역과 조화되어, 그것이 위장하게 해준다. 그 새는 주로 곤충과 연체동물을 먹는다. 그것은 또한 여러 더 작은 동물들의 알도 먹는다. 피리 물떼새가 먹이를 먹을 때가 되면, 짧게 한바탕 달리다가 멈춰서 먹이를 찾아 지면을 뒤지고, 그리고 나서 만약 아무것도 찾지 못하면 다시 떠난다. 이 새들은 주로 서식지의 변화들로 인해 멸종 위기에 있다고 여겨진다. 그 새들이 서식하는 곳에서의

증가한 인간의 활동은 그 새들이 안전하게 둥지를 틀 수 있는 것을 막았다. 피리 물떼새 개체 수가 회복되도록 도우려는 시도로 그 지역들을 보존하기 위한 보호 활동이 진행 중이다.

[어휘] piping plover 피리 물떼새 shorebird 바닷가에 사는 새
indigenous 토착의, 토종의 body of water 수역
tan 황갈색의 camouflage 위장 burst 한바탕 달리기 effort 활동, 운동

[구문분석] [4행] The colors match **the area** [where it nests], providing it with camouflage.

→ [where it nests]는 선행사 the area를 수식하며, 장소를 나타내는 관계부사 where가 이끄는 관계부사절이다.

27 안내문 정보 파악하기 정답 ④

[해설] 추가 정보와 관련된 부분인 Registration ends on May 1를 통해 등록은 5월 1일에 마감된다는 것을 알 수 있으므로, 글의 내용과 일치하지 않는 것은 ④이다.

[해석]

초보자들을 위한 영화 제작 워크숍

영화를 제작하고 싶으신가요? 당신에게 필요한 것은 당신의 휴대전화뿐입니다! 저희와 함께하셔서 당신만의 영화 영상을 만드는 방법을 배워보십시오.

장소: Walker 지역 문화 회관
날짜: 5월 10일-11일, 토요일-일요일
시간: 오전 11시에서 오후 4시
비용: 학생당 150달러

가져오실 것:
- 스마트폰 (어떤 모델이든)
- 줄거리 초안

배우실 것:
- 스토리보드 작업
- 촬영 방법
- 연출
- 영상 및 음향 편집

유의 사항:
- 저희 웹사이트 www.cinemaworkshop.com에서 등록해주십시오. 등록은 5월 1일에 마감됩니다.
- 만약 취소하셔야 한다면, 5월 6일 이전에 해주십시오. 이 날짜 이후에는 환불이 안 될 것입니다.
- 추가 문의 사항은, directorsmith@cinemaworkshop.com으로 Lewis Smith에게 연락 주십시오.

[어휘] cinema 영화 제작, 영화 community center 지역 문화 회관, 주민 센터
storyline 줄거리, 구상

[구문분석] [3행] Join us and **learn** [how to create your own cinematic video].
의문사 to부정사

→ 명사절 [how ~ video]는 동사 learn의 목적어 역할을 하며, '~하는 방법'이라는 의미의 'how + to부정사' 구문이다.

[20행] If you need to cancel, please do **so** before May 6.

→ so는 앞의 cancel을 가리킨다.

28 안내문 정보 파악하기 정답 ⑤

(해설) The Eden Book Festival is free of charge를 통해 입장료가 없다는 것을 알 수 있으므로, 글의 내용과 일치하는 것은 ⑤이다.

(해석)
Eden 도서 축제

8월 21일에서 30일까지, Eden은 일 년에 두 번 열리는 도서 축제를 Eden 시립 도서관에서 열 것입니다.

주요 활동들:
국내 최고의 신흥 작가들 세 명의 소개가 있을 것입니다. 그들은 8월 21일과 22일에 오후 2시부터 오후 5시까지 강당에서 연설을 할 것입니다. 시 낭송은 매일 오후 5시에 열릴 것입니다. 누구든지 참석하시는 것이 환영됩니다!

주요 행사:
도서 마켓은 매일 오전 8시 30분에서 오후 4시까지 열릴 것입니다. 저희는 고서와 희귀 서적뿐만 아니라 중고 도서와 신간 도서도 있을 것입니다. 여러분들은 책들을 구매하시거나 다른 수집가들과 교환하실 수 있을 것입니다.

Eden 도서 축제는 무료입니다. 간식은 구매 시 이용 가능할 것입니다. 더 많은 정보를 원하시면, www.edenbooks.com을 방문해주십시오.

(어휘) biannual 일 년에 두 번의

(구문분석) [11행] Anyone is **welcome** [to attend]!
→ [to attend]는 to부정사의 부사적 용법으로, 형용사(welcome)의 의미를 한정한다.

[15행] You will be able ①[to buy books] **or** ②[(to) exchange them] with other collectors.
→ to부정사구 ①[to buy books]와 ②[exchange them]은 접속사 or로 연결되어 병렬 구조를 이루고, 두 번째 to는 생략되었다.

29 어법상 틀린 것 찾기 정답 ②

(해설) 주어 they, 동사 would be, 주격 보어 able이 모두 있는 완전한 절을 이끌고 있고, '~에서(부터)'라는 의미가 되어야 하므로 ②의 which를 '전치사 + 관계대명사' 형태의 from which로 고쳐야 한다.

(오답분석) ①은 부사 newly의 수식을 받으면서 뒤의 명사구 Union army prisoners of war를 수식하는 역할을 하는데, Union army prisoners of war는 '풀려나는' 행위의 대상이므로 과거분사 released를 사용한 것은 어법상 적절하다. ③은 주격 관계대명사 that이 이끄는 형용사절이 수식하는 선행사가 every enlisted man인데, 'every + 명사'는 단수 취급하므로, 단수동사 was를 사용한 것은 어법상 적절하다. ④는 주격 관계대명사 who 앞의 선행사 Soldiers가 '떼지어 몰리는' 행위의 대상이므로 수동태 been packed를 사용한 것은 어법상 적절하다. ⑤는 앞 문장에서 언급된 그 자리에서 사망한 군인들 외의 다른 사람들 중 몇몇을 가리키므로 부정대명사 Others를 사용한 것은 어법상 적절하다.

(해석) 'Sultana'는 미시시피 강에서 다니던 기선이었다. 한번은, 그것의 임무는 최근에 풀려난 북부군 전쟁 포로들을 미시시피 주의 빅스버그에서 그들이 집으로 갈 수 있는 위치인 미주리 주의 세인트 루이스까지 미시시피 강을 따라 북쪽으로 이송하는 것이었다. 'Sultana'의 법정 수송 정원은 승객 376명이었지만, 정부가 무사히 돌려보내지는 모든 사병에 5달러씩, 모든 장교에 10달러씩 지

불하겠다고 제시했기 때문에 남부 연맹 지지자들은 2,500명이 넘는 군인들을 배에 타게 했다. 재앙이 닥치기 전에 그 배는 계획된 항로의 절반보다 더 적게 지났었다. 한밤중에, 보일러 중 하나가 갑자기 폭발해, 다른 두 개의 보일러를 폭발하게 만든 연쇄 작용을 일으켰다. 지나치게 혼잡한 배에서 보일러 근처에 떼지어 몰려 있던 군인들은 즉사했다. 다른 사람들은 화재나 파편으로 인해 사망했지만, 더 많은 사람들이 익사나 체온 저하로 인해 이후에 사망했다. 모두 합쳐, 거의 1,800명의 사람들이 그 비극에서 목숨을 잃었다.

(어휘) steamboat (주로 하천·연안용 등의) 기선
Union army (남북 전쟁 때의) 북부군 prisoner of war 전쟁 포로
capacity 정원, 수용력 officer 장교, 관리
Confederate 남부 연맹 지지자·군인, 동맹자 set off 일으키다, 유발하다
perish 죽다, 소멸하다 shrapnel 파편 exposure 체온 저하, 노출

(구문분석) [11행] The ship completed less than half of its intended route [**before** disaster struck].
→ [before disaster struck]은 접속사 before(~ 전에)가 이끄는 시간의 부사절이다.

[13행] In the middle of the night, one of the boilers suddenly blew up, [setting off a chain reaction that caused two other boilers to explode].
→ [setting ~ explode]는 결과를 나타내는 분사구문으로, 분사구문의 주어가 주절의 주어(one of the boilers)와 같아서 생략되었다.

30 어휘 적절성 파악하기 정답 ③

(해설) 혐오 치료는 한 개인의 바람직하지 않은 습관이나 중독을 멈추기 위해 그것을 불쾌한 것과 연관 짓게 만듦으로써 이루어진다고 했다. 따라서 의사는 환자가 술을 마실 때마다 메스꺼움이나 구토와 같이 음주에 대한 조건화된 반응을 일으키는 약을 투여한다는 맥락이 되어야 하므로, ③의 inhibit(막다, 억제하다)을 그와 반대되는 의미의 cause(일으키다, 야기하다)와 같은 어휘로 바꾸어야 문맥상 적절하다.

(오답분석) ①은 고전적 조건화가 인간의 행동을 바꿔서 바람직하지 않은 습관이나 중독을 멈추도록 돕는 치료에도 이용된다는 문맥이 되어야 하므로 alter가 오는 것이 적절하다. ⑤는 알코올 중독의 환자가 더 이상 술을 갈망하지 않고 그들의 습관을 재개할 의향이 없다는 문맥이 되어야 하므로 resume이 오는 것이 적절하다.

(해석) 고전적 조건화는 흔히 생리학자 Ivan Pavlov(이반 파블로프)의 개에 대한 실험이 연상되지만, 그것은 또한 인간의 행동을 ① 바꾸도록 고안된 치료에도 이용될 수 있다. 고전적 조건화에 근거한 치료법의 한 가지 방식은 혐오 치료로, 그것은 한 개인이 ② 바람직하지 않은 습관이나 중독을 멈추도록 돕는 데에 이용된다. 이는 그들이 그것을 불쾌한 것과 연관 짓게 만듦으로써 이루어진다. 예를 들어, 알코올 중독의 치료에 대한 미국국립보건원(NIH)의 연구들에서, 의사는 환자가 술을 마실 때마다 메스꺼움이나 구토를 ③ 막는(→일으키는) 약을 투여한다. 그 약은 보통의 경우에는 중립 자극인 음주에 대해, 아프지 않길 바라는 조건화된 반응을 일으키도록 의도되었다. 이 치료 방식에서, 환자가 술을 마시고 아파지는 과정이 ④ 반복되기 때문에, 결국에 환자는 더 이상 술을 갈망하지 않는다. 심지어 메스꺼움을 유발하는 약이 더 이상 투여되지 않을 때에도 그들의 습관을 ⑤ 재개할 의향이 없을 수도 있는데, 왜냐하면 환자는 스스로에게 물어야 하기 때문이다: 단 한 번의 음주일지라도 아픈 것 이상의 가치가 있는가?

(어휘) classical conditioning 고전적 조건화 physiologist 생리학자
aversion therapy 혐오 치료 undesirable 바람직하지 않은

nausea 메스꺼움　vomiting 구토　neutral 중립의, 중성의
crave 갈망하다　induce 유발하다　resume 재개하다

[구문분석] [10행] ~ a doctor administers drugs that cause nausea or vomiting [**whenever** the patient drinks alcohol].

→ [whenever ~ alcohol]은 복합관계부사 whenever(~할 때마다)가 이끄는 시간의 부사절로, whenever는 at any time when으로 바꿔 쓸 수 있다.

[17행] Even [**once** the nausea-inducing drugs are no longer being administered], the patient may not be willing to resume their habit because ~

→ [once ~ administered]는 접속사 once(~할 때, ~하자마자)가 이끄는 시간의 부사절이다.

31　빈칸 추론하기　정답 ⑤

[해설] 현대 미술의 거만함에 대한 반발로 발전한 팝 아트는 그것이 묘사하는 소재처럼 현대 문화의 처분 가능한 과잉을 나타내는 것을 의도했다는 내용의 글이다. 주제문을 재진술하는 빈칸 문장에서는 Andy Warhol이 미국인들이 주기적으로 구매하는 수프 캔을 그린 것은 수프 캔에 숨겨진 깊이가 있음을 시사하기 위해서가 아니라, 그것의 '무엇'을 찬양하기 위해서라고 하였다. 따라서 빈칸에는 '숨겨진 깊이'와 반대되는 ⑤ '피상'이 오는 것이 적절하다.

[오답분석] ①, ②, ③, ④은 Andy Warhol이 <캠벨 수프 통조림>을 통해 나타내고자 한 바를 숨겨진 깊이와 대조하여 설명하는 단어로 적절하지 않다.

[해석] 팝 아트는 현대 미술의 거만함에 대한 반발로 1950년대 후반과 1960년대 초반에 발전했다. 팝 아티스트들은 광고 이미지, 대량 생산된 제품, 만화책, 유명 인사들을 묘사함으로써 일상생활을 나타냈다. 그렇게 하면서, 그들은 전후 시대에 등장했던 소비자 주도의 세계를 찬양했다. 이러한 형태의 예술은 그것이 묘사하는 소재처럼 현대 문화의 처분 가능한 과잉을 나타내는 것이 가능하도록 의도되었다. 팝 아트의 가장 유명한 실천가인 Andy Warhol(앤디 워홀)은 <캠벨 수프 통조림>으로 이것을 전형적으로 보여주었고, 그것에서 그는 수백만 명의 미국인들이 주기적으로 구매하는 수프 캔의 한 종류를 그렸다. 그는 이 대량 생산된 식료품에 숨겨진 깊이가 있음을 시사하기 위해서가 아니라, 그것의 피상을 찬양하기 위해 이것을 했다. 그렇게 함으로써, Warhol은 고급문화가 일상생활과 그것을 지배했던 제품들로부터 반드시 제거되어야 할 필요는 없음을 보여주었다.

① 잠재력　　② 실현 가능성
③ 직접성　　④ 실용성
⑤ 피상

[어휘] reaction 반발, 반응　disposable 처분 가능한　excess 과잉, 지나침
practitioner 실천가, 현역　epitomize 전형적으로 보여주다

[구문분석] [9행] The most famous practitioner of pop art, Andy Warhol, epitomized this with his *Campbell's Soup Cans*, [in which he painted a type of **soup can** (that millions of Americans purchased regularly)].

→ [in ~ regularly]는 선행사 *Campbell's Soup Cans*를 수식하며, '전치사 + 관계대명사' in which가 이끄는 관계대명사절이다.

→ (that ~ regularly)는 선행사 soup can을 수식하며 목적격 관계대명사 that이 이끄는 관계대명사절이다.

32　빈칸 추론하기　정답 ①

[해설] 주제문에 해당하는 빈칸 문장에서 이력 현상이란 '무엇'에도 불구하고 계속해서 영향을 미치는 사건이라고 했다. 이력 현상의 예시로 불황 이후에 경제가 회복되었더라도 실업률이 계속해서 상승하는 것과, 주식 시장 붕괴 이후에 투자자들이 주식에 투자하기를 꺼리는 것을 언급하고 있다. 따라서 빈칸에는 ① '그것을 야기했던 요인들의 제거'가 와서 이력 현상이란 사건을 야기했던 요인들이 사라져도 그 여파가 지속되는 것이라는 의미가 되어야 한다.

[오답분석] ②의 근로자들에게 미치는 영향의 심각함에 대한 내용은 글에서 언급되고 있지 않다. ③은 글에서 언급한 skills를 사용하여 헷갈리게 하는 오답이다. ④의 변화들이 발생하는 속도는 글의 내용과 관련이 없다. ⑤은 글에서 언급된 unemployment의 반의어 employment를 사용하여 헷갈리게 하는 오답이다.

[해석] 이력 현상이란 그것을 야기했던 요인들의 제거에도 불구하고 계속해서 영향을 미치는 사건으로 정의되는 경제 용어이다. 이는 대개 붕괴나 불황과 같은 중대한 경제적 사건: 사실상 심각하고 길어지는 사건들 이후에 발생한다. 예를 들어, 불황 이후에 경제가 회복되었더라도 실업률이 계속해서 상승할 수도 있다. 이러한 추세는 앞뒤가 맞지 않는 것처럼 보일 수도 있지만, 사실 그에 대한 이유가 있다. 경제가 회복되었을 때, 근로자들은 업계들에서 일하는 데 요구되는 필수 기술들이 부족할 수 있다; 이용 가능한 전문 기술이 회사들의 새로운 요구들을 충족시키지 못하는 것이다. 이는 영국에서 불황 중에 1980년에서 1981년 동안 실업자 수가 150만에서 200만으로 증가했고, 그 후에 불황이 끝난 후에 300만으로 증가했을 때 그런 경우였다. 이력 현상은 또한 주식 시장 붕괴에도 발생할 수 있는데, 이는 투자자들이 그러한 사건 후에 돈을 다시 주식에 투자하기를 꺼리기 때문이다. 붕괴가 끝나더라도, 그 사건의 여파는 지속된다.

① 그것을 야기했던 요인들의 제거
② 근로자들에게 미치는 영향의 심각함
③ 전문 기술의 다양화
④ 변화들이 발생하는 빠른 속도
⑤ 고용 기회의 확대

[어휘] hysteresis 이력 현상　occurrence 사건, 발생　crash 붕괴, 폭락
recession 불황, 불경기　draw out 길게 하다, 끌다
explanation 이유, 설명　expertise 전문 기술, 전문 지식
aftershock 여파, 여진　[선택지] diversification 다양화, 다양성

[구문분석] [6행] For example, ①[following a recession] the unemployment rate may persist in rising ②[**even though** the economy has rebounded].

→ ①[following a recession]의 following은 '~후에'라는 의미의 전치사로 쓰였다.

→ ②[even ~ rebounded]는 접속사 even though(~라 하더라도)가 이끄는 양보의 부사절이다.

[8행] This trend might not [appear to make sense], but there is actually an explanation for it.

→ [appear ~ sense]는 'appear + to부정사(~처럼 보이다, ~인 것 같다)'의 형태로, to부정사가 주격 보어 역할을 한다.

33 빈칸 추론하기 정답 ③

(해설) 정언 명령과 가언 명령에 대한 개념을 은퇴를 위해 저축하는 것과 자선 사업에 기부하는 것을 예로 들어 설명하는 글이다. 빈칸 앞에서 저축 예금은 개인이 마음 편하게 은퇴할 충분한 돈을 갖는 것에 대해 신경을 쓰는 경우에만 필수적일 뿐인 가언 명령이고, 자신이 원하는 것을 얻는 하나의 방법이라고 했다. 따라서 주제와 관련된 빈칸에는 ③ '개인적 목표를 달성하는 데에 유익한'이라는 내용이 오는 것이 적절하다.

(오답분석) ①은 도덕적 의무가 없고 개인적 목표를 달성하는 데에 필수적인 가언 명령과 관련된 내용이 들어가야 하는 빈칸과 반대되므로 오답이다. ②의 이성은 글의 내용과 관련이 없다. ④의 가치를 평가하는 것은 글의 내용과 관련이 없다. ⑤는 글에서 언급된 save money, savings deposit 등에서 연상할 수 있는 financial circumstances를 사용하여 헷갈리게 했지만, 은퇴를 위해 돈을 저축해야 한다고 하는 가언 명령을 설명하는 글의 내용과 관련이 없으므로 오답이다.

(해석) 내가 은퇴를 위해 돈을 저축해야 한다고 말하는 것과 자선 사업에 돈을 내야 한다고 말하는 것 간에는 상당한 차이가 있다. 둘 다 재정적 책임과 관련 있는 명령이다. 하지만, 후자의 명령은 사회가 다양한 질병의 치료와 그 관계자들이 직분을 다하는 것을 위해 개인 기부자의 관대함에 의존하는 만큼 사회 전체에 영향을 미치는 도덕적 의무를 나타내는 반면, 전자의 명령은 투자를 하는 개인이 마음 편하게 은퇴할 충분한 돈을 갖는 것에 대해 신경을 쓰는 경우에만 필수적일 뿐이다. 저축 예금은 자신이 원하는 것을 얻을 하나의 방법이다. 자선은 자신의 공동체에서 가장 취약한 사람들을 보살피는 하나의 방법이다. 따라서, 저축 예금을 개설하는 것은 문제의 행위자가 그렇게 하기를 바라든 바라지 않든 따라야 하는 정언 명령이 아니라 가언 명령이고, 이는 개인적 목표를 달성하는 데에 유익한 실질적인 기본 재산이 된다.

① 양심의 명령에서 기인하는
② 이성의 적용을 통해 도달하는
③ 개인적 목표를 달성하는 데에 유익한
④ 개인의 가치의 평가에 필수적인
⑤ 특정한 재정적 상황들에서 권할 수 없는

(어휘) pertain to ~과 관련되다 remediation 치료, 교정
savings deposit 저축 예금 hypothetical 가언적인, 가설의
objective 실질적인 principal 기본 재산, (단체의) 장
categorical 정언적인, 단정적인 actor 행위자 in question 문제의
[선택지] dictate 명령 instructive 유익한 inadvisable 권할 수 없는

(구문분석) [6행] ~ society, to the extent that society depends on the generosity of private donors ①[for the remediation of various ills] **and** ②[for the functioning of its participants], whereas the former imperative is only necessary if the individual ③[making the investment] cares about having enough money to retire comfortably.

→ ①[for ~ ills]와 ②[for ~ participants]는 and로 연결된 전치사구로, 둘 다 society depends on the generosity of private donors를 수식한다.

→ if절의 주어 the individual은 현재분사구 ③[making the investment]의 수식을 받고 있다.

34 빈칸 추론하기 정답 ①

(해설) 전체를 구성하는 부분들로 나눔으로써 밝혀지는 환원주의적 패러다임이 아닌, 전체로서의 유기체에 초점을 두어야 복잡한 생물학적 체계를 제대로 이해할 수 있다는 내용의 글이다. 주제와 관련된 빈칸 문장에서는 물리학과 화학의 관점에서 모든 생물학을 설명하려는 환원주의적 패러다임이 매력적으로 보일지 몰라도, 이는 '무엇'하다고 했고, 빈칸 뒤 문장에서는 의식은 화학 작용의 연속으로 환원될 수 없는, 경험과 감정이 복잡하게 얽힌 것이라고 예를 들었다. 따라서 빈칸에는 ① '생물학적 개체들의 예상 불가능한 복잡성을 과소평가한다'는 내용이 오는 것이 적절하다.

(오답분석) ②의 다양한 역할에 대한 내용은 글에서 언급되고 있지 않다. ③은 생물학의 환원주의 패러다임이 물리학과 화학의 관점에서 모든 생물학을 설명하려는 시도라는 글의 내용과 일치하지 않는 내용이고, 다른 가능성 있는 설명을 무시한다는 내용은 글에서 언급되고 있지 않다. ④은 환원주의 패러다임이 생물학적 체계를 부분들의 구성으로 본다는 글의 내용과 일치하지 않는 내용이므로 오답이다. ⑤의 질병의 유전적 요인에 대한 내용은 글에서 언급되고 있지 않다.

(해석) 유기체가 원자와 분자로 구성되어 있다는 발견은 많은 생물학자들이 생물학적 체계들을 그것들을 구성하는 부분들로 나눔으로써 그 체계의 비밀이 밝혀질 수 있다는 환원주의적 패러다임을 채택하게 했다. 하지만, DNA의 선구자 Francis Crick(프란시스 크릭)이 한때 주장했던 것처럼 "물리학과 화학의 관점에서 모든 생물학을 설명하려는" 시도들에 달성 가능성의 유혹이 있을지 몰라도, 그것들은 생물학적 개체들의 예상 불가능한 복잡성을 과소평가한다. 하나의 예시로, 의식은 단순히 뇌 속 화학 작용들의 연속이 아니라 단순화를 허용하지 않는 경험과 감정이 복잡하게 뒤얽힌 것이다. 질병들은 단지 표적 약물의 개입이나 단 하나의 유전 인자 제거로 제거될 수 있는 증상들이 아니라, 전체론적인 전략들을 필요로 하는 비정상적인 작용의 복잡한 망이다. 미세한 화학적 또는 분자에 의한 현상들이 더 높은 층위의 모든 사건을 야기한다고 가정하기 보다, 생물학자들은 낮은 층위의 현상들에 대한 높은 층위의 원인에 초점을 맞추어야 한다. 복잡한 생물학적 체계가 정확하게 이해될 수 있는 것은 오로지 전체로서의 유기체에 초점을 둠으로써이다.

① 생물학적 개체들의 예상 불가능한 복잡성을 과소평가한다
② 체계의 개별 부분들이 다양한 역할을 한다는 것을 인정한다
③ 화학에 중점을 아주 많이 두고 다른 가능성 있는 설명들을 무시한다
④ 유기체를 생물학적 기능의 집합에 지나지 않는 것으로 여긴다
⑤ 질병을 일으키는 유전적 요인들에 집중해야 하는 필요성을 설명한다

(어휘) atom 원자 molecule 분자 unravel 밝히다, 풀다 component 구성하는
allure 유혹, 매력 attainability 달성 가능성, 획득할 수 있음
intricate 복잡한 web 뒤얽힌 것 defy 허용하지 않다, 반대하다
pharmaceutical 약학의, 제약의 abnormal 비정상적인 minute 미세한
[선택지] underestimate 과소평가하다 entity 개체 heavily 아주 많이, 몹시

(구문분석) [1행] **The discovery** [that organisms are made up of atoms and molecules] led many biologists to adopt a reductionist paradigm ~

→ [that ~ molecules]는 The discovery와 동격을 이루는 명사절이다.

[19행] **It is only** by focusing attention on the organism as a whole **that** complex biological systems can be truly understood.

→ 전치사구 by focusing attention on the organism as a whole을 강조하는 it is only ~ that (~하는 것은 오직 -이다) 강조구문이 쓰였다.

35 흐름과 관계 없는 문장 찾기 정답 ④

(해설) 어휘들의 감정적 반향이 그 어휘들의 의미보다는 오로지 그것들이 어떻게 소리가 나는지에 근거할 수 있다는 내용의 글로, 부바/키키 효과를 기반으로 한 실험 내용을 기술하고 있다. 그런데 ④은 단어의 감정적 영향이 그것이 전달되는 방식과도 관련된다는 내용이므로 핵심 소재는 같지만 주제에서 벗어나 있어 글의 흐름과 무관하다.

(오답분석) ⑤의 this는 ②와 ③에서 언급된 부바/키키 효과와 관련된 연구 내용을 가리키므로 ③ 뒤에 이어지는 게 적절하다.

(해석) 한 새로운 연구는 어휘들의 감정적 반향이 그것들의 의미보다는 오로지 그것들이 어떻게 소리가 나는지에 근거할 수 있음을 보여주었다. ① 말소리와 물체의 시각적 형태 간의 상응 관계인 "부바/키키 효과"를 기반으로 하여, Cornell 대학의 연구원들은 참가자들에게 일련의 단어에 대한 그들의 감정적 반응을 기록할 것을 요구했다. ② 그들은 'bouba'와 같은 일부 단어들이 어떻게 소리가 나는지에 근거하여 참가자들에게 둥그런 형태를 지니는 것으로 인식되었고, 그것들을 듣는 것이 진정 효과를 낸다는 것을 발견했다. ③ 반면에, 'kiki'와 같은 다른 단어들은 날카롭거나 뾰족뾰족한 것으로 생각되었고 좀 더 감정적으로 자극이 되는 것으로 기록되었다. (④ 대부분의 사람들에게, 한 단어의 감정적 영향은 그것이 그 의미와 관련되어 있는 만큼이나 전달되는 방식과도 관련된다.) ⑤ 연구원들은 이것이 감정적 반향이 유아들 사이의 언어의 부호화에 중요한 역할을 할 수 있다는 암시와 함께, 언어의 발달에서 인간의 감정이 얼마나 중요한지를 보여준다고 주장한다.

(어휘) resonance 반향, 울림 solely 오로지 significance 의미
correspondence 상응 관계, 서신 speech sound 말소리
spiky 뾰족뾰족한

(구문분석)
[13행] For most people, the emotional effect of a word is related [as much to the way in which it is delivered as] **it is** to its meaning.
→ [as ~ as]는 'as + much + 명사구 + as'(~만큼 -한)의 형태로 비교를 나타내는 구문이다.
→ it is 뒤에는 related가 생략되어 있는데, 앞에서 the emotional effect ~ is related에서 이미 언급되었기 때문이다.

[15행] The researchers claim that ~ language, [with the implication being (that emotional resonance could play a significant role in the encoding of language among infants)].
→ [with ~ infants]는 'with + 명사(구) + 분사' 형태의 분사구문으로, '~와 함께'라는 의미로 해석한다. 여기서 that절(that ~ infants)는 being의 주격 보어이다.

36 글의 순서 배열하기 정답 ③

(해설) 주어진 글은 로드 무비가 미국 영화에서 매우 친숙하고 인기 있는 장르이고 주인공이 "먼 길을 떠나는" 이동 과정이 이야기의 주요한 특징이라는 주제를 제시한다. (B)는 로드 무비가 이동에 대한 폭넓은 주제를 제시한다는 내용이고, 주어진 글 마지막에서 이동이 로드 무비 속 이야기의 주요한 특징이라고 했으므로 그 뒤에 와야 한다. (C)는 역접 연결어 Although를 통해 로드 무비가 표면적으로는 이동을 다루는 것 같아도 구도나 편집과 같은 시각적 요소들에 의존한다며 (B)의 내용에 대한 반전 설명을 하고 있으므로, 로드 무비의 사건들이 이동에 대한 주제를 제시한다고 언급하는 (B) 뒤에 오는 것이 적절하다. (A)는 Ultimately를 통해 로드 무비는 역설적으로 정지된 시각적 스타일을 통

해 이동이란 주제를 표현한다고 하며 (C)의 내용에 대한 부연 설명을 하고 있으므로, 로드 무비가 시각적 요소들에 의존한다고 한 (C) 뒤에 오는 것이 적절하다. 따라서 글의 순서로 가장 적절한 것은 ③ (B) - (C) - (A)이다.

(해석) 미국 영화에서, 로드 무비는 매우 친숙하고 인기 있는 장르로, 목적지를 향해 "먼 길을 떠나는" 한 명이나 두 명의 주인공을 보여준다. 이동은 일반적으로 이야기의 주요한 특징이다.

(B) 로드 무비 속 사건들이 이동에 대한 더 폭넓은 주제를 제시하는 것은 지극히 자연스럽다. 많은 경우, 그 영화들은 강요된 이동을 탐구한다. 도망자의 로드 무비는 일반적으로 경찰로부터 달아나는 등장인물들을 특징으로 한다. 다른 등장인물들은 아픈 친척을 만나러 가야 하는 것과 같은 상황들로 인해 강제로 이동하게 된다.

(C) 이동이 로드 무비의 표면적인 주제이지만, 영화적 표현은 단순한 스토리텔링을 넘어선다. 주제가 보통 서사적 사건들을 통해 거의 전적으로 표현되는 문학과 달리, 영화는 이미지들이 구성되는 방식인 구도와, 이미지들이 나뉘고 재조합되는 방식인 편집과 같은 시각적 요소들에 의존한다.

(A) 궁극적으로, 로드 무비의 이동이란 주제는 역설적이게도 정지된 시각적 스타일로 표현된다. 구도의 초점은 화면의 가운데를 향하게 되고, 편집은 이어지는 이미지들이 반복적일 것임을 암시한다. 이렇게 해서, 홀리게 하는 단조로움이 주인공들을 에워싸고, 그들을 달래서 정적이고 불변의 존재가 되게 한다.

(어휘) road movie 로드 무비 (장소의 이동을 따라가며 이야기가 진행되는 영화 장르)
protagonist 주인공 hit the road 먼 길을 떠나다, 여행을 떠나다
in pursuit of ~을 향하여 objective 목적, 목표 motion 이동, 움직임
manifest 표현하다 composition 구도 ensuing 이어지는, 다음의
hypnotize 홀리다 sameness 단조로움 engulf 에워싸다, 사로잡다
lull A into A를 달래서 ~하게 하다 static 정적인, 고정된
outlaw 도망자, 범법자 law 경찰, 사법 기관

(구문분석)
[13행] It is only natural [that the events in road movies serve a broader theme about mobility].
가주어   진주어(that절)
→ 가주어 it이 길이가 긴 진주어 that절 [that ~ mobility] 대신 주어 자리에 쓰인 형태이다.

[23행] ~ film depends upon visual elements such as composition, **the way** ①[that images are framed], and editing, **the way** ②[that images are split and reassembled].
→ ①[that ~ framed]와 ②[that ~ reassembled]는 방법을 나타내는 선행사 the way를 수식하며, 관계부사 how 대신 that이 쓰인 관계절이다.

37 글의 순서 배열하기 정답 ②

(해설) 주어진 글은 가설이나 이론을 고안할 때 전제 위에 전제를 더하면서 복잡성 안에서 헤매기 쉽다는 문제를 제시한다. (B)는 복잡한 예측은 검증하기 어렵기 때문에 과학자들이 흔히 단순한 설명이 최고라고 하는 오컴의 면도날 원칙에 의존한다는 내용이고, 주어진 글에서 가설이나 이론을 고안할 때 복잡성 안에서 헤매기 쉽다고 했으므로 그 뒤에 와야 한다. (A)는 역접 연결어 nevertheless를 통해 오컴의 면도날이 중요시하는 단순함이 정확성을 보장하는 것은 아니라며 (B)의 내용에 대한 반전 설명을 하고 있으므로, 오컴의 면도날 원칙을 언급하는 (B) 뒤에 오는 것이 적절하다. (C)의 this example(이 예시)은 (A)의 '1879년에 Alfred Kempe가 "4색 정리"를 증명하려고 시도한 것'을 가리키므로 (A) 바로 다음에 오는 것이 적절하다. 따라서 글의 순서로 가장 적절한 것은 ② (B) - (A) - (C)이다.

(해설) 이유가 밝혀지지 않은 현상을 설명하기 위해 가설이나 이론을 고안할 때, 전제 위에 전제를 더하면서 복잡성 안에서 헤매는 것은 매력적이다.

(B) 혼란스럽고 다면적인 현실을 반영하는 복잡한 예측은 종종 검증하기가 어렵다. 그러한 이유로, 과학자들은 흔히 오컴의 면도날의 원칙에 의존하는데, 그것은 가장 단순한 설명이 일반적으로 최고의 것이라고 말한다. 이것은 관련은 없는데 진실인 사실들이 결과에는 미미한 영향을 끼치기 때문에 그것들을 잘라내는 데에 유용할 수 있다.

(A) 그렇기는 하지만, 단순함이 정확성을 보장하는 것은 아님을 아는 것이 중요하다. 1879년에, Alfred Kempe(알프레드 캠프)는 "4색 정리"를 증명하려는 시도를 했는데, 이는 접하는 두 영역이 한 가지 색을 공유하지 않는 방식으로 지도를 채우는 데에 필요한 것은 네 가지 색이 전부라는 것이다. 그의 증명은 명쾌했지만 잘못되었다.

(C) 가장 단순한 설명을 찾는 것이 틀림없이 항상 참으로 이어졌다면 연구자들에게 훨씬 더 수월했을 것이다. 하지만, 이 예시가 보여주듯이, 오컴의 면도날은 이론의 정확성을 위한 지침이 아니라, 그것의 유효성을 확인하기 위한 기준으로서 가장 적절히 이용된다. 결국, 가정은 사실 자체가 아니라, 사실을 확인하기 위한 도구이다.

(어휘) **devise** 고안하다   **tempting** 매력적인   **compound** 더하다, 섞다
assumption 전제, 가정   **accuracy** 정확성, 정밀도   **border** 접하다
elegant 명쾌한, 단순 명료한   **messy** 혼란을 주는, 지저분한
multifaceted 다면적인   **correctness** 정확성, 단정

(구문분석)
[16행] This can be useful **for** [cutting away **facts** (that are true without being relevant)] because they have an insignificant impact on outcomes.
→ [cutting ~ relevant]는 전치사 for의 목적어 역할을 하는 동명사구이다.
→ (that ~ relevant)는 선행사 facts를 수식하며, 주격 관계대명사 that이 이끄는 관계대명사절이다.

38 주어진 문장의 위치 찾기 정답 ⑤

(해설) 주어진 문장에 명시적 단서가 없는 경우에는 글의 흐름이 끊기는 곳을 찾아야 한다. ⑤ 앞까지는 복점에서 선두에 있는 회사가 경쟁의 규칙을 세우고 코카콜라가 펩시와 시장 점유율을 두고 경쟁한다는 내용이 이어지다가 ⑤ 뒤 문장에서 선두 기업과 뒤따르는 기업이 서로에게 영향력을 행사한다는 내용이 나오고 있다. ⑤ 뒤 문장에서 역접 연결어 Yet을 통해 앞 문장에 대한 반전 설명을 하고 있지만 ⑤ 앞 문장은 ⑤ 뒤 문장에 반대되는 내용이 아니라는 점을 통해 글의 흐름이 끊겼음을 알 수 있다. 따라서 주어진 문장이 들어가기에 가장 적절한 곳은 ⑤이다.

(오답분석) ② 뒤 문장은 ① 뒤 문장에 이어서 선두 기업인 코카콜라의 영향력에 대해 보충 설명하고 있다. ③ 뒤 문장은 역접 연결어 however를 통해서 소규모 기업이 기발한 전략으로 선두 기업에 대응할 수 있다며 ② 뒤 문장에 반대되는 내용을 설명한다. ④ 뒤 문장은 ③ 뒤 문장에서 설명한 내용의 예시로 선두 기업인 코카콜라가 뒤따르는 회사였던 펩시의 전략에 어떻게 대응했는지 설명한다. 따라서 주어진 문장은 이 내용이 끝난 이후에 들어가야 한다.

(해석) 시장 점유율이 두 곳의 주요한 경쟁자들 사이에서 분배될 때, 선두에 있는 기업이 그 경쟁의 규칙들을 세우지만, 뒤따르는 기업의 잠재력을 무시하는 것은 절대로 좋은 생각이 아니다. (①) 세계의 코카콜라 회사들은 얼마나 많은 제품들을 이용 가능하게 할 것인지를 결정한다. (②) 시장에서의 그들의 영향력은 제품의 경쟁력을 높이고 경쟁자들이 그러한 결정에 대응하게 만드는 우월

한 브랜드 인지도에서 기인한다. (③) 하지만, 복점이나 다른 경쟁 모델에 있는 더 소규모의 기업은 기발한 전략으로 선두 기업이 대응하게 만들 수 있다. (④) 코카콜라는 블라인드 맛 테스트에서 더 우수한 결과를 냈다는 펩시의 주장에, 오랫동안 시장을 주도해온 그들 제조법의 생산을 줄이고 그 주요 경쟁사의 더 단 맛을 똑같이 만든 제품의 생산을 늘리는 것으로 대응했다. (⑤ 시장 경쟁의 일부 모델들은 복점에 있는 두 기업이 동시에 결정을 내린다고 제시한다.) 하지만, 실제는 선두 기업과 뒤따르는 기업이 서로에게 영향력을 행사한다는 것이고, 이는 각 기업이 상대방이 하는 것에 대응하면서 차례로 행동한다는 것을 의미한다.

(어휘) **duopoly** 복점(2개 업체에 의한 시장 독점)
simultaneous 동시에 일어나는, 동시의   **market share** 시장 점유율
discount 무시하다   **brand recognition** 브랜드 인지도
competitiveness 경쟁력   **clone** 똑같이 만들다, 복제하다
exert (영향력을) 행사하다

(구문분석)
[11행] A smaller firm in a duopoly or other competitive model, however, can force the leader to react with a clever strategy.
            동사   목적어   목적격 보어
→ 동사 force의 목적어로 the leader, 목적격 보어로 to부정사 to react가 쓰였다.

39 주어진 문장의 위치 찾기 정답 ④

(해설) 주어진 문장에 명시적 단서가 없는 경우에는 글의 흐름이 끊기는 곳을 찾아야 한다. ④ 앞까지는 <파리 대왕>은 플롯이 중심이 아니기 때문에 '데우스 엑스 마키나'가 효과가 있다는 내용이 이어지다가 ④ 뒤 문장에서 <파리 대왕>에서 중요한 건 섬과 문명 사회의 병치라는 내용이 나오고 있으므로, 글의 흐름이 끊겼음을 알 수 있다. 또한 ④ 앞 문장에서 <파리 대왕> 이야기는 플롯 중심이 아니라고 한 내용은 주어진 문장에서 The main focus here(여기서의 주안점은)로 이어지고 있으므로 주어진 문장이 들어가기에 가장 적절한 곳은 ④이다.

(오답분석) ⑤ 뒤 문장은 ④ 뒤 문장에 이어서 <파리 대왕>에서 '데우스 엑스 마키나'가 효과가 있는 이유에 대해 언급하고 있다.

(해석) '데우스 엑스 마키나'는 갑작스럽거나 신성한 사건으로 인해 겉보기에 풀 수 없는 문제가 갑자기 해결되는 문학의 플롯 장치이다. 이 기법은 상황들을 마무리하는 터무니없는 방식이라고 종종 비방된다. (①) 하지만, William Golding(윌리엄 골딩)의 1954년 고전 <파리 대왕>을 예로 들면서, 몇몇 사람들은 '데우스 엑스 마키나'가 효과적으로 이용될 수 있다고 주장한다. (②) 그 소설에서, 사람이 없는 섬에 고립되어 그들 스스로를 다스려야 했던 한 무리의 소년들이 지나가던 배에 의해 갑자기 구출된다. (③) 전형적으로, 그것은 지나치게 작위적인 해결책으로 보이기 때문에 이는 실망스러운 해결일 것이지만, 그 이야기는 플롯이 중심이 아니기 때문에 그것은 효과가 있다. (④ 여기서의 주안점은 그 소년들이 서서히 혼란과 심한 불신에 빠져들면서 인간의 정신을 탐구하는 것이다.) 따라서, 그들이 그 상황에 어떻게 빠졌거나 벗어났는지보다는, 그 무리의 갑작스러운 문명 세계로의 귀환을 섬에서의 야만적인 행위와 대비하여 병치하는 것이 중요한 것이다. (⑤) 지나가는 배의 '데우스 엑스 마키나'는 그 이야기의 도덕적인 복잡성과 주제와 관련된 내용의 효과를 약화시키지 않는다.

(어휘) **psyche** 정신, 마음   **descend into** ~에 서서히 빠져들다
paranoia 심한 불신, 편집증   **plot** 플롯, 줄거리   **divine** 신성한, 신의
inept 터무니없는, 부적절한   **driven** ~ 중심의   **juxtaposition** 병치, 병렬
savage 야만적인   **undercut** ~의 효과를 약화시키다

thematic 주제와 관련된

구문분석

[15행] Thus, the juxtaposition of ~ island is ①[what is significant] **rather than** ②[how they got into or out of the situation].
동사　주격 보어

→ ①[what is significant]는 관계대명사 what(~하는 것)이 이끄는 명사절로 be동사 is의 주격 보어 역할을 한다.

→ ②[how ~ situation]은 의문사 how가 이끄는 명사절로 전치사 rather than의 목적어 역할을 한다.

---

40 요약문 완성하기　정답 ②

해설 글의 중반부에서 Alan Turing의 튜링 테스트를 통과한 기계는 지능을 가진 것이라고 볼 수도 있다고 했고, 글의 후반부에서는 기계가 인간의 지능을 가장할 수 있다는 것이 실제로 지능을 갖게 하는 것과 동일하지 않다고 했다. 따라서 지문의 has successfully passed as human and possesses intelligence를 illusion으로, actually make it intelligent를 genuine으로 바꾸어 표현한 ②이 정답이다.

오답분석 ①의 imaginary와 ④의 fabricated는 (B)의 정답인 genuine과 반대 의미의 단어이다.

해석 기계가 지능이 있는지에 대한 질문은 수십 년 동안 철학자들을 사로잡았다. 인공 지능의 존재는 기계가 사고할 수 있을 때 인간의 지능을 유일무이하게 만드는 무언가가 있는가와 같은 철학적 의문을 제기한다. 상응하여, 인공 지능의 성공이 인간의 마음이 그저 기계의 한 종류라는 것을 의미하는가? 아마도 가장 유력한 대답은 Alan Turing(앨런 튜링)의 튜링 테스트인데, 거기서 인간이 인간과 기계 간의 대화를 통해 기계의 지능을 평가한다. 만약 그 사람이 어떤 화자가 인간이 아닌지 알 수 없다면, 그 기계는 성공적으로 인간으로서 통과했고 지능을 갖춘 것이다. 몇몇 사람들은 뇌가 과학 법칙을 따르기 때문에 마음의 작용들도 틀림없이 복제 가능할 것이므로 이러한 종류의 지능 모의실험은 불가피하다고 생각한다. 하지만, 대다수의 사람들은 이것이 기계 지능의 한 형태라는 생각을 부정하고 기계가 인간의 지능을 가장할 수 있다는 사실이 실제로 그것이 지능을 갖게 만들지 않는다고 주장한다. 그들의 주장은 인간처럼 행동하는 것은 의식을 지니는 것과 매우 다르고, 그것에 대해 우리는 여전히 거의 알지 못한다는 것이다.

↓

기계가 인간 지능에 대한 (A) 환상을 보여줄 수 있다고 해서 그것이 기계가 (B) 진짜 지능을 보여준다는 것을 의미하지는 않는다.

(A)	(B)
① 본질 ……	상상의
② 환상 ……	진짜의
③ 시작 ……	충분한
④ 모습 ……	허구의
⑤ 정의 ……	전통적인

어휘 preoccupy (마음을) 사로잡다　pose (문제 등을) 제기하나
correspondingly 상응하여　replicable 복제 가능한
simulate 가장하다, 흉내 내다

구문분석

[14행] Some believe that this sort of simulation of intelligence is inevitable, [**since**, (**as** the brain obeys the laws of science), the mind's functions must be replicable].

→ since와 as는 이유를 나타내는 부사절 접속사로, [since ~ replicable] 과 (as ~ science) 모두 이유의 부사절이다.

[21행] Their point is that acting like a human is vastly different from possessing consciousness, which [we still know very **little** about].

→ [we ~ about]은 '거의 없는'이라는 의미의 부정어 little이 쓰인 부정 구문이다.

41~42 장문 독해 1

해석 암흑 물질은 거의 틀림없이 오늘날 물리학에서 가장 흥미로운 주제이다. 우선, 이 보이지 않는 물질은 나선 은하들이 분해되지 않고 매우 빠른 속도로 계속해서 회전하기에는 (a) 불충분한 가시 질량을 포함하기 때문에 존재한다고 생각된다. 하지만, [41]우주가 암흑 물질의 (b) 징후로 가득함에도 불구하고, 그것은 여전히 수수께끼이다; 그것은 과학자들이 일반적으로 우주의 작용을 연구하기 위해 의존하는 요소들인 어떠한 전자기 방사선이나 빛도 흡수하거나, 반사하거나, 내뿜는 것 같지 않다. 암흑 물질이 우주의 전체 질량의 약 85퍼센트를 차지한다고 생각되고 가장 기초적인 단계에서 우주가 어떻게 작용하는지를 우리가 이해하는 데에 도움이 될 수 있다는 점을 고려하면, 그것을 추적하고자 하는 것이 이해가 된다. 하지만 물리학자들은 우주가 어떻게 작용하는지에 대해 현재 가장 (c) 실행 가능한 설명인 표준 모형을 통해 연구해야 하고, 그것은 물질이 4가지의 인력: 중력, 전자기, 강하고 약한 핵력과 상호 작용하는 방법에 의해 우주 내의 물질의 작용이 지배된다는 것을 보여준다. 암흑 물질과 상호 작용한다고 알려진 표준 모형의 유일한 구성 요소는 중력이지만, [42]과학자들은 중력이 암흑 물질로 하여금 가시 물질과 (d) 비슷하게 작용하게 하는지에 대해서 여전히 잘 알지 못하는데, 그것은 무리를 형성하기 위해 합쳐진다. [42]만약 암흑 물질이 가시 입자들의 작용과 다른 작용을 보인다면, 그것을 발견하려면 (e) 전통적인(→대안적인) 접근법이 필요할 수도 있다.

어휘 dark matter 암흑 물질　spiral galaxy 나선 은하　working 작용
hunt down 추적하다　viable 실행 가능한　behavior 작용, 반응
fundamental force 인력　nuclear force 핵력　component 구성 요소
pull together 합치다　cluster 무리　manifest (드러내) 보이다
[선택지] missing 보이지 않는, 분실된

구문분석

[11행] **Given that dark matter** is ~ understand how the cosmos functions at its most basic level, ①[it] makes sense to want to hunt ②[it] down.
진주어　가주어

→ Given that은 '~을 고려하면'이라는 의미의 부사절 접속사이다.

→ ①[it]은 진주어 to want to hunt it down 대신 주어 자리에 쓰인 가주어 it이고, ②[it]은 앞의 dark matter를 가리키는 지시대명사 it이다.

[23행] ~ scientists are still uncertain whether gravity causes dark matter to behave similarly to visible matter, which [gets pulled] together to form clusters.

→ [gets pulled]는 get을 이용한 수동태 'get + p.p.' 형태로, 행위의 발생이나 동작에 초점을 둔 표현이다.

41 　제목 파악하기 　정답 ④

(해설) 보이지 않는 물질인 암흑 물질이 존재한다는 많은 징후에도 불구하고 그것은 여전히 수수께끼라고 했고, 이는 암흑 물질이 어떠한 전자기 방사선이나 빛도 흡수하거나, 반사하거나 내뿜지 않기 때문이라고 했다. 따라서 글의 제목으로 가장 적절한 것은 ④ '보이지 않는 물질: 우리가 볼 수 없는 것을 우리가 찾을 수 있는가?'이다.

(오답 분석) ①, ②은 글의 일부만을 다루고 있는 오답이다. ③은 글의 핵심 어구 Standard Model을 사용하여 헷갈리게 하는 오답이다. ⑤은 글의 핵심 소재 '암흑 물질'을 사용했으나, 글에서 암흑 물질을 감지할 수 있는 기구의 개발에 대해서는 다루고 있지 않으므로 오답이다.

(해석) ① 암흑 물질이 우주를 설명하는 데에 정말로 필수적인가?
② 암흑 물질을 측정하는 새로운 방안의 추구
③ 표준 모형이 틀릴 수도 있는 이유
④ 보이지 않는 물질: 우리가 볼 수 없는 것을 우리가 찾을 수 있는가?
⑤ 암흑 물질: 그것을 감지할 수 있는 기구 개발하기

42 　어휘 적절성 파악하기 　정답 ⑤

(해설) 중력이 암흑 물질을 가시 물질처럼 작용하게 하는지에 대해서 여전히 잘 알지 못하고, 만약 가시 물질과 다른 작용을 하는 것을 발견하려면 새로운 접근법이 필요할 수도 있다는 맥락이 되어야 하므로 ⑤의 conventional(전통적인)을 그와 반대되는 의미의 alternative(대안적인, 대체의)와 같은 어휘로 바꾸어야 문맥상 적절하다.

(오답 분석) ①은 나선 은하들의 회전 속도를 볼 때, 포함하고 있는 가시 질량만으로는 불충분하므로 보이지 않는 물질이 존재한다는 문맥이 되어야 하므로 insufficient가 오는 것이 적절하다.

43~45 　장문 독해 2

(해석) (A) 첫 번째 독서 동호회 모임이었고, 회원들은 새로운 회원들을 환영하는 파티를 열기로 했다. Josh는 그의 집에서 그 행사를 열고 있었다. (a) 그는 그의 친구 Eric을 보았고 인사를 하려고 갔다. Eric은 Josh를 보고 기뻐했고 그가 누군가를 데려왔다고 말했다. Josh가 그게 누군지를 물었을 때, Eric이 그 방 반대편에서 무리 속에 서 있는 한 남자를 가리켰다. "David야"라고 그가 말했다.

(C) Josh는 David에게 걸어가서 자신을 소개했다. "우리 동호회에 온 걸 환영해요"라고 그가 말했다. "어떤 종류의 책을 읽는 것을 좋아해요?" ⁴⁴David는 그에게 혼란스러워하는 표정을 보이고는 질문에 대답하지 않았다. Josh는 아마도 ⁴⁴David가 그의 말을 듣지 못한 것이라고 생각하면서 그에게 다시 물어보기로 했다. 하지만 여전히, (d) 그는 대답을 하지 않았다. 결국, Josh는 David에게서 떠났고 일어났던 일로 인해 짜증이 났다. Eric은 David가 친절하다고 했지만, 그는 전혀 그렇게 친절해 보이지 않았다.

(B) 그날 밤이 계속되고 있을 때, Josh는 ⁴⁵Eric과 David가 농담을 하고 같이 웃는 것을 보면서 더욱더 짜증이 났다. 그는 왜 David가 (b) 그에게 말을 하지 않는 것인지 이해할 수 없었다. Josh가 Eric이 혼자 있는 것을 보았을 때, 그와 함께 그것에 대해 이야기하기로 결심했다. "네 친구 David가 좀 전에 나에게 좀 무례했어"라고 Josh가 말했다. Eric은 놀란 것처럼 보였다. "무슨 말이야?"라며 그가 물었다. Josh는 Eric이 (c) 그의 입장을 이해해 줄 것이라고 기대하면서 무슨 일이 있었는지에 대해 그에게 이야기했다.

(D) Eric은 웃기 시작했고 그것은 모두 큰 오해라고 Josh에게 말했다. "David

는 영어를 잘하지 못해"라고 그가 설명했다. "그는 아마 네 말을 이해하지 못했거나 뭐라고 말해야 할지 몰랐을 거야." David는 스페인 사람이었고, 그의 영어 실력을 향상시키려고 동호회에 가입한 것이었다. Eric은 스페인어도 해서 그들은 서로를 이해할 수 있었다. (e) 그가 이전에 David를 어떻게 떠났는지에 대해 끔찍함을 느껴, Josh는 Eric에게 그를 위해 사과를 통역해달라고 부탁했다. Eric은 기꺼이 받아들였고, 그 셋은 그 일에 대해 웃으면서 남은 밤을 보냈다.

(어휘) **point of view** 입장, 관점　**translate** 통역하다, 번역하다

(구문분석)
[9행] As the night went on, Josh became more and more annoyed as he <u>watched</u> <u>Eric and David</u> <u>joke and laugh</u> together. 　　　　동사　　　목적어　　　목적격 보어
→ 지각동사 watched의 목적어로 Eric and David, 목적격 보어로 동사원형 joke와 laugh가 쓰였다.

[11행] He didn't **understand** [why David wouldn't talk to him].
→ [why ~ him]은 의문사 why가 이끄는 명사절로 동사 understand의 목적어 역할을 한다.

43 　글의 순서 배열하기 　정답 ②

(해설) (A)는 Josh가 여는 독서 동호회 모임의 환영 파티에 Eric이 David를 데려왔다는 내용이다. (C)는 Josh가 David에게 가서 자신을 소개하고 질문을 했지만 David가 대답하지 않았다고 했으므로 Josh가 여는 파티에 Eric이 David를 데려왔다고 한 (A) 뒤에 와야 한다. (B)는 David가 말을 하지 않는 것에 대해 짜증이 난 Josh가 Eric에게 그것에 대해 이야기했다고 했으므로 Josh의 질문에 David가 대답하지 않았다고 한 (C) 뒤에 와야 한다. (D)의 it was all a big misunderstanding에서 it은 (B)의 "Your friend David was a bit rude to me earlier,"를 가리키므로 (B) 다음에 오는 것이 적절하다. 따라서 글의 순서로 가장 적절한 것은 ② (C) - (B) - (D)이다.

44 　지칭 대상 파악하기 　정답 ④

(해설) (a), (b), (c), (e)는 모두 Josh를 가리키지만 (d)는 David를 가리키므로, ④이 정답이다.

45 　세부 정보 파악하기 　정답 ②

(해설) (B)의 Eric and David joke and laugh together를 통해 Eric과 David가 농담을 주고받으며 웃었다는 것을 알 수 있는데, ②은 Josh와 David가 그랬다고 일부 정보를 잘못 나타냈으므로 글의 내용과 일치하지 않는 것은 ②이다.

정답

문제집 p. 170

18	④	19	⑤	20	②	21	③	22	⑤	23	③	24	②	25	④	26	⑤	27	②
28	④	29	①	30	⑤	31	③	32	⑤	33	①	34	⑤	35	③	36	②	37	③
38	⑤	39	②	40	③	41	⑤	42	③	43	③	44	③	45	⑤				

18 목적 파악하기　　　　정답 ④

(해설) you will need to(~해야 할 것이다)라는 표현을 이용해 공동체 텃밭에 자리를 확보하려면 다음 주에 직접 방문해서 신속하게 비용을 납부해야 함을 알려주고 있으므로, 정답은 ④이다.

(해석) Wallace 씨께

귀하께서 Lakeview 공동체 텃밭에 참여하는 데에 관심이 있다는 것을 알게 되어 기쁩니다. 저는 귀하의 신청서를 받았고 귀하가 올해에 저희의 더 큰 텃밭 중 하나를 임대하고 싶어 하신다는 것을 알았습니다. 귀하의 텃밭 자리를 확보하려면, 1년치 비용을 지금 납부하셔야 할 것입니다. 비용 납부는 귀하에게 회원권을 보장합니다. 저희는 현재 대기자 명단에 많은 지원자가 있으므로, 그것이 신속히 행해져야 한다는 점에 유의해주십시오. 저희가 텃밭이 운영되는 방식에 관해 귀하에게 더 알려드릴 수 있도록 귀하가 직접 방문하여 지불하시기를 원합니다. 다음 주에 방문해주시기를 바라며, 어떠한 문의 사항이든 주저 말고 연락 주시길 바랍니다. 저희는 귀하를 맞이하기를 고대합니다.

Mark Gonzalez 드림

(어휘) community garden 공동체 텃밭　lease 임대하다　guarantee 보장하다

(구문분석)
[10행] We would prefer that you pay in person [**so that** we can tell you more about how the garden works].

→ [so ~ works]는 접속사 so that(~하도록)이 이끄는 목적의 부사절이다. 이때 so that은 in order that으로 바꿔 쓸 수 있다.

19 심경 파악하기　　　　정답 ⑤

(해설) 심경은 간접적으로 표현된다. 글의 초반부의 I couldn't believe that my book would be going into print를 통해 'I'가 책을 출판하게 되어 신이 나 있다는 것을 알 수 있고, 마지막 문장의 I was so close, but my dream had slipped away once again을 통해 'I'가 출판이 좌절되어 실망감을 느꼈다는 것을 알 수 있으므로, 'I'의 심경 변화로 가장 적절한 것은 ⑤이다.

(해석) 대형 출판사에는 처음 와보는 것이었다. 내 책이 인쇄에 들어갈 거라는 것을 믿을 수 없었다. 책을 출판하는 것은 내가 꿈꾸던 모든 것이었다. 이전에 정말 열심히 노력하고 수도 없이 시도했으나, 결국 코앞에서 거부당할 뿐이었지만, 이번은 다를 것이다. 나는 편집자의 사무실로 안내되었고, 기운치게 걸이 들어갔다. 그러나 그녀의 얼굴을 본 순간, 나는 무언가 잘못되었음을 알았다. "죄송하지만, 저희가 이번에는 다른 작가 분과 함께하기로 결정했습니다. 걱정 마세요. 당신 실력이라면, 금방 다른 기회가 올 겁니다." 이것은 예상하지 못한 충격이었다. 나는 그것이 얼굴에 드러나지 않게 하려고 애썼다. 정말 거의 다 왔는데, 내 꿈은 또 한 번 멀어졌다.

① 질투하는 → 후회하는　　② 자신 있는 → 만족한
③ 좌절하는 → 안도하는　　④ 희망하는 → 우쭐해 하는

⑤ 신이 난 → 실망한

(어휘) publishing company 출판사　only to do 결국 ~할 뿐이다
bound 기운차게 걷다　blow 충격, 타격

(구문분석)
[3행] [Having a book published] was all I had ever dreamed
　　　　사역동사　목적어　목적격 보어
about.

→ [Having ~ published]는 문장의 주어 역할을 하는 동명사구로, 사역동사 having의 목적어로 a book, 목적격 보어로 과거분사 published가 쓰였다. 사역동사는 목적어와 목적격 보어가 수동 관계일 때, 목적격 보어로 과거분사를 취한다.

20 주장 파악하기　　　　정답 ②

(해설) 글의 마지막 문장에서 민주주의를 유지하려면 공직에 있는 정치인이 헌법에 위배되지 않는 권한을 이용하는 데에도 제도적 자제가 필요하다고 주장하고 있으므로 정답은 ②이다.

(오답분석) ①은 정치인들에게 제도적 자제가 요구된다는 글의 내용과 반대되므로 오답이다. ③은 글에서 언급된 내용이 아니다. ④의 헌법 준수를 감시하는 것은 글의 내용과 관련이 없으므로 오답이다. ⑤은 헌법에 위배되는 것이 아니더라도 민주적 절차를 방해하는 행위를 자제해야 한다는 글의 주장과 반대되는 내용이므로 오답이다.

(해석) 공직에 있는 모든 정치인이 최대 범위로 그들의 권한을 이용한다면, 그 결과로서 생기는 것은 민주주의와 거의 비슷하지 않을 것이다. 이것의 예시는 현재 미국에서 볼 수 있는데, 정치적 양극화로 인해 고위 관리들이 "헌법적 강경 태도"라는 것을 정기적으로 이용하게 되었기 때문이다. 이것은 정치적 적수가 무슨 일을 하는 데 제약을 가하기 위해 행정부를 폐쇄하는 것과 대법원을 패킹하는 것을 포함하여 대표들이 그들 권한에 있는 모든 것을 하는 경우인데, 그것은 일의 진척을 모조리 멈춰 세운다. 이러한 행위들은 엄밀히 따지면 명시적으로 금지되지 않았다는 점에서 헌법에 위배되는 것은 아니지만, 그것들은 민주적 절차를 방해하는데, 이는 많은 헌법적 견제와 균형에 의해 보호되고 특정 권한을 정치적인 주체에게 부여하도록 의도되었다. 넓은 의미로는 그렇지만, 그것들만으로 민주주의를 유지시킬 수 없다. 민주적 절차의 혜택을 위해 가능한 헌법적 권한을 이용하는 데에 자제력을 발휘하는 제도적 자제 또한 요구된다.

(어휘) polarization 양극화　hardball 강경한 태도
pack 패킹하다(자기에게 유리한 사람들로 채우다)　halt 멈추다
technically 엄밀히 따지면　unconstitutional 헌법에 위배되는
uphold 유지시키다　forbearance 자제, 관용

(구문분석)
[3행] Examples of this can be seen in America now [**as** political polarization has led officials to regularly use what is called "constitutional hardball."]

→ [as ~ hardball]은 접속사 as(~하기 때문에)가 이끄는 이유의 부사절이다.

[6행] This is when representatives do **everything in their power**, ①[including shutting down the government and packing the Supreme Court], to inhibit their political opponents from achieving anything, ②[which halts progress altogether].

→ ①[including ~ Court]는 everything in their power를 부연 설명하는 전치사구이다.

→ ②[which ~ altogether]는 be동사 is의 보어 역할을 하는 명사절 (when ~ anything) 전체를 받는 주격 관계대명사절로, 콤마 뒤에서 계속적 용법으로 쓰였다.

---

21 밑줄 의미 추론하기 정답 ③

(해설) Mundell-Fleming의 트릴레마 모델에 따르면 안정적인 환율, 자유로운 자본의 흐름, 독립적인 금융 정책을 동시에 달성하는 것은 불가능하고, 상호 배타성으로 인해 삼각형의 한 변만 달성 가능하게 만든다고 설명하고 있다. 이에 따라 정책 독립성과 고정 환율을 선택한다면 자본의 자유로운 흐름을 포기해야 하고, 자본의 자유로운 흐름과 고정 환율을 선택하면 정책 독립성을 포기해야 한다고 말하고 있다. 따라서 글의 주제를 비유적으로 표현한 the most room to move around(자유롭게 행동할 수 있는 가장 넓은 폭)가 의미하는 것은 ③ '제약받지 않는 자본의 이동과 경제적 규칙을 정할 자유'이다.

(오답분석) ①의 외국의 금융 문제에 대한 통제는 글에서 언급된 내용이 아니다. ②은 글에서 언급된 내용이 아니다. ④은 세 가지 요소를 동시에 달성하는 것은 불가능하다는 글의 내용과 반대되는 내용이므로 오답이다. ⑤은 한 가지 요소인 독립적인 정책에 대해서만 설명하고 있는데, 밑줄 친 부분이 의미하는 '자유롭게 행동할 수 있는 가장 넓은 폭'을 제공하는 것은 한 변(두 가지 요소)을 가리키므로 오답이다.

(해석) 국제 경제에 관해서라면 트릴레마가 존재한다. 완벽한 세계에서는 모든 국가가 안정적인 환율, 자유로운 자본의 흐름, 그리고 자유재량에 의한 금융 정책을 동시에 가능하게 만드는 재정의 삼위 일체에서 이익을 얻을 수 있을 것이다. Mundell-Fleming(먼델-플레밍) 트릴레마 모델에 따르면, 상호 배타성이 현실에서 주어진 어느 시점이든 트릴레마 삼각형의 한 변만 달성 가능하게 만든다. 예를 들어, 한 국가가 자율적인 금융 정책을 시행하려 한다면, 고정 환율과 자본의 자유로운 흐름을 동시에 가질 수 없다는 사실을 잘 알고 있어야 한다. 정책 독립성과 함께 고정 환율의 안정성을 누리고 싶다면, 자본이 자유로이 흐르게 할 수 없다. 또한 다른 국가들과의 자본의 자유로운 흐름을 가지는 것과 더불어 하나의 혹은 더 많은 국가와 고정 환율을 유지하기를 택하는 것은 외부 영향으로부터 자유로운 금융 정책을 거의 불가능하게 만들 것이다. 이용 가능한 선택지들을 고려할 때, 정부는 필시 자유롭게 행동할 수 있는 가장 넓은 폭을 제공하는 변을 선택할 것이다.
① 고정된 통화 가치 보장과 외국의 금융 문제에 대한 통제
② 국가 간 장기적인 환율을 예측하는 지식
③ 제약받지 않는 자본의 이동과 경제적 규칙을 정할 자유
④ 국제 경제의 세 가지 주요 요소를 활용할 능력
⑤ 외부 규제 기관의 승인을 동반하지 않는 국가 정책의 시행

(어휘) **when it comes to** ~에 관해서라면 **reap** 얻다 **trinity** 삼위 일체
exchange rate 환율 **capital** 자본 **discretionary** 자유재량에 의한
mutual 상호적인 **exclusivity** 배타성 **autonomous** 자율적인, 자주적인
next to 거의 [선택지] **set** 고정된 **unhindered** 제약받지 않는
implementation 시행, 이행 **regulator** 규제 기관

(구문분석) [3행] ~ a financial trinity that would simultaneously <u>make</u> (동사)
[<u>stable exchange rates, free-flowing capital, and discretionary</u> (목적어)
<u>monetary policy</u>] <u>possible</u>. (목적격 보어)

→ 동사 make의 목적어로 셋 이상의 어구를 나열한 [stable ~ policy], 목적격 보어로 형용사 possible이 쓰였다.

[15행] Also, ①[<u>choosing to maintain fixed exchange rates</u> (주어)
<u>with one or more countries</u>] **as well as** ②[having a free flow of capital with others] would make having monetary policy (동사) (목적어)
free from outside influences next to impossible. (목적격 보어)

→ ①[choosing ~ countries]와 ②[having ~ others]는 문장의 주어인 동명사구로, 상관접속사 A as well as B(B뿐만 아니라 A도)로 연결된 병렬 구조이다.

→ 사역동사 make의 목적어로 동명사구 having ~ influences, 목적격 보어로 next to impossible이 쓰였다.

---

22 요지 파악하기 정답 ⑤

(해설) 글의 마지막 세 문장에서 불확실성을 어떻게 대처하는지는 관용의 수준에 따라 다른데, 관용이 높은 사람들은 변덕스러운 상황을 바람직하게 여기고 두려움보다는 열린 마음으로 접근한다는 요지가 제시되어 있으므로, 이 글의 요지로 가장 적절한 것은 ⑤이다.

(오답분석) ①, ②은 글에서 언급된 내용이 아니다. ③은 예측 불가능한 상황을 바람직하게 여기는 것이 변덕스러운 상황에서 일을 처리하는 데에 도움이 될 수 있다는 글의 내용과 반대되는 내용이므로 오답이다. ④의 모호성에 대한 관용을 높이는 방법에 대해서는 글에서 언급되고 있지 않다.

(해석) 불확실성이 인간 경험의 불가피한 측면이라는 사실에도 불구하고, 사람들이 그것을 받아들이는 정도는 크게 다를 수 있다. 한 사람이 예측 불가능함을 마주하거나 모호한 정보가 주어진 상황에서 어떻게 대처하는지는 그들의 관용의 수준에 따라 다르다; 만약 그들이 수월하게 받아들이고 이러한 문제들에 중립적으로 접근한다면 그것(관용의 수준)이 높다. 그 범위의 다른 끝은 변화, 무질서, 정해진 길에서 벗어나는 것에 대한 혐오감을 수반할 것이다. 한 사람이 불확실한 환경에서 일을 완수해야 할 때, 이러한 관용의 수준이 올바른 의사 결정과 전반적인 성공을 막아 약점으로 드러날 수 있다. 심리학자 Stanley Budner(스탠리 버드너)가 말하길 모호성에 대한 높은 관용을 가진 사람들은 "예측 불가능한 상황을 바람직하게 여기는 경향"이 있기 때문에 변덕스러운 상황에서 일을 잘 할 수 있다. 신경학적 관점에서, 이것은 사람들이 확신 있게 의미를 해석하기에 불충분한 정보가 주어졌을 때, 낮은 관용을 가진 사람보다는 낮은 수준으로 불안이 유발된다는 의미이다. 따라서 그들은 두려움보다는 호기심과 열린 마음으로 문제에 접근할 수 있다.

(어휘) **uncertainty** 불확실성 **facet** 측면 **cope** 대처하다
unpredictability 예측 불가능성 **vague** 모호한 **tolerance** 관용
aversion 혐오감 **disorganization** 무질서 **stray from** ~에서 벗어나다
sound 올바른 **ambiguity** 모호성 **erratic** 변덕스러운
neurological 신경학적인 **induce** 유발하다

(구문분석) [1행] In spite of the fact that uncertainty is an inevitable facet of the human experiences, **the extent** [to which people accept it] can differ greatly.

→ [to ~ it]은 선행사 the extent를 수식하며 '전치사 + 관계대명사' to which가 이끄는 관계대명사절이다.

[11행] ~ this level of tolerance can prove to be a weakness, [preventing sound decision-making and overall success].

→ [preventing ~ success]는 이유를 나타내는 분사구문으로, 분사구문의 주어가 주절의 주어(this level of tolerance)와 같아서 생략되었다.

23　주제 파악하기　정답 ③

(해설) 첫 두 문장으로 미루어 보아 관찰을 통해 평가하고자 하는 가설들이 관찰 그 자체와 불가분하게 엮여 있는데, 이는 우리가 관찰할 때 관찰을 이해하고 해석하기 위한 맥락을 제공하는 사고 체계, 즉 '이론'을 가져오기 때문이라는 내용의 글이다. 따라서 이 글의 주제로 가장 적절한 것은 ③ '관찰이 기존의 관점과는 관계없이 존재하는 것의 불가능성'이다.

(오답분석) ①은 경쟁하는 이론들 사이 불일치를 해결할 수 없다는 글의 내용에 부합하지 않는 내용이기 때문에 오답이다. ②의 실험에서 가설을 세우는 내용은 글에서 언급된 내용이 아니다. ④의 알려지지 않은 현상은 글에서 언급된 내용이 아니다. ⑤의 새로운 결론에 이르는 것은 글에서 언급된 내용이 아니다.

(해석) 우리가 과학의 기반으로서 관찰에 기대를 건다면, 감각을 통한 자료 수집이 세계에 관한 더 종합적인 이해의 열쇠라고 믿는다면, 그러면 우리는 우리가 관찰을 통해 평가하고자 하는 가설들이 관찰 그 자체와 불가분하게 엮여 있는 현실과 씨름해야 한다. 우리는 각자 그러한 관찰을 이해하고 해석하기 위한 맥락을 제공하는 사고 체계, 즉 '이론'을 우리의 관찰에 가져온다. 경험적 자료가 논쟁의 여지가 없는 사실로 독립되어 있다고 말하는 것은 과학자의 근본적인 인간성을 간과하는 것이다. 두 관찰자는 두 개의 전혀 다른 관점에서 보는 것처럼 같은 현상을 보고 다른 두 현실을 볼 수 있다. 사실 그들은 단일한 현상으로부터 진리를 포착하고자 하면서도 다른 두 개의 현상을 볼 수 있다. 그렇다면 경쟁하는 이론들 사이의 불일치를 해결하기 위해 그저 관찰에 의존할 수 없다. 피할 수 없는 현실은 관찰이 인식에 의해 영향을 받는다는 것이다.

① 단일한 이론에 국한되었을 때 합의에 이르는 것의 불가능성
② 실험에서 가설을 세울 때 관찰의 역할
③ 관찰이 기존의 관점과는 관계없이 존재하는 것의 불가능성
④ 알려지지 않은 현상으로 인한 경험적 자료의 잘못된 해석
⑤ 현존하는 전제들로부터 새로운 결론에 이르는 것의 어려움

(어휘) observation 관찰　comprehensive 종합적인
grapple with ~과 씨름하다　inextricably 불가분하게　empirical 경험적인
uncontested 논쟁의 여지가 없는　phenomenon 현상
discern 포착하다, 알아차리다　inescapable 피할 수 없는
perception 인지　[선택지] consensus 합의
independent of ~과는 관계없이　preexisting 기존의　premise 전제

(구문분석)
[1행] If we look to observation as the foundation of science, ①[if we believe that data collection through the senses is the key to a more comprehensive understanding of the universe], then we must grapple with **the reality** ②[that the hypotheses we seek to evaluate through observation are inextricably tied to the observation itself].

→ ①[if ~ universe]는 바로 앞의 If ~ science를 부연 설명하며, 접속사 if(만약 ~하다면)가 이끄는 조건의 부사절이다.

→ ②[that ~ itself]는 the reality와 동격을 이루는 명사절이다.

[9행] ①[To suggest that empirical data stands alone as uncontested fact] is ②[to ignore the fundamental humanity of the scientist].

→ ①[To ~ fact]와 ②[to ~ scientist]는 to부정사의 명사적 용법(~하는 것)으로, 각각 문장의 주어와 be동사(is)의 주격 보어 역할을 한다.

24　제목 파악하기　정답 ②

(해설) 첫 두 문장과 마지막 문장으로 미루어 보아 문학 작품에서 다양한 목소리 혹은 관점이 작가의 목소리에 전복되지 않고 공존하는 것을 폴리포니 개념으로 설명할 수 있으며, 그것이 현실 속 사람들의 다양한 목소리를 포함하고 있다는 내용의 글이다. 따라서 글의 제목으로 가장 적절한 것은 ② '현실을 묘사하는 글쓰기: 다양한 목소리의 포괄'이다.

(오답분석) ①은 글의 일부만을 다루고 있는 오답이다. ③은 폴리포니가 구현된 문학 작품에는 작가의 목소리에 압도되지 않는 다양한 목소리가 공존한다는 글의 내용과 반대되는 내용이기 때문에 오답이다.

(해석) 러시아 철학자 Mikhail Bakhtin(미하일 바흐찐)은 전통적으로 음악적 텍스처과 관련된 폴리포니 개념을 가져와 그것을 문학에 적용했다. 폴리포니는 일부 텍스트가 어떻게 작가의 목소리에 전복되지 않는 등장인물들의 여러 개의 목소리 혹은 관점들을 포괄하는지를 설명한다. 이러한 관점들은 서로, 심지어 작가와도 불일치할 수 있어 문학 작품에 보다 균형 잡히고 다양한 특성을 빌려준다. Bakhtin은, 그가 주장하기를 "대단히 다원론적인" 세계를 묘사한 Fyodor Dostoevsky(표도르 도스토예프스키) 작품에 대한 그의 해석에 이 이론의 기초를 쌓았다. 그의 작품은 모든 것에 앞선 하나의 이야기에 압도되지 않고 오히려 현실에 퍼진 모순과 차이를 아울렀다. 그는 "Dostoevsky의 예술적 시각화 방식의 주요 범주는 진화가 아닌 공존과 상호 작용"이었다고 주장했다. 이러한 형태의 문학은, 모든 등장인물이 신봉하는 이념을 창조하려 애쓰지 않는 더 정직한 사회상을 제공했다. 사람들은 다른 견해들을 가지고 있고, 그는 그들의 목소리를 침묵시키려 하기보다는 이 사실을 인정하는 것이 낫다고 생각했다.

① 소설이 사회의 미묘한 차이를 진정 포착할 수 있는가?
② 현실을 묘사하는 글쓰기: 다양한 목소리의 포괄
③ 글에서 전지적 서술자의 목소리 우선하기
④ 주제와 관련된 표현: 소설의 무엇보다 중요한 메시지 전달하기
⑤ 일관되게 서술하기: 다양성을 포용하는 방법들

(어휘) polyphony 폴리포니(다성부 음악)　texture 텍스처(음 구성 원리)
viewpoint 관점　profoundly 대단히　pluralistic 다원론적인
overarching 모든 것에 앞선, 무엇보다 중요한　contradiction 모순
permeate ~에 퍼지다　coexistence 공존　reflection 상(像), 모습
adhere 신봉하다　divergent 다른　silence 침묵시키다
[선택지] nuance 미묘한 차이, 뉘앙스　prioritization 우선하기
omniscient 전지적인, 모든 것을 아는　thematic 주제와 관련된

(구문분석)
[6행] These viewpoints can disagree with each other, and even with the author, [loaning a piece of literature a more balanced and diverse quality].

→ [loaning ~ quality]는 결과를 나타내는 분사구문으로, 분사구문의 주어가 주절의 주어(These viewpoints)와 같아서 생략되었다.

[20행] ~ and he **thought** [(that) it was better to acknowledge this fact **rather than** to try and silence their voices].
　　　　　　　　　　　가주어　　　진주어(to부정사구)

→ [it ~ voices]는 동사 thought의 목적어 역할을 하는 명사절로, 접속사 that이 생략되었다.

→ 명사절 [it ~ voices]는 가주어 it이 길이가 긴 진주어 to부정사구(to ~ fact) 대신 주어 자리에 쓰인 형태이다.

→ to ~ voices는 to부정사의 명사적 용법(~하는 것)으로, 전치사 rather than의 목적어 역할을 한다.

25 도표 정보 파악하기　　정답 ④

(해설) 2013년에서 2018년 사이에 스페인의 쓰레기에서 발생한 온실가스 배출량은 90만 이산화탄소 환산톤 감소했으나 프랑스의 배출량은 170만 이산화탄소 환산톤이 감소했으므로 수치 표현이 잘못 반영되었다. 따라서 도표의 내용과 일치하지 않는 것은 ④이다.

(해석)
2013년과 2018년의 쓰레기에서 발생한 온실가스 배출량
(이산화탄소 환산톤, 백만)

국가	쓰레기에서 발생한 온실가스 배출량		2013-2018 (비율 변화)
	2013	2018	
미국	160.8	161.1	0
러시아	86.5	98.2	14
캐나다	27.0	27.2	1
일본	22.6	20.7	-8
영국	22.3	19.4	-13
이탈리아	18.6	18.3	-2
프랑스	19.9	18.2	-9
터키	18.2	18.1	-1
한국	16.2	17.1	6
스페인	15.0	14.1	-6
호주	12.5	12.6	1

위의 표는 선정된 나라들의 2013년과 2018년 쓰레기에서 발생한 온실가스 배출량과 두 해 사이의 비율 변화를 보여준다. ① 2013년과 2018년 모두, 미국이 쓰레기에서 발생한 가장 많은 온실가스 배출량을 기록했고, 그 뒤를 러시아와 캐나다가 따른다. ② 한편, 러시아의 쓰레기에서 발생한 온실가스 배출의 비율 변화는 14퍼센트로 가장 높았다. ③ 2013년에서 2018년 사이에 영국의 쓰레기에서 발생한 온실가스 배출량은 290만 이산화탄소 환산톤만큼 감소했다. ④ 프랑스와 스페인의 경우, 2013년에서 2018년 사이에 각 나라의 쓰레기에서 발생한 온실가스 배출량은 100만 이산화탄소 환산톤보다 적게 감소했다. ⑤ 2013년에서 2018년 사이 호주의 쓰레기에서 발생한 온실가스 배출량이 증가를 보였음에도 불구하고, 그것은 두 연도 모두 선정된 국가들 중에서 가장 낮은 순위를 차지했다.

(어휘) greenhouse gas 온실가스　emission 배출
tons of CO₂ equivalent 이산화탄소 환산톤(온실가스를 이산화탄소 배출량으로 환산한 값)

(구문분석) [14행] [**Although** the amount of GHG emissions from waste in Australia showed an increase between 2013 and 2018], it ranked the lowest among the selected countries in both years.
→ [Although ~ 2018]은 접속사 although(비록 ~이지만)가 이끄는 양보의 부사절이다.

26 세부 정보 파악하기　　정답 ⑤

(해설) Fortunately, this medical issue was resolved through surgery, and she was able to continue playing을 통해 Clara Haskil이 수술 후에도 피

아노 연주를 계속했다는 것을 알 수 있는데, 피아노 연주를 계속하지 못했다고 일부 정보를 잘못 나타냈으므로 글의 내용과 일치하지 않는 것은 ⑤이다.

(해석) 1895년 루마니아에서 태어난 Clara Haskil(클라라 하스킬)은 7세 나이에 유명한 오스트리아 작곡가 Rudolf Serkin(루돌프 제르킨)에게 피아노를 배우기 시작했다. 12세가 되었을 때, 그녀는 프랑스의 유명한 음악 학교인 파리 음악원에 입학했다. 그녀는 그녀가 15세였을때 졸업했고, 그 시점에 그녀는 유럽과 미국을 순회하기 시작했다. Haskil은 Schumann(슈만)과 Mozart(모차르트)와 같은 클래식 작곡가들의 작품에 대한 그녀의 능숙한 해석으로 널리 찬사를 받았다. 그러나 1942년에 그녀의 눈부신 경력은 거의 끝날 뻔했는데, 이때 그녀가 심각한 두통을 겪기 시작하고 의사가 한쪽 눈 시신경 뒤에서 종양을 발견했다. 다행히, 이 의학적 문제는 수술로 해결되었고 그녀는 계속 연주할 수 있었다. Haskil은 1960년 사망하기 전까지 유명한 피아니스트로 남았다.

(어휘) composer 작곡가　illustrious 눈부신　tumor 종양
optical nerve 시신경　celebrated 유명한

(구문분석) [5행] She graduated when she was 15, **at which point** she began to tour Europe and the United States.
→ at which point는 '그 시점에'라는 의미로, 여기서 관계형용사 which는 앞 문장의 의미를 반복하는 point를 수식하고 있다.

[9행] However, her illustrious career almost came to an end in **1942**, [when she began experiencing severe headaches and a doctor discovered a tumor behind the optical nerve of one eye].
→ [when ~ eye]는 선행사 1942를 수식하는 관계부사절로, 콤마 뒤에서 계속적 용법으로 쓰였다.

27 안내문 정보 파악하기　　정답 ②

(해설) For reusable items, you don't have to pay a fee를 통해 재사용이 가능한 물품은 비용을 지불하지 않아도 된다는 것을 알 수 있으므로, 글의 내용과 일치하지 않는 것은 ②이다.

(해석)
대형 폐기물 수거 서비스
Columbus 주민 센터는 발생할 수 있는 환경 오염을 최소화하기 위해 여러분께서 아래 설명을 준수해 주시길 바랍니다.

언제: 매주 수요일
어디에서: 여러분 집 앞
해야 할 일:
1) 해당 물품이 재사용이 가능한지 아닌지를 판단하세요.
2) 물품을 신고하세요.
 - 재사용이 가능한 물품의 경우, 비용을 지불하지 않아도 됩니다.
 - 재사용이 불가능한 물품의 경우, 요금 지불이 요구될 것입니다.
3) 수거 차량이 당신의 집에 방문해 물품을 수거할 것입니다.

수거 비용:
- 가전제품 (10kg 미만): 3달러
- 가전제품 (10kg 이상): 5달러
- 가구 (3kg 미만): 2달러
- 가구 (3kg 이상): 5달러

물품을 신고하려면, Columbus 주민 센터를 직접 방문하시거나 저희 웹사이트를 방문해 주세요.

어휘 collection 수거 minimize 최소화하다 register 신고하다
home appliance 가전제품 in person 직접

구문분석

[2행] The Columbus Community Center would like you to observe the following instructions **in order** [to minimize] possible environmental pollution.

→ 목적의 뜻을 분명히 하기 위해 to부정사 [to minimize] 앞에 in order 를 쓴 형태이다.

28 안내문 정보 파악하기 정답 ④

해설 수치가 포함된 부분인 The deadline for registration is October 14를 통해 등록 마감일은 10월 14일이라는 것을 알 수 있으므로, 글의 내용과 일치하는 것은 ④이다.

해석

건강을 위한 수영 프로그램

저희의 8주 종합 수영 프로그램이 여러분을 눈 깜짝할 사이에 건강하게 만들어 드립니다. 건강해지기를 원하시면, 저희 프로그램이 여러분에게 맞습니다!
* 수업은 10월 31일부터 12월 23일까지 8주간 일주일에 3일 (화요일, 목요일 그리고 토요일) 열립니다.

대상:
- 초급부터 중급 수강생까지
- 15세 이상

배울 내용:
- 새로운 영법
- 기량을 개선하는 법

추가 정보:
- 수업료는 인당 90달러입니다.
- 등록 기한은 10월 14일입니다.
- 본인의 수영복을 지참해 주세요.
- 프로그램 수강에 더해 추가로 개인 강습을 등록하실 수 있습니다.
더 많은 정보를 위해서는 www.s2fprogram.com을 방문해 주세요.

어휘 fitness 건강 comprehensive 종합적인 in no time 눈 깜짝할 사이에
swimming style 영법(泳法) form 기량 tuition fee 수업료
in addition to ~에 더하여

구문분석

[2행] Our eight-week comprehensive swim program will help you get fit in no time.
동사 목적어 목적격 보어

→ 준사역동사 help의 목적어로 you, 목적격 보어로 동사원형 get이 쓰였다. help는 목적격 보어로 to부정사도 취할 수 있으므로 to get도 쓸 수 있다.

29 어법상 틀린 것 찾기 정답 ①

해설 전치사 on의 목적어절을 이끌고 있는데, 뒤에 or를 포함한 완전한 절이 이어지고 있고 문맥상 'A인지 B인지'라는 의미가 되어야 하므로, ①의 what을 whether로 고쳐야 한다.

오답분석 ②은 전치사 rather than의 목적어로 동명사 seeking을 사용한 것은 어법상 적절하다. ③은 주어 a battle, 자동사 manifests가 모두 있는 완전한 절을 이끌고 있고, 선행사 systems를 수식하여 '~ 안에서'라는 의미가 되어야 하므로 '전치사 + 관계대명사' 형태인 in which를 사용한 것은 어법상 적절하다. ④은 see A as B(A를 B라고 여기다) 형태에서 동사 see의 목적격 보어로 쓰인 형용사 necessary를 수식하는 부사 invariably를 사용한 것은 어법상 적절하다. ⑤은 This ~ world에서 단수명사 This division이 주어이고 between ~ world는 수식어(전치사구)이므로 단수동사 has를 쓴 것은 어법상 적절하다.

해석 현대에는 권력이 강력한 행정부 아니면 보다 분산된 입법부의 손에 들어가 있어야 하는지에 대한 근본적인 의견 충돌이 있다. 그러나 이 갈등을 해결하는 대신, 대부분의 민주 국가들은 이러한 분열을 정부 구조의 일부로 만들었다. 이것은 이 부문들 간 변화하는 힘의 균형 내에서 통치권 경쟁이 나타나는 체제들을 낳는다. 많은 사람들이 보기에, 이런 방식의 통치권 분할은 위험에 효과적으로 대응할 수 없는 본질적으로 취약한 제도를 만들어서, 행정부가 속박받지 않는 힘을 쥐고 있는 보다 독재적인 체제에 대한 선호를 야기한다. 비슷하게, 국제적인 주권에 대한 인식은 국제적인 구속이 언제나 필요하다고 여기는 이들과 그것들이 국가 주권을 약화시킨다고 믿는 이들 사이에 나뉘어 있다. 국가 주권에 대한 보호주의 관점과 세계에 대한 국제주의 관점 사이 분열은 최근 몇몇 국가가 알려진 대로라면 국가 주권을 보호하는 방도로써 국제 기구와 조약을 떠나게 만들었다.

어휘 executive branch 행정부 diffuse 분산된; 분산시키다
legislative branch 입법부 democracy 민주 국가, 민주주의
split 분할; 분할하다 build A into B A를 B의 일부로 만들다
sovereignty 통치권, 주권 manifest 나타나다 inherently 본질적으로
autocratic 독재적인 tie 구속 invariably 언제나, 변함없이
dilute 약화시키다 division 분열 protectionist 보호주의의
internationalist 국제주의의 treaty 조약 purportedly 알려진 대로라면

구문분석

[16행] This division between protectionist views of national sovereignty and internationalist views of the world has lately caused some countries to abandon international
　　　　동사　　目 목적어　　　목적격 보어
organizations and treaties, purportedly as a means **of** [protecting national sovereignty].

→ 동사 caused의 목적어로 some countries, 목적격 보어로 to부정사 to abandon이 쓰였다.

→ [protecting national sovereignty]는 전치사 of의 목적어로 쓰인 동명사구이다.

30 어휘 적절성 파악하기 정답 ⑤

해설 Lucky Dog의 웨이터들이 월요일에 급여를 받는다는 조건과 Tom이 월요일에 급여를 받는다는 조건으로부터 Tom이 Lucky Dog의 웨이터라는 결론은 타당하게 도출될 수 없다고 했다. 따라서 Tom이 Lucky Dog의 웨이터라고 추정하면서 우리가 저지른 실수는 처음 두 조건의 무관한 결론을 받아들인 데에 있다는 맥락이 되어야 하므로 ⑤의 rejecting(받아들이지 않는)을 그와 반대되는 의미의 accepting(받아들이는)과 같은 단어로 바꾸어야 문맥상 적절하다.

오답분석 ③은 Tom이 월요일에 웨이터들에게 급여를 지급하는 식당들 가운데 Lucky Dog에서 일할 가능성을 배제할 수 없다는 문맥이 되어야 한다. 따라서 exclude가 오는 것이 적절하다.

해석 Tom이 Lucky Dog의 웨이터라고 해보자. 우리가 Lucky Dog의 웨이터들이 월요일에 급여를 받는다는 것을 안다면, Tom이 월요일에 급여를 받을 것

이라는 건 ① 타당한 결론이다. 그러나 우리가 Lucky Dog의 웨이터들이 월요일에 급여를 받는다는 것과 Tom이 월요일에 급여를 받는다는 것을 안다면 어떻게 될까? Tom이 Lucky Dog의 웨이터라고 추정해도 무방할까? 물론 이 결론은 앞의 두 진술로부터 ② 타당하게 도출될 수 없다. 우리가 아는 것은 우리는 Tom이 Lucky Dog의 웨이터일 수도 있다는 가능성을 ③ 배제할 수 없다는 것뿐이다. 우리는 웨이터들에게 월요일에 급여를 지급하는 다른 많은 식당들이 있을 수 있다는 점과 (그리고 Tom이 그 중 한 곳에서 일할지도 모른다) Tom이 Lucky Dog에서 일하지만 웨이터로는 아닐 가능성 (아마 점장으로) 또한 고려해야 한다. 우리의 ④ 전제는 우리가 Lucky Dog의 점장이 월요일에 급여를 받는지 아닌지를 알아내게 하지 않는다. Tom이 Lucky Dog의 웨이터라고 추정함으로써 우리가 저지른 실수는 처음 두 조건의 무관한 결론을 ⑤ 받아들이지 않은(→받아들인) 데에 있다.

[어휘] **valid** 타당한 **safe** 무방한 **assume** 추정하다 **legitimately** 타당하게 **draw** 도출하다 **exclude** 배제하다 **premise** 전제 **condition** 조건

[구문분석]

[8행] **All** ①[(that) we know] **is** ②[that we cannot exclude the possibility that Tom might be a waiter at Lucky Dog].

→ ①[we know]는 선행사 All을 수식하는 관계대명사절로, 목적격 관계대명사 that이 생략되었다. 'all + 관계사절' 구문은 보통 '유일한 것' 즉 그 외에 더 이상 없다는 부정적인 의미를 나타낸다.

→ ②[that ~ Dog]은 접속사 that이 이끄는 명사절로, be동사 is의 주격 보어 역할을 한다.

[16행] The mistake we have made by assuming Tom is a waiter at Lucky Dog is **in** [accepting an irrelevant consequence of the two initial conditions].

→ [accepting ~ conditions]는 전치사 in의 목적어로 쓰인 동명사구이다.

---

31 빈칸 추론하기   정답 ③

[해설] 주제문에 해당하는 빈칸 문장에서 도덕 판단을 내릴 때 시간 제약이 있다면 '무엇'에 의존하게 될 가능성이 더 많다고 했다. 글의 후반에서는 즉각적인 판단을 내려야 하는 경우, 그 사람의 충동이 근본적으로 도덕적인지 아닌지 드러나 도덕성이 선천적인지를 판별하는 시험대가 된다고 했다. 따라서 빈칸에는 ③ '본능'이 와서 도덕적 판단을 내릴 때 시간 제약이 있으면 본능에 의존하게 될 가능성이 더 많다는 의미가 되어야 한다.

[오답분석] ①, ⑤는 시간 제약이 있는 조건에서 도덕 판단을 내릴 경우 충동이 도덕성을 드러낸다는 글의 내용과 반대되는 내용이므로 오답이다. ②, ④에 대한 내용은 글에서 언급되고 있지 않다.

[해석] 시간 제약으로 한 사람의 온전한 도덕적 판단을 내리는 능력이 제한될 때, 그 사람은 딜레마를 해결하기 위해 본능에 의존할 가능성이 더 많다. 시간 압박이 없을 때, 의사 결정 과정에 숙고할 여지가 주어진다. 이 관찰은 인간 충동이 본래 이타적 성향으로 이어지는지를 연구할 기회를 제공한다. 연구 참가자들에게 시간 압박을 포함하거나 포함하지 않는 환경에서 가혹한 도덕적 선택을 제시함으로써, 심리학자들은 중대한 선택을 하는 개인들에 의해 비용과 편익이 분석된다는 인간 본성의 공리주의적 관점이 가치가 있는지를 판단할 수 있다. 주어진 상황의 모든 면을 고려할 시간이 있는 참가자는 아마 공리주의적 결론에 다다를 가능성이 더 많을 것이다. 반면, 즉각적인 판단을 내려야 하는 사람의 성격은 확고해져서, 그 사람의 충동이 근본적으로 도덕적인지 아닌지를 드러낸다. 궁극적으로, 시간 압박 조건은 도덕성이 선천적인지를 판별하는 시험대를 제공한다.

① 추론   ② 재능

③ 본능   ④ 지혜

⑤ 정확성

[어휘] **sound** 온전한 **constraint** 제약 **reflection** 숙고 **altruistic** 이타적인 **inclination** 성향 **stark** 가혹한 **utilitarian** 공리주의의 **human nature** 인간 본성 **consequential** 중대한 **merit** 가치 **facet** 면 **presumably** 아마 **instantaneous** 즉각적인 **crystallize** 확고해지다 **discern** 판별하다 **innate** 선천적인

[구문분석]

[5행] This observation presents an opportunity for **investigating** [whether human impulse leads naturally to altruistic inclinations].

→ [whether ~ inclinations]는 접속사 whether가 이끄는 명사절로 동명사 investigating의 목적어 역할을 한다.

[10행] ~ psychologists can determine whether **a utilitarian view of human nature**, [in which costs and benefits are analyzed by individuals making a consequential choice], bears merit.

→ 선행사 a utilitarian view of human nature를 수식하는 [in ~ choice]는 '전치사 + 관계대명사' in which가 이끄는 관계대명사절로, 콤마 뒤에서 계속적 용법으로 쓰였다.

---

32 빈칸 추론하기   정답 ⑤

[해설] 생체 역학의 확립을 통해 무대 표현의 한계를 재정립하려 한 Vsevolod Meyerhold의 연출 방식은 무대 위에 육체로서 현존하는 배우의 과장된 움직임을 통해 생각과 교훈을 전달하고자 하는 것이라는 내용의 글이다. 빈칸 앞 문장에서 육체의 현존이 가장 중요하므로 배우들은 몸짓, 자세 그리고 곡예를 통해 자신의 배역을 연기했다고 설명했다. 따라서 주제와 관련된 빈칸에는 ⑤ '생리와 꽤 직접적으로 연결되어 있다'라는 내용이 오는 것이 적절하다.

[오답분석] ①, ④은 생체 역학은 언어가 아닌 몸짓에 주목했다는 글의 내용과 반대되는 내용이므로 오답이다. ③은 글의 내용과 관련이 없다.

[해석] 배우이자 연극 연출가인 Vsevolod Meyerhold(프세볼로드 메이예르홀트)는 1920년대 초반에 그의 생체 역학 확립으로 무대 표현의 한계를 재정립하려고 했다. 순전히 각본의 대화 부분이나 독백을 통해서 감정을 전달하기보다, 이 연출 방식은 생각과 의도를 명확히 전하기 위해 과장된 움직임에 의존했다. 연극 장면에서 배우들의 육체의 현존이 가장 중요하므로, 그들은 말이나 언어를 통해서가 아니라 몸짓, 자세 그리고 곡예를 통해 자신의 배역을 연기했다. 감정은 생리와 꽤 직접적으로 연결되어 있다는 것이 Meyerhold의 신념이었다. 이는 사실적이거나 자연스러운 연출로부터 벗어나는 것이었는데, Meyerhold가 그가 보기에 너무 많은 영향력을 끼쳤던 문자로부터 연극 공연을 멀리 떨어지게 하는 데 주력했기 때문이다. 간소화한 세트와 의상과 결합된 그의 연기 방식은 관객의 관심이 격렬하고 과장된 움직임으로 무대를 가로지르는 사람들에게 머무르게 했다. 이는 그들에게 연극에서 신체의 움직임에 대한 새로운 감상을 제공했고 그 경험을 고양시켰다.

① 보다 생생한 방식으로 글을 통해 묘사되었다

② 무대에서 전달될 수 없는 방식으로 느껴졌다

③ 미학적 특성을 지지하는 관객으로부터 무시되었다

④ 큰 목소리로 나타냈을 때 가장 설득력 있게 표현되었다

⑤ 생리와 꽤 직접적으로 연결되어 있다

[어휘] **redefine** 재정립하다 **establishment** 확립, 수립 **biomechanics** 생체 역학(배우의 육체적 훈련을 중시하는 연기 이론) **dramatic** 각본의 **production** (연극의) 연출 **exaggerated** 과장된

project 명확히 전하다 **message** (작품의) 의도 **acrobatics** 곡예
presence 현존 **theatrical** 연극의 **departure** 벗어남
traverse 가로지르다 **hyperbolic** 과장된 **appreciation** 감상
bodily 신체의 **elevate** 고양시키다 [선택지] **vivid** 생생한
aesthetic 미학적인 **voice** (말로) 나타내다 **physiology** 생리(生理)

[7행] Actors did **not** perform their roles through words or language **but** through gestures, poses, and acrobatics, [their physical presence being of the utmost importance in theatrical scenes].

→ 주절에 not A but B(A가 아닌 B)의 구조가 쓰였다.

→ [their ~ scenes]는 이유를 나타내는 분사구문으로, 분사구문의 주어 (their physical presence)와 주절의 주어(Actors)가 달라서 분사구문의 주어를 생략하지 않은 독립분사구문이다.

[15행] **His method of acting** ①[(that/which was) coupled with simplified sets and costumes] **ensured** ②[that the audience's attention remained on the people who traversed the stage with wild, hyperbolic movements].

→ ①[coupled ~ costumes]는 His method of acting을 설명하는 관계절로, '주격 관계대명사(that/which) + be동사(was)'가 생략되었다.

→ ②[that ~ movements]는 접속사 that이 이끄는 명사절로, 동사 ensured의 목적어 역할을 한다.

33 빈칸 추론하기 정답 ①

(해설) 빈칸 문장에서 형식주의 전통에 속한 사람들은 자본주의 체제의 참여자들이 '무엇'에 영향받지 않고 행동할 것이라고 생각했다고 했다. 빈칸 앞에서 Karl Polanyi는 경제학의 고전적 모형은 시장 경제의 행위자들이 마치 사회적 진공 상태에 존재하듯이 행동하기를 기대한다고 언급했다고 했고, 글의 후반부에서 자본주의 이전 사회에서 경제적 활동은 다른 이들과의 관계에 의존적이라는 것을 발견했다고 설명했다. 따라서 주제와 관련된 빈칸에는 ① '보다 넓은 사회적 그리고 문화적 맥락'이 오는 것이 적절하다.

(오답분석) ②은 수요와 공급 법칙은 부자연스럽다고 본 Karl Polanyi의 견해와 반대되는 내용이므로 오답이다. ③은 토지와 노동이 경제적 상품이 아니었고 유대 관계에 의존적이었다는 글의 내용과 반대되는 내용이므로 오답이다. ④에 대한 내용은 글에서 언급되고 있지 않다. ⑤은 글에서 언급된 theoretical constructs를 사용하여 헷갈리게 하는 오답이다.

(해석) Karl Polanyi(칼 폴라니)는 1944년에 경제학의 고전적 모형은 시장 경제의 행위자들이 마치 사회적 진공 상태에 존재하듯이 행동하기를 기대한다고 언급한 것으로 유명하다. 달리 말하면, 자본주의 체제의 참여자들은 형식주의 전통에 속한 사람들에 의해 보다 넓은 사회적 그리고 문화적 맥락에 영향받지 않고 그들의 편협한 이기심에 따라 예측 가능하게 행동할 것이라고 생각되었다. (Polanyi는 부자연스러운 법칙이라고 주장할) 전능한 수요와 공급 "법칙"에 대한 이러한 집착은 살아 있는 사회적 존재를 이론적 구성 개념, 즉 자연 상태가 아닌 단지 자본주의 경제학자의 마음속에만 존재하는 '효모 에크노미쿠스'라는 포괄적인 종의 일원으로 바꾸었다. 자본 환경은 불가피하게 주변 환경에 묻어 들어 있는 관념을 뒷받침하기 위해, Polanyi는 원시 경제를 연구했고 그 안의 경제적 활동은 근본적으로 다른 이들과의 관계에 의존적이라는 것을 발견했다. 이러한 자본주의 이전 사회에서, 토지와 노동은 경제적 상품이 아니었고 친족과 공동체의 유대 관계에, 그것들이 결혼에 의한 상속이든 집안의 생득권이든, 의존적이었다. 화폐는 특정 상품 교환에 유용한 도구였지만 인간 행동의 의미를 규정하는 전형이라고는 할 수 없다.

① 보다 넓은 사회적 그리고 문화적 맥락
② 완전무결한 수요와 공급 규칙
③ 돈을 바라고 하는 토지와 노동의 열린 교환
④ 친족과 공동체의 경제적 기원
⑤ 자본주의 경제의 이론적 구성 개념

(어휘) **classical** 고전적인 **vacuum** 진공 상태 **formalist** 형식주의
narrow 편협한 **self-interest** 이기심 **fixation** 집착 **all-powerful** 전능한
demand and supply 수요와 공급 **flesh-and-blood** 살아 있는
construct 구성 개념 **generic** 포괄적인 **precapitalist** 자본주의 이전의
commodity 상품 **tie** 유대 관계 **inheritance** 상속 **birthright** 생득권
paradigm 전형 [선택지] **context** 맥락 **flawless** 완전무결한

[18행] ~ land and labor were not economic commodities but dependent on the ties of kinship and community, [be they marital inheritances or family birthrights].

→ [be ~ birthrights]는 명령문 구조로 쓰인 양보의 부사절로 'whether they are marital inheritances or family birthrights'로 바꿔 쓸 수 있다.

34 빈칸 추론하기 정답 ③

(해설) 주제문에 해당하는 빈칸 문장에서 해양 남세균의 진화 덕분에 '무엇'하는 수레바퀴가 움직이기 시작했다고 하고, 글의 후반에서 해양 남세균의 광합성 능력이 발달되면서 지구의 공기 중 산소가 늘어났고, 보다 복잡한 세포 조직을 가진 생물이 출현하고 진화했다고 설명했다. 따라서 빈칸에는 ③ '지구에 다세포 생물 형태의 발달을 가능하게 하다'가 와서 해양 남세균의 진화 덕분에 지구상 다세포 생물 형태의 발달을 가능하게 하는 수레바퀴가 움직이기 시작했다는 의미가 되어야 한다.

(오답분석) ①은 해양 남세균이 광합성 능력을 발달시킨 덕분에 공기 중 온실가스는 적어지고 산소가 많아졌다는 글의 내용과 반대되는 내용이므로 오답이다. ②의 원시 해양 생물의 광합성 과정을 바꾸었다는 내용은 글에서 언급되고 있지 않다. ④은 글의 내용과 관련이 없다. ⑤은 종속 영양 세균은 온실가스를 발생시킨다는 글의 내용과 반대되는 내용이므로 오답이다.

(해석) 약 23억 5천만 년 전, 해양 남세균의 진화 덕분에 지구에 다세포 생물 형태의 발달을 가능하게 하는 수레바퀴가 움직이기 시작했다. 이 해양 유기체는 광합성 능력을 발달시켜, 생존을 위한 투쟁에서 온실가스를 발생시키는 종속 영양 세균을 능가하게 되었다. 광합성의 부산물이 산소이기 때문에, 당시 주로 이산화탄소, 메탄, 질소로 이루어져 있던 지구의 공기는 산소로 채워지기 시작했다. 산소는 종속 영양 세균에 치명적이었기에, 그 대다수는 지구의 첫 번째 대멸종 때 없어졌다. 온실가스는 적어지고 산소는 많아지면서, 종들의 물질대사 전략이 적응하기 시작해 궁극적으로 보다 복잡한 세포 조직을 가진 생물의 출현으로 이어질 길을 닦았다고 여겨진다. 산소의 증가는 또한 3억 년 넘게 얼어붙을 정도로 지구를 식게 만들었다. 눈덩이지구라고 불리는 이 시기 동안의 환경은 수중 화산의 폭발로 끝이 났는데, 과학자들이 보기에 그것은 보다 복잡한 생물의 진화로 이어졌다.

① 공기 중 온실가스 양을 증가시키는 것을 야기하다
② 원시 해양 생물의 광합성 과정을 바꾸다
③ 지구에 다세포 생물 형태의 발달을 가능하게 하다
④ 행성 표면에 탄소가 풍부한 영역의 형성으로 이어지다
⑤ 산소를 발생시키는 지구의 종속 영양 세균 대부분을 제거하다

(어휘) **set in motion** 움직이게 하다 **oceanic** 해양의 **organism** 유기체
photosynthesize 광합성하다 **outcompete** 능가하다
byproduct 부산물 **carbon dioxide** 이산화탄소 **methane** 메탄

nitrogen 질소 toxic 치명적인 wipe out 없애다
mass extinction 대멸종 metabolic 물질대사의
pave the way 길을 닦다 Snowball Earth 눈덩이지구 eruption 폭발
[선택지] primitive 원시의 multicellular 다세포의 lifeform 생물 형태
carbon-rich 탄소가 풍부한 element (활동) 영역

(구문분석)
[12행] With less greenhouse gases and more oxygen, it is believed that the metabolic strategies of species began to adapt, [paving the way for what would eventually lead to the emergence of organisms with more complicated cellular structures].

→ [paving ~ structures]는 결과를 나타내는 분사구문으로, 분사구문의 주어가 주절의 주어(it)와 같아서 생략되었다.

35 흐름과 관계 없는 문장 찾기   정답 ③

(해설) 치매 치료 방식의 초점이 격리 수용에서 관계 유지를 통한 인간으로서의 정체성 유지로 옮겨갔다는 내용의 글이다. 그런데 ③은 치매와 같은 건강 문제를 가진 환자들이 겪는 인간 관계의 문제와 행동 불안정에 대한 내용이므로 핵심 소재는 같지만 주제에서 벗어나 있어 글의 흐름과 무관하다.

(오답분석) ①은 이전의 치매 치료 방식에서 환자들이 처했던 상황을 다루고 있으므로 앞의 두 문장과 연결된다. ②은 오늘날의 치매 치료 방식은 새로운 방식으로 옮겨갔다고 설명하고 있으므로, 19세기 치료 방법에 대해 이야기하는 ① 뒤에 오는 것이 적절하다. ④은 ②의 온전한 한 인간으로서의 환자의 지속적 지위를 지지하는 것이라는 내용에 이어서 정체성 보존에 대한 내용을 다루고 있으므로 ②과 연결된다. ⑤은 정체성 보존의 핵심은 관계를 유지하는 것이라는 ④의 내용을 뒷받침하는 문장이므로 ④ 뒤에 오는 것이 자연스럽다.

(해석) 수년간 치매 치료 방식은 환자의 정체성을 앗아가는 그것(치매)의 능력에 초점을 맞췄다. 알츠하이머병과 다른 종류의 치매에 대한 지배적인 견해는 환자의 억제된 기억과 줄어든 소통 능력이 인간성 혹은 근본적인 자아의식의 상실을 초래한다는 것이었다. ① 19세기에는, 나이와 연관된 정신적 감퇴는 정신 이상의 한 형태로 여겨졌고, 환자들은 많은 경우 정신 병원에 수용되어 그들과 가장 가까운 사람들을 볼 수 없게 되었다. ② 오늘날, 그 방식은 온전한 한 인간으로서의 환자의 지속적인 지위를 지지하는 것을 강조하는 쪽으로 옮겨갔다. (③ 그러한 건강 문제를 겪는 환자들은 많은 경우 친구 및 가족과 정상적으로 지내지 못할 뿐 아니라 행동의 불안정을 경험한다.) ④ 정체성 보존의 핵심은 관계를 유지하는 것이다. ⑤ 나이 든 사람들을 심신을 약화시키는 질병의 피해자가 아니라 사람으로 여기는 가족 혹은 보호자와 관계를 유지하게 함으로써, 그들의 존엄성과 정체성이 보존될 수 있다.

(어휘) dementia 치매 prevailing 지배적인
Alzheimer's disease 알츠하이머병 inhibited 억제된
diminished 줄어든 personhood 인간성 sense of self 자아의식
insanity 정신 이상 institutionalize 보호 시설에 수용하다
fluctuation 불안정 relate (남과) 사이좋게 지내다 conservation 보존
caretaker 보호자 debilitating 심신을 약화시키는 dignity 존엄성

(구문분석)
[13행] Patients suffering from such health conditions often experience ①[behavioral fluctuations] **as well as** ②[an inability (to relate to friends and family normally)].

→ ①[behavioral fluctuations]와 ②[an ~ normally]는 상관접속사 A as well as B(B뿐만 아니라 A도)로 연결된 병렬 구조이며, 상관접속사 not only B but (also) A로 바꿔 쓸 수 있다.

→ (to ~ normally)는 to부정사의 형용사적 용법(~할)으로, 명사 inability 를 수식한다.

36 글의 순서 배열하기   정답 ②

(해설) 주어진 글은 문화 자본이 사회적 이동성과 사회 계급의 보존 둘 다에 기여한다는 주제를 제시한다. (B)는 한 사람이 여러 활동과 정규 교육을 통해 문화 자본을 획득하며, 그것이 가족 내에서 전해진다는 내용이고, 주어진 글 마지막에서 문화 자본이 사회 계급의 유지에 기여한다고 했으므로 그 뒤에 와야 한다. (A)는 아이들이 부모로부터 문화 자본을 획득하여 식습관을 통해 문화 자본이 표현된다는 내용으로, (B)의 내용에 대한 부연 설명을 하고 있으므로 (B) 뒤에 오는 것이 적절하다. (C)의 What is served on the dinner table(저녁 식탁에 무엇이 오르는지)은 (A)의 '식습관'과 이어지는 내용이므로 (A) 바로 뒤에 오는 것이 적절하다. 따라서 글의 순서로 가장 적절한 것은 ② (B) - (A) - (C) 이다.

(해석) 프랑스 사회학자 Pierre Bourdieu(피에르 부르디외)는 문화 자본, 즉 한 사람의 능력, 교육 그리고 "고급 문화"의 다양한 요소에 대한 친숙도가 사회적 이동성과 사회 계급의 유지 둘 다에 기여한다고 주장했다.

(B) 한 사람은 독서와 여행과 같은 활동과 더불어 정규 교육을 통해 일생 동안 문화 자본을 획득할 수 있다. 그것은 또한 사회적 재생산을 달성하려는 시도로 가족 내에서 전해지는데, 이는 사회적 위치의 상속이다.

(A) 아이들은 부모로부터 문화 자본을 획득하고 이 자본은 그 사회 체제에서 더 낮은 곳에 있는 사람들로부터 그들을 구별 짓는 취향을 통해 드러난다. 이 자본의 그러한 하나의 표현은 한 사람의 식습관인데, 높은 사회 계층의 사람들이 음식과 관련하여 품질, 건강, 맛 그리고 윤리의 중요성을 강조하는 경향이 있다는 것을 연구가 보여주었기 때문이다.

(C) 그렇다면 저녁 식탁에 무엇이 오르는지는 논의 주제나 예절만큼이나 중요할 것이다. 이 모든 요소들은 특정 사회 계층의 사람들이 사회 내 그들의 지위를 공고히 하는 "세련된" 취향을 가졌다는 걸 입증하게 할 것이다.

(어휘) cultural capital 문화 자본 high culture 고급 문화
social mobility 사회적 이동성 preservation 보존
representation 표현 formal education 정규 교육
inheritance 상속, 물려받은 것 social positioning 사회적 위치
refined 세련된 position 지위

(구문분석)
[20행] [What is served on the dinner table] could then be just **as important as** the topic of discussion or etiquette.

→ [What ~ table]은 관계대명사 what(~하는 것)이 이끄는 명사절로, 문장의 주어 역할을 한다.

→ as important as는 'as + 원급 + as'의 원급 비교구문으로 '…만큼 ~한/하게'라는 의미이다.

37 글의 순서 배열하기   정답 ③

(해설) 주어진 글은 물리학에 시간 여행을 불가능하게 할 것은 없지만, 물리적이기 보다는 논리적인 장애물들이 있다는 문제를 제시한다. (B)의 The most famous ~ Paradox(가장 잘 알려진 ~ 역설)는 주어진 글의 '물리적이기보다는 논리적인 장애물들' 중 하나를 가리키므로 주어진 글 바로 다음에 오는 것이 적절하다. (C)의 It은 시간 여행의 논리적 모순의 예시인 할아버지 역설에 대해 설명하는 (B)의 전체 내용을 가리키므로 (B) 바로 다음에 오는 것이 적

절하다. (A)에서 시간은 휘어진 고리를 만들어낼 수 있다고 했으므로 it's not(그렇지 않다)은 (C) 마지막에서 if time is definitively restricted to a linear line(시간이 명확히 선형에 국한되어 있는 경우)이라는 가정을 부정하는 것을 의미하기 때문에 (C) 뒤에 이어지는 것이 자연스럽다. 따라서 글의 순서로 가장 적절한 것은 ③ (B) - (C) - (A)이다.

(해석) 이론적으로 말하면, 물리학에 시간 여행을 불가능하게 할 것은 없다. 분명 장애물들이 있지만 그것들은 물리학적이기보다는 논리적이다.

(B) 가장 잘 알려진 것은 할아버지 역설로 설명된다. 만약 당신이 과거로 거슬러 가서 당신의 할아버지를 죽인다면, 당신의 부모 중 한 명은 태어나지 못할 것이다. 결과적으로 당신도 태어나는 것이 불가능한데, 이는 당신이 애초에 과거로 거슬러 가서 당신의 할아버지를 죽일 수 없었다는 것을 의미한다.

(C) 이는 시간 여행의 논리적 모순들을 지적한다. 철학자 Tim Maudlin(팀 모들린)은 이렇게 말한다: "어떤 면에서, 그것은 마치 왜 나는 젖어 있으면서 동시에 완전히 말라 있을 수 없냐고 묻는 것과 같다." 그러나 Maudlin은 이러한 변호는 시간이 명확히 선형에 국한되어 있는 경우에만 지탱된다고 말한다.

(A) Einstein(아인슈타인)의 상대성 이론은 그렇지 않다는 것을 보여준다: 공간과 시간은 접혀서 휘어진 시간의 고리를 만들어낼 수 있다. 이 경우, "현재로 간주할 것이 없어서" 우리가 현재 일어난다고 간주하는 사건들이 미래나 과거에 일어나고 있을 가능성이 열린다.

(어휘) rule out 불가능하게 하다 obstacle 장애물
theory of relativity 상대성 이론 loop 고리 inconsistency 모순, 불일치
hold up 지탱되다 definitively 명확히, 결정적으로 restrict 국한시키다
linear 선형의

(구문분석)
[13행] In turn, it is impossible for you [to have ever been born
가주어   의미상 주어   진주어(to부정사구)
either], meaning ~
→ 가주어 it이 길이가 긴 진주어 to부정사구 [to ~ either] 대신에 주어 자리에 쓰인 구조이며, to부정사의 의미상 주어가 'for + 목적격(you)' 형태로 쓰였다.

38 주어진 문장의 위치 찾기 정답 ⑤

(해설) 주어진 문장의 this area(이 영역)로 보아, 주어진 문장 앞에는 명확한 기업 전략이 없는 기업이 어떤 영역을 떠날 수 없는지에 대한 내용이 나와야 한다는 것을 알 수 있다. 이 글에서는 ①~② 뒤 문장까지 기업이 높은 실적을 내기 위해 세 가지 전략 중 하나를 택해야 한다는 것에 대해 설명하고 있고, ③~④ 뒤 문장까지 그렇지 못한 기업은 중간 영역에서 빠져나올 수 없게 된다고 하였으므로 주어진 문장이 들어가기에 가장 적절한 곳은 ⑤이다.

(오답분석) ①~② 뒤 문장은 기업이 높은 실적을 내기 위해 세 가지 전략 중 하나를 택해야 한다는 내용이므로 주어진 문장은 이것보다 뒤에 와야 한다. ④ 뒤 문장의 Doing such a thing(그렇게 하는 것)은 ③ 뒤 문장의 '타협할 수 있다는 사고방식으로 모든 핵심 요소의 균형을 잡으려 하는 것'을 가리키고, ④ 뒤 문장은 ③ 뒤 문장에 대한 보충 설명이므로 주어진 문장은 이 내용이 끝난 이후에 들어가야 한다.

(해석) 경쟁 시장에서 기업들은 돋보이기 위해 명확한 행동 계획이 있어야 한다. 이에 관해 그것들이 내리는 결정들은 성공하거나 평범한 상태에 갇히는 결과를 낳을 수 있다. (①) Michael Porter(마이클 포터)는 높은 실적을 내는 기업을 만들고 유지시키기 위한 세 가지 전략을 보였다: 이는 원가 우위, 차별화, 집중화이다. (②) 회사는 이 접근법들 중 추구할 한 가지를 선택해야 한다. (③) 타협할 수 있다는 사고방식으로 모든 핵심 요소의 균형을 잡으려 하는 것은 많은 기업가가 저지르는 일반적인 실수다. (④) 그렇게 하는 것은 아무런 전략이

없는 것과 일치하고 기업을 "중간"이라고 알려진 곳에 빠져나올 수 없게 박히게 만들 수 있다. (⑤ 고정 장치가 아래로 누르고 있는 것처럼, 명확한 기업 전략이 없는 기업은 절대 이 영역을 떠나 위로 올라갈 수 없다.) 대신, 상당히 자주, 낮은 수익성과 소비자 수요의 피할 수 없는 변화에 대응하여 과감한 조치를 취하지 못하는 경영진의 무능함은 파산과 폐업으로 이어진다.

(어휘) anchor 고정 장치, 닻 well-defined 명확한 tactic 전략
competitive market 경쟁 시장 stand out 돋보이다
mean ~라는 결과를 낳다 mediocrity 평범
high-performing 높은 실적을 내는 cost leadership 원가 우위
compromise 타협하다 equate 일치하다 inextricably 빠져나올 수 없게
lodge 박히다, 몰아넣다 profitability 수익성 decisive 과감한
inevitable 피할 수 없는 bankruptcy 파산

(구문분석)
[1행] **As if** an anchor **were** holding it down, a business without well-defined corporate tactics can never leave this area and rise to the top.
→ 'As if + 주어 + 과거시제(were) ~, 주어 + 동사 ~' 구조의 as if 가정법 과거 문장으로, '(사실은 그렇지 않지만) 마치 ~인 것처럼'의 의미로 해석한다.

39 주어진 문장의 위치 찾기 정답 ②

(해설) ② 앞까지는 두 국가의 폭력적인 충돌은 압도적인 손실을 초래하지만 역사적 영토 소유권 주장이 그 위험을 감수하기에 충분한 이유로 간주된다는 내용이 이어지다가 ② 뒤 문장에서 경쟁을 벌이는 영토에 대한 두 당사자의 요구가 어떻게 공동의 또는 분할된 통치권의 수용으로 바뀌는지를 이해하는 것이 폭력의 비용을 피하는 데에 중요하다는 내용이 나오고 있다. ② 앞뒤의 내용이 유기적으로 연결되어 있지 않고, 주어진 문장의 some areas are regarded as indivisible(일부 지역은 분할할 수 없다고 여겨진다)은 ② 뒤 문장에서 these sorts of uncompromising, all-or-nothing demands(이러한 타협하지 않는 양자택일 식 요구)로 이어지고 있으므로 주어진 문장이 들어가기에 가장 적절한 곳은 ②이다.

(오답분석) ③~⑤ 뒤 문장은 ② 뒤 문장의 어떻게 타협하지 않는 양자택일 식 요구가 공동의 또는 분할된 통치권의 수용으로 바뀌는지에 대한 보충 설명이므로 주어진 문장은 이것보다 앞에 와야 한다.

(해석) 인간의 고통과 경제적 안보 측면에서 전쟁의 막대한 비용을 고려하면, 두 국가들이 폭력적인 충돌이 그 비용들을 감수할 가치가 있는 한계점에 도달한다는 것이 놀랍다. (①) 그러나 역사는 역사적 영토 소유권에 대한 주장이 흔히 외부 관찰자들에게는 불합리해 보일지도 모르는 생명과 재화의 압도적인 손실의 위험을 감수하기에 충분한 이유로 간주된다는 점을 보여주었다. (② 많은 뿌리 깊은 갈등이 분쟁 지역을 별개의 정치적 지역들로 나눔으로써 해결된 반면, 일부 지역은 갈등의 한쪽 혹은 양쪽에 의해 분할될 수 없다고 여겨진다.) 경쟁을 벌이는 지역에서 교전 중인 당사자들로부터의 이러한 타협하지 않는 양자택일 식 요구가 어떻게 공동의 또는 분할된 통치권의 수용으로 바뀌는지를 이해하는 것은 굉장한 폭력의 비용을 피하는 데에 중요하다. (③) 그렇다면 1998년 성금요일 협정에 뒤이어 북아일랜드에 겉보기에 지속되는 평화를 가져다준 요인들은 예루살렘 소유권을 두고 이스라엘과 팔레스타인 사이에 계속 진행 중인 충돌에 중요한 암시를 가질 수 있다. (④) 어떠한 조건에서 역사적 소유권 주장이 다른 고려 사항에 의해 완화되는가? (⑤) 그 질문에 대한 답이 폭력적 충돌의 비용이 잠재적으로 받아들여질 수 있는 손실로 여겨지는 지역들에서의 외교 전략을 결정지을 것이다.

(어휘) entrenched 뿌리 깊은 disputed territory 분쟁 지역
indivisible 분할할 수 없는 security 안보 threshold 한계점, 문지방

ground 이유, 근거 staggering 압도적인 blood 생명 treasure 재화
irrational 불합리한 uncompromising 타협하지 않는
all-or-nothing 양자택일의 contested 경쟁을 벌이는
sovereignty 통치권 intolerable 굉장한, 견딜 수 없는 diplomatic 외교의

 구문분석
[12행] **Understanding** [how these sorts of uncompromising, all-or-nothing demands from engaged parties in a contested region shift to an acceptance of shared or divided sovereignty] is essential for avoiding the intolerable costs of violence.

→ [how ~ sovereignty]는 의문사 how가 이끄는 명사절로 동명사 Understanding의 목적어 역할을 한다.

[16행] **The factors** [that brought about a seemingly enduring peace in Northern Ireland following the 1998 Good Friday Agreement], then, may have significant implications ~

→ [that ~ Agreement]는 선행사 The factors를 수식하며 주격 관계대명사 that이 이끄는 관계대명사절이다.

40 요약문 완성하기 정답 ③

해설 글의 전반부에서 연구자들이 어떤 기억은 강화되는 반면 다른 기억은 사라지는 이유를 이해하려 시도했다고 했고, 글의 후반부에서는 실험을 통해 두 종류의 뇌파는 우리가 기억할지 잊을지를 결정하는 대항하는 힘이라는 생각을 하게 되었다고 했다. 따라서 지문의 reinforced를 strengthened로, rival forces determining whether we remember or forget을 compete으로 바꾸어 표현한 ③이 정답이다.

오답분석 두 종류의 뇌파가 우리가 기억할지 잊을지를 결정하는 대항하는 힘이라고 했으므로, ②의 collaborate, ④의 compromise 그리고 ⑤의 adjust는 (B)에 들어갈 단어로 적절하지 않다.

해석 자는 동안 어떤 기억은 사라지는 반면 다른 기억은 강화되는 이유를 더 잘 이해하려는 시도로, 연구자들은 두 종류의 뇌파 패턴: 서파와 델타파에 주목했다. 실험에서 쥐들이 새로운 기술을 훈련받고 나서, 다음 날 그 기술을 떠올리는 그 동물들의 능력을 확인하기 전에 연구자들은 쥐들이 자는 동안 그들의 뇌파 패턴을 억제했다. 연구자들은 그들이 서파를 겨냥할 때마다 새로운 기술을 기억하는 쥐의 능력이 감퇴한 반면 델타파는 반대라는 것을 발견했다. 이는 서파가 기억을 확고히 하고 델타파는 그것들을 저하시킨다는, 즉 두 종류의 뇌파가 우리가 기억할지 잊을지를 결정하는 대항하는 힘이라는 생각으로 이어졌다. 연구자들은 두 종류의 뇌파의 역할 사이에 차이가 있을 것이라고 예상하지 않았다; 과거에 두 종류는 보통 동시에 나타났기 때문에 함께 분류되었다. 그러나 그들의 발견은 둘 사이에 우리가 새로운 정보를 간직하게 하는 동시에 더 이상 필요하지 않은 기억들을 정리하게 하는 미묘한 균형이 존재한다는 것을 보여준다.

↓

기억이 (A) 강화될지 아닐지를 결정하는 요인들을 이해하려고 시도하는 동안, 연구자들은 두 종류의 뇌파 패턴이 (B) 겨룬다는 것을 발견했다.

	(A)	(B)
①	건설적인	…… 요동치다
②	형성되는	…… 협력하다
③	강화되는	…… 겨루다
④	정확한	…… 타협하다
⑤	제거되는	…… 적응하다

어휘 reinforce 강화하다 brain wave 뇌파 delta wave 델타파

---

suppress 억제하다 target 겨냥하다 decline 감퇴하다
solidify 확고히 하다 degrade 저하시키다 rival 대항하는, 서로 겨루는
simultaneously 동시에 delicate 미묘한 retain 간직하다
clear out 정리하다 [선택지] fluctuate 요동치다 compete 겨루다

 구문분석
[9행] The researchers found that [**whenever** they had targeted slow oscillations], the rats' ability to recall the new skill declined, whereas the opposite was true of delta waves.

→ [whenever ~ oscillations]는 복합관계부사 whenever(~할 때마다)가 이끄는 부사절로, whenever는 at any time when으로 바꿔 쓸 수 있다.

41~42 장문 독해 1

해석 11세기에 프랑스 시인들은 'l'amour courtois' 혹은 궁정풍 연애에 대해 쓰기 시작했다. 그 용어는 순수한 낭만적 사랑은 당시 일상적이고 기본적이라 기술되었던 결혼 속 사랑과 별개라는 발상을 세계에 소개했다. 다른 문화에서 사랑의 이런 개념은 (a)전례가 거의 없었다. 그러나 일단 기술되자, 이러한 열렬한 사랑의 형태가 프랑스 사회를 휩쓸었다. 궁정풍 연애를 (b)자극한 감정은 그것을 기술할 단어가 있기 전에 존재했을까? 달리 말해, 언어는 단지 우리의 경험을 묘사하는 것인가 아니면 그것이 세상에 대한 우리의 경험을 형성하는 것일까? [41]언어 상대성의 지지자들은 그것이 형성적 역할을 한다고 주장한다; 반면 인지 심리학자들은 언어는 (c)독특한(→보편적인) 인간 이해에서 발생한다고 보기를 선호한다. 전자에 속한 이들은 독일인들이 슬플 때 정크 푸드를 먹는 것은 그것에 대한 단어('쿠머슈펙')를 가지고 있기 때문이라고 말할 것이다. [42]그러나 사실, 영어로 말하는 사람들이 그 현상을 (d)간단히 기술할 단어가 없더라도 그들도 아마 우울할 때 과식하고 싶은 충동을 상세하게 알고 있을 것이다. 우리가 쓰는 언어가 그 언어로 표현된 어떤 미묘한 차이나 세부 사항에 대한 우리의 관심을 여과하는 것을 돕는다는 점에서 우리에게 분명 영향을 미치기는 하지만, 그것이 생각을 제한한다는 관념은 받아들이기 어렵다. [41]다른 언어의 화자가 언어적으로 의사 표현을 할 때 다른 인지 과정을 거친다 하더라도, 특정 개념에 대한 단어나 구문론이 우리에게 없으면 그것에 (e)접근할 수 없다고 말할 증거는 없다.

어휘 precedent 전례 put differently 달리 말해 shape 형성하다
proponent 지지자 linguistic relativity 언어 상대성 formative 형성적인
role 기능 intimately 상세하게 acquainted 알고 있는 impulse 충동
filter 여과하다 nuance 미묘한 차이 constrain 제한하다
cognitive 인지의 linguistically 언어적으로 inaccessible 접근할 수 없는
syntax 구문론 [선택지] flaw 결함 inherent 내재하는
linguistic relativism 언어 상대주의

구문분석
[22행] While the language we speak certainly influences us **in that** it helps to filter our attention towards certain nuances and details expressed in that language, ~

→ in that은 '~라는 점에서, ~이므로'라는 의미의 부사절 접속사이다.

41 제목 파악하기 정답 ⑤

해설 궁정풍 연애라는 단어의 사례를 통해 언어 상대주의는 언어가 우리의 세상에 대한 경험을 형성한다고 주장했지만, 마지막 부분으로 미루어 보아 어떤 현상을 간단히 기술할 단어가 없어도 상세히 알고 있을 수 있으므로, 그 현상에 접근할 수 없다고 보는 것은 무리라는 내용이다. 따라서 글의 제목으로 가장 적

절한 것은 ⑤ '언어 상대주의에 내재한 결함들'이다.

[오답분석] ①의 언어의 구조에 관한 내용은 글에서 언급되고 있지 않다. ②, ③은 글의 일부만을 다루고 있는 오답이다. ④은 글에서 언급된 Courtly Love를 사용하여 헷갈리게 하는 오답이다.

[해석] ① 모든 언어가 보편적인 구조를 공유하는가?
② 언어와 사고는 서로에게 의존적이다
③ 단어들은 어디서 오는가: 언어적 역사 탐구하기
④ 사랑의 발명: 시와 궁정풍 연애
⑤ 언어 상대주의에 내재한 결함들

42 어휘 적절성 파악하기　　정답 ③

[해설] 언어가 형성적 역할을 한다고 주장하는 언어 상대주의의 지지자들과 달리 인지 심리학자들은 독일어 '쿠머슈펙'과 같은 단어가 없는 영어로 말하는 사람들도 우울할 때 과식하고 싶은 충동을 잘 알고 있을 것이라고 하며, 언어가 보편적인 인간 이해에서 발생했다고 보기를 선호했다는 맥락이 되어야 하므로 ③의 unique(독특한)를 그와 반대되는 의미의 universal(보편적인)과 같은 단어로 바꾸어야 문맥상 적절하다.

[오답분석] ①은 11세기 이후로 프랑스 사회를 휩쓴 궁정풍 연애의 개념은 11세기 이전 다른 문화권에서 찾아볼 수 없었다는 맥락이 되어야 하므로 precedent가 오는 것이 적절하다. ⑤은 독일어 '쿠머슈펙'과 같은 단어가 없는 영어로 말하는 사람들도 우울할 때 과식하고 싶은 충동을 잘 알고 있을 것이라고 했고, 특정 개념에 대한 단어나 구문론이 없다고 그것에 접근할 수 없다고 말할 증거는 없다는 문맥이 되어야 하므로 inaccessible이 오는 것이 적절하다.

43~45 장문 독해 2

[해석] (A) Harry는 시골에서 조부모님과 주말을 보내게 된 것이 기쁘지 않았다. 그들의 작은 농장은 단지 들판과 숲으로만 둘러싸여 있었고 수 마일 거리에 다른 건물은 없었다. Harry는 그가 머무르는 동안 그를 계속 바쁘게 만들 일을 찾아야 한다는 것을 알았기에, (a)그는 할아버지에게 무엇을 해야 할지 물어보았다. "우리는 산책을 가야겠구나"라고 그가 답했다. "이 지역에 아름다운 등산로들이 좀 있단다." Harry는 지루할 것 같다고 생각했지만, 어쨌든 가기로 했다.

(C) Harry와 할아버지는 큰 나무들과 나뭇잎 사이로 흘러드는 햇빛이 있는 울창한 숲을 통과해서 갔다. 작은 강이 그들이 걷는 길 옆에 흘렀고, 평화로웠지만 Harry는 거의 알아채지 못했다. 그는 계속 그의 휴대폰을 확인하고 도시에 있는 친구들에게 메시지를 보냈다. (c)그는 그가 거기에 있었으면 좋겠다고 생각하며 한숨을 쉬었다. "우리는 어디 가는 거예요?"라고 그가 물었다. Harry의 할아버지는 돌아서서 그를 보며 웃었다. "알게 될 거다."

(D) 그들은 이제 몇 시간째 걷고 있었고 마침내 큰 언덕을 오르기 시작했다. ⁴⁵Harry는 (d)그의 휴대폰을 치워 두고 가파른 경사를 오르면서 땀을 흘리고 있었다. 그들이 마침내 꼭대기에 올랐을 때, Harry는 큰 바위 위로 지쳐 쓰러졌다. 산책은 정확히 그가 예상한 대로였고 그는 그것이 거의 끝나간다는 것이 기뻤다. ⁴⁴그의 할아버지가 경치를 즐기며 (e)그만의 시간을 갖는 동안 그는 다시 휴대폰을 꺼내 게임을 하기 시작했다. "Harry야, 이리 와 봐라. 너에게 보여줄 것이 있다."라고 그가 말했다. Harry는 마지못해 일어나 할아버지가 서 있는 곳으로 걸어갔다.

(B) "얼마나 아름다운지 보렴"이라고 Harry의 할아버지가 말했다. Harry는 그의 앞에 광활하게 펼쳐진 풍경을 바라보았다. 밝은 초록색의 골짜기가 꽃들로 가득했고 영원히 이어질 듯 보였다. Harry는 광경에 감탄했고, 바로 그때

그들 위의 하늘이 얼마나 완벽하게 파란지 알아차렸다. 그는 놀라서 할아버지를 보았다. "이건 굉장해요"라고 (b)그가 말했다. "여기에 데려와 주셔서 감사해요." Harry는 그가 있는 곳에 대한 새로운 감상을 느꼈고 처음으로 그의 바로 앞에 있는 것들을 받아들이는 그만의 시간을 가졌다.

[어휘] vast 광활한　expanse 넓게 펼쳐진 것　awe 감탄, 경외감
steep slope 가파른 경사　collapse (지쳐) 쓰러지다
reluctantly 마지못해, 억지로

[구문분석] [24행] ~ although it was peaceful, [Harry **barely** took notice].
→ [Harry ~ notice]는 '거의 ~ 않다'라는 의미의 부정어 barely가 쓰인 부정 구문이다.

[35행] The walk <u>had been</u> exactly [what he had expected], and he was glad it was nearly over.
→ [what ~ expected]는 관계대명사 what(~하는 것)이 이끄는 명사절로, 동사 had been의 주격 보어 역할을 한다.

43 글의 순서 배열하기　　정답 ③

[해설] (A)는 주말 동안 시골에서 조부모님과 지내게 된 Harry가 할아버지를 따라 산책을 나서는 내용이다. (C)의 첫 문장은 Harry와 할아버지는 울창한 숲을 통과해서 갔다는 내용이므로, (C)는 주어진 글 바로 뒤에 오는 것이 적절하다. (D)에서 Harry와 할아버지가 마침내 큰 언덕의 꼭대기에 올랐다고 했으므로, (D)는 Harry가 어디 가는 건지 모르는 채 할아버지를 따라갔던 (C) 뒤에 와야 한다. (B)에서 Harry가 할아버지의 권유로 보게 된 광활한 풍경에 감탄하는 것은 (D)에서 할아버지가 보여줄 것이 있다며 Harry를 부른 다음이 되어야 하므로, (B)는 (D) 다음에 오는 것이 적절하다. 따라서 글의 순서로 가장 적절한 것은 ③ (C) - (D) - (B)이다.

44 지칭 대상 파악하기　　정답 ⑤

[해설] (a), (b), (c), (d)는 모두 Harry를 가리키지만 (e)는 할아버지를 가리키므로, ⑤이 정답이다.

45 세부 정보 파악하기　　정답 ⑤

[해설] (D)의 He pulled out his phone again and began to play a game을 통해 Harry는 언덕 꼭대기에서 휴대폰으로 게임을 했다는 것을 알 수 있는데, ⑤은 풍경 사진을 찍었다고 일부 정보를 잘못 나타냈으므로 글의 내용과 일치하지 않는 것은 ⑤이다.

정답

문제집 p. 182

18	③	19	②	20	③	21	③	22	②	23	①	24	②	25	④	26	⑤	27	⑤
28	③	29	④	30	③	31	③	32	⑤	33	④	34	④	35	②	36	⑤	37	④
38	⑤	39	④	40	②	41	①	42	⑤	43	④	44	②	45	⑤						

18 목적 파악하기 정답 ③

(해설) I was wondering if you could(~해주실 수 있을지 알고 싶었어요)를 이용해 병원의 건물 벽에 전시할 예술 작품을 제작해줄 수 있는지 문의하고 있으므로 정답은 ③이다.

(해석) Stephanie께,

오랜만이네요. 잘 지내셨나요? 화랑에서 하는 당신의 지난번 전시에 갔었는데, 정말 훌륭했어요. 저는 당신이 얼마나 바쁜지 알고 있지만, 국립 어린이 병원을 위한 새 예술 작품을 제작할 시간을 내줄 수 있을지 알고 싶었어요. 당신도 알다시피, 저는 작년 한 해 동안 국립 어린이 병원을 보수해왔어요. 저희는 지역 예술가들의 그림으로 건물의 한쪽 벽을 채우려고 계획하고 있어요. 저는 이 협업에 당신이 당신의 작품을 포함해 주기를 희망하고 있어요. 모두가 다른 예술가들의 작품과 더불어 당신의 작품을 보고 싶어 할 것이라고 확신해요. 병원에도 엄청난 영광일 거예요. 프로젝트에 대한 추가 정보를 원하면 언제든지 제게 전화하거나 이메일을 보내주세요.

Lily Myers 드림

(어휘) spare (시간을) 내주다, 할애하다 collaboration 협업, 합작

(구문분석)
[4행] ~, but I **was wondering** [if you could spare some time to create a new art piece for the National Children's Hospital].

→ [if ~ Hospital]은 접속사 if가 이끄는 명사절로, 동사 was wondering의 목적어 역할을 한다.

19 심경 파악하기 정답 ②

(해설) 심경은 간접적으로 표현된다. 글의 초반부의 Hannah walked into the lunchroom, looking around at her new classmates nervously를 통해 새로운 학교에 간 Hannah가 아직 아는 사람이 아무도 없어서 불안하고 긴장한 것을 알 수 있고, 후반부의 they were all laughing together, and Hannah felt a huge sense of relief와 Hannah smiled and said, "I think I'm going to like it here after all." 등을 통해 몇몇 친구들을 알게 되어 기뻐한 것을 알 수 있다. 따라서 Hannah의 심경 변화로 가장 적절한 것은 ②이다.

(해석) Hannah는 초조하게 새로운 학교 친구들을 둘러보면서 구내식당으로 걸어 들어갔다. 새로운 학교에서의 그녀의 첫 번째 날이었고, 그녀는 아직 아는 사람이 아무도 없었다. 모두들 이미 그들의 친구들 무리와 앉아 있었고, Hannah는 누군가에게 그들과 함께할 수 있을지 물어보기가 너무 쑥스러웠다. 그녀는 빈 테이블로 가서 혼자 앉아 한숨을 쉬었다. 이런 식으로는, 그녀는 절대 친구를 만들지 못할 것이었다. 그녀가 샌드위치를 먹기 시작한 바로 그때, 한 무리의 소녀들이 그녀 주위에 앉았고 그녀의 이름을 물어보았다. "Hannah야 만나서 반가워. 나는 Amy야. 얘는 Milly고, 얘는 Elena야." 곧, 그

들은 모두 같이 웃고 있었고, Hannah는 큰 안도감을 느꼈다. 그들은 작별 인사를 하기 전에 Hannah에게 또 그들과 시간을 보내자고 말했다. 다음 수업에 들어가면서, Hannah는 웃으며 "나는 결국에 여기가 좋아질 것 같아"라고 말했다.

① 침착한 → 쑥스러운   ② 불안한 → 기쁜
③ 짜증 난 → 자랑스러운   ④ 만족하는 → 혼란스러운
⑤ 긴장한 → 두려운

(어휘) lunchroom 구내식당 embarrassed 쑥스러운, 어색한
by oneself 혼자, 도움을 받지 않고 at this rate 이런 식으로는
hang out with ~와 시간을 보내다

(구문분석)
[1행] Hannah walked into the lunchroom, [looking around at her new classmates nervously].

→ [looking ~ nervously]는 '~하면서'라는 의미의 분사구문으로, 분사구문의 주어가 주절의 주어(Hannah)와 같아서 생략되었다.

[7행] [Just **as** she began to eat her sandwich], a group of girls sat down around her and asked her name.

→ [Just ~ sandwich]는 접속사 as(~할 때)가 이끄는 시간의 부사절이다. 이때 Just는 부사절 접속사 as를 꾸며주는 부사이다.

20 주장 파악하기 정답 ③

(해설) 글의 마지막 세 문장에서 학교의 교육 과정은 학생들이 선택 가능한 것들을 철저하게 검토하도록 도와서, 미래에 최선의 판단을 내릴 수 있는 능력을 갖추는 것을 목표로 해야 한다고 주장하고 있으므로 정답은 ③이다.

(오답분석) ①은 글의 핵심 소재 '비판적 사고'를 사용했으나, 글에서 학생 참여형 수업에 대해서는 다루고 있지 않으므로 오답이다. ②은 글에서 학생들의 미래에 도움이 되는 방식으로 수업의 목표를 개선해야 한다고 했지만, 시대의 흐름을 반영해야 한다는 내용은 다루고 있지 않으므로 오답이다. ④, ⑤은 글에서 언급된 내용이 아니다.

(해석) 학교들은 수업하는 동안 사실과 정보의 암기를 용이하게 하려고 흔히 교과 과정을 조정한다. 이는 학생들에게 창의적으로 주제들을 탐구할 자유를 주기보다는 그들이 일정 한도 내에 사고하도록 부추긴다. 주제들에 대해 신중히 평가하는 역량을 제한함으로써, 현재의 교육 제도는 학생들의 의사 결정 능력을 개선하는 것이 아니라 제한하고 있고, 이는 학생들의 미래에 해롭다. 급하게 진행되는 수업과 자료를 기반으로 성급한 판단을 하도록 압박을 받는 것은 학생들에게 이롭지 않은데, 그들은 인생 동안 중요한 선택들을 할 수밖에 없을 것이기 때문이다. 따라서, 수업은 단순히 기초 지식을 빨아들이고 수용하기를 부추기는 것 대신에 비판적 사고를 발전시키는 방식으로 접근되어야 한다. 학생들이 선택 가능한 것들을 철저하게 검토하도록 돕는 것을 목표로 하는 교과

과정은 그때가 왔을 때 자신들을 위한 최선의 판단을 내리는 데에 필요한 능력을 그들에게 제공할 것이다. 이것은 그들이 성인기에 배워야 할 것이 아니라 인생의 초기에 배워야 하는 것이다.

[어휘] tailor 조정하다, 맞추다   curricula(curriculum의 복수형) 교과 과정
facilitate 용이하게 하다   parameter 한도   refine 개선하다, 정제하다
detrimental 해로운   snap 성급한   foster 발전시키다, 조성하다
intake 빨아들임, 수용

[구문분석]
[9행] ①[Being pressured to make snap judgments based on rushed lessons and material] is not beneficial to **students**, ②[who will be forced to make significant choices throughout their lives].

→ ①[Being ~ material]은 주어 역할을 하는 동명사구이다.

→ ②[who ~ lives]는 선행사 students를 수식하는 주격 관계대명사절로, 콤마 뒤에서 계속적 용법으로 쓰였다.

[15행] A curriculum with the aim **of** [helping students
주어   동명사   목적어
consider options thoroughly] will give them the necessary
목적격 보어   동사
skills ~

→ 전치사 of의 목적어로 쓰인 동명사구 [helping ~ thoroughly]에서 동명사 helping의 목적어로 students, 목적격 보어로 동사원형 consider가 쓰였다.

---

② 사회적 기여로 좋은 평판을 얻는 것
③ 이윤을 내기에 충분한 수익을 발생시키는 것
④ 대중들 사이에서 긍정적인 평판을 얻는 것
⑤ 건전한 사업 모델을 통해 투자자들을 유인하는 것

[어휘] make ends meet 수입과 지출을 맞추다, 겨우 먹고 살 만큼 벌다
tackle (문제를) 다루다   undermine 약화시키다
strike a balance 균형을 이루다   sustain 유지하다
adhere 고수하다   precarious 불안정한, 위태로운   translate ~이 되다
sterling 훌륭한   make a living 생계를 유지하다
[선택지] publicity 평판, 홍보   sound 건전한, 건강한

[구문분석]
[6행] Social enterprises must then strike a delicate balance of being able to sustain themselves **through** ①[what they earn] ②[**while** still adhering to their mission].

→ ①[what they earn]은 관계대명사 what(~하는 것)이 이끄는 명사절로, 전치사 through의 목적어 역할을 한다.

→ ②[while ~ mission]은 분사구문의 의미를 분명하게 하기 위해 부사절 접속사(while)가 분사 앞에 온 형태이다.

[15행] Good deeds do **not always** translate to good business, though, and ~

→ not always는 '언제나 ~인 것은 아니다, 반드시 ~하는 것은 아니다'라는 의미로 부분 부정을 나타내는 구문이다.

---

21   밑줄 의미 추론하기   정답 ③

[해설] 사회적 기업들이 사회적 문제를 다루면서도 생계를 유지하고 운영을 지속하기 위해서는 목표만큼 수익도 중요하다고 말하고 있다. 따라서 글의 주제를 비유적으로 표현한 Making more than ends meet(수입과 지출을 맞추는 이상을 하는 것)이 의미하는 것은 ③ '이윤을 내기에 충분한 수익을 발생시키는 것'이다.

[오답분석] ①은 글에서 언급된 내용이 아니다. ②, ④은 많은 사회적 기업들이 훌륭한 평판에도 불구하고 운영을 지속하는 데에 어려움을 겪는다고 한 글의 내용과 반대되는 내용을 다루고 있으므로 오답이다. ⑤은 글에서 투자자들을 유인하는 것에 대해서는 언급되지 않았고, 글에서 언급된 business model을 사용하여 헷갈리게 하는 오답이다.

[해석] 수입과 지출을 맞추는 이상을 하는 것은 사회적 문제들을 다루는 것을 목표로 삼는 사회적 기업들의 장기적인 존속을 보장한다. 그들의 사업 모델은 그것에 의존한다. 하지만 그들은 이것을 도를 지나치게 할 수는 없다; 만약 그들이 이익을 극대화하는 것에 너무 중점을 둔다면, 그들은 진정한 사회적 영향력을 지닌다는 그들의 목표를 약화시킬 위험이 있다. 사회적 기업들은 그렇다면 여전히 사명을 고수하는 동시에 그들이 버는 것을 통해 스스로를 유지할 수 있는 섬세한 균형을 이루어야 한다. 실제로 공동체들을 돕는 것을 통해서 사회적 자본을 얻는 것이 점점 중요해지면서 오늘날 점점 더 많은 사업체들이 스스로가 이러한 불안정한 상황에 있음을 깨닫고 있다. 사실, 사회적 문제들을 다루는 것에 대한 기업의 헌신은 흔히 현대의 비즈니스 환경에서 그들의 성공을 결정하는 한 가지 요인이다. 그렇지만, 선행이 항상 잘 되는 사업이 되는 것이 아니고 많은 사회적 기업들이 훌륭한 평판에도 불구하고 운영을 지속하는 데에 어려움을 겪는다. <가디언>에 따르면, 사회적 기업가들의 71퍼센트가 "사회적 벤처 사업을 통해 생계를 유지하려고 분투"하며, 이러한 사업 방식을 추구하는 사람들이 직면하는 딜레마를 강조한다. 그들의 목표는 분명히 중요하지만, 수입도 마찬가지이다.

① 사업 운영비를 줄이는 방법을 찾는 것

---

22   요지 파악하기   정답 ②

[해설] 글의 마지막 세 문장에서 진정한 발전을 이루고 학계와 대중이 연구에 신뢰를 가질 수 있도록 윤리적 기준들이 연구 절차에 적용되어야 한다는 요지가 제시되어 있으므로, 이 글의 요지로 가장 적절한 것은 ②이다.

[오답분석] ①의 학문의 지속 가능한 발전은 글에서 언급된 내용이 아니다. ④의 학문의 특성에 맞는 윤리에 대해서는 글에서 언급되지 않았다. ⑤은 글이 연구 절차를 조작하는 것을 막기 위해 연구에서 규약이 지켜져야 한다고 한 것이지, 이 행위들을 규제하는 사회적 조치가 필요하다고 한 것이 아니므로 오답이다.

[해석] 윤리는 무엇이 용인되는 행동인지를 규정하고, 사람들이 옳은 것과 그른 것 사이의 중간 영역을 처리하는 것을 도울 수 있다. 다양한 직종과 기관들에는 활동과 상호 작용을 이끄는 엄격하지 않은 법률로서의 역할을 하는 다양한 윤리적 기준들이 있다. 대중의 신뢰를 쌓고 지식의 공정한 입수를 보장하기 위해 다양한 분야들은 심지어 이러한 행동 규범들을 연구에도 적용한다. 이러한 기준들은 사람들이 연구 절차를 조작하는 것을 막는다. 만약 누군가가 거짓되거나 편향된 정보를 발표하거나 다른 연구자의 연구를 도용하거나 적절한 규약에 따라 실험을 진행하지 못한다면, 이루어진 진보는 진정한 가치가 없다. 신뢰와 정직은 진정한 발전이 이루어지기 위해서 연구 절차에서 필수이다. 이는 받아야 할 누구든 인정을 받고, 연구원들 간의 협업과 협력 동안에 상호 간의 존중이 있다는 것을 의미한다. 학계와 더불어 대중이 연구에 신뢰를 가질 수 있도록 규약이 지켜져야 한다. 진실성 없이는 어떠한 진정한 것도 성취되지 않는다.

[어휘] gray area 중간 영역, 애매한 부분   navigate 처리하다, 길을 찾다
code 규범, 암호   conduct 행동, 행위   tamper with 조작하다
protocol 규약, 의례   imperative 필수의, 의무의   integrity 진실성, 정직

[구문분석]
[14행] This means that credit is given **to** [whomever it is owed to], and that ~

→ [whomever ~ to]는 복합관계대명사 whomever가 이끄는 명사절로 전치사 to의 목적어 역할을 한다.

[17행] Protocol must be followed [**so that** the public, along with the academic community, can have confidence in research].

→ [so ~ research]는 접속사 so that(~하기 위해서)이 이끄는 목적을 나타내는 부사절이다. so that은 in order that으로 바꿔 쓸 수 있다.

---

23 주제 파악하기
정답 ①

(해설) 우리의 시간에 대한 경험은 주관적이어서 시간이 사건들 간의 간격이라는 것을 이해하기 어려워하고, 과거의 사건들을 순서대로 기억하려는 우리의 능력과, 시간의 비가역성 등으로 인해 시간의 흐름이 존재한다고 느끼지만 과학적 관점에서 그러한 흐름이 존재한다는 증거가 없다는 내용의 글이다. 따라서 이 글의 주제로 가장 적절한 것은 ① '시간에 대한 우리의 잘못된 이해에 대한 가능한 설명들'이다.

(오답분석) ②은 글에서 우리가 시간의 흐름을 인식하는 데에 미치는 시계의 영향에 대해서는 설명했지만, 현재에 대한 우리의 개념을 형성하는 데에 미치는 시계의 영향에 대해서는 언급하고 있지 않다. ③은 글에서 시간에 대한 우리의 경험이 주관적이라고 했을 뿐, 주관적 경험과 객관적 경험 간의 차이에 대해서는 다루고 있지 않으므로 오답이다. ④은 글에서 언급된 내용이 아니다. ⑤은 뇌가 우리에게 일어났던 것을 이야기로 편집한다는 글의 내용과 반대되기 때문에 오답이다.

(해석) 우리는 시곗바늘의 이동에서 시간의 흐름을 알 수 있다고 생각한다. 우리가 시간이 흐른다고 말할 때, 우리는 현재의 순간이 과거의 순간으로부터 그리고 미래로 흐른다는 뜻으로 말한다. 하지만 시계들이 실제로 측정하는 것은 시간의 끊임없는 흐름이 아니라 사건들 간의 간격이다. 그것들은 출생과 죽음, 첫사랑과 결혼, 아침 식사와 점심 식사 간의 간격을 측정한다. 시간에 대한 우리의 경험은 전적으로 주관적이기 때문에, 우리는 이것을 이해하는 것을 어려워해서 시간이 흐른다는 허상을 받아들이는 것을 선택한다. 과학적 관점에서, 그러한 흐름이 존재한다는 증거가 없다. 그 허상은 과거의 사건들을 순서대로 기억하는 우리의 능력의 작용이다. 우리가 흐름이 있다고 느끼도록 우리의 뇌는 우리에게 일어났던 것을 하나의 이야기로 편집한다. 우리의 경험들에서 우리가 배우는 것은 깨진 유리잔은 다시 맞춰질 수 없고 탁자에 있는 한 잔의 차는 절대로 뜨거워지지 않는다는 것이다. 사건들의 비가역성은 우리에게 시간이 한 방향으로 움직인다는 인상을 주는데, 그것은 정확히 말하면 시간 자체의 속성은 아니다.

① 시간에 대한 우리의 잘못된 이해에 대한 가능한 설명들
② 현재에 대한 우리의 개념을 형성하는 데에 미치는 시계의 영향
③ 주관적 경험과 객관적 경험 간의 차이점들
④ 과학을 통해서 시간의 존재를 입증하는 것의 어려움
⑤ 상상의 사건들로부터 이야기를 구성하는 뇌의 능력

(어휘) hand (시계의) 바늘 interval 간격 illusion 허상, 착각 function 작용, 기능
sequence 순서 narrative 이야기, 묘사
reassemble 다시 맞추다, 재조립하다
irreversibility 비가역성, 이전 상태로 되돌릴 수 없음 attribute 속성, 자질
[선택지] flawed 잘못된, 결함 있는 conception 이해, 신념

(구문분석) [17행] The irreversibility of events gives us **the impression** ①[that time moves in one direction], ②[which is not exactly an attribute of time itself].

→ ①[that ~ direction]은 the impression과 동격을 이루는 명사절이다.
→ ②[which ~ itself]는 바로 앞의 that절 ①[that ~ direction]을 수식하는 주격 관계대명사절로, 콤마 뒤에서 계속적 용법으로 쓰였다.

---

24 제목 파악하기
정답 ②

(해설) 첫 세 문장과 마지막 세 문장으로 미루어 보아 인간이 신체적 그리고 정신적으로 기술과 결합함으로써 우리의 진화를 이끌어 가고 있고, 우리에게 영향을 미치고 있는 기계인 보철기기나 스마트폰의 예를 들며 우리가 인간이라고 말하기 어려운 전혀 다른 종으로 진화할 때까지 인간과 기술의 통합이 계속될 것이라는 내용의 글이다. 따라서 글의 제목으로 가장 적절한 것은 ② '인간과 기계 간의 경계를 모호하게 만드는 것'이다.

(오답분석) ①은 글에서 인간이 기술을 통해 진화한다고는 했지만 로봇이 인류를 대체할지에 대한 내용은 언급되지 않았으므로 오답이다. ④은 글의 일부만을 다루고 있는 오답이다.

(해석) 대부분의 역사를 통틀어, 종의 진화는 우리 인간이 거의 통제권이 없었던 과정으로, 우리 자신들보다 높은 어떠한 힘에 의해 지배되었다. 자연 선택에는 항상 오래된 생물에서 새로운 생물을 만들어내는 신과 같은 능력이 있었다. 그러나 이제, 인간은 신체적 그리고 정신적으로 기술과 융합하여 우리 자신의 진화를 이끌 방법들을 찾고 있다. 만약 그것이 공상 과학 소설처럼 들린다면, 현대의 보철 산업이 인간의 생각으로 제어 가능한 팔다리를 만들어낼 수 있다는 것을 고려해보아라. 우리의 스마트폰은 우리 신체의 연장선이 되어, 우리의 심장 박동 수를 측정하고 우리가 언제 깨어 있거나 자고 있는지를 감지하며 Socrates(소크라테스)나 Plato(플라톤)가 가능하다고 생각했던 모든 것 이상으로 우리의 정신적 역량을 확대한다. 시간이 흐르면서, 아마도 인류는 우리가 우리의 조상들이 완전히 알아보지 못할 종으로 진화할 때까지 계속해서 기술을 우리의 생명 활동에 통합시킬 것이다. 이러한 업그레이드된 형태의 인류는 결국 우리가 네안데르탈인과 공통점을 지니는 것보다 21세기의 인류와 더 적은 공통점을 지닐 수도 있다. 그 결과로 등장한 종이 인간일지는 말하기 어렵지만, 그렇더라도 불가피해 보인다.

① 기술이 진보함에 따라 로봇이 인류를 대체할 것인가
② 인간과 기계 간의 경계를 모호하게 만드는 것
③ 어떻게 스마트폰이 인류의 문명을 지배하게 되었는가
④ 자연의 신과 같은 능력: 인류 진화의 역사
⑤ 기술과의 통합의 증가하는 속도

(어휘) natural selection 자연 선택 steer 이끌다, 조종하다
merge with ~와 융합하다 prosthetics 보철(술) limb 팔다리
humanity 인류, 인간성 integrate 통합시키다 biology 생명 활동
utterly 전적으로, 완전히 inevitable 불가피한

(구문분석) [1행] Throughout most of history, the evolution of species has been **a process** [over which we humans have had little control], governed by a power higher than ourselves.

→ [over ~ control]은 선행사 a process를 수식하며, '전치사 + 관계대명사' over which가 이끄는 관계대명사절이다.

[10행] Our smartphones have become an extension of our bodies, measuring our heart rates, **sensing** [when we are awake or asleep], and expanding ~

→ [when ~ asleep]은 의문사 when이 이끄는 명사절로, 현재분사 sensing의 목적어로 쓰였다.

25 도표 정보 파악하기 정답 ④

(해설) 잘 준비가 되어 있을 때에도 학교 시험에 대해 불안을 느끼는 청소년들의 비율과 관련해서 2위를 차지한 국가는 63.9퍼센트의 캐나다가 아니라 67.7퍼센트의 미국이므로 수치가 잘못 반영되었다. 따라서 도표의 내용과 일치하지 않는 것은 ④이다.

(해석)

학교생활과 교육에 대한 청소년들의 태도

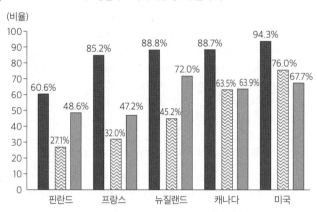

- 학교에서 우수한 성적을 원하는 청소년들
- 대학 학위를 이수하기를 바라는 청소년들
- 잘 준비가 되어 있을 때에도 학교 시험에 대해 불안을 느끼는 청소년들

위의 도표는 선정된 5개국에서의 학교생활과 교육에 대한 청소년들의 태도와 관련된 세 가지의 지수를 보여준다. ① 도표의 국가들 중에서, 핀란드가 27.1퍼센트로 대학 학위를 이수하기 바라는 청소년들의 가장 적은 비율을 나타낸다. ② 프랑스에서, 대학 학위를 이수하기 바라는 청소년들의 비율은 학교에서 우수한 성적을 원하는 청소년들의 그것(비율)의 절반보다 더 적다. ③ 미국은 학교에서 우수한 성적을 원하는 청소년들의 비율이 90퍼센트를 넘는 유일한 국가이다. ④ 잘 준비가 되어 있을 때에도 학교 시험에 대해 불안을 느끼는 청소년들의 비율과 관련해서, 뉴질랜드가 72퍼센트로 1위를 차지했고, 63.9퍼센트로 캐나다가 뒤를 이었다. ⑤ 미국을 제외한 선정된 국가들 각각에서, 잘 준비가 되어 있을 때에도 학교 시험에 대해 불안을 느끼는 청소년들의 비율은 대학 학위를 이수하기를 바라는 청소년들의 그것(비율)보다 더 높다.

(어휘) attitude 태도, 의식 index 지수, 지표 as for ~에 관해서

(구문분석) [6행] In France, [the percentage (of adolescents) (who expect to complete a university degree)] is less than half of that of adolescents who want top grades at school.
주어 / 동사

→ [the ~ degree]는 전치사구(of adolescents)와 관계대명사절(who ~ degree)을 포함하며, 전체가 문장의 주어이다.

26 세부 정보 파악하기 정답 ⑤

(해설) However, he became increasingly interested in religion ~ his writings began to focus more on theology and morality를 통해 Blaise Pascal이 종교에 점점 관심을 갖게 되면서 그의 집필이 신학과 도덕에 더 중점을 두었다는 것을 알 수 있는데, ⑤은 그 후에도 물리학 저술에 집중했다고 일부 정보를 잘못 나타냈으므로 글의 내용과 일치하지 않는 것은 ⑤이다.

(해석) Blaise Pascal(블레즈 파스칼)은 17세기 프랑스의 과학자, 수학자이자, 철학자였다. 그의 아버지는 수학에 매우 정통했고 Pascal이 어렸을 때 그를 가르

쳤다. Pascal이 16세였을 때, 그는 첫 번째 학술 논문을 썼다. 이 논문은 매우 수준이 높아 일부 사람들은 그의 아버지가 그것을 썼다고 주장했다. 1642년에, Pascal은 그의 아버지가 세금 징수하는 것을 돕기 위해 계산기를 개발했다. 그의 계산기는 그 당시에 이용 가능한 다른 어떠한 것보다도 더 선진적이었지만, 높은 가격 때문에 광범위하게 사용되지는 못했다. 1646년부터 1654년까지, Pascal은 물리학 분야에, 가장 두드러지게는 유체 역학과 관련된 영역에 중대한 기여를 했다. 하지만, 그는 1655년부터 계속 종교에 점점 더 관심을 갖게 되었고, 그의 집필은 신학과 도덕에 더 중점을 두기 시작했다. Pascal은 오래 계속되는 질병 이후 1662년에 사망했지만, 그의 저술들은 오늘날 계속해서 학자들에게 영향을 준다.

(어휘) sophisticated 수준 높은 advanced 선진적인 fluid mechanics 유체 역학 theology 신학 morality 도덕, 도덕성

(구문분석) [8행] Although his calculator was [more advanced than any other] available at the time, it did not achieve ~

→ [more ~ other]는 '비교급 + than any other (+ 단수명사)'(다른 어떤 ~보다도 더 -한)의 형태로 최상급을 나타내는 구문이다. 이 문장에서는 other 뒤에 단수명사 calculator가 생략되었다.

27 안내문 정보 파악하기 정답 ⑤

(해설) Please request a parking pass at the reception desk when you arrive를 통해 도착해서 접수처에서 주차권을 요청해야 한다는 것을 알 수 있으므로, 글의 내용과 일치하지 않는 것은 ⑤이다.

(해석)

Coleman Museum의 고고학 워크숍

올해의 워크숍은 로마의 영국 제도 정복을 다룰 것입니다. 각 세션은 이 분야의 전문가에 의해 진행될 것입니다.

일정
- 7월 15일 금요일, 오전 10시에서 오후 6시까지
- 세션별 주제와 시간의 전체 목록은 www.coleman.com/workshops 에서 이용 가능합니다.

장소
- Coleman 박물관 본관 201호

등록
- 마감일: 6월 25일
- 비용: 45달러 (대학생은 15퍼센트 할인)
- 등록하시려면 555-3939로 Denise Miller에게 연락하십시오.

주차
- 워크숍 참석자들에게는 5달러의 일일 주차료가 적용되지 않을 것입니다.
- 도착하시면 접수처에서 주차권을 요청하시기 바랍니다.

(어휘) archaeology 고고학 conquest 정복 British Isles 영국 제도 waive 적용하지 않다, 생략하다

(구문분석) [3행] Each session [will be led] by an expert in this field.

→ [will be led]는 조동사(will)가 있는 '조동사 + be + p.p.' 형태의 수동태이다.

28 안내문 정보 파악하기 정답 ③

(해설) 수치와 관련된 부분인 Prizes 항목의 First Prize: $150, Third Prize: $50를 통해 1등 상금인 150달러는 3등 상금인 50달러의 세 배임을 알 수 있으므로, 글의 내용과 일치하는 것은 ③이다.

(해석)

Norden 대학교 영어 연설 경연대회

Norden 대학교는 제4회 연례 영어 연설 경연대회를 공지하게 되어 기쁩니다. 올해의 주제는 "사회 변화에서 기술의 역할"이 될 것입니다. 현재 Norden 대학교에 등록된 학생들만 참가해 주시길 바랍니다.

장소: 대강당 - 학생회관
시간 및 날짜: 5월 15일, 오후 1시부터 오후 6시까지

연설 요건
• 전부 영어로 되고, 완전히 독창적이어야 하며, 6-8분 동안 지속되어야 합니다.

상금
• 1등: 150달러
• 2등: 100달러
• 3등: 50달러

수상자들은 5월 30일에 웹사이트에 발표될 것입니다. 개별 통보는 되지 않을 것입니다.

참고 부탁드립니다: 지원서는 4월 20일 이후에는 받아들여지지 않을 것입니다.

(어휘) venue 장소 entirely 완전히, 전부 notification 통보, 알림

(구문분석)
[2행] Norden College is **pleased** [to announce] its fourth annual English Speech Competition.
→ [to announce]는 to부정사의 부사적 용법으로 감정(pleased)의 원인을 나타낸다.

29 어법상 틀린 것 찾기 정답 ④

(해설) at the time을 통해 의료 전문가들이 세로토닌과 우울증의 연관 관계에 대한 결론에 이르렀던 과거의 특정 시점을 나타내고 있으며, 문제를 겨냥한 것이 현재와 연관된 과거의 동작이 아니라 순전히 과거의 일이므로 ④의 현재완료시제 have targeted를 과거시제 targeted로 고쳐야 한다.

(오답분석) ①은 동사 believe의 목적어 역할을 했던 that절의 주어(Serotonin)를 문장의 주어로 쓴 수동태 구문이므로 that절의 동사였던 influence를 to부정사 to influence로 쓴 것은 어법상 적절하다. ②은 2형식 동사 became의 주격 보어로 형용사 apparent를 쓴 것은 어법상 적절하다. ③은 문장의 주어 자리에 있는 It은 가주어이고 '이프로니아지드'가 세로토닌의 증가를 유발한다는 내용이 문장의 진주어가 되어야 하므로, 길이가 긴 진주어(that iproniazid ~ chemical down)를 이끌기 위해 that을 쓴 것은 어법상 적절하다. ⑤은 Drugs ~ brain에서 that ~ brain은 수식어(주격 관계대명사절)이고 복수명사 Drugs가 주어이므로 복수동사 were를 쓴 것은 어법상 적절하다.

(해석) 신경 세포들 사이에서 메시지 전송을 담당하는 뇌의 화학 물질인 세로토닌은 기분과 행동에 영향을 미친다고 여겨진다. 더 높은 수치의 이 "행복 화학 물질"은 더 명랑한 기분과 연관되는 반면, 더 낮은 수치는 반대로 우울증의 증상과 관련된다. 이러한 관련성은 폐결핵 환자들에게 '이프로니아지드'라는 약이 치료를 위해 투약되고 그 뒤에 놀라운 부작용: 명랑한 기분을 경험했던 1950년대에 처음으로 명백해졌다. '이프로니아지드'가 그 뇌의 화학 물질을 분해하는 효소의 정상적인 작용을 억제한다는 사실로 인해 '이프로니아지드'가 세로토닌의 증가를 유발한다는 것이 그러고 나서 발견되었다. 의료 전문가들은 세로토닌이 어떻게든 우울증과 불가분하게 연관된다는 결론에 이르렀고, 그 시기에 드디어 이 문제를 겨냥했던 항우울제가 개발되었다. 분자 스펀지가 뇌의 시냅스로부터 여분의 세로토닌과 같은 신경 전달 물질을 흡수하는 것을 억제하는 약물들이 만들어졌으며, 우울증의 세로토닌 결핍 이론의 타당성에 이의가 제기되었더라도 그것은 의심할 바 없이 그 질환의 치료에서 혁신으로 이어졌다.

(어휘) serotonin 세로토닌 transmit 전송하다 neuron 신경 세포, 뉴런 disposition 기분, 경향 tuberculosis 폐결핵 elevated 명랑한, 높은 inhibit 억제하다 enzyme 효소 inextricably 불가분하게 in one way or another 어떻게든 culminate in 드디어 ~이 되다 antidepressant 항우울제 molecular 분자의 neurotransmitter 신경 전달 물질 synapse 시냅스, 신경 접합부 validity 타당성 deficiency 결핍

(구문분석)
[10행] It was then discovered ①[that *iproniazid* led to an increase in serotonin due to **the fact** ②[that it inhibits the normal functioning of **the enzyme** (that breaks the brain chemical down)]].
가주어 / 진주어(that절)
→ 가주어 It이 길이가 긴 진주어 that절 ①[that *iproniazid* ~ down] 대신 주어 자리에 쓰인 형태이다.
→ ②[that it ~ down]은 the fact와 동격을 이루는 명사절이고, 명사절 안의 (that ~ down)은 선행사 the enzyme을 수식하며 주격 관계대명사 that이 이끄는 관계대명사절이다.

30 어휘 적절성 파악하기 정답 ③

(해설) "본인"은 "대리인"이 본인에게 가장 이익이 되도록 행동할 것이라고 기대하지만, 그들 사이에 이해의 충돌이 있을 때 손해를 입을 수도 있다는 내용의 글이다. 글의 마지막 부분에서 변호사가 고객이 아닌 자신의 이익을 위한 행동 방침을 권하는 상황을 예시로 든 것으로 보아, 본인-대리인 문제라고 알려진 딜레마는 대리인이 자신의 이익을 우선시할 위험이 있다는 문맥이 되어야 한다. 따라서 ③의 disregard(소홀히 하다)를 그와 반대되는 의미의 prioritize(우선시하다)와 같은 어휘로 바꾸어야 문맥상 적절하다.

(오답분석) ①은 대리인에게 본인이 지배권을 넘겨준다고 했으므로 가장 이익이 되도록 행동할 것이라는 기대를 갖는다는 문맥이 되어야 하므로 expectation이 오는 것이 적절하다. ②은 대리인이 무능했거나 이해의 충돌이 있었기 때문에 본인이 손해를 볼 것이라는 문맥이 되어야 하므로 ineffective가 오는 것이 적절하다.

(해석) 한쪽 당사자("본인")가 그들을 대신해서 행동을 취하도록 다른 당사자("대리인")를 고용할 때, 그들은 상대방이 그들에게 가장 이익이 되도록 행동할 것이라는 ① 기대를 가지고 일정한 정도의 지배권을 넘겨준다. 그렇게 함으로써 두 가지의 가능한 결과들이 있다: 본인이 대리인의 수고와 노하우에서 이익을 얻거나, 대리인이 ② 무능했거나 이해의 충돌이 있었기 때문에 손해를 입을 것이다. 본인-대리인 문제라고 알려진 딜레마는 대리인이 자신의 이익을 ③ 소홀히 할(→우선시할) 수도 있다는 위험이 있다는 것이다. 이는 양쪽 당사자들 간의 정보가 비대칭일 가능성이 있기 때문에 가능하다; 대리인은 본인보다 ④ 더 많이 아는 경향이 있고, 이는 애초에 대리인의 도움이 요구되는 이유이다. 예를 들어, 변호사는 잠재 고객에게 길고 비용이 많이 드는 행동 방침을 ⑤ 권할 수도 있는데, 고객에게 더 나은 결과를 가져올 가능성이 더 많아서가 아니라, 그것이 그 변호사에게 결과적으로 더 많은 돈을 벌 기회를 제공하기 때문이다.

principal 본인, 우두머리 agent 대리인 surrender 넘겨주다, 포기하다
suffer 손해를 입다, 고통받다 ineffective 무능한, 효과 없는
disregard 소홀히 하다 asymmetrical 비대칭적인

[구문분석]

[8행] [Known as the principal-agent problem], the dilemma is that there is a risk the agent might prioritize his or her own interests.

→ [Known ~ problem]은 과거분사(Known)로 시작하는 수동형 분사구문이다.

---

31 빈칸 추론하기
정답 ③

[해설] 글의 중반의 더미가 무엇인지에 대한 예시에서 모래 더미에서 알갱이 하나를 없애는 것은 더미가 아닌 것으로 만들지는 않지만, 계속 반복해서 한 개의 알갱이만 남았을 때 그 더미가 언제 더미가 아닌 것이 되었는지 모호하다고 했다. 따라서 주제와 관련된 빈칸에는 ③ '경계들 간의 구분'이 와서 경계들 간의 구분이 없음은 참인 진술에서 명백한 거짓으로 나아가는 타당한 주장의 연쇄를 야기한다는 의미가 되어야 한다.

[오답분석] ①, ⑤은 글의 내용과 관련이 없다. ②은 글에서 언급된 linguistic descriptions를 사용하여 헷갈리게 하는 오답이다. ④은 글에서 언급된 process와 'is repeated'를 바꿔 표현한 repetition을 사용하여 헷갈리게 하는 오답이다.

[해석] 분석 철학자들은 우리가 논리적인 현상을 완전히 비논리적인 용어들로 개념화하는 경향이 있기 때문에 세계에 대한 우리의 언어적 표현이 쓸모없다고 할 정도로 대개 모호하다고 주장한다. '연쇄 논법'의 역설을 가지고 가정을 세워보자: 더미란 무엇인가? 당신에게 모래 더미가 있고 한 번에 알갱이가 하나씩 없앤다고 해보자. 알갱이가 하나를 없애는 것은 더미를 더미가 아닌 것으로 만들지 않지만, 만약 이 과정이 충분히 반복된다면, 어느 순간에는 단 하나의 알갱이만이 남을 것이다. 한 개의 알갱이가 여전히 더미인가? 그리고 만약 아니라면, 그 더미는 언제 더미가 아닌 것이 되었는가? 관찰 가능한 현상의 범위 내에서, 어느 순간에 그 모래 더미는 알갱이가 하나가 되었는데, 이는 잘못된 결론이다. 따라서, 경계들 간의 구분이 없음은 참인 진술에서 명백한 거짓으로 나아가는 타당한 주장의 연쇄를 야기한다.

① 관련된 비유적 예시들
② 추상적인 언어적 표현들
③ 경계들 간의 구분
④ 일관된 과정의 반복
⑤ 사고의 논리적 적용

[어휘] analytical 분석적인 argument 주장, 논거
to the point of ~라고 할 정도로 formulate (가설을) 세우다, 만들어내다
sorites 연쇄 논법, 삼단 논법 heap 더미 grain 알갱이, 곡물
observable 관찰 가능한 constitute ~이 되다, 구성하다
erroneous 잘못된, 틀린 falsehood 허위
[선택지] metaphorical 비유적인 abstract 추상적인

[구문분석]

[8행] ~ yet **if** this process **is** repeated enough times, at some point, only a single grain **will remain**.

→ if가 이끄는 절이 조건의 의미를 나타내는 부사절이므로, 주절이 미래시제(will remain)이더라도 if절은 현재시제(is)를 사용한 형태이다.

---

32 빈칸 추론하기
정답 ⑤

[해설] 마케팅 담당자들은 사람들에게 선택지들이 주어지면 양극단을 피해 "딱 적당한" 것을 고르게 되는 '골디락스 효과'를 이용하고, 이에 따라 우리는 가장 비싼 상품과 가장 싼 상품을 피해 가운데 상품을 적당한 것으로 인식해서 구매한다는 내용의 글이다. 주제문에 해당하는 빈칸 문장에서는 우리는 중간 가격의 상품을 구매하고는 '무엇이 어떠하다'는 것을 알지 못한 채 합리적인 결정에 이르렀다고 생각한다고 하였다. 따라서 빈칸에는 ⑤ '우리의 선택이 다른 선택지들에 의해 틀이 잡혔다'는 내용이 오는 것이 적절하다.

[오답분석] ①의 더 비싼 물건들이 보통은 더 나은 특징들을 지니는지에 대한 내용은 글에서 언급되고 있지 않다. ②은 글에서 처음 한 선택에 대한 내용은 언급되지 않았고, 글에서 언급된 selections를 사용하여 헷갈리게 하는 오답이다. ③의 더 나은 대안을 찾을 수도 있었다는 것은 글의 내용과 관련이 없다. ④의 광범위한 계획을 요구한다는 것은 글의 내용과 관련이 없다.

[해석] 마케팅 담당자들은 우리가 선천적으로 삶의 모든 영역들에서 양극단에 저항하고 우리가 선택할 능력이 있을 때 힘을 부여받은 것으로 느껴진다는 사실을 흔히 이용한다. 그게 바로 많은 선택권들을 제시하는 마케팅 기술을 이용하는 것이 상당히 효과적인 이유이다; 우리는 자주 무언가를 구매해서 걸어나갈 것이고 그런 때의 대부분 우리의 선택은 선택권들이 주어졌을 때 "딱 적당한" 선택지들을 택한 동화 속 소녀의 이름을 따서 명명된 '골디락스 효과'에 의해 영향을 받았을 것이다. 같은 종류의 제품 3가지가 모두 다른 가격으로 주어졌을 때, 우리 중 대부분은 각각의 인식된 가치를 비교한다. 우리는 가장 비싼 상품은 너무 고급이고 가장 싼 상품은 돈에 비해 가치가 낮다고 볼 수도 있다. 하지만, 우리는 대개 중간의 상품을 질과 감당할 수 있는 비용 간에 적절한 조화를 이루는 제품으로 보고, 그래서 우리는 그것을 구매하고는 우리의 선택이 다른 선택지들에 의해 틀이 잡혔다는 것을 절대 알지 못한 채 합리적인 결정에 이르렀다고 생각한다.

① 더 비싼 물건들이 보통은 더 나은 특징들을 지닌다
② 우리의 처음 선택들이 일반적으로 가장 좋은 것들이다
③ 우리는 쉽게 더 나은 대안을 찾을 수 있었을 것이다
④ 결정을 하는 것은 광범위한 계획을 요구한다
⑤ 우리의 선택이 다른 선택지들에 의해 틀이 잡혔다

[어휘] play on 이용하다 innately 선천적으로, 타고나서 empower 힘을 부여하다
employ 이용하다, 고용하다 more often than not 자주, 대개
opt for 선택하다 strike a balance 조화를 이루다, 균형을 유지하다
affordability 감당할 수 있는 비용 [선택지] frame 틀을 잡다

[구문분석]

[8행] ~ so named for the little girl in the fairy tale who, [when (she was) presented with choices], opted for selections that were "just right."

→ [when ~ choices]는 주격 관계대명사 who와 동사 opted 사이에 접속사 when(~하면서)이 이끄는 시간의 부사절이 삽입된 형태이며, 부사절의 '주어(she) + be동사(was)'가 생략되었다.

[17행] ~ so we buy it and believe we have reached a rational conclusion, [never realizing our choice was framed by the other options].

→ [never ~ options]는 'never + 분사(realizing)' 형태로, 분사구문의 부정형이다.

33 빈칸 추론하기 정답 ⑤

(해설) 주제문에 해당하는 빈칸 문장에서 과학적 이론들은 '어떠하다'고 하고, 글의 중반에서 과학적 이론은 실험에 대한 반응으로 다듬어지는 이론들의 연속이라 했다. 또한, 빈칸 앞 문장에서는 Newton과 Einstein의 중력 이론 모두 동일한 발전의 일부이고 둘 다 완전히 폐기되지 않는다고 했다. 따라서, 빈칸에는 ⑤ '상충되는 정보의 발견에 의해 전개된다'가 오는 것이 적절하다.

(오답분석) ①은 글에서 언급된 irregularities를 사용하여 헷갈리게 하는 오답이다. ②은 과학적 이론은 실험에 대한 반응으로 다듬어지는 이론들의 연속이므로 상충되는 발견에 의해 발전된다는 글의 내용과 관련이 없다. ③, ④은 시간이 지나 대체되는 이론도 완전히 폐기되지 않는다는 글의 내용과 반대되므로 오답이다.

(해석) 과학적 연구의 과정에서, 우세한 이론이 때때로 관찰 가능한 실제와 상충하는 것은 불가피하다. 문제는 이론이 그러한 상충을 피할 정도로 충분히 설득력 있는지가 아니라, 상충이 일어났을 때 과학자들이 어떻게 대응하는지이다. 예측과 증거 간의 불일치를 발견하자마자 바로 이론을 폐기하는 것은 성급할 것이다. 과학자들이 데이터에서 변칙을 발견해서 한 이론에서 다른 이론으로 옮겨갈 때 우리는 그 과학적 방법이 이치에 맞지 않는다고 제쳐 놓아서도 안 된다. 과학적 이론은 사실상 실험에 대한 반응으로 다듬어지는 이론들의 연속이다. 분명히, 시간이 지나면서 우세한 이론이 퇴보할 때 패러다임의 전환이 발생하지만, 이러한 전환들은 닥치는 대로 이루어지지 않는다. Einstein(아인슈타인)은 Newton(뉴턴)을 대신했지만, 전지적인 우주의 힘이라는 Newton의 최초의 중력에 대한 개념은 현실이 공간을 휘게 하는 질량의 영향이라는 Einstein의 중력에 대한 관점과 일치한다는 것을 보여주는 수많은 실험들의 대상이다. 두 이론 모두 동일한 발전의 일부이고, 둘 다 완전히 폐기되지 않는다. 따라서 과학적 이론들은 상충되는 정보의 발견에 의해 전개된다.

① 변칙을 모르는 일반인들에게 받아들여지는
② 과학적 연구의 과정에 포함되는
③ 배제 과정을 통해 반증되는
④ 과학자들에 의해 번갈아 제시되고 일축되는
⑤ 상충되는 정보의 발견에 의해 전개되는

 (어휘) inquiry 연구, 탐구   conflict 상충, 충돌   discard 폐기하다
discrepancy 불일치, 차이   rash 성급한, 경솔한
dismiss ~하다고 제쳐 놓다, 일축하다
irrational 이치에 맞지 않는, 비이성적인   irregularity 변칙, 불규칙
degenerate 퇴보하다, 퇴행하다   omniscient 전지적인, 박식한
[선택지] laypeople 일반인, 비전문가   ignorant 모르는, 무지한

(구문분석)
[3행] The question is **not** ①[whether a theory is strong
　　　　　　　　　동사
enough to avoid such conflicts] but ②[how scientists respond
　　　　　　　　　　　　　　　주격 보어
when the conflicts arise].

→ ①[whether ~ conflicts]와 ②[how ~ arise]는 not A but B(A가 아니라 B)의 구조로 연결되었으며 각각 접속사 whether와 의문사 how가 이끄는 명사절로, be동사 is의 주격 보어 역할을 한다.

[7행] [**Neither** should we dismiss the scientific method as
　　　　　　　　조동사　주어　동사
irrational] when scientists move ~

→ [Neither ~ irrational]은 부정어 Neither가 문장 맨 앞에 나왔기 때문에, 주어와 조동사가 도치되어 '조동사(should) + 주어(we) + 동사(dismiss)'의 어순으로 쓰였다.

34 빈칸 추론하기 정답 ④

(해설) 선형성 개념을 받아들여 변수 하나가 약간 바뀌더라도 그 결과가 크게 다르지 않다고 보는 고전 역학과 달리, 지난 몇 십 년 동안 과학자들은 삼체 문제와 같이 변수의 작은 변화가 큰 결과를 야기할 수 있는 비선형적인 새로운 현상을 알아차렸다는 내용의 글이다. 빈칸 뒤 문장에서 동일해 보이는 원인도 매우 다른 결과로 이어질 수 있다고 하였으므로, 주제와 관련된 빈칸에는 ④ '그것들의 움직임은 사실상 완전히 예측 불가능하다'가 와서 비선형적인 삼체 문제와 같은 작용들이 이론적으로는 결정론적이더라도, 움직임은 사실상 예측 불가능하다는 의미가 되어야 한다.

(오답분석) ①의 다양한 분야에서의 적용에 대한 내용은 글에서 언급되지 않았다. ②은 글에서 언급된 deterministic을 사용하여 헷갈리게 하는 오답이다. ③은 삼체 문제에서 결과들이 초기 조건들에 매우 민감하다는 글의 내용과 반대되므로 오답이다. ⑤ 삼체 문제에서 동일해 보이는 원인도 매우 다른 결과로 이어질 수 있다는 글의 내용과 반대되므로 오답이다.

(해석) 수 세기 동안, 고전 역학은 행성, 별과 같은 물체들이 어떻게 하나의 체계 안에서 움직이는지에 대한 물리학자들의 이해를 좌우했다. 고전 역학은 선형성의 개념을 이용하는데, 이는 결과가 원인에 비례한다는 것이다. 예를 들어, 만약 당신이 원래보다 2배 더 세게 돌을 던지려고 한다면, 그것은 약 2배의 거리를 이동할 것이다. 하지만, 지난 몇 십 년 동안 과학자들은 새로운 현상을 알아차렸는데, 그 현상에서 관찰 불가능한 작은 원인이 엄청나게 큰 결과를 야기할 수 있었다. 이 현상의 그러한 한 가지 예는 삼체 문제이다. 만약 변수들 중의 하나가 약간 바뀌더라도 그 결과가 크게 다르지 않을 선형적 작용과는 달리, 삼체 문제에서는 변수의 작은 변화가 큰 결과를 야기할 수도 있다. 본질적으로, 결과들은 그것들을 야기하는 초기 조건에 매우 민감하다. 이러한 무질서하고 비선형적인 작용들이 이론적으로 결정론적이더라도, 그것들의 움직임은 사실상 완전히 예측 불가능하다. 결국, 동일해 보이는 원인도 매우 다른 결과로 이어질 수 있다.

① 그것들의 다양한 분야에서의 적용은 많은 잠재력을 가지고 있다
② 그것들의 민감성은 결정론적인 힘에 의해 주도된다
③ 그것들의 결과는 초기 조건들에 좌우되지 않는다
④ 그것들의 움직임은 사실상 완전히 예측 불가능하다
⑤ 그것들의 결과는 거의 항상 예측과 일치한다

(어휘) mechanics 역학, 기계학   proportional 비례하는
three-body problem 삼체 문제   materially 크게, 물질적으로
in essence 본질적으로   deterministic 결정론적인, 결정론자의

(구문분석)
[3행] Classical mechanics employs the concept of linearity, which is [that effects are proportional to causes].

→ [that ~ causes]는 that이 '~라는 것'의 의미로 명사절 접속사로 쓰여 완전한 절(effects ~ causes)을 이끄는 형태이다.

[5행] For example, if you [**were to throw** a stone twice as hard as normal], it would travel approximately twice the distance.

→ [were ~ normal]은 주어를 서술하는 'be + to부정사' 구문으로, 의도의 의미를 나타낸다.

35 흐름과 관계 없는 문장 찾기 정답 ②

(해설) 저널리즘에서의 풍자는 악의적이거나 잘못된 정보를 퍼뜨리려는 가짜 뉴스와 달리 유머와 비꼬기를 이용해서 현실의 문제들에 대한 사람들의 인식을 높이기 위해 의도된다는 내용의 글이다. 그런데 ②은 정치적 수사에서 과장을 인

지하는 것에 대한 내용이므로 핵심 소재는 같지만 주제에서 벗어나 있어 글의 흐름과 무관하다.

[오답분석] ③의 the two는 ① 앞 문장과 ①에서 언급한 fake news와 satire를 가리키고 있으므로 ① 뒤에 이어지는 것이 적절하다. ④, ⑤은 ③에 이어서 사람들이 가짜 뉴스와 풍자를 구별하지 못하는 것에 대한 내용을 다루고 있으므로 자연스럽게 이어진다.

[해석] 저널리즘에서의 풍자는 악의적이거나 잘못된 정보를 퍼뜨리도록 의도된 것이 아니다; 그것이 진짜는 아니지만, 유머와 비꼬기를 이용해서 현실의 문제들에 대한 사람들의 인식을 높이도록 의도된다. ① 의제를 이행하기 위해 고의로 사람들을 속이려고 만들어진 정보인 가짜 뉴스와 달리, 풍자의 목적은 사람들을 웃게 만드는 것이고, 그것이 이용하는 사실에 의거한 부정확함이 독자들에게 이해되도록 의도된다. (② 일반적인 정치적 수사가 어떻게 들리는지를 이해하고 과장을 인지할 수 있는 것이 진짜와 진짜가 아닌 것을 구별하는 데에 있어 핵심이다.) ③ 하지만, 감소하는 미디어 정보 해독력과 확증 편향과 같은 몇몇 요인들로 인해 모두가 그 둘 간의 차이를 구별할 수 있는 것은 아니다. ④ 사람들은 자주 단순히 헤드라인이 그들의 지배적인 견해와 맞는 것 같아서 뉴스의 진실성을 확인하지 않은 채 뉴스를 매우 빠르게 퍼뜨린다. ⑤ 따라서, 풍자는 심각하게 받아들여지도록 의도된 것이 아니고 독자들이 정보에 대해 이의를 제기하고 스스로 생각할 수 있게 하지만, 그것을 이해하지 못하는 사람들에게 잘못 해석되고 그 때문에 나쁜 쪽으로 여론을 형성할 수도 있다.

[어휘] satire 풍자 malicious 악의적인 genuine 진짜의, 진실한
irony 비꼼, 아이러니 agenda 의제, 안건 factual 사실에 의거한
rhetoric 수사, 미사여구 media literacy 미디어 정보 해독력
confirmation bias 확증 편향 credibility 진실성, 신뢰성
empower ~할 수 있게 하다 for the worse 나쁜 쪽으로

[구문분석]
[8행] **Understanding** [what normal political rhetoric sounds like] and being able to recognize exaggeration are key to distinguishing between what is real and what isn't.
→ [what ~ like]는 의문사 what이 이끄는 명사절로, 동명사 Understanding의 목적어로 쓰였다.

36 글의 순서 배열하기 정답 ⑤

[해설] 주어진 글은 지구는 폐쇄계라서 지구에서의 탄소의 양이 항상 동일하다는 주제를 제시한다. (C)는 문제는 지구에서의 탄소의 양을 없애는 것이 아니라 탄소 보유량의 균형을 이루는 것이라는 내용이고, 주어진 글의 마지막에서 지구에서의 탄소의 양이 항상 동일하다고 했으므로 그 뒤에 와야 한다. (B)는 then을 통해 (C)에서 언급한 퇴적물에 대한 내용을 이어가며, 이러한 퇴적물들이 탄소 불균형을 일으키는 이유와 그 영향을 설명하므로 (C) 뒤에 오는 것이 적절하다. (A)의 this disturbance in the carbon cycle(탄소 순환에서의 이러한 어긋남)은 (B)의 '탄소 분포가 불균형해지는 것'을 가리키므로 (B) 바로 다음에 오는 것이 적절하다. 따라서 글의 순서로 가장 적절한 것은 ⑤ (C) - (B) - (A)이다.

[해석] 탄소는 모든 생물에게 필요하다. 지구는 폐쇄계인데, 이는 탄소가 어떻게 분포되더라도 지구에서의 탄소의 양이 항상 동일하다는 것을 의미한다.
(C) 문제는 지구에서의 탄소의 양을 없애는 것이 아니라 지구의 탄소 보유량이 반드시 균형을 이루게 하는 것이다. 광합성이나 호흡을 통해서 탄소를 처리하는 식물과 동물들은 하나의 저장소에 해당한다. 식물과 동물들이 부패할 때 형성되는 지구 표면 밑의 퇴적물은 또 다른 저장소이다.
(B) 그 후에, 탄소의 분포는 석탄과 천연가스와 같은 지하의 퇴적물들이 탈 때 탄소를 대기로 방출하면서 불균형해진다. 거기에서, 과도한 탄소는 지구의 평

균 기온을 상승시킬 수도 있다.
(A) 탄소 순환에서의 이러한 어긋남을 바로잡기 위해, 대기 중으로 방출되는 탄소의 양은 감소되어야 한다. 숲이 대기의 탄소를 흡수할 수 있기 때문에 삼림 벌채를 늦추는 것이 도움이 될 수 있다. 하지만, 화석 연료에 대한 대안을 찾는 것 또한 필수적이다.

[어휘] living thing 생물 closed system 폐쇄계 disturbance 어긋남, 소란
deforestation 삼림 벌채, 산림 개간 absorb 흡수하다
reservoir 보유(량), 저장소 photosynthesis 광합성 respiration 호흡
decompose 부패하다

[구문분석]
[1행] Earth is a closed system, which means that the amount of carbon on the planet is always the same, [**no matter how it is distributed**].
→ [no ~ distributed]는 no matter how(어떻게 ~하더라도)가 이끄는 양보의 부사절이다.

37 글의 순서 배열하기 정답 ④

[해설] 주어진 글은 시민들의 투표보다는 선거인단의 주 대표들의 투표가 미국의 다음 대통령을 결정하는 투표라는 주제를 제시한다. (C)의 The current system(현 제도)은 주어진 글의 '선거인단의 주 대표들의 투표가 다음 대통령을 결정한다는 것'을 가리키며, 이를 통해 주어진 글의 내용에 대한 부연 설명을 하고 있으므로 주어진 글 바로 다음에 오는 것이 적절하다. (A)의 Such an idiosyncrasy(그러한 특이한 방식)는 '승자독식제'를 가리키므로 승자독식제로 인해 발생하는 문제점을 언급한 (C) 바로 다음에 오는 것이 적절하다. (B)는 미국 헌법 제정자가 그것, 즉 그 선거 제도를 마지막 순간에 서둘러 만들었다는 내용이고, (A)의 마지막에서 그 선거 제도가 신중한 설계의 결과물이었다는 생각은 사실과 거리가 있다고 했으므로 그 뒤에 와야 한다. 따라서 글의 순서로 가장 적절한 것은 ④ (C) - (A) - (B)이다.

[해석] 이 사실이 보통 간과되기는 하지만, 시민들의 투표보다는 선거인단의 주(州) 대표들의 투표가 미국의 다음 대통령을 결정하는 투표이다.
(C) 현 제도는 승자독식제에 따라서 운영된다; 한 후보가 한 주에서 표의 100퍼센트를 차지하든 50.1퍼센트를 차지하든, 그들은 그 주의 선거인단 표를 얻는다. 이는 다수의 주들은 당선이 확실하게 하여(그들은 항상 같은 당을 택한다), 선거가 결국 후보자들이 놓고 싸우는 소수의 "초접전" 주로 요약되게 된다.
(A) 일반 투표에서 이긴 후보자가 그 국가의 지난 총선거들에서 다섯 번 패배함에 따라, 그러한 특이한 방식은 무시하기가 점점 더 어려워지고 있다. 많은 사람들이 그 선거 제도가 신중한 설계의 결과물이었다고 생각하지만, 이 생각은 사실과는 거리가 있다.
(B) 미국 헌법 제정자가 그것을 마지막 순간에 서둘러 만들었고, 거의 바로 그들이 의도한 대로 작용하기를 멈추었다. 그렇다 하더라도, 그것을 헌법에 포함하는 것이 실제로 그렇지 않지만 그것이 민주 국가에서 중요한 역할을 한다고 암시한다는 잘못된 생각 때문에 그것은 선거 제도 내에 남아 있다.

[어휘] idiosyncrasy 특이한 방식 popular vote 일반 투표
general election 총선거 presume 생각하다, 추정하다 electoral 선거의
meticulous 신중한, 꼼꼼한 throw together ~을 서둘러 만들다
misguided 잘못된, 잘못 알고 있는 inclusion 포함 Constitution 헌법
winner-take-all 승자독식제 electoral vote 선거인단 투표
safe 당선이 확실한, 틀림없이 지지하는 go for ~을 택하다
come down to ~으로 요약되다 a handful of 소수의
battleground state 초접전 주(州)

구문 분석

[11행] The Founding Fathers threw it together at the last minute, and it stopped working as they intended it **to** (work) almost immediately.

→ to는 to부정사 to work에서 work가 생략된 것으로, 앞서 it stopped working에서 이미 언급되었기 때문에 생략되었다.

[13행] And yet, it has remained within the election system because of misguided **notions** [that its inclusion in the Constitution implies (that) it serves an important role in a democratic nation], when in reality it does not.

→ [that ~ nation]은 notions와 동격을 이루는 명사절이다.

→ 명사절의 동사 implies 뒤에 that이 생략된 형태이다.

---

38 주어진 문장의 위치 찾기 정답 ⑤

(해설) 주어진 문장의 this shift towards individualization(이러한 개별화로의 전환)으로 보아, 주어진 문장 앞에는 개별화로의 전환에 대한 내용이 나와야 한다는 것을 알 수 있다. 이 글에서는 ①~② 뒤 문장까지 언론의 인공지능 활용에 대해 설명하고 있고, ③~④ 뒤 문장까지 인공지능을 통해 개별화된 보도가 가능해졌다고 설명하고 있다. 그러다가 ⑤ 뒤 문장에서 신문들이 사람들의 선호에 의존한다면 중요한 기사들을 공개하지 않은 채 둘 수도 있다는 부정적인 내용이 나와 ⑤ 앞뒤의 내용이 유기적으로 연결되지 않는다는 점을 통해 글의 흐름이 끊겼음을 알 수 있다. 따라서 주어진 문장이 들어가기에 가장 적절한 곳은 ⑤이다.

(오답 분석) ② 뒤 문장의 These systems는 ① 뒤 문장의 AI systems를 가리키므로 그 뒤에 이어지는 것이 적절하다. ③ 뒤 문장은 역접 연결어 though를 통해 ② 뒤 문장에 대한 반전 설명을 하고 있으므로 자연스럽게 이어진다. ④ 뒤 문장은 인공지능을 통해 개별화된 보도가 가능해졌다는 앞 문장에 대한 보충 설명이므로 주어진 문장은 이 내용이 끝난 이후에 들어가야 한다.

(해석) 모든 업계들에 걸친 공통적인 우려는 인공지능의 커지는 중요성과 그것이 인간 근로자들을 대체하고 그로 인해 다양한 직업들을 불필요하거나 쓸모 없게 만들 가능성이다. (①) 언론계도 이에 예외가 아니며, 많은 유명한 신문들이 현재 그들의 결과물을 늘리고 개선하기 위해 인공지능 시스템들을 이용하고 있으므로, 기술이 언론의 과정에 계속해서 더욱 중요해지기만 할 것처럼 보인다. (②) 이러한 시스템들은 현재 그들이 제공받은 자료를 해석하고 주목할 만한 양상을 기술하는 것에 국한되어, 그들의 기사가 사람의 집필을 통해 표현되는 개성, 위트, 그리고 유머를 결여하게 한다. (③) 그렇지만, 인공지능은 신문들이 더 다양한 주제를 다루게 하고, 미래에는 독자들에게 좀 더 개인화된 보도로 이어져서 독자의 관심사와 관련하여 수집된 자료에 기반을 둔 기사를 작성할 수도 있을 것이다. (④) 이 "로봇 저널리즘"은 결국 제시된 정보가 어떻게 그 사람만의 인생 경험과 관련되는지 설명하면서 기사를 특정 개인에게 맞출 수 있다. (⑤ 뉴스의 전통적인 목적이 시민들에게 필수적인 정보를 제공하는 것이기 때문에 일부 언론인들은 이러한 개별화로의 전환에 대해 우려한다.) 만약 신문들이 그들의 내용을 위해 사람들의 선호에 의존한다면, 중요한 기사들을 공개하지 않은 채 둘 수도 있을 것이다.

(어휘) shift 전환, 변화 individualization 개별화 prominence 중요성, 두드러짐 redundant 불필요한 obsolete 쓸모 없는, 구식인 fundamental 중요한, 근본적인 journalistic 언론의 devoid of ~이 결여된 personalize 개인화하다 coverage 보도 tailor 맞추다 unpublished 공개되지 않은, 출판되지 않은

구문 분석

[8행] ~ and ①[with <u>many renowned papers</u> now <u>utilizing</u> AI
　　　　　　　　명사구　　　　　　　　　현재분사
systems to increase and refine their output], it seems ②[**as though** technology will only continue to become more fundamental to the journalistic process].

→ ①[with ~ output]은 'with + 명사(구) + 분사' 형태의 분사구문으로, '~이므로'라는 의미로 해석한다.

→ ②[as ~ process]는 접속사 as though(마치 ~한 것처럼)가 이끄는 양보의 부사절이다. as though는 as if로 바꿔 쓸 수 있으며 as though가 조금 더 격식 있는 표현이다.

---

39 주어진 문장의 위치 찾기 정답 ④

(해설) 주어진 문장의 Up to that point(그때까지는)로 보아, 주어진 문장 앞에는 하나의 영화를 한 번에 한 사람이 아닌 여러 사람이 볼 수 있게 하는 기술이 발명된 시점이 나와야 한다는 것을 알 수 있다. 이 글에서는 ④ 앞 문장에서 최초의 영화 상영은 Lumière 형제가 시네마토그래프를 발명한 덕분에 가능해진 업적이라고 하였고, 주어진 문장의 하나의 영화를 한 번에 한 사람만 볼 수 있었다는 내용은 ④ 뒤 문장에서 the limitations of previous technology(이전 기술의 한계)로 이어지고 있으므로 주어진 문장이 들어가기에 가장 적절한 곳은 ④이다.

(오답 분석) ①~③ 뒤 문장은 <리옹의 뤼미에르 공장문을 나서는 노동자들>을 소개한 ① 앞 문장에 대한 보충 설명이므로 주어진 문장은 이 내용이 끝난 이후에 들어가야 한다. ⑤ 뒤 문장은 Lumière 형제가 다수의 관객에게 영화를 상영할 수 있는 영화관을 곳곳에 열었다는 내용이므로 주어진 문장은 이것보다 앞에 와야 한다.

(해석) 최초의 영화는 액션이 많은 장면들이나 예상 밖의 전개와 전환들을 포함하지 않았다; 대신에, 그것은 그저 긴 하루의 근무가 끝나고 공장을 나서는 직원들을 보여주었다. 1895년에 처음으로 공개된 그 영화는 Auguste Lumière(오귀스트 뤼미에르)와 Louis Lumière(루이 뤼미에르)에 의해 제작되었으며 <리옹의 뤼미에르 공장문을 나서는 노동자들>이라고 칭해졌다. (①) 이것은 그 형제의 첫 번째 "actualités", 즉 "기록 영화"였는데, 그것은 오늘날 다큐멘터리와 비슷하게 실제 사람들과 사건들을 포함하는 장면들을 담았다. (②) 그 개념은 단순했지만 획기적이었다. (③) 어쨌든, <리옹의 뤼미에르 공장을 나서는 노동자들>은 관객에게 보여질 수 있었던 최초의 영화였다; 그 형제의 시네마토그래프라고 불리는 기기의 발명으로 인해 가능해진 위업이었다. (④ 그때까지는, 하나의 영화를 한 번에 한 사람이 보는 것만 가능했다.) 시네마토그래프는 카메라와 영사기 둘 다로 사용될 수 있었기 때문에 이전 기술의 한계를 극복했다. (⑤) <리옹의 뤼미에르 공장을 나서는 노동자들>의 성공은 그 형제가 런던, 브뤼셀, 뉴욕에 영화관을 열고 관객들이 즐길 전 세계의 일상생활의 장면들을 촬영하도록 사람들을 보내, 우리가 아는 영화 산업을 활성화시키게 했다.

(어휘) action-packed 액션이 많은, 흥미진진한 sequence 장면, 연속 twist (예상 밖의) 전개, 꼬임 actuality 기록 영화, 실재 groundbreaking 획기적인, 창시의 feat 위업, 공적 projector 영사기 jumpstart 활성화하다

 구문 분석

[4행] ~ instead, it merely showed **employees** [leaving a factory after a long day's work].

→ [leaving ~ work]는 앞의 명사 employees를 수식하는 현재분사구이다.

[21행] ~ to send people to shoot scenes of everyday life around the world <u>for audiences</u> <u>to enjoy</u>, jumpstarting cinema as we know it.
　　의미상 주어　　to부정사

→ for audiences는 'for + 명사' 형태로, to부정사 to enjoy의 의미상 주어이다.

---

40 요약문 완성하기　　　　정답 ②

(해설) 글의 중반부에서 가장 일반적으로 이용되는 분류 방식인 린네 시스템은 생물들 간 관계를 더 효율적으로 연구할 수 있게 한다고 하였고, 글의 후반부에서 린네 시스템은 또한 지구상의 모든 생명체들에 대한 이해를 제시한다고 했다. 따라서 maps ~ out을 arrangement로, allows people to study를 outline으로 바꾸어 표현한 ②이 정답이다.

(오답분석) 분류학은 식물, 동물, 미생물들에 이름을 붙이고 일정 기준에 따라 그것들을 분류한다고 했으므로 ①의 unification, ③의 illustration, ④의 connection은 (A)에 들어갈 단어로 적절하지 않다.

(해석) 지구상의 생물체가 다양한 만큼, 분류학은 그렇게 매우 다양한 생물들을 이해하고 연구하는 것을 더 용이하게 만든다. 식물, 동물, 미생물들은 이 체계에 따라서 이름이 붙여지고 분류되는데, 이 체계는 그것들의 형태, 구조, 습성, 유전학 및 생화학적 분석을 기반으로 한다. 지구에 사는 5백만에서 3천만의 예측되는 종들 중에서, 178만 종이 현재까지 확인되고 분류되었다. 이러한 목적으로 가장 일반적으로 이용되는 분류 방식은 린네 시스템인데, 이는 스웨덴의 동식물 연구가인 Carolus Linnaeus(카를로스 린네)에 의해 1750년대에 확립되었다. 그것은 생물들을 계, 강, 목, 속과 같은 그룹으로 분류한다. 그러한 분류는 사람들이 생명체들의 유사점 및 차이점뿐만 아니라 그것들 간의 관계를 더 효율적으로 연구하게 해준다. 그것은 또한 지구상의 모든 생명체가 어떻게 그리고 왜 그들이 진화한 대로 진화해왔는지를 포함해서 과학자들에게 지구상의 모든 생명체에 대한 이해를 제시하는 방식으로 식물, 동물, 미생물들을 배치한다. 이는 다른 종들뿐만 아니라 인류 자체의 기원을 이해하는 데에 핵심으로, 인간이 자연 분류상에서 어디에 들어맞는지에 대한 이해를 사람들에게 제시한다.

↓

분류학은 모든 생명체들이 어떻게 서로 관련되어 있는지를 (B) 설명하는 것을 돕는 생물학적 범주 속에 식물, 동물, 미생물들의 (A) 배치를 포함한다.

　　(A)　　　　(B)
① 통합　…… 강화하다
② 배치　…… 설명하다
③ 설명　…… 보여주다
④ 관련성 …… 과장하다
⑤ 분배　…… 숨기다

(어휘) microorganism 미생물　behavior 습성, 행동　biochemical 생화학적인　the planet 지구　naturalist 동물학 연구가, 박물학자　kingdom (동식물 분류상의) 계　class (동식물 분류상의) 강　order (동식물 분류상의) 목　family (동식물 분류상의) 속　map out 배치하다, 상세히 나타내다　natural order 자연 분류

(구문분석) [1행] ~ taxonomy <u>makes</u> <u>understanding and studying such a</u>
　　　　　　　　　　동사　　　　목적어
<u>large range of organisms</u> <u>easier</u>.
　　　　　　　　　　　　목적격 보어

→ 동사 makes의 목적어로 동명사구 understanding ~ organisms, 목적격 보어로 easier가 쓰였다.

[7행] **Of** the predicted five to thirty million species living on the planet, ~

→ 전치사 of가 문장 맨 앞에 오면 '~중에서'로 해석한다.

41~42 장문 독해 1

(해석) [41]예술가와 관람객 간의 관계는 신뢰에 기반을 둔 신성한 유대이고, 예술가의 의도의 미적 가치가 (a)참되기 위해서 예술가의 의도의 진정성에 대한 관람객의 믿음이 존중되어야 한다. 당신이 미술관 전시회에 가서 Monet(모네) 그림의 기술적 능숙함에 감탄한다고 상상해보아라. 당신은 뒤얽힌 붓놀림이 아른아른 빛나는 아침에 생생한 활기를 가져오는 풍경에 대한 그 화가의 주관적인 경험을 전달하는 방식에 사로잡힌다. 당신은 그 그림을 집에 가져오기 위해 당신 재산의 상당한 부분을 사용하지만 그것이 사실은 Monet가 만든 것이 아니었음을 다음날에 알게 될 뿐이다. 그 작품은 위작이다.

상업적 기준에 의하면, 그 가상의 위작은 어제보다 오늘 금전적 가치가 상당히 (b)더 적다. 그렇다 하더라도, 미적 관점에서 그 예술가의 실력은 (c)의심할 여지가 없다. 그 잠깐 동안의 순간을 경험한 것은 작자 불명의 수채화가이지 저명한 거장이 아니었음에도, 어제 당신을 감동시켰던 그 붓놀림은 여전히 그 순간의 본질을 담고 있다. 하지만, 하룻밤 사이에 추정되는 의도가 바뀌었다. [41, 42]어제, 그 작품은 풍경의 실체를 표현하도록 의도되었다. 오늘, 그것의 수고로운 목적은 당신을 (d)속이는 것이었다. 예술가와 관람객 간의 유대가 끊어졌기 때문에, 그 그림의 미적 매력이 회복할 수 없을 정도로 손상되었다. 작품의 (e)객관적인(→인지되는) 목적은 그것의 미적 가치의 불가분한 요소이다.

(어휘) sacred 신성한, 종교적인　sincerity 진정성, 진실성　aesthetic 미적인　honor 존중하다, 지키다　proficiency 능숙, 숙련　strike 감탄하게 하다　captivate 사로잡다, 매혹하다　intricate 뒤얽힌, 복잡한　brushwork 붓놀림, 화법　shimmer 아른아른 빛나다　sizable 상당한 크기의　counterfeit 위작; 위조의　capture 표현하다, 사로잡다　essence 본질, 정수　fleeting 잠깐 동안의　established 저명한, 확립된　design 의도하다, 설계하다　truth 실체, 진실　painstaking 수고로운, 애쓴　sever 끊다, 절단하다　irreparably 회복할 수 없을 정도로　mar 손상시키다　inextricable 불가분한, 뒤얽힌　[선택지] appraisal 평가

(구문분석) [19행] ~ moment, even if [**it was** an anonymous watercolorist **who** experienced the moment] and not an established master.

→ [it ~ moment]는 명사구 an anonymous watercolorist를 강조하는 it is(was) ~ who 강조 구문이다.

[25행] [The bond between artist and viewer having been severed], the painting's aesthetic attraction is irreparably marred.

→ [The ~ severed]는 이유를 나타내는 분사구문으로, 분사구문의 주어(The bond between artist and viewer)와 주절의 주어(the painting's aesthetic attraction)가 달라서 분사구문의 주어를 생략하지 않은 독립분사구문이다.

---

41 제목 파악하기　　　　정답 ①

(해설) 첫 문장과 마지막 부분으로 미루어 보아, 작품의 미적 가치는 예술가의 의도의 진정성에 대한 관람객의 신뢰를 바탕으로 하고 예술가와 관람객 간의 유대가 끊어지면 작품의 미적 매력이 손상된다는 내용의 글로, Monet의 위작을 산

다는 가정을 예로 들어 설명하고 있다. 따라서 글의 제목으로 가장 적절한 것은 ① '예술 작품의 가치: 뛰어난 위작들이 원작들에 비교되지 않는 이유'이다.

[오답분석] ②은 뛰어난 위작이라도 예술가와 관람객 간의 유대가 끊어지면 미적 가치가 손상된다는 글의 내용과 반대되기 때문에 오답이다. ⑤은 글의 핵심 어구 Forgeries를 사용하여 헷갈리게 하는 오답이다.

[해석] ① 예술 작품의 가치: 뛰어난 위작들이 원작들에 비교되지 않는 이유
② 진품임의 무가치함: 업적으로서의 위작
③ 교묘한 복제가 예술계에서의 엘리트주의를 거스를 수 있는가?
④ 예술 작품의 평가가 일관적이지 않고 믿을 수 없는 이유들
⑤ 뛰어난 위작을 찾아내는 것의 어려움

42 어휘 적절성 파악하기   정답 ⑤

[해설] 원본이라고 생각했던 예술 작품이 위작임을 알게 되면 그 그림의 매력이 손상되는 것처럼 예술 작품이 한 사람에게 인지되는 목적은 미적 가치의 불가분한 요소라는 맥락이 되어야 하므로, ⑤의 objective(객관적인)를 그와 반대되는 의미의 perceived(인지되는)와 같은 어휘로 바꾸어야 문맥상 적절하다.

[오답분석] ②은 예술 작품이 위작임을 알게 되면 금전적 가치가 적어진다는 문맥이 되어야 하므로 less가 오는 것이 적절하다. ③은 예술 작품이 위작임을 알게 되더라도 예술가의 실력이 뛰어나다는 것에는 의심할 여지가 없다는 문맥이 되어야 하므로 unquestionable이 오는 것이 적절하다.

43~45 장문 독해 2

[해석] (A) Jane은 Louise와 카페에 앉자마자, 무언가가 잘못되었음을 느꼈다. Louise는 말이 없었고 심란해 보였다. "너 괜찮아?"라고 Jane이 물었다. Louise는 고개를 끄덕이고는 "나는 다가오는 사진 대회가 조금 걱정될 뿐이야. 무엇을 제출해야 할지 모르겠어."라고 답했다. Jane은 사진 대회가 Louise에게 중요한 일이고 (a)그녀가 가능한 한 최고의 사진들을 제출하기를 원한다는 것을 알고 있었다.

(D) "내가 찍은 사진들 중 어느 것도 충분히 좋은 것 같지가 않아"라고 Louise가 슬프게 말했다. 그녀는 그들이 같이 살펴보기 위해 ⁴⁵색채가 풍부한 사진들 몇 장을 테이블 위에 놓았다. 그것들은 훌륭했지만, 그것들 중 어느 것도 눈에 띄지는 않았다. "내 선생님이 좋은 사진은 대비가 필요하다고 말씀하셨어"라고 Louise가 설명했다. "하지만 그 속에 여러 가지 색과 형태가 있는 (e)내 사진들은 전부 똑같아 보여. 달리 어떻게 대비를 주어야 할지 모르겠어." Louise는 한숨을 쉬었고 자신의 작품을 치웠다.

(B) ⁴⁴Jane은 그것에 대해 생각했고 "아마 너는 다른 방식으로 대비를 주는 것에 대해 생각해봐야 할 것 같아."라고 말했다. Louise는 (b)그녀에게 어리둥절한 표정을 보였다. "무슨 말이야?" Jane은 사진들을 좀 더 독특하게 만들기 위해서 여러 대상들을 보여주는 사진들을 찍을 수 있을 것이라고 그녀에게 말했다. Louise는 그녀의 제안을 생각해보고는 "좋은 생각이지만, 그래도 난 무엇을 찍을지 생각해내야 해. 게다가 사진들은 바로 며칠 뒤에 마감이라 (c)나는 시간이 많이 없어."라고 말했다.

(C) "여기 주변에서 사진 몇 장을 찍는 건 어때? 우리는 도시에 살지만, 어디에나 공원과 나무들이 있어"라고 Jane이 말했다. "너는 자연과 건물 둘 다를 같이 보여주는 사진을 찍어야 할 것 같아." Louise는 그것이 효과가 있을 수도 있다고 확신하며 그녀를 향해 활짝 웃었다. 그들은 카페에서 나간 후에, Louise가 더 많은 사진들을 찍을 수 있도록 주변을 돌아다녔다. Jane은 Louise가 그녀의 새로운 사진들에 대해 훨씬 더 만족하고 더 자신감 있다는 것을 느꼈다. (d)그녀는 "이것들이 훨씬 더 나아"라고 말했고, 그녀가 대회에서 우승하지 못

하더라도 드디어 자신의 작품을 자랑스럽다고 생각했다.

[어휘] distracted 심란한, 산만한   puzzled 어리둥절한

[구문분석]

> [1행] [As soon as Jane sat down with Louise at the café], she knew something was wrong.
> → [As ~ café]는 접속사 as soon as(~하자마자)가 이끄는 시간의 부사절이다.
>
> [30행] "I don't **think** [(that) any of the photos I've taken are good enough]," Louise said sadly.
> → 명사절 [any ~ enough]는 동사 think의 목적어로, 명사절 접속사 that이 생략되어 있다.

43 글의 순서 배열하기   정답 ④

[해설] (A)는 Jane이 다가오는 사진 대회에 대한 Louise의 걱정을 알게 되는 내용이다. (D)는 Louise가 자신의 사진들에 만족하지 못하고 있고 선생님이 말한 대비를 어떻게 표현해야 할지 모르겠다는 내용이므로, Louise가 무슨 사진을 제출해야 할지 모르겠다고 한 (A) 뒤에 와야 한다. (B)의 Jane thought about it에서 it은 (D)의 how else to make contrast를 가리키므로 (D) 다음에 오는 것이 적절하다. (C)는 Louise가 카페 주변에서 사진을 찍었고 새로운 사진들에 만족했다는 내용이므로 여러 대상을 담는 방식으로 대비를 주라는 Jane의 조언을 듣고 Louise가 무엇을 찍을지 생각해보겠다고 한 (B) 뒤에 와야 한다. 따라서 글의 순서로 가장 적절한 것은 ④ (D) - (B) - (C)이다.

44 지칭 대상 파악하기   정답 ②

[해설] (a), (c), (d), (e)는 모두 Louise를 가리키지만 (b)는 Jane을 가리키므로, ②이 정답이다.

45 세부 정보 파악하기   정답 ⑤

[해설] (D)의 She put a few colorful photographs on the table을 통해 Louise가 색채가 풍부한 사진들을 찍었다는 것을 알 수 있는데, ⑤은 사진들이 흑백이라고 일부 정보를 잘못 나타냈으므로 글의 내용과 일치하지 않는 것은 ⑤이다.

해커스

수능 독해
불변의 패턴 실전편

정답 및 해설

중·고등영어도 역시 1위 해커스

중·고등

해커스 young star

중·고등영어의 압도적인 점수 상승,
해커스 영스타 중·고등에서 현실이 됩니다.

해커스 영스타 중·고등 강의 무료체험

내게 맞는 공부법 체크! 학습전략검사

해커스 중·고등교재 무료 학습자료

보카 강의 수강생 수
1위 박가은